Fundamentals of
FORTRAN 77 Programming

A Structured Approach

Little, Brown Computer Systems Series

CHATTERGY, RAHUL, AND UDO W. POOCH

Top-down, Modular Programming in FORTRAN with WATFIV

COATS, R. B., AND A. PARKIN

Computer Models in the Social Sciences

CONWAY, RICHARD, AND DAVID GRIES

An Introduction to Programming: A Structured Approach Using PL/I and PL/C, third edition
Primer on Structured Programming: Using PL/I, PL/C, and PL/CT

CONWAY, RICHARD, DAVID GRIES, AND E. CARL ZIMMERMAN

A Primer on Pascal, second edition

CRIPPS, MARTIN

An Introduction to Computer Hardware

EASLEY, GRADY M.

Primer for Small Systems Management

FINKENAUR, ROBERT G.

COBOL for Students: A Programming Primer

FREEDMAN, DANIEL P., AND GERALD M. WEINBERG

Handbook of Walkthroughs, Inspections, and Technical Reviews: Evaluating Programs, Projects, and Products, third edition

GRAYBEAL, WAYNE, AND UDO W. POOCH

Simulation: Principles and Methods

GREENFIELD, S. E.

The Architecture of Microcomputers
The Architecture of Microcomputers, Volume I: Fundamentals

GREENWOOD, FRANK

Profitable Small Business Computing

HEALY, MARTIN, AND DAVID HEBDITCH

The Microcomputer in On-Line Systems: Small Computers in Terminal-Based Systems and Distributed Processing Networks

LEMONE, KAREN A., AND MARTIN E. KALISKI

Assembly Language Programming for the VAX-11

LIAS, EDWARD J.

Future Mind: The Microcomputer— New Medium, New Mental Environment

LINES, M. VARDELL, AND BOEING COMPUTER SERVICES COMPANY

Minicomputer Systems

MARCA, DAVID

Applying Software Engineering Principles

MASHAW, B. J.

Programming Byte by Byte: Structured FORTRAN 77

MILLS, HARLAN D.

Software Productivity

MONRO, DONALD M.

Basic BASIC: An Introduction to Programming

MOSTELLER, WILLIAM S.

Systems Programmer's Problem Solver

NICKERSON, ROBERT C.

Fundamentals of Programming in BASIC
COBOL Programming
Fundamentals of FORTRAN Programming
Fundamentals of FORTRAN Programming: A Structured Approach, third edition

PARIKH, GIRISH

Techniques of Program and System Maintenance

PARKIN, ANDREW

Data Processing Management
Systems Analysis

PIZER, STEPHEN M., WITH VICTOR L. WALLACE

To Compute Numerically: Concepts and Strategies

REINGOLD, EDWARD M., AND WILFRED J. HANSEN

Data Structures

SAVITCH, WALTER J.

Abstract Machines and Grammars

SCHNEIDERMAN, BEN

Software Psychology: Human Factors in Computer and Information Systems

SHIVA, SAJJAN G.

Computer Design and Architecture

WALKER, HENRY M.

Problems for Computer Solutions Using BASIC
Problems for Computer Solutions Using FORTRAN

WEINBERG, GERALD M.

Rethinking Systems Analysis and Design
Understanding the Professional Programmer

WEINBERG, GERALD M., AND DENNIS GELLER

Computer Information Systems: An Introduction to Data Processing

The Little, Brown Microcomputer Bookshelf

BANSE, TIMOTHY

Home Applications and Games for the Apple® II, Apple® II Plus, and Apple® IIe Computers

Home Applications and Games for the ATARI® 400™/800™, 600XL™, 800XL™, 1200XL™, 1400XL™, and 1450XLD™ Home Computers

Home Applications and Games for the Commodore 64®

Home Applications and Games for the IBM® PC and PCjr

Home Applications and Games for the VIC-20

BARNETT, MICHAEL P., AND GRAHAM K. BARNETT

Personal Graphics for Profit and Pleasure on the Apple® II Plus Computer

Personal Graphics for Profit and Pleasure on the IBM® Personal Computers

HODGES, WILLIAM S., AND NEAL A. NOVAK

Personal Finance Programs for Home Computers

LEMONE, KAREN A.

Assembly Language and Systems Programming for the IBM® Personal Computer

MORRILL, HARRIET

BASIC for IBM® Personal Computers

Mini and Micro BASIC: Introducing Applesoft®, Microsoft®, and BASIC PLUS

NAHIGIAN, J. VICTOR, AND WILLIAM S. HODGES

Computer Games for Businesses, Schools, and Homes

Computer Games for Business, School, and Home for TRS-80 Level II BASIC

ORWIG, GARY W., AND WILLIAM S. HODGES

The Computer Tutor: Apple® Computer Edition Learning Activities for Homes and Schools

The Computer Tutor: ATARI® Home Computer Edition (for the ATARI® 400/800™, 600XL™, 800XL™, 1200XL™, 1400XL™, and 1450XLD™ Home Computers)

The Computer Tutor: IBM® Personal Computer Edition (for the IBM® PC and PCjr)

The Computer Tutor: Learning Activities for Homes and Schools (for the TRS-80®, Apple®, Commodore 64™, VIC-20, and PET / CBM® Home Computers)

SIMPSON, TOM, AND SHAFFER & SHAFFER APPLIED RESEARCH & DEVELOPMENT, INC.

VisiCalc® Programming: No Experience Necessary

SHAFFER & SHAFFER APPLIED RESEARCH & DEVELOPMENT, INC.

VisiCalc® Programming: No Experience Necessary, for the Apple® II, Apple® II Plus, and Apple® IIe Personal Computers

VisiCalc® Programming: No Experience Necessary, for ATARI® 800™ and 1200XL™ Home Computers

VisiCalc® Programming: No Experience Necessary, for the IBM® Personal Computer

VisiCalc® Programming: No Experience Necessary, for the TRS-80® Model III Microcomputer

SHNEIDERMAN, BEN

Let's Learn BASIC: A Kids' Introduction to BASIC Programming on the Apple® II Series

Let's Learn BASIC: A Kids' Introduction to BASIC Programming on ATARI® Home Computers

Let's Learn BASIC: A Kids' Introduction to BASIC Programming on the Commodore 64®

Let's Learn BASIC: A Kids' Introduction to BASIC Programming on IBM® Personal Computers

WINDEKNECHT, THOMAS G.

6502 Systems Programming

Fundamentals of
FORTRAN 77 Programming

A Structured Approach
Third Edition

Robert C. Nickerson
San Francisco State University

Little, Brown and Company

Boston   Toronto

Library of Congress Cataloging in Publication Data

Nickerson, Robert C.
    Fundamentals of FORTRAN 77 programming.

    (Little, Brown computer systems series)
    Rev. ed. of: Fundamentals of FORTRAN programming.
2nd ed. c1980.
    Includes index.
    1. FORTRAN (Computer program language) I. Nickerson,
Robert C., 1946–   . Fundamentals of FORTRAN
programming. II. Title. III. Title: Fundamentals of
FORTRAN seventy-seven programming. IV. Series.
QA76.73.F25N49   1985   001.64'24   84-25111

ISBN 0-316-60653-7

Library of Congress Catalog Card No. 84-25111

ISBN 0-316-60653-7

9 8 7 6 5 4 3 2 1

HAL

Published simultaneously in Canada
by Little, Brown & Company (Canada) Limited

Printed in the United States of America

Previous editions of this book were entitled *Fundamentals of FORTRAN Programming*.

Disclaimer of Liabilities: Due care has been exercised in the preparation of this book to ensure its effectiveness. The author and publisher make no warranty, expressed or implied, with respect to the programs or other contents of this book. In no event will the authors or publisher be liable for direct, indirect, incidental, or consequential damages in connection with or arising from the furnishing, performance, or use of this book.

Preface

The objective of this book is to provide a carefully paced introduction to structured computer programming and the FORTRAN 77 language for students with a minimal mathematical background. To accomplish this objective the book systematically introduces the features of FORTRAN 77 as they are needed for various processing situations. These language features are illustrated by program examples that are drawn from nonmathematical problems that most readers will readily recognize. Structured programming concepts are developed along with, not separate from, the language features. As a result, the reader not only learns the FORTRAN 77 language but also gains an understanding of the need for and use of each language element, and learns how to develop well-structured programs in FORTRAN 77.

The book adheres strictly to FORTRAN 77 (the 1978 version of ANS FORTRAN). List-directed input and output is introduced at the beginning. Block IF statements are used for decision structures. Loop control is accomplished by standard features in FORTRAN 77. Character data processing and file processing are explained in detail. Appendix A summarizes the FORTRAN 77 language elements covered in the book. The only exception to the strict FORTRAN 77 orientation is the last section of Chapter 5 which describes WHILE loops as implemented in WATFIV-S and some other versions of FORTRAN. In addition, Appendix B briefly discusses several other versions of FORTRAN and provides a table that compares features in different versions of the language.

Language features are covered in conjunction with structured program development. Basic program structure is discussed early with complete chapters on decision logic (Chapter 4) and loop control (Chapter 5). Nested decisions and loops are described fully in these chapters. The program development process is covered in detail in Chapter 7. Topics such as program refinement, design, testing, and documentation are discussed at appropriate points. Program style and understandability are emphasized throughout the book. The use of subroutines in the top-down design and development of large programs is covered in Chapter 11. Upon completion of this book the reader should be able to develop FORTRAN 77 programs that are well structured, understandable, and correct.

The first chapter of the book introduces the basic concepts necessary to understand programming and FORTRAN 77. Chapters 2 through 6 cover the fundamental elements of the language and develop basic programming methodology. These chapters discuss input and output, arithmetic processing, decision logic, and loop control. Chapter 7 can be thought of as a capstone for these first chapters because it brings together many concepts of program development and explains them in detail. Chapter 7 is also a transition to the more advanced topics covered in Chapters 8 through 12. These chapters describe character and logical data processing, arrays, subprograms, and files (sequential and direct). The material in these advanced chapters can be read in different sequences. In addition, some of the advanced topics can be covered along with earlier chapters. (The chapter prerequisite structure is described completely in the instructor's manual.)

A number of features make the book especially useful. These include the following:

- The first section of Chapter 1 discusses essential computer concepts. This serves as an introduction to these topics for readers with no previous computer background or as a review for readers with some computer experience.
- The book emphasizes program development using interactive computer systems. Consequently, the book can be used with most micro, mini, and mainframe computers. Punched card program development is described briefly for those using this approach.
- The book is designed so that programming can begin as early as possible. After finishing Chapter 2, the reader can write complete programs of his or her own design. After each succeeding chapter, the reader can develop increasingly more complex programs.
- Many examples and illustrative programs are provided throughout the book. The examples are nonmathematical in nature and oriented toward applications the reader should easily understand. Complete lists of input data and output are shown with most sample programs.*
- Interactive program design is discussed in detail. Characteristics that make an interactive program easy to use are explained and illustrated.
- Many common algorithms are described, including algorithms for sequential and binary searching, sorting, sequential file updating, and direct file processing.
- Each chapter contains questions to review the material covered in that chapter. The answers to approximately half of the review questions are found in Appendix G.
- All chapters except the first contain a substantial number of programming problems. Most problems require only a minimal mathematical background and emphasize nontechnical areas, including business and social science. Some problems are designed for math,

---

* All names of persons, companies, and organizations in examples, problems, and questions in this book are fictitious and are used for illustrative purposes only.

science, and engineering students. The programming problems range in difficulty from relatively easy to very difficult and challenging. Test data is provided with most problems.

- Flowcharts are discussed in Appendix D. This allows this topic to be covered at the most appropriate time. The discussion in the appendix parallels the text development of the corresponding programming topics. All flowchart examples are keyed to illustrative programs in the book.
- Numerous appendices are included. In addition to those already mentioned, there are appendices covering FORTRAN-supplied functions (Appendix C), internal data representation (Appendix E), and exponential form and double precision data (Appendix F). The appendices can be used in various ways depending on the reader's needs.

An instructor's manual is available that contains teaching suggestions, course schedules, chapter objectives, lists of terms, chapter outlines, answers to review questions, and test questions and answers. Also included in the instructor's manual are overhead transparency masters for a number of illustrations from the book.

Many of the ideas for this edition of the book came from reviews by users of the second edition. I greatly appreciate their effort. The manuscript reviewers did an excellent job and their comments were especially useful. I would like to thank Robert E. Case, United States Military Academy; Steve Drasner, North Virginia Community College; Henry A. Etlinger, Rochester Institute of Technology; Maurice D. Lind, Jefferson State Junior College; Ronald D. Schwartz, Baldwin Wallace College; and Judith Watson, Virginia Polytechnic Institute, for their participation in the reviewing process. Many of their suggestions have been incorporated into the book.

Finally, I would like to thank my family for their support and help during the writing of this book.

Contents

Fundamentals of
FORTRAN 77 Programming

A Structured Approach

Chapter 1

Introduction to FORTRAN programming

A computer is a device that is used to solve problems. The process that a person goes through in instructing a computer how to solve a problem is called programming. Programming involves combining words and symbols that are part of a special language. FORTRAN is a language that is commonly used for programming solutions to many types of problems.

This book is about programming in the FORTRAN language. The book describes the main rules of FORTRAN and explains the general process of computer programming. It also presents many programming examples for different types of problems. As a result, you should not only learn the fundamentals of the FORTRAN language, but also you should gain an understanding of the programming process and an insight into different computer applications.

Chapter 1 introduces the basic concepts necessary to begin studying FORTRAN. The first section covers elementary computer concepts. We then introduce the FORTRAN language and describe the general process of programming in FORTRAN. After completing this chapter you should have the background needed to begin learning to program in FORTRAN. Later chapters go into detail about the FORTRAN language, the programming process, and computer applications.

1-1. Computer concepts

Three topics should be understood before studying FORTRAN: computers, programs, and data. Basically, a *computer* is an electronic device that processes data by following the instructions in a program. A *program* is a set of instructions that is stored in the computer and performed automatically by the computer.

Data* is facts, figures, numbers, and words that are stored in the computer and processed according to the program's instructions.

Computers

A computer consists of several interconnected devices or components. One way to view the organization of a computer is shown in Figure 1-1. In this diagram, boxes represent the different components of the computer and lines with arrowheads show the paths taken within the computer by data and program instructions. There are five basic components: the input device, the output device, the internal storage, the processor, and the auxiliary storage. Sometimes the internal storage and processor together are called the central processing unit or CPU.

Figure 1-1. The organization of a computer

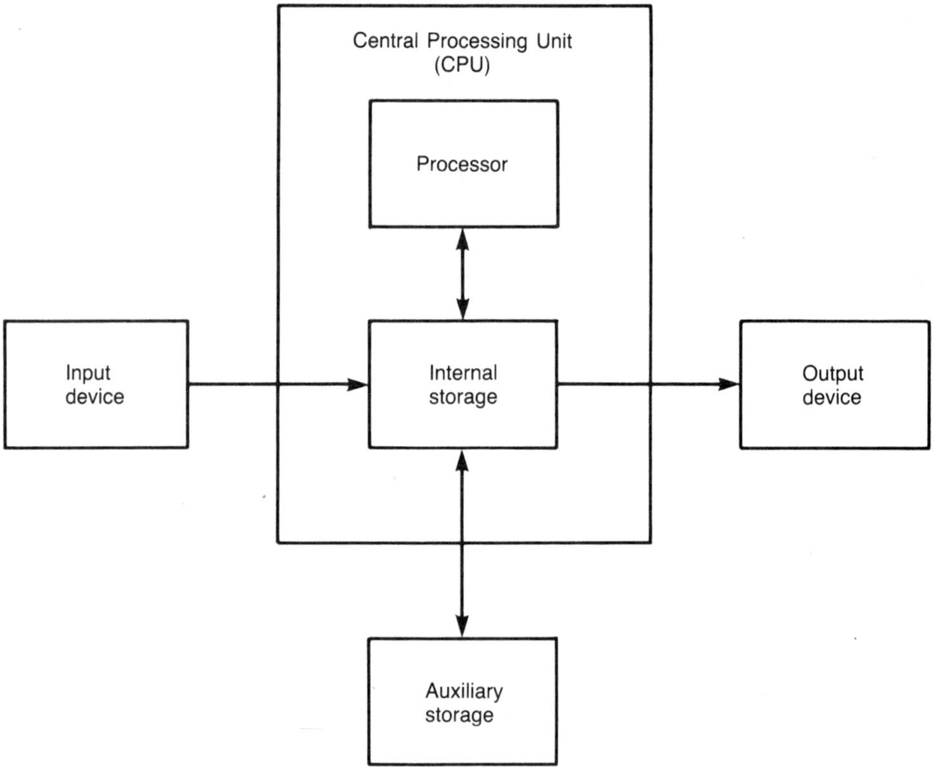

* The word "data" is most correctly used as a plural noun. The singular of data is "datum." The usual practice, however, is to use the word data in a singular rather than plural sense. We will follow that practice in this book.

Figure 1-2. A mainframe computer. This is an IBM 3081. (Photo courtesy of International Business Machines Corporation.)

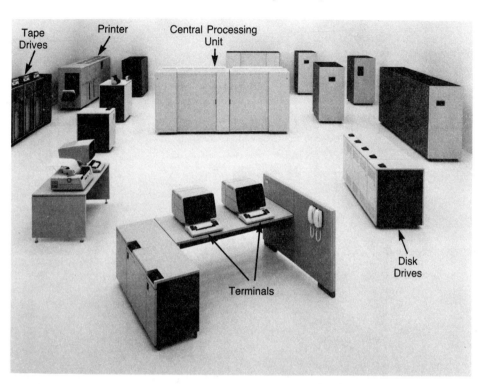

In this subsection we describe the components diagrammed in Figure 1-1. Figures 1-2, 1-3, and 1-4 show actual computers with the components discussed here.

Input and output devices. An *input device* is a mechanism that accepts data from outside the computer and converts it into an electronic form understandable to the computer. The data that is accepted is called *input data,* or simply *input.* For example, one common way to enter input into a computer is to type it with a typewriter-like *keyboard.* This keyboard is an input device. Each time a key is pressed, the electronic form of the symbol on the key is sent into the computer.

Another way to enter input into a computer is to use a device that reads the data from *punched cards* ("IBM" cards). Figure 1-5 shows an example of punched card input. The patterns of holes in the card represent different data. An input device for punched cards recognizes this data and transforms it into an electronic form understandable to the computer. Such a device is called a *card reader.*

An *output device* performs the opposite function of an input device. An output device converts data from its electronic form inside the computer

Figure 1-3. A minicomputer. This is a Digital VAX 11/785. (Photo courtesy of Digital Equipment Corporation.)

to a form that can be used outside. The converted data is called *output data,* or simply *output.* For example, one of the most common forms of output is a printed document or *report.* We often call this a computer "printout." Figure 1-6 shows an example of printed report output.

Printed output is produced by a device called a *printer,* which converts data from the computer into printed symbols to produce a paper copy of the output. Instead of being printed on paper, output is often displayed on a TV-like screen. Such a video display device is called a *CRT* for *c*athode *r*ay *t*ube (another name for a TV tube). When printer or CRT output is used with keyboard input, the devices are sometimes combined to form a unit called a *terminal.*

Input and output devices are often referred to together as input/output or *I/O* devices. Most computers have several I/O devices attached at one time. For example, a medium-sized computer may have many terminals and a printer. Some small computers, however, have only one input device and one output device (such as a keyboard and a CRT).

Figure 1-4. A microcomputer. This is an IBM Personal Computer. (Photo courtesy of International Business Machines Corporation.)

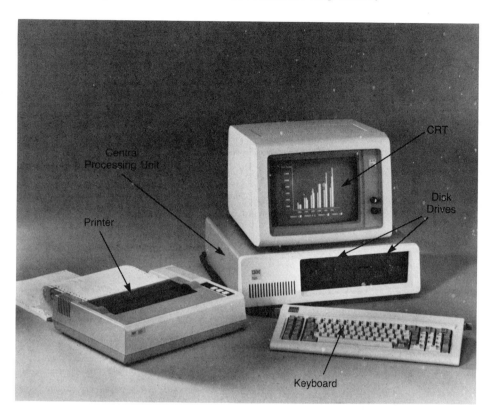

The central processing unit. Between the input devices and the output devices is the component of the computer that does the actual computing or processing. This component is the *central processing unit,* or *CPU*. (See Figure 1-1.) Input data is converted into an electronic form by an input device and sent to the central processing unit where the data is stored. In the CPU the data is used in calculations or other types of processing to produce the solution to the desired problem. After processing is completed, the results are sent to an output device where the data is converted into the final output.

The central processing unit contains two basic units: the internal storage and the processor. The *internal storage* is the "memory" of the computer. Data currently being processed is stored in this part of the CPU. Instructions in the program being performed are also stored in the internal storage.

The *processor* is the unit that carries out the instructions in the program. Among other things, the processor contains electronic circuits that do arithmetic and perform logical operations. A computer can do the basic arithmetic tasks that a human can do; that is, a computer can add, subtract,

Figure 1-5. Punched card input

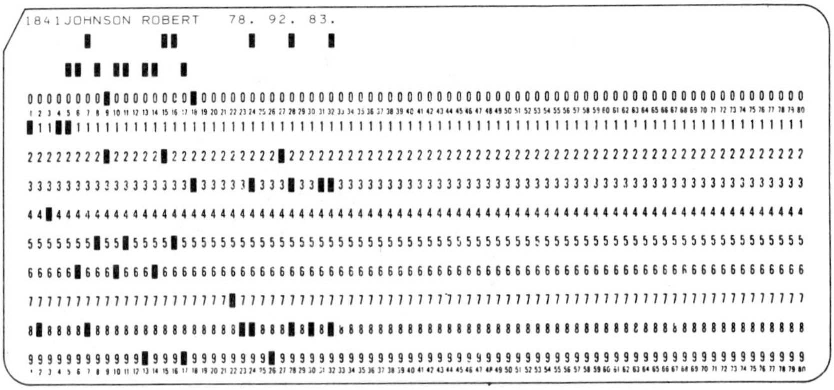

multiply, and divide. The logical operations that a computer can do are usually limited to comparing two numbers to determine whether they are equal or whether one is greater than or less than the other. Complex processing is accomplished by long sequences of these basic operations.

The processor contains electronic circuits that control the other parts of the computer. The control circuits perform their function by following the instructions in the program. The program is stored in the computer's internal storage. During processing, each instruction in the program is brought from the internal storage to the processor. The control circuits in the processor analyze the instruction and send signals to the other units based on what the instruction tells the computer to do. Performing one instruction may involve actions in any of the other parts of the computer. After one instruction in the programmed sequence is performed, the next is brought from internal storage to the processor and performed. This process continues until all the instructions in the program have been carried out.

Figure 1-6. Printed report output

TEST SCORE ANALYSIS

NUMBER	STUDENT NAME	TEST 1	TEST 2	TEST 3	TOTAL	AVERAGE
1841	JOHNSON ROBERT	78.	92.	83.	253.	84.3
1906	SMITH MARY	100.	95.	97.	292.	97.3
2133	ANDERSON RICHARD	65.	72.	57.	194.	64.7
2784	WILSON ALEX	73.	69.	78.	220.	73.3
2895	DEAN BRIAN	42.	56.	47.	145.	48.3
3047	EMERY MARY	91.	100.	92.	283.	94.3
3260	COLE JAMES	75.	78.	73.	226.	75.3
3335	GUINN DOROTHY	86.	82.	74.	242.	80.7
3819	JONES ED	71.	85.	78.	234.	78.0

Auxiliary storage. The final component of a computer is the *auxiliary storage*. This component stores data that is not currently being processed by the computer and programs that are not currently being performed. It differs from internal storage, which stores the data and instructions that are being processed at the time by the computer. Sometimes internal storage is called *primary storage* and auxiliary storage is called *secondary storage* or *mass storage.*

A common type of auxiliary storage is *magnetic disk,* or simply *disk,* which resembles a phonograph record. Disks come in different sizes: some as small as 3½ inches in diameter and others as large as 14 inches across. Some disks are made of plastic with a metallic coating; these are called *floppy disks* because they are flexible. Other disks are made of metal; these are commonly called *hard disks.* No matter what type of disk is used information is recorded on the surface of the disk by patterns of magnetism. A *disk drive* is a device for recording data on magnetic disks and for retrieving data from the disks.

Another type of auxiliary storage is *magnetic tape,* or simply *tape,* which is much like audio recording tape. Magnetic tape comes in reels of various sizes and even in cassettes and cartridges. Data is recorded on the surface of the tape by patterns of magnetism. A *tape drive* is a device that records data on magnetic tape and retrieves data from the tape.

Most computers have several auxiliary storage devices attached at one time. For example, a computer may have four disk drives and two tape drives. Other types of auxiliary storage can also be used; however, disk and tape are the most common.

Computer hardware. The physical equipment that makes up a computer system is called *hardware.* Computer hardware consists of keyboards, printers, CRTs, card readers, CPUs, disk drives, tape drives, and other pieces of equipment. Figures 1-2, 1-3, and 1-4 show typical computers with the hardware that we have described.

Figure 1-2 shows a large computer, usually called a *mainframe* computer. The computer in the figure has several CRT terminals for input and output and a printer. Auxiliary storage consists of a number of disk drives and tape drives. A computer such as this one usually executes numerous programs concurrently and can be used by many people at one time.

The computer in Figure 1-3 is commonly called a *minicomputer.* It is smaller and slower than a mainframe computer. The computer in the figure has several terminals for input and output and uses magnetic disks for auxiliary storage. This computer can process several programs at a time, and a number of people can use it simultaneously.

Figure 1-4 shows a small computer called a *microcomputer.* This computer has a keyboard for input and a CRT and printer for output. It has two disk drives that use floppy disks for auxiliary storage. (By contrast, the computers in Figures 1-2 and 1-3 use hard disks.) Most microcomputers can only execute one program and be used by one person at a time.

Programs

A computer program is a set of instructions that tell the computer how to solve a problem. A program is prepared by a person, called a *programmer,* who is familiar with the different things a computer can do. First the programmer must understand the problem to be solved. Next he or she determines the steps the computer has to go through to solve the problem. Then the programmer prepares the instructions for the computer program that solves the problem.

To illustrate the idea of a computer program, assume that we want to use a computer to solve the problem of finding the sum of two numbers. To solve this problem, the computer must go through a sequence of steps. First the computer must get two numbers from an input device. Then the numbers must be added to find their sum. Finally, the sum must be sent to an output device, such as a printer or CRT, so that we can see the result. Thus a computer program to solve this problem would have three instructions:

1. Get two numbers.
2. Add the numbers.
3. Send the result.

The instructions would be prepared in a form the computer could understand. Once this was done, the computer could perform the instructions in the program. This process is called *executing* the program.

The remainder of this subsection explains how such a program is executed, what languages are used to prepare programs, and what types of programs are needed.

Program execution. To execute a computer program the instructions in the program must be entered into the computer using an input device. For example, the instructions can be keyed in using a keyboard or they can be punched in cards and read with a card reader. The program is then stored in the computer's internal storage.

In executing a program the computer goes through the instructions one at a time in the sequence in which they are stored. For example, assume that the program to find the sum of two numbers has been entered into the computer and is stored in internal storage. The computer brings the first instruction in the program from internal storage to the processor. Then execution would proceed as follows:

1. Get two numbers. The processor examines this instruction and issues a signal to the input device that causes two numbers (input data) to be transferred to internal storage. The second instruction is then brought to the processor.
2. Add the numbers. The processor issues a signal to internal storage that causes the two numbers to be sent to the arithmetic circuit in the processor. Then the numbers are added and the re-

sult is stored in internal storage. The last instruction is then brought to the processor.

3. Send the result. The processor issues a signal to internal storage that causes the result to be transferred to the output device. Then the output device prints or displays the output data.

Two important concepts are illustrated by this example. The first is that internal storage is used to store both program instructions and data. All instructions in the program are stored in internal storage before the program begins execution. Data is brought into internal storage as the program executes.

The second important concept is that the instructions in the program are executed in the sequence in which they are written. The sequence must be such that, when executed, the problem is correctly solved. If the instructions are out of order, the computer cannot figure out what the right sequence should be. In such a case, the computer would follow the instructions in the order in which they appeared and thus would produce an incorrect result.

Computer programming languages. A program must be written in a form that a computer can understand. Every instruction must be prepared according to specific rules. The rules form a language that we use to instruct the computer. Humans use *natural languages* such as English and Spanish to communicate with each other. To communicate with a computer we use a *computer programming language.*

To write a sentence in a natural human language, we form words and phrases from letters and other symbols. The construction of the sentence is determined by the grammar rules of the language. The meaning of the sentence depends on what words are used and how they are organized. A computer programming language also has rules that describe how to form valid instructions. These rules are called the *syntax* of the language. The meanings or effects of the instructions are called the *semantics* of the language. For example, the *syntax* of a particular computer language may say that one type of instruction has the following form:

> *variable name = arithmetic expression*

That is, the instruction consists of a *variable name* followed by an equal sign and then an *arithmetic expression*. (Of course, we must know what a variable name and an arithmetic expression are in order to complete the instruction.) The *semantics* of the language tells us that this instruction means that the value of the arithmetic expression on the right of the equal sign is to be assigned to the variable name on the left. (We will study this instruction in detail in Chapter 3.)

In this book we discuss the syntax and semantics of the FORTRAN computer programming language. FORTRAN is just one of many programming languages. In fact, there are several groups of languages and many different languages in each group.

One group of languages is called *machine language,* the language in which a computer actually does its processing. To a computer, machine language is a series of electronic impulses. A programmer expresses this language symbolically by using binary numbers, which are sequences of ones and zeros (e.g., 10010110). Each type of computer has its own machine language; because there are many different types of computers, there are many machine languages. It is important to know, however, that the machine language for any particular computer is the *only language that computer can understand. Every program for that computer must be either written in its machine language, or written in another language and then translated into its machine language.*

We think of machine language as a low-level computer language because it is the basic language of a computer. There are also many *high-level languages* for computers. These languages are called high level because they are closer to languages humans use than to machine language. FORTRAN is an example of a high-level language. In some ways FORTRAN is close to mathematical language.

Although there are many high-level languages, they all have one characteristic in common: any program written in a high-level language must first be translated into the machine language of the computer being used. Only then can the program take control of the computer. For FORTRAN as well as for most other high-level languages, the translation process is called *compilation.* The translation is performed by a special computer program called a *compiler.* First a program is written in FORTRAN. Then the compiler translates the FORTRAN program into an equivalent machine language program. Finally, the machine language program is executed. (In a later section we will discuss the process of FORTRAN compilation in more detail.)

Computer software. Hardware is the general term for the physical equipment that makes up a computer system. *Software* is the term for programs used with a computer. The software for a computer is any program that can be executed by that computer.

There are two main types of software: application software and system software. *Application software* consists of programs that are written to solve specific problems. For example, a program that prepares the payroll for a business is an application program. Similarly, programs that analyze engineering problems are examples of application software.

System software refers to general programs that are designed to make the computer easier to use. A system program does not solve a problem for a specific application but rather makes it easier to develop the necessary application program. A compiler is one example of system software; it helps prepare a high-level language application program by translating that program into machine language.

Another example of system software is an *operating system.* This system is a set of programs that controls the basic operation of the computer. For example, the operating system determines where an application program is stored in the computer's internal storage. The operating system is always in control of the computer when some other program (such as a compiler or an application program) is not executing. In a later section we will see that the operating system must be given special instructions to ensure that other programs are processed properly.

FORTRAN is used for programming application software, so all of our examples will show application programs. However, we use system software — including a compiler and an operating system — to help develop application programs.

Data

Computers process data. A computer gets data from input devices and sends data to output devices. It stores data in internal storage and in auxiliary storage. It performs computations and makes logical decisions using data. The instructions in a program tell the computer how to process the data.

We must arrange or organize data so that it is easy to process. In this subsection we explain the main concepts of data organization. We also discuss data input and output and modes of data processing.

Data organization. Data is composed of symbols or *characters*. There are three basic types of characters: *numeric characters* or *digits* (0, 1, ..., 9), *alphabetic characters* or *letters* (A, B, ..., Z), and *special characters* (comma, decimal point, equal sign, and so forth). A *blank* or *space* is considered a special character; it is often very important in data processing.

Although a single character can represent data, more often groups of characters convey information. A related group of characters, representing some unit of information, is called a *field*. For example, a person's name is a field; it is a group of characters that conveys specific information. A social security number is also a field. Similarly, a person's address, pay rate, age, and marital status are fields. A field usually contains several characters, but it can consist of a single character (such as a code field for marital status).

Fields are grouped together to provide information about a single entity such as a person or event. Such a related group of fields is called a *record*. For example, all of the fields containing information about a single employee (such as employee name, social security number, address, pay rate, and so on) form an employee information record.

Finally, all of the records that are used together for one purpose are called a *file*. For example, all of the employee information records for a business make up the employee information file. The file consists of as many records as there are employees in the business.

Data input and output. Files are used for input and output data. Input data is organized as a file; the data in the file is brought into the computer through an input device. Output data is sent to an output device; all of the output data forms a file. Data stored in auxiliary storage is also organized as a file. When the data is brought from auxiliary storage to the CPU, we think of the data as forming an *input* file. Data sent from the CPU to auxiliary storage forms an *output* file.

One way to enter input data into a computer is to type lines of data using a terminal keyboard. Such an input line is divided into a certain number of *character positions,* usually a maximum of eighty. The character positions in a line are grouped to form fields. For example, if employee data is to be entered, the first nine character positions may contain the field for the employee's social security number, the next twenty positions could contain the employee name field, and so forth. An entire line, which is a group of fields, forms the employee information record. All of the lines that are entered constitute the employee information file.

Punched cards are another way to enter input data into a computer. The most common type of card is divided vertically into eighty *columns.* A character is recorded on a card by punching a pattern of holes in a column. Punching is done on a typewriter-like device called a *keypunch.* Because there are eighty columns on a card, the maximum capacity of a card is eighty characters.

When data is recorded on a punched card, the columns of the card are grouped together to form fields. For example, employee information may be punched with the employee's social security number in the first nine columns, the employee's name in the next twenty columns, and so on. Each card contains many fields and forms a separate record. All of the card records together make up a file.

Besides keyed lines and punched cards, auxiliary storage can also be used for input files. Most often the storage that is used is magnetic disk. Data is recorded on disk by patterns of magnetism that represent characters. One character is stored after another along the surface of the disk. The characters are grouped to form fields and groups of fields form records. Each record can be thought of as the equivalent of either a keyboard line or a punched card. All of the related records stored on a disk constitute a file that can be used for input.

Output data is also organized as a file. Output can be displayed on a CRT or printed by a printer. Each line that is displayed or printed is a record containing a number of fields. All the output lines on a CRT display or in a printed report form an output file.

Magnetic disk and other types of auxiliary storage can also be used for output. Records containing any number of fields can be sent to auxiliary storage. The output file consists of all the related records stored in auxiliary storage.

To summarize, input and output data are organized as files. It does not matter where the input data comes from (terminal keyboards, punched cards, magnetic disk) or where the output data goes to (printers, CRTs, magnetic disk) the data consists of fields that are grouped into records that then form files.

Data processing modes. There are two basic ways, or modes, of processing data on a computer: batch processing and interactive processing.

In *batch processing,* all the data that is to be processed is prepared in some form understandable to the computer prior to actual processing. For example, all the data may be punched in cards or stored in an auxiliary storage file. Then the batch of data is processed by the computer and the resulting output is received in a batch. An example of batch processing is the preparation of the weekly payroll for a business. At the end of the week each employee turns in a time sheet. The information from each sheet is punched into one or more cards or entered into a disk file. Once all the data is ready, it is processed by a payroll program to produce the paychecks and other payroll information.

With *interactive processing* a human interacts with the computer through a terminal or other I/O device at the time the processing is done. Each set of data is entered directly into the computer, processed, and the output is received before the next input data is supplied. An airline reservation system is an example of this type of processing. When a customer requests a ticket for a particular flight, the reservation clerk enters the information directly into the computer using a terminal. The computer processing includes determining if a seat is available on the requested flight. The output comes back immediately to the terminal so that the customer will know whether or not the reservation is confirmed.

Sometimes the term *time-sharing* is heard instead of interactive processing. In fact, time-sharing is a mechanism that a computer uses to interact with several different computer users at one time. With time-sharing the computer allows each user a small amount of time for processing before going on to the next user. In effect, the computer shares its time among the people trying to interact with it. With time-sharing, many people using different terminals can interact with the computer at the same time.

Interactive processing does not always involve time-sharing. For example, most microcomputers have only one keyboard and CRT and can interact with just one person at a time. In this situation time-sharing is not needed.

The type of programming discussed in this book may be used for both batch processing and interactive processing. Examples of both modes of processing are given in the book. As we will see, most of the techniques and concepts are applicable to batch and interactive processing.

1-2. The FORTRAN language

FORTRAN, which stands for FORmula TRANslation, was originally designed to make it easy to solve problems involving many mathematical formulas. Because of its popularity and ease of use, FORTRAN has been applied to a wide variety of computer problem-solving situations.

FORTRAN was one of the first high-level languages. Developed originally in the mid-1950s, it has undergone several modifications and improvements. (Appendix B gives a brief history of the FORTRAN language.)

Actually, there are several different "dialects" or *versions* of FORTRAN. The versions are very similar, but features in some versions are not allowed in others. Sometimes the differences are slight, but at other times they are quite significant. In any case, the version of FORTRAN used on one computer may not be identical to the version used on other computers. As a consequence, if we prepare a FORTRAN program for one computer, we may not be able to process it on a different computer without some modification.

In this book we describe the features of a version known as FORTRAN 77. (However, we will simply refer to it as FORTRAN in the text.) FORTRAN 77 is the most recent version of FORTRAN and it is used on many different types of computers. Appendix A summarizes the characteristics of this version of the language, and Appendix B contains tables that compare the features of FORTRAN 77 and several other versions of FORTRAN.

Although FORTRAN 77 is used on different computers, some of the language's features may not be the same on all computers. To answer any questions about a particular feature, consult the appropriate reference manual to determine the actual requirements.

1-3. Basic FORTRAN concepts

Figure 1-7 shows a sample FORTRAN program as the programmer would prepare it. This program performs a simple calculation to find the total and average of three numbers. In the next section we will explain how this program works. For now we are interested only in the FORTRAN concepts that this program illustrates.

Coding

When a programmer prepares a program, he or she writes on paper the words and symbols that make up the program's instructions. This process of writing the program is called *coding,* and it is usually done on special sheets of paper called *coding forms.* The program shown in Figure 1-7 is coded on such forms.

Notice that the coding form is divided into lines and that each line has eighty spaces. These spaces correspond to the character positions in a terminal line or to the columns on a punched card. In FORTRAN coding, the spaces in a line are always called *columns.* Each line of the coding form is either keyed on a terminal or punched in a card. The characters must be keyed or punched in the same positions in which they are written on the coding form.

When coding a program, it is important to distinguish between easily confused characters. For example, the letter O and the number 0 are often indistiguishable when hand written. To differentiate these and other characters,

Figure 1-7. Coding for a sample FORTRAN program

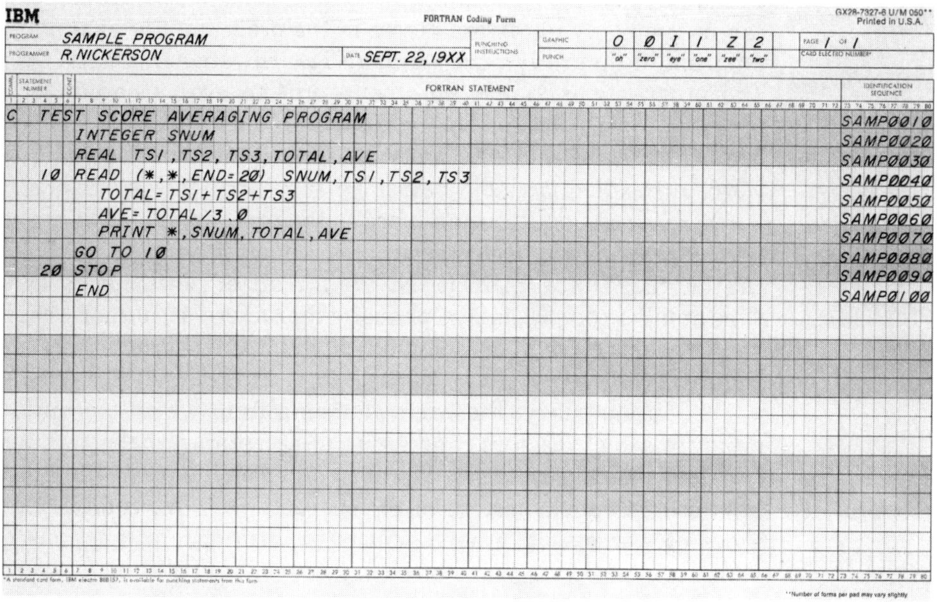
IBM FORTRAN Coding Form GX28-7327-6 U/M 050** Printed in U.S.A.

PROGRAM: SAMPLE PROGRAM
PROGRAMMER: R. NICKERSON DATE: SEPT. 22, 19XX
PUNCHING INSTRUCTIONS — GRAPHIC: O Ø I 1 Z 2; PUNCH: "oh" "zero" "eye" "one" "zee" "two"
PAGE 1 OF 1 CARD ELECTRO NUMBER*

```
C     TEST SCORE AVERAGING PROGRAM                                      SAMP0010
      INTEGER SNUM                                                      SAMP0020
      REAL TS1,TS2,TS3,TOTAL,AVE                                        SAMP0030
   10 READ (*,*,END=20) SNUM,TS1,TS2,TS3                                SAMP0040
        TOTAL=TS1+TS2+TS3                                               SAMP0050
        AVE=TOTAL/3.0                                                   SAMP0060
        PRINT *,SNUM,TOTAL,AVE                                          SAMP0070
      GO TO 10                                                          SAMP0080
   20 STOP                                                              SAMP0090
      END                                                               SAMP0100
```

*A standard card form, IBM electro 888157, is available for punching statements from this form.
**Number of forms per pad may vary slightly

the sample program in Figure 1-7 uses the conventions shown on the top right-hand part of the form.

FORTRAN statements

Each instruction in a FORTRAN program is called a *statement.* A FORTRAN statement tells the computer something about the processing that is to be done in the program. In the sample program in Figure 1-7 each line (except the first) is a statement. (We will see later that statements can be more than one line in length.) A FORTRAN *program* is a sequence of FORTRAN statements that describe some computing process. To prepare a FORTRAN program, the programmer must know how to form statements in the FORTRAN language and what each statement means.

There are many types of statements in FORTRAN. However, all statements fall into one of two broad classes — executable statements and nonexecutable statements. *Executable* statements cause the computer to perform some action. For example, a statement that tells the computer to get some input data from the input device is an executable statement because it causes the computer to do something. *Nonexecutable* statements do not cause the computer to perform an action, but rather they describe some characteristic of the program or of the data processed by the program. For example, a statement that describes the fields in an input record is a nonexecutable statement. In later chapters we will explain the various FORTRAN statements; some will be executable and some will be nonexecutable.

All FORTRAN statements are composed of words and symbols. Some words have special meaning in the language. These are called *keywords* and can be used only in certain places in the program. For example, in the sample program in Figure 1-7, the words INTEGER, READ, and STOP are keywords. The programmer makes up other words to use as names for data that the program must process. The words TOTAL and AVE in the sample program are examples of this. (Actually, as we will see in Chapter 2, these types of words are called variable names.)

The symbols that are used in the program and that make up the words in the language must come from a set of characters that is acceptable in the language. For FORTRAN, the character set consists of 49 characters. This number comprises 26 alphabetic characters, 10 numeric characters, and 13 special characters. The complete FORTRAN character set is presented in Figure 1-8.

In summary, the basic elements from which we build a FORTRAN program are characters. The group of acceptable characters in the language is called the character set. We form other elements in the language, such as keywords, from characters in the character set. We combine keywords, other types of words, and other symbols to form the instructions of FORTRAN, which are called statements. Then a sequence of statements forms a program.

The coding format

When we code a FORTRAN program, we write each statement on the coding form in a special format. Recall that a line on the coding form is divided into eighty spaces (called columns). These correspond to the eighty character positions

Figure 1-8. The FORTRAN character set

Alphabetic characters (letters):
ABCDEFGHIJKLMNOPQRSTUVWXYZ

Numeric characters (digits):
0123456789

Special characters:
    Blank (space)
= Equals
+ Plus
− Minus
* Asterisk
/ Slash
(Left parenthesis
) Right parenthesis
, Comma
. Decimal point
$ Currency symbol
' Apostrophe
: Colon

in a terminal line or the eighty columns of a punched card. The rules that describe the coding format specify in which columns the statements of the program may appear.

Each FORTRAN statement must be coded between columns 7 and 72 of the coding form. A statement must not begin before column 7 and must not extend beyond column 72. The statement may start in column 7 or it may be indented. We will see that indenting some statements can make the program easier to read. Blank spaces may be used freely to spread out the parts of the statement. This spacing is often done to improve the readability of the program.

No part of a statement may go beyond column 72. If a statement is too long to fit on one line, it must be continued onto the next line. The continued part must also be written between columns 7 and 72. There may be as many as nineteen successive continuation lines beyond the initial line of a statement. For each continuation line we must put a character in column 6. The character that is used may be any symbol in the character set except a blank or a zero. For example, Figure 1-9 shows a FORTRAN statement that is coded on three lines. The first line of the statement does not have a character in column 6 (a zero may be used for this initial line). The first continuation line has a 1 in column 6 and the second continuation line has a 2 in column 6. Any character other than a zero or blank may be used to indicate continuation, but a common practice is to number the continuation lines. Notice in Figure 1-9 that the coding on each line does not extend all the way to column 72. A statement may be broken at almost any point and continued on the next line or it may be written out to column 72 before continuing.

Any statement in a program may be given a number between 1 and 99999 called a *statement number*. The statement number must appear in columns 1 through 5. For example, in the sample program in Figure 1-7 two statements are numbered. These are the statements with the numbers 10 and 20. Although any statement in the program may be numbered, unnecessary statement numbers can make the program hard to read. However, as we will see, certain statements must be numbered. Statement numbers need not be in sequence, and no two statements can have the same number.

In addition to statements, we can put explanatory comments in a program. These comments are often used to describe the processing done in the program to make the program easier to understand. To put a comment in a program, the letter C or an asterisk (*) is placed in column 1. Then the

Figure 1-9. Continuing a statement

```
 900  FORMAT ('/            COURSE GRADE REPORT'/
     1          'ØSTUDENT          AVERAGE       LETTER'/
     2          ' NUMBER            SCORE        GRADE'/)
```

programmer may write anything he or she wishes on the line. The computer treats any line with a C or an asterisk in column 1 as a comment and not a statement. Comments may appear anywhere in the program before the last line. In the sample program in Figure 1-7, the first line is a comment.

Columns 73 through 80 are ignored by the computer and may contain any characters or may be left blank. Most often these columns are used for identifying information about the program or to number the lines for sequencing purposes. However, their use is optional. The sample program in Figure 1-8 shows how these columns can be used to identify and sequence a program.

1-4. A sample program

We can now begin to understand what the sample program in Figure 1-7 does. The purpose of this program is to find the total and average of three numbers. There are several sets of such numbers and each set represents one student's scores on three tests. The input data consists of each student's identification number and the three test scores. The program gets the student's identification number and scores from an input device, adds the scores to find the total, calculates the average by dividing the total by three, and sends the results of the calculations to an output device. It then repeats this sequence for the next student. The program stops when there is no more input data to process.

Figure 1-10 shows the input and output for this program. Part (a) of this figure gives the input data. Each line contains one student's identification number and three test scores. The corresponding output is shown in part (b). Each line in the output contains the identification number, total score, and average score. (The output from this program may appear differently on other computers.)

The first line in the sample program in Figure 1-7 is a comment that explains the purpose of the program. The next two lines are statements that

Figure 1-10. Input and output for the sample program

```
1465,100,87,95
2108,82,71,79
2462,89,81,82
3750,94,89,77
```

(a) Input data

```
1465 282. 94.
2108 232. 77.33333
2462 252. 84.
3750 260. 86.66667
```

(b) Output

specify names that will be used for data in the program. These are called the INTEGER and REAL statements, which we will discuss in detail in Chapter 2. The specified names are SNUM (the student's identification number); TS1, TS2, and TS3 (the three test scores); TOTAL (the total score); and AVE (the average).

Following the INTEGER and REAL statements is a READ statement. This statement instructs the computer to get (we usually say *read*) data from an input device and to store the data in the computer's internal storage. The data that is read is referred to by the names SNUM, TS1, TS2, and TS3. Notice that the READ statement does not give the actual values that are read. These values are the student's identification number and test scores that are to be averaged; they are input data and are read as the result of the READ statement. We will discuss the READ statement in Chapter 2.

Next in the program come two statements that perform the calculations. These are called arithmetic assignment statements, and we will explain them in detail in Chapter 3. The first arithmetic assignment statement instructs the computer to add the three test scores to find the total. The next statement tells the computer to divide the just-calculated total by three to get the average.

After these calculations are performed, the next statement, which is called a PRINT statement, tells the computer to send (we usually say *write, print,* or *display*) the results of the processing to an output device. The student's identification number and the just-calculated values of the total and average are printed. We will discuss the PRINT statement in Chapter 2.

Following the PRINT statement is a GO TO statement. This statement tells the computer to go back to the statement numbered 10 (the READ statement) and start processing over again. Thus another set of input data is read, a new total and average are calculated, and more output is printed. We will describe the GO TO statement in Chapter 2.

The sequence in this program is repeated over and over again until the end of the input data is reached. At that time, the code END = 20 in the READ statement tells the computer to go to the statement numbered 20. This is the STOP statement, which tells the computer to stop executing the program. Following the STOP statement is the END statement. The END statement indicates that no more statements are in the program. We will discuss the STOP and END statements in Chapter 2.

The INTEGER and REAL statements are nonexecutable statements because they only specify information about the program. As we will see, these statements must appear at the beginning of the program. The other statements are executable statements and are performed in the order in which they are written. This order must represent the correct sequence for solving the problem. For example, the two arithmetic assignment statements cannot be reversed because the total is used in the calculation of the average and therefore must be calculated first.

To understand this program in detail the programmer must know the rules for forming FORTRAN statements (that is, the *syntax* of FORTRAN), the meaning or effect of each statement (that is, the *semantics*), and the logic necessary to solve a problem using a FORTRAN program. Beginning with Chapter 2 we will explain these in detail. In the remainder of this chapter we cover the background necessary to prepare and execute a FORTRAN program on a computer.

1-5. Running a FORTRAN program

The program in Figure 1-7 is a complete FORTRAN program and can be processed or *run* on a computer. Running a program involves entering the program into the computer, compiling the program, and executing the program. In this section we describe how this is done. We first review program compilation and execution, and then we explain two approaches to program and data entry: keyboard input and punched card input. Finally, we discuss error detection.

Program compilation and execution

A program written in a high-level language such as FORTRAN must be translated into machine language before it can be executed on a computer. The translation process, called *compilation,* is done by a program called a *compiler.* After the program is compiled, it can be executed. The process of compilation and execution is summarized in Figure 1-11.

The FORTRAN program as it is written by the programmer is called the *source program.* The source program may be entered into the computer by keying it at a terminal, or it may be punched in cards and read by a card reader. To translate the source program into machine language, the FORTRAN compiler, which is stored in auxiliary storage, is brought into the computer's internal storage. The compiler takes control of the computer and translates the source program into machine language. The resulting machine-language equivalent of the source program is called the *object program.* The compiler may also produce some output, including a printout or CRT display of the FORTRAN program called the *source program listing* (see Figure 1-12) and a list of any errors in the program. (We will discuss errors later.)

After compilation, the object program is stored in auxiliary storage. The object program can be retained for future processing or it can be executed immediately. When the object program is to be executed, it is first brought into the computer's internal storage. The program then takes control of the computer and performs the tasks specified by the programmer. This often involves reading input data (which may come from a terminal, auxiliary storage, or a card reader), using the data in calculations and for decision making, and producing output (which may go to a terminal, printer, or auxiliary storage).

Although the translation of a FORTRAN program into an object program may seem complicated, to a large extent it is handled automatically by the

Figure 1-11. FORTRAN compilation and execution

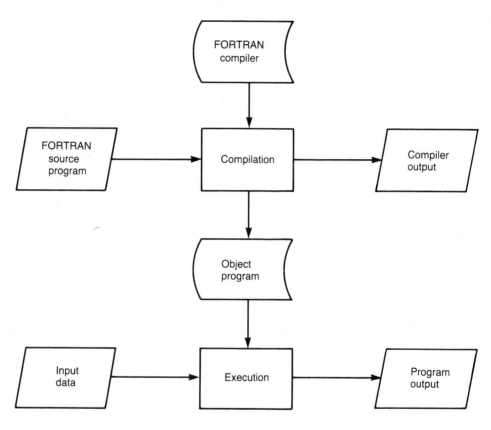

computer. Most programmers never see their object programs. The programmer prepares the FORTRAN source program, and the computer system does everything else. However, it is important to remember that the computer does not execute the source program; rather, it executes the object program that results from the compilation process.

Figure 1-12. The source program listing for the sample program

```
C   TEST SCORE AVERAGING PROGRAM                      SAMP0010
        INTEGER SNUM                                  SAMP0020
        REAL TS1,TS2,TS3,TOTAL,AVE                    SAMP0030
     10 READ (*,*,END=20) SNUM,TS1,TS2,TS3            SAMP0040
        TOTAL=TS1+TS2+TS3                             SAMP0050
        AVE=TOTAL/3.0                                 SAMP0060
        PRINT *,SNUM,TOTAL,AVE                        SAMP0070
        GO TO 10                                      SAMP0080
     20 STOP                                          SAMP0090
        END                                           SAMP0100
```

Keyboard input*

With many computers, the program and data are entered using a terminal keyboard. Before the program and data can be entered, the programmer must activate the terminal through a procedure that is usually called "logging on." The actual procedure depends on the computer being used. (With microcomputers this step is not necessary.) After the programmer has logged on, he or she can type in various instructions called *system commands*. The system commands tell the operating system what to do. (Recall that the operating system is the set of programs that control the basic operation of the computer.) For example, different system commands are used to tell the operating system to compile a program and to execute a program. System commands vary from one computer to another and are not part of the FORTRAN language.

There are two main variations on running a FORTRAN program using keyboard input. They depend on whether the program involves batch processing or interactive processing during execution. Some situations involve both interactive and batch processing in the same program. Here we describe the variations separately; other situations are just combinations of these.

Batch execution. Figure 1-13 summarizes the process of running a FORTRAN program using keyboard input and printer output with batch execution. The first step is to key in the source program. To do this, another program, called a *text editor* or *word processor,* is often used. The program is activated by typing a system command such as the word EDIT or WP. Then the source program is keyed in line for line exactly as it is coded. Each character in the source program must be keyed in at the same character position as it appears on the coding form. The RETURN key on the keyboard must be pressed after each line is typed. If a typing error is made, the text editor or word processor has special instructions for making corrections easily. To check the typing, the source program can be displayed or printed at the terminal with a system command such as the word LIST. After the source program is keyed in, it is usually stored in auxiliary storage with a system command such as the word SAVE. Storing the source program makes it available for future processing.

In addition to the source program, the input data must be keyed in. Keying the input data may also be accomplished with the aid of the text editor or word processor. Input data must be entered in a special format that depends on the program. For example, the sample program in Figure 1-7 requires input data in the form shown in Figure 1-10(a). This data would be entered by typing each line exactly as it appears in the figure. After each line is typed, the RETURN key must be pressed. Once all the data is keyed in, it is stored in auxiliary storage separately from the source program.

Whether the source program or the input data is entered first is not important. Both must be entered, however, before the program can be executed. To execute the program, the source program must first be compiled. A special

---

* This subsection can be skipped if punched card input is used.

Figure 1-13. Running a FORTRAN program using keyboard input and printer output with batch execution

Step 1: Enter the source program.

Step 2: Enter the input data.

Step 3: Compile and execute the program.

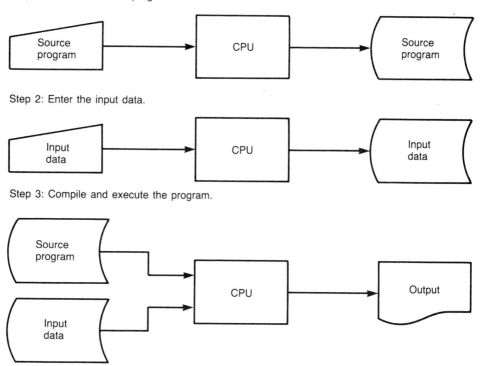

system command is used to tell the operating system to get the FORTRAN compiler. The compiler is brought into the computer's internal storage. Reading the source program from auxiliary storage, the compiler translates it into a machine-language object program. A source program listing may also be printed.

After the program is compiled, the object program can be executed. Another system command is used to initiate this phase. (Sometimes a single command tells the computer both to compile and to execute the program.) During execution, the instructions in the program are performed. Some program instructions cause input data to be read from auxiliary storage. Other instructions cause the results of processing to be printed. (In some cases the output is sent to auxiliary storage rather than being printed.) Execution continues until the program tells the computer to stop.

Interactive execution. When execution involves interactive processing, the input data is not entered until the program is executed. Figure 1-14 summarizes the process of running a FORTRAN program using keyboard input and CRT output with interactive execution. As before, the first step is to key in the

Figure 1-14. Running a FORTRAN program using keyboard input and CRT output with interactive execution

Step 1: Enter the source program.

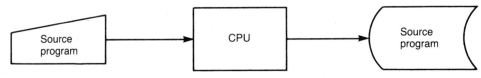

Step 2: Compile and execute the program.

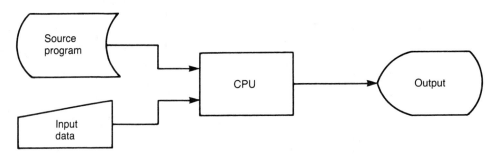

source program and store it in auxiliary storage. A text editor or word processor is usually used for entering the source program. However, the input data is not entered before the program is compiled and executed. Rather, as the program is executing, each line of input data is typed when requested by the program. (A text editor or word processor is *not* used for entering the input data.) After each set of input is entered, the corresponding output is displayed. For example, Figure 1-15 shows how the input and output for the sample program in Figure 1-7 would appear on a CRT. The lines following the question marks are the input; the other lines are the output. After the last question mark, a special key or combination of keys is pressed to cause the program to end. (We will discuss interactive input and output in more detail in Chapter 2.)

Figure 1-15. Interactive input and output for the sample program

```
? 1465,100,87,95
  1465 282. 94.
? 2108,82,71,79
  2108 232. 77.33333
? 2462,89,81,82
  2462 252. 84.
? 3750,94,89,77
  3750 260. 86.66667
?
```

Punched card input*

Figure 1-16 summarizes the process of running a FORTRAN program using punched card input and printer output. The first step is to punch the source program into cards using a keypunch. One card is punched for each line on the coding form, and the columns on the coding form correspond to the columns on the card. The program must be punched exactly as it is coded; any punching errors must be corrected before processing the program on the computer. The cards must be kept in the same order as the coded program. The source program punched into cards is often called the *source deck*.

In addition to the source deck, an *input data deck* must be prepared. Data is punched into cards in a special format that depends on the program. For example, the sample program in Figure 1-7 requires input data in the form shown in Figure 1-10(a). Each line in this figure would be punched in a separate card exactly as it appears.

* This subsection can be skipped if keyboard input is used.

Figure 1-16. Running a FORTRAN program using punched card input and printer output

Step 1: Punch the source program.

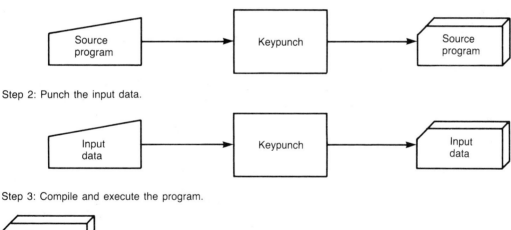

Step 2: Punch the input data.

Step 3: Compile and execute the program.

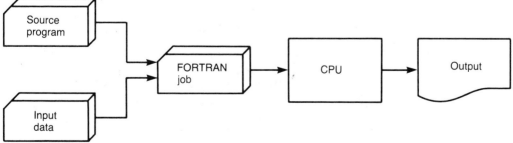

Whether the source program or the input data is punched first is not important. After the decks are prepared, they are combined to form a FORTRAN *job*. The job, consisting of both the program and the data, is run on the computer to produce the desired output.

Actually, a FORTRAN job consists of more than just the source program and the input data. Other cards, called *control records,* are required. The control records contain instructions that tell the operating system how the program is to be processed. (Recall that the operating system is the set of programs that control the basic operation of the computer.) The instructions in the control records are written in a language called *job control language* or *JCL* that is understood by the operating system. Job control language varies from one type of computer to another and is not part of the FORTRAN language. Usually, a group of control records appears at the beginning of the job, then the source program, then another group of control records, then the input data, and then a group of control records at the end of the job. (See Figure 1-17.)

The function of the control records is related to the compilation and execution of the program. Usually, the first group of control records informs the operating system that this is the beginning of a job and instructs it to get the FORTRAN compiler. The compiler is brought into the computer's internal storage. Reading the source program from auxiliary storage, the compiler translates it into a machine-language object program. In addition, the source program listing is printed. The compiler stops when it reaches the end of the source program; then the object program is ready for execution.

The group of control records following the source program tells the operating system to bring the object program into internal storage and begin executing it. During execution, the instructions in the program are performed. Because some program instructions cause input data to be read, the next group of cards in the job must contain the input data. Other program instructions cause the results of processing to be printed. This is the output from the program.

Figure 1-17. Deck setup for running a FORTRAN program using punched cards

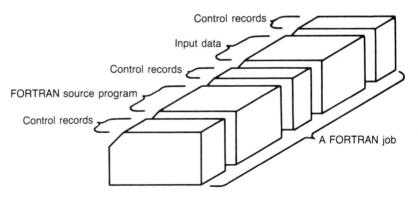

Control records

Input data

Control records

FORTRAN source program

Control records

A FORTRAN job

When the program is finished executing, the final group of control records tells the operating system that the job is finished and instructs it to go on to the next job.

Error detection

In our description of the running of a FORTRAN program, we assumed that the program contained no errors. In fact, one of the biggest problems that a programmer faces is the detection and correction of errors. More often than not, the program does not complete its run successfully. It is the programmer's responsibility to locate and correct any errors in the program.

Errors may be detected in the processing of the program at three times: during compilation, during execution, and after execution. The computer can detect errors that occur during the first two times, but the programmer must detect any errors during the third.

The computer discovers *compilation errors* during the compilation of the program. These are usually errors that the programmer has made in the use of the language and are called *syntax errors*. For example, spelling a keyword incorrectly is a syntax error. Whenever the compiler detects a compilation error, it prints or displays a message that describes the error and indicates the error's location in the program. Often the compiler finds many compilation errors in a program. Usually, all error messages appear following the source program listing that the compiler produces. Even though the compiler has found an error, it usually cannot correct the error and the program will not execute. The programmer must correct any compilation errors that are detected.

If the program has no serious compilation errors, it can be executed by the computer. During execution, other errors may appear. These are called *execution errors*. For example, an attempt to divide a number by zero causes an execution error. Whenever an execution error is detected, the computer prints or displays an error code or error message and stops executing the program. The programmer must correct the error.

The final type of error is detected only after successful compilation and execution of the program. If the output from the program does not agree with what is expected, there is a *logic error* in the program. For example, if, in the sample program in Figure 1-7, the first arithmetic assignment statement had been incorrectly coded as

```
TOTAL=TS1-TS2-TS3
```

then no compilation or execution error would be detected. The final output would be incorrect, however, because the total of three numbers is found by adding the numbers, not by subtracting them. This error is in the logic of the program. The computer cannot detect such an error because it does not know what the logic of the program should be.

It is the programmer's responsibility to detect logic errors in the program. This is done by making up input data to test the program. The programmer figures out what output the program should produce when it is executed with this test data. Then the actual output from running the program with the test data is compared with the expected output. Any discrepancy indicates an error that must be corrected. This procedure is called *program testing,* and we will have more to say about it in Chapter 7.

Any error in a computer program is called a *bug,* and the process of locating and correcting bugs in a program is called *debugging.* Only after a program has been debugged completely can the programmer be reasonably sure that the program is correct.

1-6. A preview of the programming process

In the process of preparing a computer program to solve a particular problem, the programmer performs a number of tasks. One thing that must be done is to code the program. As we have seen, coding involves writing the instructions in the program. Before coding can begin, however, the programmer must first understand the problem to be solved and then plan the solution procedure.

Understanding the problem involves determining the requirements of the problem and deciding how they can be met. The programmer must know what the program is meant to do: what output must be produced and what computations must be performed. The programmer must also decide what resources are available (including input) to meet these requirements.

Once the problem is understood, the programmer can begin to design a program to solve it. The sequence of steps necessary to solve the problem must be carefully planned. This program-designing activity does *not* involve coding the program. Before coding can start, the programmer must develop the solution procedure completely. This solution procedure is called an *algorithm.*

In general, an algorithm is a set of steps that, if carried out, results in the solution of a problem. An algorithm can be represented in many forms. For example, an algorithm may be written in English, with mathematical notation, or using a diagram. The following is an example of an English-like algorithm that corresponds to the sample program in Figure 1-7:

> Repeat the following until there is no more input data.
> Read a student's identification number and test scores.
> Compute the total and average of the test scores.
> Print the student's identification number, total, and average.

Notice that the algorithm expresses the sequence of steps that solves the problem. (A tool that is sometimes used to show an algorithm is a flowchart. Flowcharts are discussed in Appendix D.) The objective during the program-designing activity is to develop an algorithm that solves the desired problem.

After the program has been designed, it can be coded. The programmer uses his or her knowledge of the computer language, an understanding of the problem to be solved, and the program design determined previously. With this background, the programmer writes the program to solve the problem.

The next step is to test the program by running it on the computer with test data. The objective is to locate errors in the program. Testing the program in this manner will not necessarily find all the errors, but usually it will point out any serious problems. The actual process of determining the correctness of a program involves much more than just testing it on a computer. A program is correct because it makes sense logically. The programmer tries to ensure it makes sense as he or she plans and codes the program.

Finally, the programming process is completed by bringing together all the material that describes the program, called *documenting* the program. The result of this activity is the program's *documentation*. Included in the documentation is the source program listing (usually containing many comments) and any descriptions of how the program works. The purpose of documentation is to enable other programmers to understand how the program functions. Often it is necessary to return to the program after a period of time to make corrections or changes. Adequate documentation makes it much easier to understand how a program works.

Throughout much of this book we discuss the program-designing and coding activities of the programming process. However, remember that this is only part of the entire process. Chapter 7 will cover the other activities in detail.

Review questions

1. What are the five basic components of a computer?
2. Data to be processed by a computer is called _____; the result produced by a computer is called _____.
3. Name two input devices and two output devices.
4. The unit of a computer that does the actual computing or processing is the _____.
5. What units of the computer are found in the CPU?
6. What is the difference in function between internal storage and auxiliary storage?
7. Name two common forms of auxiliary storage.
8. What is a computer program?
9. What happens in the CPU during the execution of a program?
10. The rules that describe how the instructions of a computer programming language are formed are called the _____ of the language. The meanings of the instructions in a computer programming language are called the _____ of the language.
11. What is the difference between a machine-language program and a high-level language program?
12. Translation of a program written in a high-level language into machine language is called _____.

13. What is the difference between application software and system software?
14. What is an operating system?
15. What are the three types of characters that make up computer data?
16. Explain the difference between fields, records, and files.
17. Auxiliary storage is sometimes thought of as an input/output device. Why?
18. Explain the difference between batch processing and interactive processing. Give an example of each.
19. What is time-sharing?
20. Can a program that is written in FORTRAN be processed on different types of computers? Explain.
21. The process of writing on paper the instructions in a program is called _____.
22. Each instruction in a FORTRAN program is called a _____.
23. What is the difference between executable statements and nonexecutable statements?
24. What are keywords?
25. List the special characters in the FORTRAN character set.
26. In what columns of a coding form must a FORTRAN statement be coded?
27. How is a statement that is longer than one line coded in FORTRAN?
28. Must every statement in a FORTRAN program have a number?
29. How are comments placed in a program?
30. What is the difference between a source program and an object program?
31. What is the function of system commands or control records (JCL)? Are they part of the FORTRAN language?
32. Explain the difference between compilation errors, execution errors, and logic errors.
33. Explain the process of program testing.
34. An error in a program is called _____.
35. What are the five activities in the programming process?

Computer exercises

1. Investigate the computer that you will use to process programs that you prepare. Who manufactured the computer and what is its model number? What input and output devices are available? What type of auxiliary storage does it use? Is it a mainframe, mini, or microcomputer? What operating system does it use? Is it a batch processing system or an interactive system? (Some computers process in both a batch mode and an interactive mode.) What version of FORTRAN will you be using? What computer languages other than FORTRAN are available on the computer?

2. The program shown in Figure 1-7 is complete and can be run on a computer. Doing so will help you to become familiar with the structure of FORTRAN, the coding format, system commands or control records, and other aspects of running a program.

   If keyboard (terminal) input is used, key the source program exactly as it is coded in Figure 1-7. To key the program, a text editor or word processor may have to be used. List the program to get a source program listing. If batch execution is used, enter the input data exactly as shown in Figure 1-10(a). If interactive execution is used, the input data is entered later during execution as shown in Figure 1-15. Next, compile the program. If any compilation errors occur, they are probably the result of keying mistakes. Correct any errors and compile the program again. Once the program compiles without any errors, execute the program. Check the output to be sure that it is correct. (See Figure 1-10(b) or 1-15. Your output may be in a slightly different format.)

If punched card input is used, punch the source deck with the program exactly as it is coded in Figure 1-7. Then punch an input data deck with the data exactly as shown in Figure 1-10(a). Combine the source deck and the input data deck with the proper control records. The general deck setup is shown in Figure 1-17, but the specific control records depend on the computer being used. Run the program on the computer and get the printed output. Any errors that occur are probably the result of punching mistakes. Correct any errors and rerun the program. Get the source program listing and the output. Check the output to be sure it is correct. [See Figure 1-10(b). The format of your output may be slightly different.]

Chapter 2

Basic input and output programming

When we write a computer program to solve a problem, we prepare a sequence of instructions for the computer to follow. Many different sequences can be used, depending on the problem to be solved. However, one *pattern* appears over and over again. This pattern is simply

$$input \longrightarrow process \longrightarrow output$$

That is, first the computer reads some input data to be used in the problem solution. Then the processing and computation necessary to solve the problem using the input data is done. Finally, the computer writes the output data that represents the results of the processing.

For example, in Chapter 1 we saw a sample program that computes the total and average of three test scores. The first step in this program was to read the three test scores as input data. Then the processing involved calculating the total and average of the input data. Finally, the results were written out.

Many other patterns appear in computer programs, but this is one of the most common. In addition, the input, process, and output steps may each be quite complex, especially the process step.

In this chapter we discuss the input and output steps in this pattern. We describe the FORTRAN statements necessary to do basic input/output (I/O) programming. With this background you should be able to write programs that only do input and output. These steps are a necessary part of almost all programs. In the chapters that follow we will discuss the various types of processing activities that can be done and how they are coded in FORTRAN.

2-1. Introduction to FORTRAN input and output programming

To program a computer for input and output operations, we need three things:

1. A way to instruct the computer to transfer data from an input device to the CPU; that is, an *input* instruction.

2. A way to instruct the computer to transfer data from the CPU to an output device; that is, an *output* instruction.
3. A way to tell the computer the arrangement or *format* of the input and output data.

In FORTRAN there are two approaches for accomplishing these things. The main difference between the approaches involves the third item. In one approach, called *list-directed* (or *format-free*) *I/O,* the format of the input and output data is preset outside of the program. The input data must be prepared in a prescribed fashion, and the output data always appears in a particular form. In the other approach, called *formatted I/O,* the format of the input and output data is specified in the program. In this case, statements in the program indicate the arrangement of the input and output data.

List-directed I/O is easier to use for simple programs. However, because the input and output formats are preset, the programmer has very little control over how the input is read or the output is written. With formatted I/O the programmer has complete control over the input and output formats. Because of this, the programming is more complex than with list-directed I/O.

In this chapter we cover only list-directed input and output. We use this form of I/O in programs in the next few chapters. In Chapter 6 we explain formatted I/O and use it and list-directed I/O in subsequent chapters.*

To illustrate list-directed input consider the following statement:

```
READ *,A,B,I,J
```

(In writing a FORTRAN statement without a coding form, we assume that the statement begins in column 7 or beyond and that a statement number, if one exists, falls anywhere in columns 1–5.) List-directed input is accomplished by the READ statement with an asterisk (*). The asterisk is important because it indicates that the input is list-directed input and not formatted. The effect of the READ statement is to read data from an input device and to store the data in the computer's internal storage. In the example just given, the letters A, B, I, and J are symbols that tell the computer where in internal storage the input data is to be stored.

List-directed output is accomplished by the PRINT statement with an asterisk, as the following illustrates:

```
PRINT *,X,K,Y
```

Again the asterisk indicates that the output is list-directed and not formatted. The effect of the PRINT statement is to write data using an output device. The symbols X, K, and Y in the example tell the computer what data is to be written.

---

* List-directed I/O is not available in all versions of FORTRAN. If this is the case for the computer you are using, read this chapter for general concepts. Then go directly to Chapter 6 for an explanation of formatted I/O. The intervening chapters do not have to be read first.

We can see from these examples that list-directed I/O statements are fairly simple. However, before we can describe these statements in detail, we need to understand how data is stored in the computer and identified in a program.

2-2. Internal storage and FORTRAN data

To understand the effect of the FORTRAN input and output statements, we must be familiar with the internal storage component of the computer. In this section we explain the basic structure of internal storage and show the relationship to FORTRAN. We also cover two important statements — the INTEGER and REAL statements — that are used in almost all programs.

Internal storage

A computer's internal storage is a complex device composed of a large number of electronic parts. The various parts of the internal storage are grouped to form *storage locations*. One way of thinking of a computer's internal storage is in terms of a large number of boxes similar to post office boxes. Figure 2-1 illustrates this idea. Each box represents a storage location. In this example there are twelve storage locations, and in each location the computer can store only one number. Once data is placed in a storage location, it remains there for the computer to use. The data can be used over and over again without destroying it. However, if new data is placed in the same storage location, the old data is destroyed.

The computer keeps track of storage locations by giving each location

Figure 2-1. Internal storage

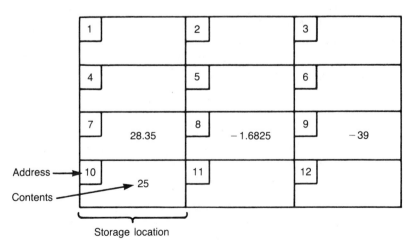

Storage location

a unique number called an *address*. In Figure 2-1 the address of each storage location is shown in the small box. Post office boxes have addresses to distinguish them. To find a specific post office box, we search through the boxes until the one with the desired address is located. Similarly, the computer identifies a particular storage location by means of its address.

It is important not to confuse a storage address with the contents of the storage location. A storage location contains data which can change from time to time. However, the address of each location is fixed. The computer uses the address to find the storage location. Once the storage location is found, the computer can put data into the location or retrieve data from the location. For example, in Figure 2-1, if the computer is told to retrieve the contents of storage location 10, it gets the number 25. Note that the number 25 is still in location 10; in retrieving data the computer does not destroy the original data. If the computer is told to put the number 35 in location 10, the value that is in this location is destroyed and replaced by the new data.

FORTRAN variables

In the simplified internal storage illustrated in Figure 2-1, there are only twelve storage locations. In actual computers there are hundreds of thousands and even millions of storage locations. For example, one common computer has about 500,000 locations in its internal storage. Other computers have several million storage locations. To keep track of that many storage locations and their addresses would be quite a complex task for a programmer. Fortunately, FORTRAN does not require the programmer to use addresses to identify locations in storage. Instead, symbolic names are used. For example, in the sample program from the previous chapter, the symbolic names TS1 and TOTAL identify two storage locations.

It is not necessary to give a symbolic name to every location in the computer's internal storage; it is only necessary to name those locations that the program uses. In fact, the programmer does not even have to worry about which storage locations and addresses are being used. The programmer merely uses a symbolic name, and the computer automatically reserves a storage location for that name and keeps track of its address. Most FORTRAN programmers think in terms of data and assign symbolic names to data used in the program. Thus the name TOTAL stands for the value that is found by adding the data referred to by the names TS1, TS2, and TS3.

A *variable* in FORTRAN is a value that is identified in a program by a symbolic name. The name that is used is called a *variable name*. Because the variable name does not specify exactly what the value is but rather specifies where it is stored, the quantity may change or vary from time to time in a program. Thus the name TOTAL may have a particular value at one point in a program and then another value later in the program. Any time that a variable name is used (for example, for output), the current value of that variable name is retrieved by the computer (without destroying it).

Any time that a value is assigned to a variable name (for example, through an input operation), the old value of that variable name is destroyed and the new value replaces it.

Figure 2-2 illustrates this concept with the variable names A, B, I, and J. Each name identifies a storage location in the computer's internal storage that contains a variable value. For example, the name A refers to location 7, which contains the value 28.35. Similarly, the other variable names refer to other storage locations. If the variable name A is used in the program, the computer goes to location 7 and retrieves the value 28.35. If a new value is assigned to A, then 28.35 is destroyed and replaced by the new value.

Variable names

It is the programmer's responsibility to select names for all variables used in a program; however, the selections must follow certain rules. In FORTRAN a variable name may be one to six characters in length. The name may contain any alphabetic or numeric characters but may not contain any special characters. The first character of the name must always be an alphabetic character. For example, the following variable names are valid:

```
TOTAL
  A
  K
EV86D
  K3
  ZZZ
```

The following variable names are invalid for the reasons given:

```
2M35      (first character is not alphabetic)
M93LZTS   (contains more than six characters)
X.95Z     (contains a special character)
```

Note that it is not just the first character that defines the variable name; it is all of the characters that make the name unique. Thus K and K3 are two separate variable names that refer to different storage locations in the computer's internal storage.

In writing a program the programmer should attempt to select meaningful variable names. This procedure helps the programmer, or anyone else who examines the program, to remember the function of each variable name.

Figure 2-2. Variable names and internal storage

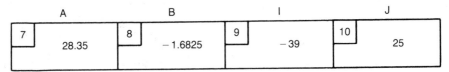

For example, in the sample program from the previous chapter the variable name TS1 stood for the score on test 1, TS2 identified the score on test 2, and TS3 stood for the score on test 3. Similarly, the name TOTAL identified the total of the test scores, and AVE stood for their average. In a business application, PRICE might stand for the unit price of an item, QTY the quantity purchased, and COST the total cost of the order. In a program that analyzes the results of a sociological questionnaire, the variable names AGE, STATUS, and SEX might identify a respondent's age, marital status, and sex, respectively. In a scientific program, PRESS might stand for the pressure and TEMP for the temperature.

FORTRAN data types

In FORTRAN, there are two basic types of numeric data — integer and real. *Integer data,* or simply *integers,* are written without decimal points; that is, as whole numbers. For example, 25 and −38 are integers. *Real data,* or just *reals,* are written with decimal points. For example, 25.0, −6.2, and .083 are real data. Integers are sometimes called *fixed-point data,* and reals are often referred to as *floating-point data.*

The distinction between integers and reals may seem trivial, but in FORTRAN it is very important. The distinction is made because the data is stored in different forms in the computer's internal storage. Integers are stored similarly to the way that they are commonly written. For example, the number 25 occupies a storage location and is stored as shown in Figure 2-3. (The actual representation of an integer is in the binary number system, but the principle is the same. Binary representation of data is discussed in Appendix E.)

Real data is stored in a form similar to scientific notation. This is known as *floating-point notation* and involves rewriting the number as a fraction times some power of ten. For example, 28.35 is written as $.2835 \times 10^2$ and .058 is $.58 \times 10^{-1}$. To remember a number in this form, we only need to remember the fraction and the exponent. For example, assume that we know that the fraction is 2835 and the exponent is 2. The decimal point is always just to the left of the fraction, and the exponent is a power of ten. Hence we know that the number must be $.2835 \times 10^2$ or 28.35. In floating-point notation this approach is used, and only the fraction and exponent are stored. In the computer the value 28.35 is stored as shown in Figure 2-4. (Appendix E discusses floating-point notation in more detail.)

It is not usually important in FORTRAN to know precisely the internal

Figure 2-3. Internal storage representation of an integer value

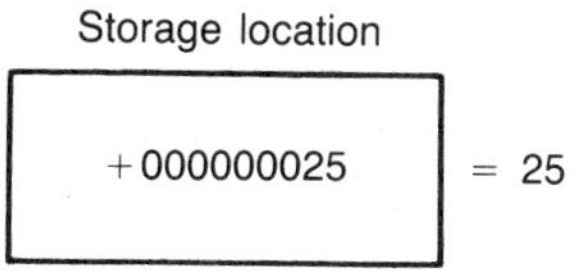

Storage location

| +000000025 | = 25 |

Figure 2-4. Internal storage representation of a real value

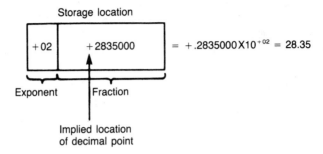

representation of integers and reals. However, it *is* important to remember that there is a difference and that the difference is significant. The difference is most important for variable names.

Data type of a variable name

A FORTRAN variable name can refer to a storage location that contains an integer or a real value. However, the computer must know what type of data is being identified by the variable name. In addition, once the computer has been told that a particular variable name refers to integer data, that same name cannot be used for real data. Similarly, a real variable name cannot be used for integer data.

In FORTRAN there are two ways of telling the computer to what type of data a variable name refers: *explicit typing* and *implicit typing*.

Explicit typing. With explicit typing the data type of each variable name is specified in an INTEGER or REAL statement. These statements have the following syntax:

> INTEGER *list*
> REAL *list*
>
> where *list* is a list of variable names
> separated by commas.

For example, the following statement identifies B, C, and VALUE as integer variable names:

    INTEGER B,C,VALUE

Similarly, the following statement declares that names ITEM and K refer to real data:

    REAL ITEM,K

Other examples of the INTEGER and REAL statements were shown in the sample program discussed in Chapter 1. (See Figure 1-12.)

There can be as many INTEGER and REAL statements in a program as we wish. For example, the following four statements could be in one program:

```
INTEGER A,B,C
REAL X,Y
REAL J
INTEGER L,M
```

In this example, two INTEGER statements declare five variable names and two REAL statements specify three variable names. The order of these statements is not important. Alternatively, the same thing could be accomplished with one REAL and one INTEGER statement as follows:

```
REAL X,Y,J
INTEGER L,M,A,B,C
```

The only restriction is that once a variable name has been listed in one of these statements, it cannot be listed again.

The INTEGER and REAL statements are called *type statements*. We will describe several other type statements in FORTRAN later. All type statements are in a broad classification of FORTRAN statements known as *specification statements*. In general, specification statements provide information about the data to be processed by a program. They are nonexecutable statements. The INTEGER and REAL statements specify that certain variable names refer to integer and real data. Such information is needed by the computer before the rest of the program is compiled. Hence all INTEGER and REAL statements, and, in fact, all specification statements, must appear at the beginning of the program, before the first executable statement.

Implicit typing. With implicit typing, type statements are not used. Rather, the type of numeric data to which a variable name refers is indicated by the first letter of the variable name. If the first letter is an I, J, K, L, M, or N, the variable name identifies an integer value. If the first letter is any other letter of the alphabet, the name refers to a real value. For example, using implicit typing the following are integer variable names:

```
I
J
K3
NUM
```

The following are real variable names using implicit typing:

```
A
X
AMT
PRICE
EV86D
```

(There is a statement, called the IMPLICIT statement, that can be used to specify different groups of letters for implicit typing. We do not cover this statement in this book.)

Use of explicit and implicit typing. Explicit and implicit typing can be used in the same program. Any variable names listed in type statements are *explicitly* typed. All other variable names are *implicitly* typed. For example, assume a program includes the following type statements:

```
INTEGER A,B
REAL I
```

In addition, assume the program uses the variable names X, Y, and J. Then, in this program, A, B, and J are integer variable names, and I, X, and Y are real variable names.

Notice that explicit typing overrides implicit typing. Thus, in this example, even though A and B are implicitly typed as real variable names, they would be integer variable names because they are listed in an INTEGER statement. Similarly, I, which is implicitly an integer variable name, would be a real variable name because it is listed in a REAL statement. All other variable names, however, are implicitly typed.

Although type statements can be used to override implicit typing of variable names, they may also list names of the same implicit type as indicated by the statement. Thus the following examples are valid type statements:

```
REAL AMT,M,L,C
INTEGER VOL,POP,I,J
```

Although AMT and C in the first statement are implicitly real variable names, they may be included in the REAL statement. Similarly, in the INTEGER statement, variable names I and J, implicitly typed as integer, are included.

We can see that mixing explicit and implicit typing can lead to much confusion. In general, one approach or the other should be selected for a program. Either *all* variable names should be explicitly listed in type statements or *all* variable names should be implicitly typed. Usually, the explicit typing approach is preferred because this allows the programmer to keep a complete list of all variable names and their types in the program. Because of this we will use explicit typing in all sample programs.

Limitations on data values

The FORTRAN language does not limit the size of numbers that can be assigned to variable names. However, computers have limited capacity, and therefore there are practical maximum and minimum values that can be stored. These limits depend on the type of computer being used.

For integer data, the maximum value on one common computer is $+2,147,483,647$ and the minimum value is $-2,147,483,648$. These seemingly arbitrary numbers result from the binary representation of integers in the computer. (See Appendix E.) Any integer value between these limits can be assigned to an integer variable name; however, if an attempt is made to store a value outside of this range, the result is unknown.

With real data the limits are not expressed as easily. Because a real value is stored in floating-point notation, limitations must be given for the exponent and for the fraction. On one common computer, the maximum exponent is approximately 75 and the minimum is about -78. The fraction can have approximately seven digits at most. These values are approximate because the internal representation is in the binary mode. (See Appendix E.) For example, 583079000000000.00 is an acceptable real number. In floating-point notation this is interpreted as $.583079 \times 10^{15}$. Notice that there are fewer than seven digits in the fraction, and the exponent is between -78 and 75. However, 39025672.53 is not acceptable. In floating-point form this value is interpreted as $.3902567253 \times 10^8$. Although the exponent is within the required range, the fraction contains more than seven digits; hence, the number cannot be stored.

It is important to know the limitations for the computer being used. Any input data that is read must be within the limits for integer or real data, as the case may be. Similarly, no attempt should be made to compute a value that violates the restrictions because no output can be produced that is not within the limits.

2-3. List-directed input and output

As we saw in Section 2-1, list-directed I/O uses the READ statement for input and the PRINT statement for output. These statements are executable statements that cause the computer to perform list-directed input or output when executed. In this section we describe these statements and explain their use.

List-directed input

The syntax of the READ statement for list-directed input is as follows:

```
READ *,list
```

where *list* is a list of variable names
separated by commas.

The asterisk indicates that list-directed input is to be used. The computer assumes that the input data comes from a standard input device such as a terminal keyboard or card reader. Auxiliary storage can also be used for list-directed input.

The list of variable names, called an *I/O list,* indicates how many values are to be read and the names that are used to refer to the values in the program. The computer automatically assigns a storage location to each variable name. When the READ statement is executed, one value for each variable name in the list is read and stored in its respective location. As an example, consider the following READ statement:

```
READ *,NUM,P,AZ
```

Three variable names are in the I/O list in this statement. Assume that the first is integer and the other two are real. Consequently three values are read with this statement: the first is an integer and the others are reals. If the three input values are 158, -17.63, and .0035, respectively, then after execution of this statement the value of NUM is 158, P is -17.63, and AZ is .0035. Notice in the READ statement that there is a comma after the asterisk and that the variable names in the list are separated by commas, but that there is no punctuation after the last variable name.

Execution of a READ statement causes one record from a file to be read. Recall from Chapter 1 that a file contains many records, and each record consists of a number of fields. With list-directed input we do not use the term *field* for the data in a record. Rather we simply refer to the data as values. (As we will see in Chapter 6, we use the term *field* with formatted I/O.) In preparing the input data the values in a record must be separated by commas or blanks. For example, an input record for the previous READ statement could have data recorded as follows:

```
158,-17.63,.0035
```

There must be a comma or a blank between each input value. Blanks can be used before or after the comma, or several blanks can be left between each value without a comma. In addition, extra blanks can appear at the beginning or end of the record. However, a blank or a comma must never be put in the middle of a value. As another example, this same data could be recorded as follows:

```
158 -17.63 ,  .0035
```

With interactive processing, a line representing the record is keyed directly into the computer in the required format. Sometimes with an interactive system, the computer displays a question mark and skips a space on the CRT when a READ statement is encountered. Then the data in the record is keyed after the question mark and the RETURN key is pressed at the end of the line. Thus the previous example might appear on the CRT as follows:

```
? 158,-17.63,.0035
```

If processing is done in a batch mode, the input data may come from auxiliary storage or from a punched card. With auxiliary storage input, each record in the file must have data recorded in the required format. With punched card input, each card is an input record with data punched in the proper format. For example, the data from the previous READ statement could be recorded in an auxiliary storage record or punched in a card as follows:

```
158,-17.63,.0035
```

If the value to be read is integer, it must not have a decimal point. A real value requires a decimal point unless the decimal point is on the right in which case it is optional. If the value is negative, a minus sign is required on the left. For a positive value, a plus sign is not needed but one may be used.

It is important that the type of the variable name and the type of the data correspond. If the variable name is integer, the value read must be integer; if the name is real, the input data must be real. Thus in the previous example, the first input value is integer and the next two are real, corresponding with the order of the variable names in the READ statement list.

As another example consider the following READ statement:

```
READ *,X,Y,K,L
```

In this example four variable names are included in the I/O list. Assume that the first two are real and the last two are integer. The following input data could be read by this statement:

```
4.53 62 18 -37
```

Blanks instead of commas are used in this example to separate values. After the READ statement reads this record, the value of X is 4.53, Y is 62., K is 18, and L is −37. Notice that the value for Y in the input data does not have a decimal point even though Y is a real variable name. This is because the decimal point, if included, would be on the right and thus it is optional.

Each READ statement causes the computer to begin reading a new record. With interactive processing, each READ statement displays a question mark and accepts an input line from the keyboard. For batch processing using auxiliary storage input, each READ statement reads a new record from an auxiliary storage file. With punched card input, a new card is read when a READ statement is executed. Thus the following statements cause two records to be read:

```
READ *,X,Y
READ *,K,L
```

The first record contains the values of X and Y; the second contains data for K and L.

If there are more values in a record than there are variable names in the READ statement list, any excess data is ignored. Thus if there are six values and only four variable names, the last two values are not read. If there are fewer values in a record than there are variable names, the computer continues to read from the next record. For example, if there are four variable names in the READ statement list and two values in each of two input records, the computer reads the data in the first record and assigns it to the first two variable names. Then the data from the second record is read and assigned to the third and fourth variable names.

List-directed output

For list-directed output, the PRINT statement is used. The syntax of this statement is as follows:

PRINT *,list

where *list* is a list of variable names
separated by commas.

The asterisk indicates list-directed output. The computer assumes a standard output device such as a printer or CRT. Auxiliary storage can also be used for list-directed output. When using the PRINT statement, we usually say the data is "printed" no matter what form the output takes.

The I/O list gives the variable names of the values to be printed. When the PRINT statement is executed, the computer prints the current value of each variable name in the list. For example, the following PRINT statement causes the computer to print two values:

PRINT *,X,I

In this example X is real and I is integer. Thus the first value printed is real and the second value is integer. If X is 4.53 and I is -37 in the computer's internal storage, execution of this statement causes the computer to print these two values. Note that commas must be used after the asterisk and between the variable names.

The way the output is printed depends on the computer being used. On some computers the values are printed close together with just a single blank space between the values. For example, the previous PRINT statement might result in the following output:

4.53 −37

On other computers the output is spread out with several blank spaces between the values and extra zeros to the right of the decimal point in a real value. This is shown in the following example:

4.530000   −37

In any case, the values are always printed left to right in the order in which the corresponding variable names appear in the PRINT statement. Thus, in the example, the value of X is printed first and then the value of I is printed. The values are always separated by one or more blank spaces to make the output readable. If the number is negative, a minus sign is printed; otherwise no sign appears.

Depending on the computer, the output may be printed on paper or displayed on a CRT. The output format is the same for both output devices. In general, execution of a PRINT statement causes one record to be printed in a file. The file may consist of printed output or a CRT display. Each record is a line that is printed or displayed. It is also possible to "print" the output in an auxiliary storage file. One record is put in the file each time a PRINT statement is executed. This allows the output to be saved for future processing. (We will discuss auxiliary storage input and output in detail in Chapter 12.)

An integer is always printed as it would normally be written, as in the earlier examples. No decimal point is printed with an integer. The output format for a real number depends on its size. If the value requires relatively few print positions, as in the previous examples, the number is printed as we would normally write it with a decimal point. As we have mentioned, with some computers extra zeros are added on the right of a real number so that all real numbers have the same number of digits. With other computers this is not the case. Note that if extra zeros are not added on the right and the number has no digits to the right of the decimal point, a decimal point is still printed.

For real numbers that require many print positions, the output appears in exponential notation. (Some versions of FORTRAN print all real output in exponential notation.) In this notation the number appears in a form somewhat similar to floating-point notation. The output consists of a real number with one digit to the left of the decimal point and several digits to the right followed by the letter E and then an exponent. For example, assume that the value of the real variable named S is 583079000000000.0. If the computer executes the PRINT statement

```
PRINT *,S
```

then the output would appear as follows:

```
5.830790E+14
```

This output is interpreted as 5.830790×10^{14}. If the value to be printed is very small, the exponent is negative. For example, if the value of the real variable named T is .00000000038045, then execution of the statement

```
PRINT *,T
```

results in the following output:

```
3.804500E-10
```

This output is interpreted as 3.804500×10^{-10}.

It is easy to convert exponential notation to our usual way of writing numbers by shifting the decimal point. If the exponent is positive, the decimal point should be shifted to the right the number of places given by the exponent. For a negative exponent, the decimal point should be shifted to the left. Thus, in the first example, the decimal point should be shifted fourteen places to the right to get the equivalent value. In the second example, the decimal point should be shifted ten places to the left.

Each PRINT statement causes the computer to start a new record, which for printer and CRT output means a new line. For example, the following statements cause two lines to be printed:

```
PRINT *,A,B,C
PRINT *,X,Y
```

The first line is printed with the values of A, B, and C. The second line contains the values of X and Y. The lines are single-spaced.

If more values are to be printed than can fit on a line, the computer automatically continues on to the next line. Thus if only eight values can be printed on a line and there are twelve variable names in the PRINT statement list, the values of the first eight variable names are printed on the first line and the last four values appear on the second line. The next PRINT statement starts printing on the third line.

List-directed character output

Most programs not only print numeric values but also print words and phrases that describe the output. Then a person reading the output will know what the data represents. Sometimes a word or phrase is printed followed by the results of a computation. At other times, headings are printed above the output. In addition, phrases are sometimes printed at the end of the output. Many variations are used to make the output more readable. In general, words and phrases printed this way are called *character output*. In this subsection we describe the FORTRAN elements necessary to produce character output using list-directed I/O.

Character output is produced by enclosing the words to be printed in apostrophes. The combination of words and apostrophes is called a *character constant*. The character constant is then included in the I/O list of the PRINT statement. When the PRINT statement is executed, the character constant is printed without the apostrophes. The values of any variable names in the I/O list are also printed.

For example, consider the following PRINT statement:

```
PRINT *,'THE SOLUTION IS ',X
```

The character constant in this statement is 'THE SOLUTION IS '. The comma separating the constant and the variable name X is required. Execution of this statement causes the phrase in the character constant to be printed followed by the value of X. If X is a real variable name with a value of

125.25, the output appears as follows:

```
THE SOLUTION IS 125.25
```

Notice that the apostrophes are not printed; only the characters between the apostrophes appear in the output. (The actual format of the output depends on the computer being used. With some computers, as in this example, an extra blank space may be required in the character constant to separate the output. With other computers this space may not be needed.)

There may be as many character constants in a PRINT statement as are needed. For example, the following statement includes two character constants:

```
PRINT *,' AMOUNT = ',AMT,' COUNT = ',KT
```

If AMT (real) is 2.58 and KT (integer) is -10, the output from execution of this statement is as follows:

```
AMOUNT = 2.58 COUNT = -10
```

A character constant by itself can be printed without printing the value of a variable name. The following statement illustrates this:

```
PRINT *,'STATISTICAL DATA'
```

The effect of executing this statement is that the only output that is printed is the characters in the character constant. This technique is often used to print headings to describe the output that follows.

Any characters may appear in a character constant. Letters, digits, and special characters, including blanks, are all permitted. If an apostrophe is to be printed, two consecutive apostrophes must be used in the character constant. For example, to print the word JOHN'S we must use the character constant 'JOHN''S'. The two consecutive apostrophes indicate that one apostrophe is to appear in that position in the actual output.

It is also possible to use a PRINT statement with nothing in its I/O list as in the following example:

```
PRINT *
```

The effect of this statement is to skip a line of output. This technique is often used to leave a blank line in a printout or on a CRT and thus to double space the output.

2-4. Writing complete FORTRAN programs

A FORTRAN program is a sequence of FORTRAN statements. Some statements in a program are nonexecutable and others are executable. The computer uses the nonexecutable statements to determine certain characteristics of the program. The computer performs the executable statements in the order in which they appear in the program. Although only the nonexecutable INTEGER and REAL statements and the executable READ and PRINT statements have been considered so far, it is possible (with the addition of two simple statements) to write complete programs.

As a first example, consider the simple problem of reading a single real value and then printing the value. The following statements accomplish this task:

```
REAL A
READ *,A
PRINT *,A
```

The REAL statement specifies that A is a real variable name. As we know, this is a type statement that must appear at the beginning of the program before the first executable statement. The READ and PRINT statements are executed in the sequence in which they are written in the program. The effect is shown in Figure 2-5. First, the READ statement causes the computer to read one number and to store it in the storage location identified by the variable name A. Then the PRINT statement causes the computer to print the value of A. Notice that the variable name used in the PRINT statement is the same as the name in the READ statement. It would not make sense to read a value for A and then print, for example, the value of B.

Termination statements

This simple program has two executable statements in it. But what does the computer do after it executes the PRINT statement? One rule in programming is that the computer must be told everything, including when to stop. For this purpose, FORTRAN uses the STOP statement. The syntax of this statement is as follows:

```
STOP
```

The statement is just the keyword STOP. Its function is to cause the computer to cease processing the present program and to go on to the next program.

Figure 2-5. Effect of execution of a simple program

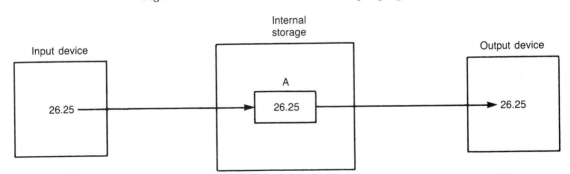

In addition to the STOP statement, every FORTRAN program must have an END statement as the last statement in the program. The syntax of the END statement is as follows:

```
END
```

Whereas the STOP statement specifies the *logical* end of the program during execution, the END statement signals the *physical* end of the program for the FORTRAN compiler. During translation of the FORTRAN source program into machine language, the compiler processes each statement in turn until it encounters the END statement. At that point the compiler knows that there are no more source statements; compilation is terminated and execution of the program can begin. (It is possible not to use a STOP statement in which case execution terminates when the END statement is reached. However, most programmers include a STOP statement to mark the logical end of the program, thus distinguishing it from the physical end.)

Illustrative programs

To complete the previous example, we add a STOP and an END statement. The result is the following complete FORTRAN program:

```
REAL A
READ *,A
PRINT *,A
STOP
END
```

The computer first reads a value for A, then prints A, and finally stops execution. As another example, the following program reads and prints two integer values:

```
INTEGER J,K
READ *,J,K
PRINT *,J,K
STOP
END
```

Finally, the following program reads and prints two real values and one integer:

```
REAL P,Q
INTEGER M
READ *,P,Q,M
PRINT *,P,Q,M
STOP
END
```

Notice in all of these examples that the type statements to specify the variable names are at the beginning of the program, the executable statements are next, and the END statement is the last statement in the program.

The order of the executable statements in a program is important. The computer executes the statements in the order in which they are written. Thus the statements must be logically arranged. For example, the following program is incorrect:

```
REAL A
PRINT *,A
READ *,A
STOP
END
```

In this example the value of A is printed before it is read, which does not make any sense.

For each input record, a separate READ statement is used. In addition, each output record requires a separate PRINT statement. For example, the following program reads two records and prints two lines:

```
REAL A,B
READ *,A
READ *,B
PRINT *,A
PRINT *,B
STOP
END
```

In this example, the first input record contains the value of A and the second record contains the value of B. The values of A and B are then printed on two successive lines. The effect of execution of this program is shown in Figure 2-6.

A program need not read all input before printing some of the output. For example, the following program reads one record and prints a line, then reads a second record and prints another line:

```
REAL A,B
READ *,A
PRINT *,A
READ *,B
PRINT *,B
STOP
END
```

The effect of execution is the same as in the previous example. (See Figure 2-6.)

A variable name may be reused after its value is no longer needed in the program. For example, the previous program could be coded as follows:

Figure 2-6. Effect of execution of a sample program

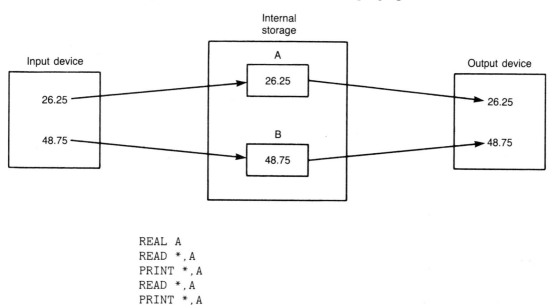

```
REAL A
READ *,A
PRINT *,A
READ *,A
PRINT *,A
STOP
END
```

In this case, the variable named A is used for both input values. The first READ and PRINT statements cause the first input record to be read, a value to be assigned to A, and that value to be printed. When the second READ and PRINT statements are executed, a second record is read. The previous value of A is destroyed and replaced with the new data and the new value is printed. This approach is acceptable in this program because the previous value has already been printed. Figure 2-7 shows what happens during execution of this program.

In a more complicated situation it may be necessary to print the output in a different order than the input. The following program reads two records and produces three lines of output:

```
INTEGER I,J,K
REAL X,Y,Z
READ *,I,J,K
READ *,X,Y,Z
PRINT *,I,X
PRINT *,J,Y
PRINT *,K,Z
STOP
END
```

The first input record contains three integer values, and the second record

Figure 2-7. Effect of execution of a sample program

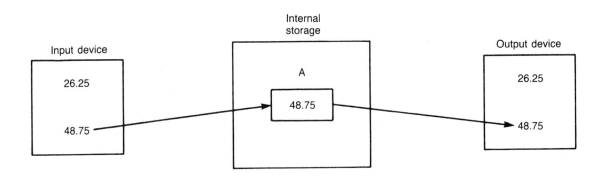

(a) Execution of first READ and PRINT statements

(b) Execution of second READ and PRINT statements

contains three reals. The output is printed with one integer and one real per line.

As another example, assume that the test score data for two students is recorded in two input records. Each record contains one student's identification number followed by his or her scores on two tests. It is necessary to list the data for the students. Each line of output should contain the data for one student. A program to accomplish this is shown in Figure 2-8(a). In this program, the variable named ID refers to the student's identification number and SCR1 and SCR2 are for the student's two test scores. Input data for the program is given in Figure 2-8(b). The output that results from running the program with this input data is shown in Figure 2-8(c). (The actual way in which the output is printed for this program may be different on other computers.)

Figure 2-8. An illustrative program

```
C  PROGRAM TO LIST TEST SCORES
      INTEGER ID
      REAL SCR1,SCR2
      READ *,ID,SCR1,SCR2
      PRINT *,ID,SCR1,SCR2
      READ *,ID,SCR1,SCR2
      PRINT *,ID,SCR1,SCR2
      STOP
      END
```

(a) The program

```
12841,98,83
20853,92,85
```

(b) Input data

```
12841 98. 83.
20853 92. 85.
```

(c) Output

Batch vs. interactive I/O

The way in which input and output is performed is different with batch processing than it is with interactive processing. Examine the two sample programs shown in Figure 2-9. (These two programs are the same as two we discussed in the previous subsection.) With batch processing, the input and output would be the same for these programs. Both programs would read

Figure 2-9. Two sample programs

```
REAL A,B
READ *,A
READ *,B
PRINT *,A
PRINT *,B
STOP
END
```

(a)

```
REAL A,B
READ *,A
PRINT *,A
READ *,B
PRINT *,B
STOP
END
```

(b)

two input records and print two lines. Figure 2-6 shows the effect of executing these programs when processed in a batch mode.

If interactive processing is used, the input and output would be different for these two programs. Figure 2-10 shows the difference. With interactive processing, each READ statement causes the computer to display a question mark on the CRT and wait for a line to be keyed. Each PRINT statement prints a line of output on the CRT. The program in Figure 2-9(a) has two READ statements followed by two PRINT statements. Thus when this program is executed, two lines must be keyed in and then two lines are printed. (See Figure 2-10(a).) The program in Figure 2-9(b) has a READ statement, then a PRINT statement, and then another set of READ and PRINT statements. With this program one line must be keyed in, then a line is printed, then another line is entered, and a final line is printed. [See Figure 2-10(b).]

Figure 2-10. Effect of interactive execution of two sample programs

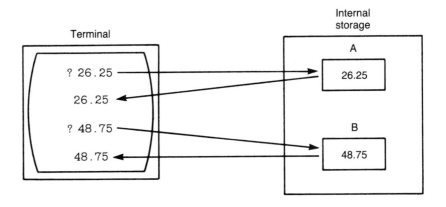

(a) Execution of the program in Figure 2-9(a)

(b) Execution of the program in Figure 2-9(b)

Usually with our illustrative programs we will show the input and the output separately. (See, for example, Figure 2-8.) This form is characteristic of batch processing. Most of these programs can also be executed in an interactive mode. We will leave it to the reader to figure out what the input and output would look like when the programs are executed interactively.

Programs with character output

So far our sample programs have printed only numeric output. As we know from Section 2-3, character output can also be printed. Character output is used for phrases that describe the output, for headings at the beginning of the output, and for other types of descriptive output.

Figure 2-11(a) shows a program that prints a descriptive phrase with each numeric value. This program is similar to the one in Figure 2-8(a) that lists student identification numbers and test scores. Notice that each PRINT statement includes appropriate phrases in the form of character constants. Figures 2-11(b) and 2-11(c) show sample input data and output for this program. (The actual format of the output for this program may be different on other computers.)

Headings can be printed by putting a PRINT statement with the desired heading before the other PRINT statements in the program. Figure 2-12 illustrates the technique with a variation of the previous example. In this program the heading 'TEST SCORE SUMMARY' is printed before any input data is read. Note that the character constant with this heading has blank spaces at the beginning so that the heading is centered above the other

Figure 2-11. An illustrative program with character output

```
C   PROGRAM TO LIST TEST SCORES
        INTEGER ID
        REAL SCR1,SCR2
        READ *,ID,SCR1,SCR2
        PRINT *,'ID = ',ID,'  1ST SCORE = ',SCR1,'  2ND SCORE = ',SCR2
        READ *,ID,SCR1,SCR2
        PRINT *,'ID = ',ID,'  1ST SCORE = ',SCR1,'  2ND SCORE = ',SCR2
        STOP
        END
```

(a) The program

```
12841,98,83
20853,92,85
```

(b) Input data

```
ID = 12841  1ST SCORE = 98.  2ND SCORE = 83.
ID = 20853  1ST SCORE = 92.  2ND SCORE = 85.
```

(c) Output

Figure 2-12. An illustrative program with character output

```
C  PROGRAM TO LIST TEST SCORES
      INTEGER ID
      REAL SCR1,SCR2
      PRINT *,'            TEST SCORE SUMMARY'
      PRINT *
      READ *,ID,SCR1,SCR2
      PRINT *,'ID = ',ID,'  1ST SCORE = ',SCR1,'  2ND SCORE = ',SCR2
      READ *,ID,SCR1,SCR2
      PRINT *,'ID = ',ID,'  1ST SCORE = ',SCR1,'  2ND SCORE = ',SCR2
      STOP
      END
```

(a) The program

```
12841,98,83
20853,92,85
```

(b) Input data

```
          TEST SCORE SUMMARY

ID = 12841  1ST SCORE = 98.  2ND SCORE = 83.
ID = 20853  1ST SCORE = 92.  2ND SCORE = 85.
```

(c) Output

output. (The number of spaces needed may differ on other computers.) Then the data is read and the other output printed. The statement

```
PRINT *
```

immediately after the PRINT statement with the heading causes a line to be skipped after the heading is printed. Thus there is a double space between the heading and the other output. [See Figure 2-12(c).] (We can use the technique described here to print headings above columns of output. However, it is often difficult to line up the headings properly because of variations in the format of list-directed output.)

Sometimes character output is printed after all other output has been printed. This is done to mark the end of the output. (Sometimes this type of output is called a *report footing*.) Figure 2-13 shows how the previous program can be modified to include such output. Two PRINT statements have been added to the program just before the STOP statement. The first causes a line to be skipped; the second prints the final line of output.

Interactive programs

Character output can help make a program that involves interactive processing easier to use. One way of doing this is to display an explanation of what input is required before the input is entered. Such an explanation is called a *prompt*. (The question mark that is displayed during interactive input is

Figure 2-13. An illustrative program with character output

```
C   PROGRAM TO LIST TEST SCORES
        INTEGER ID
        REAL SCR1,SCR2
        PRINT *,'           TEST SCORE SUMMARY'
        PRINT *
        READ *,ID,SCR1,SCR2
        PRINT *,'ID = ',ID,'  1ST SCORE = ',SCR1,'  2ND SCORE = ',SCR2
        READ *,ID,SCR1,SCR2
        PRINT *,'ID = ',ID,'  1ST SCORE = ',SCR1,'  2ND SCORE = ',SCR2
        PRINT *
        PRINT *,'END OF OUTPUT'
        STOP
        END
```

(a) The program

```
12841,98,83
20853,92,85
```

(b) Input data

```
         TEST SCORE SUMMARY

ID = 12841  1ST SCORE = 98.  2ND SCORE = 83.
ID = 20853  1ST SCORE = 92.  2ND SCORE = 85.

END OF OUTPUT
```

(c) Output

also called a prompt.) By displaying prompts at appropriate times during the execution of the program, the terminal operator is guided through the processing of the program.

As an example, Figure 2-14(a) shows a program that displays prompts for the input data. This program contains two READ statements, one to read a student's identification number and the other to read two test scores. Before each READ statement is a PRINT statement that displays a prompt. Each prompt gives clear instructions to the terminal operator about what input data should be entered. After the data has been read, the output is displayed with appropriate descriptive phrases. Figure 2-14(b) shows the interactive input and output for this program.

The program in Figure 2-14(a) is an example of a simple interactive program. Most interactive programs are much more complex. In Chapter 6 we will discuss interactive program design in more detail.

2-5. Program repetition

The programs in the previous section illustrate the use of input and output operations. Each program follows the same general pattern. That is, each program reads some input data, prints some output, and then stops. One

Figure 2-14. An interactive program

```
C  INTERACTIVE PROGRAM TO DISPLAY TEST SCORES
      INTEGER ID
      REAL SCR1,SCR2
      PRINT *,'ENTER STUDENT IDENTIFICATION NUMBER'
      READ *,ID
      PRINT *,'ENTER TWO TEST SCORES SEPARATED BY A COMMA'
      READ *,SCR1,SCR2
      PRINT *
      PRINT *
      PRINT *,'  TEST SCORE SUMMARY'
      PRINT *
      PRINT *,'  STUDENT ID:  ',ID
      PRINT *,'  1ST SCORE:   ',SCR1
      PRINT *,'  2ND SCORE:   ',SCR2
      STOP
      END
```

(a) The program

```
ENTER STUDENT IDENTIFICATION NUMBER
? 12841
ENTER TWO TEST SCORES SEPARATED BY A COMMA
? 98,83


  TEST SCORE SUMMARY

  STUDENT ID:  12841
  1ST SCORE:   98.
  2ND SCORE:   83.
```

(b) Interactive input and output

problem with this pattern is that if a lot of data is to be read and printed, the program becomes very large. For example, in the sample program in Figure 2-8 there are two READ statements, one for each input record. If there is more input data, additional READ statements are required. Thus if there are 10 or 100 or 1000 input records, an equal number of READ statements is needed. (For this program, an equal number of PRINT statements is also needed.) Obviously the size of the program gets out of hand very quickly.

In the sample program in Figure 2-8, each input record has the same type of data in the same format. That is, even though the numbers are different, the first value is always the student's identification number and the next two values are always test scores. In addition, the format of the output is the same for each line. Thus we could use just one READ statement and one PRINT statement if we had some way of causing the computer to execute these statements more than once. In fact, as we will see, we want to be able to execute the statements in a program repeatedly until there is no more input data.

One way to execute the statements in a FORTRAN program more

than once is by using a GO TO statement. The syntax of the GO TO statement is as follows:

```
GO TO n

where n is a statement number.
```

The statement number in the GO TO statement must correspond with an executable statement in the program. (Recall that any statement in a program can have a number.) For example, the following is a valid GO TO statement:

```
GO TO 50
```

The effect of the GO TO statement is to cause the computer to interrupt the normal sequential execution of the program and to continue execution at the statement whose number is given in the GO TO statement. This process of breaking execution of the program at a point and continuing elsewhere is called *branching* or *transferring control*. Thus the GO TO statement just given causes the computer to branch to statement 50.

It is possible to branch from a point in a program either in the direction of the end of the program (i.e., "down" the program) or toward the beginning of the program (i.e., "up" the program). Later we will see examples of branching down the program. For now we will concentrate on branching up.

We can modify the program in Figure 2-8 to use a GO TO statement to branch up the program and thus to execute the statements in the program repeatedly. The following is the modified program:

```
      INTEGER ID
      REAL SCR1,SCR2
   10 READ *,ID,SCR1,SCR2
         PRINT *,ID,SCR1,SCR2
      GO TO 10
      END
```

In this program the READ statement is numbered 10. Execution of the READ statement causes values to be read for ID, SCR1, and SCR2. Then the PRINT statement prints the output. Next the GO TO statement causes the computer to branch to the statement numbered 10 and to continue execution with that statement. Because statement 10 is the READ statement, the computer reads another input record. The data that is read is assigned to ID, SCR1, and SCR2, replacing the previous values that were read. Execution of the PRINT statement causes the current values of these variables to be printed on the next line. Then the GO TO statement causes the computer to repeat the program, reading another record, printing another line, and so forth. Notice that the GO TO statement causes the computer to branch to the READ statement, not to the type statements. The type statements are nonexecutable, and although they can have statement numbers, their numbers cannot be used in GO TO statements.

The statements in this program are executed over and over again. In general, a group of statements that is repeatedly executed is called a *loop*. The process of repeatedly executing the statements in a loop is called *looping*. In this example, the loop consists of the READ statement through the GO TO statement. There can be any number of statements in a loop. Usually the statements in a loop, except the first and the last, are indented to show clearly the loop in the program. We will have more to say about loops and looping in Chapter 5.

In this program there is no STOP statement. In fact, the GO TO statement is in the place where we would expect the STOP statement. Thus this program appears to have no way to terminate execution. In fact, the program will continue to execute as long as input data is supplied. The program will read an input record and print a line until there is no more input. On most computers an execution error will occur after all data is read. We need a way to end the loop when there is no more input data. There are several ways to accomplish this, but for now we will use a form of the READ statement. The syntax of this READ statement is as follows:

```
READ (*,*,END=n) list
```

where *n* is a statement number.
    list is a list of variable names
      separated by commas.

Notice that the syntax requires two asterisks and the element END = followed by a statement number, all separated by commas and enclosed in parentheses. For example, the following is a valid READ statement of this form:

```
READ (*,*,END=100) A,B,C
```

The first asterisk indicates that input is to come from a standard input device such as a terminal keyboard or a card reader or from auxiliary storage. The second asterisk specifies list-directed input. The element END = *n* is called an *end-of-file specifier*. The effect is that when the READ statement executes and no more input data is available (that is, the end of the input file has been reached), the computer branches to the statement whose number appears in the end-of-file specifier, not to the next statement in sequence. Thus, in the example just given, the computer would branch to the statement numbered 100 when there was no more input data. At all other times, when there was input to read, the computer would go on to the next statement in sequence after reading the data.

We can use this form of the READ statement in our programs to terminate execution after processing all input data. Figure 2-15(a) shows a

Figure 2-15. An illustrative program with a loop

```
C   PROGRAM TO LIST TEST SCORES
        INTEGER ID
        REAL SCR1,SCR2
    10 READ (*,*,END=20) ID,SCR1,SCR2
        PRINT *,ID,SCR1,SCR2
        GO TO 10
    20 STOP
        END
```

(a) The program

```
12841,98,83
20853,92,85
23619,78,73
28900,87,91
31072,82,87
```

(b) Input data

```
12841 98. 83.
20853 92. 85.
23619 78. 73.
28900 87. 91.
31072 82. 87.
```

(c) Output

program that reads and prints any number of records, each with a student identification number and two test scores. The end-of-file specifier in the READ statement causes the computer to branch to the statement numbered 20 when there is no more input data. Because statement 20 is the STOP statement the program terminates execution in a normal way without an error occurring.

Notice that the input data in Figure 2-15(b) includes five records. Hence five lines are printed [Figure 2-15(c)]. However, any number of input records will be read by this program. The number of lines printed will be the same as the number of records read. The program even works if there are no input records; in this case, no lines will be printed because the end-of-file specifier causes the computer to branch immediately to the STOP statement. Thus we do not need to know in advance how many input records there are; the program correctly processes any number of records.

The way in which the end of the input data is indicated depends on whether batch processing or interactive processing is used. In batch processing there is usually a special record at the end of the input file called an *end-of-file record*. (With punched card input this record is the first control record after the input data deck and must be punched along with the other control records. For auxiliary storage input, the end-of-file record is usually put in place automatically by the text editor or word processor when the file is created.) When an end-of-file record is read, it is detected by the READ statement and the computer goes to the statement whose number is given in the end-of-file specifier.

With interactive processing, a question mark is displayed each time a READ statement executes. If there is no more input, a special key or combination of keys is pressed after the question mark. (On some computers just the RETURN key is pressed. With other computers a key marked BREAK or ATTN must be pushed. On still other computers the CONTROL key must be held and another key such as C or Z pressed at the same time.) When this signal is read by the READ statement, the computer branches to the statement identified in the end-of-file specifier.

As a final example, Figure 2-16 shows a program with numeric and character output and a loop. A variation on the program in Figure 2-13, this program prints a heading, descriptive phrases for the output data, and a phrase at the end of the output. Note that the heading is printed *before* the loop. If the PRINT statement for the heading were inside the loop, the heading would be printed each time a record was read. Similarly, the final output is

Figure 2-16. An illustrative program

```
C   PROGRAM TO LIST TEST SCORES
        INTEGER ID
        REAL SCR1,SCR2
        PRINT *,'            TEST SCORE SUMMARY'
        PRINT *
10  READ (*,*,END=20) ID,SCR1,SCR2
        PRINT *,'ID = ',ID,'  1ST SCORE = ',SCR1,'  2ND SCORE = ',SCR2
        GO TO 10
20  PRINT *
        PRINT *,'END OF OUTPUT'
        STOP
        END
```

(a) The program

```
12841,98,83
20853,92,85
23619,78,73
28900,87,91
31072,82,87
```

(b) Input data

```
        TEST SCORE SUMMARY

ID = 12841  1ST SCORE = 98.  2ND SCORE = 83.
ID = 20853  1ST SCORE = 92.  2ND SCORE = 85.
ID = 23619  1ST SCORE = 78.  2ND SCORE = 73.
ID = 28900  1ST SCORE = 87.  2ND SCORE = 91.
ID = 31072  1ST SCORE = 82.  2ND SCORE = 87.

END OF OUTPUT
```

(c) Output

printed *after* the loop. Note that the end-of-file specifier causes the computer to branch to the final PRINT statements, not to the STOP statement. The pattern illustrated by this program is used often in programming.

2-6. Program style

The most important objective of the programming process is to produce a program that correctly solves the required problem. The process of program testing, discussed briefly in Chapter 1, is designed to help locate errors in a program. We will have more to say about program testing in Chapter 7.

After correctness, the most important characteristic of a program is usually its understandability. By this we mean the qualities of the program that make it understandable or readable to a human. Program understandability is important because programs are often reviewed by people other than the original programmer. For example, the programming manager may review the program to check for completeness and consistency with the problem definition. Other programmers may have to read the program to correct errors that were not detected until after the program had been in use for a while. Modifications are often necessary in the program because of changing requirements. For example, payroll programs have to be modified regularly because of changing tax structures. Sometimes the program is enhanced so that it does more than was originally planned. In all these situations, someone must look at the program often several months or even years after it was originally coded. Even if the original programmer is given the task, he or she may have difficulty remembering the program's logic unless the program is easily understood.

Program style deals with those characteristics of a program that make it more understandable to a human. Even though we have only covered a few features of the FORTRAN language, we can begin to incorporate good style into our programs. One very basic rule is to use variable names that symbolize the data to which they refer. For example, in the program in Figure 2-16 we used ID for the student's identification number. Similarly, the name SCR1 identified the first test score and SCR2 referred to the second score.

Another good style rule is to use statement numbers that increase in sequence. It is possible to use any valid statement number for any statement as long as the number is not used elsewhere in the program. However, for a large program it is often difficult to locate a particular statement if the numbers are out of sequence. Thus statement numbers that increase through the program should be used.

Indentation should be used in loops and other parts of a program that we will discuss later. Such indentation helps show the organization or structure of the statements in the program. The indentation gives a visual cue to help the programmer understand the program. We will have more to say about indentation and program structure in later chapters.

Finally, comments should be used to explain complex parts of a program. Although the examples so far have been relatively straightforward, many programs involve sophisticated processing. Comments can be used to include explanations of the processing at different points in a program.

The rules discussed here are just a few of the ways that a program can be made more understandable. As we explain other features of the FORTRAN language, we will give more rules for program style.

Review questions

1. What is the difference between list-directed and formatted I/O?
2. What symbol in the READ and PRINT statements indicates that list-directed I/O is to be used?
3. Data is stored in internal storage in _____, each of which is identified by a unique number called _____.
4. What is the syntax rule for a variable name in FORTRAN?
5. Indicate whether each of the following is a valid or invalid variable name:
   a. ZERO   d. V
   b. 37X25Z   e. TOT$
   c. BALANCE   f. A85CB7
6. What is the difference between integer and real data?
7. Code statements that explicitly type the variable names PRICE and DESC as real and the variable name QTY as integer.
8. Indicate which of the following variable names are implicitly typed as real and which are implicitly typed as integer:
   a. DESC   d. M
   b. QTY   e. LR25
   c. KOUNT   f. HELP
9. What are the limitations on data values for the computer you are using?
10. Code a list-directed input statement to read the values of PRICE, DESC, and QTY.
11. How must data be recorded for list-directed input?
12. Three input records need to be read. Each contains one real value. Code statements to read the records. Include any specification statements that are needed.
13. Code a list-directed output statement to print the values of PRICE, DESC, and QTY.
14. How many values can be printed on one line with the computer you are using?
15. Code statements to print three lines, each with one integer value.
16. What is a character constant?
17. Code a statement to print the words OUTPUT DATA followed by the values of A and B.
18. What does the following statement do?

```
PRINT *,' '
```

19. What statements can be used to terminate execution of a program?
20. The last statement of a program must be _____.
21. Code a statement that branches to the statement numbered 100.
22. A group of statements that are executed repeatedly is called a _____.
23. Code a list-directed input statement that reads the values of PRICE, DESC, and QTY and branches to statement 999 when no more input data is available.
24. Consider the program in Figure 2–15. How could this program be modified so that the output is double-spaced?
25. Why is good program style important?

Programming problems

In each of the following problems, the requirements are given for a computer program. A complete FORTRAN program should be prepared according to the requirements. The program should be fully debugged and tested on a computer using the test data given.

1. Write a FORTRAN program to list three input values. The first is real and the second and third are integers. Print the data in the same order as the input. Use the input values 98.6, 120, and 80 to test the program.

2. Input to a program consists of four integers. Write a FORTRAN program to print the input data in a column; that is, print each value on a separate line. Use the values 47, −13, 29, and 148 to test the program.

3. Write a FORTRAN program that reads two input records. The first record contains two integers and the second record has two reals. Print the data on one line with the first integer followed by the first real, then the second integer followed by the second real. Use the input values 1083, 2174, 47.49, and 63.95 to test the program.

4. The results of the analysis of a survey need to be printed. Input consists of three records, each with the following data:

      Survey number (integer)
      Number of respondents (integer)
      Percent responding (real)

Write a FORTRAN program to print the input data in three columns with the survey numbers on the first line, the number of respondents on the second line, and the percent responding on the third line. Use the following data to test the program:

Survey Number	Number Respondents	Percent Responding
146	375	46.5%
205	139	28.6%
439	643	67.3%

5. Write the program for Problem 4 with the additional requirements that the heading SURVEY ANALYSIS is printed before the other output, the words SURVEY, RESPONDENTS, and PERCENT are printed on the three lines of output, and the words END OF ANALYSIS are printed at the end of the output.

6. Write a FORTRAN program to print your name in block letters. A sample of how the output might appear is as follows:

```
    X     XXX    X   X   X   X
    X    X   X   X   X   XX  X
    X    X   X   X   X   X   X
    X    X   X  XXXXX  X X X
    X    X   X   X   X   X   X
 X  X    X   X   X   X   X  XX
   XX     XXX   X   X   X   X
```

7. A list of student grade point averages is needed. Input consists of one record for each student giving his or her identification number (integer) followed by his or her grade point average (real). An unknown number of input records is to be processed. Write a FORTRAN program that prints one line for each record, listing the data from the record. Use the following data to test the program:

Student Number	Grade Point Average
10837	2.67
14836	3.50
15006	2.99
17113	1.85
17280	3.89
19463	2.25

8. Write the program for Problem 6 with the additional requirements that the heading GPA LIST is printed before the output, the word NUMBER is printed before each student number, the word GPA is printed before each grade point average, and the words LIST COMPLETED is printed at the end of the output.

9. An unknown number of input records each contain a product number (integer), unit price (real), and quantity sold (integer). Write a FORTRAN program to list the input data. One line should be printed for each input record. Print appropriate descriptive phrases with the output. Use the following data to test the program:

Product Number	Unit Price	Quantity Sold
147	$1.29	50
153	$4.25	29
185	$2.50	138
187	$6.95	250
228	$3.49	73

10. The first input record in a file contains an automobile identification number (integer). Following this record are an unknown number of records, each containing the results of a mileage test. The first number in each record is a test number (integer), the next is a test type (integer), and the last value is the miles per gallon (real). Write a FORTRAN program that prints the words AUTOMOBILE ID NUMBER followed by the identification number on the first line of output. Then the program should list the input data with one line for

each mileage test. Print appropriate descriptive phrases with the output. Use the following input data for the program:

AUTOMOBILE ID NUMBER: 4836

Test Number	Test Type	Miles Per Gallon
1	2	23.8
2	1	18.6
3	3	28.6
4	4	31.5
5	1	17.3
6	2	24.0
7	1	19.2
8	3	26.4

Chapter 3

Arithmetic programming

With the statements discussed in Chapter 2, we can write programs that read and print data. After a program reads input data, however, it normally *processes* the data, and then prints the results. Processing includes many types of data manipulation, but one of the most common is arithmetic processing. In this chapter we describe the FORTRAN elements necessary for performing arithmetic calculations. After completing this chapter, you should be able to write programs that do arithmetic processing.

3-1. FORTRAN constants

As we saw in Chapter 2, a symbolic name for a data value that occupies a storage location is called a *variable name*. The value in that storage location — that is, the value referred to by the variable name — can change or vary as the program executes. A data value that does not change during execution of the program is called a *constant*. Like the value of a variable name, a constant occupies a storage location. But a constant is not identified by a variable name; it appears as a number in a FORTRAN statement. For example, the following are valid constants in FORTRAN:

```
482.59    0
    25    5.83
   -18    0.0
    10    -1.6258
```

Just as there are two main types of variables — integer and real — there are also two types of constants.* An *integer constant* is any numeric

---

* There are several other types of constants. We have already mentioned character constants when discussing character output. We will describe other uses of character constants and discuss other types of constants later.

value that does not have a decimal point. The following are valid integer constants:

```
     0
     1
    91
  -173
+24567
```

Commas are not permitted in any constant. For an integer constant, no decimal point is allowed. A minus sign is required if the value of a constant is negative; a plus sign is optional for positive constants. The following are invalid integer constants for the reasons given:

```
   3.2     (contains a decimal point)
  27.0     (contains a decimal point)
 5,468     (contains a comma)
```

A *real constant* is any numeric value that has a decimal point. For example, the following are valid real constants:

```
    0.0
  +58.3
    .00392
  145.
-2538.63
```

Commas are not acceptable. A minus sign is required for negative values, but a plus sign is optional for positive values. A leading zero for a value with a fractional part is also optional. Thus 0.05 and .05 are equivalent. Trailing zeros for a value with no fractional part are also optional. For example, 58., 58.0, and 58.00 are equivalent. However, a decimal point is required. Thus 58. is real and 58 is integer. The following are invalid real constants for the reasons given:

```
   265        (does not contain a decimal point)
84,532.65     (contains a comma)
  $12.75      (contains a dollar sign)
```

In Section 2-2 we discussed limitations on the size of numbers that can be assigned to variable names. These limitations also apply to constants, and they depend on the computer being used. Thus an integer constant must be within a certain range which, on one common computer, is from $+2,147,483,647$ to $-2,147,483,648$. Any integer between these values, including zero, is an acceptable integer constant. A real constant is stored in floating-point notation and so has limitations on its fraction and its exponent. On one computer a real constant can have no more than seven digits in its fraction, and its exponent must be between -78 and $+75$. Any positive or negative real constant within these limits, including zero, is valid.

3-2. Arithmetic expressions

An *arithmetic expression* is an instruction to the computer to perform arithmetic. It is not a statement by itself, but it is used to form other statements. Arithmetic expressions are formed from constants, variable names, and arithmetic operators.

Arithmetic operators and simple arithmetic expressions

Arithmetic operators are symbols that indicate what form of arithmetic is to be performed. The symbols used in FORTRAN and their meanings follow:

Arithmetic Operator	Meaning
+	Add
−	Subtract
*	Multiply
/	Divide
**	Exponentiate

To form a simple arithmetic expression using these symbols we write an unsigned constant or variable name on each side of the operator. For example, the following are valid arithmetic expressions in FORTRAN:

```
A+B
X−Y
2*K
TOTAL/3.0
X**2
```

Each of these expressions tells the computer to perform the indicated operation using the values of the variables and constants. For example, A + B means to add the value of A and the value of B. If A is 8.3 and B is 5.2, the value of A + B is 13.5. With subtraction, the value on the right of the subtraction operator is subtracted from the value on the left. X − Y means to subtract the value of Y from the value of X. Note that multiplication is indicated by the asterisk symbol. 2*K means to multiply the value of K by the constant 2. With division, the value on the left of the division operator is divided by the value on the right. TOTAL/3.0 means to divide the value of TOTAL by 3.0. Exponentiation means raise the value on the left of the operator to the power of the value on the right. X**2 means to raise the value of X to the second power (that is, square the value of X).

The addition and subtraction symbols may be used alone in front of a single constant or variable name to form an arithmetic expression. In fact, a variable name or a constant by itself is considered to be an arithmetic expression. Hence each of the following are arithmetic expressions:

```
3
J
+7.5
+P
−.0063
−A
```

In the last example, if the value of A is -6.2, the value of the arithmetic expression is $-(-6.2)$ or 6.2.

Evaluation of complex arithmetic expressions

To form more complex arithmetic expressions, several arithmetic operators are used. For example, the following are valid arithmetic expressions:

```
EL/F3+2.0
8-I*J
A*X**2+B*X-C
3.14159*R**2
-B+B/2.0/A
```

With complex arithmetic expressions, the order in which the operations are performed is very important. The order is always as follows:

1. All exponentiation is performed.
2. All multiplication and division is performed left-to-right.
3. All addition and subtraction is performed left-to-right.

For example, consider the expression

```
8.7-A*2.4/B+C**2+D
```

Figure 3-1 shows how this expression is evaluated if the value of A is 6.0, B is 4.0, C is 2.0, and D is 1.0. The expression is evaluated in this order:

1. The values of all variables are substituted in the expression.
2. The value of C is raised to the second power.
3. The value of A is multiplied by 2.4.
4. The result from Step 3 is divided by the value of B.
5. The result from Step 4 is subtracted from 8.7.
6. The result from Step 5 is added to the result from Step 2.
7. The result from Step 6 is added to 1.0.

In algebraic notation, this expression is

$$8.7 \ - \ \frac{A \ \times \ 2.4}{B} \ + \ C^2 \ + \ D$$

To change the order of evaluation, arithmetic expressions may be enclosed in parentheses and combined with other expressions. When this is done, all operations in parentheses are performed before those outside of the parentheses are performed. For example, consider the following modification of the previous expression:

```
8.7-A*2.4/(B+C**2)+D
```

The expression B+C**2 is enclosed in parentheses and is evaluated before any other operations are performed. Thus the computer first raises the value

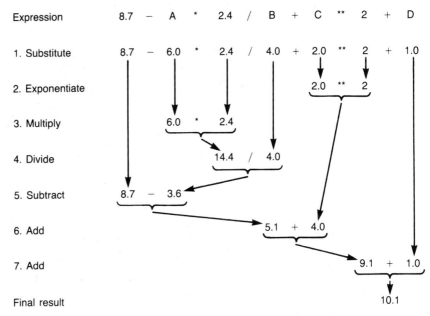

Figure 3-1. Evaluation of an arithmetic expression

of C to the second power and adds the result to the value of B. Next, the value of A is multiplied by 2.4, and the result is divided by the value of B+C**2. Finally, the other addition and subtraction are performed. Figure 3-2 shows the evaluation sequence for the data given earlier. The equivalent expression in algebraic notation is

$$8.7 - \frac{A \times 2.4}{B} + C^2 + D \qquad 8.7 - \frac{A \times 2.4}{B + C^2} + D$$

Arithmetic expressions in parentheses may be imbedded in other parenthetic expressions. When this is done, the computer evaluates the expression in the innermost parentheses before continuing with the expression in the next level of parentheses. For example, consider the expression

```
8.7-A*(2.4/(B+C**2)+D)
```

First the computer evaluates B+C**2. The result is then divided into 2.4 and the value of D is added. Then the final multiplication by the value of A and subtraction from 8.7 are performed. In algebraic notation, this expression is

$$8.7 - A \times \left(\frac{2.4}{B + C^2} + D \right)$$

Notice that when using parentheses, as in these examples, each left parenthesis

Figure 3-2. Evaluation of an arithmetic expression containing parentheses

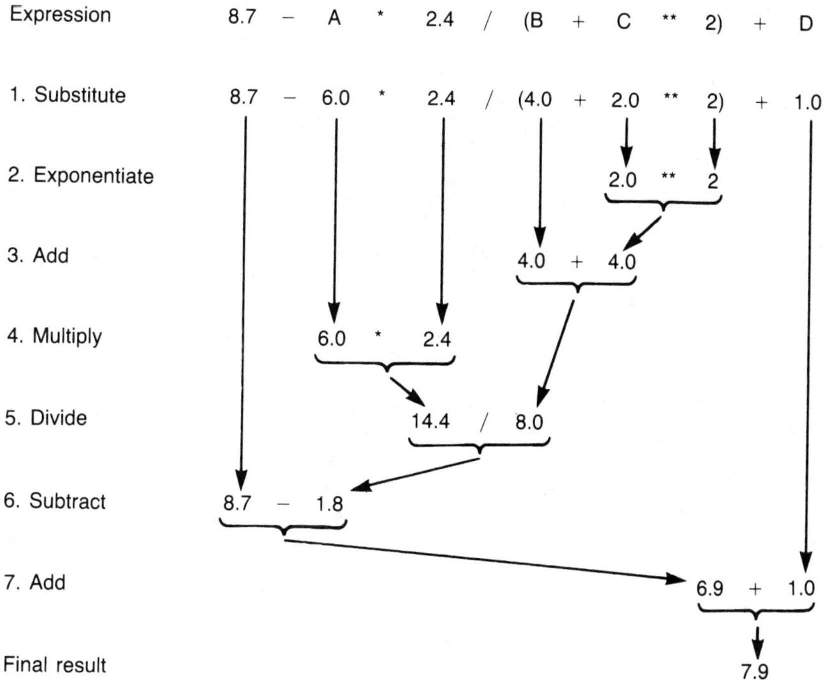

Expression	8.7 − A * 2.4 / (B + C ** 2) + D
1. Substitute	8.7 − 6.0 * 2.4 / (4.0 + 2.0 ** 2) + 1.0
2. Exponentiate	2.0 ** 2
3. Add	4.0 + 4.0
4. Multiply	6.0 * 2.4
5. Divide	14.4 / 8.0
6. Subtract	8.7 − 1.8
7. Add	6.9 + 1.0
Final result	7.9

must have a matching right parenthesis. Brackets are not allowed in arithmetic expressions in FORTRAN.

A common mistake when writing an arithmetic expression is to forget that certain operations are done before others. For example, assume that the programmer must write an arithmetic expression in FORTRAN for the algebraic expression

$$\frac{A + B}{C + D}$$

In coding the expression, the programmer may hastily write

    A+B/C+D

This is incorrect because division is done ahead of addition and thus this arithmetic expression is interpreted as

$$A + \frac{B}{C} + D$$

To force the additions to be done before the division, the programmer must use parentheses. The correct arithmetic expression is

    (A+B)/(C+D)

It is important to remember that the order of evaluations is left to right in a series of successive multiplications and divisions. Thus, in the expression

    A/B*C

the division is performed first and the result is multiplied by C. In algebraic notation, the expression is

$$\frac{A}{B} \times C$$

To write the algebraic expression

$$\frac{A}{B \times C}$$

in FORTRAN, we must use parentheses to force the multiplication to be done ahead of the division. Hence the equivalent FORTRAN expression for this example is

    A/(B*C)

The left-to-right evaluation also applies to addition and subtraction. For example, in the expression $J - K + L$ the subtraction is done first followed by the addition. If J is 3, K is 2, and L is 1, then the correct value of this expression is 2. Had we interpreted the expression incorrectly and assumed that the addition was to be done first, we would have had zero as the result. But because of the left-to-right order of evaluation, this result is incorrect. To change the order, we must use parentheses and write the expression as $J - (K + L)$.

With a series of exponentiations, the order of evaluation is right to left, the opposite of the order for the other operators. Hence the expression X**Y**Z is interpreted as X**(Y**Z). If we want to have the computer evaluate the expression left to right, we must use parentheses and write the expression (X**Y)**Z.

Unlike algebra, leaving out an arithmetic operator does not mean multiplication. For example, 3K is invalid and must be written 3*K. Similarly, parentheses may not be used to imply multiplication. For example, $(A + B)(C + D)$ is invalid and must be written as $(A + B)*(C + D)$.

Two arithmetic operators may not appear adjacent to each other. For example, $A/-B$ is invalid. However, $-B$ by itself is an arithmetic expression and therefore may be enclosed in parentheses to give meaning to the expression. This example may be written correctly as $A/(-B)$. The same does not hold true for the invalid expression $A*/B$; there is no way to make this expression meaningful.

Mode of an arithmetic expression

A final consideration in arithmetic expressions is the *mode* of the expression. The mode of an arithmetic expression is determined by the types of constants and variable names in the expression.

An *integer mode* expression contains all integer constants and variable names. The following are integer mode arithmetic expressions if we assume that all variable names are integer:

```
I+2
K3*(6-L)
MON**2+18/J
```

A *real mode* expression contains all real constants and variable names except that exponents may be integer constants, variable names, or arithmetic expressions in parentheses. The following are real mode arithmetic expressions if we assume that I is an integer variable name and all other variable names are real:

```
A+7.8*B**1.5
Y**Y-5.38
2.73/AMT**2
VALUE**(I+2)
```

Note that exponents in real mode expressions may be real or integer.

A *mixed mode* expression contains any other combination of integer and real constants and variable names. The following are mixed mode arithmetic expressions if we assume that A, B, and C are real variable names and I is integer.

```
A-2*B+3.5
C+I**2.5
4-A/B
```

Mixed mode expressions are valid in FORTRAN, but their evaluation follows complex rules. Therefore, their use should be avoided.

3-3. The arithmetic assignment statement

An arithmetic expression by itself is not a FORTRAN statement. Rather, arithmetic expressions are parts of statements that are then used in programs. The most common statement in which an arithmetic expression appears is the *arithmetic assignment statement*. This statement causes the computer to evaluate an arithmetic expression and then to assign the result to a variable name.

The syntax of an arithmetic assignment statement is as follows:

```
variable name = arithmetic expression
```

On the left of the equal sign is a single variable name; on the right is any valid arithmetic expression. For example, the following are valid arithmetic assignment statements:

```
TOTAL=TS1+TS2+TS3
AVE=TOTAL/3.0
Y=A*X**2+B*X+C
A=3.14159*(D/2.0)**2
```

In each of these, the computer uses the current values of the variable names to evaluate the arithmetic expression. Then the result is stored at the storage location identified by the variable name on the left. For example, in the statement

```
TOTAL=TS1+TS2+TS3
```

if the value of TS1 is 89.0, TS2 is 81.0, and TS3 is 82.0, then after execution of this statement the value of TOTAL is 252.0. This value replaces the previous value of TOTAL and is the value that is retrieved at any subsequent use of the variable named TOTAL.

The equal sign in an arithmetic assignment statement does not mean equality in FORTRAN; it means *assignment*. That is, the equal sign tells the computer that the value of the expression on the right is to be *assigned* to the left-hand variable name, which is why there can be only one variable name to the left of the equal sign. For example, the statement

```
A+B=X+Y
```

is invalid because it instructs the computer to assign the value of the expression $X + Y$ to the expression $A + B$. Because the left-hand expression is not a single storage location, such assignment is meaningless and therefore not allowed. A single variable name must always be on the left.

A further consequence of this concept of assignment is that some algebraically invalid equations become valid statements in FORTRAN. For example, the following statement is valid and often useful:

```
K=K+1
```

The meaning of this statement is that 1 is added to the current value of K and the result returned to the storage location reserved for K. (See Figure 3-3.) Thus the value of K is increased by 1. Similarly, the following statement

Figure 3-3. Evaluation of the statement K = K + 1

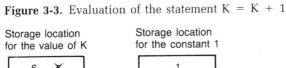

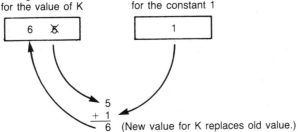

causes the current value of A to be replaced by a value that is five times as large as A:

    A=5.0*A

We can use the arithmetic assignment statement to assign a constant to a variable name or to assign the value of one variable name to another. For example, the statement

    M=3

assigns the value 3 to the variable named M. Similarly, the statement

    N=M

assigns the value of M to N. If M is equal to 3 before this statement is executed, N is 3 afterwards. Note, however, that this last assignment statement does *not* change the value of M; M is still equal to 3 after execution of the statement.

On the right of the equal sign may be an integer mode or a real mode expression. Usually the arithmetic expression is the same mode as that of the variable name on the left. This eliminates any problem with conversion from one mode to another. However, mixed mode arithmetic assignment statements are acceptable. The effect of a mixed mode statement is that the expression on the right is evaluated in the mode in which it is written. Then the result is converted to the mode of the variable name on the left. If the expression is integer and the left-hand variable name is real, the conversion involves changing the integer form of a numeric value into its real form. If the expression is real and the left-hand variable name is integer, the conversion is more complex. Because the internal representation of an integer does not allow for a fractional part, any digits to the right of the decimal point are dropped. We say the value is *truncated*. For example, consider the following statement in which K is integer and A and B are real:

    K=A+B

If the value of A is 5.0 and B is 7.8, the value of A + B is 12.8. Because this must be assigned to an integer variable name, the fractional part is dropped and K becomes 12. Although the left-hand variable name and the arithmetic expression in an arithmetic assignment statement may have different modes, the expression on the right should not be mixed mode. (See Section 3-2.)

3-4. Illustrative programs

The test score averaging program from Chapter 1 illustrates a complete program that involves arithmetic processing. The program is repeated in Figure 3-4. Note that the program involves input, arithmetic calculations, and output.

Figure 3-4. A test score averaging program

```
C   TEST SCORE AVERAGING PROGRAM
        INTEGER SNUM
        REAL TS1,TS2,TS3,TOTAL,AVE
    10 READ (*,*,END=20) SNUM,TS1,TS2,TS3
            TOTAL=TS1+TS2+TS3
            AVE=TOTAL/3.0
            PRINT *,SNUM,TOTAL,AVE
        GO TO 10
    20 STOP
        END
```

Two arithmetic assignment statements perform the calculations. These statements must be in the order listed because the result of the first calculation (TOTAL) is needed in the second calculation. The arithmetic assignment statements must come after the READ statement because the data read (TS1, TS2, and TS3) is used in the calculations. Finally, the PRINT statement must follow the arithmetic assignment statements because the results of the calculations (TOTAL and AVE) are printed in the output.

As another example of arithmetic processing, assume that we must compute the gross pay, withholding tax, and net pay for an employee. Input to the program consists of the employee's identification number (EMPID) and his or her hours worked (HOURS). The gross pay (GROSS) is to be computed at the rate of $6.50 per hour; the withholding tax (TAX) is 18 percent of the gross pay; the net pay (NET) is the gross pay less the withholding tax. Output should list the employee's identification number, gross pay, withholding tax, and net pay.

The program in Figure 3-5 satisfies these requirements. First the input data is read. Next the gross pay, withholding tax, and net pay are computed in three arithmetic assignment statements. The order of these statements is important. The gross pay must be computed first because it is needed in the calculation of the withholding tax. In addition, the tax must be computed before the net pay can be found. After all calculations are completed, the output is printed.

This program includes a loop that repeats the processing for each input record. The loop consists of the READ statement through the GO TO statement. The first time the loop is executed, the computer reads the first input record and assigns the data to EMPID and HOURS. This data is processed and one line is printed. Then the computer executes the GO TO statement, returning to the READ statement, which causes the computer to read the second input record. The data from this record is assigned to EMPID and HOURS, replacing the old values of these variables. Hence, the second time the loop is executed, the calculations use the data from the second input record; the second line printed gives the results of these calculations. Then the computer branches to the READ statement again, reads the third record, and proceeds as before. The program repeats the loop until no more input data is available.

As a final example, assume that we must calculate the floor area of

Figure 3-5. A payroll calculation program

```
C  PAYROLL CALCULATION PROGRAM
        INTEGER EMPID
        REAL HOURS,GROSS,TAX,NET
   100 READ (*,*,END=200) EMPID,HOURS
          GROSS=6.50*HOURS
          TAX=.18*GROSS
          NET=GROSS-TAX
          PRINT *,'ID = ',EMPID,'  GROSS PAY = ',GROSS,
       1          '  TAX = ',TAX,'  NET PAY = ',NET
        GO TO 100
   200 STOP
        END
```

(a) The program

```
234,32
456,48
678,36
```

(b) Input data

```
ID = 234  GROSS PAY = 208.  TAX = 37.44  NET PAY = 170.56
ID = 456  GROSS PAY = 312.  TAX = 56.16  NET PAY = 255.84
ID = 678  GROSS PAY = 234.  TAX = 42.12  NET PAY = 191.88
```

(c) Output

a room so that new carpet can be ordered. The input to the program consists of the room's length (LENGTH) and width (WIDTH) in feet. The output should be the number of square feet (SQFT) of carpet to order. The problem is complicated by the fact that we can only order a whole number of square feet and the amount ordered must be greater than or equal to the actual area. Thus, if the dimensions are 10.3 feet by 14.5 feet, then the area (10.3 × 14.5) is 149.35 square feet. We must order 150 square feet of carpet.

The program in Figure 3-6 is a solution to this problem. After reading the input data, the computer calculates the number of square feet by multiplying LENGTH by WIDTH. The result of the multiplication is a real number (149.35 in our example), but it is assigned to an integer variable name (SQFT). Hence the fraction is truncated when the assignment takes place. (Thus SQFT is 149 in our case.) To make sure that an adequate amount of carpet is ordered, we add one to SQFT before printing the result. (Thus the output is 150 square feet for the data that we are using.)*

As we can see from these examples, the arithmetic assignment statement is the basic statement that is used in FORTRAN for arithmetic processing. The statement assigns the value of an arithmetic expression to a variable name. This is one use of arithmetic expressions. Other uses will be discussed in later chapters.

---

* This program gives one extra square foot if the actual area is a whole number. A good exercise is to figure out a way to overcome this problem.

Figure 3-6. A program to calculate carpet requirements

```
C  CARPET REQUIREMENTS CALCULATION PROGRAM
      REAL LENGTH,WIDTH
      INTEGER SQFT
      READ *,LENGTH,WIDTH
      SQFT=LENGTH*WIDTH
      SQFT=SQFT+1
      PRINT *,'ORDER ',SQFT,' SQUARE FEET OF CARPET'
      STOP
      END
```

(a) The program

```
10.3,14.5
```

(b) Input data

```
ORDER 150 SQUARE FEET OF CARPET
```

(c) Output

3-5. The PARAMETER statement

Constants have many uses in a program. Sometimes a constant is a value that affects the processing in a program, but its value may need to be changed in the future. Such constants are called *parameters* of the program. For example, in the payroll calculation program in Figure 3-5, the constants for the pay rate (6.50) and the tax rate (.18) are parameters. These values determine the final result, but they may change in the future. If they do change, all statements that use these values must be modified.

Another way of using constants is to assign a name, called a *constant name,* to each constant and to use these names in place of the constants in the program. A constant name has the same syntax as a variable name (one to six alphabetic and numeric characters beginning with an alphabetic character). Each constant name has a type that is either specified explicitly in a type statement or implicitly by the first letter of the name. (See Section 2-2.) A constant name is assigned a value in a PARAMETER statement. The syntax of this statement is as follows:

```
PARAMETER (constant name=constant, constant name=constant,...)
```

For example, asume that A and B are real constant names and that K is an integer constant name. Then the following statement assigns values to these names:

```
PARAMETER (A=25.5,B=-.375,K=10)
```

The effect of this statement is to assign the value 25.5 to the constant name A, −.375 to B, and 10 to K. One or more constant names can be assigned values in a PARAMETER statement.

The type of the constant in a PARAMETER statement should correspond to the type of the constant name. In the example just given, A and B are assigned real constant values and K is assigned an integer value. If the types do not agree, the type of the constant is converted to that of the constant name as in a mixed mode arithmetic assignment statement. (See Section 3-3.)

The PARAMETER statement is a specification statement. As such it is a nonexecutable statement and must come at the beginning of the program before the first executable statement. If explicit typing is used for the constant names, the PARAMETER statement must come after the corresponding type statements. (Other type statements, however, may come after the PARAMETER statement.) A program can contain any number of PARAMETER statements.

Once a constant name is specified in a PARAMETER statement, its value cannot be changed while the program is executing. Thus a constant name cannot appear on the left of the equal sign in an arithmetic assignment statement or in a READ statement list. A constant name can be used in an arithmetic expression or in a PRINT statement list. When a constant name does appear, the value of the constant name from the PARAMETER statement is used.

Figure 3-7 shows the payroll calculation program from Figure 3-5 modified to include constant names for the pay rate (PAYRAT) and the tax rate (TAXRAT). The PARAMETER statement assigns values to these names. This statement comes after the REAL type statement that specifies the constant names. The constant names are used instead of constants in the arithmetic assignment statements that compute the gross pay and tax. Although this program is different from the earlier one, the effect of execution is identical.

Use of the PARAMETER statement and constant names provides two advantages to the programmer. One is that the program is easier to change. For example, in the program in Figure 3-7, to change the pay rate or tax rate we only have to find the PARAMETER statement and make the change

Figure 3-7. The payroll calculation program using constant names

```
C   PAYROLL CALCULATION PROGRAM
        INTEGER EMPID
        REAL HOURS,GROSS,TAX,NET,PAYRAT,TAXRAT
        PARAMETER (PAYRAT=6.50,TAXRAT=.18)
    100 READ (*,*,END=200) EMPID,HOURS
        GROSS=PAYRAT*HOURS
        TAX=TAXRAT*GROSS
        NET=GROSS-TAX
        PRINT *,'ID = ',EMPID,'  GROSS PAY = ',GROSS,
    1           ' TAX = ',TAX,'  NET PAY = ',NET
        GO TO 100
    200 STOP
        END
```

there. Without the PARAMETER statement we would have to search the entire program for the statements that use the constants. Although this is fairly easy with short programs such as our examples so far, with long programs it can be very difficult to do.

The second advantage is that using constant names usually makes a program easier to understand. For example, in the program in Figure 3-7, we know that the gross pay is found by multiplying the pay rate by the hours because we have used symbolic names throughout the assignment statement. Similarly, the program clearly indicates that the tax is the product of the tax rate and the gross pay. Thus the program is easier to read.

In general, constant names should be used for all constant values that may need to be changed in the future. Constant names usually should not be assigned to constants that will not change. For example, in the program in Figure 3-6, the constant 1 is used in the statement

```
SQFT=SQFT+1
```

Because it is unlikely that this constant will change, a constant name should not be used in its place.

3-6. FORTRAN-supplied functions

Many common processing activities are regularly required in FORTRAN programs. For example, converting a value from integer to real and finding the square root of a quantity are common tasks. To relieve the programmer of repeatedly preparing the instructions necessary to perform such activities, FORTRAN supplies special programs called functions. A *function* is a separate program that performs a special task. Each function has a name and is written in the program by coding the name of the function followed by an arithmetic expression in parentheses. The resulting reference to the function forms an arithmetic expression by itself or is used as part of a more complex arithmetic expression.

An example of a function is SQRT. This function finds the square root of a nonnegative, real value. For example, the following statement calculates the square root of the value of B and assigns the result to C:

```
C=SQRT(B)
```

It is important to remember that the SQRT function operates on nonnegative, real values. For example, if K is an integer variable name, the expression SQRT(K) should not be used. A complex arithmetic expression may be used if the expression is real and its value is nonnegative. Thus, if X and Y are real, SQRT(X + 3.5*Y) is valid and the square root of the value of the expression is found.

Functions may be used in simple or complex arithmetic expressions. For example, the following statement shows a valid use of the square root function:

```
ROOT=(-B+SQRT(B**2-4.0*A*C))/(2.0*A)
```

SQRT is just one of many FORTRAN-supplied functions. Appendix C contains a list of the functions available in FORTRAN. In the remainder of this section we describe two functions, REAL and INT, that can be used to avoid mixed mode in arithmetic expressions and arithmetic assignment statements.

The REAL function

The syntax of the REAL* function is as follows:

```
REAL (integer mode arithmetic expression)
```

The effect of this function is to change the value of the expression to real. For example, assume that M and N are integer variable names and that we must add the value of M + N to the value of the real variable A and assign the result to the real variable B. In the statement B = A + M + N the right-hand-side expression is mixed mode. Using the REAL function the statement can be coded as follows:

```
B=A+REAL(M+N)
```

The effect of using the REAL function reference in this statement is to evaluate the expression M + N and then to convert the result to a real value. The real value is then added to the value of A and the result assigned to B.

The following statements show valid uses of the REAL function (assume that W, X, Y, and Z are real and that J, K, L, and M are integer):

```
W=REAL(K-5)*6.25
Y=-2.83*REAL(3*L)+REAL(M)
X=SQRT(REAL(-K))
Z=REAL(J)
```

In all of these statements the contents of the storage locations reserved for integer variable names are not changed by the function. For example, in the last statement the value of J is converted to real only for the purpose of assigning it to the variable named Z. At the storage location reserved for the value of J, the original integer value is retained.

---

* Older versions of FORTRAN used the name FLOAT instead of REAL. This name can still be used, but it is not as descriptive as the new name.

The INT function

The syntax of the INT* function is as follows:

```
INT (real mode arithmetic expression)
```

The effect of this function is to change the value of the expression to integer. For example, consider the following statement in which K is integer and A is real:

```
K=INT(2.5*A)+7
```

In evaluating this statement, the real value of 2.5*A is calculated. The result is then converted to an integer by the INT function. Finally, the constant 7 is added to the integer value and the result assigned to K.

In converting a real value to an integer, any fractional part of the real value is dropped. That is, the value is truncated. For example, consider the following statement in which M is integer and X is real:

```
M=INT(X)
```

If the value of X is 25.83, then after execution of this statement, M is 25. If X is negative, the fraction is dropped but the sign is retained. Thus if X is −4.6, M is −4 after execution of this statement. Note that X retains its original value; conversion from one mode to another does not change the contents of the storage location reserved for the variable name.

If we must round off rather than truncate a positive real value when converting to an integer, we can use a technique called *half-adjusting*. With this technique, we add one-half (.5) to the value before using the INT function. With half-adjusting the previous statement is written as follows:

```
M=INT(X+.5)
```

For example, if X is 25.5 or greater but less than 26.0, X + .5 is 26.0 or greater. Then truncation results in the integer 26 which is assigned to M. If X is less than 25.5 but greater than or equal to 25.0, X + .5 is less than 26.0 and truncation yields 25. Hence the value of X is correctly rounded with this technique. Note that if X is negative, − .5 must be added to correctly half-adjust.

The INT function can be used in a variety of ways in a FORTRAN program. The following statements show valid uses of the INT function (assume that I, J, K, L, and M are integer and that V and W are real):

---

* Older versions of FORTRAN used the name IFIX instead of INT. This name can still be used, but it is not as descriptive as the new name.

```
I=82*INT(W)
M=INT(7.3-V*28.97)+K
L=-3*J*INT(3.0-REAL(I))
```

An illustrative program

As an example of the use of the SQRT, REAL, and INT functions, assume that the input to a program is an integer giving the number of square feet (SQFT) of carpet purchased to cover a floor. The program must compute and print the integer length of the side (SIDE) of the largest square floor that can be covered by this amount of carpet. The program in Figure 3-8 accomplishes this. After reading the value of SQFT, the program converts this value to real (RSQFT) for use with the SQRT function. The square root of RSQFT gives the length of the side of a square floor (RSIDE) that can be covered by the carpet. Converting RSIDE to integer (SIDE) gives the final result. Because only SIDE is printed, the three assignment statements can be reduced to one statement as follows:

```
SIDE=INT(SQRT(REAL(SQFT)))
```

3-7. Integer and real arithmetic

Calculations involving integers and reals differ significantly. Without going into detail, this section discusses some of the important characteristics of real and integer arithmetic.

Figure 3-8. A program to calculate floor dimensions

```
C  FLOOR DIMENSION CALCULATION PROGRAM
      INTEGER SQFT,SIDE
      REAL RSQFT,RSIDE
      READ *,SQFT
      RSQFT=REAL(SQFT)
      RSIDE=SQRT(RSQFT)
      SIDE=INT(RSIDE)
      PRINT *,'THE LENGTH OF THE SIDE IS ',SIDE
      STOP
      END
```

(a) The program

```
150
```

(b) Input data

```
THE LENGTH OF THE SIDE IS 12
```

(c) Output

Assume that J and K are integer variable names, and consider the integer expression J/K. If J is 9 and K is 5, the result of evaluating this expression is 1.8. But because the result must be integer, the fractional part is lost. Thus the actual answer is 1. Note that the result is not rounded; it is truncated. This rule, together with the rules for the order of execution of operations in an arithmetic expression, yields some peculiar results:

```
1/2=0
1/2+2/3=0+0=0
2/5*5=0*5=0
2/3*3/2=0*3/2=0/2=0
```

All of these are correct, according to the FORTRAN rules for integer arithmetic.

The truncation characteristic of integer division can be both a hindrance and an aid. For example, the program in Figure 3-9 uses this characteristic to calculate the number of dozen in a given number of eggs (NEGG). Notice that all variable names in this program are integer. The first arithmetic assignment statement calculates the number of dozen (NDOZ), truncating any fractional part. The second arithmetic assignment statement calculates the number remaining (NREM) after the calculated number of dozen are removed. If the input value is 226 eggs, the output is 18 dozen eggs with 10 eggs remaining.

Another problem that sometimes occurs with integer arithmetic is *overflow*. This occurs when the result of an arithmetic operation is greater than the maximum value that the computer can store. For example, if J is 5000 and K is 1000000, then J*K is 5000000000. For most computer systems, this is greater than the maximum integer value that can be stored; hence, an overflow condition occurs. If the result of an arithmetic calculation is less

Figure 3-9. The egg program

```
C  EGG PROGRAM
      INTEGER NEGG,NDOZ,NREM
      READ *,NEGG
      NDOZ=NEGG/12
      NREM=NEGG-NDOZ*12
      PRINT *,'THERE ARE ',NDOZ,' DOZEN WITH ',
     1        NREM,' REMAINING IN ',NEGG,' EGGS.'
      STOP
      END
```

(a) The program

```
226
```

(b) Input data

```
THERE ARE 18 DOZEN WITH 10 REMAINING IN 226 EGGS.
```

(c) Output

than the minimum acceptable value, the condition is called *underflow*. Overflow and underflow can occur in real arithmetic when the exponent of the result of a calculation is outside of the acceptable exponent range. When overflow or underflow occurs, the result of the calculation is not correct. Thus, we should try to avoid such situations.

Both integer and real arithmetic can be used in the same program. For certain types of operations, one is preferred to the other. For problems involving whole numbers, integer arithmetic is preferred because operations involving whole numbers are usually faster using integer arithmetic than using real arithmetic. Integers are most often used for counting, keeping tallies, and similar operations. If an exponent is a whole number, an integer should always be used.

Integers cannot be used when a fractional part is necessary. Reals are used whenever the result may contain an important fraction. Much larger values can be stored as reals than as integers, but for whole numbers the values are usually not as accurate as their integer equivalent because of the difference in the way reals and integers are stored in the computer's internal storage. (See Appendix E.) Thus integers should be used for whole numbers unless they are very large, in which case reals must be used.

Real numbers are often only approximately equal to the desired value. For example, the quantity one-tenth (0.1) may actually be represented as 0.09999999 in the computer. Although this is very close to 0.1, it is not exactly equal to it. Approximations such as this can create problems when many calculations are done with real numbers. In such situations the final result may not be precisely correct.

3-8. Additional list-directed I/O features

In Chapter 2 we covered list-directed input and output in detail. Several additional features that are available with list-directed I/O are helpful in more advanced programs. This section describes these features.

List-directed input features

With list-directed input any valid constant is acceptable as an input value. The only restriction is that the constant's type must be the same as the type of the variable name in the I/O list. Thus we can read integer or real data from an input record. In addition, a *null value* can be specified in a data record by keying two successive commas. In effect, the commas indicate that no value is to be read for the corresponding variable name in the I/O list. As a result, the value of the variable name is unchanged. For example, assume that the following READ statement appears in a program (A and B are real; I and J are integer):

```
READ *,A,I,J,B
```

If we wish to read the values 12.5, 63, and 85.4 for A, I, and B, respectively, but not change the value of J, we would key the input data as follows:

```
12.5,63,,85.4
```

The two commas in the place where a value for J should appear indicate that no value is to be read for J. Hence, after execution of this statement, the value of J is whatever it was before the statement was executed.

If the values to be read for several successive variables in an I/O list are the same, the value can be keyed once with a *duplication factor*. The factor indicates how many times the value is to be repeated. For example, assume that we have the following READ statement in a program (all variable names are real):

```
READ *,A,B,C,D,E
```

We wish to read the value zero for each of the five variable names in the I/O list. One way to do this is to key the input data with five zeros separated by commas or blanks. Because the same value is to be read for each of the five variable names, we can use a duplication factor of 5 in the input record. This factor is followed by an asterisk and then the constant to be duplicated, which is 0.0 in this example. Thus the input record can be keyed as follows:

```
5*0.0
```

Note that this does *not* mean to multiply 0.0 by 5. Rather, the effect is as if 0.0 were keyed in the record five times. We can use a duplication factor with any type of value. In addition, we can duplicate a null value by not keying any value after the asterisk. We can have unduplicated values along with ones with duplication factors in the same record. Thus the following input record is acceptable:

```
3.5,4*,45,3*25,2*1
```

The first value read is 3.5. Then four null values appear. Next the value 45 is read, followed by 25, which is repeated three times. Finally, two 1s are read.

Sometimes we wish to stop reading before reaching the end of the I/O list. For example, assume that we have the following statement in a program (I, J, and K are integer; X, Y, and Z are real):

```
READ *,I,J,K,X,Y,Z
```

We wish to read values for I, J, and K, but not for X, Y, and Z. In effect, we want to supply null values for X, Y, and Z. One way to do this is to key the record with extra commas for the null values as follows:

```
5,6,7,,,,
```

An easier approach is to use a slash (/) after the last value in the record. That is, the record can be keyed as follows:

```
5,6,7/
```

This has the effect of stopping execution of the READ statement after the last value has been read and assigned to its corresponding variable name.

List-directed output features

With list-directed output, any valid variable name can be used in the I/O list. We can also put any acceptable constant in the list. We have seen this already with character constants, but we can also print the value of an integer or real constant. For example, the following PRINT statement is valid:

```
PRINT *,2,I,T,98.6
```

In addition to the values of the variables I and T, the constants 2 and 98.6 are printed. We can also use expressions in the list. For example, the following PRINT statement is valid:

```
PRINT *,I+J,7.5-3.2*A
```

The effect is that each expression is first evaluated, and then the resulting value is printed.

Review questions

1. Indicate whether each of the following is a valid or invalid constant:
   a. $-.004385$
   b. 83,250
   c. 16.5%
   d. $+58213$
2. Indicate whether each of the following is an integer or a real constant:
   a. 528.378
   b. .005821
   c. $+65.$
   d. -38012
3. What is the order of evaluation of the operators in an arithmetic expression?
4. Code an arithmetic expression that is equivalent to each of the following algebraic expressions:
   a. $x^2 - 2x + 3$
   b. $\dfrac{4x}{y} + \dfrac{a}{3}$
   c. $\dfrac{a - b}{a + b}$

d. $\dfrac{\left(4 - \dfrac{x}{a + b}\right)^3}{(c - d)^2}$

5. Assume that A, B, and C are real variable names and that A is 2.0, B is 3.0, and C is 4.0. What is the value of each of the following arithmetic expressions?
   a. $A - B + C$
   b. $C/A*B$
   c. $-C + B**2$
   d. $A - B*C/A + B/C$
   e. $(A - B)*C/(A + B)/C$
   f. $(A - B)*(C/((A + B)/C))$

6. Assume that X and Y are real variable names and that M and N are integer variable names. Indicate whether each of the following arithmetic expressions is integer mode, real mode, or mixed mode:
   a. $X + Y**2$
   b. $M*N/3.$
   c. $2.5*X/(M - N)$
   d. $10*(M - N)**3$

7. What is the effect of the following statement?
   ```
   X=X/2.0
   ```

8. Code a statement to compute the miles per gallon that an automobile uses given the distance traveled and the gallons used.

9. Assume that X is a real variable name and that M is an integer variable name. If the value of X is 2.78, what is the value of M after the following statement is executed?
   ```
   M=10.0*X
   ```

10. Code a PARAMETER statement that assigns the value 3.14 to the constant named PI.

11. Code a statement that is equivalent to the following algebraic equation:

$$c = \sqrt{a^2 + b^2}$$

Use a FORTRAN-supplied function

12. Assume that I is an integer variable name with a value of 5 and that A is a real variable name. What is the value of A after execution of each of the following statements?
   a. `A=REAL(I)`
   b. `A=REAL(I)/2.0`
   c. `A=REAL(I/2)`
   d. `A=5.0*REAL(I)/REAL(2*I)`

13. Assume that A and B are real variable names with values of 2.5 and 10.0, respectively, and that I is an integer variable name. What is the value of I after execution of each of the following statements?
   a. `I=INT(A)`
   b. `I=INT(B)/INT(A)`
   c. `I=INT(B/A)`
   d. `I=INT(2.75*REAL(INT(A)))`

14. Assume that Y is a real variable name with a positive value. Code a single statement that rounds off the value of Y to one decimal position and assigns the result to the real variable named Z. For example, if the value of Y is 25.578, then Z should be assigned the value 25.6.

15. Assume that L, M, and N are integer variable names with values of 2, 3, and 4, respectively. What is the value of each of the following arithmetic expressions?
    a. L−M*N
    b. L**M**L
    c. L*M/N
    d. N/M/L

16. Code a group of statements that computes the length of a room in yards and feet given the length in feet. For example, if the length is 17 feet, the result computed should be 5 yards and 2 feet. Assume all variable names used in the statements are integer.

17. If the result of an arithmetic operation is greater than the maximum value that the computer can store, an _____ occurs.

18. A program is needed to tabulate the votes for each candidate in an election. What type of variable name (integer or real) would be best for keeping track of the vote counts? What type of variable name would be best for computing the percentage of the total vote that each candidate got?

19. In the following READ statement all variable names are integer:
    ```
    READ *,Z,Y,X,W,V,U,T,S,R,Q
    ```
    Assume that the record read by this statement has the following data recorded in it:
    ```
    2*6,,,5,3*8/
    ```
    What is the value of each variable name in the input list of the READ statement after it is executed?

20. Code a single statement that prints the value of A, the constant 8, and the value of A+8.

Programming problems

For each of the following problems, all output should be identified with appropriate headings or other descriptive phrases.

1. The annual depreciation of an asset by the straight-line method is calculated by the following formula:

$$\text{Depreciation} = \frac{\text{Cost} - \text{Salvage value}}{\text{Service life}}$$

Write a FORTRAN program that reads the cost, salvage value, and service life. Then calculate the depreciation and write the result. Test the program using $13,525.00 for the cost, $1,500.00 for the salvage value, and 7 years for the service life.

2. Fahrenheit temperature is converted to Celsius temperature by the following formula:

$$C = \frac{5}{9} \times (F - 32)$$

In this formula F is the temperature in degrees Fahrenheit, and C is the temperature in degrees Celsius. Write a FORTRAN program to read the temperature in Fahrenheit, calculate the equivalent temperature in Celsius using the preceding formula, and write the result. To test the program use the following Fahrenheit temperatures as input data:

> 78.4
> − 50
> 98.6
> 0
> 32
> 212

3. The present value P of income I received N years in the future is given by the formula:

$$P = \frac{I}{(1 + R)^N}$$

In this formula R is the discount rate expressed as a fraction (e.g., if the discount rate is 5% then R is .05). Write a FORTRAN program that computes the present value given the income, number of years, and discount rate, and prints the result. To test the program use the following input data:

Income ($)	Number of Years	Discount Rate (%)
10,000	5	10
1,200	2	5
42,365	18	12.5
6,000	20	8

4. In economic theory, supply and demand curves can sometimes be represented by the following equations:

> Supply: $P = A \times Q + B$
> Demand: $P = C \times Q + D$

In these equations, P represents the price and Q the quantity. The values of A, B, C, and D determine the actual curves.

These equations can be solved for P and Q, giving the equilibrium price and quantity for any commodity. The formulas are as follows:

$$P = \frac{C \times B - A \times D}{C - A}$$

$$Q = \frac{D - B}{A - C}$$

Write a FORTRAN program to calculate the equilibrium price and quantity for a product. Input to the program should be the values of A, B, C, and D. Output should be the price and quantity at equilibrium. Test the program with the following data:

> $A =$ .19
> $B =$ 1.20
> $C =$ − .42
> $D =$ 8.50

5. The system of linear equations

> $ax + by = c$
> $dx + ey = f$

has the following solution:

$$x = \frac{ce - bf}{ae - bd}$$

$$y = \frac{af - cd}{ae - bd}$$

Write a FORTRAN program to solve the system and to print the values of x and y. Input consists of the values of a, b, c, d, e, and f. Use the following data to test the program:

a	b	c	d	e	f
1.0	2.0	3.0	4.0	5.0	6.0
5.2	8.9	13.2	-6.3	7.2	2.1
-83.82	42.61	-59.55	14.73	5.32	-39.99
.035	-.327	1.621	.243	.006	.592

6. Several calculations are important in analyzing the current position of a company. The formulas for the calculations are as follows:

$$\text{Working capital} = \text{Current assets} - \text{Current liabilities}$$

$$\text{Current ratio} = \frac{\text{Current assets}}{\text{Current liabilities}}$$

$$\text{Acid-test ratio} = \frac{\text{Cash} + \text{Accounts receivable}}{\text{Current liabilities}}$$

Assume that the cash, accounts receivable, current assets, and current liabilities are available for input. Write a FORTRAN program to read the data, perform the preceding calculations, and print the results. Use the following data to test the program:

Cash:	10,620
Accounts receivable:	5,850
Current assets:	22,770
Current liabilities:	14,680

7. The final score for a particular test is equal to the number of questions answered correctly minus one-fourth of the number answered incorrectly. Assume that test data available for input includes the student's identification number, number correct on the test, and number incorrect, all of which are integers. Write a program to calculate the final score from this data and to print the results along with the input data. Note that the number correct and incorrect are integers and should be printed as integers but must be converted to reals before doing the calculations.

Use the following input data to test the program:

Student Number	Number Correct	Number Incorrect
1	90	10
2	75	20
3	84	0
4	57	35
5	10	50
6	95	5

8. The interest and maturity value of a promissory note can be calculated as follows:

$$\text{Interest} = \frac{\text{Principal} \times \text{Rate} \times \text{Time}}{360}$$

$$\text{Maturity value} = \text{Principal} + \text{Interest}$$

Write a FORTRAN program that reads the loan number, principal, rate (percent), and time (days), performs the preceding calculations, and prints the loan number, rate (percent), time, interest, and maturity value. Note that the rate is expressed in percent for input and output purposes but must be converted to decimal form for the calculation. Thus, if the input value for the rate is 5 (meaning 5%), this must be converted to .05 for use in the calculation. The conversion from percent to decimal form must be done within the program; the input and output of the rate should be percentages. Use the program to find the interest and maturity value of loan number 1875 which is a $450 note with a rate of 6% for 60 days.

9. An approximation to the value of sin x can be computed as follows:

$$\sin x = x - \frac{x^3}{6} + \frac{x^5}{120}$$

In this formula the angle x must be in radians (1 radian = 59.2958 degrees). Write a FORTRAN program that reads an angle in degrees and computes the sine of the angle using the preceding equation and using the FORTRAN-supplied SIN function. (The SIN function also requires that the angle be in radians.) Then the program should compute the difference between the two values for the sine. The program should print the angle in degrees, the two values for the sine, and the difference between the values. Test the program with the following angles:

    45
    0
    37.5
    90
    22

10. The payroll in a particular business is calculated as follows:
    a. Gross pay is the hours worked times the pay rate.
    b. Withholding tax is found by subtracting thirteen times the number of exemptions from the gross pay and multiplying the result by the tax rate.
    c. Social security tax is 6.05% of the gross pay.
    d. Net pay is the gross pay less all taxes.

    Write a FORTRAN program that reads an employee's identification number, hours worked, pay rate, tax rate, and number of exemptions. The program should calculate the employee's gross pay, withholding and social security taxes, and net pay and then print these results along with the employee's identification number.

    Use the following input data to test the program:

Employee Number	Hours Worked	Pay Rate	Tax Rate (%)	Number of Exemptions
1001	40	4.50	20	3
1002	36	3.75	17.5	4
1003	47	6.50	24	0
1004	25	5.25	22.5	2

11. Grade point average is calculated by multiplying the units for each course that a student takes by the numeric grade that he or she receives in the course

(A = 4.0, B = 3.0, C = 2.0, D = 1.0, F = 0.0), totaling for all courses, and dividing by the total number of units. For example, assume that a student received a C (2.0) in a four-unit course and a B (3.0) in a two-unit course. Then his or her GPA is calculated as follows:

$$\frac{4 \times 2.0 + 2 \times 3.0}{4 + 2} = 2.33$$

Write a FORTRAN program to calculate one student's GPA, given the units and grade in each of five courses that he or she took. Input for the program is the student's identification number and the units (integer) and number grade (real) for each of the five courses. Output from the program should list the student's number, total units (integer), and grade point average (real).

Test the program with data for student number 18357, who got an A in a two-unit course, a C in a three-unit course, a D in a one-unit course, a C in a four-unit course, and a B in a three-unit course.

12. A projectile that is fired with an initial velocity v at an angle θ reaches a maximum height h in time t given by the following formulas:

$$h = \frac{1}{2} \frac{v^2 \sin^2 \theta}{32}$$
$$t = \frac{v \sin \theta}{32}$$

The sine of an angle is found using the function SIN; the angle must be in radians. (One radian equals 57.2958 degrees.)

Write a FORTRAN program that reads the values of v and θ (in degrees) and computes h and t. The program should print the values of v, θ (in degrees), h, and t. Use the following input data to test the program:

Velocity	Angle
247.38	45
100.00	72.5
360.00	0
282.61	90
75.32	25.6

13. Write a FORTRAN program that converts seconds into hours, minutes, and seconds remaining. Input should be the amount of time in seconds. Output should be the number of seconds and its equivalent in hours, minutes, and seconds remaining. For example, 4372 seconds is equivalent to 1 hour, 12 minutes, and 52 seconds. Test the program using 28,635 seconds.

14. There are 3.281 feet in a meter and 0.3937 inches in a centimeter. Write a program that reads a distance in feet and inches and computes and prints the equivalent distance in meters and centimeters. Give the answer in whole meters and centimeters rounded to the nearest centimeter. Test the program with the distance 6 feet, 9 inches.

15. The percent correct for each part of a three-part test needs to be calculated. The number of questions in each part varies but is always less than 100. Write a FORTRAN program to do the necessary calculations. Input consists of one record containing the number of questions in each of three parts. Following this is one input record for each student giving the student's number followed by his or her scores on each of the three parts. The program should calculate the percent correct for each part and the percent correct on all three parts

combined. Output should give the number of questions in each part and the total number of questions for all three parts. Then for each student the output should list the number correct on each part, the percent correct on each part, and the total percent correct.

To test the program assume that Part I of the test contains 50 questions, Part II contains 90 questions, and Part III contains 40 questions. The students' results are as follows:

Student Number	Part I Correct	Part II Correct	Part III Correct
18372	37	83	28
19204	25	30	30
20013	45	87	36
21563	0	53	40

16. The economic order quantity represents the most economic quantity of inventory that should be ordered for each item in stock. The formula for calculating the economic order quantity is:

$$Q = \sqrt{\frac{2 \times R \times S}{H}}$$

In this formula Q is the quantity ordered, R is the demand rate, S is the set-up or ordering cost, and H is the inventory holding cost. If C represents unit cost, then the average cost per unit of inventory held is given by the following formula:

$$A = C + \frac{S}{Q} + \frac{H \times Q}{2 \times R}$$

Write a FORTRAN program to calculate the economic order quantity and the average cost per unit when this quantity is ordered. Read the values for R, S, H, and C. Print the values for the economic order quantity and the average cost per unit. Be sure to print the economic order quantity as a whole number, correctly rounded.

Finally, calculate the average cost per unit when the quantity ordered is 30% more than the economic order quantity. Print that quantity and the average cost. Do the same for an order quantity that is 30% less than the economic order quantity.

Use the following data to test the program:

$$R = 1025$$
$$S = \$75$$
$$H = \$60$$
$$C = \$235$$

Chapter 4

Programming for decisions

In a program containing only a sequence of input/output and arithmetic assignment statements, the statements are executed in the order in which they are written. The examples in the last two chapters illustrated this. Sometimes we wish to alter the order of the execution of the statements in a program. For example, we may want the computer to select between several sequences of statements based on some condition or to repeat a group of statements until a particular condition occurs. These activities involve controlling the order of execution within a program. The statements that are used in FORTRAN to accomplish this are called *control statements*. (The GO TO statement, discussed in Chapter 2, is an example of a control statement.)

In this chapter we begin the discussion of program control and control statements by examining programming for decision making. Decision making involves selecting between alternative sequences of statements based on some condition that occurs during the execution of the program. For example, assume that we need to write a program that calculates the tuition for a college student based on the number of units (credits) that the student is taking. If the student is taking fewer than a certain number of units (say, twelve), the tuition is calculated one way; otherwise a different calculation is used. To do this the computer must decide which of two calculations are to be performed based on a particular condition.

In this chapter we describe the FORTRAN control statements necessary for decision making and discuss related program logic. After completing this chapter you should be able to write programs using a variety of patterns of decision making. In the next chapter we discuss other aspects of program control.

4-1. The block IF statement

The main decision-making statement in FORTRAN is the block IF statement. This statement is used in conjunction with the ELSE statement and the END

IF statement. The snytax of these statements and their basic pattern is as follows:

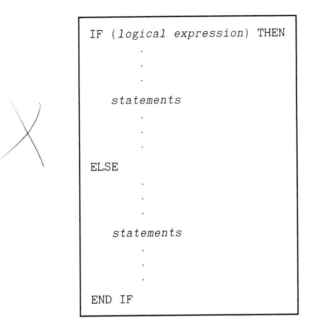

```
IF (logical expression) THEN
          .
          .
          .
       statements
          .
          .
          .
ELSE
          .
          .
          .
       statements
          .
          .
          .
END IF
```

The first statement in this group is the block IF statement. This statement contains a logical expression enclosed in parentheses. A *logical expression* is one that is either true or false. A common type of logical expression is called a *relational expression* which we describe later. (Other types of logical expressions are discussed in Chapter 8.) Following the block IF statement are any number of FORTRAN statements and then the ELSE statement which is just the keyword ELSE. After this statement comes any number of FORTRAN statements and then the END IF statement. This statement is the keywords END IF, which may also be written ENDIF.

The following is an example of the use of these statements:

```
IF (A.GT.B) THEN
   C=A-B
   PRINT *,A,B,C
ELSE
   C=0
   READ *,A,B
END IF
```

In this example, A.GT.B is a relational expression that is true if the value of A is greater than the value of B and false otherwise. Execution of the block IF statement causes the computer to evaluate the relational expression to determine whether it is true or false. Then, if the expression is true, the first group of statements, between the block IF statement and the ELSE statement, is executed and the second group of statements following the ELSE statement up to the END IF statement is bypassed. If the condition is false, the first group of statements is bypassed and the second group of statements is executed. In this example, the first arithmetic assignment statement and the PRINT statement are executed if the value of A is greater than that of B; otherwise, the second assignment statement and the READ statement are executed. After doing either group of statements, the computer goes on to the next statement following the END IF statement.

Notice in this example that the statements between the block IF and ELSE statements and between the ELSE and END IF statements are indented. This is a common style used with the block IF statement that helps the programmer see the decision logic of the program.

Any number of statements (including none) may be between the block IF statement and the ELSE statement and between the ELSE statement and the END IF statement. The computer executes all statements in one or the other of these groups of statements (but not in both) depending on the truth or falsity of the logical expression. After executing the appropriate statements, the computer goes to the next statement after the END IF statement.

Almost any type of executable statement may be used with a block IF statement. Thus, READ statements, PRINT statements, arithmetic assignment statements, STOP statements, GO TO statements, and as we shall see, other block IF, ELSE, and END IF statements may appear between block IF and ELSE statements and between ELSE and END IF statements. One exception is the END statement which can only come at the end of the program.

If a GO TO statement is used with a block IF statement, the computer may branch to another statement in the program rather than go on to the next statement following the END IF statement. For example, consider the following statements:

```
IF (A.GT.B) THEN
  C=A+B
  GO TO 50
ELSE
  PRINT *,A,B
END IF
```

In this example, if the value of A is greater than that of B, the assignment statement is executed followed by the GO TO statement which causes the computer to branch to statement 50. In this case, the computer would not go on to the next statement after the END IF statement (unless this statement were numbered 50). Although to use the GO TO statement like this is valid in FORTRAN, this is generally not a good technique because it can create very confusing logic in the program. (In Chapter 7 we will discuss the reason for this.)

GO TO statements can be used between block IF and END IF statements to branch out of a decision as just shown. However, it is not valid to use a

GO TO statement someplace else in the program to branch to a statement between a block IF statement and an END IF statement. For example, consider the following statements:

```
      IF (A.GT.B) THEN
120     PRINT *,A,B
      ELSE
140     C=B-A
      END IF
```

With this example it would not be permissible to branch to the statements numbered 120 and 140. It is also not valid to branch to an ELSE statement, and there is usually no reason to branch to an END IF statement. However, it is entirely acceptable to branch to a block IF statement.

Relational expressions

The most common type of logical expression is the relational expression. This expression compares the values of two arithmetic expressions. Values may be compared to determine whether one is greater than or less than the other, whether they are equal or not equal, or whether combinations of these conditions are true. The relational expression has a *truth value* of true or false, depending on whether the indicated comparison is correct or not correct.

The way in which the values of the arithmetic expressions are compared is given by a *relational operator*. The following are the relational operators used in FORTRAN and their meanings:

Relational Operator	*Meaning*
.LT.	Less than
.LE.	Less than or equal to
.GT.	Greater than
.GE.	Greater than or equal to
.EQ.	Equal to
.NE.	Not equal to

Notice that each relational operator begins and ends with a period.

The simplest form of a relational expression is a constant or a variable name followed by a relational operator and then another constant or variable name. For example, the following are valid relational expressions:

```
J.LT.K
6..LE.C
Q.GT.5.6
K.GE.-5
A.EQ.B
7.NE.J
```

To evaluate each of these, the values of the variables and constants are compared according to the relational operator. For example, if J is 6 and K is 5, the first expression is *false*. Similarly, if both J and K are both 6 the expression is *false*. However, if J is 6 and K is 7, the expression is *true*.

Mixed mode is allowed in relational expressions. For example, if A is integer and K is real, the expression

```
A.LT.K
```

is mixed mode because it compares a real value with an integer. However, this expression is valid. Even though mixed mode relational expressions are acceptable, they should not be used because their evaluation can be complex. Mixed mode can always be overcome by using the REAL and INT functions. Thus the previous expression can be coded

```
A.LT.REAL(K)
```

which is not mixed mode.

When comparing a real constant without decimal positions, the potential for mixed mode is particularly great. For example, if C is real, the expression

```
6.LE.C
```

is mixed mode because the first period belongs with the less than or equal to operator (.LE.) and not with the digit six. This can be overcome in this example by adding a decimal point after the number 6. The resulting expression is

```
6..LE.C
```

A better approach is to code the constant as 6.0. Then the expression is

```
6.0.LE.C
```

Relational operators may be used to compare the values of complex arithmetic expressions. For example, the following relational expressions are valid:

```
Q.GT.P-5.6
K+8.GE.-5-L
X+Y/(4.56-Z).EQ.(Z-REAL(M))
INT(A)-(I+1).NE.(K-5)
```

Notice that parentheses may be used to enclose part or all of either arithmetic expression in a relational expression.

In evaluating a relational expression containing arithmetic expressions, the computer uses the current values of the variable names to evaluate each arithmetic expression. The computer then compares the resulting values of the arithmetic expressions according to the relational operator to determine the truth value of the relational expression. If the condition specified by the relational operator is correct, the relational expression is *true*. If the condition is not correct, the relational expression is *false*. For example, consider the following relational expression (assume that N is integer):

    N-3.GE.5

If N has a value of 10, then N−3 is 7. Because 7 is greater than 5, the relational expression is true. If N has a value of 4, then N−3 is 1. Because 1 is not greater than or equal to 5, the expression is false. If N is 8, then N−3 is 5 and the relational expression is true.

A relational expression may not be written with just one arithmetic expression. For example, the following expression is invalid because it lacks an arithmetic expression on the left of the relational operator:

    .GT.P-5.6

If we had wanted to compare the value of Q with the value of P−5.6, the correct expression would have been

    Q.GT.P-5.6

In addition, the relational operator must always begin and end with a period. The following expression is invalid because the period on the right of the relational expression is missing:

    K+8.GE -5-L

This is correctly coded as

    K+8.GE.-5-L

Illustrative programs

To illustrate the use of the block IF statement and relational expressions in a program, assume that we need to write a program that calculates the tuition for a college student. The input data is the student's identification number and the number of units (credits) for which the student is enrolled. If the student is taking twelve or fewer units, the tuition is $350. However, if the student is taking more than twelve units, the tuition is $350 plus $20 per unit for all units over twelve. The program must print the identification number and tuition for each student.

The program to accomplish this requires decision making. First the input data must be read. Then the computer must examine the number of units to determine the tuition. This decison-making step can be stated as follows: If the number of units is less than or equal to twelve, the tuition is $350; otherwise, the tuition is $350 plus $20 per unit for all units over twelve. In other words, the computer must select between two ways of calculating the tuition based on a comparison between the number of units for which the student is enrolled and twelve. After the tuition is calculated, the output can be written.

The program in Figure 4-1 solves this problem. The READ statement reads the student's number (SNUM) and number of units (UNITS). Then the IF statement compares the number of units with 12.0. If UNITS is less than or equal to 12.0, the tuition (TUIT) is set equal to $350. If this condition is not true, the tuition is calculated as $350 plus $20 per unit for all units over 12.0. After determining the tuition, the PRINT statement is executed. The program has a loop so that the processing is repeated until no more input data is supplied.

As another illustration of decision making assume that we need a program to calculate employee pay. The gross pay is $6.50 per hour for the first forty hours worked and $9.75 per hour for all time over forty hours. In addition, the withholding tax is 18% of the gross pay if 40 or fewer hours are worked and 22% of the gross pay if more than 40 hours are recorded. The net pay is the gross pay less the withholding tax.

The program in Figure 4-2 satisfies these requirements. The program first reads the input data. Then the number of hours worked is compared with forty. If the hours are less than or equal to forty, the gross pay and tax

Figure 4-1. The tuition calculation program

```
C   TUITION CALCULATION PROGRAM
        INTEGER SNUM
        REAL UNITS,TUIT
    10 READ (*,*,END=20) SNUM,UNITS
        IF (UNITS.LE.12.0) THEN
          TUIT=350.00
        ELSE
          TUIT=350.00+20.00*(UNITS-12.0)
        END IF
        PRINT *,'STUDENT NUMBER = ',SNUM,'  TUITION = ',TUIT
        GO TO 10
    20 STOP
        END
```

(a) The program

```
1234,6.
3456,15.
5678,12.
7890,12.5
```

(b) Input data

```
STUDENT NUMBER = 1234   TUITION = 350.
STUDENT NUMBER = 3456   TUITION = 410.
STUDENT NUMBER = 5678   TUITION = 350.
STUDENT NUMBER = 7890   TUITION = 360.
```

(c) Output

Figure 4-2. A payroll calculation program

```
C  PAYROLL CALCULATION PROGRAM
       INTEGER EMPID
       REAL HOURS,GROSS,NET
       REAL PAYRT1,PAYRT2,TAXRT1,TAXRT2
       PARAMETER (PAYRT1=6.50,PAYRT2=9.75,TAXRT1=.18,TAXRT2=.22)
  100 READ (*,*,END=200) EMPID,HOURS
       IF (HOURS.LE.40.0) THEN
          GROSS=PAYRT1*HOURS
          TAX=TAXRT1*GROSS
       ELSE
          GROSS=PAYRT1*40.0+PAYRT2*(HOURS-40.0)
          TAX=TAXRT2*GROSS
       END IF
       NET=GROSS-TAX
       PRINT *,'ID = ',EMPID,'  GROSS PAY = ',GROSS,
      1          ' TAX = ',TAX,'  NET PAY = ',NET
       GO TO 100
  200 STOP
       END
```

(a) The program

```
234,32
456,48
678,36
789,38
890,44
```

(b) Input data

```
ID = 234  GROSS PAY = 208.  TAX = 37.44  NET PAY = 170.56
ID = 456  GROSS PAY = 338.  TAX = 74.36  NET PAY = 263.64
ID = 678  GROSS PAY = 234.  TAX = 42.12  NET PAY = 191.88
ID = 789  GROSS PAY = 247.  TAX = 44.46  NET PAY = 202.54
ID = 890  GROSS PAY = 299.  TAX = 65.78  NET PAY = 233.22
```

(c) Output

are calculated by the statements following the block IF statement up to the ELSE statement. If the hours are greater than forty, the computer calculates the gross pay and tax with the statements following the ELSE statement up to the END IF statement. After the computer calculates the gross pay and withholding tax by one of the two methods, it calculates the net pay and prints the output.

Alternative use of the block IF statement

The block IF statement may be used without the ELSE statement. The pattern is as follows:

```
IF (logical expression) THEN
                .
                .
                .
        statements
                .
                .
                .

END IF
```

Notice that there is no ELSE statement but that the END IF statement is still required. If the logical expression is true, the computer executes the statements between the block IF statement and the END IF statement and then goes on to the next statement following the END IF statement. If the expression is false, the computer bypasses these statements and goes directly to the first statement after the END IF statement.

As an example of this use of the block IF statement, consider the following statements:

```
IF (A.LE.B) THEN
    C=B-A
    PRINT *,C
END IF
```

If A is less than or equal to B, the computer executes the arithmetic assignment statement and the PRINT statement. If this condition is not true, the computer skips these statements. In either case the computer continues with the next statement following the END IF statement.

The tuition calculation program in Figure 4-1 can be modified to use the block IF statement this way. Figure 4-3 shows the modified program. In this example, the input data is read and then TUIT is set equal to 350.00.

Figure 4-3. The modified tuition calculation program

```
C   TUITION CALCULATION PROGRAM
        INTEGER SNUM
        REAL UNITS,TUIT
    10 READ (*,*,END=20) SNUM,UNITS
        TUIT=350.00
        IF (UNITS.GT.12.0) THEN
          TUIT=350.00+20.00*(UNITS-12.0)
        END IF
        PRINT *,'STUDENT NUMBER = ',SNUM,'  TUITION = ',TUIT
        GO TO 10
    20 STOP
        END
```

Next the block IF statement determines if the units are greater than twelve. If this is true, the tuition is calculated as \$350 plus \$20 per unit over twelve. This new value of the tuition replaces the previous value of TUIT. However, if the units are less than or equal to twelve, the new calculation is not done and TUIT remains equal to 350.00. Finally, the PRINT statement prints the output and the loop is repeated. Although this program is slightly different from the one in Figure 4-1, the output is identical if the same input is used.

Conditions and complements

A relational expression represents a *condition* that is either true or false. For example, the condition "the number of units is less than or equal to twelve" is represented by the relational expression UNITS.LE.12.0. Most conditions that involve a comparison of two values can be expressed in a relational expression. Chapter 8 discusses more complex conditions that can be represented in FORTRAN.

Sometimes the logic in a program is such that the *complement* of a condition is needed. The complement of a condition is the condition that is true if the original condition is false and vice versa. For example, the complement of the condition "the number of units is less than or equal to twelve" is the condition "the number of units is greater than twelve." Similarly, the complement of the condition "A is equal to B" is the condition "A is not equal to B."

For each relational operator in FORTRAN, there is another relational operator for representing the complement of the original condition, as the following table shows:

Relational Operator	Complement
.LT.	.GE.
.LE.	.GT.
.GT.	.LE.
.GE.	.LT.
.EQ.	.NE.
.NE.	.EQ.

Thus in FORTRAN the complement of the condition UNITS.LE.12.0 is UNITS.GT.12.0. Similarly, the complement of A.EQ.B. is A.NE.B.

We can rewrite most decisions using the complement of the condition. To do this, the true and false parts need to be reversed. For example, the decision in the program in Figure 4-1 can be rewritten as follows:

```
IF (UNITS.GT.12.0) THEN
    TUIT=350.00+20.00*(UNITS-12.0)
ELSE
    TUIT=350.00
END IF
```

The program with this decision gives output identical to that of the original program for the same input.

Usually the selection of the appropriate condition to use in a program is fairly straightforward. However, sometimes the programmer can choose between using a condition or its complement. In such cases the programmer should select the approach that makes the program easier to understand.

Patterns of decision making

In this section we have described two patterns of decision making. The diagram in Figure 4-4 represents the first pattern. At the point in the program where the decision is to be made, a condition is tested for its truth value. If the condition is true, one group of statements is executed; if the condition is false, another set of statements is performed. We call the statements to be executed if the condition is true the *true part* of the decision, and the statements to be executed if the condition is false the *false part*. After doing either the true part or the false part (but not both), the computer continues with the next statement. We sometimes call this a "two-sided" decision because it has both a true part and a false part. The pattern is coded in FORTRAN using a block IF statement, an ELSE statement, and an END IF statement, as shown in Figure 4-5.

Figure 4-6 shows the second pattern. This pattern also tests a condition for its truth value. If the condition is true, a group of statements (the *true part*) is executed; if the condition is false, these statements are bypassed. In either case, the computer goes on to the next statement in sequence. We sometimes call this a "one-sided" decision because there is only a true part in the decision logic. This pattern is coded in FORTRAN using a block IF

Figure 4-4. The two-sided decision pattern

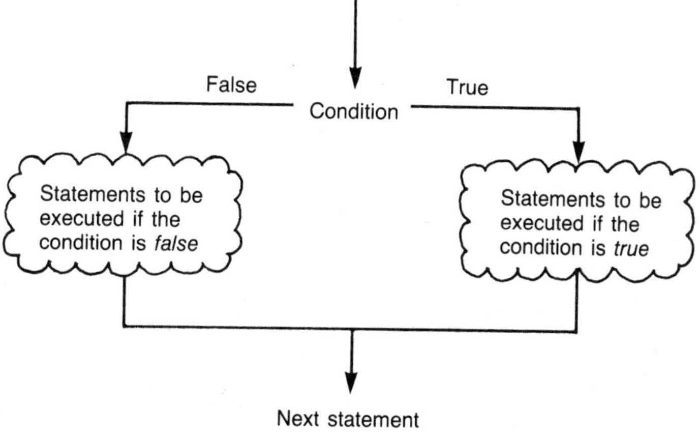

Figure 4-5. The two-sided decision pattern in FORTRAN

IF (*condition*) THEN

ELSE

END IF

Figure 4-6. The one-sided decision pattern

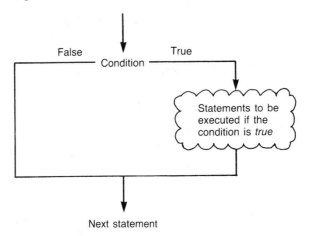

Next statement

statement and an END IF statement, but no ELSE statement, as shown in Figure 4-7.

    These two patterns form the basis for all decision making in programs. We will see many examples of their use in this book.

Figure 4-7. The one-sided decision pattern in FORTRAN

IF (*condition*) THEN

true part

END IF

4-2. Nested decisions

The true or false parts of a decision may contain any number or type of statements (with some exceptions). In fact, the true or false parts may contain other block IF statements. When a block IF statement is included within a set of statements that is executed depending on the condition in another block IF statement, we say there are *nested IF statements* and we call the pattern *nested decisions*.

Figure 4-8 shows a typical nested decision pattern. This figure is similar to Figure 4-4 except that the true and false parts are replaced by other decisions. Figure 4-9 shows the FORTRAN equivalent of this pattern. The interpretation is as follows: First, condition-1 is tested. If this condition is true, condition-2 is checked. If this second condition is true, all of the statements between the second block IF statement and the first ELSE statement are executed. We call this the *true-true part* because both conditions must be true for these statements to be executed.

If condition-2 is false (and condition-1 is true), the statements between the first ELSE statement and the first END IF statement are executed (the *true-false part*). If the original condition, condition-1, is false, the computer checks condition-3. If this condition is true, all statements between the second block IF statement and the third ELSE statement are executed (the *false-true part*). Finally, if condition-3 is false (and condition-1 is false), the statements

Figure 4-8. A nested decision pattern

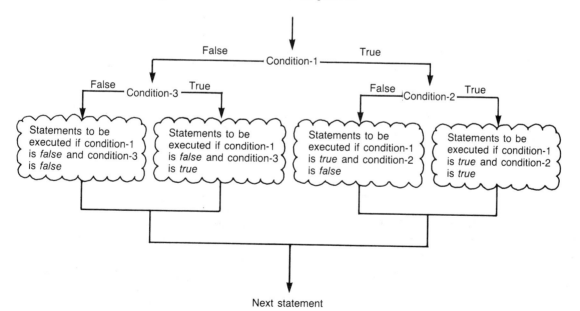

Next statement

Figure 4-9. A nested decision pattern in FORTRAN

```
IF (condition-1) THEN
    IF (condition-2) THEN
```

```
        true-true part
```

```
    ELSE
```

```
        true-false part
```

```
    END IF
ELSE
    IF (condition-3) THEN
```

```
        false-true part
```

```
    ELSE
```

```
        false-false part
```

```
    END IF
END IF
```

after the third ELSE statement up to the second END IF statement are executed. We call this the *false-false part* because both conditions must be false in order for these statements to be performed. After executing the statements in one and only one of the four "parts" in this pattern, the computer goes on to the next statement after the last END IF statement.

Notice in Figure 4-9 that each block IF statement has a matching END IF statement. The first END IF statement matches the second block IF statement. The second END IF statement goes with the third block IF statement. The last END IF statement is paired with the first block IF statement. There can never be a block IF statement without an END IF statement and vice versa. In addition, there can never be an ELSE statement without a matching block IF statement.

Each ELSE statement is paired with a block IF statement. In Figure 4-9 the first ELSE statement goes with the second block IF statement. The second ELSE statement matches the first block IF statement. The third ELSE statement is paired with the third block IF statement.

As an example of nested decisions assume that a college student's tuition is not only based on the number of units taken but also on whether or not the student is a resident of the state. If the number of units are less than or equal to twelve and the student is a state resident, the tuition is $350. If the student is not a resident (and the units are less than or equal to twelve), the tuition is $800. If the number of units is greater than twelve and the student is a resident, the tuition is $350 plus $20 for all units over twelve. For a nonresident with more than twelve units, the tuition is $800 plus $45 for each excess unit.

This problem requires first deciding if the number of units is or is not less than or equal to twelve and then in each case determining if the student is or is not a state resident. Assume that the input data is the student's identification number (SNUM), the number of units (UNITS), and a resident code (RES) which is 1 if the student is a state resident and 0 otherwise. Figure 4-10 shows a program to accomplish this. After reading the input data, the first block IF statement compares UNITS with 12.0. If UNITS is less than or equal to 12.0, the computer goes to the second block IF statement. This statement checks RES to determine whether or not the student is a state resident. If UNITS is greater than 12.0, the computer goes to the third block IF statement to check RES. The actual tuition depends on both the number of units and the residence code. After the tuition is determined, the output is printed and the loop is repeated.

Notice that indentation is used in this example to show which part belongs with which IF statement. This is especially important with nested IF statements. The indentation gives a visual clue to the program's logic.

Any type of decision (one-sided or two-sided) can be nested in another decision. The important requirements are that each block IF statement has a matching END IF statement and each ELSE statement is paired with a block IF statement. Figure 4-11 shows several valid patterns of nested decisions. Lines have been drawn in this figure to connect each block IF statement with its corresponding END IF statement.

As many decisions as the programmer needs can be nested inside each other. However, if too many decisions are nested, the program can be very difficult to understand. Usually it is best to nest no more than two or three decisions so that the logic is not too complex.

4-3. Case selection

A special type of nested decision, called *case selection,* involves selecting from among several cases. For example, assume that a student's tuition is based on the following schedule:

Units	*Tuition*
0.1 to 6.0	$200
6.1 to 12.0	$200 + $25/unit over 6
12.1 to 18.0	$350 + $20/unit over 12
18.1 and up	$470 + $15/unit over 18

Figure 4-10. A tuition calculation program with nested decisions

```
C   TUITION CALCULATION PROGRAM
        INTEGER SNUM,RES
        REAL UNITS,TUIT
    10 READ (*,*,END=20) SNUM,UNITS,RES
        IF (UNITS.LE.12.0) THEN
          IF (RES.EQ.1) THEN
            TUIT=350.00
          ELSE
            TUIT=800.00
          END IF
        ELSE
          IF (RES.EQ.1) THEN
            TUIT=350.00+20.00*(UNITS-12.0)
          ELSE
            TUIT=800.00+45.00*(UNITS-12.0)
          END IF
        END IF
        PRINT *,'STUDENT NUMBER = ',SNUM,'  TUITION = ',TUIT
        GO TO 10
    20 STOP
        END
```

(a) The program

```
1234,6.,0
2345,12.,1
3456,15.,1
4567,13.,0
5678,12.,0
6789,8.,1
7890,12.5,1
8901,18.,0
```

(b) Input data

```
STUDENT NUMBER = 1234   TUITION = 800.
STUDENT NUMBER = 2345   TUITION = 350.
STUDENT NUMBER = 3456   TUITION = 410.
STUDENT NUMBER = 4567   TUITION = 845.
STUDENT NUMBER = 5678   TUITION = 800.
STUDENT NUMBER = 6789   TUITION = 350.
STUDENT NUMBER = 7890   TUITION = 360.
STUDENT NUMBER = 8901   TUITION = 1070.
```

(c) Output

There are four cases that depend on the number of units for which the student is enrolled. We need FORTRAN statements that select the appropriate case and do the required calculation for each case.

We can use nested decisions to perform the selection process. First, we determine if the number of units is less than or equal to six. If it is, we select the first case and the tuition is $200. If the number of units is greater than six, we check to see if the number is less than or equal to twelve. If it is, the second case applies and the tuition is calculated appropriately. If the

Figure 4-11. Some valid nested decisions

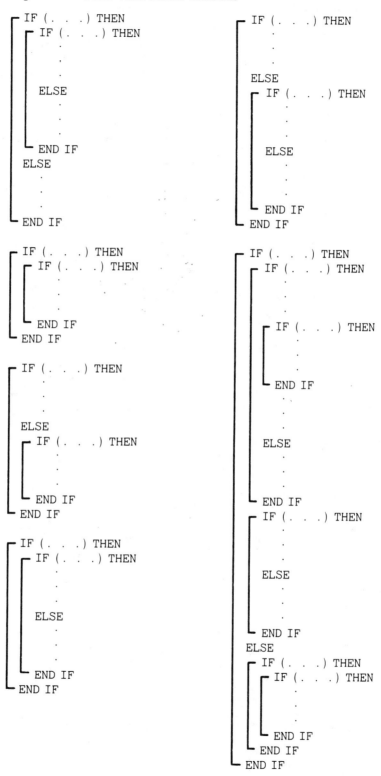

number of units is greater than twelve, we compare the number with eighteen. If it is less than or equal to eighteen, the third case is selected; otherwise, the fourth case applies.

Figure 4-12 shows how the tuition calculation can be coded using this case selection logic. The nested IF statements select the appropriate case for the tuition by comparing UNITS with 6.0, 12.0, and 18.0. The four cases for the tuition are coded in the proper places in the decision logic.

In this example all nesting is in the *false* parts of the decisions. This is characteristic of case selection. Because of this, FORTRAN provides a special statement, the ELSE IF statement, that can be used for this type of nested decision. The syntax of the ELSE IF statement is as follows:

```
ELSE IF (logical expression) THEN
```

For example, the following is a valid ELSE IF statement:

```
ELSE IF (UNITS.LE.12.0) THEN
```

This statement may appear only between a block IF and an END IF statement. Any number of ELSE IF statements may appear between these other statements. The ELSE IF statement never has a matching END IF statement; the END IF statement only goes with a block IF statement. If an ELSE statement is paired with the block IF statement, the ELSE statement must come after the last ELSE IF statement.

Figure 4-13 shows how the ELSE IF statement can be used for case selection for the tuition calculation. This figure gives the complete program for this problem. After reading the input data, the block IF statement checks the first condition. If this condition is true, the computer assigns TUIT the value of 200.00 and continues with the next statement following the END IF statement. If the first condition is false, the computer checks the condition in the first ELSE IF statement. If this condition is true, the second assignment statement calculates the tuition; otherwise, the computer checks the condition

Figure 4-12. Tuition calculation with case selection

```
IF (UNITS.LE.6.0) THEN
  TUIT=200.00
ELSE
  IF (UNITS.LE.12.0) THEN
    TUIT=200.00+25.00*(UNITS-6.0)
  ELSE
    IF (UNITS.LE.18.00) THEN
      TUIT=350.00+20.00*(UNITS-12.0)
    ELSE
      TUIT=475.00+15.00*(UNITS-18.0)
    END IF
  END IF
END IF
```

Figure 4-13. A tuition calculation program with case selection

```
C   TUITION CALCULATION PROGRAM
        INTEGER SNUM
        REAL UNITS,TUIT
    10  READ (*,*,END=20) SNUM,UNITS
        IF (UNITS.LE.6.0) THEN
          TUIT=200.00
        ELSE IF (UNITS.LE.12.0) THEN
          TUIT=200.00+25.00*(UNITS-6.0)
        ELSE IF (UNITS.LE.18.0) THEN
          TUIT=350.00+20.00*(UNITS-12.0)
        ELSE
          TUIT=470.00+15.00*(UNITS-18.0)
        END IF
        PRINT *,'STUDENT NUMBER = ',SNUM,'  TUITION = ',TUIT
        GO TO 10
    20  STOP
        END
```

(a) The program

```
1234,6.
2345,12.
3456,15.
4567,13.
5876,3.
6789,8.
7098,20.
8901,18.
9012,7.
9901,19.
```

(b) Input data

```
STUDENT NUMBER = 1234   TUITION = 200.
STUDENT NUMBER = 2345   TUITION = 350.
STUDENT NUMBER = 3456   TUITION = 410.
STUDENT NUMBER = 4567   TUITION = 370.
STUDENT NUMBER = 5876   TUITION = 200.
STUDENT NUMBER = 6789   TUITION = 250.
STUDENT NUMBER = 7098   TUITION = 500.
STUDENT NUMBER = 8901   TUITION = 470.
STUDENT NUMBER = 9012   TUITION = 225.
STUDENT NUMBER = 9901   TUITION = 485.
```

(c) Output

in the second ELSE IF statement. If none of the conditions is true, the assignment statement following the ELSE statement is executed. Notice that there are no matching END IF statements for the ELSE IF statements. The END IF statement at the end matches the block IF statement at the beginning. Also notice that the ELSE statement that goes with the block IF statement comes after all ELSE IF statements.

This example shows the usual way that indentation is used with ELSE IF statements. Some programmers, however, prefer other indentation patterns.

The example in Figure 4-13 includes an ELSE statement for the block IF statement. The statement following the ELSE statement is executed if all other cases are false. However, in some case selection situations, nothing is to be done when the other cases are not true. In such situations the ELSE statement is not included. For example, consider the following statements:

```
IF (A.EQ.1) THEN
    X=Y+Z
    B=C-D
ELSE IF (A.EQ.2) THEN
    X=Y-Z
    B=C*D
ELSE IF (A.EQ.3) THEN
    X=Y*Z
    B=C/D
END IF
```

In this example, there are three cases: A equals 1, A equals 2, and A equals 3. Different processing is done for each case. If none of these cases is true, the computer bypasses all processing in this group of statements and goes directly to the first statement following the END IF statement.

We can see from the examples that the ELSE IF statement can be extremely useful for case selection. Whenever case selection logic is required, we should consider using this statement.

4-4. The logical IF statement

Although the block IF statement is the main decision-making statement in FORTRAN, another statement, the logical IF statement, also is used in decision situations. The syntax of the logical IF statement is as follows:

```
IF (logical expression) executable statement
```

The statement begins with the keyboard IF followed by a logical expression in parentheses. After this can come any executable statement except another IF statement or a DO statement (discussed in Chapter 5). For example, the following is a valid logical IF statement:

```
IF (A.GT.B) C=A-B
```

Execution of a logical IF statement causes the computer to evaluate the logical expression and determine whether it is true or false. If the expression is true, the statement in the IF statement is executed next. If the logical expression is false, the computer bypasses this statement and continues execution with the next statement in sequence. In the previous example the computer determines if the value of A is greater than the value of B. If this condition is true, the computer executes the statement C = A − B. If A is not greater than B, the computer bypasses the statement and goes on to the next statement in sequence.

Any executable statement may be used in the logical IF statement (with the exceptions given earlier). For example, the following are valid logical IF statements:

```
IF (X.LT.Y) READ *,A,B,C
IF (K.EQ.7) PRINT *,K
IF (U.LE.12.0) GO TO 35
```

In each of these examples, the computer either executes the statement in the IF statement or bypasses it, depending on whether or not the logical expression is true. If the condition is true, the computer executes the statement in the IF statement and then goes on to the next statement in sequence unless a GO TO statement or other branching statement has been executed.

We can see that the logical IF statement creates a one-sided decision with only one statement executed when the condition is true. In fact, any logical IF statement can be coded using a block IF statement. Thus the first example in this section can be coded as follows:

```
IF (A.GT.B) THEN
    C=A−B
END IF
```

However, as we will see, in certain situations it is convenient to use a logical IF statement.

Decision logic in older FORTRAN programs

Some older programs were written in versions of FORTRAN that did not allow block IF, ELSE, ELSE IF, or END IF statements. Such programs created the same logic using a logical IF statement and GO TO statements. Although this approach should not be used today, the programmer should be familiar with it in case an older program needs to be modified.

Figure 4-14 shows the two-sided decision pattern using the block IF statement and the logical IF statement. Notice that with the logical IF statement the *complement* of the condition in the equivalent block IF statement is used. (Recall that the complement of a condition is one that is true when the original condition is false and vice versa.) The GO TO statement in the logical IF statement branches around the true part to the false part of the decision when the *complement* of the condition is *true* (that is, when the *condition* is *false*). When the *complement* of the *condition* is *false* (that is, when the *condition* is *true*), the computer goes on to the next statement after the logical IF statement which begins the true part of the decision. The GO TO statement

Figure 4-14. The two-sided decision pattern

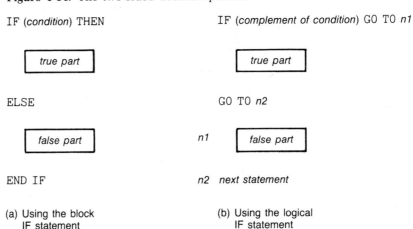

(a) Using the block
    IF statement

(b) Using the logical
    IF statement

at the end of the true part is necessary to branch around the false part when the true part is performed.

The following statements illustrate the two-sided decision pattern using a logical IF statement and GO TO statements:

```
        IF (A.LE.B) GO TO 30
          C=A-B
          PRINT *,A,B,C
        GO TO 40
    30    C=0
          READ *,A,B
    40 (next statement)
```

In this example, the first assignment statement and PRINT statement are executed if A is not less than or equal to B (that is, if A is greater than B). Then the statement GO TO 40 branches around the other statements to statement 40. If A is less than or equal to B (that is, A is not greater than B), the computer branches directly to the second assignment statement, executing it and the READ statement before going on to statement 40. Notice how indentation is used to give a visual clue to the decision logic.

Figure 4-15 shows the one-sided decision pattern using the block IF statement and the logical IF statement. Again, the complement of the condition is needed in the logical IF statement, and a GO TO statement is required to branch around the true part if the *complement* is *true* (that is, the *condition* is *false*). If the *complement* is *false* (that is, the *condition* is *true*), the computer goes on to the true part. No GO TO statement is required at the end of the true part because the computer automatically goes on to the next statement in sequence, as is desired, after executing the statements in this part. The following statements illustrate this pattern:

Figure 4-15. The one-sided decision pattern

IF *(condition)* THEN

IF *(complement of condition)* GO TO *n*

| true part |

| true part |

END IF

n   next statement

(a) Using the block
   IF statement

(b) Using the logical
   IF statement

```
     IF (A.GT.B) GO TO 50
        C=B-A
        PRINT *,C
  50 (next statement)
```

In this example, the two statements after the IF statement are executed if A is less than or equal to B, and they are bypassed if A is greater than B.

We can see from this discussion that we can code decision patterns without using block IF statements. However, the logic is more complex because of the use of complements of conditions and GO TO statements. The complexity is even greater when nested decisions or case selection are required. In general, block IF statements should always be used for decision making. However, the programmer may have to modify an older program that uses the approaches described here and hence should be familiar with them.

Review questions

1. Consider the following statements:
```
     IF (X.LT.Y) THEN
        Z=10.0
     ELSE
        Z=20.0
     END IF
```
   What is the value of Z after execution of these statements?
   a. if X is 20.0 and Y is 10.0
   b. if X is 20.0 and Y is 20.0
2. What is the meaning of each of the following relational operators?
   a. .LE.
   b. .NE.
   c. .EQ.
   d. .GT.

3. Assume that I is 2, J is 3, and K is 4. What is the truth value of each of the following relational expressions?
   a. I.GT.J
   b. K.LE.J+1
   c. 12/I+3.EQ.J**2
   d. I*J.NE.K+2
4. Code a group of statements to add 5.0 to C if A is greater than B; otherwise, add 6.0 to C.
5. Code a group of statements to assign 0.0 to S and 1.0 to T if U is less than or equal to 50.0; otherwise, assign 1.0 to S and 0.0 to T.
6. Code a group of statements to read and print the values of D and E if F is not equal to 100.0.
7. Code a group of statements to add the values of P and Q, assigning the result to R if I is greater than or equal to J.
8. What is the complement of each of the following conditions?
   a. A.EQ.B
   b. X.LE.Y
   c. P.GT.Q
   d. S.NE.T
9. Code a group of statements to assign the larger of X and Y to Z. Did you use a one-sided or two-sided decision? Code another group of statements using the other approach.
10. A program pattern in which one decision is contained in another is called
    _____ .
11. Code a group of statements to assign the value of 0, 1, 2, or 3 to I depending on the values of J and K as given in the following table:

		K	
		less than 5	5 or more
J	equal to 10	0	1
	not equal to 10	2	3

12. Code a group of statements to increase A by 1.0 if X and Y are both equal to 25.0, to increase A by 2.0 if X is equal to 25.0 and Y is equal to 35.0, to increase A by 3.0 if X is equal to 25.0 and Y is equal to neither 25.0 nor 35.0, and to assign 0.0 to A if X is not equal to 25.0.
13. Code a group of statements to assign 0.0 to S if T is equal to 2.0 and U is equal to 4.0 and to assign 2.0 to S when T is not equal to 2.0 and U is equal to 3.0.
14. Each block IF statement must have a matching _____ statement. Each ELSE statement must have a matching _____ statement.
15. A program pattern that involves picking one of several alternatives is called
    CASE SELECTION
16. Code a group of statements to assign the value to N from the following table depending on the value of M:

M	N
0	100
1 to 5	200
6, 7, or 8	300
9 or more	400

17. Code a single statement to decrease X by 2.0 if Y is less than or equal to Z.
18. Code a single statement to branch to statement 100 if K equals 0.
19. Rewrite the following group of statements without using GO TO statements:

```
      IF (X.EQ.Y) GO TO 100
        X=X+1
        Z=0
      GO TO 200
  100   Z=X+Y
        Y=X
  200 PRINT *,Z
```

20. Rewrite the following group of statements without using GO TO statements:

```
      IF (I.GE.10) GO TO 300
        I=2*I
        J=I
        PRINT *,I,J
  300 I=I-1
```

Programming problems

1. A salesperson's commission is often based on the amount that the person sold. Assume that the commission rate is 7½% if a person's sales total less than $10,000 and 9% if sales total $10,000 or more. The commission is calculated by multiplying the person's sales by the appropriate commission rate.

   Write a FORTRAN program to read the salesperson's identification number and total sales, to calculate the commission, and to print the result along with the identification number. Test the program with data for salesperson number 18735 whose sales were $11,250, data for salesperson number 27630 whose sales were $6500, and data for salesperson 31084 whose sales were $10,000.

2. A telephone company's charge for long-distance calls is based not only on distance but also on the length of time of a call. Assume that between two cities the rate is $1.10 for the first three minutes or fraction thereof, and $.40 for each additional minute. Data for a customer who made calls between these two cities consists of the customer's number and length of call.

   Write a FORTRAN program to read the customer's number and length of call, to calculate the charge, and to print the customer's number, length of call, and the charge. Use the following data to test the program:

Customer number	Length of call
9606	8
9735	3
2802	2
7921	5
1509	4
5371	1

3. Write a FORTRAN program to find the absolute value of a number. The absolute value of x is x, if x is nonnegative, and $-x$, if x is negative. Input should be the number; output should give the original number and its absolute value. Do *not* use the FORTRAN-supplied absolute value function. Use the following input data to test the program:

    25.0
    $-$ 25.0
    0.0
    $-$ 84.6
    132.5

4. A real estate office employs several salespeople. At the end of each month the total value of all property that each salesperson sold is used to calculate the person's commission. If total sales exceed $600,000, the commission is 3½% of the sales. If total sales are greater than $300,000 but not more than $600,000, the commission is 3% of the sales. Otherwise, the commission is 2½% of the sales.

    Write a FORTRAN program to read the salesperson's number and total sales, to perform the necessary commission calculation, and to print the result along with the salesperson's number and total sales.

    Use the following data to test the program:

Salesperson's number	Total sales ($)
1085	652,350
1720	142,500
2531	295,000
3007	455,500
3219	173,250
4806	682,950
6111	310,000
7932	518,000

5. An electric company charges its customers 5 cents per kilowatt-hour for electricity used up to the first 100 kilowatt-hours, 4 cents per kilowatt-hour for each of the next 200 kilowatt-hours (up to 300 kilowatt-hours), and 3 cents per kilowatt-hour for all electricity used over 300 kilowatt-hours. Write a FORTRAN program to calculate the total charge for each customer. Input to the program consists of the customer's number and kilowatt-hours used. Output from the program should list the customer's number, the kilowatt-hours used, and the total charge. Use the following data to test the program:

Customer number	Kilowatt-hours used
1065	640
2837	85
3832	220
6721	300
8475	100

6. Write a FORTRAN program to find the maximum of three numbers. Input consists of the three numbers; output should be the largest of the three. Do *not* use the FORTRAN-supplied maximum function. Use the following sets of input data to test the program:

10,25,16
17,38,41
100,52,77
$-3,-8,-1$
$0,45,-6$
$-37,0,-42$
39,39,39
14,14,8

7. Write a FORTRAN program to determine whether a student is a freshman, sophomore, junior, or senior based on the number of units (credits) that the student has completed. Input to the program consists of the student's number and the number of units completed.

   A student's classification is based on his or her units completed according to the following schedule:

Units completed	Classification
Fewer than 30 units	freshman
30 units or more but fewer than 60 units	sophomore
60 units or more but fewer than 90 units	junior
90 units or more	senior

   The output from the program should give the student's number, units completed, and the classification (FRESHMAN, SOPHOMORE, JUNIOR, or SENIOR). Use the following data to test the program:

Student number	Units completed
2352	38.0
3639	15.5
4007	29.5
4560	67.0
4915	103.5
8473	89.0

8. Write a FORTRAN program to evaluate the following function:

$$f(x) = \begin{cases} -x & \text{if } x < 0 \\ 1 & \text{if } x = 0 \\ 0 & \text{if } x > 0 \text{ and } x \leq 10 \\ 2x & \text{if } x > 10 \end{cases}$$

Input is the value of x; print the values of x and $f(x)$. Use the following data to test the program:

38.60
9.00
10.00
0.00
-45.60
0.01
-0.01
10.53

9. The basic charge for computer time is based on the number of hours of time used during the month. The schedule is as follows:

Hours used	Basic charge
0.00 to 5.00	$100
5.01 to 15.00	$100 plus $25 per hour for all time over 5 hours
15.01 and up	$225 plus $15 per hour for all time over 15 hours

In addition, a surcharge is added to the basic charge based on the priority used. The priority is indicated by a code. The surcharge is as follows:

Priority code	Surcharge
0	0
1	$50
2	$150

Write a FORTRAN program to read a customer's account number, number of hours used, and priority code; to calculate the total charge; and to print the account number and charge. Use the following data to test the program:

Account number	Hours used	Priority code
11825	3.52	0
14063	17.06	1
17185	7.93	1
19111	12.00	2
20045	5.00	1
21352	5.84	0
22841	27.94	2
23051	1.55	2
29118	15.02	0

10. Write a FORTRAN program to convert temperatures. If a temperature is entered in degrees Fahrenheit (F), it should be converted to degrees Celsius (C) and Kelvin (K). If a temperature is entered in degrees Celsius, it should be converted to Fahrenheit and Kelvin. If a temperature is entered in degrees Kelvin, it should be converted to Fahrenheit and Celsius. The following equations relate these temperature scales:

$$C = \frac{5}{9} \times (F - 32)$$
$$K = C + 273.15$$

The program should read a code indicating the temperature scale of the input and the temperature to be converted. A code of 1 means the input temperature is in Fahrenheit, 2 means it is in Celsius, and 3 means it is in Kelvin. The program should convert the input temperatures to the equivalent temperatures in the two other scales and print the results.

Use the following input data to test the program:

Code	Temperature
1	32
2	100
3	0
3	285
2	−52
1	308

11. The results of a psychological experiment need to be analyzed. Each record in an input file has information about how an individual subject in the experiment did in a series of tests. Each of the subjects took from one to four tests. The number of tests taken, the test scores, and the subject's identification code are recorded in the record. Write a FORTRAN program to calculate the average test score for each subject. The output should list each subject's identification code, the number of tests completed, the score on each test, and the average score.

Use the following data to test the program:

Identification code	Number of tests taken	Test scores
408	3	17, 16, 21
519	1	24
523	2	14, 18
584	4	22, 16, 17, 14
601	1	12
677	3	25, 23, 24
701	4	17, 18, 21, 15
713	2	13, 12

12. Write a FORTRAN program that computes the coordinates of the point of intersection of two straight lines. Assume that the lines are given by the following equations:

$$y = sx + a$$
$$y = tx + b$$

where s and t are the slopes, and a and b are the intercepts. In addition, determine the number of the quadrant (1, 2, 3, or 4) of the point of intersection. (If the point of intersection falls on an axis, use the lower quadrant number of the quadrants separated by the axis.)

The program should read the values of s, a, t, and b, do the necessary computations, and print the coordinates of the point of intersection and the quadrant number. Use the following data to test the program:

s	a	t	b
18.0	6.0	30.0	6.0
2.0	8.0	−3.0	−2.0
1.0	8.0	−2.0	−22.0
3.0	−7.0	1.0	−1.0
−0.5	−3.0	2.0	−8.0

13. Input to a payroll program consists of the employee's number, year-to-date pay, base pay rate, shift code, and hours worked. Write a FORTRAN program to

read this data; to compute the employee's gross pay, withholding tax, social security tax, and net pay; and to print these results along with the employee's number.

The gross pay is found by multiplying the hours worked by the pay rate where the pay rate is the product of the base pay rate and the shift factor. The shift factor comes from the following table:

Shift code	Shift factor
0	1.00
1	1.25
2	1.50

The withholding tax is the product of the gross pay and the tax rate. The tax rate is found from the following table:

Gross pay	Tax rate (%)
Less than $200.00	0
$200.00 to $349.99	8%
$350.00 to $499.99	12%
$500.00 to $699.99	15%
$700.00 or more	17.5%

The social security tax (F.I.C.A. tax) depends on the gross pay and the year-to-date pay. If the year-to-date pay is greater than or equal to $37,800, there is no social security tax. If the year-to-date pay plus the gross pay is less than or equal to $37,800, the social security tax is 6.7% of the gross pay. If the year-to-date pay is less than $37,800 but the sum of the year-to-date and gross pay is greater than $37,800, the tax is 6.7% of the difference between $37,800 and the year-to-date pay.

The net pay is computed by subtracting the withholding tax and social security tax from the gross pay.

Use the following input data to test the program:

Employee number	Year-to-date pay	Base pay rate	Shift code	Hours worked
1001	20,312.00	6.50	1	34.5
1002	13,888.75	5.25	0	25.0
1003	22,365.50	6.00	0	30.0
1004	35,284.25	7.25	2	38.5
1005	37,638.50	8.25	0	40.0
1006	39,465.00	10.95	2	48.0
1007	22,061.25	7.00	1	35.0
1008	37,725.00	8.00	1	40.0

14. A credit card company bases its evaluation of card applicants on four factors: the applicant's age, how long the applicant has lived at his or her current address, the applicant's income, and how long the applicant has been working at the same job. For each factor, points are added to a total as follows:

Factor	Value	Points added
Age	20 and under	−10
	21–30	0
	31–50	20
	over 50	25
At current	less than 1 year	−5
address	1–3 years	5
	4–8 years	12
	9 or more years	20
Annual	$15,000 or less	0
income	$15,001–$25,000	12
	$25,001–$40,000	24
	over $40,000	30
At same	less than 2 years	−4
job	2–4 years	8
	more than 4 years	15

Based on the point total the following action is taken by the company:

Points	Action
−19 to 20	No card issued
21 to 35	Card issued with $500 credit limit
36 to 60	Card issued with $2000 credit limit
61 to 90	Card issued with $5000 credit limit

Write a FORTRAN program to read an applicant's number, age, years at current address, annual income, and years at the same job. Then the program should evaluate the applicant's credit worthiness and print the applicant's number plus a phrase describing the action taken by the company. Use the following data to test the program:

Applicant number	Age	Years at current address	Annual income ($)	Years at same job
1234	55	10	42,000	15
2345	18	0	10,000	1
3456	35	2	32,000	4
4567	22	5	21,500	1
5678	50	1	25,000	2
6789	31	4	40,000	5

Chapter 5

Programming for repetition

As we know, a group of statements that is repeatedly executed is called a loop. In Chapter 2 we introduced the use of a loop to repeat the steps of a program so that more than one input record can be processed. We call this type of loop an *input loop* because there is an input operation within the loop. Sometimes, rather than containing an input operation, a loop just processes data. We call this type of loop a *processing loop*. We will see several examples of processing loops in this chapter.

An important concern when a loop is used in a program is how to *control* the loop, that is, how to get the computer to *stop* looping. For example, consider the tuition calculation program shown in Figure 5-1. (This is the same program as shown in Figure 4-1.) The loop in this program consists of statement 10 through the GO TO 10 statement. The computer repeats this loop as long as input data is supplied. When there is no more input data, the end-of-file specifier in the READ statement causes the computer to branch out of the loop to statement 20. Thus this loop stops repeating when the end of the input data is detected.

The loop in this program is called a *controlled loop* because there is a mechanism within the loop to stop the repetition. A loop coded without such a control mechanism is called an *uncontrolled loop*. For example, consider the following statements:

```
5 K=1
  GO TO 5
```

If these statements are executed in a program, the computer repeats the loop until stopped by something outside the program (perhaps by the computer operator). Because nothing in this group of statements causes the computer to stop repeating the loop, this is an uncontrolled loop. Uncontrolled loops should be avoided.

In this chapter we discuss programming techniques for coding controlled loops. We also describe special FORTRAN statements that are used for loop

Figure 5-1. The tuition calculation program with the input loop controlled by an end-of-file specifier

```
C   TUITION CALCULATION PROGRAM
        INTEGER SNUM
        REAL UNITS,TUIT
     10 READ (*,*,END=20) SNUM,UNITS
          IF (UNITS.LE.12.0) THEN
            TUIT=350.00
          ELSE
            TUIT=350.00+20.00*(UNITS-12.0)
          END IF
          PRINT *,'STUDENT NUMBER = ',SNUM,'  TUITION = ',TUIT
        GO TO 10
     20 STOP
        END
```

(a) The program

```
            1234,6.
            3456,15.
            5678,12.
            7890,12.5
```

(b) Input data

```
STUDENT NUMBER = 1234   TUITION = 350.
STUDENT NUMBER = 3456   TUITION = 410.
STUDENT NUMBER = 5678   TUITION = 350.
STUDENT NUMBER = 7890   TUITION = 360.
```

(c) Output

control. After completing this chapter you should be able to write programs that use a variety of loop control techniques.

5-1. Controlling loops

As we have seen, we can create a loop by using the GO TO statement to branch from the end of a group of statements to the beginning. One common technique for controlling such a loop is to use an IF statement with a GO TO statement to branch out of the loop when some condition occurs. The examples discussed in this section illustrate this approach to loop control for input loops and for processing loops.

Input loops

The program in Figure 5-1 contains a controlled input loop. Each time the loop is executed, a new input record is read. When the end-of-file record is read, the end-of-file specifier in the READ statement causes the computer to branch out of the loop.

Another technique for controlling an input loop is to use special input data at the end of the regular data. Each time an input record is read, the program checks to see if this special data has been read. If not, the program continues with the normal execution of the statements in the loop. When the special end-of-data input has been read, the program branches out of the loop.

Usually the end-of-data input contains a value that is not found in any other set of input data. We call such a value a *trailer value* or a *sentinel*. For example, in the tuition calculation program in Figure 5-1, the input consists of the student's identification number and number of units. We could use a special identification number as a trailer value. The value would have to be one that is not used in any other set of input. Then, each time that the loop is executed, we could test for this value.

We will assume that the trailer value for the tuition data is the identification number 9999. Figure 5-2 shows the program with this form of loop control. First the program reads a record with the identification number (SNUM) and the number of units. Then the program tests the value of SNUM in a logical IF statement to see if it equals the trailer value of 9999. If SNUM is *not* equal to 9999, the program continues with the next statement in

Figure 5-2. The tuition calculation program with the input loop controlled by a trailer value test

```
C   TUITION CALCULATION PROGRAM
        INTEGER SNUM
        REAL UNITS,TUIT
    10 READ *,SNUM,UNITS
        IF (SNUM.EQ.9999) GO TO 20
        IF (UNITS.LE.12.0) THEN
           TUIT=350.00
        ELSE
           TUIT=350.00+20.00*(UNITS-12.0)
        END IF
        PRINT *,'STUDENT NUMBER = ',SNUM,'  TUITION = ',TUIT
        GO TO 10
    20 STOP
        END
```

(a) The program

```
1234,6.
3456,15.
5678,12.
7890,12.5
9999,0.
```

(b) Input data

```
STUDENT NUMBER = 1234   TUITION = 350.
STUDENT NUMBER = 3456   TUITION = 410.
STUDENT NUMBER = 5678   TUITION = 350.
STUDENT NUMBER = 7890   TUITION = 360.
```

(c) Output

sequence. If the value of SNUM equals 9999, the program branches out of the loop to the STOP statement. Notice that an end-of-file specifier has not been used in the READ statement; the IF statement for the trailer value test takes its place. This IF statement comes immediately after the READ statement. We must check for the end of the input data at this point because we do not want to process the trailer value.

In this program we could have written the logical IF statement for the trailer value test as follows:

```
IF (ID.EQ.9999) STOP
```

Then statement 20, the STOP statement, would not be needed. Although this approach is appropriate for this problem, in some situations we must branch out of the loop when the trailer value has been read. This is the case when additional processing must be done after all data has been read.

When running the program in Figure 5-2, it is important that the input data contain the trailer value in the proper format. Because the READ statement contains two variable names, two values must be provided in each input record, including the record with the trailer value. Thus the last record in the input data must have 9999 for the identification number and some value for the units, even though the units are not used after the trailer value is read. In the input data in Figure 5-2(b), the last record has a value of 9999 for the identification number and 0 for the units. (Compare this input data with that in Figure 5-1(b).) When the last record is read, the program stops execution. Notice that the output for the programs in Figures 5-1 and 5-2 is identical even though the input data is slightly different.

Figures 5-1 and 5-2 show two techniques for input loop control. Often the programmer can choose which one to use. Sometimes, however, one or the other of these must be used. The programmer should be familiar with both techniques.

Processing loops

A processing loop is a loop that is controlled by some condition of the data that is processed in the loop, not by an input value. Usually within the loop, computations take place that affect the value of some variable. Each time the loop is executed, the variable is used to test whether to terminate the loop. If the loop is properly designed, the test eventually will become true and the computer will branch out of the loop.

As an example, consider the problem of determining the amount of time it will take for a bank deposit to double at a given interest rate. Assume that $1000 is put into a bank at 12 percent interest compounded annually. This means that for the first year, the interest is 12 percent of $1000, or $120 which is added to the original deposit to give an end-of-year balance of $1120. For the second year, the interest is 12 percent of $1120 or $134.40. The balance at the end of the second year is $1254.40. Thus the interest for the year is added to the balance at the end of the previous year to get the new balance, and this amount is used in the next year's interest calculation. The problem is to write a program that prints the yearly interest and the end-of-year balance for each year until the deposit has doubled to $2000 or more.

Figure 5-3(a) shows a program that accomplishes this. Notice that the program has no input instruction; this program does not require any input

Figure 5-3. The interest calculation program

```
C   INTEREST CALCULATION PROGRAM
        INTEGER YEAR
        REAL BALNC,INTRST
        BALNC=1000.00
        YEAR=1
    100 IF (BALNC.GE.2000.00) GO TO 200
        INTRST=.12*BALNC
        BALNC=BALNC+INTRST
        PRINT *,'YEAR NUMBER  ',YEAR
        PRINT *,'   INTEREST FOR YEAR: ',INTRST
        PRINT *,'   END-OF-YEAR BALANCE: ',BALNC
        PRINT *
        YEAR=YEAR+1
        GO TO 100
    200 STOP
        END
```

(a) The program

```
YEAR NUMBER  1
    INTEREST FOR YEAR: 120.
    END-OF-YEAR BALANCE: 1120.

YEAR NUMBER  2
    INTEREST FOR YEAR: 134.4
    END-OF-YEAR BALANCE: 1254.4

YEAR NUMBER  3
    INTEREST FOR YEAR: 150.528
    END-OF-YEAR BALANCE: 1404.928

YEAR NUMBER  4
    INTEREST FOR YEAR: 168.5914
    END-OF-YEAR BALANCE: 1573.519

YEAR NUMBER  5
    INTEREST FOR YEAR: 188.8223
    END-OF-YEAR BALANCE: 1762.342

YEAR NUMBER  6
    INTEREST FOR YEAR: 211.4810
    END-OF-YEAR BALANCE: 1973.823

YEAR NUMBER  7
    INTEREST FOR YEAR: 236.8587
    END-OF-YEAR BALANCE: 2210.681
```

(b) Output

data. The variable named BALNC is equal to the bank balance; initially BALNC is $1000.00. YEAR is an integer variable that counts the number of years. For the first year's calculation, YEAR is 1. The loop consists of statement 100 through the GO TO 100 statement. The IF statement, numbered 100, terminates the loop when BALNC is greater than or equal to $2000.00. Within the loop, the current year's interest (INTRST) is calculated by multiplying BALNC by .12. INTRST is then added to BALNC to give the new balance. (Recall from Chapter 3 that the statement BALNC = BALNC + INTRST adds INTRST to the old value of BALNC and assigns the result to BALNC.) Then the output is printed and YEAR is increased by 1 for the next year. The GO TO statement branches back to the beginning of the loop (which is *not* the first statement in the program). The processing is repeated as long as BALNC is less than $2000.00. The output from the program is shown in Figure 5-3(b).

Notice in this program that the statements in the loop, except for the first and the last statement, are indented. This is the style that we have used in all programs that have involved loops. Although this style is commonly used, some programmers prefer other styles. In future examples we will use the style shown here.

Besides illustrating a processing loop, the program in Figure 5-3 demonstrates the need for *initializing* variables. By this we mean assigning beginning values to variable names. We can never assume that a variable has any known value unless we assign a value to it. Thus, in the program in Figure 5-3, we cannot assume that BALNC equals 1000.00 or that YEAR is 1; these values must be assigned to the variable names at the beginning of the program. If this is not done, the computer will use whatever values happen to be in the storage locations for these variables. These values will probably be left over from some other program, and they can vary each time the program is run. (Sometimes such unknown data is called "garbage.") To avoid this situation, we must initialize variables such as BALNC and YEAR in this program.

Counting loops

A special type of processing loop, called a *counting loop,* is controlled by counting the number of times that the loop is executed and branching out of the loop when the count reaches some desired number. This approach uses a variable name as a *counter.* Before entering the loop, the counter is *initialized* to some beginning value. Each time the loop is executed, the value of the counter is *modified,* usually by increasing or *incrementing* its value by 1. Also, each time that the loop is executed, the counter is *tested* and the loop is repeated as long as the value of the counter does not exceed some final value.

As an example, the statements in Figure 5-4 show the general form of a loop that is to be executed 100 times. In this figure, the counter is the integer variable named K. Initially K is assigned the value of 1. Then K is

Figure 5-4. A counting loop

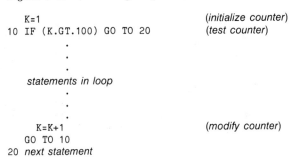

tested to determine if it is greater than 100. If this is the case, the computer branches out of the loop to the next statement following the loop. If K is less than or equal to 100, the statements in the loop are executed. At the end of the loop, the value of K is increased by 1 and the loop is repeated.

Notice in this example that the IF statement specifies that the loop is terminated when K is *greater than* 100. This is necessary to ensure that the loop is executed exactly 100 times. If the IF statement were coded so that the computer branched out of the loop when the counter *equaled* 100, the loop would be executed only 99 times.

We can modify the interest calculation program in Figure 5-3 to use this technique. Assume that we only want to print the interest and end-of-year balance for five years. The variable named YEAR may be used to count the number of years and, at the same time, the number of times that the loop is executed. The program is shown in Figure 5-5. Initially, YEAR is set equal to 1. Each time through the loop, YEAR is incremented by 1. The loop is stopped when YEAR becomes greater than 5.

Notice in these examples that the variable name used for the counter is integer. We usually select integer variable names for this purpose because integer arithmetic is usually faster and more accurate for counting purposes than real arithmetic.

As another example of this form of loop control, consider the problem of finding the total and average of ten test scores. Assume that the test scores are recorded one per record in ten records with no trailer value at the end. The program must read the data, calculate the total and average, and print the results.

One way to write the program would be to use ten variable names, one for each test score. Because such a program would be tedious to code, a better approach is to read and process the data within a loop. Although the loop in this case contains a READ statement, we cannot use a trailer value test to terminate it because there is no trailer value. However, because we know that there are exactly ten input records, we can control the loop by counting the number of times that the loop is executed.

The program is shown in Figure 5-6. The variable named TOTAL is

Figure 5-5. The interest calculation program with a counting loop

```
C   INTEREST CALCULATION PROGRAM
        INTEGER YEAR
        REAL BALNC,INTRST
        BALNC=1000.00
        YEAR=1
    100 IF (YEAR.GT.5) GO TO 200
            INTRST=.12*BALNC
            BALNC=BALNC+INTRST
            PRINT *,'YEAR NUMBER  ',YEAR
            PRINT *,'   INTEREST FOR YEAR: ',INTRST
            PRINT *,'   END-OF-YEAR BALANCE: ',BALNC
            PRINT *
            YEAR=YEAR+1
        GO TO 100
    200 STOP
        END
```
(a) The program

```
YEAR NUMBER  1
    INTEREST FOR YEAR: 120.
    END-OF-YEAR BALANCE: 1120.

YEAR NUMBER  2
    INTEREST FOR YEAR: 134.4
    END-OF-YEAR BALANCE: 1254.4

YEAR NUMBER  3
    INTEREST FOR YEAR: 150.528
    END-OF-YEAR BALANCE: 1404.928

YEAR NUMBER  4
    INTEREST FOR YEAR: 168.5914
    END-OF-YEAR BALANCE: 1573.519

YEAR NUMBER  5
    INTEREST FOR YEAR: 188.8223
    END-OF-YEAR BALANCE: 1762.342
```
(b) Output

used to accumulate the total of the test scores. Each time through the loop, the READ statement reads a test score (SCORE). Then the value of SCORE is added to TOTAL and the result is assigned to TOTAL. Note that TOTAL must be initially set equal to zero outside of the loop so that with the first execution of the loop the first test score is added to zero. Each successive time through the loop, TOTAL is increased by the value of another test score until all ten socres have been read and added.

The loop in this program is controlled by using the variable named COUNT as a counter. Initially COUNT is set equal to 1. Each time through the loop COUNT is increased by 1 and tested to see if it is greater than 10. When COUNT exceeds 10, the program branches out of the loop and calculates the average by dividing TOTAL by 10. Then the output is printed and the program terminates.

Figure 5-6. A program to find the total and average of ten test scores

```
C   TEST SCORE AVERAGING PROGRAM
        INTEGER COUNT
        REAL SCORE,TOTAL,AVE
        TOTAL=0.0
        COUNT=1
     10 IF (COUNT.GT.10) GO TO 20
          READ *,SCORE
          TOTAL=TOTAL+SCORE
          COUNT=COUNT+1
        GO TO 10
     20 AVE=TOTAL/10.0
        PRINT *,'THE TOTAL IS ',TOTAL
        PRINT *,'THE AVERAGE IS ',AVE
        STOP
        END
```

(a) The program

```
        85
        92
        77
        54
        89
        100
        72
        78
        82
        68
```

(b) Input data

```
        THE TOTAL IS 797.
        THE AVERAGE IS 79.7
```

(c) Output

This program processes exactly ten test scores. A variation on the program is to read the number of test scores to be processed from an input record that comes ahead of the other data. This record contains a count of the number of records that follow. Then the program is not limited to processing exactly ten values.

The program with this modification is shown in Figure 5-7. The first READ statement reads the number of test scores from the first record and assigns the value to the variable named NUM. [Note that the first input record in Figure 5-7(b) contains the value 12, which equals the number of records that follow.] The loop in this program is the same as that in the previous program except for the IF statement. In the IF statement, the counter is compared with NUM and the loop is terminated when COUNT is greater than the number of test scores. The average is computed by dividing TOTAL by the real equivalent of NUM.

In these examples the testing step is at the beginning of the loop.

Figure 5-7. A program to find the total and average of a given number of test scores

```
C   TEST SCORE AVERAGING PROGRAM
        INTEGER COUNT,NUM
        REAL SCORE,TOTAL,AVE
        READ *,NUM
        TOTAL=0.0
        COUNT=1
    10  IF (COUNT.GT.NUM) GO TO 20
            READ *,SCORE
            TOTAL=TOTAL+SCORE
            COUNT=COUNT+1
        GO TO 10
    20  AVE=TOTAL/REAL(NUM)
        PRINT *,'THE TOTAL IS ',TOTAL
        PRINT *,'THE AVERAGE IS ',AVE
        STOP
        END
```

(a) The program

```
            12
            91
            78
            85
           100
            73
            66
            91
            75
            77
            59
            94
            86
```

(b) Input data

```
THE TOTAL IS 975.
THE AVERAGE IS 81.25
```

(c) Output

However, this is not essential. We could put the testing step in the middle or at the end of the loop depending on the requirements of the problem. For example, Figure 5-8 shows statements for executing a loop 100 times but with the counter test at the end of the loop. Notice in this example that the loop is repeated as long as the value of the counter is *less than or equal to* 100.

We can also vary the way in which counting is done. The initial value of the counter does not have to be 1; it can be any value depending on the problem. In addition, we need not count by ones. We can modify the counter by adding or subtracting any reasonable value, including a fractional amount. The test condition is determined by the initial value of the counter, how the

Figure 5-8. A counting loop with the testing step at the end of the loop

```
    L=1                              (initialize counter)
30 first statement in loop
       .
       .
       .
   statements in loop
       .
       .
       .
    L=L+1                            (modify counter)
    IF (L.LE.100) GO TO 30           (test counter)
    next statement
```

counter is modified each time through the loop, and the number of times we wish to execute the loop.

Figure 5-9 gives several examples of counting loops that illustrate these variations. In part (a) of the figure, the integer variable named L counts from 0 to 10 by twos. The statements in this loop will be executed six times.

Figure 5-9. Examples of counting loops

```
    L=0
40 IF (L.GT.10) GO TO 50
       .
       .
       .
    L=L+2
    GO TO 40
50 next statement
```

(a)

```
    M=10
60 IF (M.LT.1) GO TO 70
       .
       .
       .
    M=M-1
    GO TO 60
70 next statement
```

(b)

```
    X=0.0
80 IF (X.GT.1.0) GO TO 90
       .
       .
       .
    X=X+.05
    GO TO 80
90 next statement
```

(c)

In part (b), M is the name of an integer variable that counts backwards from 10 to 1. This loop will be executed ten times. In part (c), a real variable named X is used to count from 0 to 1 in increments of .05. A real variable must be used in this case because the counting is being done by a fractional amount. The statements in this loop will be executed 21 times.

Patterns of loop control

The discussion and examples in this section illustrate several different patterns of loop control. In all the patterns the loop is repeated until some condition occurs that signals the end of the loop. However, the patterns vary in the placement of the end-of-loop test. Figure 5-10 summarizes the differences graphically.

Part (a) of the figure shows the basic loop pattern with the termination test in the middle of the loop. In part (b), the test is at the beginning of the loop. This pattern is called a *pretest loop*. When the test is the last statement in the loop, as in part (c) of the figure, the pattern is called a *posttest loop*. All loops in programs fall into one of these patterns. The implementation of these patterns in FORTRAN using IF and GO TO statements is shown in Figure 5-11.

5-2. Nested loops

Within a loop may be other loops. Such a combination of loops is referred to as *nested loops*. (This is similar to the idea of nested decisions discussed in Chapter 4.) Any type of loop may be nested in another loop. Thus a processing loop may be nested in another processing loop or in an input loop, and an input loop may be nested in another input loop or in a processing loop. Loops can be nested within nested loops. For example, a processing loop may be nested in another processing loop, which is nested in an input loop. There is no limit to the number of loops that can be nested.

Any of the loop patterns in Figure 5-10 may be used for nested loops. For example, Figure 5-12 shows a nested loop pattern in which a pretest loop is nested in another pretest loop. (There can also be a pretest loop nested in a posttest loop, a posttest loop nested in a basic loop, and so forth. Any combination is acceptable.) The FORTRAN equivalent of the pattern in Figure 5-12 is given in Figure 5-13. When one loop is nested within another we think of the most encompassing loop as the *outer loop* and the loop that is nested as the *inner loop*. Each repetition of the outer loop causes the statements in the inner loop to be repeated as many times as the inner loop requires.

To illustrate the use of nested loops, assume that we want to determine the amount of time that it takes a bank deposit of $1000 to double at interest rates varying from 10% to 14% in 1% increments. This is a variation of the problem solved by the program in Figure 5-3. One approach is to run the

Figure 5-10. Patterns of loop control

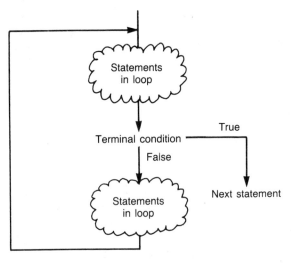

(a) Basic loop pattern

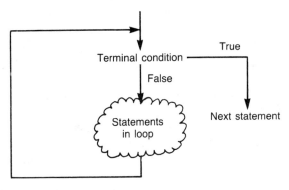

(b) Pretest loop pattern

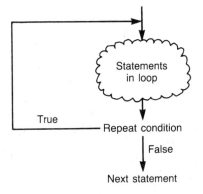

(c) Posttest loop pattern

Figure 5-11. Loop control patterns in FORTRAN

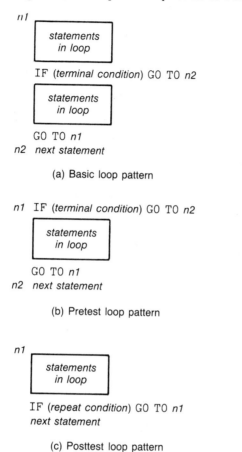

n1

statements
in loop

IF *(terminal condition)* GO TO *n2*

statements
in loop

GO TO *n1*
n2 next statement

(a) Basic loop pattern

n1 IF *(terminal condition)* GO TO *n2*

statements
in loop

GO TO *n1*
n2 next statement

(b) Pretest loop pattern

n1

statements
in loop

IF *(repeat condition)* GO TO *n1*
next statement

(c) Posttest loop pattern

program in Figure 5-3 five times, each time using a different interest rate in the calculation. A better approach is to modify the program in such a way that another loop is used to repeat the interest calculation five times, each time with a different rate. The resulting program is shown in Figure 5-14(a).

In this program the statement BALNC = 1000.00 through the GO TO 100 statement are the same as in the program in Figure 5-3 with the exception of the assignment statement that calculates the interest. In this statement the integer variable named RATE is used for the interest rate. Because RATE is an integer, it must be converted to a real value and divided by 100.0 in the interest calculation. For example, if RATE is 12, then REAL(RATE)/100.0 is .12, which is multiplied by BALNC to get INTRST. The value of RATE is controlled by a loop that surrounds these statements. Initially, RATE is set equal to 10. Each succeeding time through the loop, RATE is increased by 1. The loop is terminated when RATE becomes greater than 14. Notice that this loop also includes statements to print a heading

Figure 5-12. A nested loop pattern

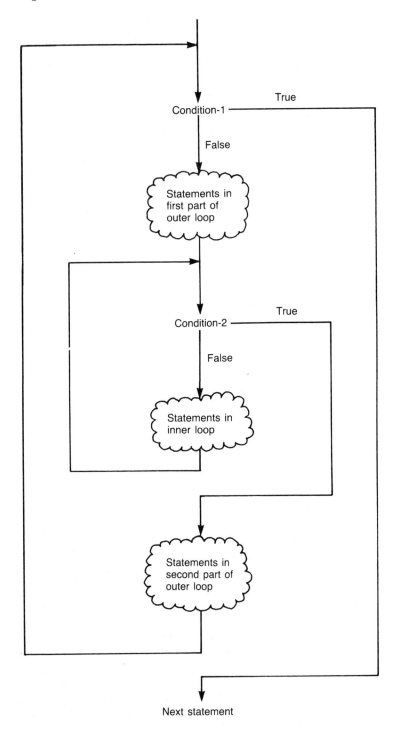

Figure 5-13. A nested loop pattern in FORTRAN

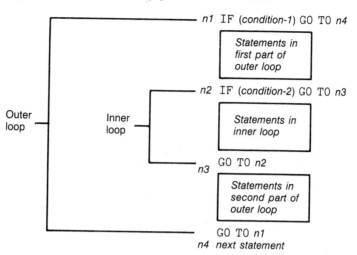

with the value of RATE. This heading is printed before each set of interest output.

In this program the inner loop (statement 100 through the GO TO 100 statement) is completely contained in the outer loop (statement 50 through the GO TO 50 statement). Each time that the outer loop is repeated, the

Figure 5-14. The interest calculation program with nested loops (Part 1 of 2)

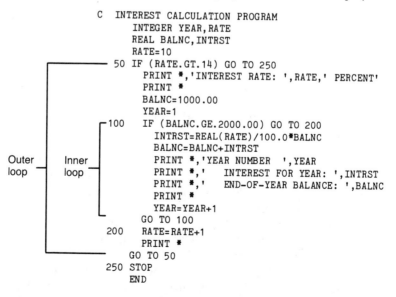

(a) The program

Figure 5-14. (Part 2 of 2)

```
INTEREST RATE: 10 PERCENT

YEAR NUMBER  1
     INTEREST FOR YEAR: 100.
     END-OF-YEAR BALANCE: 1100.
                  .
                  .
                  .

YEAR NUMBER  8
     INTEREST FOR YEAR: 194.8717
     END-OF-YEAR BALANCE: 2143.589


INTEREST RATE: 11 PERCENT

YEAR NUMBER  1
     INTEREST FOR YEAR: 110.
     END-OF-YEAR BALANCE: 1110.
                  .
                  .
                  .

YEAR NUMBER  7
     INTEREST FOR YEAR: 205.7456
     END-OF-YEAR BALANCE: 2076.160
                  .
                  .
                  .


INTEREST RATE: 14 PERCENT

YEAR NUMBER  1
     INTEREST FOR YEAR: 140.
     END-OF-YEAR BALANCE: 1140.
                  .
                  .
                  .

YEAR NUMBER  6
     INTEREST FOR YEAR: 269.5580
     END-OF-YEAR BALANCE: 2194.973
```

(b) Output

inner loop is completely executed. Because the outer loop is repeated five times, the inner loop is completely performed five times. Hence the program performs five sets of interest calculations and output but with a different interest rate used in each set of calculations. [Partial output from the program is given in Figure 5-14(b).]

This program uses indentation to show the loops and the nesting. All the statements that are in the outer loop (except the first and the last) are indented two spaces. All the statements that are in the inner loop (except the first and the last) are indented four spaces. This style gives a visual clue to the program's organization.

We can see from this example that nested loops can be very useful. They can also be difficult to understand, especially when loops are nested within other nested loops. In general, it is best to nest no more than two or three loops so that the program's logic is not too complex.

5-3. DO loops

Counting loops play an important role in programming. Section 5-1 gave several examples of the use of counting loops. Later chapters will show more examples. Because this type of loop is important, FORTRAN provides a special statement, the DO statement, to control counting loops. A loop that is controlled by a DO statement is called a *DO loop*. In this section we describe the DO statement and discuss programming with DO loops.

The basic steps for controlling a counting loop involve initializing a counter, testing the counter to determine whether the loop should be terminated, and modifying the counter after the statements in the loop have been executed. The program to find the total and average ten test scores in Figure 5-6 illustrated these steps. The main loop in this program is

```
      COUNT=1
10 IF (COUNT.GT.10) GO TO 20
      READ *,SCORE
      TOTAL=TOTAL+SCORE
      COUNT=COUNT+1
   GO TO 10
20 (next statement)
```

Using a DO loop to control this loop we can rewrite this sequence of statements as

```
      DO 20 COUNT=1,10,1
      READ *,SCORE
      TOTAL=TOTAL+SCORE
20 CONTINUE
```

The first statement in this example is a DO statement. Whenever a DO statement is used, the statements that initialize, test, and modify the counter are not needed. Instead, the DO statement combines these functions. Here the effect of the DO statement is to cause the computer to repeatedly execute the statements following the DO statement up to and including the statement numbered 20. The first time that the loop is executed, COUNT is assigned the value 1. With each succeeding execution of the loop, the value of COUNT is increased by 1. When the value of COUNT exceeds 10, the computer branches out of the loop to the next statement following the statement numbered 20. Statement 20 in this example is a CONTINUE statement, which is a special statement that is often used as the last statement in a DO loop.

The DO statement

The syntax of the DO statement is as follows:

```
DO n i=m1,m2,m3
where  n is the statement number of an executable
          statement that follows the DO statement.
       i is a variable name.
       m1, m2, and m3 are constants, variable names,
          or arithmetic expressions.
```

The effect of this statement is to cause the computer to repeatedly execute the statements following the DO statement up to and including the statement numbered n. The first time the statements are executed, i is assigned the value of $m1$. Each succeeding time the value of $m3$ is added to the value of i. In the usual use of this statement, when the value of i becomes greater than the value of $m2$, the computer goes on to the next statement following the statement numbered n.

The *range* of a DO loop is the group of statements that is to be repeatedly executed. The range begins with the first statement that follows the DO statement and ends with the statement numbered n. This last statement in the range is called the *terminal statement* or *range limit*.

The variable named i is called the *DO-variable* or *control variable*. The DO-variable is modified with each execution of the range. The values of $m1$, $m2$, and $m3$ are referred to as the *parameters* of the DO loop. The value of $m1$ is called the *initial value* or *initial parameter*. It is the value assigned to the DO-variable for the first execution of the range.

The value of $m2$ is called the *test value* or *terminal parameter*. At the beginning of the execution of the range, the value of the DO-variable is compared with the test value. In the most common use of the DO statement, if the DO-variable's value is greater than the test value, the computer branches to the next statement following the terminal statement. (We will discuss a variation of this later.)

The *increment* or *incrementation parameter* is the value of $m3$. It is the amount by which the value of the DO-variable is modified after each execution of the range. It must not be 0. The increment may be omitted from the DO statement, in which case it is assumed to be 1.

The following DO statement, from the previous example, illustrates these concepts:

```
DO 20 COUNT=1,10,1
```

The terminal statement of the loop controlled by this statement is the statement numbered 20. The DO-variable for the loop is the variable named COUNT. The initial value of the DO-variable is 1, the test value is 10, and the increment is 1. Because the increment is 1 it may be omitted and the statement may be coded as follows:

```
DO 20 COUNT=1,10
```

As another example, consider the following:

```
DO 200 I=10,20,3
```

In this example, the terminal statement is the statement numbered 200, the DO-variable is the variable named I, the initial value is 10, the test value is 20, and the increment is 3.

Variable names may be used for any or all of the parameters. For example, the following DO statement uses variable names for the initial value and the test value:

```
DO 300 K=KN,KT,5
```

When this DO statement is executed, the values of the variables KN and KT determine the initial value and the test value, respectively.

In a program that uses a DO loop, the initialization, testing, and modification of the DO-variable are not coded directly. The DO statement alone specifies these operations, but the programmer must be aware of the order in which these operations are performed. Figure 5-15 shows the pattern of execution that a DO loop usually follows. First, the DO-variable is initialized. Then the test is made to determine whether the value of the DO-variable is greater than the test value. If this test is true, the computer continues with the next statement following the terminal statement. If the DO-variable's value is not greater than the test value, the statements in the loop are executed. Then, at the end of the execution of the loop, the increment is added to the DO-variable and the loop is repeated.

Notice that this is a pretest loop pattern. Hence it is possible to code a DO loop that is never executed. For example, consider the following DO statement:

```
DO 400 J=I,M
```

If I has a value of 50 and M is 40 at the time the DO statement is executed, the initial value is greater than the test value. Hence the loop will not be executed at all. (Some older versions of FORTRAN use a posttest pattern for a DO loop, in which case the loop in the example just given will be executed once.)

The number of times that a loop is executed depends on the parameters. For example, the loop defined by the following statement is performed 50 times:

```
DO 20 COUNT=1,50,1
```

Figure 5-15. Execution of a DO loop

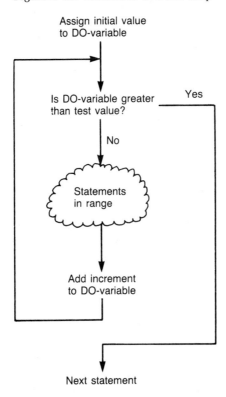

As another example, consider the following DO statement:

        DO 200 I=10,20,3

The loop described here is executed four times. The first time that the range is executed, the DO-variable has the value 10. For the second execution of the range, the DO-variable is incremented by 3 and is assigned the value 13. For the third execution of the range, the DO-variable has the value 16; for the fourth time, the DO-variable has the value 19. After execution of the range for the fourth time, the DO-variable is incremented by 3 to 22. Then the test of the DO-variable determines that its value is greater than the test value (20), and the computer branches to the next statement following the terminal statement.

The CONTINUE statement

The terminal statement in a DO loop may be any executable statement with certain exceptions such as a GO TO statement, STOP statement, block IF statement, or another DO statement. Usually programmers use a CONTINUE statement as the last statement in a DO loop. The syntax of the CONTINUE statement is as follows:

```
CONTINUE
```

If used anywhere in the program except as the terminal statement of a DO loop, the CONTINUE statement has no effect on the program. That is, the computer just passes through the CONTINUE statement to the next statement in sequence. If a CONTINUE statement is the terminal statement of a DO loop, it has the *effect* of modifying the DO-variable and repeating the loop.

The following DO loop illustrates the use of the CONTINUE statement:

```
      DO 20 COUNT=1,10
         READ *,SCORE
         TOTAL=TOTAL+SCORE
   20 CONTINUE
```

The CONTINUE statement is numbered 20 and hence is the terminal statement of the DO loop. Each time the loop is executed, the CONTINUE statement has the effect of modifying the value of COUNT and repeating the loop.

Notice in this example that we have indented the statements between the DO statement and the CONTINUE statement. This is a common style that helps set off the statements in the loop so that the program is easier to understand. Although a CONTINUE statement is not required for a DO loop, most programmers use it to clearly indicate the DO loop in the program.

Illustrative programs

A program to find the total and average of ten test scores illustrates the use of a DO loop. The complete program is shown in Figure 5-16. After initializing

Figure 5-16. A program to find the total and average of ten test scores using a DO loop

```
C   TEST SCORE AVERAGING PROGRAM
      INTEGER COUNT
      REAL SCORE,TOTAL,AVE
      TOTAL=0.0
      DO 20 COUNT=1,10
        READ *,SCORE
        TOTAL=TOTAL+SCORE
   20 CONTINUE
      AVE=TOTAL/10.0
      PRINT *,'THE TOTAL IS ',TOTAL
      PRINT *,'THE AVERAGE IS ',AVE
      STOP
      END
```

TOTAL to zero, the program accumulates the total of the ten test scores by reading each score and adding it to TOTAL in a DO loop. After the DO loop is executed ten times, the average is calculated and the results are printed. (The input and output for this program are the same as in Figure 5-6.)

A modification of this program is to read the number of test scores to be averaged from the first input record. Then this number becomes the test value for the loop. The program in Figure 5-17 illustrates the technique. Note that the value of NUM is read with the first READ statement. Then NUM is used as the test value in the DO statement. (The input and output for this program are the same as in Figure 5-7.)

In Figure 5-5 we showed a program that prints the interest and balance on an original deposit of $1000 at 12% interest compounded annually for five years. The program required a counting loop, and thus it also can be written with a DO loop. The equivalent program with a DO loop is shown in Figure 5-18. Note that the value of YEAR is controlled with the DO statement. In addition, the value of this variable is printed each time through the loop. (The output for this program is the same as in Figure 5-5.)

This example illustrates the use of the DO-variable within the range of the DO loop. Any time the DO-variable is used in the loop, its value depends on the initial value, the increment, and the number of times that the range has been executed. Figure 5-19 shows another program that uses the DO-variable within the DO loop range. This program finds the sum of the even integers from 2 to 20. In this example, the DO-variable is used in the arithmetic assignment statement that calcuates the sum. Initially zero is assigned to the variable named SUM. With the first execution of the range, the initial value of the DO-variable (2) is added to SUM and the result replaces the original value of SUM. Thus, after the first execution of the loop, SUM has a value of $0 + 2$ or 2. With each succeeding execution of the range, the current value of the DO-variable is added to SUM. After the second execution of the range, SUM has a value of $0 + 2 + 4$ or 6; after the third execution of the

Figure 5-17. A program to find the total and average of a given number of test scores using a DO loop

```
C   TEST SCORE AVERAGING PROGRAM
    INTEGER COUNT,NUM
    REAL SCORE,TOTAL,AVE
    READ *,NUM
    TOTAL=0.0
    DO 20 COUNT=1,NUM
      READ *,SCORE
      TOTAL=TOTAL+SCORE
 20 CONTINUE
    AVE=TOTAL/REAL(NUM)
    PRINT *,'THE TOTAL IS ',TOTAL
    PRINT *,'THE AVERAGE IS ',AVE
    STOP
    END
```

Figure 5-18. The interest calculation program using a DO loop

```
C  INTEREST CALCULATION PROGRAM
       INTEGER YEAR
       REAL BALNC,INTRST
       BALNC=1000.00
       DO 200 YEAR=1,5
         INTRST=.12*BALNC
         BALNC=BALNC+INTRST
         PRINT *,'YEAR NUMBER  ',YEAR
         PRINT *,'   INTEREST FOR YEAR: ',INTRST
         PRINT *,'   END-OF-YEAR BALANCE: ',BALNC
         PRINT *
   200 CONTINUE
       STOP
       END
```

Figure 5-19. A program to find the sum of the even integers from 2 to 20

```
C   PROGRAM TO SUM THE EVEN INTEGERS FROM 2 TO 20
       INTEGER SUM,I
       SUM=0
       DO 50 I=2,20,2
         SUM=SUM+I
    50 CONTINUE
       PRINT *,'THE SUM IS ',SUM
       STOP
       END
```

(a) The program

```
THE SUM IS 110
```

(b) Output

range, SUM has a value of $0+2+4+6$ or 12. This continues until, after 10 executions of the range, the value of SUM is $0+2+4+6+8+10+12+14+16+18+20$, or 110. Then the DO-variable is incremented to a value greater than the test value and the loop is terminated.

Branching and DO loops

Branching out of a DO loop is allowed at any time. For example, assume that we want to find the total and average of an unknown number of test scores. Each score is recorded in an input record. The last record has a trailer value of zero instead of a test score. If we assume that there are fewer than 100 input records, a DO loop that is executed 100 times may be used to read the data and find the total of the scores. After each record is read, a test for the trailer value must be made. When the trailer value is detected, the program must branch out of the DO loop.

Figure 5-20. A program to find the total and average of an unknown number of test scores

```
C   TEST SCORE AVERAGING PROGRAM
        INTEGER COUNT,NUM
        REAL SCORE,TOTAL,AVE
        TOTAL=0.0
        DO 20 COUNT=1,100
          READ *,SCORE
          IF (SCORE.EQ.0) GO TO 30
          TOTAL=TOTAL+SCORE
     20 CONTINUE
     30 NUM=COUNT-1
        AVE=TOTAL/REAL(NUM)
        PRINT *,'THE TOTAL IS ',TOTAL
        PRINT *,'THE AVERAGE IS ',AVE
        STOP
        END
```

(a) The program

```
89
71
92
83
75
68
98
77
0
```

(b) Input data

```
THE TOTAL IS 653.
THE AVERAGE IS 81.625
```

(c) Output

The program to accomplish this is shown in Figure 5-20.* The IF statement in the DO loop in this program checks for the trailer value and branches out of the loop when this value is read. After branching out of the loop, the number of test scores is calculated by subtracting 1 from the DO-variable. This is necessary because the DO-variable equals the last value assigned to it in the DO loop. For each record that is read, the variable is incremented by 1. Thus the DO-variable counts the number of input records. However, the record with the trailer value does not contain a test score and must not be included in the count. To correct for this, the value of the DO-variable is reduced by 1 after the program branches out of the loop. The number of test scores is then used to calculate the average score. [Note in

* Although this program is valid in FORTRAN, it violates certain principles of good program structure that are discussed in Chapter 7.

the input data in Figure 5-20(b) that there are eight records with test scores followed by a ninth record with the trailer value.]

Although branching out of a DO loop is allowed, FORTRAN does not allow branching into the range of a DO loop. Thus a GO TO statement outside of a DO loop cannot use the number of a statement in the loop.

Branching to the DO statement itself is allowed. The program can branch to a DO statement at any time and thus begin the loop processing. Branching to a DO statement from *outside* a DO loop is commonly done. In general, branching to the DO statement of a DO loop from *inside* the loop should not be done. If it is, the computer will reset the DO-variable to its initial value and restart the loop. As a consequence the loop may never terminate.

Branching to the CONTINUE statement at the end of the loop from inside the loop is acceptable. Occasionally this is necessary to bypass some statements in the loop and go directly to the incrementation of the DO-variable and repetition of the loop.

Figure 5-21 summarizes the situations described in this subsection.

Figure 5-21. Branching and DO loops. (Part 1 of 2)

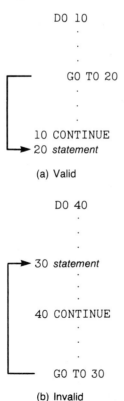

```
        DO 10
          .
          .
          .
          GO TO 20
          .
          .
          .
     10 CONTINUE
     20 statement
```

(a) Valid

```
        DO 40
          .
          .
          .
     30 statement
          .
          .
     40 CONTINUE
          .
          .
          .
          GO TO 30
```

(b) Invalid

Figure 5-21. (Part 2 of 2)

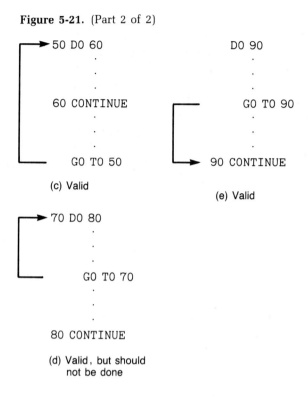

(c) Valid

(e) Valid

(d) Valid, but should
not be done

Additional DO loop rules

Within the range of a DO loop, the DO-variable cannot be used in such a way that its value is changed. For example, the following loop is invalid:

```
DO 75 J=1,10
      .
      .
      .
   J=5
      .
      .
      .
75 CONTINUE
```

In this loop the DO-variable (J) is assigned a value through the DO statement, but the value is illegally modified by the statement J = 5. This is not valid because it would affect the way the loop executes.

   The values of any variables used for the parameters of a DO statement may be modified in the loop. If this is done, the *original* values of the variables are used for loop control. For example, consider the following loop:

```
L=10
M=1
DO 85 K=1,L,M
    .
    .
    .


    L=6
    M=2
    .
    .
    .


  85 CONTINUE
```

This loop is valid. When the DO statement is executed, the test value (the value of L) is 10 and the increment (the value of M) is 1. These values are used to determine how many times the loop is executed and how the value of the DO-variable (K) is modified. This loop will be executed 10 times and K will be increased by 1 with each execution of the loop. Even though the values of L and M are changed in the loop, the original values are used for loop processing.

If a block IF statement is used in a DO loop, the corresponding END IF statement must be in the range of the DO loop. Similarly, if a DO loop is used in the true or false part of a decision associated with a block IF statement, the loop must be entirely contained in that part of the decision. Figure 5-22 shows several examples of valid and invalid combinations of DO loops and block IF statements.

Additional DO statement features

In a DO statement, the initial value, test value, and increment may be any integer or real values within the limits of the computer. This means that any of these may be positive, negative, or zero (although the increment cannot be zero), and any may have fractional parts. For example, the following DO statement is valid in FORTRAN:

```
DO 300 I=-10,0,1
```

The first time the DO loop for this statement is executed, the value of I is -10. Then 1 is added to I, making it -9 for the second execution of the loop. The value of I is incremented by 1 for each successive time through the loop. The last time the loop is executed, I is zero. The loop controlled by this statement will be executed eleven times.

Figure 5-22. Valid and invalid patterns using block IF statements and DO loops (Part 1 of 2)

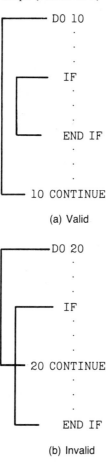

```
DO 10
   .
   .
   .
   IF
   .
   .
   .
   END IF
   .
   .
   .
10 CONTINUE
```

(a) Valid

```
DO 20
   .
   .
   .
   IF
   .
   .
   .
20 CONTINUE
   .
   .
   .
   END IF
```

(b) Invalid

If the increment is negative, the DO loop, in effect, counts backwards. For example, the following DO statement causes the value of J to be decreased by 1 each time the loop is executed:

```
DO 310 J=10,1,-1
```

If we use a negative increment, the loop terminates when the value of the DO-variable is *less than* the test value. In this example, the value of J is 1 during the last execution of the loop. Then -1 is added to J, decreasing its value to 0. Because J is now less than 1, the test value, the loop is not repeated again. This loop will be executed ten times.

A real variable name may be used for the DO-variable, and the parameters can have real values. For example, the following DO statement is valid:

```
DO 320 X=.2,1.0,.1
```

Figure 5-22. (Part 2 of 2)

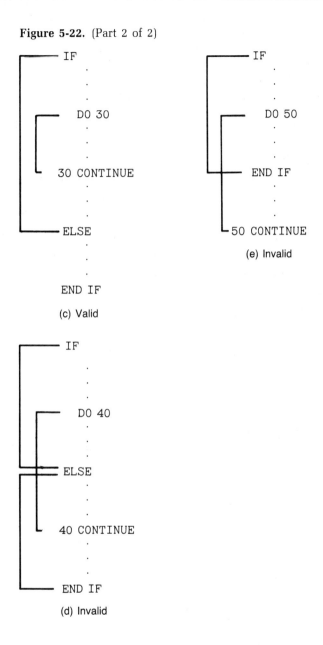

(c) Valid

(e) Invalid

(d) Invalid

The DO-variable in this example is X, a real variable name. The initial value is .2, the test value is 1.0, and the increment is .1. Thus X varies from .2 to 1.0 in increments of .1. The statements in this loop will be executed nine times. If the parameters are not the same type as the DO-variable, the effect is that they are converted to the appropriate type using the REAL or INT function. Usually we can avoid this situation by not using mixed mode in a DO statement.

As we have seen, constants or variable names may be used for the parameters. Arithmetic expressions are also allowed. The expressions may be integer or real. In evaluating the DO statement, the value of any expression is calculated at the time the statement is encountered. The resulting value is then used for loop control. For example, consider the following DO statement:

```
DO 330 Y=A,A+B,2.0*C
```

Assume that A is 5.0, B is 20.0, and C is 3.0 when this statement is executed. Then the initial value of Y is 5.0, the test value is 25.0, and the increment is 6.0.

Some versions of FORTRAN do not provide all of the features described here. In some cases the DO-variable must be an integer variable and only integer variables or constants can be used for the parameters, although the values can be positive, negative, or zero. In older versions of FORTRAN, these elements must all be integer and the parameters all must be positive. These restrictions make the DO statement less versatile.

Nested DO loops

Within the range of one DO loop there may be another DO loop. Such a combination of loops is referred to as *nested DO loops*. As an example of the use of nested DO loops, consider the problem of finding the total and average of five groups of ten test scores each. One approach is to execute the program in Figure 5-16 five separate times. Each time, the program would process a different set of input data. A better approach is to put another loop in the program to repeat the totaling and averaging statements five times. The resulting program is shown in Figure 5-23. With this program all the data can be processed at one time.

In this program, the first DO statement initializes the DO-variable CLASS to 1. Then, after printing a heading, the variable named TOTAL is assigned the value zero. The second DO statement initializes the DO-variable COUNT to 1. Next the range of the inner DO loop is executed. When the terminal statement of the inner DO loop is encountered, COUNT is incremented and the inner loop is repeated. This continues until the inner loop's DO-variable exceeds its test value. At that point, the computer executes the statements following the terminal statement of the inner DO loop. In this case, the average is computed and the output is printed. Then the terminal statement of the outer loop is encountered, the DO-variable CLASS is incremented, and the outer loop is repeated.

With the second execution of the outer DO loop, the value of the variable named TOTAL is reset to zero. Then the inner DO statement is encountered. This causes COUNT to be set to 1 and the inner loop is executed 10 times. Next the average is calculated and the PRINT statements are executed. Then the outer loop's DO-variable is incremented and the outer

Figure 5-23. A program with nested DO loops

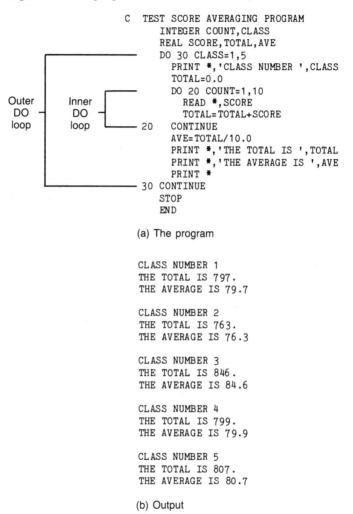

```
      C   TEST SCORE AVERAGING PROGRAM
             INTEGER COUNT,CLASS
             REAL SCORE,TOTAL,AVE
             DO 30 CLASS=1,5
                PRINT *,'CLASS NUMBER ',CLASS
                TOTAL=0.0
                DO 20 COUNT=1,10
                   READ *,SCORE
                   TOTAL=TOTAL+SCORE
      20        CONTINUE
                AVE=TOTAL/10.0
                PRINT *,'THE TOTAL IS ',TOTAL
                PRINT *,'THE AVERAGE IS ',AVE
                PRINT *
      30     CONTINUE
             STOP
             END
```

(a) The program

```
CLASS NUMBER 1
THE TOTAL IS 797.
THE AVERAGE IS 79.7

CLASS NUMBER 2
THE TOTAL IS 763.
THE AVERAGE IS 76.3

CLASS NUMBER 3
THE TOTAL IS 846.
THE AVERAGE IS 84.6

CLASS NUMBER 4
THE TOTAL IS 799.
THE AVERAGE IS 79.9

CLASS NUMBER 5
THE TOTAL IS 807.
THE AVERAGE IS 80.7
```

(b) Output

loop is repeated. This continues for a total of five times. Each time that the outer loop is executed, the statements in the inner loops are performed 10 times. [Figure 5-23(b) shows sample output from this program. The input data that produced this output consisted of 50 records each with a test score.]

We can see from the example how nested DO loops are executed. The basic rule is that each time that an outer loop is performed, the inner loop is completely executed. In the previous example, the statements in the inner loop are executed a total of 50 times.

As another example, consider the following outline of nested DO loops:

```
      DO 300 L=11,20
        DO 200 M=1,5
          DO 100 N=2,6,2
            .
            .
            .
100      CONTINUE
200    CONTINUE
300 CONTINUE
```

In this example, the innermost loop is executed three times for each execution of the intermediate loop. The intermediate loop is executed five times for each execution of the outermost loop. Because the outermost loop is executed 10 times, the intermediate loop is executed a total of 50 times (10 × 5), and the innermost loop is performed 150 times (10 × 5 × 3).

Notice that the DO-variables of the loops in a nest are different variable names. A unique name must be used for the DO-variable of each loop in a nest of DO loops. Also notice that each nested loop is indented two spaces beyond the loop in which it is nested. This is a common style for nested DO loops that helps show the organization of the program.

When using nested DO loops, the range of an inner loop must be completely contained within the range of the outer loop. Hence the following pattern of DO loops is invalid:

```
      DO 70 I=1,20
      DO 80 J=1,5
          .
          .
          .
70 CONTINUE
80 CONTINUE
```

This pattern is unacceptable because, if executed, the terminal statement of the outer loop is encountered while performing the inner loop.

Nested DO loops may have the same terminal statement. For example, the following pattern of nested loops is valid:

```
      DO 90 M=3,18,4
        DO 90 N=1,7
          .
          .
          .
   90 CONTINUE
```

This has the same effect as if each loop had a separate terminal statement. Figure 5-24 shows several valid and invalid patterns for nested DO loops.

Nested DO loops are extremely useful for manipulating certain types of data tables. We will see examples of this in Chapter 10.

Figure 5-24. Some valid and invalid patterns of nested DO loops

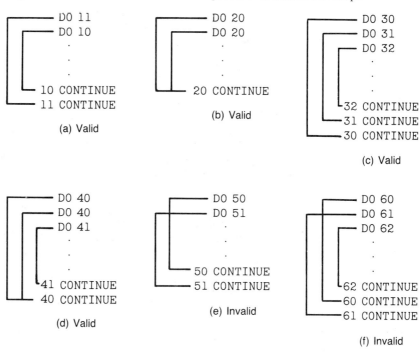

5-4. WHILE loops*

Some versions of FORTRAN provide special statements for general loop control. These are the WHILE and END WHILE statements. Together these statements are used to form a *WHILE loop*. These statements are not included in FORTRAN 77 but are available in some other versions of FORTRAN.

The syntax of these statements and their pattern of use is as follows:

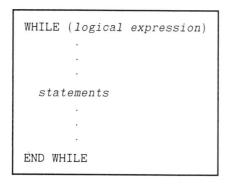

* The statements described in this section are available in the WATFIV-S version of FORTRAN. The same or similar statements are included in some other versions. This section may be skipped if these statements are not available on the computer being used.

The first statement, a WHILE statement, includes a logical expression in parentheses. Following this is the sequence of statements that is to be repeatedly executed. At the end of the loop there must be an END WHILE statement. For example, the following is a valid WHILE loop:

```
WHILE (I.LE.10)
   PRINT *,I
   I=I+1
END WHILE
```

The effect of the WHILE loop is to repeatedly execute the statements in the loop as long as the logical expression in parentheses is true. In the example just given, the PRINT and assignment statements are repeatedly executed as long as I is less than or equal to 10. As soon as the logical expression becomes false, the computer branches out of the loop and continues with the next statement following the END WHILE statement.

A WHILE loop is actually a pretest loop. The pattern is shown graphically in Figure 5-25. When a WHILE statement is encountered, the computer first evaluates the logical expression. If the expression is false, the computer branches to the next statement following the END WHILE statement. If the expression is true, the computer executes the statements in the loop up to the END WHILE statement. The logical expression is again evaluated and, if true, the loop is repeated. This continues until the logical expression becomes false; then control transfers to the statement after the END WHILE statement. Note that, because the expression is evaluated at the beginning of the loop, the loop might not be executed at all. If the logical expression is false when the WHILE statement is first encountered, the loop is bypassed completely.

With a WHILE loop we do not need IF and GO TO statements for loop control. The testing and looping functions are built into the WHILE and END WHILE statements. However, we can create the same effect using an IF statement and GO TO statements in a pretest pattern. Figure 5-26 shows the pretest loop pattern using a WHILE loop and using IF and GO TO state-

Figure 5-25. The WHILE loop pattern

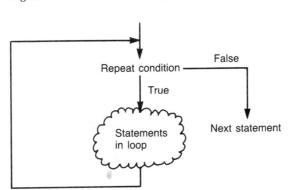

Figure 5-26. The pretest loop pattern

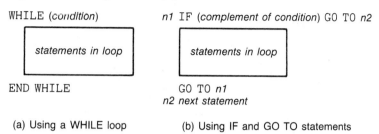

(a) Using a WHILE loop   (b) Using IF and GO TO statements

ments. Notice that, in the IF statement, we must use the complement of the condition used in the WHILE statement. As an example, the following sequence of statements is equivalent to the WHILE loop at the beginning of this section:

```
10 IF (I.GT.10) GO TO 20
      PRINT *,I
      I=I+1
   GO TO 10
20 (next statement)
```

In a WHILE loop, any number of statements may appear between the WHILE and END WHILE statements. The computer repeatedly executes all statements while the logical expression is true. The END WHILE statement is essential. If this statement is left out, the computer will not know where the end of the loop is.

Notice in our earlier example that we have indented the statements in the loop. Although indenting is not required, it is a common style that helps us to see the loop structure in a program.

Illustrative programs

We can use a WHILE loop to control any of the types of loops discussed in the previous sections. Sometimes, though, the structure of the program must be modified slightly. For example, to control an input loop with a trailer value, we must have two READ statements. One READ statement is outside the WHILE loop and reads the first input record. The other READ statement is in the WHILE loop (usually the last statement) and reads each successive input record. The logical expression in the WHILE statement checks that the trailer value has *not* been read. Figure 5-27 shows this pattern in the tuition calculation program (Figure 5-2).

In this program, the first READ statement reads the first record. The WHILE statement tests the value of SNUM to see if it is *not* equal to 9999, the trailer value. When the loop is executed, the tuition is calculated and the output is written. Then the READ statement at the end of the loop reads the *next* record. The logical expression is checked again and, if true, the loop is repeated. Finally, after the last record with actual input data has been

Figure 5-27. The tuition calculation program using a WHILE loop

```
C   TUITION CALCULATION PROGRAM
        INTEGER SNUM
        REAL UNITS,TUIT
        READ *,SNUM,UNITS
        WHILE (SNUM.NE.9999)
          IF (UNITS.LE.12.0) THEN
            TUIT=350.00
          ELSE
            TUIT=350.00+20.00*(UNITS-12.0)
          END IF
          PRINT *,'STUDENT NUMBER = ',SNUM,'  TUITION = ',TUIT
          READ *,SNUM,UNITS
        END WHILE
        STOP
        END
```

read and processed, the record with a value of 9999 for SNUM is read. Because the logical expression is no longer true, execution continues with the next statement after the END WHILE statement.

The interest calculation program in Figure 5-3 can be easily modified to use a WHILE loop. Because this program uses a pretest loop we can replace the IF statement with a WHILE statement using the complement of the condition and replace the GO TO statement with an END WHILE statement. The modified program is shown in Figure 5-28.

The program to find the total and average of ten test scores in Figure 5-6 used a pretest counting loop. We can rewrite this program easily with a WHILE loop. The result is shown in Figure 5-29. The counter must be initialized outside the loop. Within the loop, the counter is incremented. The WHILE statement causes the loop to be repeated as long as the counter is less than or equal to 10.

Figure 5-28. The interest calculation program using a WHILE loop

```
C   INTEREST CALCULATION PROGRAM
        INTEGER YEAR
        REAL BALNC,INTRST
        BALNC=1000.00
        YEAR=1
        WHILE (BALNC.LT.2000.00)
          INTRST=.12*BALNC
          BALNC=BALNC+INTRST
          PRINT *,'YEAR NUMBER  ',YEAR
          PRINT *,'   INTEREST FOR YEAR: ',INTRST
          PRINT *,'   END-OF-YEAR BALANCE: ',BALNC
          PRINT *
          YEAR=YEAR+1
        END WHILE
        STOP
        END
```

Figure 5-29. A program to find the total and average of ten test scores using a WHILE loop

```
C   TEST SCORE AVERAGING PROGRAM
      INTEGER COUNT
      REAL SCORE,TOTAL,AVE
      TOTAL=0.0
      COUNT=1
      WHILE (COUNT.LE.10)
        READ *,SCORE
        TOTAL=TOTAL+SCORE
        COUNT=COUNT+1
      END WHILE
      AVE=TOTAL/10.0
      PRINT *,'THE TOTAL IS ',TOTAL
      PRINT *,'THE AVERAGE IS ',AVE
      STOP
      END
```

Nested WHILE loops

WHILE loops may be nested. The only restriction is that each WHILE statement must have a corresponding END WHILE statement. For example, the interest calculation program in Figure 5-14 used nested loops. This program may be rewritten with WHILE loops as shown in Figure 5-30. Note that each WHILE statement has a matching END WHILE statement. The effect of execution is that the inner WHILE loop is completely executed for each repetition of the outer WHILE loop.

Figure 5-30. The interest calculation program using nested WHILE loops

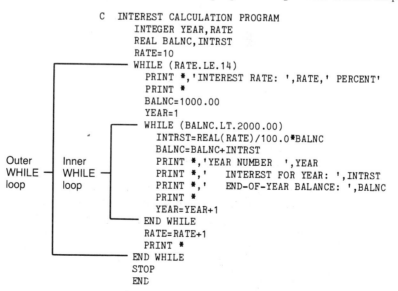

```
C   INTEREST CALCULATION PROGRAM
      INTEGER YEAR,RATE
      REAL BALNC,INTRST
      RATE=10
      WHILE (RATE.LE.14)
        PRINT *,'INTEREST RATE: ',RATE,' PERCENT'
        PRINT *
        BALNC=1000.00
        YEAR=1
        WHILE (BALNC.LT.2000.00)
          INTRST=REAL(RATE)/100.0*BALNC
          BALNC=BALNC+INTRST
          PRINT *,'YEAR NUMBER   ',YEAR
          PRINT *,'   INTEREST FOR YEAR: ',INTRST
          PRINT *,'   END-OF-YEAR BALANCE: ',BALNC
          PRINT *
          YEAR=YEAR+1
        END WHILE
        RATE=RATE+1
        PRINT *
      END WHILE
      STOP
      END
```

Outer WHILE loop / Inner WHILE loop

In all these examples of WHILE loops, note the lack of GO TO statements and statement numbers. If block IF statements and WHILE loops are used, GO TO statements are completely unnecessary and only certain statements (which we have not yet discussed) need to be numbered. In general, this greatly reduces the complexity of programs. A program written with few or no GO TO statements is generally easier to understand, debug, and modify than an equivalent program written with many GO TO statements.

Review questions

1. What is the difference between an input loop and a processing loop?
2. A loop that has no way of stopping is called _____.
3. What is a trailer value?
4. Consider the following group of statements:

```
10 READ *,A,B,C
      PRINT *,A,B,C
   GO TO 10
20 (next statement)
```

These statements are supposed to form a loop that is to be repeated until the input data contains a zero for the last value. What additional statement is needed and where should it go?

5. Each record in a file contains one integer value. Code a group of statements that counts and prints the number of records in the file up to and including the first record with a value of 100.

6. Consider the program shown in Figure 5-3. Assume that statement number 100 is changed to the following:

```
100 IF (BALNC.GE.1500.00) GO TO 200
```

How many years of output will be printed by this modified program?

7. How many lines will be printed by the following group of statements?

```
     J=20
10 IF (J.LE.3) GO TO 20
      PRINT *,J
      J=J-4
   GO TO 10
20 (next statement)
```

8. Each record in a file contains one real value. Code a group of statements to read and print the values from the first 25 records in the file. Do not use a DO statement.

9. What is the difference between a pretest and a posttest loop?

10. A program pattern in which one loop is contained within another loop is called _____.

11. Consider the following program in which all statements have been numbered for ease of reference:

```
10 INTEGER J,K
20 J=1
```

```
 30 IF (J.GT.5) GO TO 90
 40    K=20
 50    K=K-2
 60      PRINT *,J,K
 70    IF (K.GE.10) GO TO 50
 80    J=J+1
 90 GO TO 30
100 STOP
110 END
```

How many times will each of the following statements in this program be executed?

a. statement 30
b. statement 40
c. statement 50
d. statement 70
e. statement 80
f. statement 90

12. During the execution of a DO loop, when is the DO-variable tested and when is it modified?

13. Rewrite the following group of statements using a DO loop:

```
    K=5
100 IF (K.GT.15) GO TO 110
      X=X+K
      K=K+3
    GO TO 100
110 (next statement)
```

14. Rewrite the following group of statements without using a DO statement:

```
    DO 200 L=150,100,-5
      Y=Y+L
200 CONTINUE
```

15. Code a DO loop that prints the numbers 21, 18, 15, . . ., 3 in a column.

16. How many lines are printed by each of the following groups of statements?

```
a.      DO 300 K=1,10
          PRINT *,K
    300 CONTINUE
b.      DO 310 L=4,15,2
          PRINT *,L
    310 CONTINUE
c.      DO 320 M=9,-9,-3
          PRINT *,M
    320 CONTINUE
d.      DO 330 X=5.0,7.0,.25
          PRINT *,X
    330 CONTINUE
```

17. How many lines are printed by each of the following groups of statements?

```
a.      DO 410 I=1,3
          DO 400 J=4,12,2
            PRINT *,I,J
    400     CONTINUE
    410 CONTINUE
```

```
  b.      DO 430 K=1,9,3
              DO 420 L=8,2,-2
                  PRINT *,K,L
      420     CONTINUE
      430 CONTINUE
  c.      DO 460 I=10,1,-1
              DO 450 K=100,150,10
                  DO 440 M=1,2
                      PRINT *,I,K,M
      440         CONTINUE
      450     CONTINUE
      460 CONTINUE
  d.      DO 480 J=18,30,3
              PRINT *,J
              DO 470 L=-8,-18,-2
                  PRINT *,J,L
      470     CONTINUE
              PRINT *,L
      480 CONTINUE
```

18. The following are the main types of loops described in this chapter:

uncontrolled	counting	nested
input	pretest	DO
processing	posttest	

Indicate what type of loop(s) is used in each of the following groups of statements. Your answers should come from the preceding list. Some answers require more than one word (e.g., the statements may be a pretest processing loop or nested DO loops).

```
a.  10 READ *,K
           IF (X.EQ.1.0) GO TO 20
           PRINT *,X
       GO TO 10
       20 (next statement)
b.     A=-10.0
       30 PRINT *,A
           A=A+1.0
           IF (A.LE.0.0) GO TO 30
c.  40 Z=0.0
           PRINT *,Z
       GO TO 40
d.     DO 50 I=1,12,3
           PRINT *,I
       50 CONTINUE
e.     DO 70 J=1,10
           K=1
       60    IF (K.GT.5) GO TO 70
               PRINT J,K
               K=K+1
           GO TO 60
       70 CONTINUE
f.     P=1000.00
       80 IF (P.LT.50.00) GO TO 90
           P=P-.1*P
       GO TO 80
       90 (next statement)
```

19. Are WHILE loops available in the version of FORTRAN you are using?
20. Code a WHILE loop to print the numbers 21, 18, 15, ..., 3 in a column.

Programming problems

1. Write the program for Problem 2 or Problem 5 in Chapter 4 with the additional requirement that the program terminates when the customer number is 9999.
2. Write the program for Problem 4 in Chapter 4 with the additional requirement that the total commission for all salespeople is accumulated and printed at the end of the regular output. Add a record with zero for the salesperson number to control the input loop.
3. Write a FORTRAN program to create a table for converting Fahrenheit temperature to Celsius. (See Problem 2 in Chapter 3 for the appropriate conversion formula.) The table should list the Fahrenheit temperatures from 32 to 212 degrees in 2-degree increments and the equivalent of each temperature in Celsius.
4. A classic exercise in computer programming is sometimes called the "Manhattan Problem." It is based on the historical fact that in 1627 the Dutch purchased Manhattan Island from the Indians for the equivalent of $24. Currently the assessed value of Manhattan is over eight billion dollars. Did the Dutch make a good investment, or would it have been better to have deposited the original $24 in a bank at a fixed interest rate and left it for all these years?

    Assume that the original $24 used to purchase Manhattan Island was deposited in a bank that paid 3% interest compounded annually. Write a FORTRAN program to determine the account total at the end of 1986 (360 years later). Do not use an interest formula to calculate the amount at the end of the time period; instead, accumulate the total one year at a time.
5. A company agrees to pay one of its employees in grains of rice instead of money. The employee receives one grain on the first day, two grains the second day, four grains the third day, eight grains the fourth day, and so forth. In other words, each succeeding day the employee receives twice as many grains as he or she did the day before. The employee works for the company for 15 days.

    Write a FORTRAN program to determine the number of grains of rice that the employee receives on each day that he or she works. Also, accumulate the total of the rice earnings. There is no input for this program. Output should consist of 15 lines each with the day number, the number of grains received on that day, and the accumulated number of grains received to date.
6. Assume that a pair of rabbits can produce a new pair in one month's time. Each new pair becomes fertile at one month of age and begins the cycle of reproducing a new pair every month. If rabbits never die, how many pairs of rabbits are produced from a single pair in N months' time?

    If N ranges from 1 to some maximum value, the solution to this problem creates a sequence of numbers known as the Fibonacci sequence (after the Italian mathematician who first posed the problem). For $N = 1$, the value in the sequence is 1. (That is, at the end of the first month, one new pair of rabbits is produced.) For $N = 2$, the value is also 1. For any N greater than 2, the value in the sequence is the sum of the two previous values. Thus the sequence is as follows:

Number of months	Number of pairs of rabbits
1	1
2	1
3	2
4	3
5	5
6	8
7	13
.	.
.	.
.	.

Let N range from 1 to 24. Write a FORTRAN program to compute and print a table listing N and the number of rabbits produced from the original pair at the end of month N. There is no input for this program.

7. Each student in a class of 15 took examinations. Write a program to calculate the total and average test score for each student, the total and average for the entire class on each test, and the total and average of all 30 test scores. Input to the program is one record for each student with his or her identification number and score on each of the two tests. Output should list the input data and all required totals and averages. Use the following data to test the program:

Identification number	Score on first test	Score on second test
101	88	73
102	100	92
103	45	78
104	63	69
105	84	87
106	92	88
107	91	100
108	61	75
109	78	73
110	99	94
111	74	82
112	83	69
113	100	100
114	52	69
115	85	85

Notice that the data does not include a trailer value. The program should use a DO loop to process exactly 15 input records.

8. Write the program for Problem 13 in Chapter 4 with the additional requirement that the total gross pay, withholding tax, social security tax, and net pay is accumulated and printed at the end of the regular output. Add a record with 9999 for the employee number to control the input loop.

9. Write a FORTRAN program to produce a table of Fahrenheit and equivalent Celsius temperature. The equation is given in Problem 2 of Chapter 3. The program should be designed to begin the table at any initial Fahrenheit temperature, end at any final temperature, and increment between the initial and

final temperatures by any given value. Input for the program is the initial Fahrenheit temperature, the final temperature, and the increment. Use the following sets of input data to test the program:

Initial	Final	Increment
32	212	10
70	71	1
40	30	-1
-10	0	2
0	0	0

The program should terminate if the increment is 0.

10. In Problem 12 of Chapter 3 are the equations for the height h and time of travel t for a projectile fired in the air at an initial velocity v and angle θ. Let θ range from 0 to 90 degrees by 5-degree increments. Write a FORTRAN program to produce a table that lists the value of θ and the corresponding values of h and t. Use an initial velocity of 247.38 to test the program.

11. The value of e^x can be found from the following infinite series:

$$e^x = 1 + x + \frac{x^2}{2!} + \frac{x^3}{3!} + \frac{x^4}{4!} + \cdots$$

$$= 1 + \sum_{i=1}^{\infty} \frac{x^i}{i!}$$

Notice that the nth term (where the first term is 1) is the previous term times $x/(n-1)$.

An approximation to the value of e^x can be computed by carrying out this summation to a finite number of terms. Write a FORTRAN program to approximate e^x using six terms in the summation. Print the approximate value of e^x. Also compute and print the value of e^x using the EXP function. Test the program with the following values of x:

1
0
-1
2.7183
5
-5

12. A tabulation of exam scores is needed for the students in a class. The scores vary from 0 to 100. Write a FORTRAN program to determine the number of scores in the ranges 90 to 100, 80 to 89, 70 to 79, 60 to 69, and 0 to 59. Also determine the percentage of the total number of test scores that fall in each range. Print all results.

Input to the program is one record for each exam score. The last record in the file contains 999 for the exam score. Use the following exam scores to test the program:

85	100	80	76	42	65	89
91	90	37	72	83	88	69
94	85	48	66	92	45	100
73	87	70	60	80	72	59
61	78	61	91	75	78	74
82	76	75	85	91	79	75

13. The combination of n things taken k at a time is given by the following expression:

$$\frac{n!}{k!(n-k)!}$$

Write a FORTRAN program to read the values of n and k, compute the combination, and print the result. Use the following data to test the program:

n	k
10	3
2	1
5	2
8	6

14. Assume that rabbits reproduce at the rate of 20% per month until overpopulation occurs, at which time they begin dying at the rate of 15% per month. Rabbits continue to die at this rate until their population is reduced by one-third, at which time they begin reproducing again. Write a FORTRAN program to print the rabbit population for each of 48 months. Assume that there are initially 1,000 rabbits and overpopulation occurs when there are more than 3,000 rabbits.

15. A problem in timber management is to determine how much of an area to leave uncut so that the harvested area is reforested in a certain period of time. It is assumed that reforestation takes place at a known rate per year, depending on climate and soil conditions. The reforestation rate expresses this growth as a function of the amount of timber standing. For example, if 100 acres are left standing and the reforestation rate is .05, then at the end of the first year there are 100 + .05 × 100 or 105 acres forested. At the end of the second year the number of acres forested is 105 + .05 × 105, or 110.25 acres.

Assume that the total area to be forested, the uncut area, and the reforestation rate are known. Write a FORTRAN program to determine the percentage of the total area that is forested after 20 years. Output should list the input data plus the number of acres forested and the percentage of the total that this represents. Use the following data to test the program:

Area number	Total area	Uncut area	Reforestation rate
045	10,000	100	.05
083	1,000	50	.08
153	20,000	500	.10
192	14,000	3,000	.02
234	6,000	1,000	.01
416	18,000	1,500	.05
999 (trailer value)			

16. The rate of inflation is the annual percentage increase in the cost of goods and services. For example, assume that an item costs $10.00 today and the rate of inflation is 10%. Then the cost of the item in one year is 10.00 + .10 × 10.00 or $11.00. In two years the item will cost 11.00 + .10 × 11.00 or $12.10.

Write a FORTRAN program to find the cost of a $12.00 item in 15 years if the rate of inflation is 2%, 3%, 4%, and so forth up to 10%. That is, the program should give the cost after 15 years at each inflation rate. (*Hint:* Use nested DO loops.)

Also determine the overall percentage increase in the cost of the item. For example, if a $10.00 item costs $18.00 after 15 years, the percentage increase is 80%; if it costs $24.00, the overall increase is 140%. Compute the overall percentage increase for the $12.00 item after 15 years at each inflation rate.

There is no input for this program. Output should list only the final results after 15 years for each inflation rate.

Chapter 6

Formatted input and output programming

In Chapter 2 we discussed programming using *list-directed* input and output. This form of I/O is sufficient for programs that involve simple input and output. Sometimes, however, more complex I/O is required. In such situations *formatted* input and output should be used. This chapter describes formatted I/O and illustrates its use in programs. After completing this chapter you should be able to write programs that use formatted input and output.*

6-1. Formatted input/output statements

As we saw in Chapter 2 three things are needed for input and output programming:

1. An input instruction
2. An output instruction
3. A way of telling the computer the arrangement or *format* of the input and output data

With formatted I/O, the input instruction is the READ statement. For the output instruction, the WRITE statement is used. The format of the I/O data is given in the FORMAT statement. This statement is used for both input and output.

For formatted input, the READ statement is used in conjunction with the FORMAT statement. The READ statement tells the computer to read data using a specific input device and to assign the data to certain variable names. The FORMAT statement tells the computer the format or arrangement

---

* This chapter is designed so that most of it can be read after completing Chapter 2. The only topics that require an understanding of Chapters 3, 4, and 5 are the last two sample programs (Figures 6-13, 6-14, and 6-15).

of the input data. As an example, the following statements might be used for input in a typical program.

```
      READ (5,10) A,B,I,J
   10 FORMAT (F10.2,F8.4,I4,I6)
```

The READ statement is an executable statement that instructs the computer to perform an input operation. The variable names A, B, I, and J tell the computer where in internal storage the input data is to be stored. The first number in parentheses, 5, is a code that tells the computer what input device to use to read the input data. The second number in parentheses, 10, is the statement number of a FORMAT statement that corresponds to this READ statement.

The FORMAT statement is a nonexecutable statement that tells the computer the arrangement of the data in the input record. The characters in parentheses following the keyword FORMAT are codes that describe the fields in the record. (Recall that a record is composed of fields.) Note that the FORMAT statement has a statement number, 10, that corresponds to the second number in parentheses in the READ statement.

With formatted output, the WRITE statement and the FORMAT statement are used together. The WRITE statement instructs the computer to write the output using a specific output device. The data to be written is identified by variable names in the WRITE statement. The FORMAT statement tells the computer how to arrange the output data.

The following statements illustrate a typical output sequence:

```
      WRITE (6,15) X,K,Y
   15 FORMAT (1X,F12.3,I5,F8.2)
```

The WRITE statement is an executable statement that causes the computer to perform an output operation. The variable names X, K, and Y tell the computer what data is to be written. The first number in parentheses, 6, is a code that specifies the output device. The second number in parentheses, 15, is the statement number of a corresponding FORMAT statement.

The nonexecutable FORMAT statement describes the arrangement of the fields in the output record. The codes in parentheses following the keyword FORMAT specify this arrangement. The statement number of the FORMAT statement corresponds to the second number in parentheses in the WRITE statement.

Notice the similarity between the input sequence and the output sequence with formatted I/O. The READ and WRITE statements have very similar syntax. In addition, each requires a corresponding FORMAT statement. Thus the FORMAT statement is a dual-purpose statement. When used in conjunction with a READ statement, it describes the input data format; when used with a WRITE statement, it describes the arrangement of output data. The READ or WRITE statement is linked to its corresponding FORMAT statement by the number of the FORMAT statement.

In the remainder of this section we describe in detail the syntax of the READ, WRITE, and FORMAT statements.

The READ statement

The basic syntax of the READ statement for formatted input is as follows:

```
READ (i,n) list
```

where *i* is a device code.
>   *n* is the number of a FORMAT statement.
>   *list* is a list of variable names separated
>   by commas.

The *device code* (also called the *unit identifier, logical unit number,* or *data set reference number*) specifies the particular device that is used for the input data. The code for any specific input device depends on the computer system. We will use the device code 5 for the main input device, which could be a terminal keyboard or a card reader. (The code could also indicate that the input is to be read from auxiliary storage.)

Each formatted READ statement must have a corresponding FORMAT statement. The two statements are linked by the statement number of the FORMAT statement. This number must appear in parentheses, after the device code, and separated from it by a comma.

The list of variable names, called the *I/O list,* specifies how many values are to be read and the names that are to be used to refer to the values in the program. The computer automatically assigns a storage location to each variable name. When the READ statement is executed, one value for each variable name in the list is read and stored in its respective location. For example, the following READ statement causes the computer to read four values:

```
READ (5,10) AMT,B5,K,JNUM
```

The computer stores the values that are read at locations identified by AMT, B5, K, and JNUM, respectively. If the four values in the input record are 5.8, 183.52, −18, and 0, then after execution of this statement the value of AMT is 5.8, B5 is 183.52, K is −18, and JNUM is 0. Note that the variable names in the list are separated by commas, but there is no punctuation after the last variable name in the list. In this example, the device code is 5. The statement number of the corresponding FORMAT statement is 10.

Each READ statement causes the computer to begin reading a new record. Thus the following statements cause the computer to read two records:

```
READ (5,20) A
READ (5,30) X,J
```

The first record contains the value for A; the second record contains data for X and J.

The device code can be an asterisk. For example, the following READ statement is valid:

```
READ (*,40) X,Y,Z
```

When an asterisk is used for the device code, the computer assumes that the input data comes from a standard device. This is the same device that is used with the list-directed READ statement discussed in Chapter 2 (e.g., a terminal keyboard or card reader).

If an asterisk is used instead of a FORMAT statement number in a READ statement, list-directed input is specified. For example, the following is a list-directed READ statement:

```
READ (5,*) M,N
```

If a standard input device is assumed, an asterisk can also be used for the device code, as in the following example:

```
READ (*,*) M,N
```

Note that this statement is equivalent to the following list-directed READ statement:

```
READ *,M,N
```

The device code and the FORMAT statement number can be preceded by the words UNIT= and FMT=, respectively. For example, the following statement is valid:

```
READ (UNIT=5,FMT=10) AMT,B5,K,JNUM
```

When this syntax is used, the codes can be written in any order. Thus the following statement is equivalent to the example just given:

```
READ (FMT=10,UNIT=5) AMT,B5,K,JNUM
```

Note, however, that if the words UNIT= and FMT= are left out, the device code must come first followed by the FORMAT statement number.

The READ statement can include an end-of-file specifier. Recall from Chapter 2 that this specifier has the form END=n, where n is the number of another statement in the program. For example, the following READ statement includes an end-of-file specifier:

```
READ (5,50,END=100) A,B,I,J
```

The end-of-file specifier must come after the FORMAT statement number and is separated from it by a comma. (If the words UNIT= and FMT= are used

Figure 6-1. Summary of the READ statement

```
READ (UNIT=i,FMT=n1,END=n2) list
```

Notes:
1. The words UNIT= and FMT= are optional.
2. The specifier END=*n2* is optional.
3. If *i* is an *, a standard input device is used.
4. If *n1* is an *, list-directed input is used.

to identify the device code and the format statement number, respectively, then these items and the end-of-file specifier may be listed in any order.) The effect is that, if the end-of-file record is read, the computer branches to the statement whose number is given in the end-of-file specifier.

Figure 6-1 summarizes the characteristics of the READ statement.

The WRITE statement

The syntax of the WRITE statement for formatted output is as follows:

```
WRITE (i,n) list
```

where *i* is a device code.
    n is the number of a FORMAT
      statement.
    list is a list of variable names separated
      by commas.

The device code for the WRITE statement specifies the output device. We will use the device code 6 for the CRT or the printer. (This code may also indicate that the output is to be written to auxiliary storage.) As with the READ statement, the WRITE statement must have a corresponding FORMAT statement. Again the link between the two statements is the statement number of the FORMAT statement.

The I/O list gives the variable names of the values to be written. When the WRITE statement is executed, the computer writes the current value of each variable named in the list. For example, the following WRITE statement causes the computer to write three values:

```
WRITE (6,15) X,KNT,YVAL
```

If X is 25.82, KNT is 139, and YVAL is -5.6 in the computer's internal storage, then execution of this statement causes the device with code 6 to write these three values in the arrangement specified by the FORMAT statement whose number is 15.

Each WRITE statement causes the computer to start a new record (i.e., line). Hence the following statements cause the computer three records:

```
WRITE (6,25) A,I
WRITE (6,35) J
WRITE (6,45) X,Y,Z
```

The first record contains the values of A and I, the second record contains the value of J, and the third record contains the values of X, Y, and Z.

As with the READ statement, the device code in the WRITE statement can be an asterisk in which case a standard output device is assumed. For example, the following WRITE statement is valid:

```
WRITE (*,55) P,Q,R
```

The output device in this example is the same that is used with the list-directed PRINT statement discussed in Chapter 2 (e.g., a CRT or printer).

If an asterisk is used instead of a FORMAT statement number in a WRITE statement, list-directed output is specified. Thus the following is a list-directed output statement:

```
WRITE (6,*) A,B,C
```

When a standard output device is assumed, an asterisk can also be used for the device code, as in the following example:

```
WRITE (*,*) A,B,C
```

Note that this statement is equivalent to the following list-directed PRINT statement:

```
PRINT *,A,B,C
```

As with the READ statement, the words UNIT= and FMT= can be used before the device code and the FORMAT statement number, respectively, in the WRITE statement. Then these items may appear in any order. For example, the following statement is valid:

```
WRITE (FMT=15,UNIT=6) X,KNT,YVAL
```

In Section 3-8 we noted that constants and arithmetic expressions can be included in the list of a PRINT statement. Such items can also be used in a WRITE statement list. For example, the following statement is valid:

```
WRITE (6,65) 1,I,S,98.6,I+J,7.5-3.2*T
```

The effect is that all arithmetic expressions are evaluated first, and then the values of the constants, variables, and expressions are written. (A character

Figure 6-2. Summary of the WRITE statement

```
WRITE (UNIT=i,FMT=n) list
```

Notes:
1. The words UNIT= and FMT= are optional.
2. If *i* is an *, a standard output device is used.
3. If *n* is an *, list-directed output is used.

constant can also be used in a WRITE statement list. With formatted output, this requires special codes that are discussed in Chapter 8.)

Figure 6-2 summarizes the characteristics of the WRITE statement.

The FORMAT statement

A FORMAT statement must be associated with each formatted READ and WRITE statement. This statement describes the arrangement of the data in the input or output record. Internally all data is represented in a standard form. Section 2-2 briefly discussed the internal form of integer and real numbers. (A more complete discussion is contained in Appendix E.) The programmer does not need to understand the internal form of the data because the computer handles this automatically. However, the programmer must tell the computer the external form of the data, that is, the arrangement of the data in the input or output record. In the case of input, the computer must know the arrangement of the input data so that it can properly convert the data to its internal form. For output, the computer must know the external form of the output data for proper conversion from the internal form. This is the function of the FORMAT statement.

The syntax of the FORMAT statement is as follows:

```
n FORMAT (format codes)
```

where *n* is a statement number.
  format codes specify the external data format.

A statement number is required for any FORMAT statement. This same statement number must appear in the corresponding READ or WRITE statement. The *format codes* (also called *edit descriptors* or *data conversion codes*) describe how the data fields are arranged in the record and what type of conversion is to take place between the internal data representation and the external data form. A number of format codes are available in FORTRAN. In this chapter we discuss the most commonly used format codes. In Chapter 8 and Appendix F we examine other format codes.

As an example of the use of the FORMAT statement, consider the following statements:

```
      READ (5,40) A,J
   40 FORMAT (F10.2,I5)
      WRITE (6,45) A,J
   45 FORMAT (1X,F10.2,2X,I5)
```

The READ statement instructs the computer to read data for A and J using the format given in statement 40. The format codes (F10.2,I5) give the arrangement of the input data. The WRITE statement causes the computer to write the values of A and J in the format given in statement 45. The codes (1X,F10.2,2X,I5) describe the output format.

In the next few sections we describe the format codes used for input and output and discuss related topics. Then in Section 6-6 we show the use of the READ, WRITE, and FORMAT statements in complete programs.

6-2. Format codes for input

Format codes can be used to specify the arrangement of both input and output data, although their function when used for input is different than when used for output. In this section we examine the function of several codes for input. In the next section we consider the use of these codes for output.

Input records

Before describing input format codes we need to review several concepts about input records. Recall from Chapter 1 that a record is a group of fields and a field is a group of characters. (In Chapter 2 we used the term "value" instead of "field" because that is the usual terminology with list-directed I/O. With formatted I/O, the correct term is "field.") Each field in a record occupies certain *character positions*. For example, an employee's social security number may occupy the first nine character positions in a record, the employee's name may be in the next twenty character positions, and so on. (With punched card input, the character positions are called *card columns*.)

The maximum number of characters in a record depends on the type of record. With terminal keyboard input, the maximum is usually 80 characters in a line. The most common type of punched card has 80 columns, and therefore a punched card record can have at most 80 characters. With auxiliary storage input, there may be a limit on the size of a record but it is usually very large (for example, 500 characters) and therefore we usually do not have to be concerned with it.

We think of the character positions in an input record as being numbered beginning with 1 on the left and continuing to the maximum on the right. These numbers do not appear in the record (although they are usually printed on punched cards). The numbers help us identify the fields in the record. For example, we may say that one field in a record occupies character positions 1 through 10, another field is in positions 20 through 25, and so forth.

With this background about input records we can now explain format codes for input. We will see that each format code specifies a field that occupies certain character positions in a record. All the format codes taken together describe the entire record.

I-format code for input

Different format codes are used for different types of data. The I-format code is used for integer data. Only integers may be read using I-format.

The syntax of the I-format code is as follows:

> I w
>
> where w is the width of the field.

As an example of the use of I-format, consider the following READ statement and corresponding FORMAT statement:

```
    READ (5,105) K,L
105 FORMAT (I4,I5)
```

In this example, two integer variable names, K and L, are in the READ statement list. Thus two values are read. In the FORMAT statement, there are two I-format codes, I4 and I5, separated by commas. They correspond to the two input variable names, respectively. Thus the value for K is read in format I4, and that for L is read in format I5.

The numbers following the letter I specify the width of the fields in the record. The first field, containing the value for K, is four characters wide and begins in the first character position. Immediately following this field is a five-character field that contains the value for L. If the values to be read for K and L are 25 and -36, respectively, then the data is recorded in the input record as follows:

```
    123456789... (character positions)
    ┌─────┬─────┐
    │   25│  −36│
    └─────┴─────┘
```

(Note that we have listed the character positions in the record and used vertical lines to designate fields. However, none of this appears in the actual record. Only the data, the numbers 25 and -36, are in the record.) After execution of the READ statement, the values of the input variable names are as desired.

Depending on the computer being used, an input record may be keyed directly into the computer at a terminal keyboard, may be recorded in an auxiliary storage file, or may be punched in a card. In all cases the data must be recorded in the proper format. Thus, in the example just given, character positions 1 through 4 in the record must contain the value for K, and positions 5 through 9 must have the value for L. The correspondence between the variable names in the READ statement, the format codes in the FORMAT statement, and the fields in the input record must be maintained. Figure 6-3 summarizes the correspondences for this example.

In this example the selection of K and L as the integer variable names is arbitrary. The programmer may select any names as long as they are integer variable names. In addition, the locations of the fields in the input record may be different. One part of planning a program is to determine the layout of the input data. In this example, the value for K is recorded in positions 1 through 4, and the value for L is recorded in positions 5 through 9. The input record may be arranged in another manner as long as the READ and FORMAT statements correspond to the layout. For example, assume that the record has the value for L in positions 1 through 5 and value for K in positions 6 through 12. Then the READ and FORMAT statements are as follows:

```
      READ (5,106) L,K
106 FORMAT (I5,I7)
```

In this case, L is read in format I5, and K is read in format I7. Finally, note that we do not need to know the actual data values when preparing the READ and FORMAT statements. We only need to know the locations of the fields in the input record.

When an integer value is recorded in a record, it must *not* include a decimal point. If the value is negative, it must have a minus sign in front of it; if it is positive, the plus sign is optional. No commas may appear in the value. An integer should be recorded as far to the right in its field as possible. That is, integers should be *right-justified*. If an integer is not right-justified, many computers will interpret any blanks that appear in the field

Figure 6-3. Correspondence between variable names, format codes, and input fields

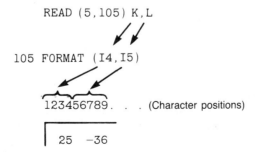

```
      READ (5,105) K,L



105 FORMAT (I4,I5)




      123456789.  .  . (Character positions)


   |  25  −36
```

after the value as zeros. For example, consider a record with data recorded as follows:

123456789......

25	−36

If the previous READ statement reads this record, many computers would interpret the value of L to be 25000 and the value of K to be −3600.

F-format code for input

When an integer value is to be read, only I-format code may be used. The F-format code is used to describe the arrangement of real data (floating-point data). Only real values may be read using F-format.

The syntax of the F-format code is as follows:

$$Fw.d$$

where w is the width of the field.
　　　d is the number of places to the right of the decimal point.

The following example illustrates the use of F-format for input:

```
   READ (5,20) X,Y,Z
20 FORMAT (F8.2,F10.4,F4.0)
```

The computer reads three real values and assigns them to the storage locations reserved for the real variables named X, Y, and Z. The three F-format codes, separated by commas, correspond to the three variable names in the input list. The value for X is read in format F8.2, Y is read in format F10.4, and Z is read in format F4.0.

Like I-format, the field width in F-format is written immediately following the letter F. Thus the value for X in the previous example occupies the first eight character positions of the input record, the value for Y is recorded in positions 9 through 18, and the value for Z is in positions 19 through 22. Because F-format is used for real data, additional information about the number of decimal positions is required. This information is coded after the field width and is separated from the field width by a decimal point. In the preceding example, the value for X has two places to the right of the decimal point, Y has four places to the right, and the value of Z has no places to the right of the decimal point. Note that, even though Z has no decimal places, it has a decimal point and is assigned to a real variable name.

To illustrate this, assume a record has data recorded as follows:

```
123456789..............
```

| 36.25 | −.2738 | 45. |

If the previous READ statement reads this record, the value of X is 36.25, Y is −.2738, and Z is 45..

When a real value is recorded in a record it often has a decimal point in the proper position, although this is not required. If the decimal point is omitted, the computer uses the F-format code to locate where the decimal point should be. For example, assume that the data in the record for the previous READ statement is as follows:

```
123456789..............
```

| 3625 | −2738 | 45 |

Then the result is the same as before. The computer examines the format codes and determines how many places should be to the right of the decimal point. For example, format code F8.2 tells the computer that there are two decimal places. The computer counts the number of places specified *from the right* and reads the value as if a decimal point were recorded in the indicated position. In this example, the value for X is read as 36.25. It is important when using this feature of the F-format that the data is right-justified. Assume, for example, that the first field is not right-justified, but instead is as follows:

```
123456789...
```

| 3625 | |

Many computers would interpret the trailing blanks as zeros, and, counting two decimal places from the right, the value read would be 36250.00.

If a decimal point is included in the data, it need not correspond with the format code, and the value need not be right-justified. For example, consider the following data:

```
123456789...
```

| 36.2587 |

The actual location of the decimal point in the field overrides the specified location in the format code, and, in this case, if format code F8.2 is used, the value read is 36.2587.

F-format and I-format may be used in the same FORMAT statement. For example, the following statements are valid (assume A and B are real, I and J are integer):

```
    READ (5,10) A,B,I,J
 10 FORMAT (F10.2,F8.4,I4,I6)
```

The values for A and B are read in formats F10.2 and F8.4, respectively; the values for I and J are read in formats I4 and I6, respectively. Care should be taken not to read a real value using I-format, or an integer value using F-format. For example, assume that the preceding READ statement is accidentally coded as follows:

```
    READ (5,10) A,I,B,J
```

In this case, an error occurs because the computer tries to read a value for the integer variable named I in format F8.4 and a value for the real variable named B in format I4.

X-format code for input

In the examples considered so far, the first input field has always begun in character position 1. If additional fields are read, they begin in the next character position following the previous field. Usually the computer begins reading in position 1 and continues through successive character positions until all of the required fields in the record are read. However, we can use X-format to have the computer skip characters. Thus fields can be spaced across the input record.

The syntax of the X-format code is as follows:

```
wX

where w is the width of the field to be skipped;
      that is, w is the number of character
      positions to be skipped.
```

For example, consider the following statements:

```
    READ (5,25) AMT,KT
 25 FORMAT (F5.2,4X,I3)
```

In this example, the value for the real variable named AMT is read in format F5.2. Then the format 4X tells the computer to skip the next four positions. Finally, the value for the integer variable named KT is read in format I3. Thus, if the values 12.58 and -10 are to be read and assigned to AMT and KT, respectively, the data in the input record would be recorded as follows:

```
123456789......
```
```
12.58    -10
```

As another example, consider the following READ and FORMAT statements:

```
    READ (5,26) ID,COST
26 FORMAT (5X,I4,1X,F10.2)
```

The format 5X tells the computer to skip the first five positions. Then the value of ID is read in format I4. Next the code 1X causes one position to be skipped. Finally, the value of the variable named COST is read in format F10.2.

Repeat specification

If an F- or I-format code is repeated successively in a FORMAT statement, the code may be written once and immediately preceded by a number that specifies the number of times that the code should be repeated. For example, in the following FORMAT statement, the FORMAT code F10.2 is repeated three times in succession:

```
55 FORMAT (F10.2,F10.2,F10.2)
```

Using a repeat specification, the statement may be shortened to

```
55 FORMAT (3F10.2)
```

The 3 in front of the format code specifies that this code should be repeated three times.

As another example, consider the following FORMAT statement:

```
56 FORMAT (F12.6,F12.6,I2,I2,I2)
```

The format F12.6 is repeated twice followed by three repetitions of I2 format. Thus the statement may be shortened to

```
56 FORMAT (2F12.6,3I2)
```

A repeat specification can be used for both input and output formats.

6-3. Format codes for output

In the last section we explained the use of I-, F-, and X-format codes for describing the arrangement of input data. In this section we discuss the use of these codes for output. First, however, we need to cover a few concepts about output records.

Output records

A record, whether input or output, is composed of fields. For input, we think in terms of the character positions of the fields in the record. In an output record we also think in terms of the character positions of the fields. With CRT output this is the usual terminology. With printed paper output we usually refer to these character positions as *print positions*. Thus with printed output we talk about printing a field in particular print positions.

The maximum number of characters in an output record depends on the output device. For most CRT output a line has 80 character positions. Thus a CRT output record can have at most 80 characters. The maximum number of print positions for a printer varies widely, but common sizes are 80, 120, and 132 print positions. No printed output record can have more characters than the number of print positions for the printer being used. (Auxiliary storage may also be used for output, in which case the maximum number of characters in a record is usually very large.)

As with an input record, we think of the character positions in an output record as being numbered beginning with 1 on the left and continuing to the maximum on the right. These numbers do not appear in the output, but when discussing output formats it is convenient to refer to numbered character positions.

Input data is read beginning with the first character position in the record. Similarly, output data is written beginning at the first position. For CRT output, the character in the first position in the output record is displayed in the first position in the line. With printed paper output this is not the case. When output is to be printed on paper, the character in the first position in the output record, as described by the FORMAT statement, is *not* printed. Rather, printing begins in print position 1 with the character in the *second* position in the output record. (See Figure 6-4.) The reason for this is that the first character in a printed output record is used to control the movement of the paper in the printer. The details of this are discussed in Section 6-5, but for now we need a way to skip the first position of the output record for printed output. The simplest approach is to use the X-format code. By using 1X as the first code in the FORMAT statement, the first position in the output record contains a blank space. Then printing begins in print position 1 with the next character.

Note that this rule only applies to output produced on a printer. For CRT output, the first character in the output record is the first character displayed. Hence 1X is not needed as the first code in the FORMAT statement for CRT output. (The same applies to auxiliary storage output.) Printed output is very common with FORTRAN programs; therefore, we will assume in most examples that the output is to be printed on paper and use an appropriate format code for the first character in the output record.

Figure 6-4. Output records and printed output

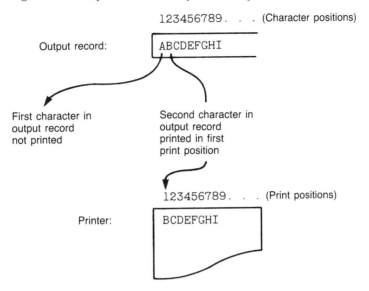

I-format code for output

As an example of output record organization and the use of the I-format code, consider the following statements (K and L are integer variable names):

```
     WRITE (6,87) K,L
  87 FORMAT (1X,I2,I4)
```

Assume that the device code 6 identifies the printer. Then the result of executing the WRITE statement is that the current values of K and L are printed. The value of K is printed in format I2, and L is printed in format I4. If this WRITE statement is executed when the values of K and L are 25 and -36, respectively, the printed output appears as follows:

```
  123456789... (print positions)
 ┌──────────────
 │ 25│ −36│
 └──────────────
```

(Note that the print positions are listed and that vertical lines are used to designate fields. However, none of this is printed by the printer.)

When the FORMAT statement is used for output, the statement describes the arrangement of the characters in the output record. In this example, the first character in the output record is a blank because the first code in the FORMAT statement is 1X. The value of K is placed in the next two positions in the output record, followed by the value of L in the next four

Figure 6-5. Correspondence between variable names, format codes, and printed output fields

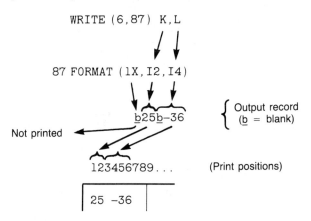

positions. Because printed output begins with the *second* position in the output record, the value of K is printed in the first two print positions and the value of L is printed in print positions 3 through 6. This is summarized in Figure 6-5.

The importance of skipping the first position in a printed output record can be seen more clearly now. Assume in this example that the 1X code had been left out, and that the statements had been coded as follows:

```
    WRITE (6,87) K,J
87 FORMAT (I2,I4)
```

In this case the value of K occupies the first two positions in the output record. However, the first character in a printed output record is not printed; printing begins with the second character. Hence, if K is 25, the 2 is not printed, and the 5 is printed in the first print position. This is summarized in Figure 6-6. Note that this applies to printed output only and does not apply to CRT output (or auxiliary storage output). With CRT output the 1X code is not needed.

When using I-format for output, the output data is automatically right-justified in its field. Because the values are integers, no decimal points are included in the output. If a value is positive, no sign is provided; if it is negative, a minus sign appears immediately to the left of the value. The minus sign occupies a character position, and enough room must be left for all digits in the value and any sign. If the field size is not large enough to contain the output, an error condition occurs. On many computer systems such an error field is filled with asterisks. For example, if the previous FORMAT statement is coded

```
87 FORMAT (1X,I2,I2)
```

Figure 6-6. Result of an incorrectly coded FORMAT statement for printed output

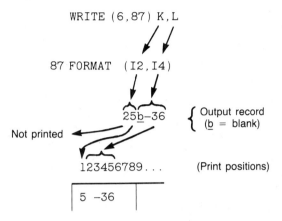

then, with K equal to 25 and L equal to −36, the resulting output appears as follows:

```
123456789...
```
```
25**
```

Because −36 requires three positions, and only two have been specified for this field in the FORMAT statement, an error occurs. Hence the field is filled with asterisks.

    The I-format code describes the external format of integer data. Internally all integer data is represented in the same general form. Thus a value that is read in one format may be written in another. For example, a value may be read in format I5 and written in format I4. In addition, there may be as many format codes in a FORMAT statement as needed. The only restriction is that the total number of characters specified for input cannot exceed the length of the input record, and that the number of output positions cannot exceed the capacity of the output record.

F-format code for output

The following example illustrates the use of F-format for output (X and Z are real variable names):

```
    WRITE (6,75) X,Z
75 FORMAT (1X,F8.2,F6.0)
```

Assume that the device code 6 identifies the printer and that the values of X and Z are 36.25 and 45., respectively. The printed output appears as follows:

```
123456789 . . . . . . . .

    36.25    45.
```

The value of X is printed in format F8.2, and Z is printed in format F6.0. Note that the input format need not agree with the output format. For example, the value of Z may be read in format F4.0 and written in format F6.0. Format codes describe the external representation of the data; internally, real data is represented in a standard form which is unrelated to the external form.

Output with F-format is always right-justified in its field. A decimal point is always included, whether or not there are places to the right of the decimal point. There should be enough field width to accommodate the value and any punctuation. The minus sign and the decimal point each require a position. In addition, on some computers a fraction is written with a leading zero. For example, assume that Y is $-.2738$ and that the following WRITE statement is executed:

```
    WRITE (6,185) Y
185 FORMAT (1X,F10.4)
```

Then with printer output the result is as follows:

```
123456789 . . .

    -0.2738
```

F-format input and output differ in that, when F-format is used for output, the number of decimal positions specified is always the controlling factor. If the number of decimal positions specified is greater than the number in the value to be written, trailing positions are filled with zeros. For example, consider the following statements:

```
    WRITE (6,410) X
410 FORMAT (1X,F12.4)
```

In this example, four decimal positions are specified, but assume that the value of X is 36.25 and thus has only two decimal positions. The resulting printed output is as follows:

```
123456789 . . . . . .

    36.2500
```

If the number of decimal positions specified is less than the actual number in the data value, the value is rounded to the specified number of decimal positions before being written. For example, assume that Y is -0.2738 and that the following statements are coded:

```
    WRITE (6,65) Y
65 FORMAT (1X,F6.3)
```

Then the printed output appears as follows:

```
    123456789...
   ┌─────────────
   │-0.274│
```

Note that -0.2738 has been rounded to -0.274 before printing.

As with input, F- and I-format may be used in the same FORMAT statement. Remember that the types of the variable names must correspond with those of the format codes. For example, consider the following statements:

```
    WRITE (6,20) A,B,I,J
20 FORMAT (1X,F10.2,F8.4,I4,I6)
```

These statements are valid *if* A and B are real variable names and I and J are integer variable names. If this is not the case, an error occurs.

Recall that constants and arithmetic expressions as well as variable names may appear in a WRITE statement list. Each constant, variable name, and expression in the list must have a corresponding format code that is of the correct type for the type of data to be written. Thus an integer constant must have a corresponding I-format code, a real expression must have a corresponding F-format code, and so on. For example, consider the following statements:

```
    WRITE (6,65) 1,I,S,98.6,I+J,7.5-3.2*T
65 FORMAT (1X,I2,I3,F4.1,F5.1,I4,F8.2)
```

Assume that I and J are integer variable names and S and T are real names. Then the integer constant 1 is written in format I2, the value of the integer variable name I is written in format I3, the value of the real variable name S is written in format F4.1, the real constant 98.6 is written in format F5.1, the value of the integer expression $I+J$ is written in format I4, and the value of the real expression $7.5-3.2*T$ is written in format F8.2. Hence the correct type of format code is used for each value to be written.

X-format code for output

As we have seen, we can use the X-format code to skip positions in an output record; in fact, X-format causes blank characters to be written. For example, the following statements cause the values of AMT and KT to be printed with five blank characters at the beginning and three blanks between the fields:

```
      WRITE (6,26) AMT,KT
   26 FORMAT (6X,F5.2,3X,I3)
```

If AMT is 12.58 and KT is −10, the printed output is as follows:

```
   123456789. . . . . . . . . .
```

	12.58	−10

Note that the first format code is 6X, even though only five blanks appear in the printed output. This is because printing begins with the second character in the output record. In previous examples we have skipped the first position in the output record with a 1X code. Here we skip five positions with a 6X code. In other words, 6X is equivalent to 1X,5X. Note, however, that if CRT (or auxiliary storage) output were used for this example, six positions would be skipped at the beginning of the output.

6-4. Formatted character output

With formatted I/O, character output can be produced by including character constants in the FORMAT statement. Recall that a character constant is a group of characters enclosed in apostrophes. When used in a FORMAT statement, the characters between the apostrophes are written when the WRITE statement that corresponds with the FORMAT statement is executed. (A character constant used in this way is also called an *apostrophe edit descriptor*.)

As an example, consider the following statements:

```
      WRITE (6,35) X
   35 FORMAT (1X,'THE SOLUTION IS',2X,F6.2)
```

The character constant 'THE SOLUTION IS' contains 15 characters (not counting the apostrophes). When this WRITE statement is executed, these 15 characters will be written followed by two blanks and then the value of X occupying six positions. If the value of X is 125.25 in the computer's internal storage, the printed output is

```
   123456789. . . . . . . . . . . . . . . .
```

THE SOLUTION IS	125.25

Note that the apostrophes are not included in the output.

The following example illustrates the use of two character constants in one FORMAT statement:

```
    WRITE (6,36) AMT,KT
36 FORMAT (1X,' AMOUNT = ',F5.2,2X,'COUNT = ',I3)
```

Assuming that the values of AMT and KT are 12.58 and -10, respectively, the printed output for this example is

```
    123456789.....................
```

| AMOUNT = |12.58| |COUNT = |-10| |

Note that the order of the character constants and format codes is important. The order must correspond with the order in which the output is to be written. Thus, in this example, a character constant is printed, followed by a numeric value in format F5.2. Then two blank spaces are left, another character constant is printed, and a final numeric value in format I3 is printed.

A list of variable names is not required in a WRITE statement. Thus we can write headings and captions without writing the value of a variable name. For example, the following sequence of statements causes the specified heading to be written:

```
     WRITE (6,101)
101 FORMAT (1X,'STATISTICAL DATA')
```

A common mistake when using character constants is to try to write more characters than there are character positions for the device being used. If we use several long character constants in one FORMAT statement, this can easily happen. This usually results in an execution error when the program is run.

Another common error occurs when we continue a FORMAT statement from one line to the next in a program. Whenever a statement is so long that it cannot fit between columns 7 and 72, the statement must be continued onto the next line. However, we do not need to fill out the line to column 72 before continuing; most statements can be broken at *almost* any point and continued onto the next line. A problem arises when we break a FORMAT statement in the middle of a character constant. In this case the statement must be carried out to exactly column 72 and continued beginning in column 7. Otherwise, the character constant will include any blank spaces up to column 72 and in column 7 or beyond.

For example, assume that a programmer wrote the FORMAT statement shown in Figure 6-7(a). In this example, column 72 in the first line is two spaces beyond the word TOTAL and there is a space in column 7 in the second line before the word IS. These three spaces would be included in the character constant between the words TOTAL and IS and would be written in the output.

Figure 6-7. Continuing a FORMAT statement

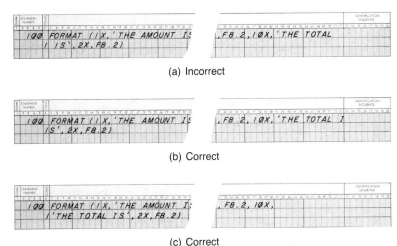

(a) Incorrect

(b) Correct

(c) Correct

To correct this example, the I of IS should be in column 72 of the first line and the S in column 7 on the next line, as shown in Figure 6-7(b). A better approach would be to only break the FORMAT statement after a comma separating format codes or character constants as shown in Figure 6-7(c). Then this type of error cannot occur.

6-5. Carriage control

As we have seen, each time the computer executes a READ statement, a new input record is read. With terminal input, each READ statement causes a new typed line to be accepted. For auxiliary storage input, a new record is read and with punched card input the next card in sequence is read. No special programming is needed to control which record is read; the computer always reads the next record in sequence.

In a similar fashion, each time the computer executes a WRITE statement, a new output record is written. For CRT input, a new line is displayed; for printer output, another line is printed. In the examples we have seen so far, the new line appears immediately after the previous line. In other words, the output lines are single spaced. Many times, however, we want to space the output in a different way, perhaps double spacing or skipping several lines. With CRT output, we can do this by displaying blank lines or by using another technique discussed later. For printer output, however, an additional programming feature is needed. This feature is called *carriage control*.

Computer output paper usually consists of individual sheets of paper connected along perforated top and bottom edges. This creates a continuous form that is moved through the printer. Figure 6-8 illustrates continuous form output and the printer mechanism that controls it. This mechanism is called a *carriage* and is similar to a typewriter carriage. As the carriage rotates, the forms move up, exposing blank paper to the printing mechanism. The carriage can move up one or more lines at a time or it can rotate until the top of the next page is reached.

FORTRAN uses special characters, called *carriage control characters,* to control carriage movement. A carriage control character is put in the first position in an output record. Recall from Section 6-3 that the character in this position is not printed. (See Figure 6-4.) Rather, the printer examines the character and interprets it as an instruction on how to move the carriage before printing the line described in the rest of the FORMAT statement. The carriage control characters in FORTRAN are as follows:

Blank — advance one line before printing (single space)
   0 — advance two lines before printing (double space)
   1 — advance to the first line of the next page before printing
   + — no advance before printing

There are several approaches to using carriage control characters. The simplest is to place a character constant at the beginning of the FORMAT statement with the appropriate carriage control character. For example, for double spacing, the correct coding for one of the previous examples is

```
35 FORMAT ('0','THE SOLUTION IS',2X,F6.2)
```

Figure 6-8. Continuous form output

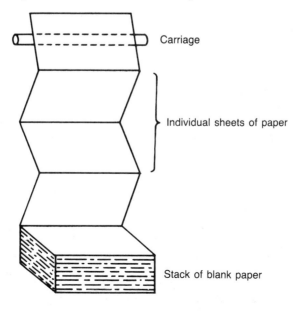

Carriage

Individual sheets of paper

Stack of blank paper

The first character of the output record is defined by the character constant '0'. Here the character is a zero, so the carriage advances two lines before printing.

For single spacing, the correct coding is

```
35 FORMAT (' ','THE SOLUTION IS',2X,F6.2)
```

Because the first character constant contains a blank (a valid character in FORTRAN), the carriage advances one line before printing.

To skip to the top of the next page before printing, the correct coding is

```
35 FORMAT ('1','THE SOLUTION IS',2X,F6.2)
```

Note that the first character (the carriage control character) is not printed; that is, the 0 or 1 in these examples does not appear in the output.

An alternative approach in these examples is to put the carriage control character in the first position in the character constant. For example, we can double space equally well with the following statement:

```
35 FORMAT ('0THE SOLUTION IS',2X,F6.2)
```

In this example, the character constant has 16 characters with zero as the first character. Because this zero is the first character in the output record, it is taken as the carriage control character by the printer.

In earlier examples of output formats, we used 1X as the first code in the FORMAT statement. This placed a blank in the first position in the output record. This is equivalent to using 'b' (b = blank) as the first item in the FORMAT statement.

Carriage control can be executed without any actual printing. For example, the following statements cause the computer to skip to the top of the next page with no printed output:

```
      WRITE (6,75)
 75 FORMAT ('1')
```

One reason that this may be done is to position the paper at the top of a new page before printing any output data. Similarly, the following statements cause the carriage to move up one line without printing anything:

```
      WRITE (6,77)
 77 FORMAT (' ')
```

6-6. Illustrative programs

As a first illustration of the use of formatted input and output in a complete program, consider the following example:

```
       INTEGER K
       REAL A
       READ (5,10) K,A
   10  FORMAT (I5,F10.2)
       WRITE (6,20) K,A
   20  FORMAT (1X,I5,5X,F10.2)
       STOP
       END
```

In this program, values for K and A are read in the format given by the FORMAT statement numbered 10. Then K and A are written using the format in the FORMAT statement numbered 20. Note that in both input and output, I-format is used for K because this variable is integer. Similarly, F-format is used in both input and output for the real variable A.

READ and WRITE statements are executable statements. The computer executes these statements in the order in which they appear in the program. FORMAT statements, however, are nonexecutable statements. They are used during input and output operations, but they are not executed by themselves. Therefore FORMAT statements do not need to be in any particular sequence and, in fact, may appear anywhere in the program before the END statement. Many programmers place all FORMAT statements together at the beginning or end of the pogram. For example, in the following program, all FORMAT statements are grouped at the end of the program, after the STOP statement and before the END statement:

```
       INTEGER K
       REAL A
       READ (5,10) K,A
       WRITE (6,20) K,A
       STOP
   10  FORMAT (I5,F10.2)
   20  FORMAT (1X,I5,5X,F10.2)
       END
```

The computer locates the appropriate FORMAT statement by the statement number given in the READ or WRITE statement. Each FORMAT statement must have a unique statement number so it can be found.

The format code that is used for a variable for input does not have to be identical to the code used for that variable for output. For example, consider the following program:

```
       INTEGER K
       REAL A
       READ (5,10) K,A
       WRITE (6,20) K,A
       STOP
   10  FORMAT (I5,F10.2)
   20  FORMAT (1X,I6,4X,F12.4)
       END
```

In this example, K is read in format I5 and written using format I6. Similarly, A is read with format F10.2 and written in format F12.4. The only restrictions are that the proper format code (I or F) must be used for the type of the variable (integer or real) and that the output format must be large enough to hold the value to be written.

Each READ and WRITE statement does not necessarily have to refer to a separate FORMAT statement. A single FORMAT statement can be referenced by several READ or WRITE statements. This would be appropriate when an input or output format is identical for several records. For example, consider the following program:

```
      INTEGER K,L
      REAL A,B
      READ (5,10) K,A
      READ (5,10) L,B
      WRITE (6,20) K,A
      WRITE (6,20) L,B
      STOP
   10 FORMAT (I5,F10.2)
   20 FORMAT (1X,I5,5X,F10.2)
      END
```

Note that FORMAT statement 10 is used with both READ statements, and that statement 20 is used with both WRITE statements. In this case, the two input records have identical formats, and the two output records have the same layout. (The same FORMAT statement may be used for both input and output, but this is rarely done because a carriage control character is usually needed for output but not for input.)

A program may use both formatted and list-directed I/O. The main requirements are that the input data for a formatted READ statement must be in the proper format as specified by the FORMAT statement, and the input data for a list-directed READ statement must be in the correct format for this type of statement. For example, consider the following program:

```
      INTEGER K,L
      REAL A,B
      READ *,K,A
      READ (5,10) L,B
      WRITE (6,20) K,A
      PRINT *,L,B
      STOP
   10 FORMAT (I5,F10.2)
   20 FORMAT (1X,I5,5X,F10.2)
      END
```

In this example K and A are read from a record in list-directed format. Then

L and B are read from the next record in the format given in FORMAT statement 10. Next a record is written with K and A in the format specified in statement 20. Finally, L and B are written in the next record in list-directed format. Note that the value of a variable may be read one way (say, using list-directed input) and written another way (for example, using formatted output).

Figure 6-9 shows another example of a program with formatted I/O. (This program is similar to the one in Figure 2-8 which used list-directed I/O.) The program reads two input records, each containing a student's identification number and two examination scores. The output lists each student's data on a separate line. Note that each FORMAT statement is used by two READ or two WRITE statements.

We can modify the program in Figure 6-9 to include a loop and put an end-of-file specifier in the READ statement. Figure 6-10 shows the resulting program. (This program is similar to the one in Figure 2-15.) This program processes as many records as there are in the input file, in contrast to the program in Figure 6-9 which only processes two records.

Statement numbers are needed in the program in Figure 6-10 not only for the FORMAT statements, but also for the READ and STOP statements. Statement numbers should always be assigned in some logical pattern. In this program we have used two-digit numbers for the executable statements and three-digit numbers for the FORMAT statements. In addition, the statement numbers are in increasing sequence. We can select statement numbers in many other ways.

Adding character output to the program in Figure 6-10 makes the output more readable. For example, Figure 6-11 shows a program which produces output with a title, headings for the columns of data, and a final output line. Note that the output for this program is all single spaced.

We can modify this program further to include carriage control. Figure 6-12 shows the final result. In this program the title is printed after skipping to the top of the next page. The column headings are double spaced after the title. The first line of data is double spaced after the column headings. This is accomplished by printing a blank line after the headings are printed. The lines of data are single spaced. The final output line is double spaced after the last line of data.

Any of the sample programs in previous chapters can be modified to use formatted I/O. For example, Figure 6-13 shows a payroll program that is based on the one in Figure 4-2. In the new program, a title line and column headings are printed for the output. In addition, each numeric value that represents a dollar amount is printed with two places to the right of the decimal point and preceded by a dollar sign. Notice that the output is much easier to read because of the use of formatted output.

Figure 6-9. An illustrative program

```
C  PROGRAM TO LIST TEST SCORES
      INTEGER ID
      REAL SCR1,SCR2
      READ (5,100) ID,SCR1,SCR2
      WRITE (6,200) ID,SCR1,SCR2
      READ (5,100) ID,SCR1,SCR2
      WRITE (6,200) ID,SCR1,SCR2
      STOP
100 FORMAT (I5,5X,2F5.1)
200 FORMAT (1X,I5,5X,F5.1,5X,F5.1)
      END
```

(a) The program

```
21167        89.5 94.0
25701        83.0 87.5
```

(b) Input data

```
21167        89.5      94.0
25701        83.0      87.5
```

(c) Output

Figure 6-10. An illustrative program with a loop

```
C  PROGRAM TO LIST TEST SCORES
      INTEGER ID
      REAL SCR1,SCR2
10 READ (5,100,END=20) ID,SCR1,SCR2
      WRITE (6,200) ID,SCR1,SCR2
      GO TO 10
20 STOP
100 FORMAT (I5,5X,2F5.1)
200 FORMAT (1X,I5,5X,F5.1,5X,F5.1)
      END
```

(a) The program

```
21167        89.5 94.0
25701        83.0 87.5
28145        87.0 76.0
30074        71.5 76.5
34230        92.0 96.0
```

(b) Input data

```
21167        89.5      94.0
25701        83.0      87.5
28145        87.0      76.0
30074        71.5      76.5
34230        92.0      96.0
```

(c) Output

Figure 6-11. An illustrative program with character output

```
C   PROGRAM TO LIST TEST SCORES
        INTEGER ID
        REAL SCR1,SCR2
        WRITE (6,150)
        WRITE (6,160)
    10 READ (5,100,END=20) ID,SCR1,SCR2
          WRITE (6,200) ID,SCR1,SCR2
          GO TO 10
    20 WRITE (6,250)
        STOP
   100 FORMAT (I5,5X,2F5.1)
   150 FORMAT (1X,5X,'TEST SCORE SUMMARY')
   160 FORMAT (1X,2X,'ID',5X,'1ST TEST',2X,'2ND TEST')
   200 FORMAT (1X,I5,5X,F5.1,5X,F5.1)
   250 FORMAT (1X,'END OF OUTPUT')
        END
```

(a) The program

```
21167      89.5 94.0
25701      83.0 87.5
28145      87.0 76.0
30074      71.5 76.5
34230      92.0 96.0
```

(b) Input data

```
        TEST SCORE SUMMARY
    ID      1ST TEST  2ND TEST
  21167       89.5      94.0
  25701       83.0      87.5
  28145       87.0      76.0
  30074       71.5      76.5
  34230       92.0      96.0
  END OF OUTPUT
```

(c) Output

6-7. Additional formatted I/O features

Several additional features for formatted I/O are often used. These are described in this section.

Group repetition

In Section 6-2 we discussed the use of the repeat specification to indicate that a format code is to be repeated. When a group of format codes is to be repeated, the group may be enclosed in parentheses and a repeat specification placed in front of the group. This is called *group repetition*. For example, consider the following FORMAT statement:

```
57 FORMAT (F8.3,I4,F8.3,I4,F12.2)
```

Figure 6-12. An illustrative program with carriage control

```
C   PROGRAM TO LIST TEST SCORES
        INTEGER ID
        REAL SCR1,SCR2
        WRITE (6,150)
        WRITE (6,160)
        WRITE (6,170)
     10 READ (5,100,END=20) ID,SCR1,SCR2
         WRITE (6,200) ID,SCR1,SCR2
        GO TO 10
     20 WRITE (6,250)
        STOP
    100 FORMAT (I5,5X,2F5.1)
    150 FORMAT ('1',5X,'TEST SCORE SUMMARY')
    160 FORMAT ('0',2X,'ID',5X,'1ST TEST',2X,'2ND TEST')
    170 FORMAT (' ')
    200 FORMAT (' ',I5,5X,F5.1,5X,F5.1)
    250 FORMAT ('0','END OF OUTPUT')
        END
```

(a) The program

```
21167       89.5 94.0
25701       83.0 87.5
28145       87.0 76.0
30074       71.5 76.5
34230       92.0 96.0
```

(b) The input

```
        TEST SCORE SUMMARY

     ID       1ST TEST   2ND TEST

   21167       89.5        94.0
   25701       83.0        87.5
   28145       87.0        76.0
   30074       71.5        76.5
   34230       92.0        96.0

   END OF OUTPUT
```

(c) Output

In this statement, the group F8.3,I4 is repeated twice. We can shorten this to the following:

```
57 FORMAT (2(F8.3,I4),F12.2)
```

Note that the F12.2 is not part of the group and therefore does not appear within the parentheses of the group.

Group repetition may also be used to repeat a character constant for output. For example, the following statements cause 80 asterisks to be printed at the top of the page:

```
   WRITE (6,58)
58 FORMAT ('1',80('*'))
```

Figure 6-13. A payroll calculation program with formatted I/O

```
C  PAYROLL CALCULATION PROGRAM
      INTEGER EMPID
      REAL HOURS,GROSS,NET
      REAL PAYRT1,PAYRT2,TAXRT1,TAXRT2
      PARAMETER (PAYRT1=6.50,PAYRT2=9.75,TAXRT1=.18,TAXRT2=.22)
      WRITE (6,900)
      WRITE (6,910)
      WRITE (6,920)
  100 READ (5,800,END=200) EMPID,HOURS
      IF (HOURS.LE.40.0) THEN
        GROSS=PAYRT1*HOURS
        TAX=TAXRT1*GROSS
      ELSE
        GROSS=PAYRT1*40.0+PAYRT2*(HOURS-40.0)
        TAX=TAXRT2*GROSS
      END IF
      NET=GROSS-TAX
      WRITE (6,930) EMPID,GROSS,TAX,NET
      GO TO 100
  200 STOP
  800 FORMAT (I3,F5.1)
  900 FORMAT ('1','                PAYROLL REPORT')
  910 FORMAT ('0','   EMPLOYEE      GROSS    WITHHOLDING      NET')
  920 FORMAT (' ','IDENTIFICATION    PAY        TAX          PAY')
  930 FORMAT (' ',5X,I3,7X,'$',F7.2,4X,'$',F6.2,4X,'$',F7.2)
      END
```

(a) The program

```
132 40.2
342 35.0
546 44.6
786 40.0
980 39.8
```

(b) Input data

```
                     PAYROLL REPORT

       EMPLOYEE      GROSS    WITHHOLDING      NET
    IDENTIFICATION    PAY        TAX          PAY
         132       $ 261.95   $ 57.63    $ 204.32
         342       $ 227.50   $ 40.95    $ 186.55
         546       $ 304.85   $ 67.07    $ 237.78
         786       $ 260.00   $ 46.80    $ 213.20
         980       $ 258.70   $ 46.57    $ 212.13
```

(c) Output

Note that we must enclose the character constant in parentheses when using a repeat specification.

A repeated group may be included within another group. We call this *nested group repetition*. For example,, the following FORMAT statement has nested group repetition:

```
59 FORMAT (2(F8.1,3(I2,I3),F8.2))
```

The innermost group (I2,I3) is repeated three times for each repetition of the outer group. Thus this statement is equivalent to the following:

```
59 FORMAT (F8.1,I2,I3,I2,I3,I2,I3,F8.2,F8.1,I2,I3,I2,I3,I2,I3,F8.2)
```

New record specification

So far, only a comma has been used in the FORMAT statement to separate format codes. We can also use a slash (/) or several slashes between format codes. Whenever the computer encounters a slash in a list of format codes, it begins a new record; that is, the computer begins reading a new input record or writing a new output record. For example, the following statements cause the computer to read four values, each from a separate record:

```
      READ (5,60) A,B,C,D
60 FORMAT (F10.2/F10.2/F10.2/F10.2)
```

In this example, the computer reads the value of A from the first 10 positions of the first input record. Then the slash in the FORMAT statement tells the computer to begin a new record. Thus the computer reads the value of B from the first 10 positions of the second record. Then the next slash starts a new record, and so on until all of the data has been read.

For printed output, the first character of a record is the carriage control character and is not printed. Thus the first character in a printed output record that follows a slash must be a carriage control character. For example, the following statements cause two lines to be printed with double spacing between the lines:

```
      WRITE (6,61) I,J,K,L
61 FORMAT ('1',2I5/'0',2I5)
```

The values of I and J are printed on the first line; the values of K and L are printed on the second line, which is double spaced after the first line. The '0' following the slash is required to control the carriage before printing the second line.

We can also use multiple slashes to skip several records. If n slashes appear at the beginning or the end of the FORMAT statement, n input records are skipped or n blank records are inserted between output records. If n slashes appear elsewhere in the statement, $n-1$ records are skipped or blank records inserted. For example, the following statements cause the computer to skip four input records, then read two values from the next record, then skip two records, and finally read one value from the last record:

```
      READ (5,62) AMT,KNT,DUE
62 FORMAT (////F6.2,I3///F10.2)
```

Underloading an I/O list

For each variable name in an input or output list, there must be a corresponding format code in the FORMAT statement. It is possible, however, to have more format codes than there are variable names. We call this *underloading* an I/O list. When this happens, the computer reads and writes only the number of values specified in the I/O list. In other words, the controlling factor is the number of variable names in the I/O list. Additional format codes in the FORMAT statement are not used (except for any character constants that are specified immediately following the last numeric code).

The advantage of underloading an I/O list is that a single FORMAT statement can be used by several READ or WRITE statements with differing numbers of variable names in their lists. As an example, consider the following statements:

```
    READ (5,15) J,B
15 FORMAT (I5,5X,F10.4)
    READ (5,16) K
16 FORMAT (I5)
```

Because the fields that contain the values of J and K are in identical positions in two separate records, both READ statements can refer to the same FORMAT statement. Thus this example can be coded as follows:

```
    READ (5,15) J,B
    READ (5,15) K
15 FORMAT (I5,5X,F10.4)
```

The first READ statement uses all of the format codes. The second READ statement has an underloaded input list and uses only the first format code.

Overloading an I/O list

The opposite of underloading is *overloading* an I/O list. In this case, more variable names appear in the I/O list than there are format codes. As before, the controlling factor is the number of variable names in the I/O list. When there is no group repetition, the rule that applies is that after the available format codes are used, the computer returns control to the beginning of the FORMAT statement, a new record is begun, and the same format codes are used again.

As an example, consider the following statements:

```
    WRITE (6,70) A,B,C,D,E
70 FORMAT ('0',F6.2,F8.3,F4.1)
```

Assume that the output is to be printed. Then, after double spacing, the value of A is printed in format F6.2, B is printed in format F8.3, and C is printed in format F4.1. At this point, no more format codes are available, so the computer returns control to the beginning of the format codes and starts a new record. Because the record is to be printed, the first character in the record is used for carriage control. Thus the '0' code causes double spacing. The D is printed in format F6.2, and E is printed in format F8.3. At this point, the execution of the WRITE statement terminates. Another way to accomplish the same thing is to use a slash in the FORMAT statement. The following statement yields the same result as before:

```
70 FORMAT ('0',F6.2,F8.3,F4.1/'0',F6.2,F8.3)
```

The advantage of the overloading technique is most apparent with large volumes of data. For example, consider the following statements:

```
    READ (5,71) Z1,Z2,Z3,Z4,Z5,Z6,Z7
71 FORMAT (F12.3)
```

This FORMAT statement, coupled with the READ statement, causes the computer to read seven records. The first record contains the value of Z1 in format F12.3. Then, because there are no more format codes, a new record containing the value of Z2 in format F12.3 is read. This continues until all variable names in the input list are satisfied.

If there is group repetition in the FORMAT statement, the computer returns control to the beginning of the last nonnested group when an I/O list is overloaded. For example, consider the following statements:

```
    READ (5,72) A1,A2,A3,A4,A5,B1,B2,B3,B4
72 FORMAT (F8.2,2(F4.2,F10.4))
```

In this example, the values of the first five variable names are read from one record. Then, because there are more variable names in the input list, the computer returns control to the beginning of the group repetition specification and reads the values for the next four variable names from a new record. In effect, this FORMAT statement is equivalent to the following:

```
72 FORMAT (F8.2,F4.2,F10.4,F4.2,F10.4/F4.2,F10.4,F4.2,F10.4)
```

6-8. Interactive program design

Most of the programs that we have discussed in this book have involved batch processing. Such programs are often designed to read input from an auxiliary storage file or from punched cards and to produce output on a printer. Although batch processing is very common with FORTRAN programs, many programs are used for interactive processing. In this type of program, the input is entered at a terminal keyboard and the output is displayed on a CRT. This section discusses the design of interactive programs and gives an example.

A program that involves interactive processing must be easy for the terminal operator to use. Basically this is accomplished by guiding the operator through the processing with messages and prompts. The operator should be told what to do at each step in the program. All input data should be requested with an appropriate prompt. All output should be provided with an adequate description. It should be assumed that the terminal operator knows nothing about computers or programming and can only follow the instructions displayed on the CRT.

Figure 6-14 shows an interactive test-score-averaging program that is designed for easy use. The terminal interaction that results from running this program is shown in Figure 6-15.

This program first displays a title so that the operator knows which program is running. Then a prompt is displayed requesting the number of test scores to be averaged. After the input is accepted, a message is displayed stating how many test scores are to be entered. Note that the input just entered (i.e., the value of NUM) is displayed in this message. This is a common technique to remind the operator of what was entered. The program then

Figure 6-14. The interactive test score averaging program

```
C   TEST SCORE AVERAGING PROGRAM
        INTEGER COUNT,NUM,RES
        REAL SCORE,TOTAL,AVE
        WRITE (*,100)
    10 WRITE (*,110)
        READ *,NUM
        WRITE (*,120) NUM
        TOTAL=0.0
        DO 20 COUNT=1,NUM
          READ *,SCORE
          TOTAL=TOTAL+SCORE
    20   CONTINUE
        AVE=TOTAL/REAL(NUM)
        WRITE (*,130) TOTAL
        WRITE (*,140) AVE
        WRITE (*,150)
        READ *,RES
      IF (RES.EQ.1) GO TO 10
      WRITE (*,160)
      STOP
  100 FORMAT ('TEST SCORE AVERAGING PROGRAM')
  110 FORMAT (/'ENTER THE NUMBER OF SCORES TO BE AVERAGED')
  120 FORMAT (/'ENTER ',I2,' TEST SCORES - ONE PER LINE')
  130 FORMAT (/'THE TOTAL IS ',F5.0)
  140 FORMAT ('THE AVERAGE IS ',F6.1)
  150 FORMAT (/'DO YOU WANT TO AVERAGE MORE SCORES?'/
     1         '(TYPE 1 FOR YES, 0 FOR NO)')
  160 FORMAT (/'END OF PROGRAM')
      END
```

Figure 6-15. Interactive input and output for the test score averaging program

```
TEST SCORE AVERAGING PROGRAM

ENTER THE NUMBER OF SCORES TO BE AVERAGED
? 5

ENTER  5 TEST SCORES - ONE PER LINE
? 100
? 85
? 79
? 96
? 62

THE TOTAL IS   422.
THE AVERAGE IS    84.4

DO YOU WANT TO AVERAGE MORE SCORES?
(TYPE 1 FOR YES, 0 FOR NO)
? 1

ENTER THE NUMBER OF SCORES TO BE AVERAGED
? 3

ENTER  3 TEST SCORES - ONE PER LINE
? 57
? 89
? 72

THE TOTAL IS   218.
THE AVERAGE IS    72.7

DO YOU WANT TO AVERAGE MORE SCORES?
(TYPE 1 FOR YES, 0 FOR NO)
? 0

END OF PROGRAM
```

accepts the required number of test scores from the keyboard, computing the total as the scores are entered. After this, the average is computed and the total and average are displayed with appropriate descriptions.

The program uses a common technique for determining whether to repeat the processing. This is shown at the end of the main loop. The technique is to ask the operator whether he or she wishes to continue. The response, RES, may be 1 or 0 in this example meaning yes or no, respectively. If RES equals 1, the computer branches to the beginning of the main loop; otherwise, a message is displayed indicating the program is finished and execution is terminated.

Note that nothing is left for the operator to figure out during the processing. All input is requested with an appropriate message; all output is displayed with an adequate description. The beginning and end of execution are clearly identified. All of this makes the program easier for the terminal operator to use.

This program uses list-directed input and formatted output. (The asterisks in the I/O statement specify standard devices, which in this case are assumed to be the terminal keyboard and CRT.) For interactive input it is usually best to use the list-directed READ statement, because then the terminal operator does not have to be concerned with the exact format of the input data. Usually output should be displayed in an exact format, so the formatted WRITE statement must be used. Note that, because the output is displayed on a CRT, carriage control cannot be used for vertical spacing. Thus the first character of each output record is *not* a carriage control character but is, in fact, the first character displayed on a line. This program uses slashes in the FORMAT statement for vertical spacing.

This program illustrates the basic principles of interactive program design. Most interactive programs use the techniques that have been described in this section.

Review questions

1. What two statements are needed for formatted input? For formatted output?
2. What device codes (unit identifiers) are used with the computer you are using?
3. Code a READ statement to read the values of PRICE, DESC, and QTY. Assume that the device code is 5 and the number of the corresponding FORMAT statement is 100.
4. Answer Question 3 assuming that a standard input device is used.
5. Answer Question 3 so that the program branches to statement 999 when there is no more input data available.
6. Code a WRITE statement to write the values of PRICE, DESC, and QTY. Assume that the device code is 6 and the number of the corresponding FORMAT statement is 200.
7. Answer Question 6 assuming that a standard output device is used.
8. Assume that an input record has the following data recorded in it:

        123456789.............

        987654321.123456789

   Assume that each of the following READ statements reads this record. Indicate the value of each variable name in the READ statement after the statement is executed. (Assume that all variable names are the correct type for the corresponding format code.)

   a.   `READ (5,300) I`
      `300 FORMAT (I4)`
   b.   `READ (5,310) L,M,N`
      `310 FORMAT (I2,I6,I1)`
   c.   `READ (5,320) A,B`
      `320 FORMAT (F8.2,F4.2)`
   d.   `READ (5,330) C,D`
      `330 FORMAT (F6.0,F8.2)`

```
e.       READ (5,340) K,X,Y
     340 FORMAT (5X,I4,3X,F2.2,1X,F4.1)
f.       READ (5,350) J,L,A,X,Z
     350 FORMAT (2I3,2F3.2,1X,F6.0)
```

9. Assume that an input record is laid out as follows:

Positions	Field
1–5	ID number (integer)
6–12	Unused
13	Status code (integer)
14–33	Unused
34–39	Sales (real, two decimal positions)

   Code statements to read this record.
10. What is the maximum number of print positions on the printer you are using?
11. The following are the values of five variable names:

$$M = 765$$
$$N = -321$$
$$S = 123.45$$
$$T = 98.7654$$
$$U = -100.0$$

   For each of the following groups of statements indicate the output that is printed in the exact print positions.

```
a.       WRITE (6,400) M,N
     400 FORMAT (1X,I5,I6)
b.       WRITE (6,410) N
     410 FORMAT (1X,I3)
c.       WRITE (6,420) S,T,U
     420 FORMAT (1X,F6.2,F8.4,F8.0)
d.       WRITE (6,430) S,T
     430 FORMAT (1X,F8.4,F6.2)
e.       WRITE (6,440) U
     440 FORMAT (1X,F6.2)
f.       WRITE (6,450) M,T,S
     450 FORMAT (3X,I3,2X,2F7.3)
```

12. Assume that an output record is laid out as follows:

Positions	Field
1–5	Blank
6	Status code (integer)
7–10	Blank
11–15	ID number (integer)
16–20	Blank
21–28	Sales (real, two decimal positions)

   Code statements to write this record.
13. Code statements to print the words OUTPUT DATA followed by the values of A and B in two fields of ten positions each. A and B are real with three digits to the right of the decimal point.
14. Code statements to print the word NUMBER in print positions 3 through 8 and the word AMOUNT in positions 12 through 17.

15. What do the following statements do?

```
    WRITE (6,500)
500 FORMAT (1X)
```

16. Code statements to do each of the following:
    a. Print the words FINAL SUMMARY at the top of a new page.
    b. Print the values of I and J after double spacing. I and J are each five-digit integers.
    c. Advance the printer five lines without printing anything. (Do not use a loop or slashes in the FORMAT statement.)
    d. Print the value of K without advancing the printer. K is a three-digit integer.

17. Three input records need to be read. Each begins with a six-digit real value with two decimal positions. Code statements to do this. (Do not use slashes in the FORMAT statement or an overloaded input list.)

18. Code statements to print three lines each with one integer in the first five print positions. (Do not use slashes in the FORMAT statement or an overloaded output list.)

19. Consider the program in Figure 6-10. How could this program be modified so that the output is double-spaced?

20. Rewrite the following FORMAT statement using group repetition:

```
510 FORMAT (I3,F6.2,I1,I3,F6.2,I1,I3,F6.2,I1,I2,F4.2,I2,F4.2)
```

21. Answer Questions 17 and 18 using slashes in the I/O lists.

22. Two records need to be written. The first contains two integers in two consecutive five-digit fields. The second contains three integers in three consecutive five-digit fields. Code a group of statements to accomplish this using only one FORMAT statement.

23. Answer Questions 17 and 18 using overloaded I/O lists.

24. What are some ways to design an interactive program to make it easy for the terminal operator to use?

Programming problems

The following problems are exercises in the topics of this chapter. In addition, many of the problems in previous chapters can be completed using formatted I/O.

1. A FORTRAN program is needed to list the data in two fields of a record. The value in the first field is integer. It is in positions 1 through 5. A real value with two places to the right of the decimal point is in positions 6 through 12.

   Write a FORTRAN program to read the data in these two fields and print the data in the same format. To test the program, use 21853 for the first field and 472.80 for the second field.

2. Three values are recorded in a record. The first and second values are integers in positions 6 and 7, and 11 and 12, respectively. The third value is real with one place to the right of the decimal point. It is in positions 14 through 18.

Write a FORTRAN program to read the values and print them with five spaces between the output fields. To test the program, let the three values be 25, 16, and 147.3.

3. Four values are recorded in a record. The first two are integer. They are in positions 11 to 14 and 16 to 18. The next value is real with three places to the right of the decimal point. It is in positions 21 to 28. The last value is real with one place to the right of the decimal point. It is in positions 31 to 34.

Write a FORTRAN program to read all four values. Then on one line print the first integer followed by the first real, then the second integer followed by the second real. Separate all output fields by three spaces. To test your program, let the four values be 1821, 793, −45.637, and 21.4, respectively.

4. Two records need to be read and printed on two separate lines. Each record has an integer and a real in format (4X,I3,3X,F6.2).

Write a FORTRAN program to read the records and print the data in the same format as the input. To test the program, use 482 and 37.35 in the first record and 913 and 125.42 in the second record.

5. Each of three input records contains data in the following format:

Positions	Field
1–3	Station number (integer)
5–10	Gallons of gasoline solid (integer)
21–25	Average price per gallon (real with one decimal position)

Write a FORTRAN program to read the data in the three records and print the data in three columns. The station numbers should be printed on the first line of the output record, the gallons of gasoline sold for each station on the second line, and the average price per gallon for each station on the third line. Use the following data to test the program:

Station	Gallons	Price
128	20,532	149.9
389	17,835	125.3
405	23,562	137.5

6. Write the program for Problem 5 with the additional requirements that the heading STATION DATA should be printed before the other output; the words STATION, GALLONS, and PRICE should be printed on the three lines of output; and the words END OF DATA should be printed at the end.

7. The results of a questionnaire survey need to be printed in sentence form. The data consists of the sample identification number, the number of questionnaires processed, and the average age of the respondents. The output should appear as follows:

```
RESULTS FROM SAMPLE XXXXX.
WITH XXX QUESTIONNAIRES PROCESSED,
THE AVERAGE AGE OF THE RESPONDENTS IS XX.X YEARS.
```

(X's represent the location of output fields.) Input data is recorded in two records. The first record contains the sample number and the number of questionnaires. The second record contains the average age.

Write a FORTRAN program to prepare the specified output from the input.

Test the program using 10083 for the sample number, 253 for the number of questionnaires, and 37.3 for the average age.

8. A summary of a student's grades is needed. The information is recorded in two records. The first record contains a one-digit value representing the semester followed by a two-digit value representing the year. The second record contains the student's identification number followed by five pairs of fields, where each pair represents a course number and the grade received in the course. The course numbers are four digits in length. The grades are each recorded in a three-column field with one decimal position. (For example, 4.0 is an A, 3.7 is an A−, 3.3 is a B+, etc.) A sample of how the output should appear is as follows:

SUMMARY OF GRADES FOR
STUDENT NUMBER 4837
SEMESTER 1   YEAR 1985

Course	Grade
1308	4.0
5872	2.3
1591	3.0
2811	2.7
4605	3.3

Write a FORTRAN program to prepare this summary of grades from the specified input. Use the data shown in the preceding sample output to test the program.

9. Input data for a program is recorded in the following format:

Positions	Field
1–5	Item number (integer)
6–10	Quantity on hand (integer)
21–25	Unit price (real, 2 decimal positions)

There is an unknown number of input records. Write a FORTRAN program that lists the input data. One line should be printed for each input record. Use the following data to test the program:

Item number	Quantity on hand	Unit price
13721	47	$4.75
19821	253	$16.95
20056	89	$28.30
21306	465	$7.56
22465	0	$63.50
22851	360	$1.29
24711	28	$12.95

[handwritten annotations: "center on main heading INVENTORY REPORT", "as^s at end Report Finishes", "right adjusted subheadings", "name", "shorts", "shirt, dress", "fancy shirt, dress", "fancy shorts", "sport coats", "handkerchief", "sport shirt", "00001 01 0.01 end"]

10. Write the program for Problem 9 with the additional requirements that the heading INVENTORY REPORT should be printed before the output; the headings ITEM NUMBER, QUANTITY, and UNIT PRICE should be printed above the columns of output; and the words REPORT FINISHED should be printed at the end.

11. Input to a program consists of several records giving information about a student's grades in the courses he or she took. The first record consists of a student's identification number (integer) in positions 1 through 5. Following this are an unknown number of course records containing data in the following format:

Positions	Field
1–4	Course number (integer)
23–25	Units (real, one decimal position)
26–28	Grade (real, one decimal position)

Course grades are expressed as numbers in the input (for example, A is 4.0, A− is 3.7, B+ is 3.3, etc.). Write a FORTRAN program to print the words STUDENT NUMBER followed by the student's identification number on the first line. Then print one line for each course record listing the data in the record with five spaces between each output field. Supply appropriate headings for the columns of output. Use the following input data to test the program:

STUDENT NUMBER: 28601

Course number	Units	Grade
1308	3.0	2.3
5872	2.0	4.0
1591	4.0	2.7
2811	3.0	3.3
4605	0.5	2.0

12. A tabulation of a statistical survey of voter preference by age groups is needed. A sample of how the output should appear follows:

AGE GROUP	18–20	21–30	31–45	46–50	OVER 60
CANDIDATE X	64.7%	59.1%	41.8%	18.2%	10.1%
CANDIDATE Y	21.5%	27.3%	43.0%	67.5%	65.3%
CANDIDATE Z	2.3%	4.2%	10.6%	10.3%	18.7%
UNDECIDED	11.5%	9.4%	4.6%	4.0%	5.9%

Write a FORTRAN program to prepare the voter preference tabulation from input data consisting of one record for each age group, giving the percentages for the four choices. In other words, there are five input records, each with four fields. Test the program with the data shown in the sample output.

13. A graphic representation of a student's class schedule is:

TIME	8–9	9–10	10–11	11–12	12–1	1–2	2–3	3–4
MONDAY	1	0	0	1	0	1	1	1
TUESDAY	0	1	1	1	0	0	0	0
WEDNESDAY	1	0	0	1	0	1	1	1
THURSDAY	0	1	1	1	0	0	0	0
FRIDAY	1	0	0	1	0	0	0	0

The digit 1 indicates hours when the student is in class; the digit 0 indicates hours when he or she is out of class.

Write a FORTRAN program that produces this graphic output. Input to the program is one record for each day with the student's study schedule for that day recorded as a series of ones and zeros. Use the data shown in the preceding graph to test the program.

14. Write an interactive FORTRAN program for Problem 14 in Chapter 4. The program should be designed to be easy for the credit card applicant to use. Appropriate prompts should be given for all input. The program should inform the applicant of the company's action after evaluating his or her credit worthiness.

Chapter 7

Program development

In previous chapters we have discussed many aspects of the process of developing computer programs. Most of the ideas about program development were presented while describing some feature of FORTRAN. In this chapter we bring together these topics and discuss program development in detail. After completing this chapter you should understand the major ideas about program development, and you should be able to apply these ideas in developing complex FORTRAN programs.

7-1. Program structure

A central aspect of program development is the concept of program structure. The *structure* of a program is the way in which the instructions in the program are organized. When a programmer develops a FORTRAN program, he or she builds a structure of FORTRAN statements. If the structure is well built, the program is likely to be correct, easy to understand, and easily modified. A poorly structured program may have errors that are difficult to detect, may be hard to read, or may be troublesome to change.

There are three basic structures of program statements, called *control structures:* the sequence structure, the decision structure, and the loop structure. In a *sequence structure,* the statements are executed in the order in which they are written, one after the other. For example, a series of assignment statements that performs some calculation is a sequence structure. A *decision structure* (also called *selection* or *alternation*) is used to decide which of two other structures is to be executed next based on some logical condition. FORTRAN uses the block IF statement to create a decision structure. If the condition in the IF statement is true, one group of statements is executed; otherwise, another set of statements is performed. (The logical IF statement also creates a decision structure.) In a *loop structure* (also called *repetition* or *iteration*), a group of statements is executed repeatedly until some condition indicates that the loop should be terminated. In FORTRAN we use a GO TO statement at the end of a set of statements to branch to the beginning and thus create a loop. The loop is controlled by checking a condition in an IF statement each time the loop is executed. (The DO statement forms a special type of loop structure. In addition, the WHILE statement, if available, creates a loop structure.)

Figure 7-1 summarizes the three basic control structures. Part (a) shows a sequence structure in which one group of statements is performed after another. In part (b), a decision structure is shown in which one of two alternative groups of statements is executed based on some condition. This is a two-sided decision. We can also create a one-sided decision by not executing any statements when the condition is false (see Figure 4-6). The loop structure in part (c) is such that a group of statements is executed, a terminal condition is checked, and then another group of statements is executed before repeating the pattern. If no statements are performed in the loop before the terminal condition is checked, the loop forms a pretest pattern [see Figure 5-10(b)]. Similarly, if the structure is such that no statements are executed after the condition is checked, the pattern is that of a posttest loop [see Figure 5-10(c)].

One characteristic that is common to all these structures is that there is only one way of entering each structure and only one way of leaving. That is, it is not possible to branch into the middle of any of the structures or to branch out of any structure in more than one place. We say that each structure has one *entry point* and one *exit point*. We will see that this is an important characteristic of these structures.

Within a structure, we can embed any other structure that we need. This is the idea of nesting that we have discussed in relation to decisions and loops. In fact, we can nest any structure within any other. For example, within a loop we may have a sequence of statements, decision structures, and other loops. Within a decision structure we can have sequences, loops, and other decisions. In terms of Figure 7-1, this means that we can substitute any structure for any block of statements within any structure.

We can use this idea of nesting to build a program as shown in Figure 7-2. In part (a) we start with a single block of statements. In part (b) we substitute a loop for this block. In part (c) we replace the statements at the beginning of the loop with a decision and we replace the statements at the end with a sequence. Finally, in part (d) we nest a loop in the decision. We can continue in this manner to build a more complex program. Note that because each structure has one entry point and one exit point, the final program has only one entry point (that is, one point where execution of the program starts) and one exit point (that is, one point where the program stops execution).

Other control structures can appear in a program. For example, the computed GO TO statement, which is not covered in this book, creates a case selection structure. The same structure, however, can be created using nested decisions. In fact, *any* other structure can be created out of the three basic

Figure 7-1. Basic control structures

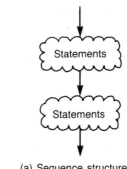

(a) Sequence structure

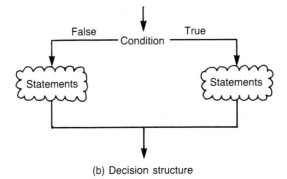

(b) Decision structure

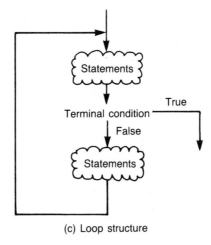

(c) Loop structure

Figure 7-2. Nested control structures

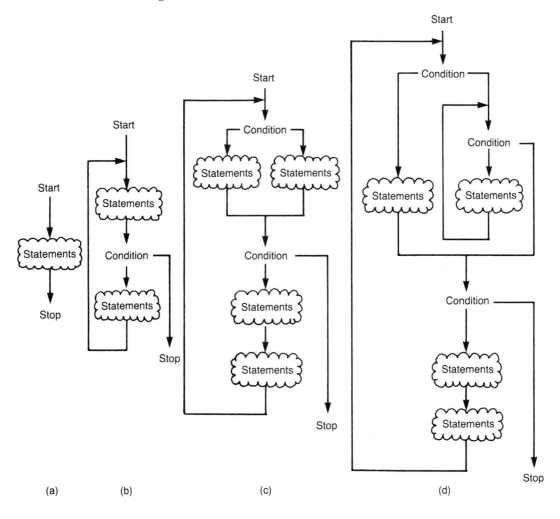

(a)   (b)   (c)   (d)

structures. This fact was proven by two computer scientists who showed that any program that has a single entry point and a single exit point can be written using just the three basic control structures.* Thus, if we know how to create these structures in a programming language, we do not need any other structures.

* C. Böhm and G. Jacopini, "Flow Diagrams, Turing Machines and Languages with Only Two Formation Rules," *Communications of the ACM,* 9, 5 (May 1966), 366–371. In proving their result, Böhm and Jacopini used a different loop structure from the one shown in Figure 7-1(c). It can be shown, however, that the general loop structure in this book can be constructed from the Böhm and Jacopini structures.

7-2. Program understandability

In Section 2-6 we discussed the importance of producing an understandable program. A program must be easily understood because people, including the original programmer, may need to correct, modify, and enhance it.

Program structure can contribute greatly to program understandability. The problem with trying to understand the logic of a complex program is that there are really two versions of the program. One is the *static* version that is represented by the listing of the program on a CRT or on paper. The other version is the *dynamic* form of the program that can only be understood by following the logic of the program as it is executed. When a programmer reads a listing, he or she is reading the static form of the program. As with the lines in a book, each statement is normally read in sequence from the top of the page down. The dynamic version may be different from the static version because the statements are not executed in the order in which they are written. To understand a program, the programmer must read the static version but interpret the program in terms of its dynamic version.

Figure 7-3 illustrates the idea of two versions of a program. In this example, GO TO statements are used to make the static and dynamic versions very different. Part (a) gives the statements in the order in which they appear in the program listing (i.e., the static version). Part (b) shows the statements in the order in which they are executed (i.e., the dynamic version). Notice that when a GO TO statement is encountered, the next statement in the dynamic version (the statement to which the program branches) is not the same as the next statement in the static version (the next statement in sequence). When the programmer reads the listing of this program, he or she has to skip all over the program to try to understand the logic rather than just reading the program from top to bottom.

We can see from this example that one of the basic principles of producing understandable programs is to make the dynamic version of the program as close as possible to the static form. Ideally the program should execute from top to bottom just as it is read. If this were the case, the program would perform only a sequence of statements (that is, there would be no decisions or loops), which would not accomplish much.

The next best situation is to have the program execute from top to bottom through a sequence of basic control structures. That is, the program first executes the statements in one structure (for example, a loop), then executes the statements in the next structure (such as a decision), and so on to the end of the program. Other structures may be nested in these structures, as we saw in the last section. This top-to-bottom execution using only the three basic control structures brings the dynamic version of the program as close as possible to the static form. In addition, we know that we can write any program using just these three structures.

The uncontrolled use of GO TO statements can greatly complicate the structure of a program. The problem with GO TO statements is that we do

Figure 7-3. Two versions of a program

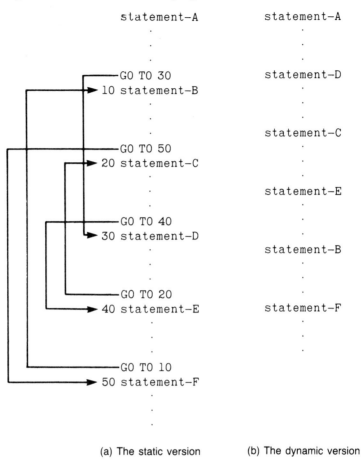

(a) The static version　　　　(b) The dynamic version

not always know where we came from. Although this may sound funny, it makes a lot of sense. For example, assume that we are trying to understand the conditions under which a particular statement is executed. If it is possible to branch to that statement from a number of different points in the program, we cannot determine how we got to the statement without going back to all of the GO TO statements that branched to it. The logic may become even more complex if there are multiple ways to get to each of these GO TO statements. (A famous letter entitled "GO TO Statement Considered Harmful" discusses this point of view.*) Sometimes a program with lots of GO TO

---

* Edsger W. Dijkstra, "GO TO Statement Considered Harmful," *Communications of the ACM,* 11, 3 (March 1968), 147–148. The letter begins with the statement, "For a number of years I have been familiar with the observation that the quality of programmers is a decreasing function of the density of *go to* statements in the programs they produce."

statements is called "spaghetti code" because lines drawn on the paper for all the branches begin to look like a bowl of spaghetti [see Figure 7-3(a)].

The ultimate solution would be to eliminate all GO TO statements in programs. In standard FORTRAN this is not possible. Although decision structures can be created without GO TO statements by using the block IF statement, loops require the use of GO TO statements. However, by using only basic loop patterns as discussed in Chapter 5 (see Figure 5-11), the logic of the program is kept as simple as possible.

In some versions of FORTRAN, WHILE statements are available for loop control. (See Section 5-4.) When this is the case, programs can be written with no GO TO statements. Then statement numbers are only needed with FORMAT statements. Figure 5-27 showed an example of such a program. (Although it is not necessary, we may also want to use DO statements for some types of loops. Then a statement number is needed for the CONTINUE statement at the end of the loop.)

To summarize, the basic approach to producing understandable programs is to design the program so that it executes from top to bottom and only uses sequences, decisions, and loops.

7-3. Program style

Program style refers to those characteristics of a program that make it easier to read and therefore easier to understand. In previous chapters we have mentioned several style rules. Some of these are listed here along with a few new rules:

1. Use meaningful variable names. This helps the programmer remember what each name refers to.
2. Use statement numbers that increase in sequence through the program. This helps the programmer locate statements in a large program.
3. Assign statement numbers in some logical pattern. For example, the statements in the first section of the program may be assigned numbers between 100 and 199, the statements in the second section may be assigned numbers between 200 and 299, and so forth for other sections of the program.
4. Put all FORMAT statements at the end of the program and number them accordingly (for example, with numbers between 900 and 999).
5. Use parentheses in expressions to show the order of evaluation even if they are not needed.
6. Indent the true and false parts of a decision and the statements in a loop. This helps the programmer see the structure of the program.
7. Always end a DO loop with a CONTINUE statement.

put FORMAT after WRITE

8. Use only the three basic control structures (sequences, decisions, and loops). Do not use the GO TO statement except when absolutely essential and then only to create basic control structures. Minimize the use of nested decisions and loops.

Following these style rules and others that we will mention later helps to make the program easier to read and understand.

Using comments

Another way of improving the readability of a program is to use comments to explain the function of different parts of the program. As explained in Chapter 1, we can place a comment anywhere in the program by putting a C in column 1. We have purposefully avoided using many comments in our illustrative programs so as to concentrate on the logic of the program. However, as programs become more complex, comments can help explain the program.

The basic principle in using comments is that each comment should explain some characteristic of the program that is not immediately obvious. Usually a comment should appear before each important loop or decision in the program to indicate the function of the code that follows. For example, consider the tuition calculation program in Figure 7-4. (This is the same program as the one in Figure 5-2.) To make this program more understandable, we might insert the following comment before statement 10:

```
C     BEGIN INPUT LOOP; REPEAT UNTIL TRAILER VALUE IS READ
```

Although we could get the information in this comment from the program, the comment makes the process of understanding the program easier. As another example we may put the following comment before the block IF statement in Figure 7-4:

```
C      CALCULATE TUITION
```

This comment describes the function of the decision structure that follows.

Figure 7-4. The tuition calculation program

```
C  TUITION CALCULATION PROGRAM
       INTEGER SNUM
       REAL UNITS,TUIT
   10 READ *,SNUM,UNITS
       IF (SNUM.EQ.9999) GO TO 20
       IF (UNITS.LE.12.0) THEN
         TUIT=350.00
       ELSE
         TUIT=350.00+20.00*(UNITS-12.0)
       END IF
       PRINT *,'STUDENT NUMBER = ',SNUM,'  TUITION = ',TUIT
     GO TO 10
   20 STOP
       END
```

A common mistake in using comments is to simply parrot the code that follows. For example, consider the following sequence that might be used in the program in Figure 7-4:

```
C       SET TUITION EQUAL TO $350.00
        TUIT=350.00
```

The comment is unnecessary because it just repeats the statement that follows. Another example of unnecessary use of comments is the following:

```
C       INCREASE I BY 1
        I=I+1
```

Again, the comment merely echoes the following statement.

Another common problem with the use of comments is that a comment may say one thing, but the program does something else. This may be because the programmer wrote the comment incorrectly or wrote a correct comment but incorrect code, or perhaps because the code was modified sometime after the original program was written. When comments are used, they must correctly describe the program. Otherwise the programmer may read the comment and think that the program does one thing, when in fact it does something else. (Because of this, some programmers advocate deleting all comments while debugging a program.)

To test if the comments in a program are sufficient, we sometimes just read the comments and not the code. If the basic logic of the program — but not the details — can be understood from the comments, the comments are usually sufficient. The problem with this test is that it may result in too many comments or comments containing too much detail. If we remember that comments should help explain difficult parts of the program but not simply repeat the code, we can achieve the best level of detail.

Besides describing how a program works, comments can be used to document important information about the program. This information includes such things as who wrote the program, when it was written, what the purpose of the program is, and what the variable names in the program mean. Usually such information is put into a block of comments at the beginning of the program. For example, Figure 7-5 shows the tuition calculation program with a block of comments at the beginning as well as with comments in the body of the program. The initial comments serve as a "preface" to the program; the other comments help explain how the program works. Notice in this example that blank comment lines (that is, lines wih just a C in column 1) are used to separate groups of comments and statements. This helps make the program more readable.

Figure 7-5. The tuition calculation program with comments

```
C
C      TITLE:  TUITION CALCULATION PROGRAM
C
C      PROGRAMMER:  ROBERT C. NICKERSON
C      DATE:  NOVEMBER 3, 19XX
C
C      PURPOSE:  THIS PROGRAM COMPUTES TUITION FOR EACH COLLEGE STUDENT
C                BASED ON THE NUMBER OF UNITS THAT THE STUDENT IS TAKING.
C
C      VARIABLE NAMES:
C          SNUM  = STUDENT IDENTIFICATION NUMBER (INPUT/OUTPUT)
C          UNITS = NUMBER OF UNITS (INPUT)
C          TUIT  = TUITION (OUTPUT)
C
C      DECLARE VARIABLES
C
       INTEGER SNUM
       REAL UNITS,TUIT
C
C      BEGIN INPUT LOOP; REPEAT UNTIL TRAILER VALUE IS READ
C
    10 READ *,SNUM,UNITS
         IF (SNUM.EQ.9999) GO TO 20
C        CALCULATE TUITION
         IF (UNITS.LE.12.0) THEN
           TUIT=350.00
         ELSE
           TUIT=350.00+20.00*(UNITS-12.0)
         END IF
         PRINT *,'STUDENT NUMBER = ',SNUM,'  TUITION = ',TUIT
       GO TO 10
C
C      END OF LOOP
C
    20 STOP
C
       END
```

7-4. Program refinement

Developing the logic of a complex program can be a difficult task. A technique that is often advocated is to develop the program through a sequence of refinement steps. The idea is to start with a general statement of what the program does and to gradually refine this statement. Each refinement should bring the program closer to the final version. The last step in the process produces the coded program. This technique is often called *stepwise program refinement*.

To illustrate this technique we consider the problem of rearranging three real values into ascending (or increasing) numerical order. This process is called *sorting*. (In a later chapter we will see how to sort large amounts of data.) We assume that the three real numbers are input data. The numbers may be in any order initially. In the program we will refer to the numbers by the variable names V1, V2, and V3. The program must rearrange the values so that V1 equals the smallest value, V2 is the middle value, and V3 equals the largest value. Finally, the sorted values must be written.

As a first step in developing the program, we write the following:

```
REAL V1,V2,V3
READ *,V1,V2,V3
Sort V1, V2, and V3 into ascending order.
PRINT *,V1,V2,V3
STOP
END
```

This program is complete except for the third line, which is written in English, not FORTRAN. If we can refine this line to a set of FORTRAN statements that accomplishes the sorting process, the program will be complete.

One way to sort the three numbers is to move the largest value to V3 and then move the next largest value to V2. If this is done without destroying any of the values, V1 will be equal to the smallest value. Hence the numbers will be sorted. For example, assume that initially the data is as follows:

$$V1 = 7.0$$
$$V2 = 9.0$$
$$V3 = 5.0$$

Moving the largest value, 9.0, to V3 results in the data being rearranged into the following order:

$$V1 = 7.0$$
$$V2 = 5.0$$
$$V3 = 9.0$$

Then moving the next largest value, 7.0, to V2 results in the following:

$$V1 = 5.0$$
$$V2 = 7.0$$
$$V3 = 9.0$$

Thus the smallest value, 5.0, is automatically moved to V1. Incorporating this refinement into our program, we get the following:

```
READ *,V1,V2,V3
Move largest value to V3.
Move next largest value to V2.
PRINT *,V1,V2,V3
```

(We will leave out the other statements until the final version of the program.)

To move the largest value to V3, we first move the larger of V1 and

V2 to V2, and then move the larger of V2 and V3 to V3. To move the next largest value to V2, we move the larger of V1 and V2 to V2. Hence the program can be refined again to the following:

```
READ *,V1,V2,V3
Move larger of V1 and V2 to V2.
Move larger of V2 and V3 to V3.
Move larger of V1 and V2 to V2.
PRINT *,V1,V2,V3
```

To move the larger of V1 and V2 to V2, we compare V1 and V2. If V1 is larger than V2, we switch the values of V1 and V2. In effect, we are asking if V1 and V2 are in proper sequence with respect to one another. If they are not, we switch their values. We do similar comparisons and switching for V2 and V3 and again for V1 and V2. Incorporating this refinement into the program, we get the following:

```
READ *,V1,V2,V3
IF (V1.GT.V2) THEN
   Switch V1 and V2.
END IF
IF (V2.GT.V3) THEN
   Switch V2 and V3.
END IF
IF (V1.GT.V2) THEN
   Switch V1 and V2.
END IF
PRINT *,V1,V2,V3
```

The only thing that remains to complete the program is to include the necessary statements to switch the values of the variables. Figure 7-6 shows how the switching is done for V1 and V2. First V1 is assigned to a temporary variable TEMP. Then V2 is assigned to V1. Finally, the value of TEMP is assigned to V2. Thus the following three statements are needed to switch the values of V1 and V2:

```
TEMP=V1
V1=V2
V2=TEMP
```

Writing similar sets of statements for the other switching steps and including these in the program, we get the final versions of the sorting program which is shown in Figure 7-7.

To illustrate how the program works, examine the following worst possible case:

```
V1 = 9.0
V2 = 7.0
V3 = 5.0
```

Figure 7-6. Switching the values of two variables

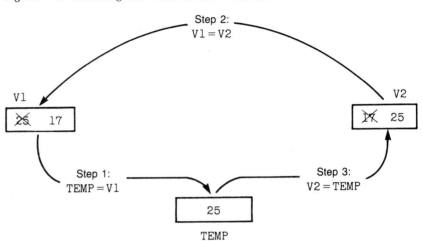

Figure 7-7. The sorting program

```
C   SORTING PROGRAM
        REAL V1,V2,V3,TEMP
        READ *,V1,V2,V3
        IF (V1.GT.V2) THEN
          TEMP=V1
          V1=V2
          V2=TEMP
        END IF
        IF (V2.GT.V3) THEN
          TEMP=V2
          V2=V3
          V3=TEMP
        END IF
        IF (V1.GT.V2) THEN
          TEMP=V1
          V1=V2
          V2=TEMP
        END IF
        PRINT *,V1,V2,V3
        STOP
        END
```

The data is completely out of order. After the first switch, the values will be as follows:

$$V1 = 7.0$$
$$V2 = 9.0$$
$$V3 = 5.0$$

That is, the larger of V1 and V2 is moved to V2. After the next switch the values will be in the following order:

$$V1 = 7.0$$
$$V2 = 5.0$$
$$V3 = 9.0$$

The larger of V2 and V3 is moved to V3. The effect of both switches is that the largest of all three is moved to V3. The final switch results in the following:

$$V1 = 5.0$$
$$V2 = 7.0$$
$$V3 = 9.0$$

The larger of V1 and V2 is moved to V2. In effect, the next largest of all three is moved to V2 and at the same time, the smallest value ends up in V1. Hence the data is sorted.

This example illustrates how the techniques of stepwise refinement can be applied to a problem solution. The technique allows the programmer to concentrate on small parts of the program in successively more detail. The programmer does not try to figure out the whole solution at one time, but rather thinks about the solution in pieces. This usually makes program development easier.

7-5. The programming process

In section 1-6 we discussed briefly the process of preparing a computer program. We mentioned five activities that make up the programming process:

1. Understand and define the problem.
2. Design the program.
3. Code the program.
4. Show that the program is correct.
5. Document the program.

In this section we discuss each of these activities in detail.

The five activities in the programming process are not necessarily performed in sequence. In fact, several activities usually take place at the same time. For example, later we will see that documenting begins when we are trying to define and understand the problem. In addition, we can begin to show correctness of the program during the designing activity. The activities are listed not in the order in which they are *started,* but rather in the order in which they are *finished.* For example, we cannot finish designing the program until we have finished understanding and defining the problem. However, we may have started the designing activity before the first activity is finished. Similarly, we cannot complete final coding until program design is done, we cannot show that the program is correct until coding is completed, and we cannot finish the documentation until all other activities have been completed.

Problem definition

The first activity in the programming process is to understand and carefully define the problem to be solved. Often the most difficult step is to recognize that a problem exists for which a programmed solution is appropriate. However, the programmer usually is not responsible for recognizing the need for a program to solve a problem. Most often the programmer receives a general statement of the problem, either verbally or in writing, and begins the programming process from that point.

At first the programmer should try to understand the problem as a whole. What does the problem require? This usually involves determining what output is to be produced. What data is available? This question involves determining what input data is to be processed. The programmer tries to get a general understanding of the problem as a whole without going into details about the input, the output, and the processing.

After the programmer has a general understanding of the problem, he or she should refine the problem definition to include specific information about the input and output data, the calculations, and the logical operations. The programmer should continue refining the problem definition until he or she obtains sufficient detail to begin designing a solution. At a minimum the problem definition should give the following:

1. What output is to be produced and what its layout is.
2. What input data is available and what its layout is.
3. What computations are to be performed.
4. What logical conditions affect processing.

Sometimes the programmer may have difficulty understanding a problem. When this happens, it often helps to isolate parts of the problem and work with each part separately. Another approach is to think of a simpler but similar problem and try to understand it first. The programmer may get some insight from the simpler problem that helps explain the more complex problem.

Some problems cannot be solved with a computer. In mathematics some problems do not have exact solutions. Some problems may be too large for a computer or take too long to solve. Problems that cannot be solved do not often arise. However, in defining a problem, we still must be sure that it is reasonable to attempt a programmed solution.

To illustrate the programming process, consider a variation of the test score averaging problem discussed in previous chapters. The problem is to calculate a weighted average of three test scores for each student in a course. We assume that the best test score counts 50%, the next best score is weighted 35%, and the worst test score counts 15%. In addition to calculating the weighted average, the corresponding letter grade must be determined. The letter grade is based on a straight percentage scale (that is, 90 to 100% is an A, 80 to 89% is a B, 70 to 79% is a C, 60 to 69% is a D, and 59% or less is an F). Finally, the overall average score for all students in the course must be calculated and all results must be printed in a report.

Already we begin to understand the problem. We need a program to produce a printed report that gives the weighted average and letter grade for each student in a course plus the overall average score for all students. The input to the program must include three test scores for each student. In addition, the student to whom the scores belong must be identified in some way (such as by a student identification number). The program must determine which is the best test score, which score is worst, and which score falls in between. Then the program must apply the appropriate percentages to arrive at the average. The program must also determine into which grade category the average falls so that the appropriate letter grade can be printed. To find the overall average test score, the program must accumulate the total of the students' average scores and count the number of students in the course. Then, after processing all the student data, the program must compute the overall average by dividing the total of the students' average test scores by the total number of students.

We can refine the problem definition at this point to specify input and output formats. We may even assign variable names to the input and output data. An acceptable input format is as follows:

Field positions	Field	Variable name	Type
1–4	Identification number	IDNUM	Integer
5–8	First test score	SCORE1	Real
9–12	Second test score	SCORE2	Real
13–16	Third test score	SCORE3	Real

For real values we need to be concerned with the number of decimal positions. In this example, we assume that each test score has zero places to the right of the decimal point.

For the output format, we must be concerned with the print positions in which the data is printed. A useful tool is a piece of graph paper or a special form called a *print chart* on which we can sketch the output. Figure 7-8 shows the output format for this program on a print chart. The numbers across the top give the print positions. Headings and other nonvariable output are written on the chart exactly as they are to be printed. Variable information, such as the student's identification number, average score, and letter grade are indicated by Xs in the print positions in which they are to be printed. Sketching the output format first on a chart such as this makes coding the necessary FORMAT statements much easier.

A question that we have not considered is how to control the input loop. As we have seen, there are a number of techniques for loop control. We will assume in this problem that the last input record contains 9999 in the student identification number field and we will use this to control the loop.

At this point we understand fairly well what is required of the program.

Figure 7-8. A print chart

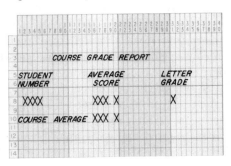

However, we may have to come back to the problem definition later if we discover things we do not understand.

Program design

After carefully defining the problem, we can begin to design an appropriate program. The objective during the program designing activity is to devise a plan for a program that solves a problem. This does not mean that the program is coded at this stage. Before coding can begin, we must develop a solution procedure. The procedure should, of course, be correct.

As we noted in Section 1-6, a procedure for solving a problem is called an algorithm. An algorithm is a set of instructions that, if carried out, results in the solution of a problem. An algorithm may be written in English, described in mathematical notation, or expressed in a diagram. A recipe to bake a cake is an algorithm in a form that is understandable to a cook. A computer program written in a programming language is an algorithm.

During the program design activity, the programmer develops an algorithm to solve the problem. This is usually the most difficult task in the programming process and there are many strategies that can help. It is important that the programmer have a repertoire of algorithms upon which he or she can draw. Then, when a problem or a part of a problem requires a particular algorithm, the programmer quickly can supply the appropriate procedure.

When the algorithm is not known, the programmer must devise one of his or her own. The use of stepwise program refinement, discussed in the last section, can help in designing an algorithm. In addition to producing the needed algorithm, this process leads naturally to the use of basic control structures in nested patterns as discussed in Section 7-1. If the programmer sticks with the basic control structures during the refinement process, the final program will have a single entry point and a single exit point and will flow from top to bottom through a sequence of loops and decisions. Thus this program refinement strategy not only helps in developing an algorithm, but it also leads to the most understandable program.

Sometimes devising an algorithm for a problem is difficult. When this happens, it often helps to think of a related problem and try to develop an algorithm for it. Another approach is to simplify the problem by discarding some of the conditions and then try to develop an algorithm for the simpler version. Sometimes the programmer must go back to the problem definition and see if anything has been left out. Any of these approaches may help the programmer develop an algorithm for the problem.

If the program will be especially large, dividing the program into sections or *modules* often helps. Each module performs some function related to the overall processing of the program. The advantage of this modular programming is that each module can be worked on separately. The programmer can develop an algorithm for each module without worrying about the logic of the other modules. In addition, the programmer can code and test each module before going on to the next module. Thus errors are isolated and easier to locate with modular programming.

When programming in a modular fashion, each module can be thought of as a subalgorithm. The logic of a module can be developed through stepwise refinement. Using only the three basic control structures results in a module with only one entry point and one exit point. The exit point for one module then leads to the entry point of the next module, and thus the complete program is a sequence of modules. (A related idea is the use of subprograms to divide a program into modules. FORTRAN subprograms are discussed in Chapter 11.)

When developing an algorithm, the programmer must keep in mind the structure of the data. Although we have only worked with simple data structures so far, we already can see that an algorithm cannot be developed without knowing how the data is going to be organized. For example, the programmer must know the organization of the input and output files before developing an algorithm to do the necessary processing. In later chapters we will discuss more complex data structures, and we will see that the algorithm depends on the structure of the data. Thus the development of an algorithm is *not* independent of the development of the data structure.

Many times the programmer develops alternative algorithms, and then must select one of the algorithms. The objective is to select the best algorithm that correctly solves the problem. However, which algorithm is "best" is often difficult to determine. The first criterion is always correctness: does the algorithm correctly solve the problem? The second criterion is usually the understandability of the algorithm: How easy is it for a programmer to understand how the algorithm works? Another criterion that may be important is the efficiency of the algorithm: How fast will the resulting program execute and how much storage space will it occupy? In many situations these questions are not important. In some cases, such as when a very large problem is being solved or a small computer is being used, efficiency is important.

To illustrate the program designing activities we continue with the development of the grade-report program. We will use the technique of stepwise program refinement discussed in the last section to derive the algorithm for this program. Recall that in this technique we start with a general statement of what the program does, that is, the general statement of the program's algorithm. Then we refine this statement gradually until we reach the final algorithm.

The most general statement of the algorithm for the grade-report program is as follows:

Produce the grade report.

Although this is a very simple statement, it expresses what the program is to do. The next step is to determine what is necessary to accomplish this.

We know that the input file consists of a sequence of student records each containing three test scores. The output is to be a report with headings, data for each student giving the student's weighted average score and letter grade, and a final line with the overall course average. Thus, to produce this output from the input, we can refine the general statement of the algorithm given earlier to the following:

Write the report headings.
Process the input data to produce the output for each student.
Determine and write the overall course average.
Stop.

The second step needs to be refined further. We know that the computer must read and process the input data in a loop until it reads the trailer value. Within the loop, the computer must read a record, calculate the weighted average, and write the output with the appropriate letter grade. Thus we can refine this step to the following:

Begin loop.
    Read an input record.
    If the trailer value is read, exit from the loop.
    Calculate the weighted average score.
    Determine the grade category based on the average and write
        the output with the appropriate letter grade.
End loop.

Note that we have clearly indicated that this is a loop and that the loop is terminated when the computer reads the record with the trailer value.

The step to calculate the weighted average score needs further refinement. Recall that the average score is found by taking 50% of the best test score, 35% of the next best, and 15% of the worst score. Hence we must determine the best score, the next best score, and the worst score. Thus we could refine this step as follows:

Find the best score.
Find the next best score.
Find the worst score.
Compute the weighted average score.

However, we can easily do the first three steps by sorting the test scores into ascending order. Thus we can express the algorithm as follows:

Sort the test scores into ascending order.
Compute the weighted average score.

Because we already know a sorting algorithm for three numbers, we can use this algorithm in the first step. Thus the refinement of the average calculation is complete (except for the final coding).

We also have to refine the step that determines the grade category and writes the output. Because there are five grade categories, we can think of this as a selection process and state it as follows:

Select the appropriate grade category:
90–100: Write output with grade "A".
80–89: Write output with grade "B".
70–79: Write output with grade "C".
60–69: Write output with grade "D".
0–59: Write output with grade "F".

Although this does not look like one of the three basic control structures, we know that we can code it using nested decisions.

The last step that must be refined is that of determining and writing the overall course average. To compute this value we have to count the number of students and accumulate the total of the average test scores. The variables used for the totals must be initialized before the input loop. The totals must be accumulated in the input loop. After the input loop is terminated, the overall course average must be computed and the final input with this average must be written.

Incorporating all of the refinements discussed here we get the algorithm shown in Figure 7-9. The final program can be coded from this algorithm.

The algorithm in Figure 7-9 is written in a semi-English, semi-programming language style. Sometimes this way of writing an algorithm is called *pseudocode*. Pseudocode has no rules; any written language for describing an algorithm can be thought of as pseudocode. Some programmers use an outline form and others prefer a form that looks more like a programming language. Pseudocode has many variations, and any style that works for the programmer is acceptable.

Another technique for expressing an algorithm is to represent it graphically in a *flowchart*. In Appendix D we discuss program flowcharts in detail and give numerous examples.

Program coding

The objective of the program coding activity is to code a program in a specific programming language that follows the algorithm developed in the previous activity. In effect, this is the last step in the program refinement.

Figure 7-9. The algorithm for the grade-report program

Write the headings.
Initialize the totals.
Begin loop.
      Read an input record.
      If the trailer value is read, exit from the loop.
      Sort the test scores into ascending order.
      Compute the weighted average score.
      Accumulate the total number of students and the total average score.
      Select the appropriate grade category:
            90–100: Write output with grade "A".
            80–89: Write output with grade "B".
            70–79: Write output with grade "C".
            60–69: Write output with grade "D".
              0–59: Write output with grade "F".
End loop.
Compute the course average.
Write output with the course average.
Stop.

Each part of the algorithm must be translated into a group of statements. The final code is correct if the algorithm is correct and the translation is done correctly.

Sometimes during the coding activity an error is discovered in the algorithm's logic. When this happens, the programmer must go back and redesign the program. It may even be necessary to return to the problem definition and work forward again if a serious error or misunderstanding is discovered.

During program coding, the style rules discussed in Section 7-3 should be followed. This helps make the program more readable and the structure more understandable. Comments should be included as the program is coded. When the coding activity is complete, the program should be in its final form (except for the correction of possible errors).

The coding for the grade report program is shown in Figure 7-10. Each step in the algorithm is translated into one or more FORTRAN statements. For example, the sorting step results in 15 statements, whereas the average calculation requires only one statement. Note that the comments in the body of the program closely follow the algorithm given in Figure 7-9. This is a common way of using comments in a program. Notice also the use of introductory comments in the program.

The program is built from the basic control structures discussed in Section 7-1. The program begins with a sequence consisting of steps to write the headings and initialize the totals. Then comes an input loop that is terminated when a trailer value is read. The loop contains a sequence of decisions for sorting, a calculation step for the average, steps to accumulate the totals, and a nested decision for the output. Finally, a sequence calculates and writes the overall average. Style rules have been followed to make the program more readable and understandable.

Figure 7-10. The grade-report program (Part 1 of 2)

```
C     TITLE:  GRADE REPORT PROGRAM
C
C     PROGRAMMER:  ROBERT C. NICKERSON
C     DATE:  NOVEMBER 10, 19XX
C
C     PURPOSE:  THIS PROGRAM COMPUTES A WEIGHTED AVERAGE OF .
C               TEST SCORES AND ASSIGNS AN APPROPRIATE LETTER GR.
C               FOR EACH STUDENT IN THE COURSE.  THE PROGRAM ALSO
C               DETERMINES THE OVERALL AVERAGE SCORE FOR ALL STUDENTS.
C
C     VARIABLE NAMES:
C         IDNUM  = STUDENT'S IDENTIFICATION NUMBER (INPUT/OUTPUT)
C         SCORE1 = SCORE ON FIRST TEST (INPUT)
C         SCORE2 = SCORE ON SECOND TEST (INPUT)
C         SCORE3 = SCORE ON THIRD TEST (INPUT)
C         STUAVE = STUDENT'S WEIGHTED AVERAGE SCORE (OUTPUT)
C         CRSAVE = OVERALL COURSE AVERAGE (OUTPUT)
C         TOTSTU = TOTAL NUMBER OF STUDENTS (INTERNAL)
C         TOTAVE = TOTAL AVERAGE SCORE (INTERNAL)
C         TEMP   = TEMPORARY VARIABLE (INTERNAL)
C
C     DECLARE VARIABLES
C
      INTEGER IDNUM,TOTSTU
      REAL SCORE1,SCORE2,SCORE3,STUAVE,CRSAVE,TOTAVE,TEMP
C
C     WRITE HEADINGS
C
      WRITE (6,900)
C
C     INITIALIZE TOTALS
C
      TOTSTU=0
      TOTAVE=0.0
C
C     BEGIN INPUT LOOP; EXIT WHEN TRAILER VALUE IS READ
C
  100 READ (5,800) IDNUM,SCORE1,SCORE2,SCORE3
      IF (IDNUM.EQ.9999) GO TO 500
C
C     SORT TEST SCORES INTO ASCENDING ORDER
C
      IF (SCORE1.GT.SCORE2) THEN
        TEMP=SCORE1
        SCORE1=SCORE2
        SCORE2=TEMP
      END IF
      IF (SCORE2.GT.SCORE3) THEN
        TEMP=SCORE2
        SCORE2=SCORE3
        SCORE3=TEMP
      END IF
      IF (SCORE1.GT.SCORE2) THEN
        TEMP=SCORE1
        SCORE1=SCORE2
        SCORE2=TEMP
      END IF
```

Figure 7-10. (Part 2 of 2)

```
C
C          CALCULATE STUDENT'S WEIGHTED AVERAGE SCORE
C
           STUAVE=.15*SCORE1+.35*SCORE2+.50*SCORE3
C
C          ACCUMULATE TOTALS
C
           TOTSTU=TOTSTU+1
           TOTAVE=TOTAVE+STUAVE
C
C          SELECT GRADE CATEGORY AND WRITE OUTPUT
C
           IF (STUAVE.GE.90.0) THEN
C            GRADE IS "A"
             WRITE (6,910) IDNUM,STUAVE
           ELSE IF (STUAVE.GE.80.0) THEN
C            GRADE IS "B"
             WRITE (6,920) IDNUM,STUAVE
           ELSE IF (STUAVE.GE.70.0) THEN
C            GRADE IS "C"
             WRITE (6,930) IDNUM,STUAVE
           ELSE IF (STUAVE.GE.60.0) THEN
C            GRADE IS "D"
             WRITE (6,940) IDNUM,STUAVE
           ELSE
C            GRADE IS "F"
             WRITE (6,950) IDNUM,STUAVE
           END IF
C
       GO TO 100
C
C      END OF LOOP
C
C      CALCULATE AND WRITE OVERALL COURSE AVERAGE
C
   500 CRSAVE=TOTAVE/REAL(TOTSTU)
       WRITE (6,960) CRSAVE
C
       STOP
C
C      INPUT FORMAT
C
   800 FORMAT (I4,3F4.0)
C
C      OUTPUT FORMATS
C
   900 FORMAT ('1        COURSE GRADE REPORT'/
      1        '0STUDENT        AVERAGE        LETTER'/
      2        ' NUMBER          SCORE         GRADE'/)
   910 FORMAT ('  ',I4,10X,F5.1,10X,'A')
   920 FORMAT ('  ',I4,10X,F5.1,10X,'B')
   930 FORMAT ('  ',I4,10X,F5.1,10X,'C')
   940 FORMAT ('  ',I4,10X,F5.1,10X,'D')
   950 FORMAT ('  ',I4,10X,F5.1,10X,'F')
   960 FORMAT ('0COURSE AVERAGE ',F5.1)
C
       END
```

The steps in this program can be accomplished in alternative ways, depending on the language features that are available. For example, if the WHILE statement is available, the program can be written using a WHILE loop for the input loop. Another example is the way in which the letter grade is printed. Using some language features discussed in Chapter 8, these steps can be simplified. The programmer should be familiar with as much of the programming language as possible and use those features that make the program easiest to code and as understandable as possible.

Program correctness

In Section 1-5 we discussed the three types of errors that can occur in a program. These are compilation errors, execution errors, and logic errors. The compiler detects compilation errors during the compilation of the program. An error message is printed for each compilation error. To correct such errors, the programmer must interpret the error message and make appropriate changes in the source program. Compilation errors usually result from the misuse of the programming language. Because the computer detects these errors, they are usually easy to correct.

Execution errors occur during the execution of the program. The program will not execute if it has any serious compilation errors. Any execution error is the result of some condition that can be detected only during execution. Some examples of execution errors are dividing by zero, attempting to read when there is no more input data, and calculating a number that is too large for a variable. When such an error is detected, the computer normally stops execution of the program and prints an error message explaining the cause of the error. The programmer must interpret the error message and make the necessary correction.

Even if the program compiles and executes without errors, it still may not be correct. Errors may exist in the logic of the program. These are the most difficult errors to detect. The usual approach is to make up test data and determine by hand what output is expected from the data. Then the program is run with the test data and the actual output is compared with the expected output. If the outputs do not agree, there is an error which must be located and corrected.

A program testing procedure such as this only shows the *presence* of errors, not their *absence*. To show that a program is correct, we must show that under all circumstances the program produces the correct result. To do this using test data would require running the program with all possible combinations of data and comparing the output with the expected output calculated by hand. In addition to being an enormous task, this would be senseless because then we would have calculated all possible outputs by hand and would no longer need a program (except, perhaps, to check our hand calculations). Thus we need some other way to show that the program is logically correct.

"Proving" program correctness. One way to show that a program is correct is to use a mathematical proof of correctness. This approach is usually very complex and tedious and few programmers know what is involved. However, we can informally "prove" a program's correctness through the stepwise program refinement process. Recall that in this approach we start with a general statement of the solution and then refine this statement by determining what things must be done to accomplish it. At each step in the development we refine the statements of the previous step until we reach the coded program. To show that a program is correct, we need to show that each refinement accomplishes the task specified at the previous step.

As an example, consider the sorting program developed in Section 7-4. The problem is to sort three numbers into ascending sequence. The first step in the refinement includes the following statement:

Sort V1, V2, and V3 into ascending order.

We assume that this is a correct definition of the problem and begin to refine it. The refinement results in the following:

Move largest value to V3.
Move next largest value to V2.

We can say that the program is correct at this point because we know that to sort the values we only need to do the two things just listed. We then refine each of these two things separately and show that each refinement is a correct way of accomplishing the task that is being described. Thus we can refine the preceding statements to the following:

Move larger of V1 and V2 to V2.
Move larger of V2 and V3 to V3.
Move larger of V1 and V2 to V2.

Then the program is correct at this level of refinement. We continue in this manner, showing that each successive step is a correct refinement of the previous step. Finally, we code the program, and, if there are no coding errors, the coded program is logically correct.

This method of showing program correctness through stepwise refinement is a very important part of programming. Most programmers do this even though they may not think they are "proving" that the program is correct. In fact, we did this when we developed the grade report program. If we do this stepwise development carefully and explicitly, we greatly reduce the chance of serious logic errors in the program. Thus the careful development of the program is the most important step in the programming process.

Program testing. Even if a program is developed in the manner described here, logic errors may occur. Often small things are forgotten or a logical step in the development is passed over too quickly. Therefore a thorough testing of the program should be performed to try to bring out any hidden errors. The programmer should be merciless in his or her testing of the program. Some organizations have a different programmer do the testing because the original programmer may feel the program has few errors and thus may not test the program thoroughly. The objective of program testing is to force errors to reveal themselves.

If the program is written in a modular fashion (i.e., in sections), each module can be tested separately. Sometimes testing can begin on an incomplete program by inserting simple modules, that do nothing, for incomplete parts of the program. (These are sometimes called *stubs*.) After the modules are tested separately, the interaction between the modules can be tested. Pairs of modules can be tested, then three modules at a time, and so forth until finally the entire program is tested as a whole.

The first tests of the program should be simple to make sure that the program works in the simplest cases. Obvious errors such as misspelling of headings or alignment of columns can be corrected at this point. Then more complex tests can be performed.

At a minimum every statement in the program should be executed at least once using test data and the results compared with the expected output. However, this strategy will not catch all obvious errors. For example, consider the following sequence of statements from the payroll program in Figure 4-2:

```
IF (HOURS.LE.40.0) THEN
   GROSS=PAYRT1*HOURS
   TAX=TAXRT1*GROSS
ELSE
   GROSS=PAYRT1*40.0+PAYRT2*(HOURS-40.0)
   TAX=TAXRT2*GROSS
END IF
```

To test this section of code we might supply two sets of test data, one with the hours equal to 35.0 and the other with the hours equal to 45.0. These data would cause every statement in this sequence to be executed at least once. However, the sequence may still be in error. For example, assume that the IF statement had been incorrectly coded as follows:

```
IF (HOURS.LT.40.0) THEN
```

Testing with only the two sets of input would not detect this error. We must also test the case where the hours are equal to 40.0.

We now have three sets of test data for this program. Even with these data, errors may still be present. For example, the following erroneous IF statement would not be detected with these test data:

```
IF (HOURS.LE.41.0) THEN
```

What we need is a test case that is just greater than 40.0, such as 40.1. Then this error would be detected.

From this example we can see the beginning of a general strategy for generating test data for the parts of programs that involve decisions. In this example the number of hours can range from zero to some practical limit such as 80. We can divide this range into two subranges based on the calculations that are to be performed. If the hours are between 0 and 40, one set of calculations should be performed. If the hours are greater than 40 but less than or equal to the upper limit, another set of calculations should be done. Then the testing strategy is as follows: for each subrange, test the program with the maximum and minimum values in the subrange and with some representative value within the subrange. Applying this strategy to the payroll example we would test the program with the hours equal to 0.0, 35.0, 40.0, 40.1, 45.0, and 80.0. If this part of the program works for each of these cases, we can be reasonably sure that it will work for other cases.

To create test data for the grade-report program is more complex. The best approach is to analyze the different parts of the program separately and to design appropriate test data for each part. We can apply the previous strategy to the grade selection algorithm in the program. Note that the grade is based on the average test score. The actual grade depends on which of the following ranges the average falls into:

> 90–100
> 80–89
> 70–79
> 60–69
> 0–59

We must select input data for the three test scores that will generate values for the average that are equal to the maximum and minimum value in each range and to values in between each set of limits. This results in 15 test cases in all.

The sorting algorithm is more complex. We notice that the algorithm does not depend on whether any of the test scores are equal. (That is, if we made a mistake and used the relational operator .GE. instead of .GT. in any of the IF statements in this part of the program, we would get the same result.) Hence for testing purposes we can assume that each score is different. Then we have six possible cases to test, based on the relative values of SCORE1, SCORE2, and SCORE3. These cases are as follows:

Smallest		*Largest*
SCORE1	SCORE2	SCORE3
SCORE1	SCORE3	SCORE2
SCORE2	SCORE1	SCORE3
SCORE2	SCORE3	SCORE1
SCORE3	SCORE1	SCORE2
SCORE3	SCORE2	SCORE1

We must supply input test data for each of these cases. We can combine these six cases with the fifteen needed for the grade selection algorithm. We need one additional case with 9999 for the student's identification number to test the termination condition of the input loop.

A complete set of input data that satisfies these requirements is given in Figure 7-11. Tests number 2, 3, 5, 6, 8, and 9 correspond with the six cases just listed for the sorting algorithm. For each set of data, the expected output is shown. In addition, the overall course average is given. The test data should be shuffled so that the tests are not done in any particular order (except for the trailer value test). Then the program should be run with the data and the actual output compared with what is expected. Any discrepancy indicates an error. The output from running the program with this data is shown in Figure 7-12. Notice that all test cases are correct.

The tests listed here will not detect all errors. For example, the tests will not detect errors that might result from using invalid input data, such as negative test scores or scores greater than 100. In general, we should make up special tests for the worst possible cases. Errors often occur at the beginning or end of processing. Hence special tests should be made with the first and last input record. Tests should be made to see what happens when there is too much or too little data. The program should be run without any input data to see what happens. Every possible worst case that can be thought of should be tested.

Debugging. When an error is detected, the programmer must locate the cause of the error in the program and correct it. This is the debugging process.

Figure 7-11. Test data and expected output from the grade-report program

	Input Test Data				Expected Output	
Test number	Student ID	First score	Second score	Third score	Average	Grade
1	1001	100	100	100	100.0	A
2	1002	83	93	100	95.0	A
3	1003	70	96	90	90.0	A
4	1004	90	90	89	89.9	B
5	1005	83	73	90	85.0	B
6	1006	86	60	80	80.0	B
7	1007	79	80	80	79.9	C
8	1008	73	80	63	75.0	C
9	1009	76	70	50	70.0	C
10	1010	70	69	70	69.9	D
11	1011	80	50	50	65.0	D
12	1012	45	75	45	60.0	D
13	1013	75	55	21	59.9	F
14	1014	40	40	70	55.0	F
15	1015	0	0	0	0.0	F
16	9999	0	0	0	—	—

Course average: 71.6

Figure 7-12. Output from the grade-report program

COURSE GRADE REPORT

STUDENT	AVERAGE	LETTER
NUMBER	SCORE	GRADE
1006	80.0	B
1011	65.0	D
1002	95.0	A
1009	70.0	C
1015	.0	F
1004	89.9	B
1005	85.0	B
1013	59.9	F
1008	75.0	C
1001	100.0	A
1012	60.0	D
1010	69.9	D
1003	90.0	A
1007	79.9	C
1014	55.0	F

COURSE AVERAGE   71.6

Testing involves determining if errors are present; *debugging* is the process of finding and correcting errors.

Testing each section (or module) of a program separately helps isolate errors. The program can be run with just one section, then the second section can be added, the program rerun, and so forth for the other sections. Any errors that occur can usually be found in the section most recently added to the program.

Because many errors are the result of incorrect input data, a good practice during debugging is to print all input data immediately after reading it. This is called *echo printing,* and it allows the programmer to check that the desired input data has been read. Another technique is to print the values of variables that are not used for input or for output (i.e., internal variables). This lets the programmer check the results of various intermediate calculations.

A common debugging technique is called *tracing.* The idea is to show the actual order of execution of various parts of the program. This can be done by inserting WRITE or PRINT statements at different points in the program. The statements should print simple phrases that identify where in the program each statement is located. This allows the programmer to compare the actual sequence of execution with what was expected.

The techniques discussed here can help detect and locate errors in a program. However, if a program has been developed by following a logical, systematic approach, errors should be at a minimum. The programmer must take whatever steps are necessary to guarantee that his or her program is correct. A program is correct when there are no logic errors as well as no compilation and execution errors.

Program documentation

Documentation for a program provides information so that others can understand how to use the program and how the program works. Documentation that explains how to use a program is mainly for computer operators and others who need to run the program. This is called *operator documentation* or *user documentation,* depending on to whom it is directed. Included in this documentation are instructions for setting up the computer to run the program, a description of the input data to use and the output to expect, and other information necessary for proper execution of the program. Documentation that explains how the program works is provided for programmers in the event that errors in the program must be corrected or modifications in the program need to be made. This is called *program documentation.* In this section we are concerned with this type of documentation.

Documenting the program begins during the problem definition activity. Any written specifications of the program prepared at this stage are part of the documentation. For example, input and output layouts are developed during problem definition and are usually included in the final documentation. During the program designing activity, various tools may be used including pseudocode and flowcharts. Final, neatly prepared versions of these are usually part of the documentation. Listings of the test data used and sample outputs for each set of test data are also normally included in the final documentation.

This type of documentation is external to the program. Much of the documentation can be included within the program itself. This is the primary purpose of comments in the program. As we have seen, comments can be used to describe the general features of the program and the detailed logic of the algorithm. A program listing with good comments in it is an important part of the documentation. The grade-report program in Figure 7-10 illustrates such a program.

A complete documentation package for a program might include the following:

1. A program summary or abstract that provides a brief statement of the purpose of the program and a short description of the program's input, output, and processing. This summary is very often included as comments in the program and may also be written or typed on a separate piece of paper or on a form to be included with the documentation.
2. Detailed descriptions of the input, output, and other data for the program. These descriptions may include the layouts of input and output records, print charts for all reports, a list of all variable names and their types (integer or real), and descriptions of the data to which the variable names refer.
3. Documents that describe the program's algorithm. These documents may include pseudocode, flowcharts, and any other documents that help to explain how the program works. A written

narrative of any particularly complex part of the algorithm may also be included.

4. A summary of any error messages that may be printed. A program very often includes statements to check for various errors or exceptions that are detected during execution. A message is usually printed when such an error occurs. Although the error message should completely describe the condition that occurred, it is usually a good idea to summarize the error messages in the documentation and provide additional explanations of what caused each error.

5. Documentation of the testing that was done on the program. This documentation includes lists of test data used with the program and the output that resulted from each test run. These items provide information for programmers who modify the program in the future so that they can run the same tests with the modified program and check that the same output is produced.

6. A record of any modifications that have been made in the program. A programmer who makes a change in a program should record the date, the nature of the change, and his or her name. As with the program summary, this is often included as comments in the program.

7. The source program listed. As noted earlier, the documentation must include, at a minimum, a current listing of the program with appropriate comments.

The complete set of documents should be bound together with a title page and a table of contents. There should be one binder for each program, and the entire library of program documentation should be the responsibility of one or more documentation librarians. If a program is changed, the documentation must be updated. No programmer should ever think his or her job done until the final documentation is prepared or appropriately modified.

7-6. Conclusion

Computer programming is a process that includes several activities. One common misconception is that programming involves only the activity of writing the program. As we have seen, the writing activity — which is called coding — is just one part of the programming process. When we use the word "programming," we mean the entire set of activities associated with preparing a computer program. This includes the five activities discussed in the last section.

The approach to programming emphasized in this book is commonly called *structured programming*. There is some disagreement about what is meant by structured programming; a single definition does not exist. However, most people agree that structured programming involves a systematic process resulting in programs that are well structured, that are easily understood, maintained, and modified, and that can be shown to be correct.

In this chapter we stressed developing programs through stepwise refinement. This approach helps us show the correctness of a program. Using the three basic control structures leads to programs that are well structured and easy to understand and change. The style rules discussed in this chapter also help produce readable programs. All of this is part of structured programming.

Structured programming should not be confused with the idea of a *structured program*. Generally, a structured program is one that contains only the three basic control structures. Producing a structured program is one of the goals of structured programming. However, structured programming involves much more than this.

Structured programming is really just good programming. By following the guidelines presented in this chapter, the programmer can produce good, correct programs.

Review questions

1. What are the three basic control structures in programming?
2. What type of control structure is formed by each of the following groups of statements?
   a. `IF (A.GT.B) THEN`
      `    C=D`
      `   END IF`
   b. `    DO 100 I=1,10`
      `        PRINT *,I`
      `   100 CONTINUE`
   c. `A=5`
      `PRINT *,A`
   d. `200 READ *,X`
      `        IF (X.EQ.0) GO TO 210`
      `        GO TO 200`
      `   210 (next statement)`
3. Why is it important that each basic control structure have a single entry point and a single exit point?
4. What principle of good program structure is violated by the program in Figure 5-20?
5. When we read the statements in a program in the order in which they are written on paper, we are reading _____ version of the program. When we read the statements in the program in the order in which they are executed, we are reading the _____ version of the program.
6. Why can the uncontrolled use of GO TO statements make a program difficult to understand?
7. Give three rules of good program style.

8. What is wrong with the following?

```
C PRINT THE VALUES OF A, B, AND C
        PRINT *,A,B,C
```

9. The process of developing a program by starting with a general statement of the problem and successively refining the statement until a program solution is obtained is called _____.

10. Consider the program shown in Figure 7-7. Assume that the input data is the numbers 8, 12, and 4. What is the value of all variables in the program after each statement in the program between the READ and PRINT statements is executed?

11. Which activity in the programming process is begun during problem definition but finished after all other activities are completed?

12. At a minimum, what should be determined during the problem definition activity?

13. A set of instructions that, if carried out, results in the solution of a problem is called _____.

14. It has been said that the most important step in the programming process is the design step. Why?

15. Program testing can show that a program is correct. True or false?

16. Assume that the value of X can range from 100 to 200. Design test data following the strategy discussed in the chapter that tests the following program:

```
        INTEGER X,Y
    10  READ (*,*,END=20) X
            IF (X.LE.125) THEN
                Y=1
            ELSE
                Y=0
            END IF
            GO TO 10
    20  STOP
        END
```

17. What is the difference between program testing and debugging?

18. What is the purpose of program documentation?

19. What is the difference between coding and programming?

20. What is structured programming?

Programming problems

1. In the economic measurement of consumer behavior the price elasticity of demand for a product is given by the following expression:

$$-\frac{(Q_2 - Q_1)/Q_1}{(P_2 - P_1)/P_1}$$

In this expression, Q stands for quantity sold and P for price.

If the elasticity is less than 1, the demand is said to be *inelastic*. If the elasticity equals 1, the demand is said to be *unit elastic*. If elasticity is greater than 1, the demand is *elastic*.

Write a FORTRAN program to calculate the elasticity of demand for a particular product. Input is the product number and the relevant prices and quantities. Output from the program should be the product number, the elasticity of demand, and a statement of whether the demand is elastic, inelastic, or unit elastic.

Use the following data to test the program:

Product number	P_1	Q_1	P_2	Q_2
103	25.00	100	17.50	135
108	20.00	200	10.00	300
112	125.00	35	95.00	37
115	32.50	512	27.00	713
128	44.00	80	33.00	100
132	15.75	72	10.25	63
999	(trailer value)			

Note that the data includes a trailer value that should be used to terminate processing.

2. A classic problem in computer programming is the "automatic change-maker" problem. The problem involves determining the breakdown of a customer's change into various denominations.

Write a FORTRAN program to solve the automatic change-maker problem. The program should read a customer's number, the amount of the customer's bill, and the cash payment. Then the program should print the number, the amount of the bill, the payment, and the change, if any. If there is no change or if the payment is less than the bill, appropriate messages should be printed.

For each transaction in which there is change, show the number and kind of each denomination in the change. The total number of bills and coins should be kept to a minimum. Assume that only pennies ($.01), nickels ($.05), dimes ($.10), quarters ($.25), and one dollar bills are available for change.

Use the following data to test the program:

Customer's number	Customer's bill ($)	Payment ($)
1234	3.59	5.00
2345	8.00	8.00
3456	14.95	14.00
4567	21.03	25.00
5678	9.95	50.00
6789	.29	1.00
	.00	(trailer value)

3. A theater sells tickets for $5.00 and averages 100 tickets sold for each performance. At this rate the theater's cost per patron is $2.00. The theater manager estimates that for each $.25 reduction in ticket price the number of tickets sold will increase by 30 and the theater's cost per patron will increase by $.10.

Write a FORTRAN program to calculate and print a table listing the ticket price, the number of tickets sold, the gross revenue (ticket price multiplied by the number of tickets sold), the theater's total cost (cost per patron times number of tickets sold), and the net profit (revenue minus theater's total cost) for each ticket price ranging from $5.00 to $3.00.

As the ticket price decreases from $5.00 to $3.00, the profit steadily increases to a maximum and then starts to decrease. Use this fact to print the phrase MAXIMUM PROFIT on the line in the table that corresponds to the greatest profit.

4. Write a FORTRAN program that finds the day of the week for any date in the twentieth century. Input to the program is the month, day, and year of any date between 1900 and 1999. The month should be numeric and the year should be two digits. For example, January 21, 1946, should be entered as 01 21 46. Output should give the day of the week for the given date (e.g., MONDAY).

The procedure to find the day of the week is as follows. Add the year, one fourth of the year (truncated), the day of the month, and the code for the month from the following table:

Month	Code
June	0
Sept., Dec.	1
April, July	2
Jan., Oct.	3
May	4
Aug.	5
Feb., March, Nov.	6

If the year is a leap year (that is, if it is evenly divisible by four), the code is one less for January and February.

From the sum subtract two and divide the result by seven. The remainder from the division is the day of the week with 0 denoting Saturday, 1 Sunday, 2 Monday, and so forth.

For example, the day of the week for January 21, 1946, is found as follows:

Year	46
¼ of year	11
Day of month	21
Code	3
Subtotal	81
Subtract	2
Total	79

Dividing 79 by 7 gives 11 with a remainder of 2. Hence, January 21, 1946, was a Monday.

Test the program with the following dates:

October 25, 1978
March 7, 1944
December 6, 1973
April 18, 1906
January 1, 1984
February 29, 1952

Use a trailer value to terminate the program.

5. Write a FORTRAN program to print student grade reports. Input to the program consists of a varying number of course grade records for each student. Each record contains the student's identification number, course identification number, course units, and numeric course grade (equal to 4, 3, 2, 1, or 0). The

input data is arranged in ascending numerical sequence by the students' identification numbers.

The program must calculate the grade point average (GPA) for each student. This is done by multiplying the number of units for each course by the grade, totaling for all courses, and dividing by the total number of units taken.

The output from the program should list for each student the student's identification number, the number of units and grade for each course that the student took, and the student's GPA. In addition, if the GPA is 3.5 or greater, the message HONOR LIST should be printed. If the GPA is less than 1.5, the message PROBATION should be printed.

Design appropriate input data that thoroughly tests the program. Note that the number of courses taken by a student varies.

6. Given the slopes, s and t, and intercepts, a and b, of two lines, that is, the lines whose equations are

$$y = sx + a$$

$$y = tx + b$$

compute the coordinates of the point of intersection of the lines. Then print the name of the quadrant (FIRST, SECOND, THIRD, FOURTH) in which the point lies. If the point of intersection falls on an axis, print the name of the axis (X-AXIS or Y-AXIS). If the point of intersection is the origin, print the word ORIGIN. Include a provision in the program to check if the lines are parallel (i.e., $s = t$, $a \neq b$) or if the equations are for the same line (i.e., $s = t$, $a = b$) and print an appropriate phrase if either case holds.

Input to the program is the data identification number (integer) and the values of s, a, t, and b (each real with two places to the right of the decimal point). Use the following data to test the program:

ID	s	a	t	b
101	2.00	8.00	−3.00	−2.00
102	4.38	4.25	−7.11	−18.92
103	.50	3.50	−.75	16.00
104	.50	0.00	−.50	0.00
105	.38	−15.79	.38	−28.35
106	.50	5.00	−.50	5.00
107	.50	5.00	−.50	−5.00
108	−5.63	28.91	6.21	14.35
109	4.87	.08	4.87	.08
110	−.50	−5.00	.50	−5.00
111	.50	−5.00	−.50	5.00
112	−.03	−16.92	1.72	24.38
113	−1.00	−4.00	−2.00	6.00

At the end of the input data place a trailer value of 999 in the ID field and use this to stop processing.

7. Write a FORTRAN program to calculate the accumulated amount of a bank deposit at any interest rate for any period of time. Input to the program is the depositor's number, the amount of his or her deposit, the interest rate the deposit earns, and the number of years that he or she leaves the deposit. The basic problem assumes that interest is compounded annually. This means that

the interest earned in one year is added to the deposit and is multiplied by the annual interest rate to get the next year's interest. For example, if the initial deposit is $1000, the interest rate is 5%, and the deposit is left for 3 years, then the first year's interest is $1000 × .05 = $50. At the end of the first year, the accumulated amount of the deposit is $1000 + $50 = $1050. Interest for the second year is $1050 × .05 = $52.50. The accumulated amount of the deposit at the end of the second year is $1050 + $52.50 = $1102.50. The third year's interest is $1102.50 × .05 = $55.12. Thus the accumulated amount of the deposit at the end of 3 years is $1102.50 + $55.12 = $1157.62.

The following are the requirements for this program:

a. Read and print the input data. Output should include appropriate titles to identify each item.

b. For each set of input data, print, below appropriate headings, the year and the accumulated amount of the deposit at the end of the year. Assume that the deposit is made at the beginning of year 1. Then the accumulated amount of the deposit at the end of year 1 is the amount of the deposit plus the interest for that year. Continue the process for the other years, making sure that the interest is compounded annually.

c. In part (b), we assumed that interest was compounded only once a year. It is possible to compound interest more frequently by incorporating a "compounding factor" into the program. This factor represents the number of times per year that interest is to be compounded. For example, a compounding factor of 4 means that interest is compounded four times per year (i.e., every 3 months). A compounding factor of 1 means that interest is compounded once per year (i.e., annually). When interest is compounded more than once a year, the interest rate used in the calculation is the annual interest rate divided by the compounding factor. For example, if the annual interest rate is 5% and the compounding factor is 4, then the interest rate used to calculate interest every 3 months is .05/4 = .0125. Interest is calculated at this rate four times a year. Each time the interest is calculated, it is added to the deposit to get a new accumulated deposit that is used for the next interest calculation. Calculate the accumulated amount of the deposit at the end of each year for each set of input data, assuming compounding factors of 2, 4, 8, and 12. Note that these compounding factors are not input data but must be generated in the program. For each compounding factor, print the factor and the *final* accumulated amount of the deposit with appropriate titles. Thus, in addition to the output already described, there will be four additional lines of output for each set of data.

Use the following data to test the program:

Depositor's number	Amount of deposit ($)	Interest rate (%)	Time (years)
10851	1000.00	5	3
13751	1000.00	4½	3
18645	1000.00	5¼	3
19541	50.00	3¾	25
24712	3500.00	6¾	10
24839	3500.00	7	10
26213	3500.00	7¼	10
28721	3500.00	7	5

8. In a geographic area the population in each of three socioeconomic groups is increasing at a known percentage rate per year. Current total population of the area and distribution (percent) of the population among the three groups is also known. Several things can be determined from this information, including the expected population in each group after a certain amount of time and the total population of the area.

Assume that the following information for each geographic area is recorded in a record: the area's code number, the current total population of the area, the percentage of the current population that makes up each of the three socioeconomic groups, and the annual growth percentage rate of each group. Write a FORTRAN program to process these data according to the following specifications:

a. Read and print the input data with appropriate headings.

b. For each group calculate the current population and the expected population after 10 years. For example, if the current population of an area is 5000 and a group comprises 20% of that population, then the current population of the group is 1000. If the growth rate is 5%, then after one year the population of the group is 1000 + .05 × 1000 or 1050. After two years, the population is 1050 + .05 × 1050 or 1103. This continues for 10 years. Also calculate the total population of the area after 10 years and the percentage of the total that each socioeconomic group comprises. Print all results with appropriate headings.

c. In part (b) we assumed that the growth rate for each group would remain constant. It may be that these growth rates are decreasing by some percentage rate each year. Repeat the calculations for part (b), assuming the growth rate decreases by .1% per year until the growth rate reaches 2.1% or less, at which time it levels off. For example, if the growth rate this year is 2.7%, next year it will be 2.6%. The following year it will be 2.5%. This continues until the growth rate reaches 2.1% at which time it levels off at 2.1% for the remainder of the 10-year period. If the growth rate is currently 2.1% or less, the rate remains unchanged for the entire 10-year period. Do this three more times using .2%, .25%, and .35% to decrease the growth rate.

Use the data in the following table to test the program:

Code	Current total population	Distribution of current population (%) Group A	Group B	Group C	Annual growth rate (%) Group A	Group B	Group C
1083	14,283	35	59	6	4.1	5.2	4.9
1215	21,863	37	42	21	5.8	5.1	5.9
1371	8,460	73	0	27	2.4	0.0	3.1
1462	5,381	55	41	4	3.7	4.2	4.2
1931	12,845	90	9	1	1.9	2.2	2.8

9. Develop a FORTRAN program to help reconcile your checkbook each month.

10. Develop a FORTRAN program to compare your expenses each month with your budget for various items (e.g., rent, food, transportation, etc.).

11. Develop a FORTRAN program to compute depreciation schedules for an asset using the straight-line method, the double declining balance method, and the sum-of-years'-digits method.

12. Write a FORTRAN program to produce a home mortgage payment schedule.

Input to the program should be the amount of the loan, the monthly payment, the annual interest rate, and the number of months that the loan runs. Output should be a table that gives for each month the amount of the payment applied to the principal, the amount applied to interest, and the balance due after the payment. Yearly totals of interest paid should also be printed. Assume that the first payment is due at the end of January.

13. Write the program for Problem 12 with the additional requirement that the input includes the month and year of the first payment. Then the totals for the first and last year may not necessarily represent twelve months of payments.

14. Write a FORTRAN program to find the definite integral of the function $f(x) = e^x$ between the limits a and b. Use the trapezoidal method described in many calculus textbooks. Input to the program should be the values of a and b. Output should be the definite integral of the function between a and b.

Chapter 8

Character and logical data

A computer can process many types of data. In previous chapters we concentrated on two types of numeric data — integer and real — but there are other numeric data types. (In Appendix F we discuss one of these — double precision data.) In addition, computers can process nonnumeric data including character data and logical data. Character data consists of words and symbols; logical data involves true and false values. In this chapter we describe character and logical data and discuss FORTRAN statements for processing these types of data. After completing this chapter you should be able to write programs that process character and logical data.*

8-1. Input and output of character data

In earlier chapters we discussed input and output of numeric data. We also covered character output, which involves producing output consisting of words and symbols. Such output is character data. It is also possible to read character data and to write the same data. This type of I/O is required in many programs. For example, the input to a payroll program may include an employee's name. This data, which is character data, must be read and then printed along with the results of the payroll calculations. In this section we describe list-directed and formatted input and output of character data. First, however, we must understand character variables.

---

* This chapter is designed so that parts of it can be read earlier. The first and second subsections of Section 8-1 can be covered along with Chapter 2 and the third subsection can be covered along with Chapter 6. Sections 8-2 and 8-4 can be covered with Chapter 4.

Character variables

A *character variable* is character data that is identified by a *character variable name*. The name is formed just like a numeric variable name. To indicate that the name refers to character data instead of to integer or real numeric data, the name must be specified in a CHARACTER statement.

The syntax of the CHARACTER statement is as follows:

```
CHARACTER list
    or
CHARACTER*l list
```

where *list* is a list of variable names separated by
        commas. Each name in the list may
        optionally be followed by *l.
    l is an unsigned positive integer.

The effect of this statement is to specify that the variable names in the list are character variable names. The CHARACTER statement is a type statement. (Recall that the REAL and INTEGER statements are also type statements.) All type statements must appear at the beginnning of the program before the first executable statement. The order of the type statements does not matter.

In its simplest form the CHARACTER statement consists of the keyword CHARACTER followed by a list of variable names separated by commas. For example, the following statement identifies the names A, B, I, and J as character variable names:

```
CHARACTER A,B,I,J
```

In the program, these names would refer to character data and could not be used for numeric data.

Each character variable has a *length* associated with it. The length is the maximum number of characters that can be assigned to the variable. For example, if a character variable has a length of 10, any group of 10 or fewer characters can be assigned to the variable. The length of each character variable is indicated by the CHARACTER statement. If the statement is written in its simplest form, the length of each variable is 1. Thus in the previous example the character variable names A, B, I, and J can each refer only to one character.

To indicate lengths longer than 1, two approaches are possible. The first is to follow the keyboard CHARACTER with an asterisk and then a length expressed as an unsigned positive integer. The length applies to each variable name in the list. For example, the following CHARACTER statement specifies names for three character variables each of length 12:

```
CHARACTER*12 X,Y,Z
```

Another approach is to include a separate length specification for each variable. Each variable name in the list is followed by an asterisk and then a length. The following statement illustrates this approach:

```
CHARACTER NAME*18,DATE*6
```

This statement specifies two character variable names: NAME, of length 18, and DATE, of length 6.

The two approaches for specifying length can be used in the same statement. Any variable name without its own length specification has the length given after the keyword CHARACTER. Other variable names have the length specification given with the name. For example, in the following statement P has a length of 8, Q and R have lengths of 10, and S has a length of 2:

```
CHARACTER*10 P*8,Q,R,S*2
```

Character variable names are used for input and output of character data and for processing character data. The remainder of this section describes character data I/O, and subsequent sections discuss character data processing.

List-directed I/O of character data

With list-directed I/O, character data is read and printed by using character variable names in the READ and PRINT statements. All character variable names must first be specified in CHARACTER statements. Values for character variable names are read with the READ statement. The values are printed using a PRINT statement. As an example, the following simple program reads a four-character value, assigns it to the variable named N, and then prints the value of N:

```
CHARACTER*4 N
READ *,N
PRINT *,N
STOP
END
```

Notice that N is first specified as a character variable name in a CHARACTER statement. Then the input and output are performed.

Character input data must be enclosed in apostrophes. As we saw in Section 2-3, this is called a character constant. For example, if the value to be read for N in the previous program is JOHN, then this value must be recorded in the input record as 'JOHN'. In this example the value is the same length (4) as the character variable. If the input value has fewer characters than the length of the character variable, the value is assigned to the leftmost part of the variable and blanks are added on the right to fill out the entire length. Thus, in the previous example, if the input data is 'ED', the value of N after execution of the READ statement is EDbb (b = blank). If the input value has more characters than the length of the character variable, the left part of the input data is assigned to the variable. For example, if the input is 'SALLY', the value of N after execution of the device in the previous program is SALL.

With character data output, the value that is printed is whatever the variable is equal to. In the previous example, if N is equal to JOHN, this is the value printed. Note that surrounding apostrophes are *not* printed. If extra blanks have been added because the input data is shorter than the length of the character variable, these blanks appear in the output.

Any printable characters can be used in character data. If an apostrophe is to be included within character input data, it must be represented by two successive apostrophes. For example, if the value to be read by the previous program is ED'S, the input data must be 'ED''S'. The value of N will be ED'S after execution of the READ statement. Notice that the apostrophe counts as one of the characters and thus the value's length is four in this example. When printed, the value of N will appear as ED'S with a single apostrophe.

More than one character value can be read or written with one statement. In addition, character and numeric data can be read and written with the same statement. For example, the following program reads and writes two character values and one numeric value:

```
REAL GPA
CHARACTER NAME*18,DATE*14
READ *,NAME,DATE,GPA
PRINT *,NAME,DATE,GPA
STOP
END
```

Input data for this program must be separated by commas or blanks. For example, the following would be acceptable input for this program:

```
'JOHN SMITH','AUG 5, 1966',3.45
```

The output appears as

```
JOHN SMITH        AUG 5, 1966   3.45
```

(The actual format of the output may be different on different computers.)

Figure 8-1 shows a program that includes list-directed character I/O. (This program is similar to the one in Figure 2-16.) The input to the program consists of one record for each student with the student's identification number, name, and scores on two tests. The student's name is character data; all other input values are numeric data. Note in the input data in Figure 8-1(b) that the student's name is enclosed in apostrophes but the other data is not. The program reads and prints the data in each input record. The program also uses character constants to print headings and other descriptive output.

Figure 8-1. An illustrative program with list-directed character I/O

```
C  PROGRAM TO LIST STUDENT NUMBERS, NAMES, AND TEST SCORES
      INTEGER ID
      REAL SCR1,SCR2
      CHARACTER*12 NAME
      PRINT *,'                    TEST SCORE SUMMARY'
      PRINT *
   10 READ (*,*,END=20) ID,NAME,SCR1,SCR2
      PRINT *,'ID = ',ID,'  NAME = ',NAME,
     1        '  1ST SCORE = ',SCR1,'  2ND SCORE = ',SCR2
      GO TO 10
   20 PRINT *
      PRINT *,'END OF OUTPUT'
      STOP
      END
```

(a) The program

```
12841,'JOHN DOE',98,83
20853,'MARY ROE',92,85
23619,'ARTHUR SMITH',78,73
28900,'SALLY JONES',87,91
31072,'ROBERT JACKSON',82,87
```

(b) Input data

```
                   TEST SCORE SUMMARY

ID = 12841  NAME = JOHN DOE      1ST SCORE = 98. 2ND SCORE = 83.
ID = 20853  NAME = MARY ROE      1ST SCORE = 92. 2ND SCORE = 85.
ID = 23619  NAME = ARTHUR SMITH  1ST SCORE = 78. 2ND SCORE = 73.
ID = 28900  NAME = SALLY JONES   1ST SCORE = 87. 2ND SCORE = 91.
ID = 31072  NAME = ROBERT JACKS  1ST SCORE = 82. 2ND SCORE = 87.

END OF OUTPUT
```

(c) Output

List-directed character I/O can be used in programs that involve batch or interactive processing. All of the rules are the same. With interactive input this can create a problem because the terminal operator must remember to enclose any character data in apostrophes. Because errors could be made in doing this, it is usually best not to use list-directed input for character data in an interactive program. Instead, formatted input should be used.

Formatted I/O of character data

With formatted character I/O, character variable names are used in READ and WRITE statements. All character variable names must first be specified in CHARACTER statements. The A-format code is used in the FORMAT statement to describe the input or output format. (The A signifies *alphanumeric data,* which is another name for character data.) The syntax of the A-format code is as follows:

> A or A*w*
>
> where *w* is the width of the field.

A-format code may be used for both input and output.

When the A-format code is used without a width specification, the field width is given by the length of the character variable. For example, consider the following program:

```
      CHARACTER*4 N
      READ (5,100) N
      WRITE (6,200) N
      STOP
100   FORMAT (A)
200   FORMAT (1X,A)
      END
```

This program reads a character data field for N in A-format and then writes the value of N. Because the format code does not specify a width, the field width is assumed to be the length of the character variable named N. In this case the length is 4. Hence the first four characters in the input record are read and assigned to N. Assume that the input data is recorded as

123456789...

| JOHN |

Then the value of N after execution of the READ statement is JOHN. (Note that the character data is *not* enclosed in apostrophes. Apostrophes around character input data are only used with list-directed input.) The WRITE statement writes the value of N in the first four positions. (The 1X code is used to skip the first character in the output record.) The printed output from this program is

123456789...

| JOHN |

If a field width is given in the A-format code, it indicates the width of the input or output field. When the width is the same as the length of the character variable, the code functions the same as if it did not have a field width. Thus, if the code A4 were used in the two FORMAT statements in the previous program, the result would be the same.

If the field width in the A-format code is less than the character variable's length, only the number of characters indicated by the width are read or written. For input, the data is read and assigned to the left-most part of the character variable with blanks added on the right to fill out the variable. For example, consider the following statements:

```
      CHARACTER*4 N
      READ (5,101) N
101 FORMAT (A2)
```

In this example N has a length of 4 but its value is read in format A2. Assume that the input data is recorded as

```
    123456789...
   ┌─────────
   │ ED|
   │
```

The READ statement reads the first two characters in the input record, assigns the data to N, and fills out the value of N with blanks. Hence N is equal to EDbb (b = blank) after execution of the READ statement. On output, only the left-most characters of the variable are printed up to the width given in the A-format code. Thus, if N is equal to JOHN and we write it in format A2, only the letters JO are written.

If the field width is greater than the length of the character variable, then, for input, the entire field is read. However, the value assigned to the variable is taken from the right-most part of the field. For example, consider the following statements:

```
      CHARACTER*4, N
      READ (5,103) N
103 FORMAT (A10)
```

In this example N is of length 4, but the field is 10 characters wide. Assume that the input data is recorded as

```
    123456789....
   ┌─────────────
   │ JOHN SMITH|
   │
```

All 10 characters are read from the record, but only the right-most 4 are assigned to N. Hence, after execution of the READ statement, N has a value of MITH. On output, if the field width is greater than the length of the character variable, the data is written right-justified. For example, assume that the following statements appear after the preceding READ statement:

```
      WRITE (6,105) N
105 FORMAT (1X,A8)
```

Then the printed output is

```
    123456789...
   ┌─────────
   │    MITH|
   │
```

In most cases the situations discussed in the last two paragraphs should be avoided. This can be done by ensuring that the length of the character variable is the same as the field width given in the A-format code.

A character constant can be included in a WRITE statement if a corresponding A-format code appears in the FORMAT statement. The effect is the same as if the character constant were used in the FORMAT statement. To illustrate this, consider the following statements from an example in Section 6-4:

```
      WRITE (6,35) X
   35 FORMAT (1X,'THE SOLUTION IS',2X,F6.2)
```

These statements can be rewritten with the character constant in the WRITE statement instead of in the FORMAT statement. The modified statements are

```
      WRITE (6,35) 'THE SOLUTION IS',X
   35 FORMAT (1X,A,2X,F6.2)
```

In this case, the character constant 'THE SOLUTION IS' is written in format A and the value of X is written in format F6.2. Note that we could use format A15 for the character constant because the constant contains 15 characters. If we had used an A-format code with a width not equal to 15, the rules discussed earlier for field widths that are less than or greater than the character data's length would apply.

Figure 8-2 shows a program with formatted character I/O. (This program is similar to the one in Figure 6-12.) Input to the program consists of one record for each student giving the student's identification number in positions 1 through 5, name in positions 6 through 17, and scores on two tests in positions 18 through 22 and 23 through 27, respectively. Output consists of a main heading, headings for the columns of output, one line for each input record giving the input data, and a final output line. Note that the program uses A-format for input and output of the student's name, and I- and F-format for the other data. In addition, character constants are included in some FORMAT statements to write the headings and other descriptive output.

Formatted character I/O can be used effectively in programs that involve batch or interactive processing. With interactive input, character data can be entered at the terminal as we would normally write it. For example, consider the program in Figure 8-3. This program displays prompts requesting a person's first and last names. After each prompt the respective data is read and assigned to a character variable name. The first name can be up to 8 characters long and the last name can be at most 10 characters long. (Note that no apostrophes are used around the character input data.) Finally, the input data is displayed with an appropriate message. Although this program is very short, it illustrates the idea of interactive I/O that involves character data.

Figure 8-2. An illustrative program with formatted character I/O

```
C   PROGRAM TO LIST STUDENT NUMBERS, NAMES, AND TEST SCORES
        INTEGER ID
        REAL SCR1,SCR2
        CHARACTER*12 NAME
        WRITE (6,150)
        WRITE (6,160)
        WRITE (6,170)
     10 READ (5,100,END=20) ID,NAME,SCR1,SCR2
          WRITE (6,200) ID,NAME,SCR1,SCR2
        GO TO 10
     20 WRITE (6,250)
        STOP
    100 FORMAT (I5,A12,2F5.1)
    150 FORMAT ('1',13X,'TEST SCORE SUMMARY')
    160 FORMAT ('0',2X,'ID',8X,'NAME',8X,'1ST TEST',2X,'2ND TEST')
    170 FORMAT (' ')
    200 FORMAT (' ',I5,3X,A12,5X,F5.1,5X,F5.1)
    250 FORMAT ('0','END OF OUTPUT')
        END
```

(a) The program

```
21167MIKE JOHNSON 89.5 94.0
25701SUE ROBERTS  83.0 87.5
28145JANET WONG   87.0 76.0
30074BRIAN DAVIS  71.5 76.5
34230BETH LEE     92.0 96.0
```

(b) Input data

```
               TEST SCORE SUMMARY

     ID         NAME       1ST TEST  2ND TEST

    21167    MIKE JOHNSON     89.5      94.0
    25701    SUE ROBERTS      83.0      87.5
    28145    JANET WONG       87.0      76.0
    30074    BRIAN DAVIS      71.5      76.5
    34230    BETH LEE         92.0      96.0

END OF OUTPUT
```

(c) Output

8-2. Comparing character data

One of the important uses of character data is in relational expressions. Character constants and variable names can appear on both sides of a relational operator. The result is that the character data is compared to determine the truth value of the relational expression. All six of the relational operators discussed in Section 4-1 can be used with character data. For example, the

Figure 8-3. An interactive program with formatted character I/O

```
C  INTERACTIVE PROGRAM TO DISPLAY A NAME
       CHARACTER FIRST*8,LAST*10
       WRITE (*,100) 'WHAT IS YOUR FIRST NAME?'
       READ (*,110) FIRST
       WRITE (*,100) 'WHAT IS YOUR LAST NAME?'
       READ (*,120) LAST
       WRITE (*,130) 'YOUR NAME IS',FIRST,LAST
       STOP
  100 FORMAT (A)
  110 FORMAT (A8)
  120 FORMAT (A10)
  130 FORMAT (/A,1X,A8,1X,A10)
       END
```

(a) The program

```
WHAT IS YOUR FIRST NAME?
? JAMES
WHAT IS YOUR LAST NAME?
? JOHNSON

YOUR NAME IS JAMES    JOHNSON
```

(b) Interactive input and output

following are valid relational expressions (assuming all variable names are of character type):

```
NAME.EQ.'JOHN'
RES.NE.'YES'
    S.LT.T
  'A'.LE.B
'WXYZ'.GT.U
   V.GE.'AA'
```

This section explains the meaning of such expressions.

Equal comparison

When the .EQ. or .NE. relational operator is used with character data, a comparison is made to determine if the data consists of identical characters in identical positions. If they do, the values are equal. However, if they are not identical, they are not equal. For example, in the expression NAME.EQ.'JOHN', if the value of NAME is JOHN, the expression is true, but if the name is JEAN, the expression is false.

Figure 8-4 shows an example of the use of this type of comparison in a program that determines tuition for a college student. In this example, each input record contains a student's identification number and his or her home state which is a two-character value. Tuition is based on whether or not the

Figure 8-4. A tuition calculation program with character data comparison

```
C  TUITION CALCULATION PROGRAM
      INTEGER SNUM
      REAL TUIT
      CHARACTER*2 STATE
   10 READ (*,*,END=20) SNUM,STATE
      IF (STATE.EQ.'CA') THEN
         TUIT=350.00
      ELSE
         TUIT=850.00
      END IF
      PRINT *,'STUDENT NUMBER = ',SNUM,'  TUITION = ',TUIT
      GO TO 10
   20 STOP
      END
```

(a) The program

```
2345,'CA'
4567,'IL'
6789,'CA'
8901,'NY'
```

(b) Input data

```
STUDENT NUMBER = 2345  TUITION = 350.
STUDENT NUMBER = 4567  TUITION = 850.
STUDENT NUMBER = 6789  TUITION = 350.
STUDENT NUMBER = 8901  TUITION = 850.
```

(c) Output

student is a California resident. If the student is a state resident the tuition is $350.00. Out-of-state residents pay a tuition of $850.00. The tuition is determined in the IF statement by comparing the character variable named STATE with the character constant 'CA'. Note that we could have used the .NE. relational operator in this example. Then the IF statement would be coded as

```
IF (STATE.NE.'CA') THEN
   TUIT=850.00
ELSE
   TUIT=350.00
END IF
```

All types of characters — letters, digits, and special characters including blanks — can be compared. For example, the following expression is valid (assuming ID is a character variable name):

```
ID.EQ.'X3 $5'
```

This expression is true if the value of ID is the characters X, 3, blank, $, and 5 in that order. As another example, the following relational expression determines if the character variable named XCODE, which has a length of 4, is not equal to all blanks:

```
XCODE.NE.'    '
```

Note that the character constant in this case contains all blank spaces.

If the character data values being compared are not the same length, blanks are added on the right of the shorter value until it is the same length as the longer one. Then the comparison is made. Thus the previous example could be coded with just one blank in the character constant as follows:

```
XCODE.NE.' '
```

No matter what the length of XCODE, the character constant will be extended with blanks on the right until it is the same length as XCODE before the comparison is done.

When comparing character data it is important to use only character constants and variable names. We cannot compare character data with numeric (integer or real) data. For example, if AMT is a character variable name, the following relational expression is invalid because 123 is a numeric constant:

```
123.EQ.AMT
```

This does not mean, however, that we cannot determine if AMT equals 123. To do this we must make 123 a character constant by putting apostrophes around it. Hence the following relational expression is valid:

```
'123'.EQ.AMT
```

Greater than and less than comparison

When the relational operator is .LT., .LE., .GT., or .GE., the evaluation of the relational expression is based on an ordering of the characters, which is called the *collating sequence*. If we just consider the letters of the alphabet, the collating sequence is the same as the alphabetical order. That is, one character value is less than another if it appears before the other in an alphabetized list. Thus JEAN is less than JOHN which is less than MARY. Hence the expression NAME.LT.'JOHN' is true if NAME is JEAN, but false if it is MARY.

The way the computer evaluates this is by comparing the data character-for-character, left-to-right. As soon as the computer finds two corresponding characters that are not equal to each other, the computer determines which value is the greater on the basis of which of the unequal characters comes later in the alphabet. Thus, in comparing JEAN and JOHN, the computer examines the first character of each and determines that they are equal. It then compares the second character of each and determines that they are not equal. Then, because letter O comes later in the alphabet than E, the computer indicates that JOHN is greater than JEAN.

If a blank is included in the data, the blank is considered to be less than any other character. Thus JOHNbb (b = blank) is less than JOHNNY. As with equal comparisons, when the character data being compared are of unequal length, the shorter value is extended with blanks until the values are of equal length before the comparison is made. Thus, in comparing JON with JOHN, the former would be extended to JONb (b = blank) and then the comparison would be made. In this case, JONb would be greater than JOHN because the third character of JONb is greater than the third character of JOHN.

When character data consists entirely of numeric characters, the data is evaluated in the same way as alphabetic data. The collating sequence is such that 0 is less than 1, 1 is less than 2, and so forth up to 9. Thus 123 is less than 456 as we would expect. However, because a blank is less than any other character, b9 is less than 8b.

If greater than or less than comparisons are used between character data consisting of both letters and digits or containing special characters, the result depends on the computer being used. This is because different computers use different collating sequences for these characters. Thus, in general, we cannot say whether X37Z is greater than or less than XM7Z. The answer depends on whether the digit 3 is greater than or less than the letter M in the collating sequence of the computer being used. Other examples of character data comparison are shown in Figure 8-5.

Figure 8-5. Examples of character data comparison

Relational expression	Truth value
`'ED JONES'.LT.'ED SMITH'`	true
`'EDWARD JONES'.LT.'ED SMITH'`	false
`'1234'.GT.'4567'`	false
`'1234'.GT.' 4567'`	true
`'MARY '.EQ.'MARY'`	true
`'MARY '.EQ.' MARY'`	false
`'    '.NE.' '`	false
`'X37Z'.NE.'3AY7'`	true

8-3. Processing character data

So far we have only used character data for input and output and in comparisons. Character data can also be processed much like we process numeric data. In this section we describe the FORTRAN elements needed for processing character data.

The character assignment statement

Character data can be assigned to a character variable name with an assignment statement. The syntax is as follows:

```
character variable name = character expression
```

On the left of the equal sign must be a character variable name; on the right must be a character expression. A *character expression* is an expression that has a character value. So far the only things we have described that can be used for character expressions are character constants and character variable names. Later we will see that more complex character expressions can be created.

To illustrate the character assignment statement, assume that STATE1 and STATE2 have been specified as character variable names in a CHARACTER statement. Then the following are valid character assignment statements:

```
STATE1='CALIF'
STATE2=STATE1
```

The effect of the first statement is that the value of the character constant 'CALIF' is assigned to the character variable named STATE1. The second statement causes the value of STATE1 to be assigned to STATE2.

If the length of the character value on the right of the equal sign in a character assignment statement is the same as the length of the character variable on the left, the assignment takes place as we would expect. That is, the character data identified on the right is assigned to the variable name on the left. If the length of the element on the right is *less* than the length of the variable on the left, the character data is assigned to the left part of the left-hand variable and blanks are added on the right to fill out this variable. That is, the character data is left-justified and blanks are added on the right. For example, if STATE1 has a length of 10, then, after execution of the first assignment statement just given, STATE1 will be equal to CALIF*bbbbb* (*b* = blank). When the length of the right-hand element is *greater* than the length of the variable, the effect is that the extra characters on the right are truncated before the assignment takes place. Thus, if STATE2 in the example has a length of 3, then, after execution of the second assignment statement, STATE2 will have a value of CAL.

Any type of character data can be assigned to a character variable. The data may consist of alphabetic, numeric, and special characters, including blanks. For example, if ACODE is a character variable name, the following statement is valid:

```
ACODE='P85 Q'
```

It is possible to assign all blanks to a character variable. For example, assume that BDATA is a character variable name. Then the following statement assigns blank spaces to this variable:

```
BDATA='
```

It is important to distinguish between character constants and numeric (i.e., integer and real) constants and between character variable names and variable names for numeric data. For example, assume that A is a character variable name and B is a numeric variable name and consider the following statements:

```
A='15'
B=15
```

The first statement assigns a character constant to a character variable name; the second statement assigns a numeric constant to a numeric variable name. Even though the characters in the constants are the same (i.e., 15), they represent different types of data. The character constant ('15') can be assigned only to a character variable name and the numeric constant (15) can be assigned only to a numeric variable name. In addition, character constants and variable names *cannot* be used in calculations; only numeric constants and variable names can be used for this purpose.

To illustrate the use of the character assignment statement, Figure 8-6 shows a program that sorts three names into alphabetical order. In Section 7-4 we discussed a program that sorts three numbers into ascending numerical order (see Figure 7-7). By using character variable names instead of numeric variable names, we have a program that sorts character data. The program in Figure 8-6 reads three character values that represent names. The values may be in any order initially. Through a series of comparisons, the values are switched until they are arranged in the required sequence. The switching is done with character assignment statements.

The PARAMETER statement with character data

We can use the PARAMETER statement to assign values to constant names for character data. The syntax is the same as the PARAMETER statement for numeric data (see Section 3-5) except that character constant names and character constants must be used. A *character constant name* has the same syntax as a character variable name and must be specified in a CHARACTER statement before it is used in a PARAMETER statement.

Figure 8-6. A program to sort three names

```
C   PROGRAM TO SORT THREE NAMES
      CHARACTER*4 NAME1,NAME2,NAME3,TEMP
      READ *,NAME1,NAME2,NAME3
      IF (NAME1.GT.NAME2) THEN
        TEMP=NAME1
        NAME1=NAME2
        NAME2=TEMP
      END IF
      IF (NAME2.GT.NAME3) THEN
        TEMP=NAME2
        NAME2=NAME3
        NAME3=TEMP
      END IF
      IF (NAME1.GT.NAME2) THEN
        TEMP=NAME1
        NAME1=NAME2
        NAME2=TEMP
      END IF
      PRINT *,NAME1,'  ',NAME2,'  ',NAME3
      STOP
      END
```

(a) The program

```
'MARY','JOHN','JEAN'
```

(b) Input data

```
JEAN  JOHN  MARY
```

(c) Output

As an example, consider the following statements:

```
CHARACTER NAME*4,STATE*2
PARAMETER (NAME='JOHN',STATE='CA')
```

The CHARACTER statement specifies that NAME and STATE are of type character and have lengths of 4 and 2, respectively. The PARAMETER statement indicates that these are constant names with values of JOHN and CA, respectively. Note that we must use character constants in the PARAMETER statement because the constant names are of type character.

Substrings

A *substring* is a group of one or more adjacent characters in a character data value.* For example, consider the character data NEW YORK. The following are substrings of this:

---

* Often a character data value is called a *string*. Hence a substring is a part of a string.

```
       NEW
       OR
       YORK
       EW YO
        W
       NEW YORK
```

Note that any single character of a character data value is a substring, and that the entire character data is a substring of itself. In addition, any group consisting of characters that are adjacent to each other forms a substring. If characters are not adjacent to each other, they do not form a substring. Thus NOR is *not* a substring of NEW YORK even though the characters come from the data.

In FORTRAN a substring is identified by a *substring name*. A substring name is formed from a character variable name followed by the position of the substring enclosed in parentheses. For example, the following are valid substring names:

```
       STATE1(1:3)
       STATE2(5:8)
       STATE2(2:6)
```

The characters in a string are assumed to be numbered from left to right beginning with one for the first character. In a substring name the first number in parentheses gives the position of the first character in the substring and the second number specifies the position of the last character in the substring. The numbers must be separated by a colon. Thus, in the first example we are naming the substring consisting of the first character in STATE1 through the third character. If STATE1 equals CALIF, then STATE1(1:3) is CAL. In the second example, we are referring to the fifth through eighth characters in STATE2. If STATE2 equals NEW YORK, then STATE2(5:8) is YORK. (Note that the blank counts as one of the characters in the string.) The final example identifies the substring consisting of characters 2 through 6 of STATE2. For our data, STATE2(2:6) would be EW YO.

To identify a substring at the beginning of a character data value, we can leave out the first term in parentheses. Thus we could code our first example as STATE1(:3). Similarly, when the end of the character data is desired, the last term can be left out. We can code our second example as STATE2(5:) because we want the last part of STATE2 beginning with the fifth character. A substring consisting of a single character is indicated by a substring name with the same beginning and ending positions. Thus STATE1(3:3) refers to the third character in STATE1. Other examples of substring names are shown in Figure 8-7.

We can use integer variable names to identify beginning and ending positions in a substring name. For example, assuming that I and J are integer names, the substring name S(I:J) is valid and refers to the Ith through Jth

Figure 8-7. Examples of substring names

CHARACTER*10 ST
ST='WASHINGTON'

Substring name	Substring
ST(3:7)	SHING
ST(1:4) ST(:4)	WASH
ST(8:10) ST(8:)	TON
ST(5:5)	I

characters of S. Other examples are as follows (assume that I, J, K, L, and M are integer and T, U, V, W, and X are character type):

```
T(4:M)
U(L:8)
V(:K)
W(J:)
X(I:I)
```

In the last example, the Ith character is identified by the substring name. As we will see, this is often a useful form for a substring name.

Any integer arithmetic expression can be used in a substring name. For example, the name $S(J-2:3*I+1)$ is valid if I and J are integer. Expressions are first evaluated and then the values are used to identify the substring. In general the values in a substring name must be between 1 and the length of the string, and the first value (the starting position) must be less than or equal to the second value (the ending position).

Substring names can be used any place in a program that a character variable name can appear. Thus we can use substring names in READ, PRINT, and WRITE statements, character assignment statements, and IF statements. For example, the following are all valid uses of substring names (assuming I is integer and all other variables are character):

```
READ (5,100) S(5:10),T(4:I)
WRITE (6,200) STATE1,STATE2(5:)
U(4:6)='AND'
T(2:2)=S(4:4)
IF (RES(3:5).NE.'YES') THEN
```

The INDEX function

Sometimes it is useful to be able to locate a substring in a character data value. This can be done with the INDEX function. This function searches through character data for a substring. If the substring is found, the function gives the position of the first character in the substring. This position is an integer value. If the substring is not found, the function returns a value of zero. For example, consider the following statement:

```
LOC=INDEX(S,'END')
```

The INDEX function searches through the character data named S for the substring END. If END is found, it returns the position of the first character of the substring, and in this case the value is assigned to the integer variable named LOC. For example, if S has the value THE END IS NEAR, then INDEX will return the number 5 because END begins in the fifth position. If the substring appears more than once in the data, only the first occurrence is found. If the substring cannot be found, INDEX indicates a value of zero.

In using the INDEX function, the first entry in parentheses identifies the character data to be searched and the second entry is the substring to be located. Either entry may be a character constant, character variable name, or substring name.

The LEN function

Sometimes when manipulating character data we need to know the length of the data. We can get this information from various sources in the program. However, it is often easiest to determine the length with the LEN function. For example, the following statement assigns the length of the character data identified by the name S to the integer variable named LS:

```
LS=LEN(S)
```

If S is of length 8, LS will be equal to 8 after execution of this statement. The entry in parentheses may be a character variable name, character constant, or a substring name. For example, we can use LEN(S(5:)) to determine the length of the substring beginnning with the fifth character through the end of the character data named S. The result of the LEN function is an integer value.

Concatenation of character data

Concatenation is the operation of putting together two character data values to form one. For example, concatenating the character data ABC and XYZ produces ABCXYZ. To concatenate two values in FORTRAN we use the *concatenation operator*. This operator consists of two slashes (//). For example, to concatenate ABC and XYZ, we can write the following:

```
'ABC'//'XYZ'
```

On each side of the concatenation operator may be a character constant, character variable name, or substring name. For example, each of the following is a valid use of the concatenation operator (assuming S, T, U, and V are character variable names):

```
S//T
U//'1234'
'MY '//V
U(4:7)//S(:3)
V(4:)//T
```

In each of these cases a new character data value is formed consisting of the character data identified by the constant, variable name, or substring name on the left of the operator followed by the data identified on the right. Thus if S equals ABC and T equals XYZ, then S//T is ABCXYZ and T//S is XYZABC.

Character expressions

When we use a concatenation operator we form a type of character expression. In general, a *character expression* is a character constant, character variable name, substring name, or any of these in conjunction with the concatenation operator. We also can have multiple concatenations in a character expression. For example, the following is a valid character expression:

```
U//'ABC'//T(6:12)//S
```

The character values identified in the expression are concatenated from left to right. Other examples of character expressions involving concatenation are shown in Figure 8-8.

A character expression by itself is not a FORTRAN statement. Rather it is used as part of a statement. For example, we may assign the value of a character expression to a character variable name with a character assignment statement. Thus the following is a valid FORTRAN statement (assume all variable names are character type):

```
S=T//U//V
```

Figure 8-8. Examples of character expressions

```
CHARACTER*10 ST
ST='WASHINGTON'
```

Character expression	Result
ST//' STATE'	WASHINGTON STATE
'GEORGE '//ST	GEORGE WASHINGTON
ST(:4)//ST(5:7)//ST(8:)	WASHINGTON
ST(:3)//' '//ST(5:5)//ST(8:8)//'?'	WAS IT?
ST(10:10)//ST(9:9)//ST(8:8)	NOT

The character data identified in the character expression are concatenated and the resulting string is assigned to S. We can also use a character expression in a relational expression. For example, consider the following relational expression:

```
U//V//W(:10).EQ.A//'AA'
```

The character data in each of the character expressions are concatenated. The resulting character values are then compared to determine if they are equal.

As an example of the use of a character expression consider the problem of rearranging the order of a person's name. Assume that LSTNAM, FSTNAM, and MI are character variable names that identify a person's last name, first name, and middle initial, respectively. The problem is to create a character value consisting of the person's first name followed by a space, then the person's middle initial followed by a period and a space, and then the person's last name. The result should be assigned to the character variable named NAME. The following statement accomplishes this:

```
NAME=FSTNAM//' '//MI//'. '//LSTNAM
```

Note that we must put the period and spaces in the proper place in the expression so that the final result is the way we want it.

An illustrative program

To illustrate some of the character data processing features discussed here we consider a text analysis program. Input to the program is a line of text (that is, a sentence) up to 80 characters long that ends with a period. The program must count the number of blank spaces in the line and print this count along with the original text.

Figure 8-9 shows a program that accomplishes this. The program first specifies that LINE is a character variable name of length 80. Then a line of text is read and assigned to LINE. If the first five characters of the line consist of the word STOP followed by a period, the program terminates. That is, STOP with a period serves as a trailer value. If the trailer value is not read, the line is written and a counter (COUNT) is set equal to 0. The program then enters a loop that is executed once for each character in the line. Each time through the loop, the next character in the line is examined to determine if it is a period. This is done by using the substring name LINE(I:I) where I is an integer variable that is initially one and is incremented by one each time the loop is executed. Thus, when I is one, LINE(I:I) identifies the first character in the data; when I is two, LINE(I:I) refers to the second character; and so forth for the other values of I. If LINE(I:I) is not a period but is a blank, the counter (COUNT) is incremented. This is repeated for each I until a period is found. After branching out of the loop, the program

Figure 8-9. A text analysis program

```
C   TEXT ANALYSIS PROGRAM
        CHARACTER*80 LINE
        INTEGER COUNT,I
    10 READ (5,100) LINE
        IF (LINE(1:5).EQ.'STOP.') GO TO 40
        WRITE (6,200) LINE
        COUNT=0
        I=1
    20  IF (LINE(I:I).EQ.'.') GO TO 30
            IF (LINE(I:I).EQ.' ') THEN
                COUNT=COUNT+1
            END IF
            I=I+1
            GO TO 20
    30   WRITE (6,210) COUNT
        GO TO 10
    40 STOP
   100 FORMAT (A80)
   200 FORMAT ('0',A80)
   210 FORMAT (' THERE ARE ',I2,' BLANKS IN THIS LINE.')
        END
```

(a) The program

```
        NOW IS THE TIME.
        FOUR SCORE AND SEVEN YEARS AGO.
        THE END.
        HELP.
        STOP.
```

(b) Input data

```
NOW IS THE TIME.
THERE ARE  3 BLANKS IN THIS LINE.

FOUR SCORE AND SEVEN YEARS AGO.
THERE ARE  5 BLANKS IN THIS LINE.

THE END.
THERE ARE  1 BLANKS IN THIS LINE.

HELP.
THERE ARE  0 BLANKS IN THIS LINE.
```

(c) Output

writes the value of COUNT which is the count of the number of blanks in the line.

This program illustrates one use of the character manipulation features in FORTRAN. There are many other interesting and practical applications of character data processing. Some of these are discussed in the programming problems at the end of the chapter.

8-4. Logical expressions

There are several types of expressions in FORTRAN. In Chapter 3 we discussed arithmetic expressions. An arithmetic expression is formed from numeric constants and variables, and arithmetic operators. The evaluation of an arithmetic expression results in a numeric value.

Relational expressions were discussed in Chapter 4. A relational expression is formed by combining arithmetic expressions with relational operators. A relational expression has a *truth value;* that is, it is either true or false.

Relational expressions are used in *logical expressions.* In fact, a relational expression by itself is one form of a logical expression. More complex logical expressions are formed by combining several relational expressions with logical operators. The resulting expression is then evaluated to determine its truth value.

Logical operators and simple logical expressions

The *logical operators* used in FORTRAN and their meanings are as follows:

Logical Operator	*Meaning*
.AND.	Are both expressions true?
.OR.	Is one or the other expression or both true?
.NOT.	Is the expression not true?

Note that each logical operator begins and ends with a period.

The following logical expression uses the .AND. logical operator:

```
A.GT.B.AND.C.LT.5.1
```

Another way to code such expressions is to enclose the relational expressions in parentheses as in the following example:

```
(A.GT.B).AND.(C.LT.5.1)
```

This form yields the same result and is usually easier to understand.

In evaluating a logical expression with an .AND. operator, the truth values of the relational expressions are determined first. In the previous expression it is determined whether the value of A is greater than the value of B and whether the value of C is less than 5.1. Then the logical operator .AND. determines whether both relational expressions are true. If they are, the logical expression is true. If one or the other of the relational expressions or both are false, the logical expression is false.

Figure 8-10. Truth tables for the logical expressions

A	B	A.AND.B	A	B	A.OR.B	A	.NOT.A
T	T	T	T	T	T	T	F
T	F	F	T	F	T	F	T
F	T	F	F	T	T		
F	F	F	F	F	F		

The .OR. logical operator works differently than the .AND. operator. The following logical expression illustrates its use:

    (5.EQ.K).OR.(X.NE.Y)

Again, the truth values of the relational expressions are evaluated first. Then the logical operator .OR. determines whether one or the other relational expression or both are true. If one of these conditions exists, the logical expression is true. Only if both relational expressions are false is the logical expression false.

The .AND. and .OR. operators each require that two relational expressions be evaluated. The logical operator .NOT. is used with only one relational expression. The following logical expression uses the .NOT. operator:

    .NOT.(D+E.GE.8.69)

In evaluating this logical expression, the value of the relational expression must first be determined. Then the .NOT. operator determines whether the relational expression is not true — in other words, false. If the relational expression is false, the logical expression is true. On the other hand, if the relational expression is true, the logical expression is false.

Logical operations can be summarized most easily with *truth tables*. Such tables show all possible combinations of truth values for relational expressions and the resulting truth values of the logical expessions. Figure 8-10 shows the truth tables for the .AND., .OR., and .NOT. logical operators. In this figure, A and B represent relational expressions with the values true or false.

Evaluation of complex logical expressions

Simple logical expressions of the type shown so far may be combined to form complex logical expressions. The following examples are valid logical expressions:

    (K.GT.7).AND..NOT.(A.LT.5.)
    (C.EQ.X).OR.(M.LT.N).OR..NOT.(A-5.5.GT.Z)
    3.7.NE.W.AND.4.2.NE.X.OR.3.7.NE.Z

Note that the only times that two logical operators may appear one after the other are in the following cases:

```
.AND..NOT.
.OR..NOT.
```

Any other combination of two logical operators is invalid. Three operators in sequence should never be coded.

In evaluating a logical expression the computer performs the operations in the following order:

1. Arithmetic expressions are evaluated to determine their numeric values.
2. Relational expressions are evaluated to determine their truth values.
3. Logical operators are evaluated in the following order:
   .NOT.
   .AND.
   .OR.

For example, consider the following logical expression:

```
A-5.5.LT.B.OR..NOT.6.3+C.GT.D.AND.12.5.EQ.E
```

First, the arithmetic expressions $A - 5.5$ and $6.3 + C$ are evaluated. Then the truth values of the relational expressions are determined. There are three relational expressions in this example:

```
A-5.5.LT.B
6.3+C.GT.D
12.5.EQ.E
```

Next, the truth value of

```
.NOT.6.3+C.GT.D
```

is determined. Then the .AND. logical operator is evaluated in the expression

```
.NOT.6.3+C.GT.D.AND.12.5.EQ.E
```

Finally, the .OR. operator is evaluated, yielding the truth value of the logical expressions. These steps are shown in Figure 8-11.

Parentheses may be used to modify the order in which operations are performed in a logical expression. Any logical expression that is contained in parentheses is evaluated before operations outside of the parentheses are performed. To illustrate, the following expression is a modification of the previous example:

```
A-5.5.LT.B.OR..NOT.(6.3+C.GT.D.AND.12.5.EQ.E)
```

Figure 8-11. Evaluation of a logical expression

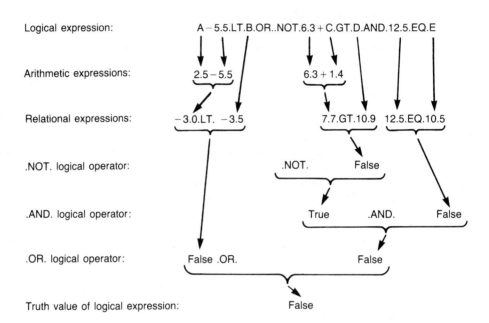

Values of variable names: A = 2.5, B = −3.5, C = 1.4, D = 10.9, E = 10.5

Logical expression: A − 5.5.LT.B.OR..NOT.6.3 + C.GT.D.AND.12.5.EQ.E

Arithmetic expressions: 2.5 − 5.5   6.3 + 1.4

Relational expressions: − 3.0.LT. −3.5   7.7.GT.10.9 12.5.EQ.10.5

.NOT. logical operator: .NOT.   False

.AND. logical operator: True   .AND.   False

.OR. logical operator: False .OR.   False

Truth value of logical expression: False

In this example, the truth value of the parenthetic expression is determined first. This includes the evaluation of the relational expressions within the parentheses and the .AND. operator. Then the operations outside of the parentheses are performed in the appropriate order. Figure 8-12 shows the evaluation steps for this example.

Extra parentheses are often used to clarify the meaning of a logical expression even though the order of evaluation of the expressions is not changed. For example, the following logical expression is evaluated in the same order as the previous example:

```
((A−5.5).LT.B).OR.(.NOT.(((6.3+C).GT.D).AND.(12.5.EQ.E)))
```

The primary use of logical expressions is in block and logical IF statements. In Chapter 4 we used only relational expressions in IF statements. In fact, any logical expression may be used in an IF statement. For example, the following are valid IF statements:

```
IF ((K.LE.5).OR.(M.LE.5)) THEN
IF (.NOT.((A.GT.B).AND.(A.GT.C))) THEN
IF((K1.EQ.1).OR.(K1.EQ.2).AND..NOT.(K2.EQ.1))PRINT *,X,Y
```

Figure 8-12. Evaluation of a logical expression containing parentheses

Values of variable names: A = 2.5, B = − 3.5, C = 1.4, D = 10.9, E = 10.5

Logical expression: A − 5.5.LT.B.OR..NOT.(6.3 + C.GT.D.AND.12.5.EQ.E)

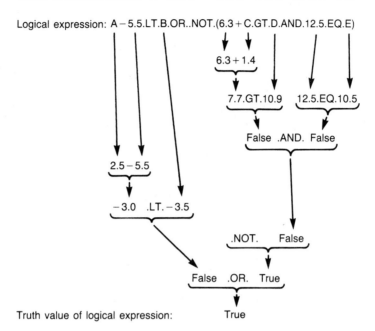

Truth value of logical expression: True

In each of these, the truth value of the logical expression is evaluated first. Then, if the expression is true, the statements in the true part of the decision are executed next. If the logical expression is false, these statements are skipped.

An illustrative program

As an example of the use of logical expressions in a program, consider a variation on the tuition calculation program discussed in Section 4-1 (see Figure 4-1). As before, we assume that the tuition is based on the number of units that the student is taking. However, the tuition is reduced by $250.00 for a scholarship if the student's identification number is between 3000 and 5999. The program for this problem is shown in Figure 8-13. Notice how the .AND. logical operator is used to test the identification number to see if it falls in the appropriate range.

Logical expressions are used in other statements besides the IF statement. For example, logical expressions are used in the WHILE statement, if it is available. Logical expressions are also used with several other logical programming features discussed in the following section.

Figure 8-13. A tuition calculation program

```
C   TUITION CALCULATION PROGRAM
        INTEGER SNUM
        REAL UNITS,TUIT
    10 READ (*,*,END=20) SNUM,UNITS
        IF (UNITS.LE.12.0) THEN
           TUIT=350.00
        ELSE
           TUIT=350.00+20.00*(UNITS-12.0)
        END IF
        IF ((SNUM.GE.3000).AND.(SNUM.LE.5999)) THEN
           TUIT=TUIT-250.00
        END IF
        PRINT *,'STUDENT NUMBER = ',SNUM,'  TUITION = ',TUIT
        GO TO 10
    20 STOP
        END
```

(a) The program

```
1234,6.
3456,15.
5678,12.
7890,12.5
```

(b) Input data

```
STUDENT NUMBER = 1234  TUITION = 350.
STUDENT NUMBER = 3456  TUITION = 160.
STUDENT NUMBER = 5678  TUITION = 100.
STUDENT NUMBER = 7890  TUITION = 360.
```

(c) Output

8-5. Processing logical data

As we know, decisions in a program are based on the truth or falsity of an expression. *True* and *false* are logical values. Logical data is data that can only have one of these values. In this section we discuss logical data processing in FORTRAN.

Logical constants and variable names

Integer and real constants and variable names are used to identify numeric data. Logical constants and variable names refer to logical data. A *logical constant* is a fixed truth value that is used in a statement. In FORTRAN, logical constants are coded .TRUE. and .FALSE.. Notice that each constant begins and ends with a period.

A *logical variable* is logical data that is identified by a *logical variable name*. The value of a logical variable may be either true or false. A logical variable name refers to the logical data. To specify a logical variable name, we use the LOGICAL statement. The syntax of this statement is as follows:

> LOGICAL *list*
>
> where *list* is a list of variable names separated
> by commas.

For example, the following statement identifies the names LA, P, and W2 as logical variable names:

```
LOGICAL LA,P,W2
```

Note that a variable name that has been specified as logical type cannot be used to refer to any other type of data. The LOGICAL statement is a type statement and therefore must appear at the beginning of the program before the first executable statement.

Logical constants and variable names may be used in logical expressions. For example, assume that the variable names LA, LB, and LC have been specified as logical type. Then the following are valid logical expressions (other variable names are numeric):

```
.TRUE.
LA
LB.OR.LC
(X*B).GT.-W.AND.LA
LC.AND..NOT.(LA.OR.(X.EQ.5))
```

A logical expression containing logical constants and variable names is evaluated following the same rules discussed in Section 8-4. Such a logical expression can be used in IF and other statements.

The logical assignment statement

An arithmetic assignment statement assigns the numeric value of an arithmetic expression to a numeric variable name. A logical assignment statement assigns the truth value of a logical expression to a logical variable name. The syntax of a logical assignment statement is as follows:

> *logical variable name = logical expression*

On the left of the equal sign must be a logical variable name. On the right is a logical expression. The following are examples of logical assignment statements (assume that LA, LB, and LC are logical variable names and other names are numeric):

```
LC=.FALSE.
LB=LA
LA=LC.AND..NOT.LB
LC=X.LT.Y
LB=((S*5.2).GE.7.3).OR.LB
LA=.NOT.LB
```

The expression on the right of the equal sign in a logical assignment statement must be a logical expression or the statement is invalid. For example, if LA is a logical variable name, the following statement is not valid because the expression on the right is an arithmetic expression:

```
LA=X*Y-3.5
```

Similarly, the variable name on the left of the equal sign in a logical assignment statement must be of logical type. The following example is invalid because it attempts to assign a logical value to a numeric variable name (X):

```
X=(K.EQ.5).OR.LB
```

One use of logical assignment statements is to save the result of a logical expression so that the expression need be evaluated only once. For example, assume that the expression

```
(N.EQ.1).OR.(N.EQ.2)
```

is used in several IF statements. We can reduce the coding required for the program by assigning the value of this expression to a logical variable name, then testing the variable name in the IF statements. The following statements illustrate this approach:

```
LOGICAL SAVE
        .
        .
        .
SAVE=(N.EQ.1).OR.(N.EQ.2)
        .
        .
        .
IF (SAVE) THEN
        .
        .
        .
IF (SAVE) THEN
        .
        .
        .
IF (SAVE) THEN
```

Each IF statement tests to see if the value of the logical variable named SAVE is true or false. Because SAVE equals the truth value of the logical expression (N.EQ.1).OR.(N.EQ.2), this is equivalent to testing this expression in the IF statements.

A similar use of the logical assignment statement is to set a flag in a program. A *flag* (also called a *signal* or a *switch*) is used to identify whether or not some condition has occurred during the processing of the program. For example, a flag may be used to signal the end of the input file.

When a flag is needed, a logical variable name can be used. The flag is usually assigned an initial value of false, indicating that the condition to be flagged has not occurred. Then at the appropriate points in the program, the condition can be checked and, if true, the flag is assigned a value of true. At any time during the processing, the flag can be tested to see whether or not the condition is true.

To illustrate this approach, assume that we need to flag the end-of-file condition in a program. Then the following statements might appear at appropriate points in the program:

```
LOGICAL EOF
EOF=.FALSE.
   .
   .
   .

READ (6,100) ID,...
IF (ID.EQ.9999) EOF=.TRUE.
   .
   .
   .

IF (EOF) WRITE (6,220) TOTAL
   .
   . .
   .

IF (EOF) THEN
```

In the sequence, EOF is the flag. Initially EOF is false. Each time an input record is read, we check the value of ID for a trailer value (9999) and set EOF to true when the end of the input file is reached. Then we test EOF in IF statements at various other points in the program.

The PARAMETER statement with logical data

The PARAMETER statement can be used to assign logical values to constant names for logical data. The syntax of the PARAMETER statement is the same as for numeric data (see Section 3-5) except that logical constant names and logical constants must be used. A *logical constant name* has the same syntax as a logical variable name and must be specified in a LOGICAL statement before it is used in a PARAMETER statement.

As an example, consider the following statements:

```
LOGICAL EOF,TOP
PARAMETER (EOF=.FALSE.,TOP=.TRUE.)
```

The LOGICAL statement specifies that EOF and TOP are of logical type. The PARAMETER statement indicates that these are constant names with values of false and true, respectively. Note that logical constants are used in the PARAMETER statement because the constant names are logical.

List-directed I/O of logical data

Logical data can be read and printed with list-directed I/O. To do this, logical variable names are used in the READ and PRINT statements. To illustrate, consider the following simple program:

```
LOGICAL X,Y,Z
READ *,X,Y,Z
PRINT *,X,Y,Z
STOP
END
```

This program causes three logical data values to be read and printed. Note that the variable names are specified in a LOGICAL statement at the beginning of the program.

Logical data can be recorded in several ways in input records. The basic rule is that each logical value must begin with a T or F (representing true or false) optionally preceded by a period. Any other characters can follow the T or F. For example, the input data for the previous program could be recorded as follows:

```
T,.FALSE.,TRUE
```

After this data is read, the value of X will be true, Y will be false, and Z will be true. Note that the first letter indicates the truth value. This first letter must be a T or F. The only character other than a blank space that can come before the T or F is a period. Any other symbol before the T or F causes an error. Thus the following input data is valid:

```
YES,NOT TRUE,$TRUE
```

After the T or F, however, can be any characters. Thus, the following data is valid:

```
TRUTH,FAILURE,.T$X37Z
```

Logical data is printed as the letter T or F. For example, assume that the previous program is executed and input data is supplied that causes X to be true, Y to be false, and Z to be true. Then the output appears as follows:

    T F T

Note that the output is separated by blank spaces. (The output format may be different on different computers.)

Formatted I/O of logical data

With formatted I/O, logical data is read and written by using logical variable names in READ and WRITE statements. In the FORMAT statement, input and output fields of logical data are specified by the L-format code. With this code, logical data can be read and assigned to logical variable names. Similarly, the values of logical variable names can be written in a format specified by the L-format code. The syntax of the L-format code is as follows:

> Lw
>
> where w is the width of the field.

For input, the L-format code specifies a field of w characters that must contain a T (true) or F (false) as the first nonblank character or a period as the first nonblank character followed by a T or F. Any other characters may follow the T or F. Blanks preceding the T or F and the characters following are optional. The T or F indicates the truth value of the field.

As an example, assume that A, B, and C have been declared as logical variable names. The following statements cause values to be read from a record and assigned to these names:

        READ (5,10) A,B,C
    10 FORMAT (L2,L3,L7)

The first input field is two positions wide; the second field occupies three positions; the third field is seven positions wide. The truth values of the fields are assigned to the logical variable names A, B, and C, respectively. Data may be recorded in the field in a variety of forms; the following is one possibility:

        123456789......

        | T | F | .FALSE. |

In this case, the value assigned to A is true; B and C are given values of false. The same values result if the data is recorded as follows:

```
123456789......
┌─────────────────────┐
│ T │.FX│ FT          │
```

Note that it is the *first nonblank* character (optionally preceded by a period) that indicates the truth value; other characters in the field have no effect on the value of the field. This first character must be a T or F; otherwise, an error occurs. Thus the following data results in an error when the third field is read:

```
123456789......
┌─────────────────────┐
│ TRFAI│.NOT T.        │
```

For output, only the character T or F is written, right-justified in the field. For example, consider the following statements:

```
    WRITE (6,20) A,B,C
20 FORMAT (1X,3L4)
```

In this case, the truth values of A, B, and C are each written in a four-position field. The first three positions in each field are blank. The last position contains a T or F, depending on the truth values of the logical variable names. If the value of A is true and the values of B and C are false, the printed output appears as

```
123456789......
┌─────────────────────┐
│  T│  F│  F           │
```

An illustrative program

To illustrate the logical programming features described in this section, consider the problem of analyzing the results of a true-false questionnaire. The input data consists of the respondent's identification code and the answers to four questions. Each answer is a T or F recorded in a one-position field. A program is needed to print the identification code and answers to the second two questions for all respondents who answered true to the first two questions. In addition, a count of the number of respondents who answered true to the first two questions or to the second two questions is needed.

Figure 8-14 shows the program for this problem. Note the use of L-format code for input and output of logical data. (We could also have used list-directed I/O.) The logical input data is read from four one-position fields. Logical output data is written in two fields of one position each. A logical

Figure 8-14. A program to analyze a true-false questionnaire

```
C  QUESTIONNAIRE ANALYSIS PROGRAM
      LOGICAL ANS1,ANS2,ANS3,ANS4,RES
      INTEGER IDCODE,COUNT
      WRITE (6,200)
      COUNT=0
   10 READ (5,100) IDCODE,ANS1,ANS2,ANS3,ANS4
         IF (IDCODE.EQ.9999) GO TO 20
         RES=ANS1.AND.ANS2
         IF (RES) THEN
            WRITE (6,210) IDCODE,ANS3,ANS4
         END IF
         IF (RES.OR.(ANS3.AND.ANS4)) THEN
            COUNT=COUNT+1
         END IF
      GO TO 10
   20 WRITE (6,220) COUNT
      STOP
  100 FORMAT (I4,4L1)
  200 FORMAT ('1','RESPONDENTS WHO ANSWERED TRUE TO QUESTIONS 1 AND 2'/
     1        '0','  ID CODE     QUESTION 3     QUESTION 4'/)
  210 FORMAT (' ',3X,I4,11X,L1,14X,L1)
  220 FORMAT ('0','NUMBER OF RESPONDENTS WHO ANSWERED TRUE TO'/
     1        ' ','QUESTIONS 1 AND 2 OR TO QUESTIONS 3 AND 4:',1X,I3)
      END
```

(a) The program

```
1234TFTF
2345FFFF
3456TTFF
4567FFTT
5678FTFT
6789TTFT
7890TTTT
8901TFFT
9012FTTT
9999FFFF
```

(b) Input data

```
RESPONDENTS WHO ANSWERED TRUE TO QUESTIONS 1 AND 2

 ID CODE     QUESTION 3     QUESTION 4

  3456          F             F
  6789          F             T
  7890          T             T

NUMBER OF RESPONDENTS WHO ANSWERED TRUE TO
QUESTIONS 1 AND 2 OR TO QUESTIONS 3 AND 4:    5
```

(c) Output

assignment statement is used to determine if the responses to the first two questions are both true. The result is assigned to the logical variable named RES. This name is then used in two IF statements to test for this true condition.

Review questions

1. Code a statement that specifies that CNTRY and LANG are character variable names of lengths 15 and 10, respectively.
2. Code a statement to read the values of CNTRY and LANG described in Question 1 using list-directed input.
3. How must character data be recorded in an input record when the data is to be read using list-directed input?
4. Code a statement to print the values of CNTRY and LANG described in Question 1 using list-directed output.
5. Code statements to read the values of CNTRY and LANG described in Question 1 using formatted input. Assume that the values for CNTRY and LANG are recorded in successive fields of 15 and 10 positions, respectively.
6. Answer Question 5 assuming that the input data is recorded in fields of 12 and 20 positions, respectively.
7. Code statements to write the values of CNTRY and LANG described in Question 1 using formatted output. Write the value of CNTRY in positions 1 through 15 and the value of LANG in positions 21 through 30.
8. Code formatted output statements to write a line with the word COUNTRY in positions 5 through 11 and the word LANGUAGE in positions 22 through 29. Put the character constants for the heading in the WRITE statement.
9. Assume that A, B, and C are character variable names and the value of A is AL, B is ALAN, and C is ALFRED. What is the truth value of each of the following relational expressions?
    a. A.EQ.B
    b. B.NE.C
    c. C.EQ.'ALFRED'
    d. A.LT.B
    e. B.GE.C.
    f. A.LE.'AL'
10. What is the collating sequence for the computer you are using?
11. Assume that MCODE is a character variable name and NUM is an integer variable name. Code a group of statements that increases NUM by 1 if MCODE equals M, decreases NUM by 1 if MCODE equals D, and assigns 0 to NUM if MCODE equals S.
12. Code statements that assign MEXICO and SPANISH to CNTRY and LANG described in Question 1.
13. Code a statement that assigns 12345 to the character variable named ID.
14. Assume that A is a character variable name of length 5. What is the value of A after each of the following statements is executed? Be sure to indicate any blank spaces.

a. A='ABCDE'
b. A='THE'
c. A='OUTPUT'
d. A='95.75'

15. Assume that CNTRY and LANG described in Question 1 are character constant names. Code a PARAMETER statement that assigns the values USA and ENGLISH to these names.

16. Assume that W is a character variable name with a value of XYZ123ABC. What is the value of each of the following substring names?
    a. W(3:7)
    b. W(1:3)
    c. W(7:9)
    d. W(5:5)
    e. W(:4)
    f. W(6:)

17. Assume that V is a character variable name with a value of PA37Qb4X. (The b stands for a blank space; there are no other blanks besides the one shown.) What is the value of each of the following?
    a. INDEX (V,'7Q')
    b. INDEX (V,'QU')
    c. LEN(V)
    d. LEN(V(INDEX(V,'Q'):))

18. The operation of joining together two character data values to form one is called _____. The symbol used for this operation in FORTRAN is _____.

19. Assume that X, Y, and Z are character variable names and that X is XYZ, Y is 123, and Z is ABC. What is the value of each of the following character expressions?
    a. Z//X
    b. X//' '//Y//' '//Z
    c. Z//'DEF'
    d. Z(:1)//Y(2:2)//X(3:)

20. Assume that I, J, and K are integer variable names with values of 5, 6, and 7, respectively. What is the truth value of each of the following logical expressions?
    a. I.EQ.5.AND.J.LT.8
    b. J.GT.4.OR.K.LE.7
    c. I.LE.6.AND.J.EQ.6.AND.K.EQ.6
    d. I.GE.8.OR.J.LT.5.OR.K.EQ.7
    e. I.NE.5.OR.J.EQ.5.AND. K.GT.5
    f. I.EQ.5.AND..NOT.J.LT.7.OR.K.GT.6
    g. I.GT.4.AND.(J.GT.6.OR.K.LT.8)
    h. .NOT.(I.EQ.5.OR.K.LT.6)

21. Code a group of statements using only one IF statement that prints the value of A if I or J is 5 and at the same time K is 10.

22. Code a statement that specifies that RESP and CHCK are logical variable names.

23. Consider RESP and CHCK described in Question 22. Code statements that assign a value of true to RESP and the truth value of the expression A greater than B to CHCK.

24. Code a group of statements that increases A by 1 if both RESP and CHCK described in Question 22 are true.
25. Assume that CHCK described in Question 22 is a logical constant name. Code a PARAMETER statement that assigns a value of false to this name.
26. Code a statement to read the values of RESP and CHCK described in Question 22 using list-directed input.
27. How must logical data be recorded in an input record when the data is to be read using list-directed input?
28. Code a statement to print the values of RESP and CHCK described in Question 22 using list-directed output.
29. Assume that the values of RESP and CHCK described in Question 22 are recorded in five- and four-position fields, respectively, in an input record. Code statements to read the values of these variable names using formatted input.
30. Code statements to write the values of RESP and CHCK described in Question 22 using formatted output. The value of RESP should be written in positions 1 and 2. The value of CHCK should be written in positions 3 through 7.

Programming problems

1. Write a FORTRAN program to read and print a list of names. Supply six to eight names as test data for the program.
2. Write a FORTRAN program to read a name of up to six characters. Then print the name on a diagonal. For example, the name ROBERT should print as follows:

Supply several names to test the program.
3. Write the program for Problem 2 or 5 in Chapter 4 with the additional requirement that the customer's name is read and printed. Supply appropriate names with the test data.
4. Write the program for Problem 4 in Chapter 7 with the additional requirement that the month is entered as character data (e.g., JANUARY).
5. A market research survey gave a number of customers a choice of two brands for each of five products and asked the customers to indicate their preference. If a customer preferred the first brand over the second, his or her response was recorded as X in a record. If the second brand was preferred, the response was recorded as Y. After the survey was completed, each record contained a two-position customer code and one position for each product with X or Y.

   A FORTRAN program is needed to analyze the results of this survey. The program should determine which customers preferred the first brand for the first or second product, and print — for these customers only — the customer's code and preferences for the last three products. In addition, a count of the number of customers who preferred the first brand for any of the five products should be kept and printed at the end. Supply appropriate headings for all output.

Use the following data to test the program:

Customer's code	Brand preferences
11	XYXYX
12	YYYYY
13	XXYXX
14	XYYYY
15	YYYYY
16	YYXXX
17	XYXYY
18	YYYYY
19	XXYXY
20	YYXYY
00 (trailer value)	

6. A six-question multiple-choice test needs to be graded. Each question can be answered A, B, C, D, or E. The correct answers are recorded in the first record of a file. On each succeeding record is a student's name and his or her answers to the six questions. Write a FORTRAN program to determine the number of correct answers for each student. The output should give the correct answers followed by each student's name, his or her answers, and the number of correct answers. Supply appropriate headings for all output data.

Use the following data to test the program:

CORRECT ANSWERS: BECADC

Student's name	Student's answers
JONES	AECBDC
SMITH	BECADC
JOHNSON	EABADC
DOE	BCDEAB
ANDREWS	EDACBD
COLE	CECADC
EMERY	BEEADC

7. Write a FORTRAN program to compute final grades for a course. Input to the program in the student's identification number and five letter grades. In the program, convert each grade to its equivalent numerical grade according to the following table:

A+	4.3	C	2.0
A	4.0	C−	1.7
A−	3.7	D+	1.3
B+	3.3	D	1.0
B	3.0	D−	0.7
B−	2.7	F+	0.3
C+	2.3	F	0.0

The lowest of the five grades should be dropped and the remaining four should be averaged (weighted equally). Compute the numeric average and determine the final letter grade according to the following scale (where G is the numerical grade):

$3.5 \leq G$	A
$2.5 \leq G < 3.5$	B
$1.5 \leq G < 2.5$	C
$0.5 \leq G < 1.5$	D
$G < 0.5$	F

Output from the program should give the student's identification number, numerical grade, and letter grade with appropriate descriptive phrases. Use the following data to test the program:

Student number	Grades
1015	B,C +,B +,A −,C −
1130	A,C −,C,D,D +
1426	B −,A −,B +,A +,A
1703	C,F +,D,F,D −
1933	A +,A +,A,A,A +

8. Write a FORTRAN program to compute the average length of the words in a line of text. Assume that the line only contains alphabetic characters and blanks. Use the following lines to test the program:

> NOW IS THE TIME FOR ALL GOOD MEN
> THE QUICK BROWN FOX JUMPED OVER THE LAZY DOG
> FOUR SCORE AND SEVEN YEARS AGO
> PETER PIPER PICKED A PECK

9. Write a FORTRAN program to count the number of times that the word THE occurs in a line of text. Assume that the line only contains alphabetic characters and blanks. Use the following lines to test the program:

> THE MAN WONDERED WHETHER THE THEATER WAS THERE
> THEN THE MAN THOUGHT THAT IT WAS HERE
> BUT IT WAS NOT THERE
> THE THE THE TITHE THE THE THE

10. Write a FORTRAN program that reads a person's name with the last name first followed by a comma and a space and then the first name. The length of the last name and the first name can vary but the complete name is at most 18 characters long. After reading the data, the program should rearrange and print the name with the first name first, a space, and then the last name. Use the following input data to test the program:

> WASHINGTON, GEORGE
> ADAMS, JOHN
> JEFFERSON, THOMAS
> MADISON, JAMES
> MONROE, JAMES

11. A palindrome is a word, phrase, or number that reads the same forward or backward. For example, RADAR is a palindrome. Write a FORTRAN program that reads a character data value containing at most 25 characters and deter-

mines if it is a palindrome. Print the character data and a statement as to whether or not it is a palindrome. Test the program with the following data:

> RATS STAR
> MOM
> PALINDROME
> A
> 11/5/11
> ABLE WAS I ERE I SAW ELBA
> ABABAB
> 1991

12. Write a FORTRAN program to read a title of up to 40 characters and then print the title centered within 60-character margins. Use the following titles to test the program:

> FUNDAMENTALS OF COMPUTER PROGRAMMING
> A TALE OF TWO CITIES
> MOBY DICK
> MACBETH
> THE HOUND OF THE BASKERVILLES

13. Write a FORTRAN program to read two words and a line of text. Then the program should create a new line by replacing every occurrence of the first word in the text with the second word. Finally, the program should print the new line. Assume that the line of text contains only alphabetic characters and blank spaces.

    Use the following data to test the program:

> THE A
> NOW IS THE TIME FOR THE BEGINNING
> FOX RABBIT
> THE QUICK BROWN FOX JUMPED
> FOUR SEVEN
> FOUR SCORE AND FOUR EQUALS MORE THAN FOUR
> THAT WHICH
> WHICH ONE WAS IT

14. Write a FORTRAN program to right-justify a line of text (i.e., align the right margin). Input to the program should be a line of no more than 40 characters including blanks. Output from the program should be the same line with the first word beginning in position 1 and the last word ending in position 40 (i.e., left- and right-justified). This may involve inserting extra blanks between words so that the line is properly aligned.

    Make up several lines of input to test the program. One test line should be exactly 40 characters long. All other test lines should be less than 40 characters long. At least one line should be less than 30 characters long.

15. The roman numeral system uses the following seven symbols: M (value 1000), D (value 500), C (value 100), L (value 50), X (value 10), V (value 5), and I (value 1). The arabic value of each symbol is shown in parentheses. The value of a roman numeral expressed as an arabic numeral is found by adding the arabic value of each roman symbol. However, if a C, X, or I is to the left of a symbol with a greater value, then the arabic value of C, X, or I is subtracted. For example, roman MCDLXXVI is 1476 in the arabic system.

Write a FORTRAN program to convert roman numerals to arabic numerals. The program should read a roman numeral of up to 14 symbols, determine the equivalent in the arabic system, and print the roman numeral and its arabic equivalent. The arabic equivalent of a roman numeral can be determined by examining each character in the roman numeral and its relation to other characters.

Use the following data to test the program:

> CMXCIX
> MDCCLXVI
> DCCCXXXIV
> MMDCCCLXXXVIII
> MCMLXXIV
> MCDXLII
> CCIII
> MMDXXII

16. In one business the commission paid to each salesperson is based on the product line sold and the total amount of sales. Assume that the product line is indicated by a code that can be either 5, 8, or 17. If the code is 5 or 8, the commission rate is 7½% for the first $5000 of sales and 8½% for sales over $5000. However, if the product-line code is 17, the commission rate is 9½% for the first $3500 of sales and 12% for sales over $3500.

    Write a FORTRAN program to determine the commission for each salesperson. Input is the salesperson's number, product-line code, and total sales. Output should be the salesperson's number, total sales, and commission with appropriate headings.

    Use the following data to test the program:

Salesperson's number	Product-line code	Total sales ($)
101	17	2250
103	5	4000
117	8	7350
125	5	6500
138	17	6375
192	8	8125
203	8	3250
218	5	5000
235	5	5250
264	17	4150
291	17	750
999 (trailer value)		

17. A student is placed on the Dean's list of a college if his or her grade point average (GPA) is above a certain level. The minimum GPA necessary to make the Dean's list depends on the student's year in college. A freshman must have a 3.70 GPA or higher to make the Dean's list. For a sophomore the minimum GPA is 3.50. Juniors and seniors require a 3.30 GPA or better to make the Dean's list.

    Write a FORTRAN program to print data for all students who are on the Dean's list. Input for the program is one record for each student indicating the student's identification number, year in school (1=freshman, 2=sophomore, 3=junior, 4=senior), and his or her grade point average. Output should consist of the student's number and GPA for the Dean's list students only. Supply appropriate headings for the output data.

Use the following data to test the program:

Student number	Year	GPA
1012	2	3.61
1385	1	2.63
1472	3	3.95
1981	2	3.30
2061	4	2.91
2111	4	3.30
2385	1	3.85
2500	1	3.75
2911	2	3.50
3047	3	3.28
3568	3	3.00
3910	4	3.35
9999 (trailer value)		

18. The annual bonus paid to each employee of an organization is based on the number of years of service and the age of the employee. If the employee has 5 to 9 years of service and is between 25 and 34, the annual bonus is $200. If he or she is 35 or older with 5 to 9 years of service, the bonus is $400. If the years of service are between 10 and 19 and the age is less than 40 years, the bonus is $400. If the employee is 40 or older with 10 to 19 years of service, the bonus is $500. If he or she has 20 or more years of service, no matter what age, the bonus is $600. For other employees, there is no annual bonus.

Write a FORTRAN program to determine the annual bonus for each eligible employee in the organization. Input for the program is one record for each employee with his or her identification number, age, and number of years of service. Output should include the employee's number and bonus only for those employees who receive a bonus. Supply appropriate headings for the output.

Use the following data to test the program:

Employee's number	Age	Years of service
1001	38	12
1121	52	28
1305	42	16
1457	29	8
1689	29	3
1810	37	9
1925	42	20
2008	33	10
2025	24	5
2133	54	23
2485	49	19
2561	24	6
2610	33	5
9999 (trailer value)		

19. In a political survey a number of people were given six statements about a political candidate's involvement in illicit campaign practices. Each person was asked to indicate whether he or she felt each statement was true or false. The responses for each person were recorded in a record.

    A FORTRAN program is needed to analyze these data. The program should determine the answers to the following questions:
    a. What percentage of the people in the survey felt that the first two statements were true and the remainder false?
    b. What percentage felt that all six statements were true?
    c. What percentage felt that all six were false?
    Output should give the answers to these questions with appropriate descriptive headings.
    Use the following data to test the program:

    SURVEY RESPONSES

TFTFFF	TTFTFF
TTFFFF	TTFFFF
TTTTTT	TTFFFF
FFTTFF	FFFFFF
FFFFFF	TFFFFF
TTFTFT	TTTTTT
FTFTFF	TTFFFF
FFFFFF	FTFFFF
TTFFFF	FFFFFF

20. An employee satisfaction survey asked every employee of an organization to indicate whether each of four working conditions was true or false. The results of the survey were recorded with one record for each employee.

    Write a FORTRAN program to determine how many employees answered true to all four conditions, how many answered true to any three conditions, how many responded true to any two conditions, and how many felt only one condition was true. Print the totals with appropriate headings.
    Use the following data to test the program:

    EMPLOYEES' RESPONSES

TTFF	FTFF	FFFF
TFTT	FFFT	TFFF
TFFF	TTTT	FFFT
FTTT	TTFT	FTFF
FFFF	FTTF	TTTT
TTTF	FTFT	FTFF
TTFF	TTTT	FFFF

21. Figure 8-10 shows the truth tables for the basic logical expressions. Sometimes it is necessary to develop a truth table for more complex logical expressions. For example, here is a truth table for the expressions A.OR.B.AND.C:

A	B	C	A.OR.B.AND.C
T	T	T	T
T	T	F	T
T	F	T	T
T	F	F	T
F	T	T	T
F	T	F	F
F	F	T	F
F	F	F	F

Write a FORTRAN program to print a truth table for the expression

A.AND..NOT.B.OR.B.AND.C

(*Hint:* This problem can be most easily solved by using nested DO loops and the .NOT. logical operator to change the value of a logical variable name.)

There is no input for this program. Output for the program should list the truth table with appropriate headings.

22. A five-question true-false test needs to be graded. The correct answers are recorded in the first record of a file. On each succeeding record are a student's number and his or her answers to the five questions. Write a FORTRAN program to determine the number of correct answers for each student. The output should give the correct answers followed by each student's number, his or her answers, and the number of correct answers. Supply appropriate headings for all output data.

Use the following data to test the program:

CORRECT ANSWERS: FTTFT

Student's number	*Student's answers*
101	FTFFT
102	TTTFF
103	TFFTF
104	FTTFT
105	TFTFT
106	FTTTT
107	FTFTF
108	TFFTF
109	FTTFT
999	(trailer value)

Chapter 9

Arrays

In many programs it is necessary to store and process a large amount of data. For example, we may need to process a list of 50 numbers, all of which must be available in the program at the same time. Using the techniques that we have discussed so far, a separate variable name would have to be used for each number in the list. Thus we would need 50 variable names.

Another approach to this type of problem is to identify the entire list of data by a single name. Then we can refer to each value in the list by indicating its position in the list. A list of data like this is called an array. In this chapter we examine the use of arrays in FORTRAN. After completing this chapter you should be able to write programs that process arrays of data.

9-1. Arrays and array elements

An *array* is a group of data values that is identified in a program by a single name. An array may be thought of as a list or table of data. An array may contain data of any type: integer, real, character, or logical. However, all data values in any one array must be of the same type. Thus one array may contain a group of integer values, but another array is needed for a list of real numbers.

A name that identifies an array is called an *array name*. An array name must follow the rules for variable names and must be the same type as the data in the array. As an example, Figure 9-1 shows an array of 10 real values which are identified by the array name A.

Each value in an array is called an *array element*. In the array in Figure 9-1, the number 23.2 is an array element. Similarly, 17.5, −10.8, and so forth are each elements of the array A. There are 10 elements in this array.

Figure 9-1. An array

The array A

23.2
17.5
− 10.8
6.3
31.0
− 4.0
5.7
13.8
20.5
16.2

In a program the elements of an array are numbered — the first element in an array is numbered 1, the second is numbered 2, and so forth through the array. Figure 9-2 shows the elements of the array A and the corresponding element numbers. Element number 1 in this array is 23.2, element number 2 is 17.5, and so on up to element number 10 which is 16.2. The element numbers do not actually appear in the array, but the computer keeps track of the elements by their numbers.

In a program, an array element is identified by coding the name of the array followed immediately by the number of the element in parentheses. Figure 9-3 shows how this is done for the array A. The first element in this array is identified by A(1), the fifth element is A(5), and the last is A(10). A

Figure 9-2. Element numbers for an array

Element
numbers   The array A

Element numbers	The array A
1 →	23.2
2 →	17.5
3 →	− 10.8
4 →	6.3
5 →	31.0
6 →	− 4.0
7 →	5.7
8 →	13.8
9 →	20.5
10 →	16.2

Figure 9-3. Element names for an array

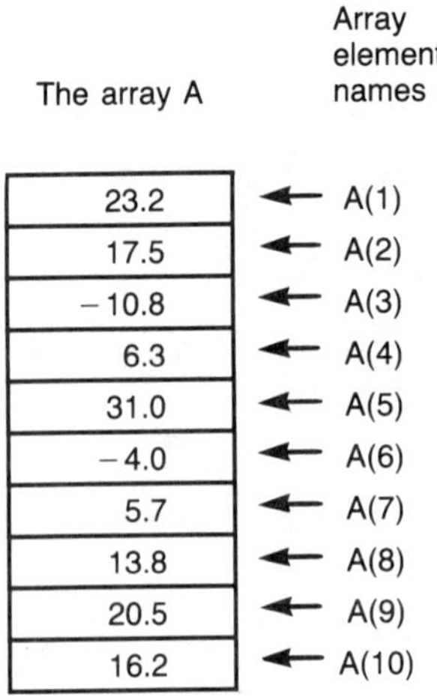

name of this sort is called an *array element name* (or sometimes a *subscripted variable name*). The number in parentheses following the array name is called a *subscript*. An array element name such as A(5) is read "A sub five."

It is important not to confuse an array element with its subscript. A subscript specifies which value in an array is being identified. The actual value is the array element. Thus A(5) identifies the fifth value in the array A. The corresponding array element from Figure 9-3 is 31.0.

The data in an array is referred to collectively by an array name. An array name, however, may not be used by itself in a FORTRAN program except in a few specialized situations. An array name must normally be followed by a subscript to identify which element of the array is being identified. An array element name may be used like any variable name. Thus array element names may be used in READ, PRINT, and WRITE statements and in arithmetic expressions. For example, assume that X and Y are the names of arrays of 20 elements each. Then the following statements are valid examples of the use of array element names:

```
READ (5,10) X(1),Y(1)
W=X(5)+X(6)+X(7)
WRITE (6,20) X(5),X(6),X(7),W
Y(3)=X(2)*Y(1)/3.5
IF (X(15).GE.Y(10)) THEN
PRINT *,X(20),Y(20)
```

Dimensioning arrays

Before a FORTRAN compiler can translate a source program into machine language it must have information about any arrays that are used in the program. The compiler must know what names are array names and the number of elements in each array. The procedure to do this is sometimes called *dimensioning* an array because the size of the array is specified. Among other things, dimensioning causes storage locations to be reserved for the array. (Note, however, that dimensioning does not cause initial values to be assigned to the elements of the array.)

The easiest way to dimension an array is to specify the number of elements in the array in a type statement. This number comes after the array name and is enclosed in parentheses. For example, consider the following type statements:

```
INTEGER K(15),X(20)
REAL A(10)
```

The effect of these statements is to specify three arrays named K, X, and A. The array named K has 15 integer elements, X has 20 integer elements, and A has 10 real elements. Note that specifying these names with an array size is what identifies them as array names and not variable names. Thus the names K, X, and A may refer only to arrays in the program that contain these type statements and not to nonarray data.

As many arrays as are needed may be specified in a program. Several type statements may be used and these statements may also include variable names. For example, the following statements may be used in a program:

```
REAL Y(20),Z(20),P,Q
INTEGER B,C,M(25)
REAL N(200)
```

These statements cause Y, Z, M, and N to be specified as arrays, and P, Q, B, and C to be declared as variable names of the types indicated.

The DIMENSION statement. Another way to dimension arrays is with the DIMENSION statement. The syntax of this statement is as follows:

> DIMENSION a1(k1),a2(k2),...,an(kn)
>
> where a1,a2,...,an are array names.
>   k1,k2,...,kn are integer constants indicating the
>   number of elements in the respective arrays.

use type statements instead

For example, the following DIMENSION statement describes three arrays:

```
DIMENSION A(10),X(20),K(15)
```

The first array is named A and it has 10 elements. The second array is X with 20 elements. The third array is K with 15 elements. Note that if a name is specified in a DIMENSION statement, it cannot be used as a simple variable name in the program. Thus, in this example, the names A, X, and K may refer only to arrays.

The DIMENSION statement is a specification statement. Therefore, it is a nonexecutable statement that must come at the beginning of the program before the first executable statement. Any number of DIMENSION statements can appear in a program.

When the DIMENSION statement is used, the type of data in the array may be specified implicitly or explicitly. Recall from Section 2-2 that implicit typing is indicated by the first letter of the name. (If the first letter is I, J, K, L, M, or N, the name is integer. If the first letter is any other letter, the name is real.) Thus, in the example of the DIMENSION statement just given, A and X are implicitly typed as real and K is implicitly integer.

If we wish to use explicit typing for array names that are dimensioned in a DIMENSION statement, the names must also appear in type statements. For example, to explicitly type K and X as integer and A as real and to specify these as array names in a DIMENSION statement, we would code the following:

```
DIMENSION A(10),X(20),K(15)
INTEGER K,X
REAL A
```

The DIMENSION statement specifies that the names are array names that identify arrays of certain sizes. The INTEGER and REAL statements specify their types. The order of these statements is not important. Note that type statements do *not* give the array size. In fact, it is invalid to dimension the same array in a DIMENSION statement and in a type statement in a program.

As we have seen, we can dimension arrays in two ways — using type statements and using DIMENSION statements. Because it is simpler and clearer, we prefer to dimension arrays with type statements rather than with DIMENSION statements. However, many existing programs use DIMENSION statements and thus the programmer should be familiar with this statement.

Subscripts

A subscript indicates which element of an array is being identified. As we have seen, a subscript may be an integer constant. A subscript may also be an integer variable name. For example, A(I) is a valid array element name (assuming I is integer). This is read "A sub I." The element of an array A that is being identified by this name depends on the value of I. For example, if the value of I is 3, the third element of the array A is identified by the name A(I).

The use of a variable name as a subscript is a powerful technique in FORTRAN programming. For example, assume that 10 real values are recorded in input records. A program is needed to store the 10 values in an array, accumulate the totals of the values, write the array data, and then write the

Figure 9-4. An array processing program

```
C   PROGRAM TO TOTAL THE ELEMENTS OF AN ARRAY
        INTEGER J
        REAL A(10),TOTAL
        (Read data for array)
        TOTAL=0.0
        DO 100 J=1,10
          TOTAL=TOTAL+A(J)
    100 CONTINUE
        (Write array data)
        WRITE (6,320) TOTAL
        STOP
    320 FORMAT ('0','TOTAL ',F6.1)
        END
```

total. The program in Figure 9-4 shows how this can be done. This program is complete except for the input and output of the array data. (Input and output of array data is discussed in the next section.)

In this program the total of the array elements is accumulated by successively adding each element to the variable named TOTAL and storing the result as the value of TOTAL. This is accomplished in a DO loop by using the DO-variable as the subscript for the array element name. Initially the value of TOTAL is set to 0. With the first execution of the loop, the value of the DO-variable J is 1, and the value of A(1) is added to TOTAL. The second execution of the loop causes the value of A(2) to be added to TOTAL. This continues for the remaining executions of the loop. Upon completion of the DO loop, the value of the variable named TOTAL is

```
0.0+A(1)+A(2)+A(3)+A(4)+A(5)+A(6)+A(7)+A(8)+A(9)+A(10)
```

In addition to integer constants and variable names, subscripts may be integer arithmetic expressions. For example, the following array element names use expressions as subscripts (assume that all variable names are integer):

```
A(I+2)
A(J-3)
A(8*K-3)
A(L**2+2*M-1)
```

The value of a subscript expression is determined by the current values of the variable names in the expression. For example, if the value of L is 2 and M is 3, the last array element name in the preceding list refers to the ninth element of array A. Note that whether the subscript is a constant, variable name, or arithmetic expression, it must have an integer value.

Dimension bounds

If an array is dimensioned as we have described earlier, any subscript used with the array name must have a value between 1 and the number of elements in the array. For example, assume that the array A is dimensioned as follows:

```
REAL A(10)
```

Then a subscript for this array must be an integer between 1 and 10. We say that the *lower dimension bound* is 1 and that the *upper dimension bound* is 10. We also can specify a lower dimension bound that is not 1. In fact, the lower and upper dimension bounds can be specified as any integer values — positive, negative, or zero — as long as the lower dimension bound is less than or equal to the upper bound.

The lower and upper dimension bounds for an array are indicated by an *array declarator* in the type or DIMENSION statement that dimensions the array. An array declarator consists of an array name followed by the lower and upper dimension bounds separated by a colon and enclosed in parentheses. The lower dimension bound and colon may be left out, in which case the array declarator is of the form we have used so far. As an example of array declarators with both dimension bounds, consider the following statements:

```
REAL C(5:10)
INTEGER L(0:7),Y(-10:-1)
```

These statements specify three arrays. The first, C, has a lower dimension bound of 5 and an upper bound of 10. Hence it has six elements. The array L has eight elements with a lower dimension bound of 0 and an upper bound of 7. The array Y has a lower bound of -10 and an upper bound of -1. Hence it has ten elements.

Whenever an array is dimensioned with lower and upper dimension bounds, the array name must be used with a subscript value that falls within the bounds. Thus, in the example just given, we could use C(7) in the program but not C(3) because 3 is less than the lower dimension bound for the array C. Similarly, L(0), L(7), Y(-3), and Y(-1) are valid but L(-2), L(8), Y(-12), and Y(0) are invalid with this example.

When processing an array in a DO loop, we often use an initial value and a test value that correspond to the dimension bounds. For example, to total the elements of the array Y, which has a lower dimension bound of -10 and upper bound of -1, we can write the following:

```
TOTAL=0.0
DO 100 J=-10,-1
   TOTAL=TOTAL+Y(J)
100 CONTINUE
```

Note in this example that the DO-variable J is incremented from -10 to -1 which corresponds to the dimension bounds of the array Y.

Finally, when we dimension an array, if we do not include a lower dimension bound, it is assumed to be 1. This is the way we dimensioned arrays in our discussion earlier in this section.

9-2. Input and output of array data

Many techniques can be used for input and output of array data. One technique is to list each array element name in the READ, PRINT, or WRITE statement. For example, assume that B is the name of a five-element real array. The following statements cause the data from a record to be read using formatted input and assigned to the array elements:

```
    READ (5,11) B(1),B(2),B(3),B(4),B(5)
 11 FORMAT (5F8.2)
```

We could also do this using list-directed input as follows:

```
READ *,B(1),B(2),B(3),B(4),B(5)
```

Similarly, the array data could be printed using formatted output with the following statements:

```
    WRITE (6,21) B(1),B(2),B(3),B(4),B(5)
 21 FORMAT (1X,5F8.2)
```

We could also do this using list-directed output as follows:

```
PRINT *,B(1),B(2),B(3),B(4),B(5)
```

The problem with this technique is that if the array is very large, the READ, PRINT, or WRITE statement list is quite long and tiresome to code. This section presents a number of other techniques for input and output of array data and describes the use of each technique with formatted I/O. Most of the techniques can also be used with list-directed I/O. Any differences between formatted and list-directed input and output are explained.

The short-list technique

An array name may be used in a READ or WRITE statement list without a subscript. When this is done, *all* of the data for the array is read or written. For example, the following statement has the same effect as the previous formatted READ statement that reads the five elements of the array B:

```
READ (5,11) B
```

Similarly, the previous WRITE statement that wrote the five elements of B may be coded as follows:

```
WRITE (6,21) B
```

In both examples, the presence of the array name, B, indicates that data for *all* elements in the array is to be read or written. This approach is sometimes called the *short-list technique* because the input or output list is short in comparison to a list of all array element names.

The short-list technique may be used only for the input or output of an entire array. If only part of an array is to be read or written, we must use some other approach. For example, assume that only the first three elements of the array B are to be read. Then we cannot use the short-list. Instead, we could use the following statements:

```
    READ (5,12) B(1),B(2),B(3)
12 FORMAT (3F8.2)
```

If array elements are to be read or written in any order other than in sequence of ascending subscripts, we cannot use the short-list technique. For example, assume that the elements of B are to be written in reverse order. Again, we cannot use the short-list technique, but we could use the following statements:

```
    WRITE (6,22) B(5),B(4),B(3),B(2),B(1)
22 FORMAT (1X,5F8.2)
```

Another situation in which we cannot use the short-list technique is when other data is to be read or written between the elements of an array. For example, assume that M and N are the names of two three-element arrays. The data for M and N is recorded in alternating fields in a record. Thus the first field contains the value of M(1), the second field contains N(1), the third field contains M(2), and so forth. If the READ statement is coded as

```
    READ (5,13) M,N
```

then all elements of M are read before the elements of N are read. To read the data in the required order, the array element names must be listed alternately as in the following READ statement:

```
    READ (5,13) M(1),N(1),M(2),N(2),M(3),N(3)
```

List-directed I/O. The short-list technique can be used with list-directed READ and PRINT statements. For example, the following statements use this technique for list-directed input and output of the array B:

```
    READ *,B
    PRINT *,B
```

The first statement reads all the data for B, and the second statement prints all the data.

Multiple records

Assume that the data for the five elements of the array named B is recorded in five records. One way to read this data is to use a slash in the FORMAT statement to indicate a new record. (The use of a slash to start a new record was described in Section 6-7.) For example, the following statements may be used to read the data:

```
    READ (5,14) B(1),B(2),B(3),B(4),B(5)
 14 FORMAT (F8.2/F8.2/F8.2/F8.2/F8.2)
```

Because the entire array is read in the normal order in this example, the short-list technique may be used with the same FORMAT statement. Thus these statements could be coded as

```
    READ (5,14) B
 14 FORMAT (F8.2/F8.2/F8.2/F8.2/F8.2)
```

For output, this approach may be used to write the array data in separate records. For example, the following statements write the elements of the array B in five records:

```
    WRITE (6,24) B
 24 FORMAT (1X,F8.2/1X,F8.2/1X,F8.2/1X,F8.2/1X,F8.2)
```

The short-list technique is used in this example.

In some cases, the programmer can take advantage of the technique of overloading the I/O list. (This technique was described in Section 6-7.) In this approach there are more entries in the input or output list than there are format codes in the FORMAT statement. When additional format codes are needed, control returns to the beginning of the last major group or, if no group repetition exists, to the beginning of the format codes. Then a new record is begun, and the same format codes are used again. For example, data for the array named B may be read from five records with the following statements:

```
    READ (5,15) B(1),B(2),B(3),B(4),B(5)
 15 FORMAT (F8.2)
```

The value of B(1) is read from the first record. Then, because there are no more entries in the input list, control returns to the beginning of the FORMAT statement and the value of B(2) is read from a second record. This continues until data for all array element names in the input list have been read.

This approach, coupled with a short-list, makes an extremely powerful yet easy-to-code technique for input and output of array data. For example, the following statements have the same effect as the previous example:

```
    READ (5,15) B
 15 FORMAT (F8.2)
```

Although it appears that only the data for a single variable is to be read, the fact that B is a five-element array (as indicated when the array was dimensioned) causes five values to be read. The same technique can be used for output. For example, the following statements write the elements of B in five records:

```
      WRITE (6,25) B
25 FORMAT (1X,F8.2)
```

List-directed I/O. The technique described here does not work with list-directed I/O because no FORMAT statement is used. However, the same effect can be accomplished with list-directed input. For example, the following list-directed READ statement reads five values:

```
READ *,B(1),B(2),B(3),B(4),B(5)
```

If each value is recorded in a separate record, this statement reads five records. Alternatively, in this situation we could have used the short-list technique as in the following example:

```
READ *,B
```

If each record had only one value, five records would be read.

This technique does not work for list-directed output. For example, consider the following PRINT statement:

```
PRINT *,B(1),B(2),B(3),B(4),B(5)
```

This does *not* cause five lines to be printed. Rather, it causes five values to be printed on one line. The same result occurs with the short-list technique as illustrated in the following statement:

```
PRINT *,B
```

Again, the data for the array is printed on one line, not on separate lines.

Looping techniques

Another approach to the problem of reading and writing multiple records is to use a loop to control the input or output operation. For example, the following sequence of statements uses a DO loop to control the number of records that are read:

```
      DO 50 I=1,5
         READ (5,160) B(I)
   50 CONTINUE
  160 FORMAT (F8.2)
```

The DO-variable is used as the subscript of the array element name. With each execution of the loop, the READ statement is executed and a new record is read. Thus, with the first execution of the loop, the value of B(1) is read. Then, during the second execution of the loop, the DO-variable is incremented and the value of B(2) is read. This continues until the loop is terminated. This looping technique also can be used for output. For example, the following statements cause the data in the array B to be written in five records:

```
      DO 60 I=1,5
         WRITE (6,260) B(I)
   60 CONTINUE
  260 FORMAT (1X,F8.2)
```

Using a loop to control the input and output of array data is most useful for large arrays when the data is to be read or written in an unusual order. For example, assume that the first 100 elements of the integer array M are recorded with two elements per record. The data can be read by using a DO loop that is executed 50 times as illustrated by the following statements:

```
      DO 70 J=1,99,2
         READ (5,170) M(J),M(J+1)
   70 CONTINUE
  170 FORMAT (2I6)
```

With each execution of the DO loop, two elements of the array are read. The use of the DO-variable in the subscripts J and J+1 causes the data to be assigned to the proper array element names.

As another example of the use of the looping technique, consider the problem of printing two arrays in adjacent columns. Assume that X and Y are the names of two 20-element arrays. The following statements cause the data in the arrays to be printed in columns along with another column for the value of the DO-variable:

```
      DO 80 L=1,20
         WRITE (6,280) L,X(L),Y(L)
   80 CONTINUE
  280 FORMAT (1X,I3,2F8.2)
```

If array data is to be read until a trailer value is detected, a looping technique must be used. For example, assume that the array named N has at most 150 elements. Each element is recorded in a separate record. The last record contains a trailer value of zero in the field for the array element. To read the data, a loop must be used with a test for the trailer value included in the loop. The following statements accomplish this:

```
      INTEGER N(151),J
      J=1
   90 READ (5,190) N(J)
         IF (N(J).EQ.0) GO TO 95
         J=J+1
      GO TO 90
   95 (next statement)
  190 FORMAT (I5)
```

Note in this example that N is dimensioned with 151 elements. This is because there can be at most 150 elements read for N plus the trailer value. When the loop is terminated, J is equal to the number of elements read plus one for the trailer value. Hence, to find the actual number of data values in the array, J must be decreased by 1.

List-directed I/O. The looping technique can be used with list-directed I/O. For example, the following statements cause five records to be read:

```
      DO 55 I=1,5
         READ *,B(I)
   55 CONTINUE
```

Similarly, five lines are printed with the following statement:

```
      DO 65 I=1,5
         PRINT *,B(I)
   65 CONTINUE
```

Note that this is the only way that the array data can be printed on five separate lines using list-directed I/O; the short-list technique cannot be used for this.

Implied-DO lists

For input or output of partial or whole arrays, a DO loop may be implied in a READ or WRITE statement list. This is called an *implied-DO list*. For example, the input list in the following statement consists of an implied-DO list:

we will use often

```
      READ (5,31) (B(I),I=1,4,1)
```

The implied-DO list must be enclosed in parentheses. Within the parentheses is a list of variable and array element names separated by commas with a comma following the last name. In this example, one name, B(I), is in the list. Following this, the DO-variable and parameters are specified as in a DO statement. In this example, the DO-variable is the variable named I, the initial value of the DO-variable is 1, the test value is 4, and the increment is 1. As in a DO statement the increment may be omitted, in which case the computer assumes it is 1. The keyword DO and the terminal statement number are not included in an implied-DO list. The range is the list of variable and array element names. The function of the parameters is the same as in a DO loop. Thus this example has the effect of causing the values of B(1), B(2), B(3), and B(4) to be read in that order.

The parameters of an implied-DO list may be any constants, variable names, or expressions with values within the appropriate limits. For example, consider the following WRITE statement:

```
      WRITE (6,41) (AMT(J),J=10,LIM,2)
```

In this statement the initial value of the DO-varable is 10, the test value is the value of the variable named LIM, and the increment is 2. If LIM is 18, this statement causes the values of AMT(10), AMT(12), AMT(14), AMT(16), and AMT(18) to be written. It is important to ensure that the value of a subscript for an array element name does not exceed the array bounds. In this example, if AMT is the name of an array with a lower bound of 1 and an upper bound of 25, a test value greater than 25 results in an error.

An implied-DO list does not necessarily cause data to be read or written in the same manner as a regular DO loop. This depends on the way in which the FORMAT statement is coded. For example, consider the following sequence of statements:

```
      DO 20 I=1,4
         READ (5,33) B(I)
   20 CONTINUE
   33 FORMAT (F8.2)
```

In this case, four records are read and the data assigned to the first four elements of the array named B. The same effect can be accomplished using an implied-DO list as follows:

```
      READ (5,33) (B(I),I=1,4)
   33 FORMAT (F8.2)
```

In this case, the input list is overloaded because four values are to be read, but the FORMAT statement contains only one format code. Thus the data is read from four records. If all four values are recorded in one record, the following statements may be used:

```
      READ (5,34) (B(I),I=1,4)
   34 FORMAT (4F8.2)
```

The same effect cannot be accomplished with a regular DO loop because each execution of the DO loop's range causes a new record to be read.

A READ or WRITE statement list may contain several implied-DO lists as well as other variable and array names. For example, consider the following READ statement:

```
READ (5,32) ID,SN,(N(J),J=1,10),(A(J),J=1,5)
```

With this statement a total of 17 values are read.

More than one variable or array element name may be included in the list of an implied-DO list. For example, the following statements cause values for the first 50 elements of the array M to be read:

```
      READ (5,17) (M(J),M(J+1),J=1,49,2)
   17 FORMAT (2I6)
```

Because the input list is overloaded in this example, two values are read from each input record. As another example, consider the following statements:

```
WRITE (6,28) (L,X(L),Y(L),L=1,20)
28 FORMAT (1X,I5,2F8.2)
```

In this example, the variable named L is included in the implied-DO list. Because this is also the DO-variable of the loop, the printed output consists of three columns, one listing the value of L, and the other two giving the values of elements of the arrays X and Y.

Using an implied-DO list is a versatile technique for input and output of array data. Whenever an entire array is to be read or written in sequence, the short-list technique is more efficient. An implied-DO list is most useful for the input or output of partial arrays or several alternating arrays. If it can be used, an implied-DO list is preferred over a regular DO loop. In some situations neither the short-list technique nor an implied-DO list can be used. For example, if a test for a trailer value is needed in an input routine, a regular loop must be used.

List-directed I/O. Implied-DO lists can be used with list-directed READ and PRINT statements. For example, the following statements are valid:

```
READ *,(B(I),I=1,4)
PRINT *,(B(I),I=1,4)
```

The first statement causes four values to be read. If the values are all recorded in one record, only one record is read. However, if the data is recorded in four separate records, all four records are read. The second statement causes four values to be printed. The data is printed on one line, not on four lines.

A complete program

We can now complete the program shown in Figure 9-4. Recall that this program finds the total of ten real values. The program is not complete because the array input and output is not included.

Figure 9-5 shows the program with the necessary input and output statements using formatted I/O. The array input data is assumed to be recorded in ten records. The short-list technique is used for the input operation. Ten records are read because the FORMAT statement that corresponds with the READ statement has only one format code and hence the input list is overloaded. Also, the array is printed using the short-list technique. Again, the corresponding FORMAT statement has only one numeric format code. Hence each value in the array is written in a separate record.

List-directed I/O. The previous example can be coded using list-directed I/O. The program is shown in Figure 9-6. Note that a list-directed READ statement with a short-list is used to read the array data. Because each input value is

Figure 9-5. An array processing program with formatted I/O

```
C   PROGRAM TO TOTAL THE ELEMENTS OF AN ARRAY
        INTEGER J
        REAL A(10),TOTAL
        READ (5,200) A
        TOTAL=0.0
        DO 100 J=1,10
          TOTAL=TOTAL+A(J)
    100 CONTINUE
        WRITE (6,300)
        WRITE (6,310) A
        WRITE (6,320) TOTAL
        STOP
    200 FORMAT (F5.1)
    300 FORMAT ('1','ARRAY DATA'/)
    310 FORMAT (' ',2X,F5.1)
    320 FORMAT ('0','TOTAL ',F6.1)
        END
```

(a) The program

```
        23.2
        17.5
       -10.8
         6.3
        31.0
        -4.0
         5.7
        13.8
        20.5
        16.2
```

(b) Input data

```
    ARRAY DATA

        23.2
        17.5
       -10.8
         6.3
        31.0
        -4.0
         5.7
        13.8
        20.5
        16.2

    TOTAL   119.4
```

(c) Output

Figure 9-6. An array processing program with list-directed I/O

```
C  PROGRAM TO TOTAL THE ELEMENTS OF AN ARRAY
        INTEGER J
        REAL A(10),TOTAL
        READ *,A
        TOTAL=0.0
        DO 100 J=1,10
          TOTAL=TOTAL+A(J)
    100 CONTINUE
        PRINT *,'ARRAY DATA'
        PRINT *
        DO 150 J=1,10
          PRINT *,A(J)
    150 CONTINUE
        PRINT *
        PRINT *,'TOTAL ',TOTAL
        STOP
        END
```

recorded in a separate record, ten records are read. However, a looping technique is used to print the array. This is necessary so that each element of the array is printed on a separate line. The input data and output from this program is essentially the same as that of the program in Figure 9-5.

9-3. Array processing techniques

Arrays are one of the most powerful features of the FORTRAN programming language. With the proper use of loops and subscripts, extensive processing can be accomplished with just a few statements. This section illustrates a number of array processing techniques. Although many of the examples may seem simple, the techniques appear often in complex array processing programs. For the examples, we assume that X, Y, and Z are real arrays with 20 elements each and that I, J, K, and L are integer variables.

Initializing an array

Often we must set each element of an array to an initial value. For example, assume that the elements of array X must be initialized to 0, and the elements of Y and Z are each to be assigned an initial value of 1. Then the three arrays may be initialized in one loop as follows:

```
      DO 110 I=1,20
        X(I)=0.0
        Y(I)=1.0
        Z(I)=1.0
  110 CONTINUE
```

Copying an array

After the data has been read for an array, sometimes we must copy the data into another array. As a result, the original data can be saved in one array while it is manipulated or modified in the other. For example, assume that data has been read for array X. Then the data is copied into array Y by the following statements:

```
      DO 120 J=1,20
         Y(J)=X(J)
  120 CONTINUE
```

Copying an array in reverse order

Occasionally we need a copy of the array data with the elements in reverse order. To do this, the first element of one array is assigned to the last element of another array, the second element of the first array is assigned to the next-to-last element of the other array, and so forth until the last element of the first array is assigned to the first element of the other array. Thus the subscript of one array must be incremented from 1 to the maximum, while the subscript of the other array is decremented from the maximum to 1. The following statements accomplish this for arrays X and Y:

```
      J=20
      DO 130 I=1,20
         Y(J)=X(I)
         J=J-1
  130 CONTINUE
```

Note that the variable named J is initialized to 20 and then decreased by 1 with each execution of the DO loop. At the same time, the DO-variable I is increased from 1 to 20. Thus, with the first execution of the DO loop, X(1) is assigned to Y(20). Then the value of J is decremented to 19 and the value of the DO-variable is incremented to 2. The second execution of the loop causes the value of X(2) to be assigned to Y(19). This continues until the last execution of the loop when the value of X(20) is assigned to Y(1).

Processing corresponding elements of two arrays

Often we need to process corresponding elements of two arrays. For example, we may have to add corresponding elements of the X and Y arrays, assigning the results to the Z array. The following statements show how this is done:

```
      DO 140 K=1,20
         Z(K)=X(K)+Y(K)
  140 CONTINUE
```

Counting specific values in an array

On occasion we must determine how many times a particular value occurs in an array. For example, we may need to know the number of elements of Y that are 0. The following statements accomplish this (assume that NUM is integer):

```
      NUM=0
      DO 150 I=1,20
         IF (Y(I).EQ.0.0) THEN
            NUM=NUM+1
         END IF
  150 CONTINUE
```

At the end of execution of this sequence, the variable named NUM will be equal to the number of elements of Y that are equal to 0. A similar situation occurs when we want to know the number of elements in two arrays that are equal. For example, we may want to know how many corresponding elements of X and Z are the same. The following statements accomplish this:

```
      NUM=0
      DO 160 J=1,20
         IF (X(J).EQ.Z(J)) THEN
            NUM=NUM+1
         END IF
  160 CONTINUE
```

Finding the largest or smallest element of an array

Sometimes we want to locate the largest or smallest element in an array. For example, assume we have to find the smallest element in the array X. The following statements accomplish this (assume that SMALL is real):

```
      SMALL=X(1)
      DO 170 L=2,20
         IF (X(L).LT.SMALL) THEN
            SMALL=X(L)
         END IF
  170 CONTINUE
```

Initially we assume that the first element of the array is the smallest and its value is assigned to the variable named SMALL. Then this value is compared with each succeeding element to determine if there is one smaller. If an element is smaller, its value is assigned to SMALL, replacing the previous value. If an element is not smaller than the current value of SMALL, this assignment is bypassed. At the end of the execution of the loop, the value of the variable named SMALL equals the smallest element of the array. The same basic technique is used to find the largest element of an array.

9-4. Searching and sorting

Two common problems in array processing are searching and sorting. *Searching* involves locating a specific value in an array. *Sorting* is the process of re-arranging the data in an array into a specific order. In this section we describe algorithms for searching and sorting.

Searching

Many situations involve searching. In the simplest case, a value is given and the first occurrence of an equivalent value is to be located in an array. For example, assume that X is a real array with 20 elements. The following statements search this array for the first element whose value is equal to that of V (assume that V is real and I is integer):

```
       I=1
    10 IF (X(I).EQ.V) GO TO 20
          I=I+1
          GO TO 10
    20 WRITE (6,300) I
   300 FORMAT ('VALUE FOUND AT ELEMENT',I2)
```

In this sequence, I is used as a subscript. Initially I is 1, and each time through the loop I is increased by 1. The loop is terminated when X(I) is equal to V. The value of I at this time is the number of the first element in X that has a value equal to V. This value of I is written when the loop is terminated.

The problem with this sequence of statements is that it does not take into account the case where the value of V is not in the array. However, we can modify the statements to print a message if the value is not found. The sequence of statements shown in Figure 9-7 accomplishes this. In this sequence the loop is terminated when X(I) equals V *or* when I equals 20. The latter case occurs when we reach the end of the array. After branching out of the loop, we must see if the value was actually found or if the loop was terminated without finding the value. If X(I) is equal to V, the value has been found and the corresponding array element number is written. If X(I) is not equal to V when the loop is terminated, the value was not found and an appropriate message is written.

Many times we need to search one array and retrieve the corresponding element of another array. For example, we may wish to search array X for value V and write the corresponding value of array Y when V is found. To do this, the only modification in the sequence of statements in Figure 9-7 is that Y(I) is written instead of I.

To illustrate the use of searching in an actual program, consider the problem of locating the price of an item in a table. Figure 9-8 shows a table of item numbers and prices. The program must store the pricing table in two

Figure 9-7. A sequential search algorithm

```
      INTEGER I
      REAL X(20),V
        .
        .
        .
      I=1
   10 IF ((X(I).EQ.V).OR.(I.EQ.20)) GO TO 20
         I=I+1
      GO TO 10
   20 IF ((X(I).EQ.V) THEN
         WRITE (6,300) I
      ELSE
         WRITE (6,310)
      END IF
  300 FORMAT (' VALUE FOUND AT ELEMENT ',I2)
  310 FORMAT (' VALUE NOT FOUND')
        .
        .
        .
```

arrays, one for the item numbers and one for the prices. Then the program must read an item number and a value that represents the quantity of the item purchased, locate the item's price in the table, and compute the cost by multiplying the price by the quantity. Figure 9-9 shows the program that accomplishes this.

At the beginning of the program the pricing table data is read into two arrays, one for the item numbers (ITNUM) and one for the prices (PRICE). Then the program reads an item number (INUM) and quantity (QTY). (Note that the first ten records in the input data consist of the data for the pricing table and the remaining records each contain an item number and quantity field.) Next the program searches the item number array for an element that is equal to INUM. The program assumes that the item numbers are in increasing order in the array and branches out of the searching loop when ITNUM(I) is either equal to INUM or greater than INUM. This latter case occurs when the search has gone beyond the value of INUM in the array. (If the item

Figure 9-8. A pricing table

Item Number	Unit Price
1001	$2.95
1023	$3.64
1045	$2.25
1172	$0.75
1185	$1.50
1201	$1.95
1235	$4.85
1278	$9.95
1384	$6.28
1400	$4.75

Figure 9-9. A pricing program with a sequential search

```
C  PRICING PROGRAM WITH A SEQUENTIAL SEARCH
       INTEGER ITNUM(10),I,INUM
       REAL PRICE(10),QTY,COST
       DO 100 I=1,10
         READ (5,300) ITNUM(I),PRICE(I)
   100 CONTINUE
   200 READ (5,310) INUM,QTY
       IF (INUM.EQ.9999) GO TO 230
       I=1
   210   IF ((ITNUM(I).GE.INUM).OR.(I.EQ.10)) GO TO 220
         I=I+1
       GO TO 210
   220   IF (ITNUM(I).EQ.INUM) THEN
         COST=PRICE(I)*QTY
         WRITE (6,400) INUM,COST
       ELSE
         WRITE (6,410) INUM
       END IF
       GO TO 200
   230 STOP
   300 FORMAT (I4,F5.2)
   310 FORMAT (I4,F4.0)
   400 FORMAT (' ','ITEM ',I4,' COST ',F7.2)
   410 FORMAT (' ','ITEM ',I4,' NOT FOUND')
       END
```

(a) The program

```
1001 2.95
1023 3.64
1045 2.25
1172 0.75
1185 1.50
1201 1.95
1235 4.85
1278 9.95
1384 6.28
1400 4.75
1172  10
1400   5
1025  25
1438  15
1001 100
0985  20
1384   1
9999   0
```

(b) Input data

```
ITEM 1172 COST    7.50
ITEM 1400 COST   23.75
ITEM 1025 NOT FOUND
ITEM 1438 NOT FOUND
ITEM 1001 COST  295.00
ITEM  985 NOT FOUND
ITEM 1384 COST    6.28
```

(c) Output

numbers are not in increasing order, the greater than or equal to condition would have to be changed to an equal to condition.) The loop is also terminated if the end of the array is reached without finding INUM (that is, when I is equal to 10). After leaving the loop, the program checks to see if ITNUM(I) equals INUM. If this condition is true, PRICE(I) is multiplied by QTY to get the cost and the result is written. Otherwise, a message indicating that the item was not found is written. Then the input loop is repeated.

The example illustrates a common algorithm for "table look-up," the process of looking something up in a table. In this algorithm the array elements are searched in sequence. This approach is called a *sequential search*. In a sequential search we begin by looking at the first element of the array, then we examine the second element, then the third, and so forth until the desired element is found or until we can determine that the item is not in the array.

Binary search

Another algorithm for searching for an element in an array is called a *binary search*. In a binary search the array elements that are searched *must* be in ascending or descending order. We will assume that the elements of the array to be searched are in ascending order. Then, with a binary search, we first check the *middle* element of the array and determine if this is the desired element. If it is not, we determine if the element we want is located before or after the middle element. We then search the appropriate half of the array by examining the middle element of that half. Again we determine whether the element is the one we want or whether to search before or after the middle element. We continue to search by examining the middle of smaller and smaller sections of the array until the desired element is found or until we can determine that the element is not in the array.

To illustrate this algorithm, assume that the 20 elements of the array X are in ascending order. We wish to use a binary search to locate the element with a value equal to V. The sequence of statements shown in Figure 9-10 accomplishes this. In this sequence BOT equals the number of the bottom element of the part of the array being searched and TOP equals the number of the top element. Initially these are 1 and 20, respectively. The number of the middle element of the part of the array being searched is computed and assigned to MID. Notice that MID is calculated by dividing the sum of BOT and TOP by 2. Because this involves integer division, any fraction in the quotient is truncated. Each time through the loop the program checks to see if X(MID) equals V and branches out of the loop if this is the case. If V is not found, the program checks to see if X(MID) is less than V. If this is the case, BOT is assigned a value of one more than MID. If X(MID) is greater than V, TOP is MID minus 1. Then a new MID is computed and the process is repeated. The loop terminates either when the desired element is found, in which case the value of MID is the number of the element, or when BOT is greater than TOP, in which case the element is not in the array. Figure 9-11 shows how a binary search compares with a sequential search.

Figure 9-10. A binary search algorithm

```
      INTEGER BOT,TOP,MID
      REAL X(20),V
         .
         .
         .
      BOT=1
      TOP=20
   10 MID=(BOT+TOP)/2
         IF ((X(MID).EQ.V).OR.(BOT.GT.TOP)) GO TO 20
         IF (X(MID).LT.V) THEN
            BOT=MID+1
         ELSE
            TOP=MID-1
         END IF
      GO TO 10
   20 IF (X(MID).EQ.V) THEN
         WRITE (6,300) MID
      ELSE
         WRITE (6,310)
      END IF
  300 FORMAT (' VALUE FOUND AT ELEMENT ',I2)
  310 FORMAT (' VALUE NOT FOUND')
         .
         .
         .
```

We can use a binary search algorithm in the pricing program. Figure 9-12 shows the complete program. Note that after the appropriate item is found, the cost is determined by multiplying PRICE(MID) by QTY. Also note that the output from this program is the same as that of the sequential search program (Figure 9-9).

For large arrays, a binary search is much faster than a sequential search. For example, if an array contains 1000 elements, a sequential search will require an average of 1000/2 or 500 repetitions of the loop. Using a binary search, the loop will be repeated no more than $\log_2 1000$ or about 10 times. For large arrays, the extra complexity required to program a binary search results in considerable savings in program execution time.

Sorting

Sorting is the process of rearranging a set of data into a particular order. For example, given a list of numbers, we may wish to sort the numbers into ascending or descending order. Many times we need sorted data. For instance, we may want to produce a list of students in a class in order by student identification number. The student data requires sorting if it is not already in the desired order. In the last subsection we saw that an array must be in ascending or descending order if the binary search algorithm is to be used. If the array is not in the appropriate order, it must be sorted before it can be searched.

Figure 9-11. Sequential vs. binary search

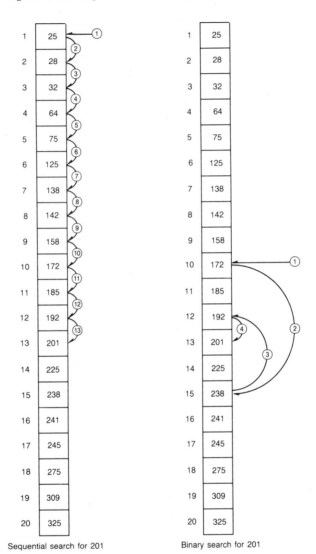

Sequential search for 201   Binary search for 201

Figure 9-12. A pricing program with a binary search (Part 1 of 2)

```
C  PRICING PROGRAM WITH A BINARY SEARCH
      INTEGER ITNUM(10),I,INUM,BOT,TOP,MID
      REAL PRICE(10),QTY,COST
      DO 100 I=1,10
        READ (5,300) ITNUM(I),PRICE(I)
  100 CONTINUE
  200 READ (5,310) INUM,QTY
      IF (INUM.EQ.9999) GO TO 230
      BOT=1
      TOP=10
  210   MID=(BOT+TOP)/2
        IF ((ITNUM(MID).EQ.INUM).OR.(BOT.GT.TOP)) GO TO 220
        IF (ITNUM(MID).LT.INUM) THEN
          BOT=MID+1
        ELSE
          TOP=MID-1
        END IF
      GO TO 210
  220   IF (ITNUM(MID).EQ.INUM) THEN
          COST=PRICE(MID)*QTY
          WRITE (6,400) INUM,COST
        ELSE
          WRITE (6,410) INUM
        END IF
      GO TO 200
  230 STOP
  300 FORMAT (I4,F5.2)
  310 FORMAT (I4,F4.0)
  400 FORMAT (' ','ITEM ',I4,' COST ',F7.2)
  410 FORMAT (' ','ITEM ',I4,' NOT FOUND')
      END
```

(a) The program

```
                    1001 2.95
                    1023 3.64
                    1045 2.25
                    1172 0.75
                    1185 1.50
                    1201 1.95
                    1235 4.85
                    1278 9.95
                    1384 6.28
                    1400 4.75
                    1172   10
                    1400    5
                    1025   25
                    1438   15
                    1001  100
                    0985   20
                    1384    1
                    9999    0
```

(b) Input data

Figure 9-12. (Part 2 of 2)

```
ITEM 1172 COST    7.50
ITEM 1400 COST   23.75
ITEM 1025 NOT FOUND
ITEM 1438 NOT FOUND
ITEM 1001 COST  295.00
ITEM  985 NOT FOUND
ITEM 1384 COST    6.28
```

(c) Output

There are many algorithms for sorting. In this subsection we discuss *bubble sorting.* (This type of sorting is also called *pushdown sorting, interchange sorting,* and *exchange sorting.*) As we will see, bubble sorting gets its name from the fact that data "bubbles" to the top of the array.

The basic technique in bubble sorting is to compare adjacent elements of the array to be sorted. If any two adjacent elements are found to be out of order with respect to each other, they are interchanged (that is, their values are switched). For example, assume that the array B has five elements that are to be sorted into ascending order (smallest to largest). Then the following loop passes through the array once, exchanging elements that are not in the proper order:

```
DO 10 I=1,4
   IF (B(I).GT.B(I+1)) THEN
     T=B(I)
     B(I)=B(I+1)
     B(I+1)=T
   END IF
10 CONTINUE
```

Note that the loop is repeated *four* times (one less than the number of elements in the array). Each time through the loop, B(I) is compared with B(I+1). Thus the first time through the loop, B(1) is compared with B(2). Then B(2) is compared with B(3). Next B(3) and B(4) are compared. Finally, B(4) and B(5) are compared. If any two adjacent elements are not in ascending order, they are switched. (See Section 7-4 for a discussion of switching the values of two variables.) Figure 9-13 shows what takes place with each execution of this loop for a particular set of data.

Figure 9-13. Pushing the largest element to the end of an array

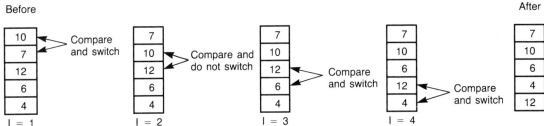

This loop causes the largest element of the array to be "pushed down" to the last position in the array. At the same time, smaller elements start to "bubble up" to the top of the array. We now must repeat the loop to cause the next largest elements to be pushed to the next-to-last position in the array. Then the loop must be repeated for the next-to-next-largest element, and so forth. In all, this loop must be repeated four times. The last time, the smallest element will automatically end up in the first position of the array. This repeated execution of the loop can be accomplished by nested DO loops as follows:

```
      DO 20 J=1,4
        DO 10 I=1,4
          IF (B(I).GT.B(I+1)) THEN
            T=B(I)
            B(I)=B(I+1)
            B(I+1)=T
          END IF
10      CONTINUE
20 CONTINUE
```

Figure 9-14 shows how the array appears after each execution of the outer loop. Note that large values in the array are "pushed down" and small values "bubble up."

We can make the algorithm more efficient by recognizing that, with each successive pass through the inner loop, one less comparison is required. This is because once the largest element has been pushed to the end of the array we do not need to include it in any subsequent comparisons. The same holds true for the next largest element and so forth. The following sequence of statements includes this modification:

```
      DO 20 K=4,1,-1
        DO 10 I=1,K
          IF (B(I).GT.B(I+1)) THEN
            T=B(I)
            B(I)=B(I+1)
            B(I+1)=T
          END IF
10      CONTINUE
20 CONTINUE
```

Figure 9-14. Sorting a five-element array

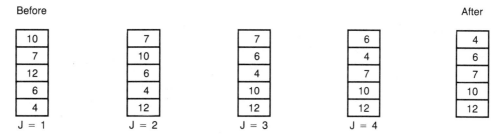

Note that the test value for the inner loop is the value of the variable named K. This variable is decremented from 4 to 1. When K is 4, the inner loop is executed four times. When K is 3, the inner loop is done three times. K is one less for each successive time through the inner loop. Hence one less comparison is done with each repetition of the loop.

We can use bubble sorting to sort the pricing table used in the examples in the previous subsection. This would be required if a search is to be done and the table is not read in ascending order by item number. The only modification we need is that each time two item numbers are found out of sequence and are switched, the corresponding prices are also switched. This is to maintain the relationship between the item numbers and prices. The program in Figure 9-15 sorts the pricing table. The input to this program consists of the data for the pricing table in any order; the output is the pricing data in increasing order by item number. Note that the statements to do the sorting could be included in the programs in Figures 9-9 and 9-12 between statements 100 and 200.

Figure 9-15. A program to sort a pricing table (Part 1 of 2)

```
C   PROGRAM TO SORT A PRICING TABLE
        INTEGER ITNUM(10),TEMPIT,I,K
        REAL PRICE(10),TEMPPR
C   TABLE INPUT
        DO 100 I=1,10
          READ (5,300) ITNUM(I),PRICE(I)
     100 CONTINUE
C   SORTING ALGORITHM
        DO 160 K=9,1,-1
          DO 150 I=1,K
            IF (ITNUM(I).GT.ITNUM(I+1)) THEN
              TEMPIT=ITNUM(I)
              ITNUM(I)=ITNUM(I+1)
              ITNUM(I+1)=TEMPIT
              TEMPPR=PRICE(I)
              PRICE(I)=PRICE(I+1)
              PRICE(I+1)=TEMPPR
            END IF
     150    CONTINUE
     160 CONTINUE
C   TABLE OUTPUT
        WRITE (6,400)
        DO 200 I=1,10
          WRITE (6,410) ITNUM(I),PRICE(I)
     200 CONTINUE
C
        STOP
C
     300 FORMAT (I4,F5.2)
     400 FORMAT ('1','ITEM NUMBER     UNIT PRICE'/)
     410 FORMAT (' ',3X,I4,11X,F5.2)
        END
```

(a) The program

Figure 9-15. (Part 2 of 2)

```
1235 4.85
1278 9.95
1045 2.25
1400 4.75
1201 1.95
1001 2.95
1023 3.64
1185 1.50
1384 6.28
1172 0.75
```

(b) Input data

ITEM NUMBER	UNIT PRICE
1001	2.95
1023	3.64
1045	2.25
1172	.75
1185	1.50
1201	1.95
1235	4.85
1278	9.95
1384	6.28
1400	4.75

(c) Output

The examples so far demonstrate *ascending* order sorts. To sort an array into descending order, the greater-than condition in the IF statement must be changed to a less-than condition. The effect then is to push the smaller elements to the end of the array and to "bubble" the larger elements up to the beginning of the array.

Bubble sorting is just one of many ways to sort an array. A number of algorithms are considerably faster than bubble sorting for large arrays. These algorithms are also more difficult to program. As the programmer finds more situations that require sorting, he or she should explore other techniques.*

9-5. The DATA statement

Very often we need to initialize the elements of an array at the beginning of a program. We could use a technique such as the one shown in Section 9-3. However, sometimes it is more convenient to use a special statement, called the DATA statement, to initialize the array. The syntax of the DATA statement

* Most textbooks on data structures include sections on sorting. A very complete reference is by Donald Knuth entitled *The Art of Computer Programming, Vol. 3, Sorting and Searching*, published by Addison-Wesley, Reading, Mass., 1973.

is as follows:

DATA *list/data/,list/data/,...*

where *list* is a list of variable, array, or array element
names separated by commas.
data is a list of constants separated by commas.

Note that the commas after the slashes are optional. This statement can be used to assign initial values to simple variables as well as to array elements. In this section we first show how the DATA statement is used for initializing variables and then explain its use with arrays.

Initializing variables with a DATA statement

Assume that we need to assign the value 0 to the integer variable named I, and the value 2.0 to the real variables named A, B, and C. This can be accomplished by a series of arithmetic assignment statements such as the following:

```
I=0
A=2.0
B=2.0
C=2.0
```

With the DATA statement, I, A, B, and C can be initialized to the desired values as follows:

```
DATA I/0/,A/2.0/,B/2.0/,C/2.0/
```

In this statement each variable name is listed, followed by its initial value enclosed in slashes, with commas separating the variable names. The end result of this statement is the same as the preceding arithmetic assignment statements. However, the way in which the variable names are initialized is different. The arithmetic assignment statements cause variable names to be initialized when the program is executed. The assignment statements require instructions in the object program and time during execution to initialize the data. The DATA statement is more efficient because no object program instructions are needed and the initialization is completed before the program begins executing.

The previous example shows one form of the DATA statement. Another way to code this statement is to list several variable names together, followed by the corresponding initial values enclosed in slashes. For example, the following statement initializes the variable names I, A, B, and C to the desired values:

```
DATA I,A,B,C/0,2.0,2.0,2.0/
```

Whenever the DATA statement is used in this form, each variable name is assigned the corresponding value in the list of data. Thus I is assigned the value 0, A is assigned the value 2.0, and so forth.

When several variable names are to be initialized to the same value, the value may be preceded by a repeat count instead of being repeatedly listed. The repeat count is an integer constant and an asterisk. For example, the entry 3*2.0 in a DATA statement means to repeat the value 2.0 three times. Thus the previous example may be shortened to

```
DATA I,A,B,C/0,3*2.0/
```

When using the DATA statement in any of these forms, it is important that the number of variable names corresponds to the number of constants. For example, consider the following DATA statement that initializes three groups of variable names:

```
DATA X,Y,Z/2*7.5,0.0/,K,L/3*5/,E,F,G/4.5,3.7/
```

The first group contains three variable names as does the list of constants when the repeat count is taken into consideration. The second group contains two variable names, but the list of constants indicates three values. This results in an error. Similarly, the last group is erroneous because there are three variable names but only two constants.

Any type of data may be initialized with the DATA statement as long as the data type of the constant and the type of the variable name correspond. Thus an integer variable name must correspond to an integer constant and a real variable name must have a corresponding real constant.

DATA statements may be placed anywhere in the program after the specification statements and before the END statement. The usual practice is to place all DATA statements immediately after the specification statements and before the first executable statement.

Character variables in a DATA statement. Character variables can be initialized in a DATA statement. The variable name must have been specified previously in a CHARACTER statement. Character constants are then used for the initial values. For example, consider the following DATA statement (assume that all variable names are character type):

```
DATA STATE1,STATE2/'CALIF','NEW YORK'/X,Y,Z/3*' '/
```

In this example, STATE1 is initialized to CALIF; STATE2 is initialized to NEW YORK; and X, Y, and Z are each initialized to one blank space. Note that if the length of the character variable is not the same as the length of the character constant, blanks are added or characters are truncated on the right as with the character assignment statement. (See Section 8-3.)

Logical variables in a DATA statement. Logical variables can be initialized with the DATA statement by using logical constants. For example, assume that LB, LC, and LD are logical variable names. Then the following statement initializes LB to the value true and LC and LD to false values:

```
DATA LB,LC,LD/.TRUE.,2*.FALSE./
```

Initializing array elements with a DATA statement

Array elements can be initialized in a DATA statement by listing each array element name. For example, the following statement assigns the value 0.0 to each of the first three elements of the real array named AMT:

```
DATA AMT(1),AMT(2),AMT(3)/3*0.0/
```

To initialize the entire array, the array name can be used without a subscript. The effect is to cause the entire array to be initialized to the indicated values. For example, consider the following statement:

```
DATA AMT/25*0.0/,K/10*0,5*1/
```

Here we assume that AMT is the name of a 25-element real array and that K is a 15-element integer array. The effect of this DATA statement is to initialize all elements of AMT to 0.0 and to assign 0 to the first 10 elements of K and 1 to the remaining five elements.

Implied-DO lists are also allowed in the DATA statement. For example, consider the following statement:

```
DATA (X(I),I=2,20,2)/10*1.0/
```

This statement causes X(2), X(4), X(6), and so forth up to X(20) to be each initialized to 1.0. As another example, consider the following statement:

```
DATA A,B,(K(J),M(J),J=1,10)/2.5,3.5,20*0/
```

This statement causes A and B, which we assume are simple variables, to be initialized to 2.5 and 3.5, respectively, and causes the first 10 elements of K and M to be initialized to 0.

9-6. Character data arrays

An array may contain character data if it is declared in a CHARACTER statement. For example, the following statement specifies a character data array with 20 elements:

```
CHARACTER CA(20)
```

Recall from Section 8-1 that the CHARACTER statement not only indicates that a name refers to character data but also gives the length of the data. With an array of character data, each element in the array has the same length. In the example just shown, because an explicit length is not given, each element is assumed to have a length of 1. When a length specification is given, it may appear after the word CHARACTER or after the dimension of the array. For example, consider the following statement:

```
CHARACTER*10 CB(30),CC(100)*20
```

This statement specifies two character arrays. The first, CB, has 30 elements each of length 10. The second array, CC, contains 100 elements each with a length of 20.

A character array element name is subscripted just like a numeric array element name. For example, CB(5) refers to the fifth element of the character array named CB. Similarly, CB(J) identifies the Jth element. When a substring name is used, the position of the substring follows the subscript. For example, CB(15)(3:8) refers to the third through eighth characters of the fifteenth element of the array CB.

A subscripted character array name or substring name may be used in a character expression just like a character variable name. For example, the following statements use character array element names:

```
CB(5)=CB(4)
IF (CB(30)(1:3).EQ.'END') THEN
WRITE (6,200) (CB(I),I=1,10)
CC(I)=CB(I)//CB(I+1)
```

To illustrate the use of character arrays in a program, assume that each of 50 records contains the name of a state and its population. This data must be stored in two arrays, one for the state names and one for the population, to create a population table. Next a record must be read with any state's name. Then the population table has to be searched to find and print the state's population. Figure 9-16 shows a program to accomplish this. Note that the input data contains 50 records with state names and populations, followed by a group of records just containing state names. The population table, created from the first group of 50 records, is searched for each state in the second group of records.

9-7. Logical data arrays

Section 8-5 described the use of the LOGICAL type statement to declare logical variable names. This statement is also used to dimension arrays that contain logical data. For example, the following statement declares that the name LA identifies a 20-element array of logical data:

```
LOGICAL LA(20)
```

A logical array name may be subscripted like any other array name to identify an element of an array. For example, LA(1) is the name of the first element in the logical array LA. Similarly, LA(I) identifies the Ith element.

Figure 9-16. A program to look up state populations (Part 1 of 2)

```
C  STATE POPULATION LOOK-UP PROGRAM
      CHARACTER*14 STATE(50),STA
      INTEGER POP(50)
      DO 100 I=1,50
         READ (5,300) STATE(I),POP(I)
 100  CONTINUE
 200  READ (5,310) STA
      IF (STA.EQ.' ') GO TO 230
      I=1
 210  IF ((STATE(I).EQ.STA).OR.(I.EQ.50)) GO TO 220
         I=I+1
      GO TO 210
 220  IF (STATE(I).EQ.STA) THEN
         WRITE (6,400) STATE(I),POP(I)
      ELSE
         WRITE (6,410) STA
      END IF
      GO TO 200
 230  STOP
 300  FORMAT (A14,I8)
 310  FORMAT (A14)
 400  FORMAT (' ',A14,' HAS A POPULATION OF ',I8)
 410  FORMAT (' ',A14,' IS AN INVALID STATE NAME')
      END
```

(a) The program

```
ALABAMA        3890000
ALASKA          400000
ARIZONA        2718000
ARKANSAS       2286000
CALIFORNIA    23669000
COLORADO       2889000
CONNECTICUT    3108000
DELAWARE        595000
FLORIDA        9740000
GEORGIA        5464000
HAWAII          965000
IDAHO           944000
     .
     .
     .
VERMONT         511000
VIRGINIA       5346000
WASHINGTON     4130000
WEST VIRGINIA  1950000
WISCONSIN      4705000
WYOMING         471000
CALIFORNIA
WASHINGTON
SOUTH VIRGINIA
HAWAII
WEST CAROLINA
WYOMING
```

(b) Input data

Figure 9-16. (Part 2 of 2)

```
CALIFORNIA      HAS A POPULATION OF 23669000
WASHINGTON      HAS A POPULATION OF  4130000
SOUTH VIRGINIA  IS AN INVALID STATE NAME
HAWAII          HAS A POPULATION OF   965000
WEST CAROLINA   IS AN INVALID STATE NAME
WYOMING         HAS A POPULATION OF   471000
```

(c) Output

A logical array element name may be used in a logical expression in the same manner as a logical variable name. For example, the following are valid statements that use logical array element names:

```
IF (LA(3).AND.LA(4)) THEN
LA(5)=LA(6)
WRITE (6,200) LA(I),LA(I+1)
LA(1)=.NOT.LA(2).AND.LA(3).OR.LA(4)
```

As an example of a program that uses logical arrays, consider the problem of analyzing the results of a true-false questionnaire. Assume that the questionnaire contains 20 questions and the answer to each question is recorded as a T or F in the first 20 positions of a record. The program in Figure 9-17 reads the questionnaire answers by using the short-list technique, counts the number of true answers by using the array element name as a logical expression in an IF statement, and writes the result.

Figure 9-17. A program to analyze a true-false questionnaire

```
C  QUESTIONNAIRE ANALYSIS PROGRAM
      LOGICAL ANS(20)
      INTEGER COUNT,I
      READ (5,100) ANS
      COUNT=0
      DO 10 I=1,20
        IF (ANS(I)) THEN
          COUNT=COUNT+1
        END IF
   10 CONTINUE
      WRITE (6,200) COUNT
      STOP
  100 FORMAT (20L1)
  200 FORMAT (' ','NUMBER OF TRUE ANSWERS IS ',I3)
      END
```

(a) The program

```
TFFTTTFTFTTFFTTFFFTFF
```

(b) Input data

```
NUMBER OF TRUE ANSWERS IS   9
```

(c) Output

Review questions

1. Define each of the following terms:
   a. array
   b. array name
   c. array element
   d. array element name
2. Code statements to specify that S is a 50-element array of integer data and T is a 50-element array of real data. Do not use a DIMENSION statement.
3. Answer Question 2 using a DIMENSION statement.
4. Consider the array A shown in Figure 9-1. Assume that J and K are integer variable names and that J is 4 and K is 3. What is the value of each of the following array element names?
   a. A(9)
   b. A(J)
   c. A(J + K)
   d. A(J/K)
5. Code a statement to specify that U is an array of real data with a lower dimension bound of 10 and an upper dimension bound of 30.
6. Consider the array U defined in Question 5. Assume that L is an integer variable name with a value of 25. Indicate whether or not each of the following array element names is valid.
   a. U(1)
   b. U(L)
   c. U(L − 10)
   d. U(2*L − 20)
7. Code a statement to multiply the first two elements of the array U defined in Question 5 and assigns the result to the last element of U.
8. Code a group of statements to read the data for the array S defined in Question 2. Assume that each element in the array is in a separate input record.
9. Code the answer to Question 8 assuming that each input record contains 10 elements of the array.
10. Code a group of statements to write the elements of the array S defined in Question 2 in a column in reverse order.
11. Code a group of statements to write the elements of the array S defined in Question 2 in two adjacent columns. The first column should contain the elements S(1) through S(25). The second column should contain the elements S(26) through S(50).
12. Code a group of statements to assign the numbers 1, 2, . . . , 50 to the corresponding elements of the array S defined in Question 2.
13. Code a group of statements to find the total of the odd-numbered elements of the array S defined in Question 2.
14. Consider the arrays S and T defined in Question 2. Code a group of statements to search the array S for all elements equal to R. Each time an element of S equal to R is found, write the corresponding element from the array T.
15. Code the answer to Question 14 with the modification that only the first element of the array S equal to R is to be found. If no such element is found, write an appropriate message. Use a sequential search.

16. Assume that the elements of the array S defined in Question 2 are in decreasing order. Code a group of statements that uses a binary search to search S for an element equal to R. If such an element is found, write a message indicating this. If no such element is found, write an appropriate message.

17. Consider the sorting algorithm discussed in Section 9-4 and the 5-element array B shown in Figure 9-13. This figure gives the order of the data in B for each value of I during the *first* execution of the sorting loop. Draw the equivalent figure for the *second* execution of the sorting loop.

18. Consider the program shown in Figure 9-15. What modification would have to be made in the program for a descending order sort?

19. Code a DATA statement to initialize the integer variables named J, K, and L to 1, 2, and 3, respectively, and the real variables named X and Y to 2.5 and 7.5, respectively.

20. Consider the arrays S and T defined in Question 2. Code a DATA statement to initialize the elements of S to 0 and the odd-numbered elements of T to 0.0.

Programming problems

1. Write a FORTRAN program to read hourly temperatures for a day into a 24-element array. The first element of the array gives the temperature at 1:00 A.M., the second element is the temperature at 2:00 A.M., and so forth. Note that the thirteenth element is the temperature at 1:00 P.M. Then search the array for the maximum and minimum temperatures. Print these temperatures along with the times at which they occur. Supply appropriate input data to test the program.

2. An inventory table contains information about the quantity of inventory on hand for each item stocked. Assume that there are 15 items in the inventory. The inventory data is recorded in 15 records each containing an item number and the quantity of the item that is in stock. The data is in increasing order by item number.

   Write a FORTRAN program to do the following:

   a. Read the inventory table into two arrays, one for the item numbers and one for the quantities. Then print the inventory data in columns below appropriate headings.

   b. Read a record containing an item number, an amount received, and an amount sold. Search the inventory table for the corresponding item using either a sequential search or a binary search. Then update the quantity on hand by adding the amount received to the amount from the table and subtracting the amount sold. Repeat this step until 9999 is read for an item number. Be sure to account for the case where the item is not in the table.

   c. After all items have been updated print the inventory data in columns below appropriate headings.

Use the following data for the inventory table:

Item number	Quantity on hand
1102	100
1113	25
1147	37
1158	95
1196	225
1230	150
1237	15
1239	105
1245	84
1275	97
1276	350
1284	82
1289	125
1351	138
1362	64

Use the following data to update the inventory:

Item number	Quantity received	Quantity sold
1230	25	100
1113	0	15
1255	16	42
1289	50	0
1405	26	5
1102	100	75
1239	25	25

3. Figure 9-18 shows the tax rate schedule used to compute income tax for a single taxpayer. The tax is based on the individual's taxable income. For example, if the taxable income is $17,500, the income tax is $2097 plus 24% of the difference between $17,500 and $15,000, or $2697.

Write a FORTRAN program to read the tax rate schedule into several arrays. One approach is to use three arrays, one for the first column, and two for the third column. Then the program should read a taxpayer identification number and taxable income, compute the income tax, and print the results.

Use the following data to test the program:

Taxpayer number	Taxable income
1234	$ 17,500
1332	6,200
1424	10,201
2134	1,500
2432	47,300
3144	154,000
3223	23,350

Figure 9-18. Tax rate schedule

Schedule X
Single Taxpayers

Use this Schedule if you checked **Filing Status Box 1** on Form 1040—

If the amount on Form 1040, line 37 is: Over—	But not over—	Enter on Form 1040, line 38	of the amount over—
$0	$2,300	—0—	
2,300	3,400	.......11%	$2,300
3,400	4,400	$121 + 13%	3,400
4,400	8,500	251 + 15%	4,400
8,500	10,800	866 + 17%	8,500
10,800	12,900	1,257 + 19%	10,800
12,900	15,000	1,656 + 21%	12,900
15,000	18,200	2,097 + 24%	15,000
18,200	23,500	2,865 + 28%	18,200
23,500	28,800	4,349 + 32%	23,500
28,800	34,100	6,045 + 36%	28,800
34,100	41,500	7,953 + 40%	34,100
41,500	55,300	10,913 + 45%	41,500
55,300	....	17,123 + 50%	55,300

4. Write a FORTRAN program to find the mean and standard deviation of the heights of the students in a class. If there are n students with heights x_i, $i = 1, \ldots, n$, the formulas for the mean and standard deviation are as follows:

$$\text{mean} = \bar{x} = \frac{\sum_{i=1}^{n} x_i}{n}$$

$$\text{standard deviation} = s = \sqrt{\frac{\sum_{i=1}^{n}(x_i - \bar{x})^2}{n}}$$

Test the program for a class of 25 students with the following heights in inches:

70	62	71	67	67
69	74	63	70	68
71	70	69	68	73
75	77	66	69	74
67	60	72	71	64

5. The results of a random survey of the households in an area of a city have been recorded in a file. Each record in the file contains information about one household in the area. An identification number, the annual income of the

head of the household, and the number of people living in the household are recorded in each record. The last record in the file has 9999 in the identification number field. Write a FORTRAN program to analyze these data according to the following specifications:

a. Read the survey results into three arrays, one for the identification numbers, one for the annual incomes, and one for the number of people living in the households. Assume that no more than 50 households are in the survey and dimension all arrays accordingly. However, there may be fewer than 50 records, so a count of the number of records must be kept as the data is read. Finally, print the array data in columns below appropriate headings.

b. Calculate the average income and average number of people for all households. Print the results with appropriate headings.

c. Print the identification number and annual income of all households whose income is below average.

d. Determine the percentage of the households in the area that have incomes below the poverty level. The poverty level depends on the number of people living in the household. If there is one person, the poverty level income is $6500. If there are two people, the poverty level is $8500. For a household with more than two people, the poverty level is $8500 plus $950 for each additional person.

Use the following data to test the program:

Identification number	Annual income	Number of people
1101	$10,750	3
1020	5,250	2
1083	8,000	5
1141	8,500	1
1157	14,300	4
1235	9,000	6
1347	10,350	7
1508	4,350	1
1512	6,900	3
1513	7,600	4
1584	8,385	2
1631	6,300	2
1690	17,200	4
1742	15,350	5
1755	5,700	1
1759	8,300	3
1809	10,250	1
1853	12,500	2
1899	14,000	6
1903	2,500	1
1952	5,250	3
9999	(trailer value)	

6. This problem involves analyzing product sales information. Input consists of the identification number and quantity sold for each of 25 products. Write a FORTRAN program to do the following:

a. Read the identification numbers and quantities into two arrays. After all data has been read, print the arrays in columns below appropriate headings.
b. Calculate and print the average of the quantities sold.
c. Determine the number of products whose sales fall into each of the following categories:

> 500 or more
> 250 to 499
> 100 to 249
>   0 to 99

Print the results with appropriate headings.
d. Sort the quantity array into descending order (largest to smallest) using the bubble sorting algorithm. Note that there are two arrays, although only the quantity array is to be sorted. However, whenever two elements of the quantity array are out of order and need to be switched, the corresponding identification numbers must be switched. After the array is sorted, print the two arrays in columns with appropriate headings.
e. Sort the identification number array into ascending order (smallest to largest). Again note that any exchange of elements in one array must be accompanied by an exchange of corresponding elements in the other array. After the array is sorted, print the two arrays in columns below appropriate headings.

Use the following data to test the program:

Identification number	Quantity sold
208	295
137	152
485	825
217	100
945	250
607	435
642	500
735	36
300	163
299	255
435	501
116	75
189	0
218	63
830	617
695	825
708	416
325	99
339	249
418	237
225	712
180	328
925	499
455	240
347	378

7. Merging is the process of bringing together two lists of data to form one. For example, consider the following lists of five numbers each:

List 1	List 2
2	1
3	6
5	8
8	9
10	12

When these two lists are merged they form the following list:

Merged list

1
2
3
5
6
8
8
9
10
12

Note that the original lists are in increasing order and so is the merged list.

Write a FORTRAN program to read two lists of 15 numbers each. The numbers may be in any order initially. The program should sort each list into increasing order and then merge the two lists to form one list of 30 numbers. Finally, the program should print the original two lists, the sorted lists, and the merged list.

Use the following data to test the program:

List 1	List 2
100	53
87	85
91	92
52	98
63	63
39	75
85	89
91	96
82	81
99	62
73	69
57	85
82	91
85	80
78	71

8. Write a FORTRAN program to read student test score data into an array, calculate the mean (average) of the test scores, tabulate the test scores, sort the test scores into descending order, and find the median (middle value) of the test scores.

Test scores are recorded one per record along with a student identification number for each test score. There are an unknown number of records. The last record does not contain a test score but has 999 in the student identification number field. Use this trailer value to control the input process. Assume that there are no more than 99 test scores and dimension any arrays accordingly.

Prepare the program according to the following specifications:

a. Read the identification numbers and the test scores into two separate arrays. The records must be counted as they are read to determine how many test scores are to be processed. Finally, list, below appropriate headings, the data in the identification number and test scores arrays. At the end, print a statement of the number of test scores in the data.

b. Accumulate and print the total of the test scores. Calculate and print the mean of the test scores. The mean is the average of a set of data values, which is found by dividing the total by the number of values.

c. Tabulate (count) the number of scores that fall into each of the following categories:

$$90-100$$
$$80-89$$
$$70-79$$
$$60-69$$
$$0-59$$

Print the results with appropriate titles.

d. Sort the test scores into descending order (largest to smallest). Print a list of the identification numbers and the test scores in descending order. Use the bubble sorting algorithm to sort the test score data. Note that there are two arrays, although only the test score array is to be sorted. However, when two elements of the test score array are out of order and need to be switched, the corresponding identification numbers must be switched.

e. Determine and print the median of the test scores. The median is the middle value of a set of data; 50 percent of the data values are greater than or equal to the median and 50 percent are less than or equal to the median. To determine the median, the data must first be sorted into ascending or descending order. Then the median is the middle value of the sorted data for an odd number of values or the average of two middle values for an even number of items. Be sure to make the program sufficiently general to handle both cases.

Use the following input data to test the program:

Identification number	Test score	Identification number	Test score	Identification number	Test score
282	99	283	83	240	73
115	75	116	72	145	74
124	76	123	71	267	74
215	77	114	74	294	91
275	69	287	96	232	75
208	78	201	79	206	75
225	85	242	71	150	76
113	77	119	63	133	83
205	76	142	78	255	70
122	89	219	84	250	77
137	78	248	72	210	70
185	75	173	79	233	80
235	100	261	85	166	71
138	74	265	71	202	61
298	74	281	72	176	81
217	62	139	55	257	72
104	82	141	73	256	14
108	73	266	65	230	73
191	79	110	81	129	89

9. Each state has a two-letter abbreviation authorized by the U.S. Postal Service. For example, the abbreviation for California is CA; the abbreviation for New York is NY. (See a Zip Code directory for a complete list.)

Write a FORTRAN program to read a complete table of state abbreviations and corresponding state names. Use one array for the abbreviations and another array for the names. Then print the arrays below appropriate headings. Next, read a state abbreviation and search the table for the corresponding state's name. Print the abbreviation and the name. Repeat this part of the program until an abbreviation of XX is read. Supply appropriate input data to test the program.

10. Write a FORTRAN program to read an array of 20 names and sort the names into alphabetical order. Each name is recorded in a record and consists of the last name, a comma, a space, and then the first name. Separate the names into two arrays before doing the sorting and then reconstruct the names in the appropriate format after the sorting is completed. Print the sorted array of names. Supply an appropriate list of 20 names to test the program.

11. A 25-question true-false test needs to be scored. The correct answers to the questions are recorded in the first record of a file. Following this is one record for each student with the student's number and his or her answers to the questions. Write a FORTRAN program to correct each student's answers. The program should print the student's number. Below this, listed in adjacent columns, should be the correct answers, the students answers, and an X opposite any incorrect answers. At the end of this, the program should print the percentage of the answers that are correct.

Use the following data to test the program:

Correct Answers: *FTTTFFTFTTFTFFFFTFTTFFTFFT*

Student's number	Student's answers
11301	FTTFTFTFTTTFTFFTFTTFFFTFT
11302	FFTTTTFFTTFTTFFTTFTFFTFFF
11303	FTTTFFTFTTFTFFFTFTTFFTFFT
11304	TFTTFFTFTTTFFFFFFTTFTTFTT
11305	TTTTFFFFTTFTFFFFTFTFFFTFFT
11306	FFFFFFTFTTTTTFFFTFFTFTFFF
11307	TTTFFFFTTTFTFFFFTTFTFTTFFT
11308	FTFTFTFTFTFTFTFTFTFTFTFTF
11309	TFTFTFTFTFTFTFTFTFTFTFTFT
11310	TTTTTTTTTTTTTTTTTTTTTTTTT
11311	FFFFFFFFFFFFFFFFFFFFFFFFF

12. Using the data in Problem 11, write a FORTRAN program to determine the percentage of the students in the class who got each question correct. That is, determine and print the percentage of the students who got the first question correct, the percentage who got the second question correct, and so forth.

Chapter 10

Multidimensional arrays

The type of array described in Chapter 9 is called a *one-dimensional array*. This is because we think of the data in the array as being organized in one direction, such as a column. (See Figure 9-1.) FORTRAN also allows two-, three-, and even higher dimensional arrays. In this chapter we examine multidimensional arrays and their use in FORTRAN. After completing this chapter you should be able to write programs that process multidimensional arrays.

10-1. Two-dimensional array concepts

A *two-dimensional array* is usually thought of as a table of data organized into rows and columns. Figure 10-1 shows a two-dimensional array of four rows and three columns. In an actual case, this data may represent the test scores of four students on three different exams. For example, the data in row 1 represents the three test scores of student number 1. The score on the first test for this student is 91; this score is found in column 1 of row 1. In row 1, column 2, is this student's score on the second test (78). This student's third test score is in row 1, column 3. Similarly, test scores for the other students are found in the other rows.

As with one-dimensional arrays, a two-dimensional array is given a name that refers to the whole array. For example, the array in Figure 10-1 could be named SCR. To locate an element in a two-dimensional array, both the row number and column number of the element must be given. A two-dimensional array element name is formed from the array name and *two* subscripts; the subscripts are separated by commas and enclosed in parentheses. The first subscript is the row number of the element; the second subscript is the column number. Thus, for the SCR array in Figure 10-1, the element in row 1, column 2, is named SCR(1,2). Similarly, the name of the element in

Figure 10-1. A two-dimensional array

Column numbers

	1	2	3
1	91	78	85
2	95	90	96
3	85	100	89
4	69	75	68

Row numbers

row 3, column 1, of this array is SCR(3,1). Figure 10-2 shows the names of all elements in this two-dimensional array.

Dimensioning two-dimensional arrays

Like one-dimensional arrays, a two-dimensional array must be dimensioned in the program. This can be done either with a type statement or with a DIMENSION statement. The maximum value of each subscript must be given when dimensioning the array. For example, the test score array illustrated previously can be specified as follows:

```
REAL SCR(4,3)
```

The first number in parentheses is the number of rows; the second number indicates the number of columns. Such an array is said to be a "four-by-three" array. Because the array is dimensioned in a REAL statement, it contains real data.

Both one- and two-dimensional arrays may be dimensioned in the same statement. For example, the following statement describes three integer arrays:

```
INTEGER S(10,10),LIST(12,2),X(20)
```

Figure 10-2. Element names for a two-dimensional array

Column numbers

	1	2	3
1	SCR(1,1)	SCR(1,2)	SCR(1,3)
2	SCR(2,1)	SCR(2,2)	SCR(2,3)
3	SCR(3,1)	SCR(3,2)	SCR(3,3)
4	SCR(4,1)	SCR(4,2)	SCR(4,3)

Row numbers

The first two arrays specified in this statement, S and LIST, are two-dimensional and the last array, X, is one-dimensional.

The following statement illustrates the use of the DIMENSION statement to dimension two-dimensional arrays:

```
DIMENSION X(8,12)
```

This array contains eight rows and twelve columns. The type of data in the array depends on whether implicit or explicit typing is used. (See Section 9-1.)

When a two-dimensional array is dimensioned as in our examples so far, the lower dimension bounds of the subscripts are 1. If lower dimension bounds other than 1 are required, these are given for each subscript. For example, the following statement declares a two-dimensional array with lower and upper bounds:

```
REAL B(5:10,0:8)
```

This array contains six rows numbered 5, 6, . . . , 10, and nine columns numbered 0, 1, . . . , 8.

Subscripts for two-dimensional arrays

Subscripts for two-dimensional arrays must follow the rules for one-dimensional array subscripts. The important difference is that there must be two subscripts instead of one. Two-dimensional array subscripts may be integer constants, variable names, and arithmetic expressions. For example, the name SCR(I,J) indicates the element in the Ith row and Jth column (assuming I and J are integer). The value of a subscript must never be less than its lower dimension bound or greater than its upper dimension bound.

Two-dimensional array element names can be used like any variable names. For example, all of the following statements are valid (assuming I, J, and K are integer and SCR is a two-dimensional array):

```
READ (5,100) SCR(1,1),SCR(1,2),SCR(1,3)
SCR(I,J)=SCR(J,K)+SCR(K,I)
WRITE (6,200) SCR(J+2*K,I-J)
IF (SCR(I,3).GE.90.0) THEN
```

To illustrate the processing of a two-dimensional array in a program, assume that we need to find the total of all of the elements in the test score array SCR discussed earlier. Figure 10-3 shows a program that does this. The program is complete except for the input and output of the array data, which we will discuss later.

In this program, the two-dimensional array is processed using two DO loops in a nested pattern. The DO-variable of the outer loop is used as the subscript that indicates the row number. This DO-variable is incremented

Figure 10-3. A two-dimensional array processing program

```
C   PROGRAM TO TOTAL ALL ELEMENTS OF A TWO-DIMENSIONAL ARRAY
        INTEGER I,J
        REAL SCR(4,3),TOTAL
        (Read data for array)
        TOTAL=0.0
        DO 210 I=1,4
          DO 200 J=1,3
            TOTAL=TOTAL+SCR(I,J)
    200   CONTINUE
    210 CONTINUE
        (Write array data)
        WRITE (6,430) TOTAL
        STOP
    430 FORMAT ('0','    TOTAL OF ALL SCORES ',F6.0)
        END
```

from 1 to 4. The DO-variable of the inner loop is used as the subscript for the column number. This DO-variable is incremented from 1 to 3. In the inner loop, an element of the array is added to the total (which is initially zero). For each repetition of the outer loop, the inner loop is executed three times, causing the elements of one row of the array to be added to the total. After four repetitions of the outer loop, the elements in all four rows will have been added to the total.

The loop pattern in this example is commonly used in processing two-dimensional arrays. We will see more examples of its use later.

Two-dimensional character data arrays

Two-dimensional arrays may contain any type of data, including character data. A two-dimensional array of character data is dimensioned in a CHARACTER statement. For example, the following statement dimensions an array of character data called NAME:

```
CHARACTER*10 NAME(20,2)
```

This array has twenty rows and two columns. Each element of the array has a length of ten characters.

Two-dimensional character array element names can be used like any character variable names. The important thing to remember is that two subscripts are always required. If a substring name is needed, the substring position comes after the subscripts. The following are examples of valid uses of two-dimensional character array element names (assuming I and J are integer):

```
NAME(J,2)=NAME(I,2)
IF (NAME(I,J)(1:4).EQ.'JOHN') THEN
WRITE (6,300) NAME(5,2)(I:J)
NEWNAM=NAME(1,1)//NAME(2,1)
```

Two-dimensional logical data arrays

Two-dimensional arrays may contain logical data. Such an array is dimensioned in a LOGICAL statement. For example, the following statement specifies that ANS is a two-dimensional logical array with ten rows and four columns:

```
LOGICAL ANS(10,4)
```

A two-dimensional logical array element name can be used like any logical variable name. For example, the following statements are valid (assuming I and J are integer):

```
IF (ANS(I,J)) THEN
ANS(I,1)=ANS(I,2).AND.ANS(I,3)
READ (5,400) ANS(1,1),ANS(1,2)
```

10-2. Processing two-dimensional arrays

As we have seen, a two-dimensional array can be processed using a nest of two DO loops. (See Figure 10-3.) This is a very common technique. The DO-variable of the outer loop is used as one subscript in the array element name and the DO-variable of the inner loop is used as the other subscript. With appropriate parameters for each loop, part or all of the array can be processed. In this section we show a number of examples that use this and other techniques for two-dimensional array processing. We will use the four-by-three test score array named SCR described earlier in our examples. We assume that I, J, and K are integer variable names.

Initializing a two-dimensional array

Very often we must initialize all elements of an array. For example, assume we have to set each element of the test score array to zero. The following statements accomplish this:

```
      DO 110 I=1,4
        DO 100 J=1,3
          SCR(I,J)=0.0
100     CONTINUE
110 CONTINUE
```

In this example, as in the example in Figure 10-3, the DO-variable for the outer loop is used as the row subscript in the array element name. The DO-variable for the inner loop is used as the column subscript. The nested loops cause all possible combinations of subscripts to be used in the assignment statement. Hence each element of the array is initialized to zero.

Totaling the elements in each row or column of a two-dimensional array

Sometimes we must find the total of the elements in each row or column of a two-dimensional array. For example, to find the average of the test scores for each student, we must first determine the total of the elements in each row. This can be accomplished most easily by using a one-dimensional array of four elements to accumulate the totals of the rows. Assume that this array is named ROW and has been properly dimensioned in a REAL statement. Because the ROW array is used to accumulate totals, it must first be initialized to zero. Then the elements in each row of the test score array are successively added to the appropriate element of the ROW array. The following statements show how this is done:

```
      DO 200 I=1,4
         ROW(I)=0.0
  200 CONTINUE
      DO 220 I=1,4
         DO 210 J=1,3
            ROW(I)=ROW(I)+SCR(I,J)
  210    CONTINUE
  220 CONTINUE
```

When this sequence of statements has been executed, the elements of the one-dimensional ROW array will contain the totals of the elements in each row of the two-dimensional test score array.

A similar approach may be used to calculate the total of the elements of each column of the test score array. Assume that COL has been specified in a REAL statement as a one-dimensional array with three elements. After setting the elements of COL to zero, the following sequence of statements accumulates the total of each column of the test score array and assigns the results to elements of the COL array:

```
      DO 300 J=1,3
         COL(J)=0.0
  300 CONTINUE
      DO 320 J=1,3
         DO 310 I=1,4
            COL(J)=COL(J)+SCR(I,J)
  310    CONTINUE
  320 CONTINUE
```

Note in this example that the outer loop of the nested DO loops controls the column number. The inner loop controls the row number and is executed four times for each execution of the outer loop. At the end of the execution of this sequence of statements, the elements of the COL array contain the totals of the columns of the test score array.

Counting specific values in a two-dimensional array

As with one-dimensional arrays, sometimes we need to determine how many times a particular value occurs in a two-dimensional array. For example, the following statements count the number of elements of the test score array that are equal to 100 (assume that NUM is integer):

```
      NUM=0
      DO 410 I=1,4
        DO 400 J=1,3
          IF (SCR(I,J).EQ.100.0) THEN
            NUM=NUM+1
          END IF
 400    CONTINUE
 410 CONTINUE
```

In this example, NUM, which is initially zero, is incremented by 1 each time an element of the array satisfies the condition in the IF statement. When these statements have been executed, NUM will equal the number of elements of the test score array that equal 100.

A more complex example involves counting the number of rows in the test score array that have all elements equal to 100. The following statements show how this can be done (assume that COUNT and ALL are integer):

```
      COUNT=0
      DO 510 I=1,4
        ALL=1
        DO 500 J=1,3
          IF (SCR (I,J).NE.100.0) THEN
            ALL=0
          END IF
 500    CONTINUE
        IF (ALL.EQ.1) THEN
          COUNT=COUNT+1
        END IF
 510 CONTINUE
```

In this example, the variable ALL is used to indicate whether or not all elements in a row equal 100. Before checking each row, that is, before the inner loop is executed, ALL is set to 1. While checking the elements in a row in the inner loop, ALL is set to 0 if any element of that row is found that is not equal to 100. After all the elements in a row have been checked, the value of ALL is tested. If ALL equals 1, indicating that all elements in the row were 100, COUNT is increased by 1. At the end of execution, COUNT will equal the number of rows in the test score array that have all elements equal to 100.*

> * The variable ALL in this example is used to signal the presence or absence of a condition. In Section 8-5 we noted that a variable used like this is called a flag. This would be an appropriate place to use a logical variable instead of an integer variable and logical constants instead of 1 and 0.

Searching a two-dimensional array

In searching a two-dimensional array we may wish to locate all occurrences of a specific value. To do this, we include a test for the value in the nested DO loops. For example, assume that we need to determine the student number and test number for any student who got a score of 90 or higher on any test. The following statements accomplish this:

```
      DO 610 I=1,4
         DO 600 J=1,3
            IF (SCR(I,J).GE.90.0) THEN
               WRITE (6,910) I,J
            END IF
600      CONTINUE
610 CONTINUE
```

In this example, the WRITE statement is executed only if the student's test score is 90 or higher. The current values of the DO-variables for each DO loop are written and indicate the student number and test number.

Many times when we search a two-dimensional array we search one column (or row) for a specific value and use the information from the other columns (or rows). For example, assume that we wish to calculate and write the average of the second and third test scores for each student that got 70 or higher on the first test. The following statements accomplish this:

```
      DO 700 I=1,4
         IF (SCR(I,1).GE.70.0) THEN
            AVE=(SCR(I,2)+SCR(I,3))/2.0
            WRITE (6,920) I,AVE
         END IF
700 CONTINUE
```

In the IF statement, SCR(I,1) refers to the Ith element in the first column of the array. Hence, each time through the loop, we check the first score for a student to see if it is greater than or equal to 70. If this is the case, we average the other two scores for that student and write the student number and average.

Sorting the elements in a row or column of a two-dimensional array

We can sort the elements in one row or column of a two-dimensional array. If it is necessary to maintain the correspondence between elements in a row or column during the sorting process, then any time two elements in one row or column are switched, the corresponding elements in the other rows or columns must be switched. For example, the following sequence of statements sorts the first column of the test score array into descending order:

```
        DO 820 K=3,1,-1
          DO 810 I=1,K
            IF (SCR(I,1).LT.SCR(I+1,1)) THEN
              DO 800 J=1,3
                T=SCR(I,J)
                SCR(I,J)=SCR(I+1,J)
                SCR(I+1,J)=T
800           CONTINUE
            END IF
810       CONTINUE
820 CONTINUE
```

The sorting is done on the first column because the second subscript of each array element name in the IF statement is 1. The innermost loop is used to switch all elements of two rows if the elements in the first column are out of order with respect to each other.

10-3. Input and output of two-dimensional array data

In this section we describe several techniques for input and output of two-dimensional array data. We explain the use of each technique with formatted I/O, but most of the techniques also can be used with list-directed I/O. We will use the four-by-three test score array SCR in our examples.

Looping techniques

Loops are commonly used for input and output of two-dimensional array data. Sometimes nested DO-loops are used, but often a DO loop is coupled with an implied-DO list in the READ or WRITE statement. The DO loop varies one subscript, whereas the implied-DO list varies the other subscript.

As an example, assume that the entire test score array is recorded in four records with the three elements of each row in each record. Then the following sequence of statements can be used to read the array data:

```
        DO 120 I=1,4
          READ (5,810) (SCR(I,J),J=1,3)
120 CONTINUE
810 FORMAT (3F4.0)
```

This input sequence involves an implied-DO list in a READ statement that is within a regular DO loop. With each execution of the regular loop, the READ statement causes one row of the array to be read. To do this, we use the DO-variable of the regular DO loop as the row number of the array element name and the DO-variable of the implied-DO list as the column number.

We can use this same approach to write the data with one row of the array in each output record. The following statements accomplish this:

```
      DO 130 I=1,4
         WRITE (6,930) (SCR(I,J),J=1,3)
  130 CONTINUE
  930 FORMAT (1X,3F4.0)
```

Nested implied-DO lists

Another way to read or write a two-dimensional array is to use two implied-DO lists, one within the other. Such a configuration is called *nested implied-DO lists*. As an example, the following statements cause the test score data to be read from four records, each containing three test scores:

```
      READ (5,800) ((SCR(I,J),J=1,3),I=1,4)
  800 FORMAT (3F4.0)
```

The outer list of the nest uses the variable named I as the DO-variable. It is executed four times. The inner list is

```
(SCR(I,J),J=1,3)
```

This list is completely executed for each execution of the outer list. Each time the DO-variable of the outer list is incremented, the inner list causes three values to be read and assigned to the elements in a row in the array. The row number is specified by the DO-variable of the outer list; the column number is given by the DO-variable of the inner list.

In this example we assume that the array data is to be read by rows; that is, each input record contains one row of the array. Sometimes the data must be read by columns. For example, assume that each column of the test score array is recorded in one record. There are three input records with four test scores in each record. The following READ statement uses nested implied-DO lists to read this data:

```
      READ (5,820) ((SCR(I,J),I=4),J=1,3)
  820 FORMAT (4F4.0)
```

Notice here that the inner list controls the row number, whereas the outer list indicates the column number. Thus with each execution of the outer list, one column is read.

We can use nested implied-DO lists for output as well as for input of two-dimensional array data. For example, the following statements cause the test score data to be written with one column in each output record:

```
      WRITE (6,940) ((SCR(I,J),I=1,4),J=1,3)
  940 FORMAT (1X,4F4.0)
```

The short-list technique

To use the short-list technique for input and output of two-dimensional array data, the data must be arranged by *columns* because the data is stored in

Figure 10-4. Storage order of the elements of a 4-row, 3-column array

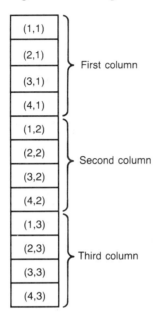

order by columns in the computer's internal storage. For example, Figure 10-4 shows the order in which the elements of the test score array are stored. Note that the data for the first column is stored first, followed by the data for the second column, and then the third column's data.

To illustrate the use of the short-list technique, consider the following statements:

```
      READ (5,820) SCR
      WRITE (6,940) SCR
  820 FORMAT (4F4.0)
  940 FORMAT (1X,4F4.0)
```

The READ statement and its FORMAT statement cause three records to be read, each containing the data for one column of the array. Similarly, the WRITE statement and its FORMAT statement cause three records to be written, each containing the data for one column of the array.

The short-list technique cannot be used if the data must be read or written by rows. In this case, one of the previous techniques must be used. In addition, the short-list technique can be used only if the entire array is to be read or written. Input and output of partial arrays must be accomplished by some other approach.

A complete program

We can now complete the program shown in Figure 10-3. Recall that this program finds the total of all elements in the test score array. To complete the program we need to include the statements necessary to read and write the array data.

The final program is shown in Figure 10-5. The array input data is assumed to be recorded in four records, each containing the three elements in one row of the array. A DO loop and an implied-DO list in a READ statement control the input operation. The array output is written in a similar format. Again a DO loop and an implied-DO list are combined in the output sequence. Note in the WRITE statement that writes the test score data that the DO-variable of the DO loop is included in the output list. This DO-variable corresponds to the row number of the array which is also the student number. Because the DO-variable is in the output list, the student number is written in each output record. [See Figure 10-5(c).]

This program uses formatted I/O, but it can be modified for list-directed I/O. The array input and output sequences would be the same, except that the list-directed READ statement and the PRINT statement would be used.

10-4. An illustrative program

To illustrate some of the two-dimensional array processing techniques discussed in this chapter, consider a program that tabulates test scores. Assume that twelve students are in a class and each student took four tests. We need a program that counts, for each test, the number of scores between 90 and 100, between 80 and 89, between 70 and 79, and between 0 and 69. In addition, we need the total number of test scores that fell in each range for all tests.

Figure 10-6 shows a program that accomplishes this. In this program, SCORE is a twelve-by-four real array that contains the test score data. The four-by-four array named COUNT is used to keep count of the number of test scores in each range. The first row of this array is used for the number of scores between 90 and 100 on each of the four tests, the second row is used for the number of scores between 80 and 89 on each test, and so on. Finally, the four-element, one-dimensional array named TOTAL is used for the total number of test scores in each range on all tests.

At the beginning of the program, the test score data is read into the SCORE array using a looping technique. Then the elements of the COUNT array are initialized to zero. This is necessary because these elements are used to count the number of test scores in each range. Next, nested DO loops cause the elements of the SCORE array to be checked one at a time. Within the DO loops, nested IF statements determine in which range a test score falls. Once this is determined, the appropriate element of the COUNT array is incremented.

After all elements of the SCORE array have been checked, the totals of the counts for each range are accumulated. This is done by totaling the elements in each row of the COUNT array. The TOTAL array is used to

Figure 10-5. A two-dimensional array processing program with formatted I/O

```
C  PROGRAM TO TOTAL ALL ELEMENTS OF A TWO-DIMENSIONAL ARRAY
      INTEGER I,J
      REAL SCR(4,3),TOTAL
      DO 100 I=1,4
        READ (5,400) (SCR(I,J),J=1,3)
  100 CONTINUE
      TOTAL=0.0
      DO 210 I=1,4
        DO 200 J=1,3
          TOTAL=TOTAL+SCR(I,J)
  200   CONTINUE
  210 CONTINUE
      WRITE (6,410)
      DO 300 I=1,4
        WRITE (6,420) I,(SCR(I,J),J=1,3)
  300 CONTINUE
      WRITE (6,430) TOTAL
      STOP
  400 FORMAT (3F4.0)
  410 FORMAT ('1','            TEST SCORES'/
     1          '0','STUDENT    TEST 1   TEST 2   TEST 3'/)
  420 FORMAT (' ',3X,I1,8X,F4.0,4X,F4.0,4X,F4.0)
  430 FORMAT ('0','    TOTAL OF ALL SCORES ',F6.0)
      END
```

(a) The program

```
91. 78. 85.
95. 90. 96.
85.100. 89.
69. 75. 68.
```

(b) Input data

```
                    TEST SCORES

        STUDENT    TEST 1   TEST 2   TEST 3

           1         91.      78.      85.
           2         95.      90.      96.
           3         85.     100.      89.
           4         69.      75.      68.

        TOTAL OF ALL SCORES   1021.
```

(c) Output

accumulate the totals. Note that the elements of the TOTAL array are first initialized to zero.

The final steps in the program involve printing the output. First, headings are printed. Then the elements of the COUNT array are printed with the columns of the array on separate lines. Each column of this array represents the counts of the number of test scores in each range on one test. The test number is printed on the left by using the DO-variable of the DO

Figure 10-6. An illustrative program (Part 1 of 2)

```
C     TEST SCORE TABULATION PROGRAM
C
      REAL SCORE(12,4)
      INTEGER COUNT(4,4),TOTAL(4),I,J
C
C     READ TEST SCORE ARRAY DATA
C
      DO 100 I=1,12
         READ (5,500) (SCORE(I,J),J=1,4)
  100 CONTINUE
C
C     COUNT TEST SCORES IN EACH RANGE
C
      DO 210 I=1,4
         DO 200 J=1,4
            COUNT(I,J)=0
  200    CONTINUE
  210 CONTINUE
      DO 260 I=1,12
         DO 250 J=1,4
            IF (SCORE(I,J).GE.90.0) THEN
               COUNT(1,J)=COUNT(1,J)+1
            ELSE IF (SCORE(I,J).GE.80.0) THEN
               COUNT(2,J)=COUNT(2,J)+1
            ELSE IF (SCORE(I,J).GE.70.0) THEN
               COUNT(3,J)=COUNT(3,J)+1
            ELSE
               COUNT(4,J)=COUNT(4,J)+1
            END IF
  250    CONTINUE
  260 CONTINUE
C
C     ACCUMULATE TOTALS IN EACH RANGE
C
      DO 300 I=1,4
         TOTAL(I)=0
  300 CONTINUE
      DO 360 I=1,4
         DO 350 J=1,4
            TOTAL(I)=TOTAL(I)+COUNT(I,J)
  350    CONTINUE
  360 CONTINUE
C
C     WRITE OUTPUT
C
      WRITE (6,600)
      DO 400 J=1,4
         WRITE (6,610) J,(COUNT(I,J),I=1,4)
  400 CONTINUE
      WRITE (6,620) TOTAL
C
      STOP
C
  500 FORMAT (4F4.0)
  600 FORMAT ('1','                TEST SCORE SUMMARY'/
     1        '0','            90-100   80-89   70-79    0-69'/)
  610 FORMAT (' ','TEST ',I1,4X,I2,7X,I2,6X,I2,6X,I2)
  620 FORMAT ('0','TOTALS',3X,I3,6X,I3,5X,I3,5X,I3)
      END
```

(a) The program

Figure 10-6. (Part 2 of 2)

```
 74. 84. 86. 77.
100. 94. 95. 89.
 82. 87. 87. 91.
 35. 48. 52. 63.
 85. 84. 75. 72.
 91. 84. 72. 95.
 72. 78. 81. 69.
 84. 75. 80. 79.
 70. 69. 72. 73.
 55. 72. 70. 38.
 90. 95. 91. 82.
 75. 81. 78. 72.
```

(b) Input data

TEST SCORE SUMMARY

	90-100	80-89	70-79	0-69
TEST 1	3	3	4	2
TEST 2	2	5	3	2
TEST 3	2	4	5	1
TEST 4	2	2	5	3
TOTALS	9	14	17	8

(c) Output

loop in the WRITE statement list. Finally, the elements of the TOTAL array are printed at the end of the output. A short-list technique is used for this output.

10-5. Initializing two-dimensional arrays with a DATA statement

A DATA statement may be used to initialize the elements of a two-dimensional array. One way to do this is to list each array element name in the DATA statement. For example, the following statement sets each element of the two-by-three array named X to zero:

```
DATA X(1,1),X(1,2),X(1,3),X(2,1),X(2,2),X(2,3)/6*0.0/
```

The array name may be used without a subscript. Then we can initialize the entire array X to zero as follows:

```
DATA X/6*0.0/
```

When this technique is used, the array is initialized in order by columns (the same order that is used for the short-list I/O technique). Because of this, we have to be careful in coding the DATA statement. For example, if we wished to set the elements of the first row of the array X to zero and the second row to one, we would use the following statement:

```
DATA X/0.0,1.0,0.0,1.0,0.0,1.0/
```

The alternating zeros and ones are necessary to initialize the array properly.

Implied-DO lists can also be used to initialize two-dimensional arrays with a DATA statement. Usually the lists are nested to produce the desired effect. For example, the following statement initializes the elements of the first row of X to zero and the second row to one:

```
DATA ((X(I,J),J=1,3),I=1,2)/3*0.0,3*1.0/
```

In this statement the outer list controls the row number and the inner list controls the column number.

10-6. Three-dimensional arrays

A *three-dimensional array* may be thought of as a group of data organized into levels, where the data in each level is arranged in rows and columns. These levels can be imagined as planes or surfaces, where each plane contains a two-dimensional array. Figure 10-7 shows a three-dimensional array of four rows, three columns, and three levels. This data could represent test scores for four students (rows) on three tests (columns) in each of three different classes (levels). Thus the element 85 in the third row and first column of the second level represents the test score of student number three on the first exam in the second class.

Each element of a three-dimensional array is identified by three subscripts that are separated by commas, are enclosed in parentheses, and follow the array name. The subscripts represent the number of the row, column, and level, respectively. For example, assume that the array shown in Figure 10-7 is named TS. Then the element in row three, column one, level two is named TS(3,1,2). Figure 10-8 shows the names of all elements in this three-dimensional array.

Subscripts for a three-dimensional array must follow the rules for one- and two-dimensional array subscripts, except that there always must be three subscripts. Thus subscripts may be integer constants, variable names, or arithmetic expressions. For example, the array element name TS(I,J,K) indicates the element in the Ith row, Jth column, and Kth level. The value of a subscript must not be less than its lower dimension bound or greater than its upper dimension bound.

Any array used in a program must be dimensioned in a type statement or a DIMENSION statement. With three-dimensional arrays, the bounds of

Figure 10-7. A three-dimensional array

Column numbers

	1	2	3
1	72	63	68
2	75	78	76
3	83	83	85
4	87	95	100

Row numbers

Third level

	1	2	3
1	73	79	65
2	100	92	89
3	85	79	88
4	63	82	79

Second level

	1	2	3
1	91	78	85
2	95	90	96
3	85	100	89
4	69	75	68

First level

all three subscripts must be specified. For example, the following statement dimensions the three-dimensional test score array:

```
REAL TS(4,3,3)
```

The entries in parentheses give the number of rows, columns, and levels, respectively, in the array. This array is said to be a "four-by-three-by-three" array. Because it is specified in a REAL statement, the array contains real data.

Lower dimension bounds may be given as in the following example:

```
INTEGER X(0:5,-3:3,11:20)
```

This statement specifies an integer array with six rows, seven columns, and ten levels. The following example shows the use of the DIMENSION statement for dimensioning three-dimensional arrays:

```
DIMENSION Y(10,5,2)
```

Figure 10-8. Element names for a three-dimensional array

Column numbers

	1	2	3	
1	TS(1,1,3)	TS(1,2,3)	TS(1,3,3)	
2	TS(2,1,3)	TS(2,2,3)	TS(2,3,3)	Third level
3	TS(3,1,3)	TS(3,2,3)	TS(3,3,3)	
4	TS(4,1,3)	TS(4,2,3)	TS(4,3,3)	

Row numbers

	1	2	3	
1	TS(1,1,2)	TS(1,2,2)	TS(1,3,2)	
2	TS(2,1,2)	TS(2,2,2)	TS(2,3,2)	Second level
3	TS(3,1,2)	TS(3,2,2)	TS(3,3,2)	
4	TS(4,1,2)	TS(4,2,2)	TS(4,3,2)	

	1	2	3	
1	TS(1,1,1)	TS(1,2,1)	TS(1,3,1)	
2	TS(2,1,1)	TS(2,2,1)	TS(2,3,1)	First level
3	TS(3,1,1)	TS(3,2,1)	TS(3,3,1)	
4	TS(4,1,1)	TS(4,2,1)	TS(4,3,1)	

This statement dimensions a ten-by-five-by-two array. Its type depends on whether implicit or explicit typing is used.

When using large arrays in a program, it is possible to exceed the computer's internal storage capacity. For example, consider the arrays specified by the following statement:

```
INTEGER D(400,400),A(10000),M(10,100,100)
```

The first array contains 160,000 elements (400×400), the second array has 10,000 elements, and the third array contains 100,000 elements ($10 \times 100 \times 100$). Thus these three arrays contain a total of 270,000 elements, which exceeds the capacity of the internal storage of many computers.

Processing three-dimensional arrays

As with two-dimensional arrays, a three-dimensional array is usually processed by using nested DO loops. With a three-dimensional array three loops are required, one to control each subscript. For example, the following sequence of statements uses three nested DO loops to initialize the elements of the four-by-three-by-three test score array TS to zero (assume that I, J, and K are integer):

```
      DO 120 I=1,4
        DO 110 J=1,3
          DO 100 K=1,3
            TS(I,J,K)=0.0
100       CONTINUE
110     CONTINUE
120 CONTINUE
```

The DO-variable of the inner loop is used in the array element name to indicate the level number. The DO-variables of the intermediate and outer loops specify the column and row numbers, respectively.

To accumulate the total score of all tests for each student in each class, we can use a two-dimensional array for the results. The subscripts of this array indicate the student number and class number. Assume that STOT is the name of a two-dimensional real array of four rows and three columns. In the following sequence of statements the elements of STOT are first set to zero. Then the total for each student in each class is accumulated and the result is assigned to the appropriate element of STOT.

```
      DO 210 I=1,4
        DO 200 K=1,3
          STOT(I,K)=0.0
200     CONTINUE
210 CONTINUE
      DO 240 I=1,4
        DO 230 K=1,3
          DO 220 J=1,3
            STOT(I,K)=STOT(I,K)+TS(I,J,K)
220       CONTINUE
230     CONTINUE
240 CONTINUE
```

In the second set of nested DO loops in this example, the inner loop controls the column number, whereas the intermediate and outer loops control the level and row numbers, respectively. Thus, with each complete execution of the inner loop, the total of the elements in one row of one level is accumulated.

If we need the total of all test scores for each class, we can use a one-dimensional array to store the results. For example, assume that CTOT has been specified as the name of a three-element, one-dimensional real array. The following statements set the elements of CTOT to zero and then accumulate the total for each class, assigning the result to the appropriate element of CTOT:

```
      DO 300 K=1,3
        CTOT(K)=0.0
300 CONTINUE
      DO 330 K=1,3
```

```
      DO 320 I=1,4
        DO 310 J=1,3
          CTOT(K)=CTOT(K)+TS(I,J,K)
310       CONTINUE
320     CONTINUE
330 CONTINUE
```

In this sequence of statements, the outer loop of the nest of DO loops controls the level number. The intermediate and inner loops control the row and column numbers, respectively. So with each complete execution of the intermediate and inner loops, the total of the elements in one level is accumulated.

To search a three-dimensional array for all occurrences of a specific value, a test for the value is included in the nested DO loops. For example, the following statements locate all students who received a score of 90 or higher on any test in any class:

```
      DO 420 I=1,4
        DO 410 J=1,3
          DO 400 K=1,3
            IF (TS(I,J,K).GE.90.0) THEN
              WRITE (6,900) I,J,K
            END IF
400       CONTINUE
410     CONTINUE
420 CONTINUE
```

In this example, the current values of the three DO-variables are written if the test score is greater than or equal to 90. The DO-variables represent the student number, test number, and class number, respectively.

Input and output of three-dimensional array data

Input and output of data for a three-dimensional array may be accomplished in a number of ways. In the following discussion we show several techniques using formatted I/O, but most of the techniques can also be used with list-directed I/O.

As a first example, assume that the data for the four-by-three-by-three test score array TS is recorded with the elements of one row in each input record. The first four records contain the data for the first level, the next four records have the second level's data, and the last four records contain the third level's data. To read this data, a nest of two DO loops and an implied-DO list may be used as follows:

```
      DO 110 K=1,3
        DO 100 I=1,4
          READ (5,800) (TS(I,J,K),J=1,3)
100     CONTINUE
110 CONTINUE
800 FORMAT (3F3.0)
```

The implied-DO list in the READ statement controls the column number for the array element name. The inner loop of the nested DO loops controls the row number, and the outer loop indicates the level number. With each execution of the READ statement, one record is read and the data assigned to the elements in one row of the three-dimensional array. In all, twelve records are read because the READ statement is executed twelve times.

The approach shown here can also be used to write three-dimensional array data. For example, the following statements write the test score array with one row in each output record:

```
      DO 210 K=1,3
         DO 200 I=1,4
            WRITE (6,900) (TS(I,J,K),J=1,3)
200      CONTINUE
210 CONTINUE
900 FORMAT (1X,3F5.0)
```

Three nested implied-DO lists may be used to read or write data for a three-dimensional array. The following statements use this approach to read the test score data in the same format as in the previous input sequence:

```
      READ (5,800) (((TS(I,J,K),J=1,3),I=1,4),K=1,3)
800 FORMAT (3F3.0)
```

The outer implied-DO list uses the DO-variable K to control the level number. The intermediate list uses the DO-variable I to control the row number. The inner implied-DO list causes three values to be read and assigned to the elements in one row of the array.

If the data to be read is recorded with each column of the array in a record, the order of the loops is different. Assume that the input data consists of nine records. The first three records each contain four fields with the data for one column of the first level. The next three records contain the data for the second level. The third level's data is contained in the last three records. The following statements read the data in the specified order:

```
      READ (5,810) (((TS(I,J,K)I=1,4),J=1,3),K=1,3)
810 FORMAT (4F3.0)
```

Note that the innermost implied-DO list controls the row number, the intermediate list controls the column number, and the outer list controls the level number. Thus each execution of the inner list causes the data for one column in one level to be read.

If the data is arranged by columns within levels as described in the previous paragraph, the short-list technique may be used. For example, the following statements have the same effect as the previous example:

```
      READ (5,810) TS
810 FORMAT (4F3.0)
```

Figure 10-9. Storage order of the elements of a 4-row, 3-column, 3-level array

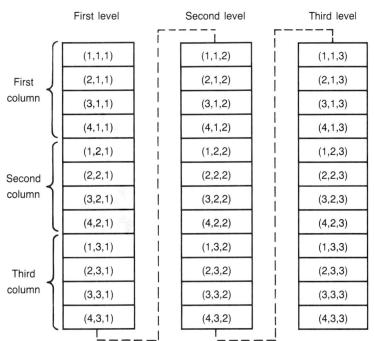

In general, when the short-list technique is used, all of the array data is read or written in an order such that the first subscript is incremented through its values before the second subscript is incremented, which, in turn, is incremented before the third subscript is incremented. Thus the data for a three-dimensional array is read by columns within each level because this is the order in which the elements in the array are stored in the computer's internal storage. (See Figure 10-9.) Note, however, that if the array data is in some order other than this or if only part of the array data is to be read or written, the short-list technique cannot be used.

Initializing three-dimensional arrays with a DATA statement

As with two-dimensional arrays, the DATA statement may be used to initialize the elements of a three-dimensional array. The array element names may be listed individually in the DATA statement, the array name may be given by itself, or implied-DO lists (usually nested to three levels) may be used. The only difficulty arises when the array name is used by itself. Then the order in which the elements are initialized is by columns within levels. For example, the following statement sets each element of the first and third levels of the four-by-three-by-three test score array TS to zero and each element of the second level to 100:

```
DATA TS/12*0.0,12*100.0,12*0.0/
```

The data in this example must be listed in the order shown so that the elements of the array are properly initialized.

Higher dimensional arrays

FORTRAN allows arrays of more than three dimensions. Arrays of up to seven dimensions are permissible. In a four-dimensional array, four subscripts are needed and the bounds of all four subscripts must be specified when the array is dimensioned. Similar rules apply to five-, six-, and seven-dimensional arrays. Although we cannot visualize an array with more than three dimensions, the computer can store such an array. The principles behind the processing techniques that we have described for two- and three-dimensional arrays apply to higher dimensional arrays.

Review questions

1. What are the differences between one-dimensional arrays and two-dimensional arrays?
2. Consider the two-dimensional array SCR shown in Figure 10-1. Assume that I, J, and K are integer variable names and that I is 2, J is 3, and K is 4. What is the value of each of the following array element names?
   a. SCR(3,2)
   b. SCR(K,1)
   c. SCR(I,J)
   d. SCR(I*J − 4,K/2)
3. a. Code a statement to specify that A is a two-dimensional array of real data with five rows and twenty columns.
   b. How many elements are there in this array?
4. a. Code a statement to specify that B is a two-dimensional array of integer data with lower and upper dimension bounds for the rows of 0 and 10, respectively, and lower and upper dimension bounds for the columns of 51 and 75, respectively.
   b. How many elements are in this array?
5. Consider the array A defined in Question 3. Code a statement that adds the first element of the first row of this array and the third element of the second row and assigns the result to the last element of the fourth row.
6. Code a group of statements to initialize the elements of the array A defined in Question 3. Assign 1.0 to the elements in the first row of A, 2.0 to the ele-

ments in the second row, and so forth up to the fifth row in which the elements should be assigned the value 5.0. Do not use a DATA statement.

7. Code a group of statements to determine how many corresponding elements in the first two rows of the array A defined in Question 3 are equal.

8. Code a group of statements to find the largest element in the array A defined in Question 3. Assign the value of the largest element to ALARG.

9. Code a group of statements to search the array A defined in Question 3 for the first element in each row that is equal to the value of AVAL. If such an element is found, write an appropriate message. If no element in a row is equal to AVAL, write a message indicating this.

10. Code a group of statements to sort the elements in each row of the array A defined in Question 3 into decreasing order.

11. Assume that an input file contains five records each with twenty fields in format (20F4.1). Code a group of statements to read the records in the file and assign the data in each record to a row of the array A defined in Question 3.

12. Code a group of statements to write the data in the array A defined in Question 3 with the last column on the first line, the next-to-last column on the second line, and so forth.

13. In what order must the elements of a two-dimensional array be arranged in an input file for the data to be read using the short-list technique?

14. Answer Question 6 using a DATA statement.

15. Consider the three-dimensional array TS shown in Figure 10-7. Assume that I, J, and K are integer variable names and that I is 2, J is 3, and K is 4. What is the value of each of the following array element names?
    a. TS(1,3,3)
    b. TS(K,J,I)
    c. TS(J,1,J)
    d. TS($2*I-1,K-2,J/I$)

16. a. Code a statement to specify that C is a three-dimensional array of integer data with ten rows, five columns, and six levels.
    b. How many elements are in this array?

17. Code a group of statements to initialize the elements in the array C defined in Question 16. Assign the value 0 to the elements in the first level, the value 1 to the elements in the second level, and so forth up to the sixth level in which the elements should be assigned the value 5.

18. Code a group of statements to determine if all of the corresponding elements in the first and last levels of the array C defined in Question 16 are equal. If this is the case, write an appropriate message; otherwise, write a different message.

19. In what order must the elements of a three-dimensional array be arranged in an input file for the data to be read using the short-list technique?

20. Code a group of statements to write the elements of the array C defined in Question 16 with each row on a separate line. All of the rows in the first level should be written first, then the rows in the second level, and so forth.

Programming problems

1. A company sells five products with four models for each product. The following table gives the unit price of each model of each product:

$6X, 4(F6.2, 4X)$

		MODEL NUMBER			
		1	2	3	4
	1	10.50	16.25	21.00	23.75
	2	4.95	5.95	6.50	6.95
PRODUCT	3	.38	.47	.59	.62
NUMBER	4	8.75	8.95	9.10	9.22
	5	1.52	1.75	1.95	2.25

The pricing table is recorded in the first five records of a file. Each record has the prices for the four models of one product. Following the data for the table is one record for each sale made during the week with the customer number, the item number, and the quantity sold. The first digit of the item number represents the product number; the second digit is the model number.

Write a FORTRAN program to read the pricing table and store it in a two-dimensional array. Then print the pricing table with appropriate headings. Next, calculate the sales amount for each customer by multiplying the unit price from the table by the quantity sold. Below appropriate headings print the customer number, item number, quantity sold, unit price, and sales amount.

To test the program use the data in the preceding pricing table and the following sales data:

Customer number	Item number	Quantity
10113	21	10
11305	54	35
11412	11	100
22516	23	125
11603	42	75
11625	41	65
11735	33	50
11895	13	130
11899	24	20
11907	52	82

$(6X, I5, 1X, I2, 4X, I4)$

2. Data for Problem 8 of Chapter 9 consists of one record for each student in a class with the student's number and score on a test. The first digit of the student's number indicates his or her year in school (1 = freshman, 2 = sophomore). A tabulation of test scores by score category for each year is needed. The score categories are 90 to 100, 80 to 89, 70 to 79, 60 to 69, and 0 to 59.

Write a FORTRAN program to create a two-dimensional array of five rows and two columns where the rows represent the score categories and the columns indicate the year in school. That is, the array should appear as follows:

	Freshman	Sophomore
90–100		
80–89		
70–79		
60–69		
0–59		

Tabulate the number of scores that fall into each classification. Print the results of the tabulation with appropriate headings. After the data has been tabulated, determine the total number of freshmen and the total number of sophomores who took the test. Print the result. Use the data for Problem 8 of Chapter 9 to test the program.

3. Write a FORTRAN program to create a two-dimensional table of the number of freshman, sophomore, junior, and senior students in each major field. Also accumulate the totals for each year in school, the totals for each major field, and the total number of students. Print the table in the following format:

		Year in school			
Major field	Freshman	Sophomore	Junior	Senior	Totals
Business					
Social Science					
Humanities					
Physical Science					
Engineering					
TOTALS					

Input for the program is one or more records for each department with the department number recorded in positions 1 to 3, and digits ranging from 1 to 4 in positions 6 to 80. Department numbers are as follows:

101 Business
102 Social Science
103 Humanities
104 Physical Science
105 Engineering

Each position between 6 and 80 has one student's year in school. Use the digits 1, 2, 3, and 4 to represent freshman, sophomore, junior, and senior, respectively. There may be more than one record for any department. If data for fewer than 75 students is recorded in a record, remaining fields are filled with zeros. The input records are in no particular order.

To test the program, prepare data with at least two records for each department. Some records should not be entirely filled with the digits 1, 2, 3, or 4, but should have 0's in the last 10 to 20 positions.

4. A computer can analyze the data gathered from scouting a football team. In a simple system, assume that the scout records four characteristics of each offen-

sive play. The characteristics are the down, the yards to go for a first down, the type of play (0 indicates a pass; 1 indicates a run), and the number of yards gained or lost (a negative value indicates lost yardage). The information for each play is recorded in a separate record. In all, 25 plays are to be analyzed.

Write a FORTRAN program to read the scouting data and store it in a two-dimensional array of twenty-five rows and four columns. Each column represents one of the characteristics of the play. Print the data in columns with appropriate headings. Then find and print the answers to the following questions:
a. What were the average yards gained per play?
b. What were the average yards gained per running play?
c. Of all running plays, what percentage gained yardage, what percentage lost yardage, and what percentage gained zero yardage?
d. What were the average yards gained per passing play?
e. What percentage of the plays were passes?
f. What percentage of first-down plays were passes?
g. What percentage of second-down plays were passes?
h. What percentage of third-down plays were passes?
i. Of third-down plays with less than five yards to go, what percentage were passes?

Use the following data to test the program:

Down	Yards to go	Play	Gain (+) or loss (−)
1	10	Run	+4
2	6	Pass	0
3	6	Pass	+8
1	10	Run	−3
2	13	Run	+8
1	10	Run	0
2	10	Pass	+8
3	2	Pass	+15
1	10	Pass	+12
1	10	Run	−15
2	25	Pass	+5
3	20	Pass	0
1	10	Run	+2
2	8	Run	+4
3	4	Run	+1
1	10	Pass	0
2	10	Run	+6
3	4	Pass	+12
1	10	Pass	0
2	10	Run	+6
3	4	Run	+2
1	10	Pass	−3
2	13	Run	−5
1	10	Run	+2
2	10	Run	−16

5. The equation of a straight line is $y = mx + b$, where m is the slope and b is the y-intercept. A graph of this line can be easily created by calculating y for different values of x and plotting the resulting pairs of numbers. For example, if the slope of a line is 1 and the y-intercept is -2, the equation of the line is $y = 1x - 2$. Starting with x equal to 1 and increasing x by 1, each time calculating y from the equation, the following pairs of numbers result:

x	1	2	3	4	5	6	7	8
y	-1	0	1	2	3	4	5	6

These pairs are plotted on graph paper to plot the line.

One way to use a computer to represent a graph is to use a two-dimensional array of integer values. Initially, the array should contain all zeros. Then, if y equals some value j when x equals i, the (j, i) element of the array is set equal to 1. Through proper manipulation of output, a digitized graph is printed. For example, the equation $y = 1x - 2$ would appear as follows:

GRAPH OF THE LINE $Y = 1X - 2$

Y VALUES
```
8     0 0 0 0 0 0 0 0
7     0 0 0 0 0 0 0 0
6     0 0 0 0 0 0 0 1
5     0 0 0 0 0 0 1 0
4     0 0 0 0 0 1 0 0
3     0 0 0 0 1 0 0 0
2     0 0 0 1 0 0 0 0
1     0 0 1 0 0 0 0 0
      1 2 3 4 5 6 7 8
```
X VALUES

Write a FORTRAN program to plot a graph using this technique. Input for the program is one record for each equation to be plotted with the slope and intercept.

Print each graph on a separate page. Supply headings and x and y values, as in the example, with the exception that x and y should continue to 20. Thus a two-dimensional array of dimension (20, 20) is needed. Note that only positive x and y values are used. If a resulting pair contains a nonpositive value or a value that exceeds 20, no attempt should be made to plot it.

Test the program with the following equations:

$$y = -2x + 16$$
$$y = 1x - 5$$

A modification of this problem is to include negative x and y values in the graph. A further modification is to use blanks instead of zeros, and asterisks or some other symbol instead of the digit 1.

6. A two-dimensional array is a computer representation of the general mathematical concept of a matrix. A matrix is an ordered set of data arranged in rows and columns. If a matrix has m rows and n columns, we say it is an $m \times n$ matrix (pronounced "m by n"). For example, the following is the representation of a general 2×3 matrix:

$$\mathbf{A} = \begin{bmatrix} a_{11} & a_{12} & a_{13} \\ a_{21} & a_{22} & a_{23} \end{bmatrix}$$

The following properties of matrices are used in this problem:

a. Two matrices of the same size (i.e., the same number of rows and columns) are equal if and only if corresponding elements of the two matrices are equal. That is, given an $m \times n$ matrix $\mathbf{A}$ and an $m \times n$ matrix $\mathbf{B}$, then $\mathbf{A} = \mathbf{B}$ if and only if $a_{ij} = b_{ij}$ for all i between 1 and m and all j between 1 and n.

b. The product of a matrix and a constant (called a scalar) is a new matrix each of whose elements is the product of the constant and the corresponding element of the original matrix. That is, given an $m \times n$ matrix $\mathbf{A}$ and a constant c, a new matrix $\mathbf{B}$ equal to c times $\mathbf{A}$ is defined as $b_{ij} = c \cdot a_{ij}$ for all i and j.

c. The sum of two matrices of the same size is a new matrix each of whose elements is the sum of the two corresponding elements of the original matrices. That is, given an $m \times n$ matrix $\mathbf{A}$ and an $m \times n$ matrix $\mathbf{B}$, then a new $m \times n$ matrix $\mathbf{C} = \mathbf{A} + \mathbf{B}$ is defined as $c_{ij} = a_{ij} + b_{ij}$ for all i and j.

Write a FORTRAN program that reads two matrices and determines whether they are equal. If they are equal, an appropriate message should be printed, one of the matrices should be multiplied by 2, and the result printed. If they are not equal, a message should be printed, the matrices should be added, and the result printed. The program should then repeat the process for a new pair of matrices.

Assume that no matrix has more than 10 rows or 8 columns and dimension all arrays accordingly. Record each row of a matrix in a separate record. The first record of each set of data should contain the size of the matrices to be processed (rows and columns). Following this record should be the data for two matrices.

Use the following sets of data to test the program:

I. $\mathbf{A} = \begin{bmatrix} 8.35 & 6.24 \\ 7.91 & -5.32 \end{bmatrix}$ $\mathbf{B} = \begin{bmatrix} 8.35 & 6.24 \\ 7.91 & -5.32 \end{bmatrix}$

II. $\mathbf{A} = \begin{bmatrix} 1.62 & 4.35 & -2.13 & 7.62 \\ -8.35 & -12.72 & 6.51 & 8.39 \\ -1.82 & 4.21 & 7.83 & -0.71 \end{bmatrix}$

$\mathbf{B} = \begin{bmatrix} -4.71 & 5.63 & 7.81 & -1.22 \\ 17.39 & 8.42 & 5.61 & -2.22 \\ -5.81 & 3.92 & 8.35 & 1.11 \end{bmatrix}$

7. The product of the $l \times m$ matrix $\mathbf{A}$ with elements a_{ik} and the $m \times n$ matrix $\mathbf{B}$ with elements b_{kj} is an $l \times n$ matrix $\mathbf{C}$ with elements c_{ij} given by the following formula:

$$c_{ij} = \sum_{k=1}^{m} a_{ik} b_{kj}$$

Write a FORTRAN program to read two matrices, find their product, and print the result. Test the program with the following matrices:

$$A = \begin{bmatrix} 2 & -3 & 1 \\ -5 & 6 & 4 \\ -1 & 0 & 5 \\ 3 & -2 & -4 \end{bmatrix} \qquad B = \begin{bmatrix} 7 & 0 & 3 & -4 & -2 \\ 4 & 6 & -6 & -1 & 5 \\ -5 & -3 & 1 & 2 & -7 \end{bmatrix}$$

8. A method of solving simultaneous linear equations is called the Gauss elimination method. It is described in many algebra textbooks. Write a FORTRAN program that uses this method to solve the following system of four equations in four unknowns:

$$
\begin{aligned}
1.00x_1 + 7.30x_2 + 12.60x_3 + 11.20x_4 &= 31.30 \\
0.20x_1 - 4.74x_2 - 6.78x_3 - 36.82x_4 &= -76.82 \\
-0.20x_1 - 1.46x_2 + 0.88x_3 - 15.84x_4 &= -38.90 \\
0.30x_1 + 2.29x_2 + 4.03x_3 + 1.79x_4 &= 6.17
\end{aligned}
$$

9. In the data processing department of a particular organization there are three basic job functions — Systems Analysis, Programming, and Operations. For each function there are four levels — Manager, Senior, Junior, and Trainee. Write a FORTRAN program to read the job functions into a three-element one-dimensional array, and the levels into a four-element, one-dimensional array. Then create from these arrays a job category array of three rows and four columns containing all possible combinations of functions and levels. For example, element (1, 1) in the array should contain the following:

Systems Analysis — Manager

Finally, print the array in an appropriate format.

10. An airline flies between six cities. Whether or not there is a direct flight from one city to another is indicated in the following table:

		To					
		1	2	3	4	5	6
	1	F	T	T	F	F	T
	2	T	F	T	F	F	T
From	3	F	F	F	T	F	F
	4	F	T	F	F	T	F
	5	F	T	F	T	F	F
	6	F	T	F	F	T	F

On the left and across the top are the numbers of the cities. If there is a T at the intersection of a row and column, there is a direct flight from the city marked on the left to the city indicated at the top. An F indicates that there is no direct flight between the two cities.

The information for this table is recorded in the first six records of a file. Recorded in each record is the data for one row of the table. Following the table data is one record for each customer with the customer's number and his or her request for a flight pattern. The flight pattern indicates the cities between which the customer wishes to fly. For example, a pattern of 13426 indicates that the customer wishes to fly from city 1 to city 3, then from city 3 to city 4, then to city 2, and finally to city 6. The maximum number of cities in a flight pattern is five. If the customer has fewer than five cities in his or her pattern, the remaining numbers are zero. Thus a pattern of 62000 indicates that the customer wishes to fly from city 6 to city 2 and does not wish to continue beyond that.

Write a FORTRAN program to read the data for the flight table. Print the table with appropriate headings. Then determine if each customer's requested flight pattern is possible. Print the customer's number, his or her requested flight pattern, and a statement of whether or not a ticket may be issued for the desired pattern.

To test the program use the data in the previous flight table and the following customer data:

Customer number	Flight pattern
10123	13426
11305	62000
13427	42320
18211	52500
19006	34212
20831	65426
21475	32000
22138	43621
24105	13424
24216	65231
25009	34250

11. A telephone company charges varying rates for a long distance call between two cities. The rate charged depends on the time of day the call is made and how the call is placed. There is a fixed charge for the first three minutes and a charge for each additional minute or fraction thereof. The following table outlines the rate structure:

| How placed | Time of day | | | |
	Day	Evening	Night	Weekend
Direct-dialed	.79	.58	.52	.49
	.26	.23	.21	.15
Station-to-station — operator assisted	.95	.73	.64	.57
	.30	.25	.24	.21
Person-to-person	1.55	1.55	1.55	1.55
	.52	.52	.52	.52

For any given time of day and method of placing the call, two figures are shown. The top figure represents the charge for the first three minutes or fraction thereof; the bottom figure represents the charge for each additional minute or fraction thereof. For example, a night call that is station-to-station, operator-assisted is charged $.64 for the first three minutes, and $.24 for each additional minute.

The rate table is recorded in the first six records of a file. Each record contains four fields with the charge for a different time of day in each field. The first three records contain the basic three-minute charges for the different ways of placing the call. The second three records contain the charges for additional time. Following the data for the rate table is one record for each customer with the customer number, "how placed" code, "time of call" code, and length of call in minutes and fraction of minute. The "how placed" codes are as follows:

1 Direct-dialed
2 Station-to-station, operator-assisted
3 Person-to-person

The "time of call" codes are as follows:

1 Day
2 Evening
3 Night
4 Weekend

Write a FORTRAN program to read and print the rate table. Use a three-dimensional array. Supply appropriate descriptive headings for the table output. Then determine the charge for each customer. Print the customer's number, the length of call, and the charge with appropriate headings.

To test the program, use the data in the preceding rate table and the following customer data:

Customer number	"How placed"	"Time of call"	Length
9606	1	1	3.84
2160	3	4	2.50
6100	2	2	3.00
1820	3	3	4.00
9215	2	1	8.50
2111	1	3	6.32
1452	2	3	2.15
6658	1	2	1.05
1138	3	2	9.72
6886	2	4	6.35
3552	3	1	3.51
7111	1	4	5.75

12. Data on the age, sex, and marital status of students in the freshman class of a small college are recorded in a file. Each record contains a student number, age, sex (1 = male, 2 = female) and marital status (1 = single, 2 = married).

A tabulation of the number of students in different age groups for each sex and marital status is needed. The results are to be presented in the following form:

	Single		Married	
Age	Male	Female	Male	Female
18 and under				
19 or 20				
21 and over				

Write a FORTRAN program to create a three-dimensional array to store the tabulated data. The array should have three rows, two columns, and two levels. The subscript of an array element should indicate age group, sex, and marital status, respectively. Print the results of the tabulation in the form shown.

From the three-dimensional array create a two-dimensional array of the number of students in each age group for each sex. Print the data in the array in an appropriate format.

Finally, from the two-dimensional array create a one-dimensional array of the number of students in each age group. Print this array data with appropriate headings.

Use the following data to test the program:

Student number	Age	Sex	Marital status	Number	Age	Sex	Marital status
1001	19	1	1	1021	19	1	2
1002	17	2	1	1022	26	2	2
1003	18	2	1	1023	23	2	2
1004	22	1	2	1024	17	1	1
1005	20	2	2	1025	18	1	1
1006	18	1	1	1026	21	1	2
1007	27	2	1	1027	26	2	1
1008	17	2	1	1028	25	1	2
1009	17	1	1	1029	28	2	2
1010	18	2	1	1030	21	1	1
1011	19	1	2	1031	25	2	1
1012	20	2	2	1032	20	2	1
1013	17	1	1	1033	19	1	1
1014	18	1	2	1034	18	1	1
1015	18	1	1	1035	17	1	1
1016	20	2	1	1036	16	2	1
1017	23	1	1	1037	23	2	2
1018	20	2	1	1038	24	2	2
1019	25	2	2	1039	20	1	1
1020	17	2	1	1040	16	2	1

Chapter 11

Subprograms

The types of programs that we have discussed so far are called *main programs*. Another type of program is called a subprogram. A *subprogram* is a separate program that is executed along with a main program. In this chapter we discuss the programming and use of subprograms. After completing this chapter you should be able to write FORTRAN subprograms and execute them along with a main program.

11-1. Subprogram concepts

Often, when writing a program, we find that a set of computations must be performed at various points with different data at each point. For example, assume that we need to find the maximum of three real values several times in a main program. The first time, the maximum of the values of A, B, and C is needed. Later in the program, the maximum of the values of X, Y, and Z is required. Perhaps at another time, the maximum of three other real values is needed. To find the maximum of three values requires several statements in FORTRAN. Each time that a maximum is needed, the statements must be coded at that point in the program. The statements are basically the same at each point, only the variable names for the data change. It would simplify program preparation if the necessary statements could be coded once and then referred to each time that the computation is needed. The effect of referring to the statements would be the same as if the statements were placed in the program at the point of reference.

This is the idea of a subprogram. A subprogram is a set of FORTRAN statements that can be referred to by another program. The program that refers to a subprogram is known as the *calling program*. The calling program may be a main program or another subprogram. When a subprogram is referred to, it is said to be *called* by the calling program. The effect of calling a subprogram is the same as if the statements in the subprogram were coded in the calling program at the point where the subprogram is called.

Figure 11-1 illustrates these concepts. In this figure the main program calls the first subprogram three times. Each time the subprogram is called, the main program branches to the subprogram, then the instructions in the subprogram are executed, and finally the subprogram branches back to the main program at the point where it was called. The second subprogram in Figure 11-1 is called by the first subprogram. Thus the first subprogram is not only called by the main program, but it is also the calling program for the second subprogram.

Usually a subprogram requires that the calling program supply the data to be used for computations in the subprogram. Such data is said to be *passed* to the subprogram by the calling program. For example, if a subprogram is used to find the maximum of three values, the data passed to the subprogram must be three values. In Figure 11-1 the first subprogram is called at three points, hence data must be passed to it three times. After a subprogram completes its computations, the results are usually passed to the calling program before the subprogram branches back. Such data is said to be *returned* to the calling program. For example, in a subprogram that finds the maximum of three values, the value returned to the calling program is the maximum.

A subprogram cannot be executed by itself. It can be executed only if it is called from another program. Although the calling program need not be a main program, there must be a main program that begins calling the subprograms. Thus, although the first subprogram in Figure 11-1 calls the second subprogram, the first cannot be executed without being called by another program — in this case by the main program. In FORTRAN an *executable program* consists of one main program plus any number, including none, of subprograms.

Figure 11-1. Subprogram concepts

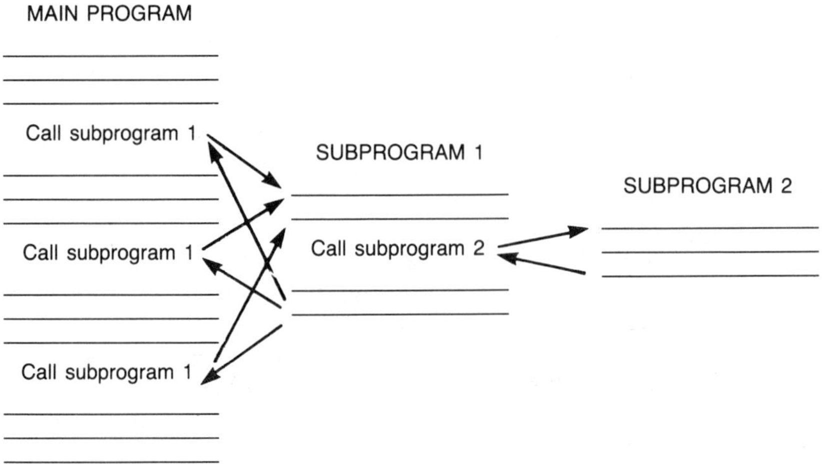

Using subprograms has several advantages. When a set of computations needs to be performed several times, using a subprogram saves on coding effort because the programmer writes the statements in the subprogram only once. Using a subprogram may save internal storage space because the subprogram appears only once in internal storage even though it is called several times. The development of large programs is often simplified by using subprograms because a large program can be prepared by coding and testing each subprogram separately. Then a main program links the subprograms together by calling each subprogram in turn.

Types of subprograms

FORTRAN has two basic types of subprograms: functions and subroutines. Their primary difference, besides the way in which they are coded, is the number of values that may be returned from the subprogram to the calling program. *Function subprograms,* or simply *functions,* return *one* value to the calling program. For example, a function subprogram that finds the maximum of three real values returns one value, the maximum, to the calling program. In Chapter 3 several FORTRAN-supplied functions were discussed. SQRT, INT, and REAL are functions because each supplies the calling program with one value. Appendix C contains a complete list of FORTRAN-supplied functions.

With a *subroutine subprogram,* or simply *subroutine,* more than one value may be returned to the calling program. For example, a subprogram may be prepared to find the largest and the smallest values from a set of three real values. In this case two values are returned to the calling program; hence a subroutine must be used. In another situation we may wish to use a subroutine to sort the data in an array of 50 numbers into ascending order. The entire array must then be returned to the calling program. Sometimes a subroutine does not return any values to the calling program. For example, a subroutine may be used to write output data in a special format. In this case, the data to be written is passed to the subroutine, but no values are returned to the calling program. In any situation where *one and only one* value is to be supplied to the calling program, a function or subroutine may be used. If no values, or if more than one value, are to be returned to the calling program, a subroutine must be used.

11-2. Functions

A function subprogram begins with a special statement, the FUNCTION statement, and ends with an END statement. Between these are other FORTRAN statements including another special statement, the RETURN statement. Figure 11-2 shows an example of a function that finds the maximum of three real values. In this section we describe the statements used in a function and explain how a function is called. We use the example in Figure 11-2 in our discussion.

Figure 11-2. The MAXVAL function that finds the maximum of three real values

```
      REAL FUNCTION MAXVAL(A,B,C)
C  FUNCTION TO FIND THE MAXIMUM OF THREE REAL VALUES
      REAL A,B,C,BIG
      BIG=A
      IF (B.GT.BIG) THEN
        BIG=B
      END IF
      IF (C.GT.BIG) THEN
        BIG=C
      END IF
      MAXVAL=BIG
      RETURN
      END
```

The FUNCTION statement

The first statement in a function subprogram must be a FUNCTION statement. The syntax of this statement is as follows:

> *type* FUNCTION *name*(*a1,a2,...,an*)
>
> where *type* is a type (e.g., INTEGER, REAL).
> *name* is the function's name.
> *a1,a2, . . . ,an* are dummy arguments.

The FUNCTION statement has several purposes. One is to give the *name* of the function. Each function must have a name, which must follow the rules for FORTRAN variable names. The name is coded after the keyword FUNCTION in the FUNCTION statement. The name of the function in Figure 11-2 is MAXVAL.

The FUNCTION statement also indicates the *type* of data to be returned to the calling program. This type is specified by the word INTEGER, REAL, CHARACTER*l (where l is the length), or LOGICAL before the keyword FUNCTION. In effect, we are saying that the name of the function is of the indicated type. For example, the function in Figure 11-2 returns a real value to the calling program; that is, MAXVAL is of type real. As another example, the following FUNCTION statement could be used for a function that returns an integer value:

```
INTEGER FUNCTION FUN1(I,J)
```

This statement specifies that FUN1 is the name of a function of type integer. Function names may be real, integer, character, or logical type.

Implicit typing may be used for real and integer function names. Then the type is given by the first letter of the function name (i.e., I through N for integer, any other letter for real). The FUNCTION statement does not have to begin with INTEGER or REAL. For example, we could use the name RMAX for the function that finds the maximum of three real values. The FUNCTION statement would be coded as follows:

```
FUNCTION RMAX(A,B,C)
```

In addition to the name and type of the function, the FUNCTION statement includes a list of names, separated by commas and enclosed in parentheses. These are called the *dummy arguments* of the function, and they indicate the names used in the subprogram for the data passed to it by the calling program. For example, the function in Figure 11-2 finds the maximum of three real values. The dummy arguments specify the variable names used in the function for the three real values. These names are A, B, and C. As another example, consider an integer function named FUN2. Assume that this function receives two integer and two real values from the calling program. Then the FUNCTION statement could be

```
INTEGER FUNCTION FUN2(X,Y,S,T)
```

The names of the dummy arguments are X, Y, S, and T. We assume the first two are for the integer data and the second two are for the real values.

A function may have no dummy arguments. This would be true if no data were passed to the function, for example, if the function simply read a value. When there are no dummy arguments, the parentheses are still required in the FUNCTION statement even though there are no names between them. For example, assume that the real function FUN3 has no dummy arguments. Then the FUNCTION statement would be as follows:

```
REAL FUNCTION FUN3()
```

Statements in a function

Any FORTRAN statement except another FUNCTION statement (or a SUB-ROUTINE statement that is described later) may appear in a function subprogram. However, certain statements are required. First, type statements are needed for the dummy arguments. These statements come after the FUNCTION statement and before the first executable statement in the function. For example, in the function in Figure 11-2, the dummy arguments A, B, and C are of type real and are specified in a REAL statement. As another example, the function FUN2 that was just described has two integer arguments, X and Y, and two real arguments, S and T. Therefore it would contain the following type statements:

```
INTEGER X,Y
REAL S,T
```

Implicit typing may be used for dummy arguments in which case type statements for the arguments are not needed in the function.

A second requirement is that the function must contain at least one statement that uses the name of the function as a variable name in such a way that a value is assigned to the name. This is because the name of the function is used to return a value to the calling program. The value to be returned must be assigned to the function name at some point in the function. In the function in Figure 11-2, the maximum value of the three arguments must be assigned to the name MAXVAL. In this function, an arithmetic assignment statement is used to supply a value for the function name. In other functions the name may be assigned a value through a READ statement or by using the name on the left-hand side of a character or logical assignment statement.

Another statement needed in a function is the RETURN statement. The syntax of this statement is as follows:

```
RETURN
```

This is a control statement that, when executed, causes the computer to branch from the function to that point in the calling program where the function is called. At the same time, the value assigned to the function name is returned to the calling program. In effect, the RETURN statement is the logical end of a function, just as the STOP statement is the logical end of a main program. The RETURN statement may appear anywhere in the function, and there may be more than one RETURN statement depending on the logic of the function.

Finally, the last statement in a function must be an END statement. This statement signals the physical end of that function. When a function is prepared for processing on a computer, it is compiled separately from the main program and other subprograms. The compiler must be able to recognize the end of the subprogram; this is the purpose of the END statement. (It is possible to not use a RETURN statement in a function, in which case control returns to the calling program when the END statement is reached. However, most programmers include a RETURN statement to show explicitly the logical end of the function.)

With the additional statements described here we now can understand how the function in Figure 11-2 works. Recall that the purpose of this function is to find the maximum of three real values. The logic of this function assumes that the value of A is the maximum. This value is assigned to the variable named BIG. (Note that BIG is specified in the REAL statement.) The value of BIG is then compared to the values of B and C. If either is larger than the current value of BIG, the larger value is assigned to BIG. Finally, the value of BIG is assigned to the name of the function, MAXVAL. The RETURN statement then causes control to return to the calling program.

Figure 11-3. A variation of the MAXVAL function

```
      REAL FUNCTION MAXVAL(A,B,C)
C  FUNCTION TO FIND THE MAXIMUM OF THREE REAL VALUES
      REAL A,B,C
      MAXVAL=A
      IF (B.GT.MAXVAL) THEN
        MAXVAL=B
      END IF
      IF (C.GT.MAXVAL) THEN
        MAXVAL=C
      END IF
      RETURN
      END
```

This function can be simplified by substituting MAXVAL for the variable named BIG. The resulting function is shown in Figure 11-3. The variable BIG is no longer needed. This function satisfies the requirement that the name of the function must be assigned a value before the function returns to the calling program.

Calling a function

A function is called from another program by using the function's name in an expression. Values for the function's arguments are also supplied when the function is called. (A FORTRAN-supplied function, such as SQRT, is called in the same way.) As an example, assume that we need to assign the maximum of the value of X, the value of Y, and 25.0 to the variable named M1. (X, Y, and M1 are real variable names.) Using the MAXVAL function in Figure 11-2 or 11-3, this can be accomplished with the following arithmetic assignment statement:

```
M1=MAXVAL(X,Y,25.0)
```

The values for the function's arguments that are supplied when the function is called are referred to as *actual arguments*. They are enclosed in parentheses and separated by commas after the function name. The actual arguments must correspond in number, type, and order to the dummy arguments. Because there are three dummy arguments for the MAXVAL function (number), there must be three actual arguments. Since the dummy arguments are real (type), the actual arguments must be real. In this example, the order of the arguments does not matter, but with many functions the order is important. The actual arguments must be assigned values before the function is called.

Figure 11-4 summarizes the effect of calling a function subprogram. When a function is called, the values of the actual arguments are assigned to the dummy arguments, and control is transferred to the function. Thus, in Figure 11-4, the value of X in the calling program is assigned to the

Figure 11-4. Calling a function subprogram

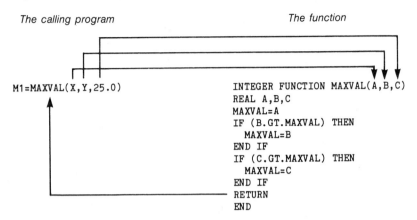

variable named A in the function, the value of Y in the calling program is assigned to B in the function, and 25.0 is assigned to C in the function. This process has the effect of passing data to the subprogram. The program then branches to the function, and the statements in the function are executed by using the dummy arguments to refer to the data. When the RETURN statement is executed, control returns to the calling program at the point where the function was called. The function returns a value to the calling program, which is used to complete the expression in which the function was called. Execution of the program then continues in its normal sequence. In Figure 11-4, the value returned is the maximum of the argument values. The arithmetic assignment statement in which the function is called is completed before going on to the next statement in the calling program.

Actual arguments may be variable names, constants, or expressions. Arrays as arguments are discussed later. The only restriction is that the actual arguments correspond in number, type, and order to the dummy arguments. In other words, the number of actual arguments must be the same as the number of dummy arguments, corresponding actual and dummy arguments must be of the same type, and the actual arguments must be in the same order as the dummy arguments. For example, consider the following FUNCTION statement:

```
INTEGER FUNCTION FUN2(X,Y,S,T)
```

This function uses four dummy arguments. We assume that the first two arguments are integer and the second two are real. Whenever this function is called, the actual arguments must correspond to the dummy arguments. They need not be the same variable names; they may be other variable names, constants, or expressions. But they must correspond in number, type, and order to the dummy arguments. Thus this function may be called by the following statement (assuming I and K are integer and S is real):

```
X=FUN2(I,K+5,S,7.6)
```

With this function call, the value of I in the calling program is assigned to X in the function; the value of K + 5 is calculated in the calling program and assigned to Y in the function; the value of S in the calling program is assigned to S in the function; and 7.6 is assigned to T in the function. Note that the variable names in the calling program may be the same or different from the names used in the function.

If a function has no dummy arguments, no actual arguments are used when the function is called. The parentheses, however, are still needed after the function name. For example, consider a real function named FUN3 which has no dummy arguments. This function may be called by the following statement:

```
Y=FUN3()
```

The parentheses are needed to indicate that FUN3 is a function name and not a variable name.

A function may be called only as part of an expression. The expression may include just the function call, or it may include other operations and function calls. The expression may be used in any statement that permits expressions of its type. For example, assume that the real functions FUN4 and FUN5 have been properly coded. Each requires two real arguments. The following are valid examples of the use of these functions (assuming all variables are of type real):

```
X=FUN4(X,Y)+FUN5(A,B)
IF (FUN4(C,D).GE.7.5) THEN
A1=A2+FUN5(A3,FUN4(A4,A5))
WRITE (6,100) 2.5*FUN4(P,Q)
```

The calling program

A program that calls a function may be a main program or it may be another subprogram (function or subroutine). In the calling program, certain restrictions apply. First, the name of the function must be specified in a type statement (unless implicit typing is used). For example, if a program calls the MAXVAL function, which returns a real value to the calling program, this function name would have to be specified as follows:

```
REAL MAXVAL
```

Note that the function name's type is specified by a type statement in the calling program, not in the subprogram; the FUNCTION statement specifies the type of the function name in the subprogram.

Variable names that are used in actual arguments must be declared in type statements in the calling program (unless implicit typing is used). This is as we would expect because these names are used in the calling program. However, the types of the dummy arguments are *not* specified in

Figure 11-5. A main program that calls the MAXVAL function

```
C  MAIN PROGRAM THAT CALLS THE MAXVAL FUNCTION
      REAL MAXVAL,X,Y,Z,M1,M2
      READ (5,100) X,Y,Z
      M1=MAXVAL(X,Y,25.0)
      M2=MAXVAL(X+Y,Z,3.0*X)
      WRITE (6,200) M1,M2
      STOP
  100 FORMAT (3F5.1)
  200 FORMAT (' FIRST MAXIMUM ',F5.1,' SECOND MAXIMUM ',F5.1)
      END
```

the calling program. Type statements for the dummy arguments are only included in the function.

To illustrate a calling program, Figure 11-5 shows a main program that calls the MAXVAL function twice. Note that the name MAXVAL is specified in a REAL statement along with the variable names used in the actual arguments and other variable names. The function is called in two arithmetic assignment statements.

Subprogram and main program independence

All subprograms (functions or subroutines) and main programs are independent of one another in the computer's internal storage. Each subprogram is stored in a separate part of the computer's memory; the main program is separate from all subprograms. There is no connection between the various programs in internal storage until one program calls another.

The consequence of this independence is that variable names and statement numbers used in a subprogram have no relation to variable names and statement numbers in other subprograms or in the main program. For example, if we use the variable name A in a subprogram, we can use the same name in a main program and the computer treats the names as if they were completely different. As another example, assume that a statement numbered 10 is in a subprogram and also in a main program. The statement

```
GO TO 10
```

in the subprogram means branch to statement 10 in that program, not to statement 10 in the main program. Thus the computer treats the programs as if they were completely independent of each other.

Compiling and executing a main program and subprograms

Recall that an executable program consists of one main program and any number of subprograms. To compile and execute a main program with one or more subprograms (functions or subroutines), we may need special system commands or job control language. Sometimes each program must be compiled separately. Then a special command is used to link the programs together before execution. At other times the main program and its subprograms can all be compiled together and then executed with no additional commands needed. The way in which a main program and its subprograms are compiled and executed depends on the computer being used.

Arrays as arguments of a function

An array name may be used as a dummy argument of a function. Then the corresponding actual argument should also be an array name. (The exceptions to this are beyond the scope of this book.) Calling a function with an array name as an argument causes the entire array to be passed to the function. The array name that is used as a dummy argument must be dimensioned in the function; the name of the actual array argument must be dimensioned in the calling program. The sizes of the array arguments normally should be the same. For example, the function in Figure 11-6 finds the smallest element of a 20-element array. (The logic used in this function is discussed in Section 9-3.) Note that the array name is used as a dummy argument; it is dimensioned in the function before the first executable statement. The function name SMALL is assigned the value of the smallest element of the array. The actual array argument is dimensioned in the calling program. For example, the main program in Figure 11-7 calls the function SMALL twice to find the

Figure 11-6. The SMALL function that finds the smallest element of a 20-element array

```
      REAL FUNCTION SMALL(X)
C  FUNCTION TO FIND THE SMALLEST ELEMENT OF AN ARRAY
      REAL X(20)
      INTEGER L
      SMALL=X(1)
      DO 100 L=2,20
        IF (X(L).LT.SMALL) THEN
          SMALL=X(L)
        END IF
  100 CONTINUE
      RETURN
      END
```

Figure 11-7. A main program that calls the SMALL function

```
C  MAIN PROGRAM THAT CALLS THE SMALL FUNCTION
      REAL X(20),Y(20),SX,SY,SMALL
      READ (5,100) X
      SX=SMALL(X)
      READ (5,100) Y
      SY=SMALL(Y)
      WRITE (6,200) SX,SY
      STOP
  100 FORMAT (10F3.0)
  200 FORMAT (' SMALLEST ELEMENTS ARE ',F4.0,1X,F4.0)
      END
```

Figure 11-8. The SMALL function with an adjustable array dimension

```
      REAL FUNCTION SMALL(X,N)
C  FUNCTION TO FIND THE SMALLEST ELEMENT OF AN ARRAY
      INTEGER N,L
      REAL X(N)
      SMALL=X(1)
      DO 100 L=2,N
        IF (X(L).LT.SMALL) THEN
          SMALL=X(L)
        END IF
  100 CONTINUE
      RETURN
      END
```

smallest element in each of two arrays. The actual arguments used when the function is called are array names that are dimensioned at the beginning of the calling program.

The size of an array used as an argument of a function need not be specified precisely in the function. Instead, the dimension bounds may be passed to the subprogram by the arguments. (If lower and upper dimension bounds are used, two values must be passed to the function; if only an upper dimension bound is needed, one value must be passed.) This is known as an *adjustable dimension*. When this technique is used, the dummy arguments that represent the array's dimension bounds must be integer variable names. The same names must be used in place of the array's dimension bounds in the type or DIMENSION statement in the function. The names must be specified as integer type prior to being used in this way. For example, the function SMALL may be modified to find the smallest element of an array of unknown size as shown in Figure 11-8. Note in this function that the array name and a variable name representing the array's size are dummy arguments. The variable name is specified as integer at the beginning of the function. Then the name is used in the REAL statement for the array's upper dimension bound.

In the calling program the dimension bounds for the actual array must be specified precisely and this information must be passed to the function. For example, the function in Figure 11-8 may be used to find the smallest element of a 50-element array named A. The calling program would contain the following statements:

```
REAL A(50)
   .
   .
   .
SA=SMALL(A,50)
   .
   .
   .
```

Note that array A is specified as having 50 elements and that this information is passed to the function as one of the arguments.

11-3. Subroutines

In many ways a subroutine subprogram is similar to a function. Like a function, a subroutine requires a name to identify it, a list of dummy arguments, a RETURN statement, and an END statement. In addition, a subroutine is called by supplying actual arguments and transferring control to the subroutine. When the execution of the statements in a subroutine has been completed, control returns to the calling program.

A subroutine differs from a function in the way in which the values are returned to the calling program. A function returns a value through the name of the function, whereas a subroutine uses arguments to return values. Because there may be several arguments, more than one value may be returned to the calling program.

A subroutine begins with a special statement, the SUBROUTINE statement, and ends with an END statement. Between these are other FORTRAN statements including RETURN statements. An example of a subroutine is shown in Figure 11-9. This subroutine finds the sum and difference of two real values. In this section we describe the statements used in a subroutine and explain how a subroutine is called. We use the example in Figure 11-9 in our discussion.

The SUBROUTINE statement

The first statement in a subroutine subprogram must be a SUBROUTINE statement. The syntax of this statement is as follows:

SUBROUTINE name(a1,a2,...,an)

where *name* is the subroutine's name.
     a1,a2,...,an are dummy arguments.

Figure 11-9. The CALC subroutine that finds the sum and difference of two real values

```
      SUBROUTINE CALC(A,B,SUM,DIF)
C  SUBROUTINE TO FIND THE SUM AND DIFFERENCE OF TWO REAL VALUES
      REAL A,B,SUM,DIF
      SUM=A+B
      DIF=A-B
      RETURN
      END
```

The name of a subroutine must follow the rules for variable names. Unlike a function, no data type is associated with the name because the name is not used to return a value to the calling program. The dummy arguments may be variable or array names. (The use of arrays as arguments of a subroutine is discussed later.) Data is both passed to the subroutine and returned to the calling program by means of the arguments.

The subroutine in Figure 11-9 illustrates these ideas. The name of this subroutine is CALC. The dummy arguments are A, B, SUM, and DIF. The first two dummy arguments are used to pass values to the subroutine and the other two arguments are used to return data to the calling program. This subroutine returns the sum (SUM) and difference (DIF) of two real values (A and B).

A subroutine does not have to have dummy arguments. This would be true if no data were passed to the subroutine and no data were returned to the calling program, for example, if the subroutine simply printed a heading. When there are no dummy arguments, the parentheses are *not* used in the SUBROUTINE statement (unlike a function with no dummy arguments). For example, if the subroutine SUB1 has no arguments, its SUBROUTINE statement would be

```
SUBROUTINE SUB1
```

Statements in a subroutine

Any FORTRAN statement, except another SUBROUTINE statement or a FUNCTION statement, may appear in a subroutine. Like a function, certain statements are needed. First, the dummy arguments must be specified in type statements (unless implicit typing is used). The type statements come after the SUBROUTINE statement and before the first executable statement in the subroutine. For example, in the subroutine in Figure 11-9, the dummy arguments A, B, SUM, and DIF are all specified in a REAL statement.

Unlike a function, the name of the subroutine must *not* be used as a variable name within the subroutine. Instead, the subroutine must contain statements that assign values to the dummy arguments that return data to the calling program. This may be accomplished through assignment or READ statements. For example, the subroutine in Figure 11-9 assigns the sum of A and B to SUM and the difference of these variables to DIF.

As with a function, there should be at least one RETURN statement to cause the subroutine to branch back to the calling program. Finally, the last statement in a subroutine must be an END statement. These are illustrated in the subroutine in Figure 11-9.

Calling a subroutine

A subroutine subprogram is called with a CALL statement. This is a control statement that passes actual arguments to the subroutine and then branches to the subroutine. The syntax of the CALL statement is as follows:

> ```
> CALL name(al,a2,...,an)
> ```
>
> where *name* is the name of a subroutine.
>   *a1,a2,...,an* are actual arguments that correspond in
>   number, type, and order to the dummy arguments of
>   the called subroutine.

As an example of a CALL statement, assume that a program must calculate the sum and difference of the values of X and Y, and assign the results to S and D, respectively. The following CALL statement may be used to call the CALC subroutine in Figure 11-9:

```
CALL CALC(X,Y,S,D)
```

The effect of this statement is summarized in Figure 11-10. First, the values of the actual arguments are assigned to the dummy arguments. The values of *all* actual arguments are passed to the subroutine, even though some arguments may have meaningless values in the calling program. Thus, in this example, the value of X in the calling program is assigned to A in the subroutine, the value of Y is assigned to B, and the values of S and D are assigned to SUM and DIF, respectively, in the subroutine. Then control transfers to the first executable statement of the subroutine.

When the RETURN statement in the subroutine is executed, the process is reversed. Figure 11-11 summarizes the process. First the values of *all* dummy arguments are returned to the calling program. Thus, for the example of the CALC subroutine, the value of A in the subroutine is assigned to X in the calling program, the value of B is assigned to Y, and SUM and DIF are assigned to S and D, respectively, in the calling program. Then control returns to the next statement following the CALL statement in the calling program.

The actual arguments used when a subroutine is called may be variable names, constants, or expressions. A constant or expression may be used as

Figure 11-10. Calling a subroutine subprogram

The calling program   *The subroutine*

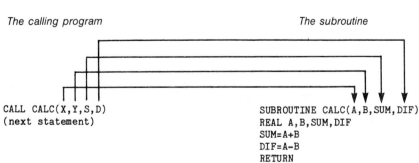

```
CALL CALC(X,Y,S,D)            SUBROUTINE CALC(A,B,SUM,DIF)
(next statement)              REAL A,B,SUM,DIF
                              SUM=A+B
                              DIF=A-B
                              RETURN
                              END
```

Figure 11-11. Returning to a calling program from a subroutine subprogram

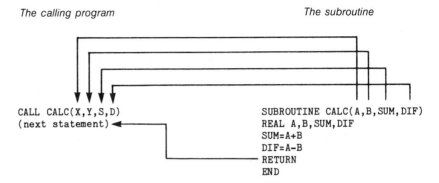

The calling program   The subroutine

```
CALL CALC(X,Y,S,D)          SUBROUTINE CALC(A,B,SUM,DIF)
(next statement)            REAL A,B,SUM,DIF
                            SUM=A+B
                            DIF=A-B
                            RETURN
                            END
```

an actual argument only if the corresponding dummy argument is not used in any way that changes its value in the subroutine. For example, with the CALC subroutine, constants and expressions may be used for actual arguments corresponding to the dummy arguments of A and B but not to SUM and DIF.

As with functions, the actual arguments of a subroutine must agree in number, type, and order with the dummy arguments. Thus, to call the CALC subroutine in Figure 11-9, four real arguments must be provided. The first two must represent the data to be used in the calculation, the third actual argument must be for the sum, and the fourth must be for the difference.

If a subroutine has no dummy arguments, no actual arguments are needed when the subroutine is called and the parentheses are not used after the subroutine name in the CALL statement. For example, assume that SUB1 is a subroutine with no dummy arguments. The following statement would call this subroutine:

```
CALL SUB1
```

The calling program

A calling program for a subroutine may be a main program or another subprogram (subroutine or function). In the calling program, variables used in the actual arguments must be specified in type statements (unless implicit typing is used). However, the types of the dummy arguments are not specified in the calling program. Type statements for the dummy arguments are only included in the subroutine. Unlike functions, the name of the subroutine is not listed in a type statement in the calling program. This is because the subroutine's name does not have a data type associated with it.

Figure 11-12 shows a main program that calls the CALC subroutine. Note that the variables X, Y, S, and D, which are used in the actual arguments, are all specified in a REAL statement. The subroutine is called twice using different sets of actual arguments.

Figure 11-12. A main program that calls the CALC subroutine

```
C  MAIN PROGRAM THAT CALLS THE CALC SUBROUTINE
      REAL X,Y,S,D
      READ (5,100) X,Y
      CALL CALC(X,Y,S,D)
      WRITE (6,200) S,D
      CALL CALC(2.0*X,3.0*Y,S,D)
      WRITE (6,210) S,D
      STOP
  100 FORMAT (2F4.0)
  200 FORMAT (' FIRST SUM ',F4.0,' FIRST DIFFERENCE  ',F4.0)
  210 FORMAT (' SECOND SUM ',F4.0,' SECOND DIFFERENCE ',F4.0)
      END
```

Arrays as arguments of a subroutine

Array names may be used as dummy arguments in a subroutine. The arrays then must be dimensioned in the subroutine. For example, Figure 11-13 shows a subroutine that finds the sum and difference of corresponding elements of two 20-element arrays. The dummy arguments are the names of four arrays: AA, BA, SUMA, and DIFA. The elements of the first two arrays are used in the calculation of the elements of the second two arrays. Note that all arrays are dimensioned in a REAL statement.

To call a subroutine that uses array names as dummy arguments, the corresponding actual arguments in the CALL statement should be array names. (The exceptions to this are beyond the scope of this book.) The actual argument arrays must be dimensioned in the calling program. For example, to call the CALCA subroutine in Figure 11-13, the calling program could include the following statements:

```
REAL XA(20),YA(20),SA(20),DA(20)
         .
         .
         .
CALL CALCA(XA,YA,SA,DA)
         .
         .
         .
```

Figure 11-13. The CALCA subroutine with arrays as arguments

```
      SUBROUTINE CALCA(AA,BA,SUMA,DIFA)
C  SUBROUTINE TO FIND THE SUM AND DIFFERENCE
C  OF CORRESPONDING ELEMENTS OF TWO ARRAYS
      REAL AA(20),BA(20),SUMA(20),DIFA(20)
      INTEGER I
      DO 100 I=1,20
        SUMA(I)=AA(I)+BA(I)
        DIFA(I)=AA(I)-BA(I)
  100 CONTINUE
      RETURN
      END
```

The data for all actual array arguments would be passed to the subroutine and assigned to the dummy array arguments. When the RETURN statement in the subroutine is executed, the values of all dummy array arguments would be sent back to the actual array arguments in the calling program.

As with functions, adjustable dimensions may be used for arrays that are arguments of subroutines. In such a situation, arguments are used for the dimension bounds of the arrays.

11-4. The COMMON statement

Arguments are one way to pass data between a subprogram and a calling program. Another approach is to declare a common area in the computer's internal storage that both the calling program and the subprogram use. The variable and array names used in the subprogram are related to the corresponding names in the calling program because they refer to the same storage locations. To specify a common area, we use the COMMON statement in both the calling program and the subprogram. The COMMON statement is a specification statement that must precede the first executable statement in any program or subprogram.

The storage area that the COMMON statement creates is known as a *common block*. Within the block may be storage for any type of data: integer, real, character, or logical. If a common block is given a name, it is called a *named common block;* a common block without a name is called a *blank common block*.

Incorrect use of the COMMON statement can lead to errors that are difficult to debug. Because of this and for other reasons, many programmers prefer not to use the COMMON statement. When using the COMMON statement, special care should be taken to avoid errors.

Blank common blocks

The syntax of the COMMON statement for a blank common block is as follows:

> COMMON *list*
>
> where *list* is a list of variable and array names separated by commas.

For example, the following COMMON statement may be used in the CALC subroutine (Figure 11-9) that finds the sum and difference of two real values:

```
COMMON A,B,SUM,DIF
```

This statement causes the variable names listed to refer to the first four storage locations in the common block.

In the calling program there must be a similar COMMON statement listing the variable names used for the actual data. For example, the following COMMON statement could appear in the program that calls CALC:

    COMMON X,Y,S,D

This statement in the calling program causes the variable names listed to refer to the same four storage locations as the names in the COMMON statement in the subroutine. Thus these two COMMON statements, the first in the subroutine and the second in the calling program, cause variable names X and A to refer to the same storage location, the names Y and B to refer to the same location, the names S and SUM to identify the same location, and the names D and DIF to identify the same location. This is summarized in Figure 11-14.

The order in which the variable names are coded in the COMMON statements specifies which names correspond. For example, assume that the COMMON statement in the program that calls the CALC subroutine is coded as

    COMMON Y,X,S,D

Then the correspondence of variable names in the calling program and subprogram is not the same as before. In this case, Y and A refer to the same location, X and B identify the same location, and S, D, SUM, and DIF are as before. This may or may not be correct, depending on what the programmer wishes to accomplish.

Any variable or array name specified in a COMMON statement must not appear in the argument list of a subprogram. In the examples of the CALC subroutine, because all the arguments are in the common block, no argument list is used. Thus subroutine CALC is coded as shown in Figure 11-15. The program that calls this subroutine requires the following

Figure 11-14. Correspondence of variable names in a common block

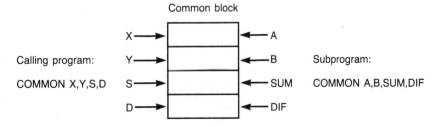

Figure 11-15. The CALC subroutine with a COMMON statement

```
      SUBROUTINE CALC
C   SUBROUTINE TO FIND THE SUM AND DIFFERENCE OF TWO REAL VALUES
      REAL A,B,SUM,DIF
      COMMON A,B,SUM,DIF
      SUM=A+B
      DIF=A-B
      RETURN
      END
```

statements:

```
COMMON X,Y,S,D
      .
      .
      .
CALL CALC
      .
      .
      .
```

In effect, the data is passed between the subprogram and the calling program by means of the common block.

In this example, all arguments of the subroutine are in a common block. Hence no argument list is used in the SUBROUTINE statement nor in the CALL statement. When all arguments of a function are in a common block, no argument list is used either. But as we know, the parentheses in the FUNCTION statement and those following the function name when the function is called are still required. For example, the function MAXVAL in Figure 11-3 would begin as follows if all arguments were in a common block:

```
REAL FUNCTION MAXVAL()
REAL A,B,C
COMMON A,B,C
```

To call this function, we would use a statement such as

```
M1=MAXVAL()
```

Note that parentheses with nothing between them are used in both the FUNCTION statement and the function reference. These parentheses are only needed with a function, not with a subroutine.

Using a common block has two main advantages: the object program requires less storage space and the program executes faster. These advantages result because no special instructions are needed to pass data between a calling program and a subprogram. When using an argument list, the object program includes instructions that make the actual arguments available to the subprogram. These instructions require storage space and must be executed each time the subprogram is called. When a common block is used, these instructions are not needed. Hence the program as a whole requires less storage and executes faster.

When using a common block, it is important that corresponding variable names be of the same type. For example, assume that the following COMMON statement appears in a main program and that M and N are integer and W and X are real:

```
COMMON M,N,W,X
```

In this case, the first two locations in the common block contain integer data, and the next two locations contain real data. Any COMMON statement in a subprogram called by this program must specify the same types of variable names in the same order.

A common block may be used with several subprograms. In this case the main program must assign names to all locations in the common block. Each subprogram requires a COMMON statement with a list of the names that it uses, plus any additional names needed to align the data in the common block. To illustrate, assume that a main program calls two subroutines, SUB1 and SUB2. The first subroutine requires three real values from the main program; the second subroutine uses two integer values. If no argument lists are used, the variable names for all values must be specified in the COMMON statement in the main program. For example, the following COMMON statement may be used in the main program (assume that A, B, and C are real; and I and J are integer):

```
COMMON A,B,C,I,J
```

Subroutine SUB1 requires a COMMON statement with names for the real values. Because these occupy the first three locations of the common block, no additional names are needed. Hence the following COMMON statement could be used in SUB1 (assume that X, Y, and Z are real):

```
COMMON X,Y,Z
```

Subroutine SUB2 must be able to refer to the two integer values in the common block. Therefore three real variable names must be specified so that the integer names used in the subroutine are properly aligned with the integer data in the common block. That is, a COMMON statement of the following form would be used in SUB2 (assume that R, S, and T are real; and K and L are integer):

```
COMMON R,S,T,K,L
```

This is summarized in Figure 11-16.

Figure 11-16. Correspondence of variable names in a common block referenced by two subprograms

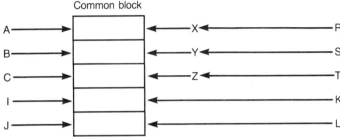

Arrays in common blocks

If an array name is specified in a COMMON statement, the entire array is stored in the common block. The size of the array in the subprogram must be the same size as the corresponding array in the calling program. For example, assume that the following statements appeared in a subprogram:

```
REAL C(5),D(5)
COMMON C,D
```

The effect of these statements is to assign the elements of array C to the first five locations in the common block and the elements of array D to the next five locations. In a calling program, the sizes of the corresponding arrays must be similarly specified. The following statements may appear in the calling program:

```
REAL W(5),X(5)
COMMON W,X
```

The correspondence between the array elements is shown in Figure 11-17. If the sizes of the arrays are not correctly specified, correspondence of array elements is affected. For example, assume that the REAL and COMMON statements in the main program are coded as follows:

```
REAL W(7),X(5)
COMMON W,X
```

Then the correspondence between the array elements in the calling program and the subprogram is as shown in Figure 11-18.

If adjustable dimensions are used, an argument list is required. An

Figure 11-17. Correspondence of array elements in a common block

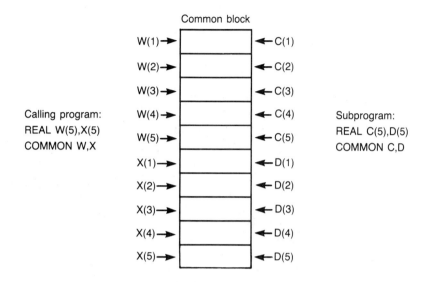

Figure 11-18. Correspondence of array elements in a common block where the array sizes do not agree

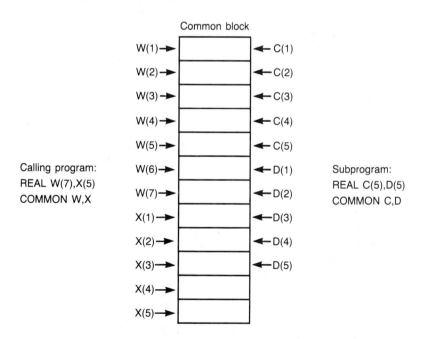

array with an adjustable dimension cannot be specified with a COMMON statement.

Arrays that are stored in a common block may be dimensioned in the COMMON statement. For example, the arrays named C and D, each with five elements, may be specified as follows:

```
COMMON C(5),D(5)
```

This eliminates the need for dimensioning the arrays in a type statement or a DIMENSION statement. If explicit typing is used, the array names must also be listed in a type statement. For example, if C and D are real arrays, the following statement should be used in addition to the COMMON statement just given:

```
REAL C,D
```

Named common blocks

The syntax of the COMMON statement for named common blocks is as follows:

COMMON /*name*/*list*/*name*/*list*/...

where *name* is a common block name.
   list is a list of variable and array names separated by commas.

A common block name must follow the rules of variable names. Although only one blank common block is allowed, there may be any number of named common blocks.

As an example, the following COMMON statement specifies two named common blocks:

```
COMMON /B1/A,B,C/B2/I,J
```

The first block, named B1, contains locations for three values. The values are identified by variable names A, B, and C. The block named B2 contains two locations for the variables named I and J.

The advantage of using named common blocks is that a subprogram need only specify variable and array names for the data in the named blocks that are used by the subprogram. For example, assume that the previous COMMON statement is contained in a main program that calls two subroutines. The first subroutine requires three values from the main program that are contained in the block named B1. In this subroutine, the COMMON statement need only specify names for the data in the B1 common block. Thus the following COMMON statement may be used:

```
COMMON /B1/X,Y,Z
```

Figure 11-19. Correspondence of variable names in named common blocks

Main program: Subroutine SUB1:   Subroutine SUB2:
COMMON /B1/A,B,C/B2/I,J   COMMON /B1/X,Y,Z   COMMON /B2/K,L

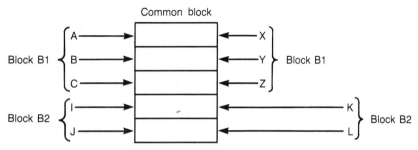

Note that the block name must be the same as the name used in the calling program but the variable names may be different.

The second subroutine uses the data found in the block named B2. Thus in this subroutine the following COMMON statement may be used:

```
COMMON /B2/K,L
```

The correspondence of variable names in named common blocks is summarized in Figure 11-19.

If both blank and named common blocks are required, the blank common block is declared first in the COMMON statement. For example, consider the following statement:

```
COMMON M,PL,N(10)/RES/AMT(100)/DAT/IM,W
```

This statement specifies a blank common block containing storage for the variables named M and PL and for the 10-element array named N. In addition, the common block named RES contains a 100-element array named AMT, and the block named DAT contains storage for data named IM and W.

11-5. Statement functions

Function subprograms and FORTRAN-supplied functions are two types of FORTRAN functions. Another type of function is a statement function. Statement functions differ from function subprograms in that a statement function is only one statement long and is coded as part of the calling program. No FUNCTION statement is used; no RETURN or END statement is required. Instead, each function consists of one statement function statement.

The syntax of a statement function statement is as follows:

```
name(a1,a2,...,an)=expression
```

where *name* is the function's name.
    a1,a2,...,an are dummy arguments.
    expression is an arithmetic, logical, or character
        expression.

The name of a statement function must indicate the type of data to be returned to the calling program. Therefore the name must have been specified previously in an appropriate type statement (unless implicit typing is used). The dummy arguments may be any variable names. Array names are not allowed as dummy arguments in a statement function. The expression type must agree with the type of the function's name. An integer or real statement function requires an arithmetic expression. A character expression may be used only with a character function. A logical function name requires a logical expression.

A statement function is coded in the program that calls the function. All statement functions used in a program must appear after the specification statements and before the first executable statement. A statement function is called in the same way that a function subprogram is called. The statement function's name is used in an expression, and actual arguments are supplied. As with function subprograms, the actual arguments must agree in number, type, and order with the dummy arguments. The actual arguments may be variable names, array element names, constants, and expressions, but may not be array names. After the expression in the statement function is evaluated, the resulting value is assigned to the name of the function, and control returns to the point where the function is called.

As an example of a statement function, assume we must prepare a program that calculates, at a number of points, the average of three test scores. If we do not use a function, we must code the appropriate formula in the program each time the average is to be calculated. A function subprogram may be prepared and called when needed, but this requires coding a complete function that contains only one calculation. If we use a statement function, the advantages of a function subprogram are gained without coding a complete function.

The following statement function may be used to average three test scores:

```
AVE(TS1,TS2,TS3)=(TS1+TS2+TS3)/3.0
```

The name of the function is AVE. This name should be specified in a REAL statement. The dummy arguments are TS1, TS2, and TS3; they represent the test scores to be averaged. These names should also be specified as real. The arithmetic expression uses the dummy arguments to perform the necessary calculations.

To call the statement function, actual arguments must be supplied when the function is used. For example, if the three test scores to be averaged are named T1, T2, and T3, the following statement may be used to find their average:

```
A1=AVE(T1,T2,T3)
```

This statement executes the statement function, substituting the values of T1, T2, and T3 for TS1, TS2, and TS3, respectively.

As another example, assume that six test scores need to be averaged. The names of the scores are S1, S2, S3, S4, S5, and S6. To average these scores, the following statement may be used:

```
A2=(AVE(S1,S2,S3)+AVE(S4,S5,S6))/2.0
```

The statement function is called twice. First, the average of S1, S2, and S3 is calculated. Then S4, S5, and S6 are averaged. The two averages are added and the result is divided by 2.0 to get the average of all six scores.

11-6. Program development revisited

In Chapter 7 we discussed several aspects of program development. These included program structure, style, and understandability, and the activities in the programming process. We saw that following the guidelines in Chapter 7 resulted in programs that were well structured, easily understood, and correct.

As programs become larger, their development becomes more complex. In Chapter 7 we mentioned the idea of modular programming in which a large program is divided into sections or modules. Each module performs some function related to the overall processing of the program. The modules for a program can be developed separately and then brought together to form a complete program after all the modules are finished. Subprograms give us a convenient mechanism for modularizing a program. The approach is to code each module as a separate subprogram. Then the main program is composed of a series of calls to the subprograms.

An illustrative program

To illustrate this approach to program development consider the problem of updating a pricing table. In an example in Section 9-4 we used a table that consisted of two 10-element arrays, one for item numbers and one for the corresponding unit prices (see Figure 9-8). Assume now that some of the prices in the table have changed. We need a program to make appropriate modifications in the table, that is, to *update* the data in the table. In addition, we want a printed copy of the table before and after the changes are made.

We can see that the program must do the following:

1. Read the pricing table.
2. Print the pricing table.
3. Update the pricing table.
4. Print the updated table.

Following our approach of using subprograms to modularize a program, we can code each of these steps as a separate subroutine. However, because the second and fourth steps both involve printing the pricing table, we only need three subroutines: one to read the pricing table, one to print the table, and one to update the table. The main program calls these three subroutines in order and then calls the printing subroutine again to print the updated table.

Assume that we have coded the three subroutines and named them TABIN, TABOUT, and UPDATE, respectively. Each subroutine requires two 10-element arrays as arguments, one for the item numbers and one for the prices. The main program to call these subroutines in the proper sequence is shown in Figure 11-20. Note the simplicity of this program; it is just a sequence of four CALL statements with the necessary arguments.

The input and output subroutines can be coded fairly easily. Each involves a loop to read or write the elements of the two arrays. The subroutines are shown in Figures 11-21 and 11-22. Notice that we have used the same

Figure 11-20. The main program for the table updating program

```
C
C  MAIN PROGRAM FOR THE PRICING TABLE UPDATE PROGRAM
C
      INTEGER ITNUM(10)
      REAL PRICE(10)
      CALL TABIN(ITNUM,PRICE)
      CALL TABOUT(ITNUM,PRICE)
      CALL UPDATE(ITNUM,PRICE)
      CALL TABOUT(ITNUM,PRICE)
      STOP
      END
```

Figure 11-21. The table input subroutine

```
      SUBROUTINE TABIN(ITNUM,PRICE)
C
C  THIS SUBROUTINE READS THE PRICING TABLE.
C
      INTEGER ITNUM(10),I
      REAL PRICE(10)
      DO 100 I=1,10
        READ (5,200) ITNUM(I),PRICE(I)
  100 CONTINUE
      RETURN
  200 FORMAT (I4,F5.2)
      END
```

Figure 11-22. The table output subroutine

```
      SUBROUTINE TABOUT(ITNUM,PRICE)
C
C  THIS SUBROUTINE PRINTS THE PRICING TABLE BELOW APPROPRIATE HEADINGS.
C  THE TABLE IS PRINTED IN FOUR COLUMNS.
C
      INTEGER ITNUM(10),I
      REAL PRICE(10)
      WRITE (6,200)
      DO 100 I=1,5
        WRITE (6,210) ITNUM(I),PRICE(I),ITNUM(I+5),PRICE(I+5)
  100 CONTINUE
      RETURN
  200 FORMAT ('1','                          PRICING TABLE'/
     1         '0','ITEM NUMBER    UNIT PRICE    ITEM NUMBER',
     2         '    UNIT PRICE'/)
  210 FORMAT (' ',3X,I4,10X,F5.2,10X,I4,10X,F5.2)
      END
```

names for the arrays in the main program and the subroutines, although this
is not necessary. However, it is necessary that the arrays be dimensioned in
the subroutines.

The updating process has not been fully defined. Assume that new
prices along with corresponding item numbers are recorded in a series of
input records. Any number of changes need to be made, and the input data
is not in any particular order. The last input record contains 9999 in the item
number field.

The updating subroutine must do the following until there is no more
input data:

1. Read an item number and new price.
2. Find the corresponding item in the pricing table.
3. Make the necessary change in the pricing table.

Assume that we have a function named LOCTN that returns the location
(that is, the element number) of a given value in a 10-element array of
integers. The arguments of the function are the value to be found and the
name of the array. If the value is found, the function returns its location;
otherwise, it returns a value of zero.

We can use this function in the UPDATE subroutine as shown in
Figure 11-23. First, an input record is read with an item number and new
price. Then the check for the trailer value is made. Next, the LOCTN function
is called and the returned value is assigned to LOC. We then test LOC to
see if it is zero. If it is not equal to zero, the new price is assigned to PRICE(LOC),
thus modifying the pricing table; if LOC equals zero, an error message is
printed. This subroutine also counts the number of prices that are updated
and prints this count after finishing all the updating.

The only thing that remains to complete the program is to develop
the LOCTN function. This function searches a 10-element array for a given

Figure 11-23. The table updating subroutine

```
      SUBROUTINE UPDATE(ITNUM,PRICE)
C
C  THIS SUBROUTINE READS AN ITEM NUMBER AND NEW PRICE, LOCATES THE
C  CORRESPONDING ITEM IN THE PRICING TABLE, AND MODIFIES THE PRICE.
C
      INTEGER ITNUM(10),I,INUM,LOC,LOCTN,COUNT
      REAL PRICE(10),PRIX
      COUNT=0
      WRITE (6,300)
  100 READ (5,200) INUM,PRIX
        IF (INUM.EQ.9999) GO TO 110
        LOC=LOCTN(INUM,ITNUM)
        IF (LOC.NE.0) THEN
          PRICE(LOC)=PRIX
          COUNT=COUNT+1
        ELSE
          WRITE (6,310) INUM
        END IF
      GO TO 100
  110 WRITE (6,320) COUNT
      RETURN
  200 FORMAT (I4,F5.2)
  300 FORMAT ('1','PRICING TABLE UPDATE')
  310 FORMAT ('0','ITEM ',I4,' NOT FOUND')
  320 FORMAT ('0',I3,' PRICES UPDATED')
      END
```

value. We could use a sequential search, or a binary search if the array is in ascending order. We will assume that this is not necessarily the case and search sequentially. The function is shown in Figure 11-24. Note that if the number is found in the table, the name of the function (LOCTN) is assigned the subscript of the matching element; otherwise, the name is assigned a value of zero.

Figure 11-24. The item locating function

```
      INTEGER FUNCTION LOCTN(NUM,TAB)
C
C  THIS FUNCTION RETURNS THE LOCATION OF NUM IN TAB.
C  IF NUM CANNOT BE FOUND, ZERO IS RETURNED.
C
      INTEGER NUM,TAB(10),I
      I=1
  100 IF ((NUM.EQ.TAB(I)).OR.(I.EQ.10)) GO TO 110
        I=I+1
      GO TO 100
  110 IF (NUM.EQ.TAB(I)) THEN
        LOCTN=I
      ELSE
        LOCTN=0
      END IF
      RETURN
      END
```

The main program in Figure 11-20 and the subprograms in Figures 11-21, 11-22, 11-23, and 11-24 form an executable program to update the pricing table. In processing these on a computer, the main program and the subprograms would be entered and compiled. Execution would begin with the first statement in the main program. Sample input and output for the program is shown in Figure 11-25. Note in the output that four of the prices in the second pricing table, which is printed after the updating takes place, are different from those in the first pricing table.

Top-down program development

One advantage of using subprograms to modularize a program is that we can develop the program in a *top-down* fashion. Top-down program development includes top-down design, coding, and testing.

Top-down design is similar to the idea of stepwise program refinement that we discussed in Section 7-4. We start by designing the overall logic of the program. Each basic function that the program is to perform becomes a subprogram. The main program contains a series of calls of the subprograms. (There may be other statements in the main program besides those that call subprograms. For example, loop control or decision-making statements may be needed to control the order of execution of the subprograms.) We then design each subprogram in a similar top-down fashion. Eventually we reach the point where we can code the basic operations of the program.

One way of displaying the top-down design of a program is to draw a diagram that shows the relationship between the main program and the subprograms. Figure 11-26 shows such a diagram for the table-updating program. This is sometimes referred to as a *calling hierarchy* or *structure diagram*. The box at the top represents the main program. Each box below signifies a subprogram. A line connects two programs if one program calls the other. Thus Figure 11-26 shows that the main program calls TABIN, TABOUT, and UPDATE, and that UPDATE calls LOCTN.

This diagram also shows how we can think of the program in terms of *levels*. At the highest level we can think of the program as the sequence of activities that take place in the main program. If we wish, we can just understand the program at this level and we do not have to examine any of the subprograms. However, to understand the program at a lower level, we can look at the subprograms that are called by the main program. Even lower, we can examine the next level of subprograms, and so forth until we reach the bottom of the diagram.

Besides designing the program in a top-down fashion, we can also follow a *top-down coding* and *testing* pattern. In this approach, we code the main program first. Then, for each subprogram called by the main program, we code a "dummy" subprogram called a *stub* that simulates, but does not actually perform, the function of the subprogram. Often each stub just contains

Figure 11-25. Input and output for the table updating program

```
1001 2.95
1023 3.64
1045 2.25
1172 0.75
1185 1.50
1201 1.95
1235 4.85
1278 9.95
1384 6.28
1400 4.75
1172 0.95
1400 5.00
1027 3.79
1450 9.25
1001 3.20
0985 1.00
1384 5.75
9999 0.00
```

(a) Input data

PRICING TABLE

ITEM NUMBER	UNIT PRICE	ITEM NUMBER	UNIT PRICE
1001	2.95	1201	1.95
1023	3.64	1235	4.85
1045	2.25	1278	9.95
1172	.75	1384	6.28
1185	1.50	1400	4.75

PRICING TABLE UPDATE

ITEM 1027 NOT FOUND

ITEM 1450 NOT FOUND

ITEM 985 NOT FOUND

  4 PRICES UPDATED

PRICING TABLE

ITEM NUMBER	UNIT PRICE	ITEM NUMBER	UNIT PRICE
1001	3.20	1201	1.95
1023	3.64	1235	4.85
1045	2.25	1278	9.95
1172	.95	1384	5.75
1185	1.50	1400	5.00

(b) Output

Figure 11-26. The calling hierarchy for the table updating program

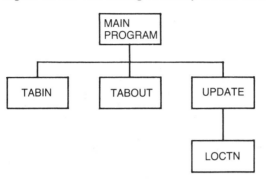

a statement that prints a message indicating that the stub has been called. We then can run the main program with the incomplete subprograms to test the logic of the main program. Next we follow the same procedure for the first subprogram, coding stubs for any subprograms that it calls. We then test the main program with the completed first subprogram. This process is repeated for all subprograms until the complete program is coded and tested.

An alternative coding and testing strategy is called *bottom-up coding and testing*. In this approach we design the program in a top-down fashion but start coding and testing with the lowest level subprograms. This requires writing main programs called *exercisers* to call and test the subprograms. We build the program from the bottom up until we reach the top level, which is the main program.

Reusing subprograms

Another advantage of using subprograms to modularize a program is that subprograms may often be used in other programs. For example, assume that we need a program to compute the cost of various items by multiplying the quantity purchased by the price. Because we already have a subroutine to read the pricing table and one to locate an item in the table, we can use these in a pricing program. The main program to do this is shown in Figure 11-27. The program first reads the pricing table using the TABIN subroutine. It then reads an item number and quantity and checks for a trailer value. Next the program uses the LOCTN function to find the desired item in the table. The returned value is then checked to see if the item was found. If it was found, the price for the item is multiplied by the quantity to get the cost and the output is printed. If the item was not found, an error message is printed. This main program, together with the TABIN and LOCTN subprograms, forms a complete pricing program.

The examples in this section show us that using subprograms has a number of advantages. In fact, most large programs are developed in the manner described here. For any complex program, the programmer should consider using the techniques in this section.

Figure 11-27. The main program for the pricing program

```
C
C  MAIN PROGRAM FOR THE PRICING PROGRAM
C
       INTEGER ITNUM(10),INUM,LOC,LOCTN
       REAL PRICE(10),QTY,COST
       CALL TABIN(ITNUM,PRICE)
  100  READ (5,200) INUM,QTY
       IF (INUM.EQ.9999) GO TO 110
       LOC=LOCTN(INUM,ITNUM)
       IF (LOC.NE.0) THEN
          COST=PRICE(LOC)*QTY
          WRITE (6,210) INUM,COST
       ELSE
          WRITE (6,220) INUM
       END IF
       GO TO 100
  110  STOP
  200  FORMAT (I4,F4.0)
  210  FORMAT (' ','ITEM ',I4,' COST ',F7.2)
  220  FORMAT (' ','ITEM ',I4,' NOT FOUND')
       END
```

Review questions

1. What is the difference between a subprogram and a main program?
2. When a subprogram is referenced in a program we say it is _____.
3. Data is _____ to a subprogram from a calling program; data is _____ to a calling program from a subprogram.
4. What is an executable program in FORTRAN?
5. What is the main difference between functions and subroutines?
6. The first statement in a function must be _____; the first statement of a subroutine must be _____.
7. What statement causes execution of a function or a subroutine to terminate?
8. The last statement of a function or subroutine must be _____.
9. The arguments used in a FUNCTION statement or SUBROUTINE statement are called _____ arguments. Those used when the function or subroutine is called are referred to as _____ arguments. The two sets of arguments must agree in _____, _____, and _____.
10. Code a function to compute Z as follows: if X is less than Y, then Z is Y minus X; if X is greater than Y, then Z is X minus Y; if X is equal to Y, then Z is 30. Assume that all variables are integer.
11. Code a main program that reads the values of A and B, calls the function defined in Question 10 using A and B for X and Y, respectively, assigns the result of the function call to C, and writes the value of C.
12. Code a function to find the total of the elements of a 25-element array of real data.
13. Code a main program that reads a 25-element array, calls the function defined in Question 10 to find the total of the elements in this array, and writes the result.

14. Answer Question 12 using an array with an adjustable dimension.
15. Code a subroutine to find X^2 and X^3 where X is a real number.
16. Code a main program that reads a value for A, calls the subroutine defined in Question 15 to find A^2 and A^3, and writes the results.
17. What is the next statement executed after a RETURN statement in a subroutine is executed?
18. Code a subroutine to find the total and average of the elements of a 25-element array of real data.
19. Code a main program that reads a 25-element array, calls the subroutine defined in Question 18 to find the total and average of the elements in this array, and writes the results.
20. Code the answers to Questions 15 and 16 using a blank common block for all arguments.
21. Modify your answer to Question 20 to use a named common block.
22. Code a statement function that computes the value of A given by the following formula:

$$A = B(1 + R)^Y$$

All variables in the function are real, except Y which is integer.
23. Code a statement to call the statement function defined in Question 21 using 1000.00 for B, .1 for R, and 5 for Y.
24. What is meant by top-down design?
25. Draw a calling hierarchy diagram for the program in Figure 11-27.
26. What is meant by top-down coding and testing?

Programming problems

1. Write a FORTRAN function subprogram to find the balance in a bank account given the initial balance, the interest rate, and the number of years since the initial amount was deposited. Assume that interest is compounded annually. Write a main program to read the initial balance, interest rate, and number of years; call the function; and write the balance computed by the function. Test the program with several sets of input data.
2. Write a FORTRAN function subprogram to find the Nth Fibonacci number. (Problem 6 in Chapter 5 describes Fibonacci numbers.) Write a main program to read a value of N, call the function, and write the result. Test the program with N equal to 5, 12, 1, 25, 2, 8, and 3.
3. Write a FORTRAN function subprogram to find e^x using the series given in Problem 11 of Chapter 5. Write a main program to read a value of x, compute e^x using the function, and print the result. Test the program with several values of x.
4. The factorial of a positive integer n, written $n!$, is $n \times (n - 1) \times (n - 2) \times \cdots \times 2 \times 1$. For example, 5! is $5 \times 4 \times 3 \times 2 \times 1 = 120$. Write a FORTRAN function subprogram to find the factorial of a positive integer. Then write a function that uses the factorial function to find the combination of n

things taken k at a time. The combination is given by the following expession:

$$\frac{n!}{k!(n-k)!}$$

Note that the combination function calls the factorial function three times. Finally, write a main program to read the values of n and k, call the combination function to find the combination of n things taken k at a time, and write the result. Use the following data to test the program:

n	k
6	3
10	9
4	1
7	2

5. Problem 4 in Chapter 7 describes an algorithm for finding the day of the week given any date in the twentieth century. Code this algorithm as a FORTRAN function subprogram. The arguments of the function are the month, day, and year. The function should return a character data value that gives the corresponding day of the week. Write a main program to read a date, call the function, and write the day of the week. Use the data in Problem 4 of Chapter 7 to test the function.

6. Problem 17 in Chapter 8 gives the requirements for a student to be on the Dean's list of a college based on the student's year in school and his or her GPA. Write a FORTRAN function subprogram that accepts the student's year and GPA, and returns the logical value TRUE if the student should be placed on the Dean's list and the value FALSE if the student should not be on the list. Write a main program to read the data given in Problem 17 of Chapter 8, call the function, and write a message indicating whether or not the student should be on the Dean's list.

7. Write a FORTRAN function subprogram that returns the logical value TRUE if a given character data value is a palindrome and FALSE if the data is not a palindrome. (Problem 11 in Chapter 8 describes palindromes.) Write a main program to read a character data value, call the function to determine if the data is a palindrome, and write the character data and a statement as to whether or not it is a palindrome. Use the data in Problem 11 of Chapter 8 to test the program.

8. The tuition charged a student at a small private college is based on the number of units (credits) that the student takes during a quarter. The tuition charge is $200 plus $25 per unit for each of the first eight units and $32.50 per unit for all units taken over eight. Write a FORTRAN function subprogram to determine the tuition charge given the number of units.

   Write a main program to read student data consisting of the student number, the units taken during the Fall quarter, the units taken during the Winter quarter, and the units taken during the Spring quarter. Using the function described in the previous paragraph, calculate the tuition for each quarter. Also calculate the total tuition for the year. Write these results along with the student number.

   Use the following input data to test the program:

Student number	Fall quarter	Units taken Winter quarter	Spring quarter
1018	7.0	18.0	15.0
1205	15.0	12.5	6.0
1214	15.5	15.5	15.5
1218	8.0	7.0	5.0
1293	8.5	7.5	4.0
1304	6.0	6.0	6.0
1351	10.5	18.5	0.0
1354	0.0	15.0	6.0

9. Write a FORTRAN function subprogram to determine the expected population of a group in ten years given the current population and the annual growth rate. Write a main program to read population data for two socioeconomic groups in each area of a city. The input data consists of the area number, the current population and growth rate for group A, and the current population and growth rate for group B. Using the function subprogram, calculate the expected population of each group in ten years. Write the area number, the expected population of each group, and the total expected population for the area.
   Use the following data to test the program:

Area number	Group A Current population	Growth rate	Group B Current population	Growth rate
001	14,500	3.5%	6,300	4.1%
002	18,251	2.3%	2,215	2.9%
003	6,205	4.0%	8,132	3.9%
004	3,738	5.4%	12,730	2.7%
005	12,100	3.0%	10,150	3.0%

10. Problem 10 in Chapter 4 describes a program to convert a temperature from Fahrenheit to Celsius and Kelvin, from Celsius to Fahrenheit and Kelvin, and from Kelvin to Fahrenheit and Celsius. Write a FORTRAN subroutine subprogram to do the required conversion. The subroutine needs four arguments: the code for the scale of the temperature passed to the subroutine, the Fahrenheit temperature, the Celsius temperature, and the Kelvin temperature. Note that the arguments used to pass a temperature to the subroutine depend on the value of the argument for the code. The other arguments are used to return the temperature in the other two scales to the calling program.
   Write a main program to read the code and temperature, call the subroutine, and write the temperature in all three scales. Use the data in Problem 10 of Chapter 4 to test the program.

11. Write a FORTRAN subroutine subprogram to find the total and average of up to four test scores. The subroutine receives the number of test scores (1 to 4) and the scores from the calling program and returns the total and average of the scores.
   This subroutine is to be used in a program that analyzes the results of a psychological experiment. Each subject in the experiment is given two series of tests with up to four tests in each series. The results of the tests were recorded in records in the following format:

Positions	Field
1–3	Subject of identification code
4	Number of tests in first series
5–6	
7–8	
9–10	Test scores in first series
11–12	
13	Number of tests in second series
14–15	
16–17	
18–19	Test scores in second series
20–21	

Write a main program to read the test score data and use the subroutine just described to find the total and average of the test scores in each series. This requires two calls of the subroutine. Then find the total and average of all test scores in the two series with a third call of the subroutine. Write all results with appropriate headings.

Use the following input data to test the program:

Identifi- cation Code	First series		Second series	
	Number of tests	Test scores	Number of tests	Test scores
408	3	17, 16, 21	2	22, 24
519	1	24	3	17, 23, 16
523	2	14, 18	4	25, 14, 17, 19
584	4	22, 16, 17, 14	4	18, 17, 17, 21
601	1	12	2	11, 9
677	3	25, 23, 24	1	25
701	4	17, 18, 21, 15	2	21, 13
713	2	13, 12	3	18, 18, 12

12. Adding amounts of time expressed in hours and minutes requires special manipulation because there are 60 minutes in an hour. Write a FORTRAN subroutine subprogram that accepts two amounts of time and determines their sum. For each time accepted by the subroutine and for their sum, two arguments are needed, one for the hours and the other for the minutes. Thus this subroutine requires six arguments in all.

Write a main program that reads an employee number and the time that the employee worked on each day of the week in the following format:

Positions	Field
1–5	Employee number
6–9	Time worked on Monday
10–13	Time worked on Tuesday
14–17	Time worked on Wednesday
18–21	Time worked on Thursday
22–25	Time worked on Friday

The first two positions of each time field contain the hours; the next two positions give the minutes. Using the subroutine described in the previous paragraph, calculate the total time worked by the employee for the week. This required four calls of the subroutine. Write all input data and the total of the times with appropriate headings.

Use the following data to test the program:

Time worked

Employee number	Monday	Tuesday	Wednesday	Thursday	Friday
10011	0800	0730	0800	0730	0730
10105	0745	0755	0630	0500	0845
10287	1000	0805	0625	0800	0715
10289	0945	0800	0610	0830	0000
10304	0000	0000	0800	0825	0745
10455	0635	0840	0000	0000	1155

13. Write the following FORTRAN subprograms:
    a. CHRG(THERM). This is a function subprogram that determines the total gas utility charge based on the number of gas therms used (THERM). (Gas consumption is measured in therms.) The charge is $.09 per therm for the first 200 therms, $.08 per therm for the next 300 therms, $.07 per therm for the next 500 therms, and $.065 per therm for all gas used over 1000 therms. The value returned to the calling program should be the total charge.
    b. OUTPT(CUSNO,THERM,CHARG). This is a subroutine subprogram that prints with appropriate headings the customer number, the gas used in therms, and the charge for one month.

    Write a main program to read the customer number and the gas consumed for three separate months. Then, through three separate calls of the function CHRG, calculate the charge for each of the three months. Write the results for each month using three calls of the subroutine OUTPT.

    Use the following data to test the program:

Customer number	First month	Second month	Third month
11825	425	172	253
13972	665	892	1283
14821	45	572	313
19213	1562	973	865
28416	200	500	1000
31082	0	300	600

14. Many introductory calculus textbooks describe a technique for numerical integration of a function in which the area under the curve is divided into a number of rectangles. Then the total area of all rectangles approximates the definite integral of the function. Write a FORTRAN function subprogram that uses this rectangular method to find:

$$\int_a^b x^2 \, dx$$

The arguments of the function are the limits of integration (a and b) and the number of rectangles that are to be used in the approximation.

Write a main program that uses the subprogram to repeatedly integrate the function between the limits $a = 0$ and $b = 3$. Start with two rectangles, then use four, then eight, and so forth, each time doubling the previous number until 8192 are used. For each case, print the number of rectangles, the definite integral, and the error, that is, the difference between the correct integral (which is 9) and the computed value.

Finally, use the function to find

$$\int_{-2}^{1} x^2 \, dx + \int_{.75}^{1.25} x^2 \, dx$$

Use 256 rectangles. All output should be through the main program, not the subprogram.

15. Assume that F, G, and H are polynomials defined as

$$F(X) = A(1) + A(2)*X + A(3)*X**2 + ... + A(N+1)*X**N$$
$$G(X) = B(1) + B(2)*X + B(3)*X**2 + ... + B(M+1)*X**M$$
$$H(X) = C(1) + C(2)*X + C(3)*X**2 + ... + C(L+1)*X**L$$

Note that the degrees of these polynomials are N, M, and L, respectively. Assume a maximum of 20 for each of these and dimension any arrays accordingly. Note also that the coefficient of X**I has a subscript I+1.

Write the following FORTRAN subprograms:

a. INPUT(A,N). This is a subroutine that reads an array A of the coefficients of a polynomial of degree N. Input data should include a record with the degree of the polynomial followed by a record or records with the coefficients. Note that a polynomial of degree N has N+1 coefficients.

b. OUTPUT(A,N). This is a subroutine that prints the array A of the coefficients of a polynomial of degree N. Arrange and label the coefficients neatly.

c. SCALM(A,N,D,C). This is a subroutine that multiplies a polynomial of degree N with array A of coefficients by the constant D and returns a polynomial of degree N with array C of coefficients.

d. ADDP(A,N,B,M,C,L). This is a subroutine that adds a polynomial of degree N with coefficient array A and a polynomial of degree M with coefficient array B, and returns a polynomial with coefficient array C of degree L.

Write a main program that uses these subroutines to do the following:

> Read F(X)
> Print F(X)
> Read G(X)
> Print G(X)
> Compute H(X) = F(X) + 2*G(X)
> Print H(X)
> Compute a new F(X) = 3*H(X)
> Print the new F(X)

Use the following data to test your program:

Polynomial F(X)	Polynomial G(X)
N = 5	M = 2
A(1) = 1.0	B(1) = −7.0
A(2) = 17.6	B(2) = 3.1
A(3) = 0.0	B(3) = −1.0
A(4) = 2.0	
A(5) = −3.6	
A(6) = 1.0	

16. Problem 8 in Chapter 9 involves writing a program to process student test score data. Rewrite this program as the following series of FORTRAN subprograms:

    a. IN(ID,TEST,COUNT). This is a subroutine that reads identification numbers and test scores into two arrays named ID and TEST, respectively. The subroutine must count the data as it is read to determine how many test scores are to be processed (COUNT). The value of COUNT should not include the record with the trailer value.

    b. OUT(ID,TEST,COUNT). This is a subroutine that prints in columns below appropriate headings the array of identification numbers and test scores.

    c. MEAN(TEST,COUNT). This is a function that calculates the mean of the test scores. The mean is the average of the test scores.

    d. TAB(TEST,COUNT,C1,C2,C3,C4,C5). This is a subroutine that tabulates (that is, counts) the number of test scores in various categories. The subroutine should determine the number of scores in each of the following categories:

    > 90–100
    > 80–89
    > 70–79
    > 60–69
    > 0–59

    C1 returns the number of scores in the first category (90–100), C2 returns the number of scores in the second category, and so forth through C5.

    e. SORTT(ID,TEST,COUNT). This is a subroutine that sorts the *test score array* into descending order (largest to smallest). The correspondence between the identification number array and the test score array must be maintained during the sorting.

    f. MED(TEST,COUNT). This is a function that determines the median of the test scores. The function should handle two cases: an even number of test scores and an odd number of test scores.

    In addition to the subprograms, write a main program that uses the subprograms to process the test score data. The main program should call the subprograms in the following order:

    > IN
    > OUT
    > MEAN
    > TAB
    > SORTT
    > OUT
    > MED

    Note that, after sorting, the program should use the OUT subroutine to print the arrays. The main program also requires other output operations. The main program must print the mean after MEAN is called, print the tabulated data after TAB is called, and print the median after MED is used. All output should be printed with appropriate headings or descriptive comments. Use the data in Problem 8 of Chapter 9 to test the program.

17. Write the IN and OUT subroutines described in Problem 16. Then write the following FORTRAN subprograms:

    a. SORTI(ID,TEST,COUNT). This is a subroutine that sorts the *identification number array* into ascending order. Note that as the ID array is rearranged, the TEST array must also be rearranged to maintain the correspondence between the two arrays.

b. SEARCH(ID1,TEST1,FOUND,ID,TEST,COUNT). This is a subroutine that searches the ID array for the element that corresponds to ID1 and sets TEST1 equal to the corresponding element of TEST. If ID1 is found in ID, the logical variable FOUND is set equal to TRUE; otherwise, FOUND is set equal to FALSE. This subroutine may use a binary search or a sequential search. In either case, assume that the ID array has been sorted previously into ascending order.

Write a main program that calls the subprograms in the following order:

> IN
> OUT
> SORTI
> OUT
> SEARCH

The SEARCH subprogram should be called within an input loop that reads an identification number, calls SEARCH, and then prints either the corresponding test score or a message indicating that the identification number was not found. This loop should terminate when an identification number equal to 999 is read. (These subroutines can be added to those from Problem 16 and the main program can be extended to meet the additional requirements.)

To test the program, use the identification numbers and test scores in Problem 8 of Chapter 9. This data should terminate with a trailer value. Following this should be data to test the SEARCH subroutine terminated with another trailer value. Use the following identification numbers for this:

> 202
> 137
> 195
> 298
> 248
> 104
> 173
> 101
> 150
> 299
> 233
> 138

18. Problem 6 in Chapter 10 describes some operations using matrices (i.e., two-dimensional arrays). Refer to that problem and write the following FORTRAN subprograms:

a. GET(A,M,N). This is a subroutine that reads a matrix A with M rows and N columns.

b. PUT(A,M,N). This is a subroutine that prints the M $\times$ N matrix named A in an appropriate format.

c. EQUAL(A,B,M,N). This is a function that returns the truth value TRUE if the M $\times$ N matrices A and B are equal and returns FALSE if they are not equal.

d. SCMLT(C,A,M,N). This is a subroutine that multiplies the M × N matrix A by C.

e. ADDM(A,B,C,M,N). This is a subroutine that adds the M × N matrices A and B, assigning the sum to the M × N matrix C.

Write a main program that uses these subprograms to process two matrices according to the requirements in Problem 6 of Chapter 10. Use the data in that problem to test the program.

Chapter 12

Files

In Chapter 1 we discussed the auxiliary storage component of a computer. (See Figure 1-1.) Two common types of auxiliary storage are magnetic disk and magnetic tape. Auxiliary storage is used to store data that is not currently being processed in the computer's internal storage. When data in auxiliary storage is needed for processing, it is brought into internal storage. Similarly, internal storage data that needs to be saved for future processing is sent to auxiliary storage.

Data stored in auxiliary storage is organized as files. As we know, a file consists of records and records contain fields. When processing the data in an auxiliary storage file, the computer reads or writes the records in the file one at a time. In other words, auxiliary storage data is processed just like other input and output data.

One main reason for using an auxiliary storage file is that the data in the file can be processed easily in several programs. For example, if student test scores are kept in an auxiliary storage file, one program can compute totals and averages for each student, another program can tabulate data for all students, and a third program can produce grade reports. These programs can be run without reentering the data for each program.

In this chapter we discuss the programming necessary for processing auxiliary storage files. We describe how such files are created and how information is retrieved from a file. We also explain how to modify data in a file. After completing this chapter you should be able to write FORTRAN programs that process auxiliary storage files in several ways.*

---

* You may already have used auxiliary storage files for simple input and output. The topics in this chapter go beyond this basic use of these files.

12-1. File concepts

Several concepts about files must be understood before discussing file processing in FORTRAN. In this section we cover these concepts.

Auxiliary storage characteristics

Magnetic disk and magnetic tape are the two most common types of auxiliary storage. Here we describe the important characteristics of each.

Magnetic disk. A magnetic disk is a flat round platter (like a phonograph record) made of metal or plastic and covered with a special magnetic coating. (See Figure 12-1.) The surface of a disk is organized into concentric circles called *tracks* (similar to the grooves in a phonograph record). Data is stored on a disk by recording patterns of magnetism along the tracks of the disk. Data that is stored on a disk can be changed by erasing the previous magnetic

Figure 12-1. Magnetic disk storage

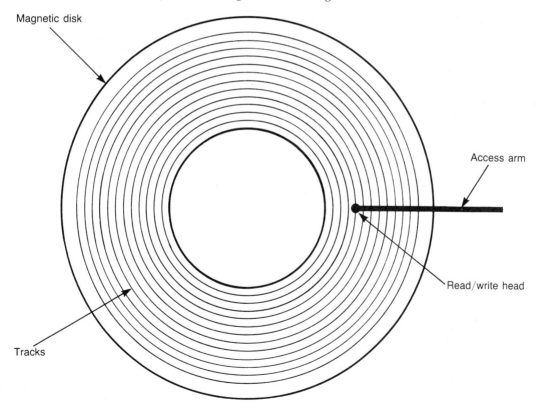

patterns and replacing them with new ones. Data can be retrieved from a disk by sensing the magnetic patterns along the tracks.

A *disk drive* is used both to record data on a disk and to retrieve data from a disk. In a disk drive, the disk rotates at a high speed. While the disk is rotating, an *access arm* comes out of the side of the disk drive. At the end of the access arm is a *read/write head*. The access arm can position the read/write head over any track of a disk. As the disk rotates, data can be written on a track by sending signals to the read/write head. Similarly, as the disk rotates, the data that is stored on a track can be read by the read/write head. When data is written on the surface of a disk, any data already existing in the same place is destroyed. However, when data is read from a disk, the data is not destroyed.

Some disk storage systems consist of a single disk and one access arm that allows data to be read from or written on one side of the disk. Other systems have two access arms, one for each side of the disk. Still other types of disk storage consist of several disks stacked on top of each other (called a *disk pack*) with an access arm for each side of each disk.

No matter what disk storage system is used, the records in a disk file are stored on a group of tracks on one or more disks. To retrieve the data from a disk file, the disk drive can position the read/write head at the first track of the file and read the data one record at a time, moving the read/write head from track to track. This is called *sequential access* because the disk drive goes through the records in the file in the sequence in which they are stored. The disk drive also can move the read/write head to any track and read the records stored there without going through the records on other tracks. This is called *direct access* (or *random access*). The records in the file are read directly by moving the read/write head forward or backward to any track in the file.*

Magnetic tape. The magnetic tape used with computers is similar to audio recording tape. It is made of a plastic material covered with a special magnetic coating. Usually magnetic tape comes in an open reel, but cassette and cartridge tape are also used. Data is stored on a tape by recording magnetic patterns on the surface of the tape. Data is retrieved from a tape by sensing the magnetic patterns.

A *tape drive* is used both to record data on a tape and to retrieve data from the tape. Figure 12-2 shows the important parts of a tape drive that uses open reels. The tape is fed from a supply reel, past a mechanism that includes a read/write head, and onto a take-up reel. As the tape moves past the read/write head, data can be read from the tape or written on the tape. When data is read from a tape, the original data is not destroyed. When data is written on a tape, the old data is erased and replaced with the new data.

The records in a tape file are stored one after the other along the

---

* Other types of auxiliary storage also allow direct access, but magnetic disk is the most common.

Figure 12-2. Magnetic tape storage

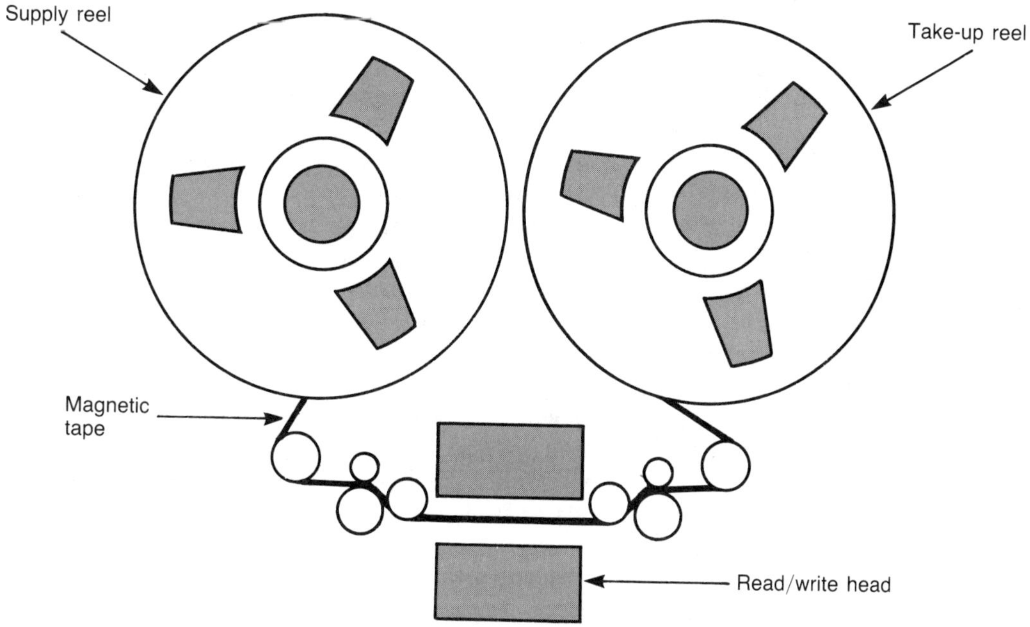

surface of the tape. To read the records in a file, the tape drive starts with the first record in the file and reads the data in the order in which it is stored. As with magnetic disks, this is called *sequential access*. The tape drive cannot go forward without reading the records along the way, and it usually cannot go backwards. Thus, unlike magnetic disks, records in a tape file cannot be read directly. (The tape can be rewound so that reading can start again at the beginning.)

As we can see, magnetic disk and magnetic tape are similar in many ways and different in other ways. Both use patterns of magnetism to store data. Both erase data when new data is written but do not destroy data when existing data is read. Both allow records in a file to be accessed sequentially. With magnetic disk, records in a file can be accessed directly; with magnetic tape, direct access is not possible.

File types

The two types of file access — sequential and direct — yield two basic types of files — sequential files and direct (or random) files. In a *sequential file* records are stored in sequence, one after the other in auxiliary storage. The records in a sequential file must be read in the order in which they are stored. That is, first the program must read the first record in the file, then it must read the second record, and so on. To read the fifth record in a sequential file, the first four records must be read. Thus the records in a sequential file are accessed sequentially. In general, records in a sequential file cannot be accessed in any order other than that in which they are stored. (There may be exceptions to this depending on the computer system being used.)

In a *direct file* (also called a *random file*) the records are identified by numbers. The first record is number 1, the second record is number 2, and so on. To read a record in a direct file, the program must specify the number of the desired record. For example, to read the first record in the file the program must specify that record number 1 is to be read. Once the record number is given, however, that record can be read without reading other records in a file. For example, the program can read record number 5 in the file without reading the first four records. Thus the records in a direct file can be accessed directly. In general, a direct file can only be accessed directly. (There may be exceptions to this depending on the computer system being used.)

A sequential file can be stored on magnetic disk or magnetic tape. If a sequential file is stored on disk, it is accessed sequentially even though magnetic disk allows direct access. A direct file can only be stored on magnetic disk because the file is accessed directly. A direct file cannot be stored on magnetic tape.

File processing

We need to be able to do several things when we use auxiliary storage files. One is to *create* a file. That is, we need to be able to put initial data into a file. The data must come from some other source, such as from keyboard input, punched cards, or another auxiliary storage file. To create a file, the data must first be brought into the computer's internal storage and then sent to the file. This is shown in Figure 12-3. Notice that *input* data must be obtained from another source and that *output* data is sent to the file. Usually this is done one record at a time.

After a file is created, we can *access* the data in the file. As we have discussed already, this involves retrieving records from the file, one record at a time. Each record that is retrieved is processed in internal storage and output is produced. This is shown in Figure 12-4. The *input* data is from the file and the *output* data may be printed, displayed on a CRT, or sent to another auxiliary storage file.

We often need to *update* the data in a file; that is, to change the data

Figure 12-3. Creating a file

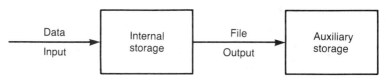

Figure 12-4. Accessing a file

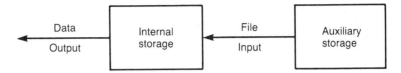

Figure 12-5. Updating a file

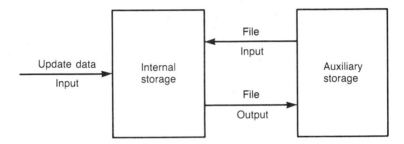

in one or more records in the file. The objective is to bring the file data up to date. Figure 12-5 shows the process. The information that describes the required updating is *input* data to the program. This data may come from keyboard input, punched cards, or another auxiliary storage file. The file to be updated contains records with data to be changed. This is also *input* data because each record must be brought into internal storage so that the necessary updating can take place. After the data is updated, the *output* data for the modified file is sent to auxiliary storage.

In all the processing situations described here, data must be transferred between internal storage and the file in auxiliary storage. Data can be processed only if it is in the computer's internal storage. The process of bringing data into internal storage from a file is an *input* operation. The process of sending data from internal storage to a file is an *output* operation. Usually input and output of file data is done one record at a time.

The next section describes statements for sequential file processing. Section 12-3 discusses sequential file creation and access, and Section 12-4 covers sequential file updating. Finally, the last section discusses direct file processing.

12-2. Statements for sequential file processing

In this section we describe the FORTRAN statements used for sequential file processing. These are the OPEN, CLOSE, READ, WRITE, ENDFILE, REWIND, and BACKSPACE statements.

The OPEN statement

Before a file can be processed, it must be "opened." Opening a file makes the file ready for processing. To open a file, we use an OPEN statement. The syntax of this statement is as follows:

> OPEN (UNIT=i,FILE='$name$',ACCESS='SEQUENTIAL',
>   FORM='FORMATTED',STATUS='$status$')
>
> where i is a device code (unit identifier).
> $name$ is the file name.
> $status$ is NEW or OLD.

For example, to open a particular file, we could use the following statement:

```
       OPEN (UNIT=1,FILE='FILEX',ACCESS='SEQUENTIAL',
     1       FORM='FORMATTED',STATUS='NEW')
```

In the OPEN statement, the device code specifies the auxiliary storage device that stores the file. In the example just given, the device code is 1. This may refer to a disk or a tape; the meaning of the code depends on the computer being used. The word UNIT= before the device code is optional. If it is not included, the device code must be the first item listed in the OPEN statement.

Each file stored in auxiliary storage must have a unique name, because many files may be stored in auxiliary storage and names are needed to distinguish the files. In the OPEN statement, the file name must be listed after the word FILE=. The name must be enclosed in apostrophes. In the example, the name FILEX is used for the file.

As we know, a sequential file is accessed sequentially. This must be specified in the OPEN statement. The word SEQUENTIAL enclosed in apostrophes following the word ACCESS= means that the file will be accessed sequentially. (Later we will see that a different word is used with direct access.)

Two forms of records can be stored in files: formatted and unformatted. Formatted records are the form we have been using in this book. These include records read and written using formatted I/O and using list-directed I/O. Formatted records are stored in the formats we have described in earlier chapters. Unformatted records are different. They are stored in a special format that depends on the computer being used. We will only use formatted records for files in this chapter. This is specified in the OPEN statement by the word FORMATTED, enclosed in apostrophes, following the word FORM=.

The final item in the OPEN statement gives the "status" of the file. When we are creating a file, that file is a new file. This is specified by using the word NEW, enclosed in apostrophes, after the word STATUS=. To access an existing file, we use the word OLD for the status. (Other entries are possible for the status, but NEW and OLD are the most common.)

The items in the OPEN statement may be listed in any order (with the possible exception of the device code, as discussed earlier). The items must be separated by commas and enclosed in parentheses.

A file must be opened before it can be processed, but a file only needs to be opened once in a program. The OPEN statement usually appears at the beginning of the program before the input/output loop. We will see examples of this later.

A program can process several files at the same time. When this is done each file must be opened with a separate OPEN statement. In addition, each file must be associated with a different device code. For example, assume that we wish to access an old file named FILEY and create a new file called FILEZ. Then two OPEN statements such as the following would be needed:

```
    OPEN (UNIT=2,FILE='FILEY',ACCESS='SEQUENTIAL',
1       FORM='FORMATTED',STATUS='OLD')
    OPEN (UNIT=3,FILE='FILEZ',ACCESS='SEQUENTIAL',
1       FORM='FORMATTED',STATUS='NEW')
```

FILEY is associated with device 2 and FILEZ is associated with device 3. These device codes must correspond to the auxiliary storage device used for the files.

In previous chapters we described input and output using the main I/O devices associated with the computer (e.g., keyboard or punched card input and CRT or printer output). In fact, this type of I/O involves sequential files. These files do not have to be opened in the program, rather they are opened automatically just before the program begins execution. (The term that is sometimes used is that the devices associated with these files are *preconnected*.)

The CLOSE statement

After a file has been processed, it must be "closed." Closing a file makes the file no longer available for processing. The statement that accomplishes this is the CLOSE statement. The syntax of this statement is as follows:

```
CLOSE (UNIT=i)
```

where i is a device code (unit identifier).

For example, to close a file associated with device 1, we would use the following statement:

```
CLOSE (UNIT=1)
```

The word UNIT= is optional in the CLOSE statement.

A file only needs to be closed once in a program, after it has been processed. The CLOSE statement usually appears at the end of the program after the input/output loop and before the STOP statement. If several files are used in a program, each must be closed with a separate CLOSE statement. Files that use the main I/O devices as discussed in earlier chapters are not closed in the program. Rather, these files are closed automatically after execution of the program stops.

The READ statement

To read a record in a file, the READ statement is used. The syntax of this statement for sequential files is the same as we discussed in Chapter 6. For reference, the syntax is as follows:

```
READ (UNIT=i,FMT=n1,END=n2) list
```

where *i* is a device code (unit identifier).
  n1 is the number of a FORMAT statement or an asterisk (*).
  n2 is the number of an executable statement.
  list is a list of variable names separated by commas.

The device code in the READ statement must be the same code used in the OPEN statement for the file. Either formatted or list-directed input may be used, depending on how the data in the records in the file is formatted. An end-of-file specifier (END = *n2*) is usually used because we need a way to detect the end of the file.

As an example, assume that each record in FILEY on device 2 has two fields. The first is a five-character field that contains an integer number. The second is a ten-character field that contains a real number with two places to the right of the decimal point. Assume that the necessary OPEN statement has been executed. Then the following statements read a record from this file (assume that K is integer and X is real):

```
      READ (2,100,END=99) K,X
100 FORMAT (I5,F10.2)
```

Note that the device code used in the READ statement is 2. The computer knows that this code refers to FILEY because the code is associated with this file name in the OPEN statement. Note also that a FORMAT statement is needed to specify the format of the records in the file.

As is always the case, the words UNIT = and FMT = are optional in the READ statement. Thus we could code the previous example as

```
      READ (UNIT=2,FMT=100,END=99) K,X
```

If the data is stored in a format acceptable for list-directed input, a list-directed READ statement may be used. For example, the following statement would read a record from the file associated with device 2 in list-directed format:

```
READ (2,*,END=99) K,X
```

A device code is still required so that the computer knows which file to access.

Each time a READ statement is executed, one record is read from the file. Input starts with the first record in the file and proceeds sequentially through the records. When the end of the file is reached, the computer branches to the statement whose number is given in the end-of-file specifier (if one is present).

The WRITE statement

The WRITE statement is used to write a record in a file. The syntax of this statement for sequential files is the same as we described in Chapter 6. For reference, the syntax is as follows:

```
WRITE (UNIT=i,FMT=n) list
```

where *i* is a device code (unit identifier).
  n is the number of a FORMAT statement or an asterisk (*).
  list is a list of constants, variable names, or expressions separated by commas.

As with the READ statement, the device code used in the WRITE statement must be the same code used in the OPEN statement for the file. Formatted or list-directed output may be used.

To illustrate the WRITE statement, assume that we need to write a record in FILEZ on device 3. Each record in this file has three fields. The first is an eight-character field that contains a real number with no places to the right of the decimal point. The other two fields contain integer numbers and are six and four characters long, respectively. (Assume that the OPEN statement for the file has been executed.) The following statements write a record in this file (assume that A is real and M and N are integer):

```
    WRITE (3,200) A,M,N
200 FORMAT (F8.0,I6,I4)
```

Note that the device code in the WRITE statement is 3. Because this code is associated with the file named FILEZ in the OPEN statement, the record is written in this file.

The FORMAT statement in this example does not include a code for a carriage control character. Carriage control characters are only used for printed output files.

As with the READ statement we could use the words UNIT= and FMT= in the WRITE statement. Thus this example could be coded as

```
WRITE (UNIT=3,FMT=200) A,M,N
```

To store the data in a list-directed format, we can use a list-directed WRITE statement. For example, the following statement would write a record in the file associated with device 3 in list-directed format:

```
WRITE (3,*) A,M,N
```

Each time a WRITE statement is executed, one record is written in the file. The first record written becomes the first record in the file. Each successive record that is written follows the previous record.

The ENDFILE statement

A sequential file should have an end-of-file record as its last record. Recall that an end-of-file record is a special record that marks the end of a file. It is used during an input operation to determine if the end of the file has been reached. If a READ statement reads an end-of-file record, the computer branches to the statement whose number is given in the end-of-file specifier. (If there is no end-of-file specifier in the READ statement, an execution error usually occurs when an end-of-file record is read.) If an end-of-file record does not exist and a READ statement attempts to read past the last data record in the file, the program terminates with an execution error. Using an end-of-file record in a sequential file avoids this situation.

The program must write the end-of-file record in the file using the ENDFILE statement. The syntax of this statement is as follows:

```
ENDFILE (UNIT=i)
```

where i is a device code (unit identifier).

For example, the following statement causes an end-of-file record to be written in the file associated with device 1:

```
ENDFILE (UNIT=1)
```

The word UNIT= is optional in this statement.

The ENDFILE statement is only used when a file is being created. (There are exceptions to this that are beyond the scope of this book.) It usually appears after the input/output loop, just before the CLOSE statement for the file.

The REWIND statement

Sometimes the records in a file need to be processed several times. For example, we may need to read the records in a file once to produce some output and then process the records again to do something else. One way that this can be accomplished is by using the REWIND statement. The syntax of this statement is as follows:

> REWIND (UNIT=*i*)
>
> where *i* is a device code (unit identifier).

For example, the following is a valid REWIND statement:

    REWIND (UNIT=3)

The word UNIT= is optional in this statement.

The REWIND statement causes the computer to go back to the beginning of the file that is associated with the device identified in the statement. For example, consider the following statements:

    READ (2,100,END=99) K,X
    REWIND (UNIT=2)
    READ (2,100,END=99) L,Y

Assume that the first READ statement reads the tenth record in the file associated with device 2. Then the REWIND statement repositions the computer at the beginning of that file. Consequently the second READ statement reads the first record in the file.

The REWIND statement is useful when we need to process the data in a sequential file more than once. By using the REWIND statement after a file has been processed, we can start processing from the beginning of the file again.

The BACKSPACE statement

The REWIND statement causes the computer to go back to the beginning of the file; the BACKSPACE statement causes the computer to go back one record in the file. This would be used to read or write a record again. The syntax of the BACKSPACE statement is as follows:

> BACKSPACE (UNIT=*i*)
>
> where *i* is a device code (unit identifier).

For example, the following is a valid BACKSPACE statement:

```
BACKSPACE (UNIT=1)
```

The word UNIT= in this statement is optional.

The BACKSPACE statement backs up one record in the file that is associated with the device identified in the statement. For example, consider the following statements:

```
WRITE (3,200) A,M,N
BACKSPACE (UNIT=3)
WRITE (3,200) X,K,L
```

The first WRITE statement causes the next record in the file associated with device 3 to be written. Then the BACKSPACE statement goes back to that record in the file. Finally, the second WRITE statement writes the same record again. The effect is that the record is written twice.

The BACKSPACE statement is useful when we need to return to a previous record, but not to the beginning of the file. For the latter case, we should use the REWIND statement. (The BACKSPACE statement may not be valid for some types of auxiliary storage.)

12-3. Sequential file creation and access

Program logic for sequential file creation and access is fairly straightforward. Such a program normally involves a loop that processes the records in the file one at a time in the order in which they are stored. In fact, almost all illustrative programs in previous chapters have used this logic. In this section we discuss several examples of programs that create and access sequential files.

Creating a sequential file

To illustrate the program logic for creating a sequential file, assume that we need a file of inventory data. Inventory is the stock of goods that a business has on hand. Each record in the inventory file contains information about one item that the business stocks. Each record contains four fields. The first is a four-character field that contains the item's identifying number. The second is a ten-character field that contains the item's name. The third is a six-character field that contains a real number with two decimal positions representing the item's unit price. The fourth is a five-character field that contains an integer number representing the stock on hand of the item.

Figure 12-6 shows a program that creates the inventory file named INVEN. The file is associated with device 1 in the OPEN statement. This

Figure 12-6. A program to create an inventory file

```
C  PROGRAM TO CREATE A SEQUENTIAL INVENTORY FILE
       INTEGER ITNUM,STOCK,COUNT
       REAL PRICE
       CHARACTER*10 DESC
       OPEN (UNIT=1,FILE='INVEN',ACCESS='SEQUENTIAL',
     1       FORM='FORMATTED',STATUS='NEW')
       COUNT=0
 100   READ (5,200) ITNUM,STOCK,PRICE,DESC
       IF (ITNUM.EQ.9999) GO TO 150
       WRITE (1,210) ITNUM,DESC,PRICE,STOCK
       COUNT=COUNT+1
       GO TO 100
 150   ENDFILE (UNIT=1)
       CLOSE (UNIT=1)
       WRITE (6,220) COUNT
       STOP
 200   FORMAT (I4,6X,I3,1X,F5.2,1X,A10)
 210   FORMAT (I4,A10,F6.2,I5)
 220   FORMAT ('1','INVENTORY FILE CREATED WITH ',I3,' RECORDS')
       END
```

statement also specifies that the file access is SEQUENTIAL, the records in the file are FORMATTED, and the file status is NEW. Note that the OPEN statement appears at the beginning of the program, before the input loop.

The READ statement (numbered 100) reads the data for the new file from the computer's main input device. The program reads one record at a time. We assume that the last record has a trailer value of 9999 for the item number field. The input loop is terminated when the trailer value is detected. If no trailer value is read, the WRITE statement writes a record in the new file. Note that different formats are used for the input and output data, but this is not required. The formats may be the same or different depending on the program requirements.

After the trailer value is read, the program branches out of the loop to the ENDFILE statement. This statement causes an end-of-file record to be written in the new file. Then the file is closed.

This program counts the number of records that are written in the new file. After the file is created, this count is written using the computer's main output device.

Figure 12-7 shows sample input and output for this program. Note that the input data contains a trailer value, but the file that is created does not. The new file has an end-of-file record which does not appear in the listing of the file. The figure also shows the printed output from the program which indicates that ten records were written in the new file.

Accessing a sequential file

A program that accesses a sequential file may process all the records in a file or it may process just certain records. Figure 12-8 shows a program that illustrates the first case. This program prints a report giving the value of the

Figure 12-7. Input and output for the inventory file creation program

1001	15	2.95	SCREWS	
1023	7	3.64	NAILS	
1045	0	2.25	BOLTS	
1172	32	0.75	WASHERS	
1185	4	1.50	NUTS	
1201	11	1.95	HOOKS	
1235	3	4.85	GLUE	
1278	0	9.95	CLAMP	
1384	12	6.28	HANGER	
1400	0	4.75	TAPE	
9999	0	0.00	X	

1001SCREWS	2.95	15
1023NAILS	3.64	7
1045BOLTS	2.25	0
1172WASHERS	.75	32
1185NUTS	1.50	4
1201HOOKS	1.95	11
1235GLUE	4.85	3
1278CLAMP	9.95	0
1384HANGER	6.28	12
1400TAPE	4.75	0

(a) Input data   (b) File output

INVENTORY FILE CREATED WITH 10 RECORDS

(c) Printed output

stock on hand for each item in the inventory file. The stock value is the product of the price and the stock on hand. One line is printed in the report for each record in the file. Sample input and output for the program are shown in Figure 12-9.

The OPEN statement in this program is the same as before except that the status is OLD because the file already exists. Again note that the OPEN statement is at the beginning of the program, before the loop. In the loop the READ statement reads one record from the file. The same format must be used for input as was used when the file was created. Thus the programmer must know the length, type, and location of each field in a record that the program reads. If the format is not correct, the data will not be read properly and an execution error may occur.

Figure 12-8. A program to process all records in an inventory file

```
C   PROGRAM TO COMPUTE THE VALUE OF EACH ITEM
C    IN THE SEQUENTIAL INVENTORY FILE
      INTEGER ITNUM,STOCK
      REAL PRICE,VALUE
      CHARACTER*10 DESC
      OPEN (UNIT=1,FILE='INVEN',ACCESS='SEQUENTIAL',
     1     FORM='FORMATTED',STATUS='OLD')
      WRITE (6,300)
  100 READ (1,200,END=150) ITNUM,DESC,PRICE,STOCK
      VALUE=PRICE*REAL(STOCK)
      WRITE (6,310) ITNUM,DESC,VALUE
      GO TO 100
  150 CLOSE (UNIT=1)
      STOP
  200 FORMAT (I4,A10,F6.2,I5)
  300 FORMAT ('1','          INVENTORY VALUE REPORT'/
     1        '0','ITEM NUMBER   DESCRIPTION   STOCK VALUE'/)
  310 FORMAT (' ',3X,I4,7X,A10,5X,F8.2)
      END
```

Figure 12-9. Input and output for the program that processes all records in an inventory file

INVENTORY VALUE REPORT

			ITEM NUMBER	DESCRIPTION	STOCK VALUE
1001SCREWS	2.95	15	1001	SCREWS	44.25
1023NAILS	3.64	7	1023	NAILS	25.48
1045BOLTS	2.25	0	1045	BOLTS	.00
1172WASHERS	.75	32	1172	WASHERS	24.00
1185NUTS	1.50	4	1185	NUTS	6.00
1201HOOKS	1.95	11	1201	HOOKS	21.45
1235GLUE	4.85	3	1235	GLUE	14.55
1278CLAMP	9.95	0	1278	CLAMP	.00
1384HANGER	6.28	12	1384	HANGER	75.36
1400TAPE	4.75	0	1400	TAPE	.00

(a) File input   (b) Printed output

After a record is read, the stock value is computed. Then the WRITE statement prints a line on the computer's main output device containing the item number, description, and stock value. The loop is repeated until the end-of-file record is read. When the program branches out of the loop, the file is closed. Note that there is no ENDFILE statement in this program. This statement is only used when the file is being created, not when it is being accessed. (There are exceptions to this for specialized processing.)

The program in Figure 12-8 processes all records in the file. To illustrate the case where only certain records are processed, assume that we need to print a report listing the item number and description for each item in the inventory file that has a stock on hand of zero. Figure 12-10 shows a program that accomplishes this. Sample input and output for this program are shown in Figure 12-11.

Figure 12-10. A program to process selected records in an inventory file

```
C   PROGRAM TO LIST THE ITEMS IN THE SEQUENTIAL
C   INVENTORY FILE THAT ARE OUT OF STOCK
      INTEGER ITNUM,STOCK
      CHARACTER*10 DESC
      OPEN (UNIT=1,FILE='INVEN',ACCESS='SEQUENTIAL',
     1      FORM='FORMATTED',STATUS='OLD')
      WRITE (6,300)
  100 READ (1,200,END=150) ITNUM,DESC,STOCK
        IF (STOCK.EQ.0) THEN
          WRITE (6,310) ITNUM,DESC
        END IF
      GO TO 100
  150 CLOSE (UNIT=1)
      STOP
  200 FORMAT (I4,A10,6X,I5)
  300 FORMAT ('1','THE FOLLOWING ITEMS ARE OUT OF STOCK'/
     1         '0','    ITEM NUMBER   DESCRIPTION'/)
  310 FORMAT (' ',8X,I4,7X,A10)
      END
```

Figure 12-11. Input and output for the program that processes selected records in an inventory file

THE FOLLOWING ITEMS ARE OUT OF STOCK

```
1001SCREWS      2.95   15          ITEM NUMBER    DESCRIPTION
1023NAILS       3.64    7
1045BOLTS       2.25    0             1045         BOLTS
1172WASHERS      .75   32             1278         CLAMP
1185NUTS        1.50    4             1400         TAPE
1201HOOKS       1.95   11
1235GLUE        4.85    3                (b) Printed output
1278CLAMP       9.95    0
1384HANGER      6.28   12
1400TAPE        4.75    0
```

(a) File input

This program has some characteristics in common with the previous one. Both programs have an OPEN statement to open the file and a READ statement to read a record from the file. Also in both programs the input loop repeats until the end-of-file record is read. However, several differences exist between the programs. First, the program in Figure 12-10 only reads three fields from each record in the file. Because the price field is not needed in this program, it is skipped in the FORMAT statement (numbered 200) with an X-format code. In addition, this program only prints output for certain records in the file. The IF statement in the input loop determines if the stock on hand is zero. The WRITE statement is executed only if this is true.

The program in Figure 12-10 reads all the records in the inventory file, but only processes certain ones (i.e., those with a stock field equal to zero). All records in the file must be read because we do not know which records to process. The program must go through all the records to locate those that satisfy the required condition.

The examples in this section illustrate programs that create and access sequential files. Many programs that process sequential files are similar to those shown here.

12-4. Sequential file updating

File updating involves changing the data in a file. For example, data in the inventory file discussed in the last section may need to be updated periodically to reflect changes in the stock on hand. To update a file, we must locate each record in the file that is to be modified. After a record is found, individual fields in the record can be changed.

Sequential file updating concepts

When updating a sequential file we normally cannot change existing data in the file. This is because once a sequential file is created, the data in the file usually cannot be modified. Therefore, to update a sequential file we must create a *new* (updated) file which contains all of the data from the *old* (non-updated) file with any changes made in the data. (There may be exceptions to this depending on the computer system being used.)

We call the file to be updated the *old master file* because the data in it is the main or "master" data and the data has not been updated (i.e., it is "old" data). The records in this file are called *old master records*. The updated file is called the *new master file*. This file contains data from the old master file that has been modified. The records in this file are called *new master records*. The data that indicates what modifications are to be made in the master file is called *transaction data* because it represents events or "transactions" that have taken place and that need to be reflected in the master file. The transaction data may be stored in a file (the *transaction file* containing *transaction records*) or it may be entered interactively as the updating program executes.

To illustrate these concepts, assume that we need to update the stock on hand in the inventory file discussed in the last section. Updating involves subtracting any amount withdrawn from stock and adding any amount added to stock. The old master file is the inventory file. The transaction data includes the amount withdrawn and the amount added to stock for each item to be updated. For example, if the stock on hand for an item in the old master file is 7 and the transaction data indicates that the amount withdrawn for the item is 4 and the amount added is 15, then the new stock on hand is 7 minus 4 plus 15 or 18. This is the amount that would go into the new master file for this item. The new master file would be the same as the old master file, except for changes such as this.

When updating a file we must have a way to determine which records are to be updated. We usually do this by including a field in the master records that uniquely identifies each record. Such an identifying field is called a *key field*. For example, in the inventory file, the key field is the item number. Each record in the inventory file has a unique value in this field. The transaction data for updating this file would have to have the values of the key fields of the records to be updated. Thus, to update the stock on hand in the inventory file, each set of transaction data would have to include a field for the item number, the amount withdrawn from stock, and the amount added to stock. We call the key field in the master file the *master key* and that in the transaction data the *transaction key*.

One requirement for the sequential file updating algorithm that we will be discussing in this section is that the master records and the transaction data must be in *increasing* order by key field. For example, the records in the inventory file and the transaction data must be in increasing order by item number. If the data is not in this order, the updating algorithm will not work. (A slight variation of the algorithm is needed if the data is in decreasing order by key field.)

Usually the transaction data does not contain transactions for each record in the old master file. In the inventory example there would be no transaction data for an item if stock was not withdrawn or added. In such a case, however, the record from the old master file must still be put in the new master file; otherwise, the record would be lost from the file.

There can also be transaction data for records that do not exist in the master file. This would be the case if an error were made in the transaction data or if a corresponding record had not yet been added to the master file. If such a situation occurs, a message should be printed or displayed indicating the condition so that corrective action can be taken.

An illustrative program

Figure 12-12 shows a program that updates the inventory file. Sample input and output for this program is shown in Figure 12-13. The old master file is the file named INVEN created by the program in Figure 12-6. This file is opened with a status of OLD in the update program. The new master file is named NEWINV. It is opened with a status of NEW. Note that these files are associated with device 1 and device 2, respectively. When more than one file is open at a time in a program, each file must be associated with a different device code.

The transaction data for the update program is read from a file associated with the computer's main input device. Each transaction record consists of an item number, the amount withdrawn from inventory, and the amount added to inventory. The last record in the transaction file contains a trailer value of 9999 in the item number field.

The basic logic of the algorithm used in the program in Figure 12-12 is to read a transaction record and then to read the records in the old master file until a record is located with the same key field as that of the transaction record. When such a record is found, the data in the old master record is updated. This process is repeated for each transaction record until all transaction records have been read.

The program in Figure 12-12 begins by reading one transaction record and one master record. In this program we must determine if the end of the transaction file and the end of the master file have been reached. The end of the transaction file is detected when the item number from a transaction record (TINUM) equals 9999. This is the trailer value that signals the end of this file. The end of the master file is detected when the end-of-file record in the master file is read. For reasons that we will see soon, we wish to set the item number from the master record (MINUM) equal to 9999 when the end-of-file record is read.* This is accomplished by statement sequences such

---

* This assumes no other record in the master file has 9999 in its item number field.

Figure 12-12. A program to update an inventory file (Part 1 of 2)

```
C
C       SEQUENTIAL INVENTORY FILE UPDATING PROGRAM
C
        INTEGER MINUM,STOCK,TINUM,WTHDRW,ADDTN
        REAL PRICE
        CHARACTER*10 DESC
C
C       OPEN OLD MASTER FILE AND NEW MASTER FILE
C
        OPEN (UNIT=1,FILE='INVEN',ACCESS='SEQUENTIAL',
       1      FORM='FORMATTED',STATUS='OLD')
        OPEN (UNIT=2,FILE='NEWINV',ACCESS='SEQUENTIAL',
       1      FORM='FORMATTED',STATUS='NEW')
C
C       READ TRANSACTION RECORD
C
        READ (5,400) TINUM,WTHDRW,ADDTN
C
C       READ OLD MASTER RECORD
C
        READ (1,410,END=110) MINUM,DESC,PRICE,STOCK
           GO TO 120
   110     MINUM=9999
   120     CONTINUE
C
   200 IF ((TINUM.EQ.9999).AND.(MINUM.EQ.9999)) GO TO 300
        IF (TINUM.EQ.MINUM) THEN
C
C          UPDATE STOCK ON HAND
C
           STOCK=STOCK-WTHDRW+ADDTN
C
C          WRITE NEW MASTER RECORD
C
           WRITE (2,410) MINUM,DESC,PRICE,STOCK
C
C          READ TRANSACTION RECORD
C
           READ (5,400) TINUM,WTHDRW,ADDTN
C
C          READ OLD MASTER RECORD
C
           READ (1,410,END=210) MINUM,DESC,PRICE,STOCK
              GO TO 220
   210        MINUM=9999
   220        CONTINUE
C
        ELSE
           IF (TINUM.GT.MINUM) THEN
C
C             WRITE NEW MASTER RECORD
C
              WRITE (2,410) MINUM,DESC,PRICE,STOCK
C
C             READ OLD MASTER RECORD
C
              READ (1,410,END=230) MINUM,DESC,PRICE,STOCK
                 GO TO 240
   230           MINUM=9999
   240           CONTINUE
```

Figure 12-12. (Part 2 of 2)

```
C
          ELSE
C
C            WRITE ERROR MESSAGE
C
             WRITE (6,500) TINUM
C
C            READ TRANSACTION RECORD
C
             READ (5,400) TINUM,WTHDRW,ADDTN
C
          END IF
        END IF
      GO TO 200
C
C     WRITE END-OF-FILE RECORD IN NEW MASTER FILE
C     CLOSE OLD MASTER FILE AND NEW MASTER FILE
C
  300 ENDFILE (UNIT=2)
      CLOSE (UNIT=1)
      CLOSE (UNIT=2)
C
      STOP
C
  400 FORMAT (I4,2I3)
  410 FORMAT (I4,A10,F6.2,I5)
  500 FORMAT (' ','ITEM ',I4,' NOT IN FILE')
      END
```

Figure 12-13. Input and output for the program that updates an inventory file

1001SCREWS	2.95	15		1001SCREWS	2.95	15
1023NAILS	3.64	7		1023NAILS	3.64	18
1045BOLTS	2.25	0		1045BOLTS	2.25	0
1172WASHERS	.75	32		1172WASHERS	.75	2
1185NUTS	1.50	4		1185NUTS	1.50	4
1201HOOKS	1.95	11		1201HOOKS	1.95	26
1235GLUE	4.85	3		1235GLUE	4.85	3
1278CLAMP	9.95	0		1278CLAMP	9.95	0
1384HANGER	6.28	12		1384HANGER	6.28	12
1400TAPE	4.75	0		1400TAPE	4.75	0

(a) Old master file input   (c) New master file output

```
1023  4 15
1172 30  0
1193 12 20
1201  0 15
1225  0 30
1235  0  0
9999  0  0
```

ITEM 1193 NOT IN FILE
ITEM 1225 NOT IN FILE

(b) Transaction data input

(d) Printed output

as the following:

```
      READ (1,410,END=110) MINUM,DESC,PRICE,STOCK
          GO TO 120
110     MINUM=9999
120     CONTINUE
```

In this sequence, when the end-of-file record is read, the end-of-file specifier in the READ statement causes the computer to branch to statement 110 and MINUM is assigned a value of 9999. If the end-of-file record is not read, the computer goes on to the next statement in sequence which is a GO TO statement that branches around the assignment statement. The CONTINUE statement only serves as a place to branch to in this sequence. (Recall that if a CONTINUE statement is used anywhere in a program except as the terminal statement of a DO loop, the computer just passes through the statement to the next statement in sequence.)*

The main loop in the program is repeated until the end of the transaction file and the end of the master file have been reached; that is, until TINUM equals 9999 and MINUM equals 9999. In the loop, a nested decision is used to determine what to do next based on how the item numbers compare. To see how this works, assume that the transaction file and master file contain records with the following item numbers (EOF means end-of-file record):

TINUM	MINUM
1023	1001
1172	1023
1193	1045
9999	1172
	1185
	1201
	1235
	EOF

Because the first transaction record and the first master record are read before the loop is entered, TINUM is 1023 and MINUM is 1001 when the nested decision in the loop is first reached. Then the conditions in the decision and subsequent input result in the following steps with each repetition of the loop. (In the following comparisons, TINUM is on the left and MINUM is on the right.)

1. 1023>1001:
     Write new master record (MINUM = 1001).
     Read next old master record (MINUM = 1023).
2. 1023 = 1023:
     Update stock on hand.

* This technique does not have to be used if the last record in the master file contains a trailer value of 9999 in its item number field.

Write new master record (MINUM = 1023).
Read next transaction record (TINUM = 1172).
Read next old master record (MINUM = 1045).

3. 1172>1045:
Write new master record (MINUM = 1045).
Read next old master record (MINUM = 1172).

4. 1172 = 1172:
Update stock on hand.
Write new master record (MINUM = 1172).
Read next transaction record (TINUM = 1193).
Read next old master record (MINUM = 1185).

5. 1193>1185:
Write new master record (MINUM = 1185).
Read next old master record (MINUM = 1201).

6. 1193<1201:
Write error message.
Read next transaction record (TINUM = 9999).

7. 9999>1201:
Write new master record (MINUM = 1201).
Read next old master record (MINUM = 1235).

8. 9999>1235:
Write new master record (MINUM = 1235).
Read next old master record (EOF record read; MINUM assigned value of 9999).

After the last step is completed, both TINUM and MINUM equal 9999 and the loop is terminated.

In this example, the end of the transaction file is reached before the end of the old master. At that time TINUM becomes 9999, and all subsequent values of MINUM are less than this value. As a consequence, the remaining old master records are written in the new master file. Had the end of the old master file been reached first, MINUM would be assigned a value of 9999 and all subsequent values of TINUM would be less than this. In this case, an error message would be written for each of the remaining transaction records.

A file-updating program such as this is used whenever the data in a sequential file changes. Additional statements can be included in the program to add new records to the file and to delete out-of-date records. These would be required in a complete file maintenance program.

12-5. Direct files

As we know, records in a sequential file are read or written sequentially. Whenever we use a READ or WRITE statement with a sequential file, we mean read or write the *next* record in sequence. The computer remembers

Figure 12-14. A direct file of student data

Record
numbers   Records

1	JOHNSON ROBERT 78. 92. 83.
2	SMITH MARY 100. 95. 97.
3	ANDERSON RICHARD 65. 72. 57.
4	WILSON ALEX 73. 69. 78.
5	DEAN BRIAN 42. 56. 47.
6	EMERY MARY 91.100. 92.
7	COLE JAMES 75. 78. 73.
8	GUINN DOROTHY 86. 82. 74.
9	JONES ED 71. 85. 78.

what record was last read or written, so it can determine what the next record is. (When a sequential file is first opened or when it is rewound, the "next" record is the first record in the file.)

With a direct file we can read or write records directly without going through other records in the file. In FORTRAN this is accomplished by identifying each record by a *record number*. The record numbers begin with 1 for the first record and increase through the file. To read or write a record in a direct file, we specify the number of the record to be read or written. For example, we can tell the computer to read record 5 or write record 8. We can read or write any record in a direct file as long as we know the record number.

Figure 12-14 shows an example of a direct file. The records in this file contain data about students. Each record has a student's name and scores on three tests. Each record is identified by its record number. (Notice that the record numbers are similar to subscripts discussed in Chapter 9.) To store the data for Mary Smith in the file, we would tell the computer to write record number 2 in the file. Similarly, to retrieve the data for James Cole, we would tell the computer to read record number 7 from the file.

Statements for direct file processing

In this subsection we describe the FORTRAN statements used for direct file processing. These are the OPEN, CLOSE, READ, and WRITE statements. The syntax of these statements is similar to that used for sequential file processing. (The ENDFILE, REWIND, and BACKSPACE statements are only used with sequential files.)

The OPEN statement. The syntax of the OPEN statement for a direct file is as follows:

```
OPEN (UNIT=i,FILE='name',ACCESS='DIRECT',
      FORM='FORMATTED',STATUS='status',RECL=l)
```

where *i* is a device code (unit identifier).
    name is the file name.
    status is NEW or OLD.
    l is the record length.

The rules for the device code, file name, record form, and file status are the same in this OPEN statement as in the OPEN statement for a sequential file. The only differences are with the file access and in a new entry that gives the record length.

A direct file is accessed directly. This must be specified in the OPEN statement by the word DIRECT enclosed in apostrophes following the word ACCESS = .

All records in a direct file must be the same length. (This is not required for sequential files.) The length of the records must be specified in the OPEN statement. The length is given in characters and comes after the word RECL= in the statement.

To illustrate the OPEN statement for a direct file, assume that FILEA is the name of an existing direct file. It is associated with device 3. Each record in the file is 20 characters long. Then the following statement opens this file:

```
     OPEN (UNIT=3,FILE='FILEA',ACCESS='DIRECT',
   1       FORM='FORMATTED',STATUS='OLD',RECL=20)
```

In this statement the file access is DIRECT and the record length is 20.

The CLOSE statement. The CLOSE statement for a direct file is identical to that of a sequential file. For reference, the syntax is as follows:

```
CLOSE (UNIT=i)
```

where *i* is a device code (unit identifier).

For example, to close the direct file associated with device 3, we would use the following statement:

```
CLOSE (UNIT=3)
```

The READ statement. The syntax of the READ statement for a direct file is as follows:

READ (UNIT=*i*,FMT=*n*,REC=*r*) *list*

where *i* is a device code (unit identifier).
     n is the number of a FORMAT statement.
     r is an integer constant, variable name, or expression.
     list is a list of variable names separated by commas.

The device code, FORMAT statement number, and input list in this statement follow the same rules as for a sequential file READ statement. Note that the words UNIT= and FMT= are optional. The main difference between the READ statement for a direct file and that for a sequential file is the entry REC=*r*. This entry is called a *record specifier,* and it gives the number of the record to be read. Following the word REC= must be an integer constant, variable name, or expression with a value of 1 or more but not greater than the number of records in the file. When the READ statement executes, the record with the number given by the value of the record specifier is read. (If the value of the record specifier is not between 1 and the number of records in the file, an execution error usually occurs.)

    As an example of a READ statement for a direct file, assume that a file named FILEA is a direct file in which each record contains two ten-character fields. The first field contains a real number with four decimal positions and the second contains an integer number. Assume that the file has been opened and is associated with device 3. Then the following statements read the fifth record in this file (assume that Z is real and L is integer):

```
      READ (3,100,REC=5) Z,L
100 FORMAT (F10.4,I10)
```

    In this example, an integer constant (5) is used in the record specifier to identify which record is to be read. We could also use an integer variable name. For example, assume that NUMREC is an integer variable name. Then the following statements accomplish the same thing as the previous example:

```
      NUMREC=5
      READ (3,100,REC=NUMREC) Z,L
100 FORMAT (F10.4,I10)
```

An integer expression can also be used in the record specifier as in the following partial example (assume that I is integer):

```
      READ (3,100,REC=2*I+1) Z,L
```

If I has a value of 2 before this statement is executed, the fifth record in the file will be read.

An end-of-file specifier is not allowed with a READ statement for a direct file because there is no end-of-file record in a direct file. Thus there is no way of detecting the end of a direct file (unless a trailer value is used in the last record).

Records in direct files can only be read and written using formatted I/O. List-directed I/O is not permitted with direct files.

The WRITE statement. The syntax of the WRITE statement for a direct file is as follows:

WRITE (UNIT=*i*,FMT=*n*,REC=*r*) *list*

where *i* is a device code (unit identifier).
     n is the number of a FORMAT statement.
     r is an integer constant, variable name, or expression.
     list is a list of constants, variable names, and
          expressions separated by commas.

The rules for the device code, FORMAT statement number, and output list are the same as those for a sequential file WRITE statement. Note that the words UNIT= and FMT= are optional. The record specifier (REC=*r*) must give the number of the record to be written. This may be specified by an integer constant, variable name, or expression with a value of 1 or more.

To illustrate the WRITE statement for a direct file, assume that we need to write a record in the file named FILEB. Each record contains three integer fields of five characters each. Assume that the file has been opened and is associated with device 4. Then the following statements write the tenth record in this file (assume that all variable names are integer):

```
      WRITE (4,200,REC=10) M1,M2,M3
  200 FORMAT (3I5)
```

In this example an integer constant is used to identify the record. We could also use an integer variable name or expression. The following example shows the use of a variable name to identify the record to be written (assume that RECID is integer):

```
      RECID=10
      WRITE (4,200,REC=RECID) M1,M2,M3
  200 FORMAT (3I5)
```

The effect of these statements is the same as the previous example.

Creating a direct file

When creating a direct file, each record must be written in the file by specifying its record number. The records for the file may be written in sequence or they may be written in some other order. For example, we could create a direct file by first writing record number 1, then record number 2, then record number 3, and so on. Alternatively, we could first write record number 5, then record number 8, then record 2, etc. Because the file is a direct file, records can be written in any order.

To illustrate a program for creating a direct file, assume that a file of student data is needed. Each record in the file contains four fields. The first field, which is 16 characters long, is the student's name. The other three fields, which are each 4 characters long, are the scores for the student on three tests. Note that there is no number to identify the student in the records in this file. Instead we use the record number as the student's identifying number. (We could have student numbers in the file, but then we would need some way of associating each student number with a record number. Techniques for doing this are beyond the scope of this book.)

Figure 12-15 shows a program that creates the student data file. The name of the file that is created is STUDAT. It is associated with device 3 in the OPEN statement. Note in the OPEN statement that the file access is DIRECT, the records in the file are FORMATTED, and the file status is NEW because the file is being created. Each record in the file contains one 16-character field and three fields with 4 characters each. Hence there are 28 characters in each record. This is specified in the record length entry in the OPEN statement. Note that the file is opened at the beginning of the program, before the input loop.

The READ statement (numbered 100) reads the data for the new file

Figure 12-15. A program to create a student data file

```
C   PROGRAM TO CREATE A DIRECT FILE OF STUDENT DATA
        INTEGER SNUM
        REAL TS1,TS2,TS3
        CHARACTER*16 NAME
        OPEN (UNIT=3,FILE='STUDAT',ACCESS='DIRECT',
       1      FORM='FORMATTED',STATUS='NEW',RECL=28)
        SNUM=0
    100 READ (5,200,END=150) NAME,TS1,TS2,TS3
        SNUM=SNUM+1
        WRITE (3,210,REC=SNUM) NAME,TS1,TS2,TS3
        GO TO 100
    150 CLOSE (UNIT=3)
        WRITE (6,300) SNUM
        STOP
    200 FORMAT (4X,A16,3F4.0)
    210 FORMAT (A16,3F4.0)
    300 FORMAT ('1','STUDENT DATA FILE CREATED WITH ',I3,' RECORDS')
        END
```

Figure 12-16. Input data and printed output for a student data file creation program

```
JOHNSON ROBERT   78. 92. 83.
SMITH MARY      100. 95. 97.
ANDERSON RICHARD 65. 72. 57.
WILSON ALEX      73. 69. 78.
DEAN BRIAN       42. 56. 47.
EMERY MARY       91.100. 92.
COLE JAMES       75. 78. 73.
GUINN DOROTHY    86. 82. 74.
JONES ED         71. 85. 78.
```

(a) Input data

```
STUDENT DATA FILE CREATED WITH   9 RECORDS
```

(b) Printed output

from the computer's main input device. An input loop is used that terminates when all data has been read. Each set of data that is read is written as a record in the new file. Slightly different formats are used for input and output although the formats may be the same in some programs. The variable named SNUM, which represents the student number, is used in the WRITE statement to specify which record is to be written. Initially SNUM is 0. Just before each record is written, SNUM is increased by 1. Hence the records are written in sequence: first record number 1 is written, then record number 2 is written, and so on. After the input loop terminates, the file is closed. Then the current value of SNUM is printed to give a count of the number of records written in the file. Note that no end-of-file record is written; end-of-file records are only used with sequential files.

Sample input data and printed output for this program are shown in Figure 12-16. The printed output indicates that nine records were written in the file. The file output for this program is the student data file shown in Figure 12-14.

Accessing a direct file

A program that accesses a direct file may process all of the records in the file or it may process only selected records. In both cases, each record that is processed must be accessed by specifying its record number. If all records are to be accessed, all record numbers must be specified in some logical order. If selected records are to be accessed, only the numbers of those records need to be given.

Figure 12-17 shows a program that processes all records in the student data file created in the last subsection. The OPEN statement in this program is the same as in the program that created the file, except the file status is OLD because the file already exists. Note that the record length in the OPEN statement must be the same as when the file was created.

Figure 12-17. A program to process all records in a student data file

```
C   PROGRAM TO COMPUTE THE TOTAL AND AVERAGE OF THE TEST SCORES
C   IN EACH RECORD IN THE DIRECT FILE OF STUDENT DATA
        INTEGER SNUM,NUMREC
        REAL TS1,TS2,TS3,TOTAL,AVE
        CHARACTER*16 NAME
        PARAMETER (NUMREC=9)
        OPEN (UNIT=3,FILE='STUDAT',ACCESS='DIRECT',
     1       FORM='FORMATTED',STATUS='OLD',RECL=28)
        WRITE (6,300)
        WRITE (6,310)
        DO 100 SNUM=1,NUMREC
           READ (3,200,REC=SNUM) NAME,TS1,TS2,TS3
           TOTAL=TS1+TS2+TS3
           AVE=TOTAL/3.0
           WRITE (6,320) NAME,TOTAL,AVE
100     CONTINUE
        CLOSE (UNIT=3)
        STOP
200     FORMAT (A16,3F4.0)
300     FORMAT ('1',13X,'TEST SCORE ANALYSIS')
310     FORMAT ('0','STUDENT NAME',7X,'TOTAL SCORE',3X,'AVERAGE SCORE'/)
320     FORMAT (' ',A16,6X,F5.0,10X,F5.1)
        END
```

To read a record we must specify the record number in the READ statement. In this program SNUM is used for the record number. Because we wish to process all records in the file, SNUM must be incremented through all of its values. This is accomplished with a DO loop. In the DO loop, SNUM is incremented from 1 to the number of records in the file. This latter value is given by the constant named NUMREC. NUMREC is assigned a value of 9 in the PARAMETER statement because there are nine records in the file. We must know how many records are in the file to write a program such as this. (We cannot use an end-of-file check to end processing because there is no end-of-file record in a direct file.)

Within the DO loop a record is read from the direct file. Then the total and average of the test scores from the record are computed and the results, along with the student's name, are printed. Sample output from this program is shown in Figure 12-18. This output was produced using the student data file shown in Figure 12-14.

To illustrate the case where we wish to process selected records in a direct file, assume that we need an interactive program that accesses specific records in the student data file. Input to the program is the student's number which, as we know, is also the record number. The program must access the desired record, determine the total and average of the test scores in the record, and display the results along with the student's name. The program must handle the case where an invalid student number is entered.

Figure 12-19 shows a program that accomplishes this. Sample interactive input and output for this program is shown in Figure 12-20. The student data file in Figure 12-14 was used to produce the output shown.

Figure 12-18. Printed output from the program that processes all records in a student data file

```
                    TEST SCORE ANALYSIS

STUDENT NAME          TOTAL SCORE    AVERAGE SCORE

JOHNSON ROBERT           253.           84.3
SMITH MARY               292.           97.3
ANDERSON RICHARD         194.           64.7
WILSON ALEX              220.           73.3
DEAN BRIAN               145.           48.3
EMERY MARY               283.           94.3
COLE JAMES               226.           75.3
GUINN DOROTHY            242.           80.7
JONES ED                 234.           78.0
```

Figure 12-19. A program that processes selected records in a student data file

```
C  PROGRAM TO COMPUTE THE TOTAL AND AVERAGE OF THE TEST SCORES
C   IN SELECTED RECORDS IN THE DIRECT FILE OF STUDENT DATA
      INTEGER SNUM,NUMREC
      REAL TS1,TS2,TS3,TOTAL,AVE
      CHARACTER*16 NAME
      PARAMETER (NUMREC=9)
      OPEN (UNIT=3,FILE='STUDAT',ACCESS='DIRECT',
     1      FORM='FORMATTED',STATUS='OLD',RECL=28)
      WRITE (*,300)
  100 WRITE (*,310)
      READ *,SNUM
      IF (SNUM.EQ.999) GO TO 150
      IF ((SNUM.GE.1).AND.(SNUM.LE.NUMREC)) THEN
         READ (3,200,REC=SNUM) NAME,TS1,TS2,TS3
         TOTAL=TS1+TS2+TS3
         AVE=TOTAL/3.0
         WRITE (*,320) NAME
         WRITE (*,330) TOTAL
         WRITE (*,340) AVE
      ELSE
         WRITE (*,350)
      END IF
      GO TO 100
  150 WRITE (*,360)
      CLOSE (UNIT=3)
      STOP
  200 FORMAT (A16,3F4.0)
  300 FORMAT ('TEST SCORE ANALYSIS PROGRAM')
  310 FORMAT (/'ENTER STUDENT NUMBER OR 999 TO END')
  320 FORMAT (/'STUDENT NAME   ',A16)
  330 FORMAT ('TOTAL SCORE    ',F5.0)
  340 FORMAT ('AVERAGE SCORE  ',F5.1)
  350 FORMAT (/'INVALID STUDENT NUMBER')
  360 FORMAT (/'END OF PROGRAM')
      END
```

Figure 12-20. Interactive input and output for the program that processes selected records in a student data file

```
TEST SCORE ANALYSIS PROGRAM

ENTER STUDENT NUMBER OR 999 TO END
? 5

STUDENT NAME    DEAN BRIAN
TOTAL SCORE     145.
AVERAGE SCORE    48.3

ENTER STUDENT NUMBER OR 999 TO END
? 1

STUDENT NAME    JOHNSON ROBERT
TOTAL SCORE     253.
AVERAGE SCORE    84.3

ENTER STUDENT NUMBER OR 999 TO END
? 12

INVALID STUDENT NUMBER

ENTER STUDENT NUMBER OR 999 TO END
? 8

STUDENT NAME    GUINN DOROTHY
TOTAL SCORE     242.
AVERAGE SCORE    80.7

ENTER STUDENT NUMBER OR 999 TO END
? 999

END OF PROGRAM
```

In the program in Figure 12-19 a loop is repeated for each record that is processed. At the beginning of the loop, a prompt is displayed and the student number for the desired record is read. The loop is terminated if the student number is 999. In the loop, the program determines whether the student number that was entered is valid, that is, whether the number is between 1 and the number of records in the file. (Again, the number of records in the file is given by a constant named NUMREC which is assigned a value in a PARAMETER statement.) If a valid student number was entered, the record for that student is read, the total and average of the test scores are computed, and the output is displayed. If an invalid student number was entered, an error message is displayed.

This program does not process the records in the file in any preset order. Each record is accessed directly based on the student number that is entered. This is illustrated in the interactive I/O in Figure 12-20 where record 5 is accessed first, then record 1 is processed, and then record 8 is accessed. The records in a direct file can be accessed in any order.

Updating a direct file

There are several differences between updating direct files and sequential files. In sequential file updating, a new file is created with the updated data because the data in a sequential file usually cannot be changed once the file is created. In a direct file, however, data can be changed without creating a new file. This is done by reading the record to be changed, making changes in the data in the record, and then writing the new record in the same location in auxiliary storage from where it was read. When the new record is written, the old record is erased and the file is updated. Thus sequential file updating requires two master files, the old master file and the new, whereas direct file updating only requires one master file.

Another difference is that with sequential file updating the master records and the transaction data must be in order by key field. With direct file updating these requirements are not necessary. Because the records in a direct file can be read and written in any order, records in a direct file do not have to be updated in sequence. Hence the order of the records in the file and the order of the transaction data are not important.

Figure 12-21 shows an interactive program that updates test scores in the direct file of student data created earlier. The interactive input and output for this program is shown in Figure 12-22. The student data file in Figure 12-14 was used during the updating process. Figure 12-23 shows the student data file after the updating was completed.

In the program in Figure 12-21 the student data file, which is the master file, is opened with a file status of OLD because the file already exists. Updating is accomplished in a loop that is repeated for each student record to be updated. At the beginning of the loop, the student number for the record to be updated is read. If this number is 999, the loop is terminated. Otherwise, the program determines if the student number is valid. If a valid student number is read, updating proceeds; otherwise, an error message is displayed.

In the record updating process, the master record for the student whose number was entered is read from the direct file. The data from this record is displayed. Then the transaction data is read and processed. Transactions for this program involve changes in scores on tests. The number of the test with a score to be changed is read. If this number is valid, the score on that test is changed; otherwise, an error message is displayed. To change the test score, a new score is read. Then the appropriate test score in the master record that was read earlier is assigned the new score. Finally, updating is completed by writing the new master record in the direct file. Note that the record number in the direct file WRITE statement is identified by SNUM, which is also used in the direct file READ statement. Because the value of SNUM is not changed between the READ and WRITE statements, the same record number is used for both input and output. Hence the original record is destroyed when the record is written. It is replaced by the new, updated record.

Figure 12-21. A program to update a student data file (Part 1 of 2)

```
C
C     DIRECT STUDENT DATA FILE UPDATING PROGRAM
C
      INTEGER SNUM,NUMREC,TSTNUM
      REAL TS1,TS2,TS3,NEWSCR
      CHARACTER*16 NAME
      PARAMETER (NUMREC=9)
C
C     OPEN MASTER FILE
C
      OPEN (UNIT=3,FILE='STUDAT',ACCESS='DIRECT',
     1      FORM='FORMATTED',STATUS='OLD',RECL=28)
C
      WRITE (*,300)
  100 WRITE (*,310)
C
C        READ STUDENT NUMBER FOR RECORD TO UPDATE
C
         READ *,SNUM
C
         IF (SNUM.EQ.999) GO TO 150
         IF ((SNUM.GE.1).AND.(SNUM.LE.NUMREC)) THEN
C
C           READ MASTER RECORD TO UPDATE
C
            READ (3,200,REC=SNUM) NAME,TS1,TS2,TS3
C
            WRITE (*,320) NAME
            WRITE (*,330) TS1,TS2,TS3
C
C           READ AND PROCESS TRANSACTION DATA
C
            WRITE (*,340)
            READ *,TSTNUM
            IF ((TSTNUM.GE.1).AND.(TSTNUM.LE.3)) THEN
              WRITE (*,350) TSTNUM
              READ *,NEWSCR
C
C             UPDATE TEST SCORE
C
              IF (TSTNUM.EQ.1) THEN
                TS1=NEWSCR
              ELSE IF (TSTNUM.EQ.2) THEN
                TS2=NEWSCR
              ELSE IF (TSTNUM.EQ.3) THEN
                TS3=NEWSCR
              END IF
C
C             WRITE UPDATED MASTER RECORD
C
              WRITE (3,200,REC=SNUM) NAME,TS1,TS2,TS3
C
              WRITE (*,360) TSTNUM
            ELSE
C
C             WRITE ERROR MESSAGE (INVALID TEST NUMBER)
C
              WRITE (*,370)
            END IF
```

Figure 12-21. (Part 2 of 2)

```
        ELSE
C
C         WRITE ERROR MESSAGE (INVALID STUDENT NUMBER)
C
          WRITE (*,380)
        END IF
      GO TO 100
  150 WRITE (*,390)
C
C     CLOSE MASTER FILE
C
      CLOSE (UNIT=3)
C
      STOP
C
  200 FORMAT (A16,3F4.0)
  300 FORMAT ('TEST SCORE UPDATING PROGRAM')
  310 FORMAT (/'ENTER STUDENT NUMBER OR 999 TO END')
  320 FORMAT (/'STUDENT NAME    ',A16)
  330 FORMAT ('SCORE ON TEST 1 ',F4.0/
     1         'SCORE ON TEST 2 ',F4.0/
     2         'SCORE ON TEST 3 ',F4.0)
  340 FORMAT (/'ENTER TEST NUMBER')
  350 FORMAT (/'ENTER NEW SCORE FOR TEST ',I1)
  360 FORMAT (/'SCORE ON TEST ',I1,' UPDATED')
  370 FORMAT (/'INVALID TEST NUMBER')
  380 FORMAT (/'INVALID STUDENT NUMBER')
  390 FORMAT (/'END OF PROGRAM')
      END
```

Figure 12-22. Interactive input and output for the program that updates a student data file (Part 1 of 2)

```
TEST SCORE UPDATING PROGRAM

ENTER STUDENT NUMBER OR 999 TO END
? 5

STUDENT NAME    DEAN BRIAN
SCORE ON TEST 1 42.
SCORE ON TEST 2 56.
SCORE ON TEST 3 47.

ENTER TEST NUMBER
? 2

ENTER NEW SCORE FOR TEST 2
? 60

SCORE ON TEST 2 UPDATED

ENTER STUDENT NUMBER OR 999 TO END
? 1

STUDENT NAME    JOHNSON ROBERT
SCORE ON TEST 1 78.
SCORE ON TEST 2 92.
SCORE ON TEST 3 83.
```

Figure 12-22. (Part 2 of 2)

```
ENTER TEST NUMBER
? 4

INVALID TEST NUMBER

ENTER STUDENT NUMBER OR 999 TO END
? 1

STUDENT NAME     JOHNSON ROBERT
SCORE ON TEST 1  78.
SCORE ON TEST 2  92.
SCORE ON TEST 3  83.

ENTER TEST NUMBER
? 3

ENTER NEW SCORE FOR TEST 3
? 81

SCORE ON TEST 3 UPDATED

ENTER STUDENT NUMBER OR 999 TO END
? 12

INVALID STUDENT NUMBER

ENTER STUDENT NUMBER OR 999 TO END
? 8

STUDENT NAME     GUINN DOROTHY
SCORE ON TEST 1  86.
SCORE ON TEST 2  82.
SCORE ON TEST 3  74.

ENTER TEST NUMBER
? 1

ENTER NEW SCORE FOR TEST 1
? 93

SCORE ON TEST 1 UPDATED

ENTER STUDENT NUMBER OR 999 TO END
? 999

END OF PROGRAM
```

This program updates the student data in any order. For example, the interactive I/O in Figure 12-22 shows that the first record updated is for student number 5, then student number 1's record is updated, and finally the record for student number 8 is updated. In the updated file in Figure 12-23 we can see that the third test score in record 1 is 81, the second score in record 5 is 60, and the first score in record 8 is 93. These differ from the

Figure 12-23. The student data file after being updated

Record
numbers   *Records*

#	Record
1	JOHNSON ROBERT 78. 92. 81.
2	SMITH MARY 100. 95. 97.
3	ANDERSON RICHARD 65. 72. 57.
4	WILSON ALEX 73. 69. 78.
5	DEAN BRIAN 42. 60. 47.
6	EMERY MARY 91.100. 92.
7	COLE JAMES 75. 78. 73.
8	GUINN DOROTHY 93. 82. 74.
9	JONES ED 71. 85. 78.

original file shown in Figure 12-14 and reflect the changes resulting from the interactive execution of the program in Figure 12-22.

This program shows one approach for updating a direct file. Many programs use a similar approach, but other techniques are also used. Direct file updating programs can vary considerably depending on the updating requirements.

Review questions

1. What is a track on a magnetic disk? What is a read/write head?
2. When data is written on a disk or tape, existing data is _____ (destroyed/not destroyed). When data is read from a disk or tape, the data is _____ (destroyed/not destroyed).
3. Explain the difference between sequential access and direct access. What type of access can be used with magnetic disk? with magnetic tape?
4. What is the difference between a sequential file and a direct file?
5. When a file is created, the file data is _____ (input/output) data.
6. When a file is accessed, the file data is _____ (input/output) data.
7. When a file is updated, the data in the file to be updated is _____ (input/output) data and the new, updated data for the file is _____ (input/output) data.
8. Assume we must create a sequential file named AFILE. Each record in the file will have three 10-character fields with integer data. Code statements to do each of the following:

  a. Open the file.
  b. Store one record in the file.
  c. Put an end-of-file record in the file.
  d. Close the file.

9. Assume that a sequential file named BFILE already exists. Each record in the file has four fields of 5 characters each. The first two fields contain real data with one decimal position. The other two fields contain integer data. Code statements to do each of the following:
   a. Open the file.
   b. Retrieve one record from the file.
   c. Backspace one record in the file.
   d. Rewind the file.

10. Why is an end-of-file record needed in a sequential file?

11. What is the difference between data in a master file and transaction data?

12. What is a key field?

13. What is the importance of the master key and the transaction key in sequential file updating?

14. Consider the sequential file updating program in Figure 12-12 and the input data shown in Figure 12-13(a) and (b). In processing this data, how many times will each of the following statements in the program be executed?
    a. `STOCK=STOCK-WTHDRW+ADDTN`
    b. `READ (1,410,END=210) MINUM,DESC,PRICE,STOCK`
    c. The second WRITE statement of the form
       `WRITE (2,410) MINUM,DESC,PRICE,STOCK`
    d. The second READ statement of the form
       `READ (5,400) TINUM,WTHDRW,ADDTN`

15. All records in a direct file must be the same length. True or false?

16. Assume we must create a direct file named CFILE. Each record in this file contains five 3-character fields of integer data. Code statements to do each of the following:
    a. Open the file.
    b. Store the fifth record in the file.
    c. Close the file.

17. Assume that a direct file named DFILE already exists. Each record in the file has three fields. The first two fields are 10 characters long and contain integer data. The last field has 5 characters. It contains real data with two decimal positions. Code statements to do each of the following:
    a. Open the file.
    b. Retrieve the tenth record from the file.

18. Can the ENDFILE, BACKSPACE, and REWIND statements be used with a direct file?

19. What are the differences between updating a direct file and updating a sequential file?

20. Consider the direct file updating program in Figure 12-21 which updates the direct file in Figure 12-14. For the interactive input shown in Figure 12-22, how many times will each of the following statements in the program be executed?
    a. `READ (*,SNUM)`
    b. `READ (3,200,REC=SNUM) NAME,TS1,TS2,TS3`
    c. `WRITE (3,200,REC=SNUM) NAME,TS1,TS2,TS3`
    d. `WRITE (*,380)`

Programming problems

1. Write a FORTRAN program to create a sequential file of payroll data. Each record in the file contains a field for the employee's number, employee's name, hourly pay rate, number of exemptions, and year-to-date gross pay. The records are in increasing order by employee number. Store the following data in the file:

Employee number	Employee name	Hourly pay rate	Number of exemptions	Year-to-date gross pay
1234	SMITH	7.25	2	23,528.32
1345	JONES	8.12	2	38,452.00
1456	BROWN	7.75	0	37,352.25
1567	JOHNSON	6.75	3	20,295.30
1678	ANDREWS	7.20	5	34,252.85
1789	MCDONALD	8.10	0	37,025.00
2123	WHITE	6.90	1	25,302.00
2234	KNIGHT	7.25	1	37,705.41
2345	DAVIS	12.15	6	44,505.25
2456	EMERY	6.00	3	37,225.36
2567	HOLT	7.50	0	32,250.00
2678	COLE	8.00	3	19,845.00

2. Write a FORTRAN program to list the payroll file created in Problem 1. Supply appropriate headings and print one line for each record in the file.
3. Write a FORTRAN program to print the employee number and name for each employee in the payroll file created in Problem 1 who has zero exemptions.
4. Write a FORTRAN program to search for and print an employee's record from the payroll file created in Problem 1 given the employee's number. Test the program for several employees. Be sure to test the case where there is no matching employee number in the file. (*Hint:* The program will have to rewind the file after each search so that the next search begins with the first record in the file.)
5. Write a FORTRAN program to process payroll transaction data along with the payroll file created in Problem 1. Transaction data consists of the employee's number and hours worked for several employees. The data is in increasing order by employee number. The program should produce a payroll summary report. The report should list the following fields for each employee for which there is transaction data: employee number, employee name, gross pay, withholding tax, social security tax, net pay, and new year-to-date gross pay. Supply appropriate headings for the columns of output. If there is transaction data for an employee for whom there is no record in the payroll file, print the employee's number and an appropriate message. The gross pay, withholding tax, social security tax, net pay, and new year-to-date gross pay are computed as follows:
   a. Gross pay is hours times rate with "time and one-half" for all hours over 40 worked in a week.
   b. Withholding tax = 22.5% of [gross pay − (exemptions × 13.5)].
   c. Social security tax is 6.7% of gross pay. Employees are exempt from social security tax once their year-to-date gross exceeds $37,800.

d. Net pay is gross pay less withholding tax and social security tax.

e. New year-to-date gross pay is the year-to-date gross pay from the payroll file plus the current gross pay.

Use the following transaction data to test the program:

Employee number	Hours worked
1345	35
1678	40
1789	50
1890	37
2234	42
2235	40
2456	45
2460	48
2567	20

6. Write the program for Problem 5 with the additional requirement that a new payroll file is created. The new payroll file should be the same as the old payroll file, except that the year-to-date gross pay is updated to the new year-to-date gross pay where appropriate. Write another program to list the new payroll file after it is created. (This can be a modified version of the program for Problem 2.)

7. Write a FORTRAN program to create a file of test score data. Each record in the file has two fields: an identification number field and a test score field. The records in the file are not in any particular order. Store the data given in Problem 8 of Chapter 9 in the file.

8. Write a FORTRAN program to print the data in the test score file created in Problem 7.

9. Write a FORTRAN program to search for and print any test score in the test score file created in Problem 7 given an identification number. Test the program with several identification numbers. Be sure to test the case where there is no matching identification number in the file. (*Hint:* The program will have to rewind the file after each search so that the next search begins with the first record in the file.)

10. Write a FORTRAN program to process the data in the test score file created in Problem 7 as follows:

a. Accumulate and print the total of the test scores.

b. Calculate and print the mean (average) of the scores.

c. Determine and print the number of scores that fall into each of the following categories:

    90–100
    80–89
    70–79
    60–69
    0–59

11. Write a FORTRAN program to create a sorted test score file from the file created in Problem 7. The data in the sorted file should be in ascending order by identification number. (*Hint:* Retrieve all of the records in the file, storing the data in two arrays in the program. Then sort the identification number array.

Finally, store the sorted data in a new file.) Write another program to print the sorted test score file. (This can be a modified version of the program for Problem 8.)

12. Write a FORTRAN program to update the sorted test score file created in Problem 11. Updating involves changing the test score in any matching record in the file to the new score given in the transaction data. Use the following transaction data to test the program:

Identification number	New test score
133	92
185	70
192	83
206	85
230	68
255	75
273	81
294	100

Write another program to print the updated file. (This can be a modified version of the program written for Problem 8.)

13. Write a FORTRAN program to create a direct name-and-address file. Each record in the file has five fields: name, street address, city, state, and zip code. Supply a list of 10 to 20 names and addresses to store in the file.

14. Write a FORTRAN program to print "mailing labels" from the records in the name-and-address file created in Problem 13. Each mailing label consists of three lines with the name on the first line; the street address on the second line; and the city, state, and zip code on the third line.

15. Write a FORTRAN program to print any name and address from the file created in Problem 13 given the record number. Test the program with several record numbers. Be certain to test the case where there is no record in the file.

16. Write a FORTRAN program to update the name and address file created in Problem 13. Updating involves changing the street address, city, state, or zip code but not the name. Test the program by making several changes in the file. Write another program to print the updated file. (This can be a modified version of the program written for Problem 14.)

Appendix A

Summary of FORTRAN 77

This appendix summarizes the syntax of the FORTRAN 77 language described in this book. Major differences for other versions of FORTRAN are outlined in Appendix B. FORTRAN-supplied functions for FORTRAN 77 and other versions of FORTRAN are listed in Appendix C.

The information in this appendix is given in three tables:

Table 1: Basic Elements of FORTRAN
Table 2: FORTRAN Statements
Table 3: Format Codes

Each entry in the tables describes the syntax of a language element, shows an example, and gives the section or sections in the text in which the element is discussed. Some elements are listed more than once in a table. Each listing describes a different form of the element.

The version of FORTRAN used with a particular computer may not include all the elements listed in this appendix, may have additional items not listed, or may use a syntax different from that given here. Consult the appropriate reference manual for detailed information about the version of FORTRAN being used.

Table 1. Basic elements of FORTRAN

Element	Syntax	Example	Section reference
arithmetic expression	an integer or real constant, constant name, or function reference, or any group of these combined with arithmetic operators and possibly parentheses	36.3 $-$K X+(Y$-$2.5)*Z 5.5+SQRT(A+3.2)	3-2, 3-6
arithmetic operator	+, $-$, *, /, **	+	3-2
array element name (one-dimensional)	an array name followed by an integer constant, variable name, or arithmetic expression in parentheses	X(5)	9-1
array element name (multidimensional)	an array name followed by two to seven integer constants, variable names, or arithmetic expressions in parentheses	Y(5,10)	10-1, 10-6
array name	(*same as* variable name)	X	9-1
character constant	a group of characters enclosed in apostrophes	'THE TOTAL IS'	2-3
character constant name	(*same as* variable name)	NAME	8-3
character expression	a character constant, constant name, variable name, or substring name or any group of these combined with the concatenation operator	MONTH//' FIRST'	8-3
character variable name	(*same as* variable name)	MONTH	8-1
concatenation operator	//	//	8-3
constant	(*see* character constant, integer constant, logical constant, real constant)		3-3
constant name	(*same as* variable name; *see also* character constant name, logical constant name)	PRICE	3-5
integer constant	a number without a decimal point	25	3-1

Element	Syntax	Example	Section reference
logical constant	.TRUE., .FALSE.	.TRUE.	8-5
logical constant name	(same as variable name)	YES	8-5
logical expression	a relational expression, logical constant, logical constant name, or logical variable name combined with logical operators and possibly parentheses	(X.EQ.Y).OR.(Z.GT.0.0) RESP.AND.YES	8-4, 8-5
logical operator	.AND., .OR., .NOT.	.OR.	8-4
logical variable name	(same as variable name)	RESP	8-5
real constant	a number with a decimal point	83.75	3-1
relational expression	an arithmetic expression followed by a relational operator followed by an arithmetic expression	A+B.GE.3.5	4-1
relational expression	a character expression followed by a relational operator followed by a character expression	MONTH.EQ.'JANUARY'	8-2
relational operator	.LT., .LE., .GT., .GE., .EQ., .NE.	.GE.	4-1
statement number	a number between 1 and 99999	100	1-3
substring name	a character variable name followed by the beginning and ending position of the substring, separated by a colon and enclosed in parentheses	MONTH(1:5)	8-3
variable name	one to six alphabetic and numeric characters beginning with an alphabetic character (see also character variable name, logical variable name)	AMT X27YZ3	2-2

467

Table 2. FORTRAN statements

Statement	Syntax	Example	Section reference
arithmetic assignment	*variable name* = *arithmetic expression*	A=B+C	3-3
assignment	(*see arithmetic assignment, character assignment, logical assignment*)		
BACKSPACE	BACKSPACE (UNIT=*i*)	BACKSPACE (UNIT=3)	12-2

block IF/ELSE/END IF	IF (*logical expression*) THEN
	  statements
	ELSE
	  statements
	END IF
		IF (A.GT.B) THEN
		  C=A−B
		ELSE
		  C=B−A
		ENDIF
			4-1

block IF/END IF	IF (*logical expression*) THEN
	  statements
	END IF
		IF (A.GT.B) THEN
		  C=A−B
		END IF
			4-1

block IF/ELSE IF/ ELSE/END IF	IF (*logical expression*) THEN
	  statements
	ELSE IF (*logical expression*) THEN
	  statements
	.
	.
	.
	ELSE
	  statements
	END IF
		IF (A.GT.B) THEN
		  E=A−B
		ELSE IF (A.GT.C) THEN
		  E=A−C
		ELSE IF (A.GT.D) THEN
		  E=A−D
		ELSE
		  E=0
		END IF
			4-3

block IF/ELSE IF/ END IF	IF (*logical expression*) THEN
	  statements
	ELSE IF (*logical expression*) THEN
	  statements
	.
	.
	END IF
		IF (I.LT.J) THEN
		  M=1
		ELSE IF (I.LT.K) THEN
		  M=2
		ELSE IF (I.LT.L) THEN
		  M=3
		END IF
			4-3

CALL	CALL *name*(*a1,a2,...,an*)	CALL SUBA(M,N,Y)	11-3
CHARACTER	CHARACTER *list* CHARACTER*l *list*	CHARACTER P,MONTH*10,R CHARACTER*5 S,T,U*3,V*15	8-1, 9-6, 10-1

Statement	Syntax	Example	Section reference
character assignment	*character variable name = character expression*	MONTH='FEBRUARY'	8-3
CLOSE (sequential and direct)	CLOSE (UNIT=*i*)	CLOSE (UNIT=3)	12-2, 12-5
COMMON	COMMON *list* COMMON */name/list/name/list/...*	COMMON A,B,C COMMON /BLOCKA/A,B,C/BLOCKB/I,J	11-4
CONTINUE	CONTINUE	100 CONTINUE	5-3
DATA	DATA *list/data/,list/data/,...*	DATA X,Y,Z/2*5.0,6.0/,I/10/	9-5, 10-5, 10-6
DIMENSION	DIMENSION *array declarators*	DIMENSION D(100),J(10:30),E(5,20)	9-1, 10-1, 10-6
DO	DO *n i=m1,m2,m3*	DO 100 K=1,15,2	5-3
ELSE	(*see block IF*)		
ELSE IF	(*see block IF*)		
END	END	END	2-4
END IF	(*see block IF*)		
ENDFILE	ENDFILE (UNIT = *i*)	ENDFILE (UNIT=3)	12-2
FORMAT	*n* FORMAT (*format codes*)	100 FORMAT (I5,2F8.2) 200 FORMAT ('1',F10.4,2X,F6.3,2X,2I8)	6-1
FUNCTION	*type* FUNCTION *name(a1,a2,...,an)*	INTEGER FUNCTION FUNB(A,B,K)	11-2
GO TO	GO TO *n*	GO TO 100	2-5
IF	(*see block IF, logical IF*)		
INTEGER	INTEGER *list*	INTEGER K,L,S	2-2, 9-1, 10-1, 10-6
LOGICAL	LOGICAL *list*	LOGICAL RESP,YES	8-5, 9-7, 10-1
logical assignment	*logical variable name = logical expression*	YES=.TRUE.	8-5
logical IF statement	IF (*logical expression*) *executable statement*	IF (X.EQ.5) X=X+1	4-4
OPEN (direct)	OPEN (UNIT=*i*,FILE='*name*', ACCESS='DIRECT', FORM='FORMATTED', STATUS='*status*',RECL=*l*)	OPEN(UNIT=2,FILE='DIRFL', 1 ACCESS='DIRECT', 2 FORM='FORMATTED', 3 STATUS='NEW',RECL=72)	12-5

Statement	Syntax	Example	Section reference
OPEN (sequential)	OPEN (UNIT=i,FILE='name', ACCESS='SEQUENTIAL', FORM='FORMATTED', STATUS='status')	OPEN (UNIT=3,FILE='SEQFL', 1 ACCESS='SEQUENTIAL', FORM='FORMATTED', STATUS='OLD')	12-2
PARAMETER	PARAMETER (constant name=constant, constant name=constant,...)	PARAMETER (PRICE=3.95,RATE=.06)	3-5, 8-3, 8-5
PRINT (list-directed)	PRINT *,list	PRINT *,N,U,K,L	2-3
READ (direct)	READ (UNIT=i,FMT=n,REC=r) list	READ (3,100,REC=10) S,M,V	12-5
READ (formatted, sequential)	READ (UNIT=i,FMT=n1,END=n2) list	READ (5,100) S,M,V READ (5,100,END=50) S,M,V READ (UNIT=3,FMT=100,END=50) S,M,V	6-1, 12-2
READ (list-directed)	READ *,list	READ *,S,M,V	2-3
READ (list-directed)	READ (*,*,END=n) list	READ (*,*,END=50) S,M,V	2-5
REAL	REAL list	REAL M,N,X,V	2-2, 9-1, 10-1, 10-6
RETURN	RETURN	RETURN	11-2
REWIND	REWIND (UNIT=i)	REWIND (UNIT=3)	12-2
statement function	name(a1,a2,...,an)=expression	TOTAL(A,B,C,D)=A+B+C+D	11-5
STOP	STOP	STOP	2-4
SUBROUTINE	SUBROUTINE name(a1,a2,...,an)	SUBROUTINE SUBA(J,L,X)	11-3
WRITE (direct)	WRITE (UNIT=i,FMT=n,REC=r) list	WRITE (2,200,REC=15) N,X,K,L	12-5
WRITE (formatted, sequential)	WRITE (UNIT=i,FMT=n) list	WRITE (6,200) N,X,K,L WRITE (UNIT=2,FMT=200) N,X,K,L	6-1,12-2

Table 3. Format codes

Code	Type of data	Syntax	Example	Section reference
apostrophe	character	group of characters enclosed in apostrophes	'THE TOTAL IS'	6-4
A-format	character	A or Aw	A5	8-1
D-format	double precision	D$w.d$	D14.6	Appendix F
E-format	real (exponential form)	E$w.d$	E10.4	Appendix F
F-format	real	F$w.d$	F10.2	6-2, 6-3
I-format	integer	Iw	I5	6-2, 6-3
L-format	logical	Lw	L3	8-5
X-format	blanks	wX	3X	6-2, 6-3

Appendix B

FORTRAN version differences

Researchers at the IBM Corporation developed the first version of FORTRAN in the mid 1950s. FORTRAN became available for use with the IBM 704 computer early in 1957. Since that time FORTRAN has undergone several modifications and improvements. In 1958 a version called FORTRAN II became available. In 1962, FORTRAN IV was developed. (For a more complete discussion of the early history of FORTRAN see Jean Sammet's book, *Programming Languages: History and Fundamentals,* published by Prentice-Hall, Inc., in 1969.)

Although these early versions of FORTRAN had many common characteristics, they were sufficiently different in that a program written in one version could not ordinarily be processed as if it were written in another version. For example, a program written in FORTRAN IV could not normally be run as a FORTRAN II program. A further problem was that each computer manufacturer usually made modifications in the language for use with the computers manufactured by that company. For example, the version of FORTRAN IV used on computer A might have some characteristics different from the version of FORTRAN IV used on computer B. Thus, although a program was written in what was supposed to be a common language, it usually could not be used on different computers without some modification.

In an attempt to overcome this problem of incompatibility between different versions of FORTRAN, the American National Standards Institute (ANSI) developed American National Standard (ANS) FORTRAN in 1966. This standard version of FORTRAN brought together the most commonly used characteristics of the versions of FORTRAN IV found on different computers. The objective was to have each computer manufacturer implement precisely the ANSI version of FORTRAN so that programs written in this version could be used on any computer without modification.

ANSI also developed a subset of ANS FORTRAN called ANS Basic FORTRAN. This version was similar to FORTRAN II, and it was designed to be used with computers that were too small to implement the full ANS FORTRAN. All of ANS Basic FORTRAN, however, was contained in the full ANS FORTRAN, so that a program written in the basic version could be processed as a full FORTRAN program (but not necessarily conversely).

Subsequent to the development of these ANSI versions of FORTRAN in 1966, most computer manufacturers implemented one or both of these. Even though these were standardized languages, computer manufacturers still made small modifications in their form of FORTRAN. Hence not all implementations of ANS FORTRAN or ANS Basic FORTRAN were entirely compatible.

In 1978 ANSI published a revised version of standard FORTRAN known as FORTRAN 77 (because the development of the language was completed in 1977). This version of FORTRAN contains many features that are not available in the 1966 language. A program written in the older language can usually be processed as a FORTRAN 77 program because there are very few differences in the common features of the languages. A program written in FORTRAN 77 that uses any of the new features cannot be processed as a 1966 FORTRAN program.

Along with FORTRAN 77, ANSI published a less complete version of the language called Subset FORTRAN 77. As with the earlier versions of the language, the subset is compatible with the full version but not conversely. Subset FORTRAN 77 was designed for use on smaller computers.

Most computer manufacturers have implemented a version of FORTRAN 77, either the full version, the subset, or a version in between. Some manufacturers still provide a version based on the 1966 FORTRAN and many existing FORTRAN programs are written in this version. The programmer should be aware of which version of the language he or she is using and should determine the particular characteristics of that version.

One other version of FORTRAN that is sometimes used was developed at the University of Waterloo in Canada. It is called WATFIV for WATerloo Fortran IV. WATFIV is actually a modification of a previous version called WATFOR (for WATerloo FORtran). Although WATFIV is similar to the 1966 ANS FORTRAN, it includes special features that are useful for beginning students of programming. The most recent version of WATFIV is commonly called WATFIV-S. It includes all of the features of WATFIV plus a number of control structures and other elements not usually found in FORTRAN. (Some of the features of WATFIV-S are included in FORTRAN 77.)

In this book we describe the most commonly used features of full FORTRAN 77. Many of these features are compatible with Subset FORTRAN 77, with the 1966 versions of FORTRAN, and with WATFIV-S. However, not all features of FORTRAN described in the text are found in all of these versions of FORTRAN.

This appendix contains a table that summarizes the differences between the versions of FORTRAN described here. Specifically, the table lists differences between the following versions of FORTRAN:

ANS FORTRAN 77
ANS Subset FORTRAN 77
ANS FORTRAN, 1966 Version
ANS Basic FORTRAN, 1966 Version
WATFIV-S

Differences are listed by the chapter in which reference to the FORTRAN characteristic is first made. In the table, YES means the feature or characteristic is included or required in the version of FORTRAN, NO means the element is not included or required, and N.A. means "not applicable."

Even though a version of FORTRAN listed in this appendix includes or requires a particular feature, the syntax and semantics of that feature may be different from that described in the text. In addition, the version of FORTRAN used with a particular computer may be different than that described here. Consult the appropriate reference manual for information about the version of FORTRAN being used.

The following publications give further details about the versions of FORTRAN listed in this appendix:

> *American National Standard Programming Language FORTRAN,* X3.9-1978. New York: American National Standards Institute, Inc., 1978. This publication describes both FORTRAN 77 and Subset FORTRAN 77.
> *American National Standard FORTRAN,* X3.9-1966. New York: American National Standards Institute, Inc., 1966.
> *American National Standard Basic FORTRAN,* X3.10-1966. New York: American National Standards Institute, Inc., 1966.
> *WATFIV Implementation and User's Guide.* Waterloo, Ontario: University of Waterloo, 1969.

FORTRAN version differences

	Full FORTRAN 77	Subset FORTRAN 77	Full FORTRAN (66)	Basic FORTRAN (66)	WATFIV-S
Chapter 1: Introduction to FORTRAN Programming					
Character set contains:					
Currency symbol ($)	YES	NO	YES	NO	YES
Apostrophe (')	YES	YES	NO	NO	YES
Colon (:)	YES	NO	NO	NO	NO
Maximum continuation lines	19	9	19	5	Varies
Maximum statement number	99999	99999	99999	9999	99999
Asterisk for a comment line	YES	YES	NO	NO	NO
Chapter 2: Basic Input and Output Programming					
Maximum number of characters in a variable name	6	6	6	5	6
INTEGER and REAL statements	YES	YES	YES	NO	YES
List-directed I/O	YES	NO	NO	NO	YES[1]
Chapter 3: Arithmetic Programming					
Mixed mode arithmetic expressions	YES	YES	NO	NO	YES
PARAMETER statement	YES	NO	NO	NO	NO
Chapter 4: Programming for Decisions					
Block IF/ELSE/ELSE IF/END IF statements	YES	YES	NO	NO	YES
Relational expressions	YES	YES	YES	NO	YES
Mixed mode in relational expressions	YES	YES	NO	N.A.	YES
Logical IF statement	YES	YES	YES	NO[2]	YES
Chapter 5: Programming for Repetition					
DO loop:					
Pre-test/post-test	Pre	Pre	Post	Post	Post
Nonpositive parameters	YES	YES	NO	NO	NO
Noninteger DO-variable and parameters	YES	NO	NO	NO	NO
Expressions for parameters	YES	NO	NO	NO	NO
WHILE loop	NO	NO	NO	NO	YES

FORTRAN version differences

	Full FORTRAN 77	Subset FORTRAN 77	Full FORTRAN (66)	Basic FORTRAN (66)	WATFIV-S
Chapter 6: Formatted Input and Output Programming					
UNIT=, FMT=	YES	NO	NO	NO	NO
End-of-file specifier	YES	YES	NO	NO	YES
* in place of device code	YES	YES	NO	NO	NO
* in place of FORMAT statement number	YES	NO	NO	NO	YES
Constants and expressions in WRITE statement	YES	NO	NO	NO	YES
Excess fractional digits rounded on output	YES	YES	YES	NO	YES
Character constant in FORMAT statement	YES	YES	NO[3]	NO[3]	YES
Carriage control	YES	YES	YES	NO	YES
Nested group repetition	YES	YES	YES	NO	YES
Chapter 8: Character and Logical Data					
Character data type (CHARACTER statement, character variables and constants)	YES	YES	NO	NO	YES
Character data I/O:					
List-directed	YES	NO	N.A.	N.A.	YES
Formatted (A-format code)	YES	YES	YES[4]	N.A.	YES
Character data comparison	YES	YES	N.A.	N.A.	YES
Character assignment statement	YES	YES	N.A.	N.A.	YES
Substrings	YES	NO	N.A.	N.A.	NO
Concatenation	YES	NO	N.A.	N.A.	NO
Logical expressions	YES	YES	YES	NO	YES
Logical data type (LOGICAL statement, logical variables and constants)	YES	YES	YES	NO	YES
Logical assignment statement	YES	YES	YES	N.A.	YES
Logical data I/O:					
List-directed	YES	NO	NO	N.A.	YES
Formatted (L-format code)	YES	YES	YES	N.A.	YES
Chapter 9: Arrays					
Generalized subscript expressions	YES	YES	NO[5]	NO[5]	YES
Lower dimension bound declared	YES	NO	NO	NO	NO
DATA statement	YES	YES	YES	NO	YES

FORTRAN version differences

	Full FORTRAN 77	Subset FORTRAN 77	Full FORTRAN (66)	Basic FORTRAN (66)	WATFIV-S
Placement of DATA statement before executable statements required	NO	YES	NO	N.A.	NO
Non-subscripted array name in DATA statement	YES	YES	NO	N.A.	YES
Implied-DO list in DATA statement	YES	NO	NO	N.A.	YES
Chapter 10: Multidimensional Arrays					
Maximum number of dimensions	7	3	3	2	7
Chapter 11: Subprograms					
Explicit typing of function names	YES	YES	YES	NO	YES
Character type functions	YES	NO	N.A.	N.A.	NO
Adjustable dimensions	YES	YES	YES	NO	YES
Named common	YES	YES	YES	NO	YES
Array size specified in COMMON statement	YES	YES	YES	NO	YES
Chapter 12: Files					
Sequential files	YES	YES	YES	YES	YES
Direct files	YES	YES	NO	NO	YES
OPEN statement (sequential)	YES	NO	NO	NO	NO
OPEN statement (direct)	YES	YES	N.A.	N.A.	NO
CLOSE statement	YES	NO	NO	NO	NO

[1] In WATFIV-S, the asterisk is not used in list-directed I/O. For example, the following statements could be used for input and output:

```
READ, A,B,C
PRINT, A,B,C
```

Note that the comma is still required.

[2] In Basic FORTRAN (66), decision making is accomplished with the arithmetic IF statement. The statement is available in other versions of FORTRAN, but the use of the block IF or logical IF statements is generally preferred.

[3] In Full and Basic FORTRAN (66), character output is accomplished using H-format code. This code is also available in other versions of FORTRAN, but use of character constants is generally preferred.

[4] In Full FORTRAN (66), A-format code is available, but numeric variables must be used to identify the data.

[5] In Full and Basic FORTRAN (66), subscripts are limited to the following forms:

k
v
$v+k$
$v-k$
$c*v$
$c*v+k$
$c*v-k$

where v is an integer variable name.

c and k are unsigned integer constants.

Appendix C

FORTRAN-supplied functions

This appendix contains a table listing the functions that are supplied in the FORTRAN language. The table indicates which of the following versions of FORTRAN includes each function:

ANS FORTRAN 77
ANS Subset FORTRAN 77
ANS FORTRAN, 1966 Version
ANS Basic FORTRAN, 1966 Version
WATFIV-S

(See the introductory remarks in Appendix B for a discussion of these versions of FORTRAN.) The functions in the version of FORTRAN available with a particular computer may be different from those listed here. Consult the appropriate reference manual for information about the version of FORTRAN being used.

FORTRAN-supplied functions

General function	Definition	Name	Number of arguments	Type of arguments	Type of value returned	Full FORTRAN 77	Subset FORTRAN 77	Full FORTRAN (66)	Basic FORTRAN (66)	WATFIV-S
Square root	Square root of argument	SQRT[1]	1	Real	Real	×	×	×	×	×
		DSQRT	1	Double	Double	×		×		×
		CSQRT	1	Complex	Complex	×		×		×
Integer conversion	Convert argument to integer	INT[1]	1	Real	Integer	×	×	×		×
		IFIX	1	Real	Integer	×	×	×	×	×
		IDINT	1	Double	Integer	×		×		×
		INT[2]	1	Complex	Integer	×				
Real conversion	Convert argument to real	REAL[1]	1	Integer	Real	×	×	×		×
		FLOAT	1	Integer	Real	×	×	×		×
		SNGL	1	Double	Real	×		×		×
		REAL[2]	1	Complex	Real	×				×
Double precision conversion	Convert argument to double precision	DBLE[1]	1	Real	Double	×		×		×
		DBLE	1	Integer	Double	×				
		DBLE[2]	1	Complex	Double	×				
Complex conversion	Convert argument to complex	CMPLX[1]	1 or 2[3]	Real	Complex	×		×		×
		CMPLX	1 or 2[3]	Integer	Complex	×				
		CMPLX	1 or 2[3]	Double	Complex	×				
Absolute value	Absolute value of argument	IABS	1	Integer	Integer	×	×	×	×	×
		ABS[1]	1	Real	Real	×	×	×	×	×
		DABS	1	Double	Double	×		×		×
		CABS[4]	1	Complex	Real	×		×		×
Maximum	Maximum value of arguments	MAX0[5]	≥2	Integer	Integer	×		×		×
		AMAX1	≥2	Real	Real	×	×	×		×
		DMAX1	≥2	Double	Double	×	×	×		×
		AMAX0	≥2	Integer	Real	×		×		×
		MAX1	≥2	Real	Integer	×	×	×		×
Minimum	Minimum value of arguments	MIN0[6]	≥2	Integer	Integer	×		×		×
		AMIN1	≥2	Real	Real	×	×	×		×
		DMIN1	≥2	Double	Double	×	×	×		×
		AMIN0	≥2	Integer	Real	×		×		×
		MIN1	≥2	Real	Integer	×	×	×		×
Truncation	Truncate fractional part of argument	AINT[1]	1	Real	Real	×	×	×		×
		DINT	1	Double	Double	×		×		×
Transfer of sign	Sign of argument 2 times absolute value of argument 1	ISIGN	2	Integer	Integer	×		×		×
		SIGN[1]	2	Real	Real	×	×	×	×	×
		DSIGN	2	Double	Double	×		×		×

479

General function	Definition	Name	Number of arguments	Type of arguments	Type of value returned	Full FORTRAN 77	Subset FORTRAN 77	Full FORTRAN (66)	Basic FORTRAN (66)	WATFIV-S
Remaindering	Remainder of argument 1 divided by argument 2	MOD[1] AMOD DMOD	2 2 2	Integer Real Double	Integer Real Double	× × ×	× ×	× × ×		× × ×
Positive difference	Argument 1 minus minimum of arguments 1 and 2	IDIM DIM[1] DDIM	2 2 2	Integer Real Double	Integer Real Double	× × ×	× ×	× ×		× ×
Nearest whole number	Round to nearest whole number	ANINT[1] DNINT	1 1	Real Double	Real Double	× ×	×			
Nearest integer	Round to nearest integer	NINT[2] IDNINT	1 1	Real Double	Integer Integer	× ×	×			
Double precision product	Product of arguments	DPROD	2	Real	Double	×				
Imaginary part of complex argument	Obtain imaginary part of complex argument	AIMAG	1	Complex	Real	×		×		×
Conjugate of a complex argument	Obtain conjugate of a complex argument	CONJG	1	Complex	Complex	×		×		×
Length	Length of a character string	LEN	1	Character	Integer	×				
Convert to character	Character equivalent of integer	CHAR	1	Integer	Character	×				
Convert to integer	Integer equivalent of character	ICHAR	1	Character	Integer	×	×			
Index of substring	Location of substring argument 1 in string argument 2	INDEX	2	Character	Integer	×				
Lexically greater than or equal	Argument 1 ≥ argument 2[7]	LGE	2	Character	Logical	×	×			
Lexically greater than	Argument 1 > argument 2[7]	LGT	2	Character	Logical	×	×			

480

General function	Definition	Name	Number of arguments	Type of arguments	Type of value returned	Full FORTRAN 77	Subset FORTRAN 77	Full FORTRAN (66)	Basic FORTRAN (66)	WATFIV-S
Lexically less than or equal	Argument 1 $\leq$ argument 2[7]	LLE	2	Character	Logical	X	X			
Lexically less than	Argument 1 $<$ argument 2[7]	LLT	2	Character	Logical	X	X			
Sine	sin(argument)	SIN[1]	1	Real	Real	X	X	X	X	X
		DSIN	1	Double	Double	X		X		X
		CSIN	1	Complex	Complex	X		X		X
Cosine	cos(argument)	COS[1]	1	Real	Real	X	X	X	X	X
		DCOS	1	Double	Double	X		X		X
		CCOS	1	Complex	Complex	X		X		X
Tangent	tan(argument)	TAN[1]	1	Real	Real	X	X			X
		DTAN	1	Double	Double	X				X
Arcsine	arcsin(argument)	ASIN[1]	1	Real	Real	X	X			X[9]
		DASIN	1	Double	Double	X				X[10]
Arccosine	arccos(argument)	ACOS[1]	1	Real	Real	X	X			X[11]
		DACOS	1	Double	Double	X				X[12]
Arctangent	arctan(argument)	ATAN[1]	1	Real	Real	X	X	X	X	X
		DATAN	1	Double	Double	X		X		X
	arctan(argument 1/ argument 2)	ATAN2[1]	2	Real	Real	X	X	X		X
		DATAN2	2	Double	Double	X		X		X
Hyperbolic sine	sinh(argument)	SINH[1]	1	Real	Real	X	X			X
		DSINH	1	Double	Double	X				X
Hyperbolic cosine	cosh(argument)	COSH[1]	1	Real	Real	X	X			X
		DCOSH	1	Double	Double	X				X
Hyperbolic tangent	tanh(argument)	TANH[1]	1	Real	Real	X	X	X	X	X
		DTANH	1	Double	Double	X		X		X
Exponential	$e^{argument}$	EXP[1]	1	Real	Real	X	X	X	X	X
		DEXP	1	Double	Double	X		X		X
		CEXP	1	Complex	Complex	X		X		X
Natural logarithm	$\log_e$(argument)	ALOG[8]	1	Real	Real	X	X	X	X	X
		DLOG	1	Double	Double	X		X		X
		CLOG	1	Complex	Complex	X		X		X
Common logarithm	$\log_{10}$(argument)	ALOG10[1]	1	Real	Real	X	X	X	X	X
		DLOG10	1	Double	Double	X		X		X

[1] In Full FORTRAN 77, these are *generic names*. A generic name may be used with any type of argument that is consistent with the function. For example, SQRT is a generic function name and may be used for the square root of a real, double precision, or complex argument. Generic names are only available in Full FORTRAN 77.

[2] INT, REAL, or DBLE when used with a complex argument returns the real part of a complex number.

[3] If CMPLX has two arguments, the result is argument 1 plus argument 2 times $\sqrt{-1}$. With Full FORTRAN 77, one argument may be used. In this case, the result is argument 1 plus zero times $\sqrt{-1}$.

[4] CABS returns $\sqrt{(\text{real part})^2 + (\text{imaginary part})^2}$.

[5] The generic function name is MAX. It may be used to find the maximum of integer, real, or double precision arguments, returning the same type value as the arguments.

[6] The generic function name is MIN. It may be used to find the minimum of integer, real, or double precision arguments, returning the same type value as the arguments.

[7] The lexical order is determined from the ASCII code.

[8] The generic function name is LOG.

[9] The function name in WATFIV-S is ARSIN.

[10] The function name in WATFIV-S is DARSIN.

[11] The function name in WATFIV-S is ARCOS.

[12] The function name in WATFIV-S is DARCOS.

Appendix D

Flowcharts

A tool that is often used to help design a computer program and to document a program is a *program flowchart* or, simply, a *flowchart*. A flowchart is a diagram of the logic in a computer program. For example, Figure D-1 shows a flowchart of the test score averaging program in Chapter 1 (Figure 1-12). This program reads a student's identification number and three test scores, calculates the total and average of the scores, and prints the student's number and the results of the calculations. The flowchart in Figure D-1 depicts the sequence of steps that the program goes through. The flowchart is drawn using special symbols for the steps in the program. Within each symbol is written a phrase that describes the activity at that step. The lines connecting the symbols show the sequence in which the activities take place.

While designing a program the programmer may prepare rough flowcharts of how he or she thinks the program should work. Sometimes several flowcharts are drawn so that different designs can be compared. After working out the program logic with the rough diagrams, the programmer draws a final flowchart from which he or she can code the program directly.

During program testing, errors may be detected in the logic. Then changes need to be made, not only in the program, but also in the flowchart. The final flowchart should depict precisely the logic in the completed program. This flowchart serves as documentation to help other programmers understand the program's logic.

Essential elements of flowcharts

In a flowchart, the shape of the symbol indicates the type of activity that is to take place. Figure D-2 shows the standard program flowchart symbols adopted by the American National Standards Institute (ANSI). The *process symbol* is used to represent any general processing activity such as an arithmetic

Figure D-1. Flowchart for the test score averaging program in Chapter 1 (Figure 1-12)

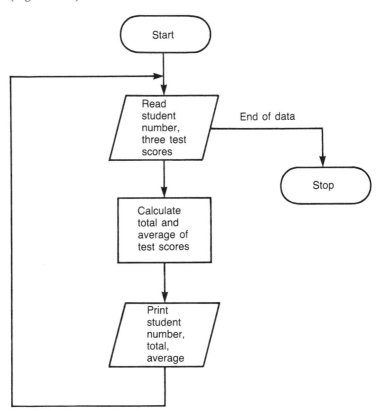

calculation or data manipulation. The *input/output symbol* is used for any step that involves input or output. The *decision symbol* is used whenever a decision is made in the program. The *terminal point symbol* appears at the beginning and end of the flowchart. The *connector symbol* connects parts of a flowchart. Finally, *flowlines* show the direction of the flow of logic in the flowchart.

Figure D-3 shows a flowchart that uses some of these symbols. This is the flowchart of a program in Chapter 2 that lists two students' identification numbers and test scores along with a heading and a final output line (Figure 2-13). The terminal point symbol marks where the flowchart logic starts and where it stops. The input/output symbol shows where each set of input data is read and where each output line is printed. Within each symbol is written a brief phrase (*not* a FORTRAN statement) that describes the processing at that step in the program. Note that no symbols correspond to the nonexecutable type statements in the program (the INTEGER and REAL statements). Usually a flowchart only includes symbols for the executable statements in the program.

Figure D-2. ANSI flowchart symbols

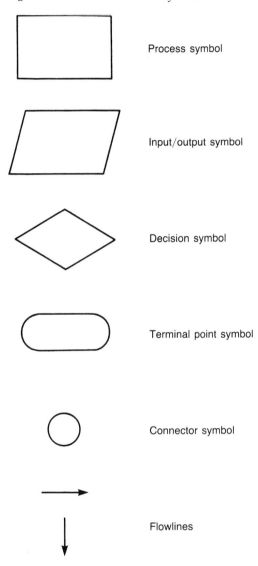

Process symbol

Input/output symbol

Decision symbol

Terminal point symbol

Connector symbol

Flowlines

Flowlines connect the symbols to show the sequence in which the steps in the program take place. If we begin with the symbol marked START and follow the flowlines through the flowchart to the STOP symbol, we can understand the logic of the program.

Another example of a flowchart is shown in Figure D-4. This is the flowchart of the program that lists any number of students' identification numbers and test scores along with a heading and final output line (Figure 2-16). This figure shows how a loop is represented in a flowchart. A loop is

Figure D-3. Flowchart for an illustrative program in Chapter 2 (Figure 2-13)

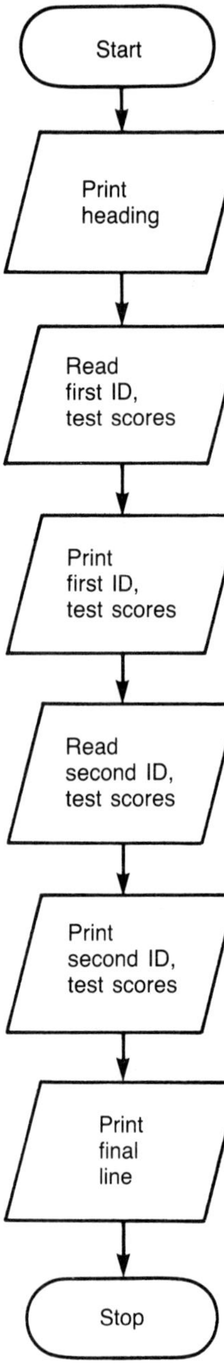

Figure D-4. Flowchart for an illustrative program in Chapter 2 (Figure 2-16)

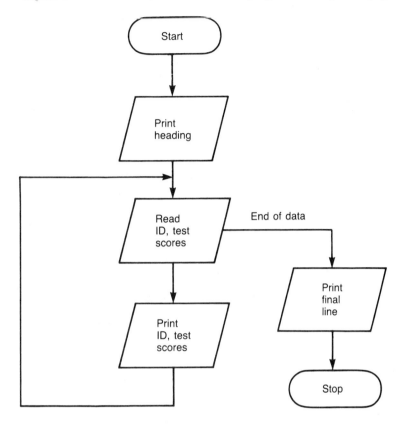

indicated by a flowline that extends from the end of the loop to its beginning. Note that there is no separate symbol for a GO TO statement; a flowline indicates branching from one point to another. In the program the loop is terminated when the end of the input data is reached. Because the READ statement in the program detects this condition, the flowchart shows the condition by a flowline leaving the symbol for the input operation. This flowline is labeled to clearly indicate that it should only be followed when the end of the input data is reached. Note that the step for printing the heading appears *before* the loop begins and that the step for printing the final output line comes *after* the loop terminates.

Flowcharts with arithmetic calculations

The process symbol is used in a flowchart for any step that involves an arithmetic calculation. A general description or a detailed specification of the calculation may be written in the symbol. The flowchart in Figure D-1 for the test score averaging program illustrates the first case. The process symbol in this flowchart includes a general statement that the total and average are to be calculated at a particular point in the program logic. It is assumed that the reader of the flowchart knows how to do the calculations. Note that the process symbol in this example corresponds to two arithmetic assignment statements in the program. Each flowchart symbol need not represent only one statement in a program; a symbol often corresponds to several statements.

Figure D-5 shows a flowchart of the payroll calculation program in Chapter 3 (Figure 3-5). This flowchart includes a detailed specification of each

Figure D-5. Flowchart for the payroll calculation program in Chapter 3 (Figure 3-5)

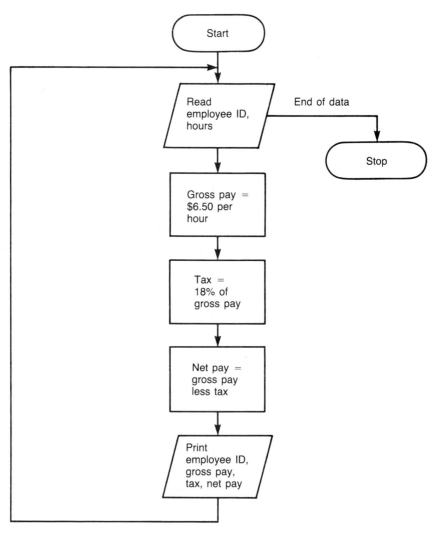

computation. The reader of the flowchart knows exactly what is done at each step in the program. Note that the flowchart steps for the computations are in the same order as the arithmetic assignment statements in the program.

Flowcharts with decisions

The flowchart of a program that includes a decision must show the condition that effects the decision and give the alternatives. As an example, the flowchart in Figure D-6 shows the logic in the tuition calculation program discussed

Figure D-6. Flowchart for the tuition calculation program in Chapter 4 (Figure 4-1)

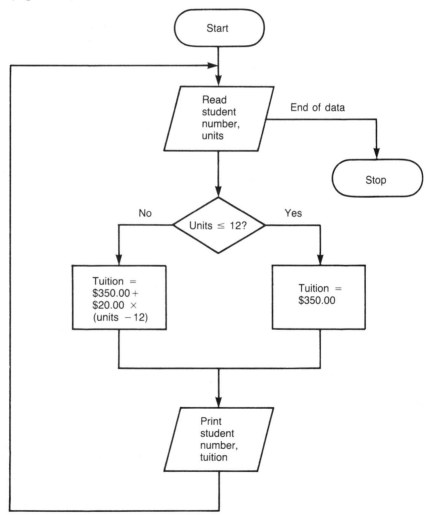

in Chapter 4 (see Figure 4-1). The decision symbol is used for the test (condition) of whether the number of units is less than or equal to 12. Whenever a decision symbol is used, two or more flowlines *must* leave the symbol. These lines represent the possible answers (alternatives) to the question asked in the symbol. The flowlines leaving a decision symbol *must* be labeled with the possible answers. The decision symbol in Figure D-6 asks whether the number of units is less than or equal to 12 and the possible answers, yes or no, are written above the flowlines leaving the symbol.

This flowchart depicts the basic two-sided decision logic discussed in Chapter 4. If a condition is true, one thing is done; otherwise, something else is done. After doing the necessary processing, the logical flow comes together to continue on to the next step.

A one-sided decision can also be represented in a flowchart. Figure D-7 shows an example of this pattern for the modified tuition calculation program (Figure 4-3). Note that if the condition is true, the tuition calculation step is done; otherwise, this step is bypassed. The logical flow comes together after the processing step is either done or bypassed.

Nested decisions

Nested decisions can be depicted in a flowchart. Figure D-8 shows a flowchart for the tuition calculation program with nested decisions (see Figure 4-10). Note that after the first decision is made, a second decision is required. The nesting of the decisions shows up very clearly in the flowchart.

This flowchart also shows the use of the connector symbol. This symbol is used when it is necessary but inconvenient to connect distant parts of a flowchart with a flowline or when a flowchart must continue on to another page. The connector symbol appears once where the flow logic leaves one part of the chart and again where the logic enters the other part. Within each set of connectors is placed an identifying letter or number. In Figure D-8 the letter A identifies the pair of connectors. If another set of connector symbols is needed for another part of the flowchart, a different letter or symbol such as B is used.

Case selection

Case selection can be shown in a flowchart using a series of nested decisions. Alternatively, one decision symbol can be used with multiple flowlines leaving it. Each flowline represents a different case and is labeled accordingly. Figure D-9 shows how this is done in a flowchart for the tuition calculation program with case selection (Figure 4-13). Note that the decision symbol gives the variable that determines which case is to be selected. The lines leaving the symbol are labeled with the possible cases. (In this figure a single line leaves the decision symbol and then splits into the four different cases. Alternatively, four separate lines may come out of the decision symbol.)

Figure D-7. Flowchart for the modified tuition calculation program in Chapter 4 (Figure 4-3)

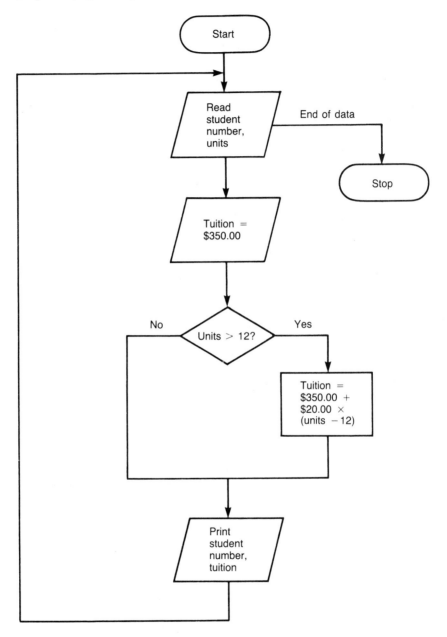

Figure D-8. Flowchart for the tuition calculation program with nested decisions in Chapter 4 (Figure 4-10)

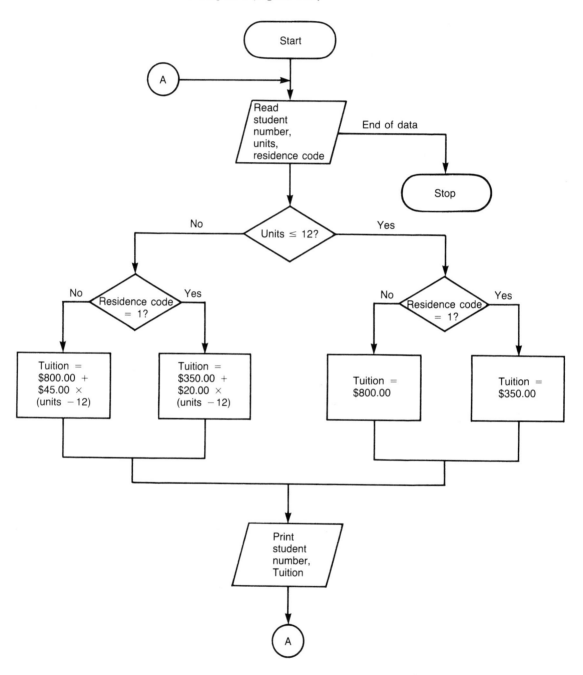

Figure D-9. Flowchart for the tuition calculation program with case selection in Chapter 4 (Figure 4-13)

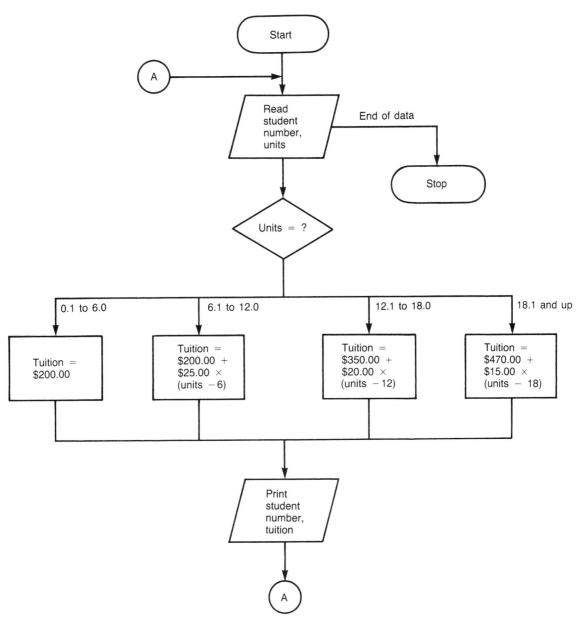

Flowcharts with loops

When one of the techniques discussed in Chapter 5 is used to control a loop, a decision within the loop usually indicates the condition that terminates the loop. For example, Figure D-10 shows the flowchart for the tuition calculation program with the input loop controlled by a trailer value (Figure 5-2). The first step after the input operation is to check for the trailer value. If the student number is 9999, the processing stops. This step is shown in the flowchart by a decision symbol.

Figure D-11 shows the flowchart for the interest calculation program with a processing loop (Figure 5-3). The loop terminates when the bank balance becomes greater than or equal to $2000, as shown in the flowchart by the decision step at the beginning of the loop. Note that the balance and year are initialized before the loop is begun.

When a program includes a counting loop, the corresponding flowchart must show the steps that initialize the counter, test the counter, and modify the counter. Figure D-12 is a flowchart of the program that finds the total and average of ten test scores (Figure 5-6). The loop is executed exactly ten times. The counter is initialized to one before the loop is entered. Each time through the loop, the counter is tested to determine if it is greater than ten. At the end of the loop, the counter is increased by one.

Nested loops

Nested loops can be shown in a flowchart. Figure D-13 gives a flowchart for the interest calculation program with nested loops (Figure 5-14). The flowchart clearly shows that the inner loop is completely contained in the outer loop. The conditions that terminate the loops are also shown clearly.

DO loops

There is no standard way to flowchart a DO loop. The DO statement alone implies all the operations necessary to control a counting loop. One approach is to show the initialization, testing, and modification of the DO-variable explicitly in the flowchart. This can be cumbersome when many loops are involved. Another approach is shown in Figure D-14 which is the flowchart of the program that finds the total and average of ten test scores using a DO loop (Figure 5-16). In this flowchart a special symbol is used for the DO statement. The symbol shows the initialization of the DO-variable (COUNT = 1), the testing of the variable (COUNT>10?), and the modification of the DO-variable (COUNT = COUNT + 1). The loop is repeated until the test becomes true.

Figure D-10. Flowchart for the tuition calculation program with the input loop controlled by a trailer value in Chapter 5 (Figure 5-2)

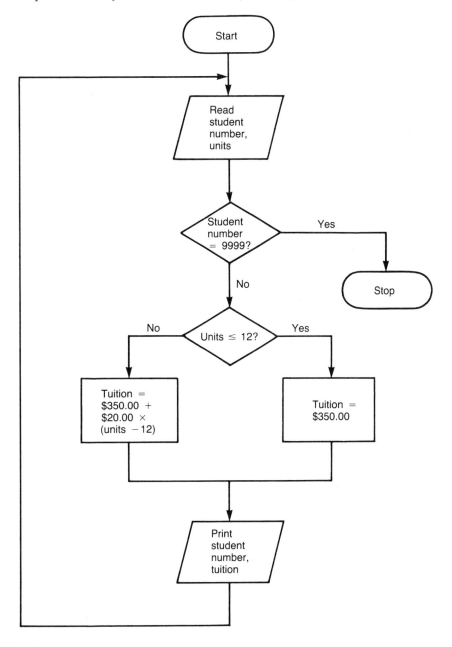

Figure D-11. Flowchart for the interest calculation program in Chapter 5 (Figure 5-3)

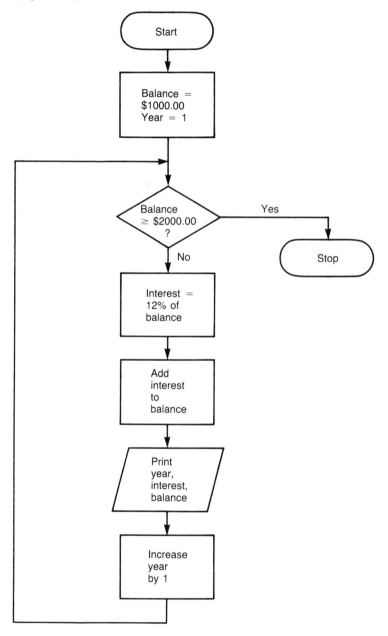

Figure D-12. Flowchart for the program to total and average ten test scores in Chapter 5 (Figure 5-6)

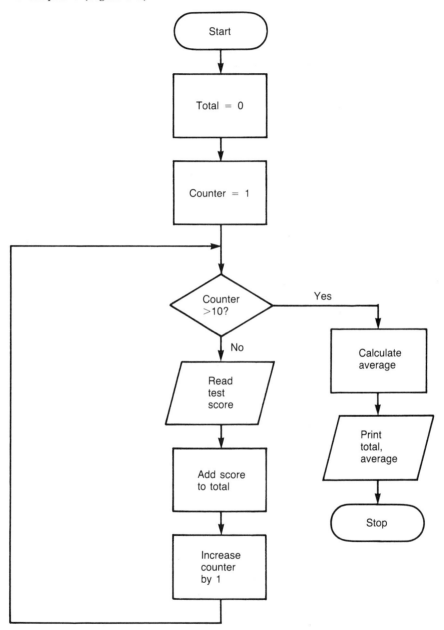

Figure D-13. Flowchart for the interest calculation program with nested loops in Chapter 5 (Figure 5-14)

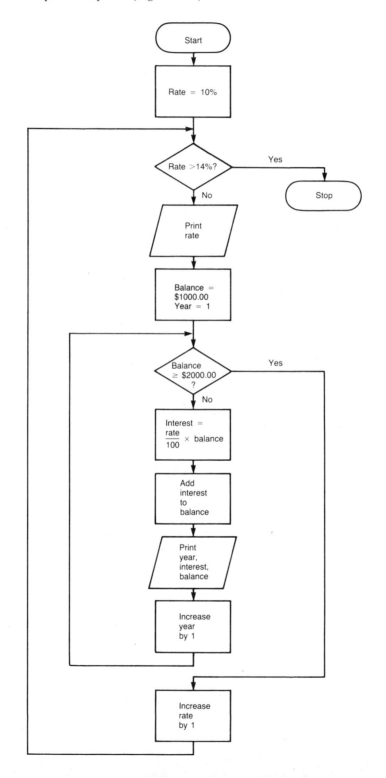

Figure D-14. Flowchart for the program to total and average ten test scores using a DO loop in Chapter 5 (Figure 5-16)

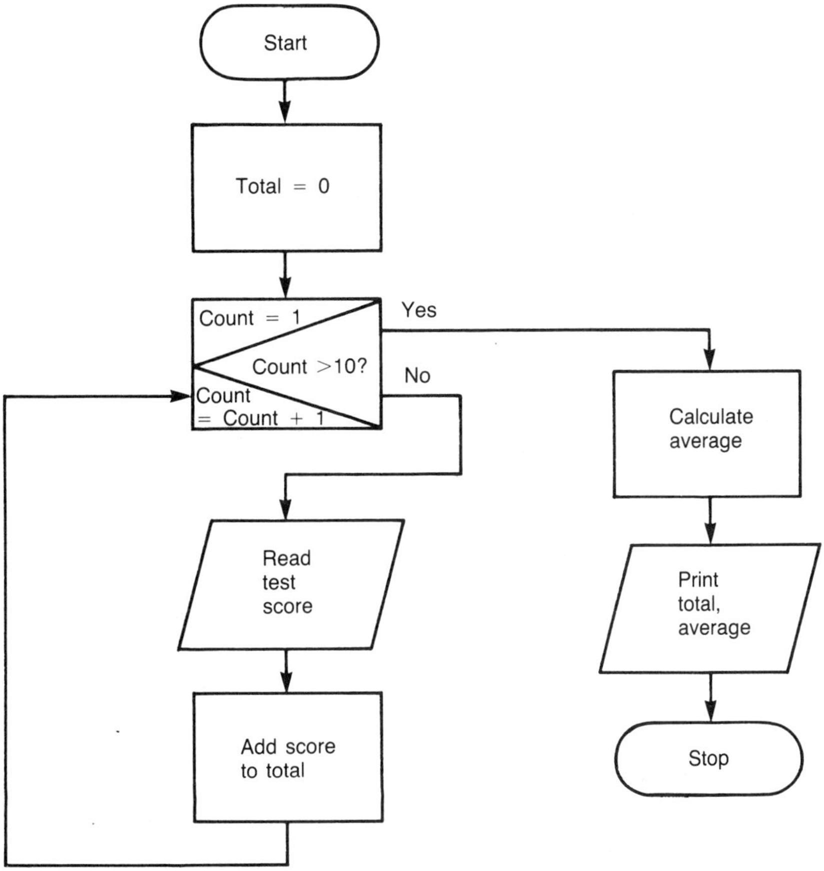

Flowcharts for advanced programs

The flowcharts shown in this appendix illustrate basic concepts. Flowcharts for more complex programs are drawn in a similar manner. Such complex flowcharts often cover many pages. Several good books describe both elementary and advanced flowcharts.*

* A complete discussion of flowcharts can be found in Marilyn Bohl's book, *Flowcharting Techniques,* published by Science Research Associates, Inc., Palo Alto, California, 1971.

Appendix E

Data representation

To program in FORTRAN, little knowledge of the internal organization of the computer is needed. In fact, in Chapter 1 we discussed only briefly the physical components of a computer before going on to programming concepts. Some understanding of the internal structure of the computer, however, helps explain some of the characteristics of FORTRAN. In particular, it is useful to understand the way data is represented in the internal storage of the computer. In this appendix we discuss data representation and its relationship to FORTRAN.

Data representation concepts

Humans usually represent data by using *characters*. In the Western world the character set consists of the *alphabetic characters* (A, B, ..., Z), the *numeric characters* (0, 1, ..., 9), and a number of *special characters* ($, + / etc.). Computers, however, cannot use human characters to represent data. A computer's internal storage is composed of a large number of electronic circuits where each circuit has only two states — "on" and "off." An example of a common electronic circuit that has only two states is a light bulb. Like a circuit in a computer, a light bulb can be only on or off. Humans use over 100 common characters to represent data. If a single circuit in a computer were used to represent any character, that circuit would have to have over 100 different states. Because a computer's circuit is a two-state device, it is not possible to represent any human character with a single circuit.

How, then, do computers store data? The answer is that computers use a series of electronic circuits in a particular pattern of on/off states to represent data. A computer processes data (that is, characters) by converting the data to its two-state representation. For output, the computer converts the results of its processing from the two-state internal representation to human characters.

Data represented in this two-state manner is said to be in the *binary mode*. For ease of presenting data in the binary mode on paper, the digit "1" is used to represent the "on" state and the digit "0" is used for the "off" state. The characters "1" and "0" are called the *binary digits* or *bits*. Internally, all data is stored as bits.

Number systems

To understand how data is represented in the binary mode, we must first consider number systems. A *number system* is a way of expressing quantities. Most humans use the *decimal number system*. Computers express quantities by using the *binary number system*.

The decimal number system

Consider the decimal number 285. What does this number really mean? We can think of 285 as 200 plus 80 plus 5. But 200 is 2 times 100, 80 is 8 times 10, and 5 is 5 times 1. Finally, 100 is 10 times 10 or 10^2, 10 is 10^1, and 1 is 10^0. Thus 285 can be interpreted as follows:

$$285 = 200 + 80 + 5$$
$$= (2 \times 100) + (8 \times 10) + (5 \times 1)$$
$$= (2 \times 10^2) + (8 \times 10^1) + (5 \times 10^0)$$

[It is appropriate at this time to review briefly the concept of raising a number to a power. Any number raised to a power means multiply the number by itself the number of times specified in the power; that is, use the number as a factor the number of times given by the power. For example, 6^4 means use 6 as a factor 4 times:

$$6^4 = 6 \times 6 \times 6 \times 6 = 1296$$

As other examples consider the following:

$$10^2 = 10 \times 10 = 100$$
$$10^3 = 10 \times 10 \times 10 = 1000$$
$$10^4 = 10 \times 10 \times 10 \times 10 = 10,000$$
$$2^2 = 2 \times 2 = 4$$
$$2^3 = 2 \times 2 \times 2 = 8$$
$$2^4 = 2 \times 2 \times 2 \times 2 = 16$$
$$2^5 = 2 \times 2 \times 2 \times 2 \times 2 = 32$$

A number raised to the first power is just that number. For example, 6^1 is 6, 10^1 is 10, and 2^1 is 2. Finally, a number raised to the zero power is one.

This is true for any number except zero. (0^0 is indeterminate.) For example, 6^0 is 1, 10^0 is 1, and 2^0 is 1.]

As another example of a decimal number, consider 4096:

$$4096 = 4000 + 000 + 90 + 6$$
$$= (4 \times 1000) + (0 \times 100) + (9 \times 10) + (6 \times 1)$$
$$= (4 \times 10^3) + (0 \times 10^2) + (9 \times 10^1) + (6 \times 10^0)$$

Notice how the digit zero can be used to hold a place in the number without adding value to the number. In this example zero holds the 100's place. Because zero times any number is zero, it does not increase the value of the number.

These examples illustrate the basic concepts of a number system. A number system is composed of a set of *digits*. In the decimal number system the digits are 0, 1, 2, 3, 4, 5, 6, 7, 8, and 9. The number of digits is called the *base* of the number system. There are ten digits in the decimal number system because the base of the system is ten. A *number* is a quantity that is represented by a *numeral* composed of a string of digits. For example, the decimal numeral 285 is composed of digits that are acceptable in the decimal number system. This numeral represents the number two-hundred eighty-five. The digits in a numeral occupy positions that have value. The *position values* (also called *place values*) of a number system are successive powers of the base. Considering only whole numbers, the right-most position has a value of the base to the zero power, the next position to the left has a value of the base to the first power, the next position has a value of the base to the second power, and so forth. Thus the position values for the decimal number system are as follows:

$$\ldots 10^5 \quad 10^4 \quad 10^3 \quad 10^2 \quad 10^1 \quad 10^0$$

A numeral is interpreted in a number system as the sum of the products of the digits in the numeral and their corresponding position values. Thus 285 is interpreted as a decimal number as follows:

Digits:	2	8	5
Position values:	10^2	10^1	10^0
Interpretation:	$(2 \times 10^2) + (8 \times 10^1) + (5 \times 10^0)$		

The interpretation of the numeral is found by multiplying the digits in the numeral by their corresponding position values and then adding the results. Note that the right-most digit occupies the 10^0 position and the position values increase to the left.

As another example, consider 4096:

Digits:	4	0	9	6
Position values:	10^3	10^2	10^1	10^0
Interpretation:	$(4 \times 10^3) + (0 \times 10^2) + (9 \times 10^1) + (6 \times 10^0)$			

Note how the digit zero holds a place in the numeral without adding value to the number.

In summary, a number system is composed of a set of digits. The base of the system is the number of digits that are acceptable in the system. The position values are successive powers of the base. A numeral is a string of digits that represents a number or quantity. A numeral can be interpreted as the sum of the products of the numeral's digits and their position values.

Although we have made a distinction here between a numeral and a number, the distinction is rarely made in practice. Most often we use the word "number" whether we mean the "quantity" or the representation of the quantity by a "numeral." We will follow this practice in the remainder of this appendix. The meaning of the term should be evident from the context in which it is used.

The binary number system

Computers do not use the decimal number system to express quantities. Because a computer uses two-state electronic circuits, it requires a number system that has only two digits. Such a system is the *binary number system*.

The base of the binary number system is two. The digits of the binary number system are 1 and 0. These are the binary digits or bits that correspond to the "on" and "off" states of a computer's circuits. The position values are successive powers of the base:

$$\ldots 2^5 \quad 2^4 \quad 2^3 \quad 2^2 \quad 2^1 \quad 2^0$$

A number in any number system can be composed only of digits acceptable to the system. Thus a binary number can be composed only of the digits 1 and 0. For example, 10011 is a binary number (read "one-zero-zero-one-one"). To interpret a binary number, each digit is multiplied by its corresponding position value and the results are totaled. Thus the binary number 10011 can be interpreted as follows:

Digits:	1	0	0	1	1
Position values:	2^4	2^3	2^2	2^1	2^0
Interpretation:	(1×2^4) +	(0×2^3) +	(0×2^2) +	(1×2^1) +	(1×2^0)

Because the position values are expressed in the decimal system, such an interpretation results in converting the binary number to its equivalent in the decimal number system:

$$\begin{aligned} 10011 &= (1 \times 2^4) + (0 \times 2^3) + (0 \times 2^2) + (1 \times 2^1) + (1 \times 2^0) \\ &= (1 \times 16) + (0 \times 8) + (0 \times 4) + (1 \times 2) + (1 \times 1) \\ &= 16 + 0 + 0 + 2 + 1 \\ &= 19 \end{aligned}$$

Thus 10011 in the binary system is equivalent to 19 in the decimal number system.

A special notation is sometimes used to distinguish numbers in different number systems. In this notation the base of the number system is written as a subscript immediately following the number. Thus, 10011_2 is a base 2 or binary number and 19_{10} is a base 10 or decimal number. This notation, though not required, is important when there may be confusion about the base of the number. For example, consider the number 10. This may represent a decimal number ("ten") or a binary number ("one-zero"). However, 10_{10} is not equivalent to 10_2 ($10_2 = (1 \times 2^1) + (0 \times 2^0) = 2_{10}$). Therefore, to avoid confusion this special notation is used to indicate what type of number is being expressed.

As a final example, consider the binary number 110101. This number can be interpreted as follows:

$$
\begin{array}{lcccccc}
\text{Digits:} & 1 & 1 & 0 & 1 & 0 & 1 \\
\text{Position values:} & 2^5 & 2^4 & 2^3 & 2^2 & 2^1 & 2^0 \\
\text{Interpretation:} & (1 \times 2^5) + & (1 \times 2^4) + & (0 \times 2^3) + & (1 \times 2^2) + & (0 \times 2^1) + & (1 \times 2^0) \\
& = (1 \times 32) + & (1 \times 16) + & (0 \times 8) + & (1 \times 4) + & (0 \times 2) + & (1 \times 1) \\
& = 32 + & 16 + & 0 + & 4 + & 0 + & 1 \\
& = 53
\end{array}
$$

Thus 110101_2 is equivalent to 53_{10}.

Decimal to binary conversion

So far, we have only shown how to convert a binary number to its decimal equivalent. The inverse, that of converting a decimal number to its binary equivalent, is only slightly more complex. There are a number of quick techniques for this. The technique discussed here, though not the fastest, is based on the underlying nature of number systems.

To convert a decimal number to its binary equivalent, the largest power of two that is less than or equal to the decimal number is first found. Then the maximum significant position value in the binary equivalent of the decimal number is that power of two. Working backwards toward 2^0, the next significant position value is found. This value is the next power of two that is less than or equal to the original decimal number minus the position value that has already been used. This continues until the 2^0 position is reached, or until the remainder from subtracting significant position values from the original number is zero.

For example, consider the decimal number 21. The largest power of two that is less than or equal to 21 is 2^4 or 16. Thus there is 1×2^4 in 21. Subtracting 2^4 from 21 leaves 5. The largest power of two that is less than or equal to 5 is 2^2 or 4; there is 1×2^2 in 5. Subtracting 2^2 from 5 leaves 1. The largest power of two that is less than or equal to 1 is 2^0 or 1; there is 1×2^0 in 1. Subtracting 1 from 1 leaves 0 and there are no more significant position values. Thus in 21 there is 1×2^4, 1×2^2, and 1×2^0. The intermediate position values (2^3 and 2^1) are held by the digit 0. Therefore, the binary equivalent of 21_{10} is 10101_2. These calculations can be summarized as follows:

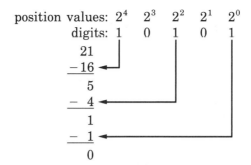

As another example, consider the decimal number 54. The largest power of two that is less than or equal to 54 is 2^5 or 32. Working backwards from 2^5 to 2^0, the following is obtained:

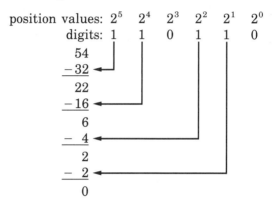

Thus 54_{10} is equivalent to 110110_2.

Fractions

So far we have only described how whole numbers (integers) are represented in the binary number system. As we know, computers also can process numbers with fractional parts. Thus we need some way of expressing fractions as binary numbers.

In the decimal number system, the position values of the digits to the *right* of the decimal point are *negative* powers of ten. That is, the position values of the fractional part are as follows:

$$10^{-1} \quad 10^{-2} \quad 10^{-3} \quad 10^{-4} \quad 10^{-5} \ldots$$

(A number to a negative power is one over the number to the absolute value of the power. Thus, 10^{-3} is $1/10^3$ or $1/1000$ or .001.) To illustrate the use of these position values, consider the decimal number 5.625. This number is interpreted as follows:

Digits: 5   6   2   5

Position values: 10^0 10^{-1} 10^{-2} 10^{-3}

Interpretation: $(5 \times 10^0) + (6 \times 10^{-1}) + (2 \times 10^{-2}) + (5 \times 10^{-3})$

With the binary number system the position values of the bits to the right of the *binary point* (which is the equivalent of the decimal point in the binary system) are negative powers of the base two. That is, the position values of the right-hand bits are as follows:

$$2^{-1} \quad 2^{-2} \quad 2^{-3} \quad 2^{-4} \quad 2^{-5} \ldots$$

These correspond to the following values:

$$2^{-1} = \tfrac{1}{2} = .5$$
$$2^{-2} = \tfrac{1}{4} = .25$$
$$2^{-3} = \tfrac{1}{8} = .125$$
$$2^{-4} = \tfrac{1}{16} = .0625$$
$$2^{-5} = \tfrac{1}{32} = .03125$$

To interpret a binary number with a fractional part we follow the usual approach. For example, the binary number 101.101 is interpreted as follows:

Digits: 1   0   1   1   0   1

Position values: 2^2 2^1 2^0 2^{-1} 2^{-2} 2^{-3}

Interpretation: $(1 \times 2^2) + (0 \times 2^1) + (1 \times 2^0) + (1 \times 2^{-1}) + (0 \times 2^{-2}) + (1 \times 2^{-3})$

$= (1 \times 4) + (0 \times 2) + (1 \times 1) + (1 \times .5) + (0 \times .25) + (1 \times .125)$

$=$ 4   +   0   +   1   +   .5   +   0   +   .125

$=$ 5.625

Thus 101.101_2 is equivalent to 5.625_{10}.

To convert a decimal number with a fractional part to its binary equivalent, we follow the procedure of finding the largest power of two as described earlier. For example, the following summarizes the conversion of 3.3125 to a binary number:

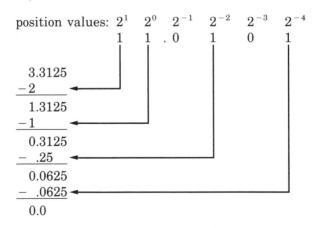

position values: 2^1 2^0 2^{-1} 2^{-2} 2^{-3} 2^{-4}

      1   1 . 0   1   0   1

```
 3.3125
-2
 1.3125
-1
 0.3125
- .25
 0.0625
- .0625
 0.0
```

Thus 3.3125_{10} is equivalent to 11.0101_2.

One problem with decimal to binary conversion involving a fractional part is that an exact equivalent of the decimal fraction does not always exist in the binary number system. For example, consider the decimal number 0.2. If we try to convert this number to binary, we get the following:

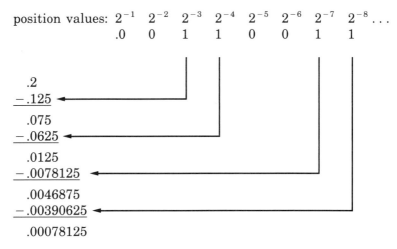

position values: 2^{-1} 2^{-2} 2^{-3} 2^{-4} 2^{-5} 2^{-6} 2^{-7} 2^{-8} ...

.0 0 1 1 0 0 1 1

```
   .2
 -.125
  .075
 -.0625
  .0125
 -.0078125
  .0046875
 -.00390625
  .00078125
```

We can see that, although we have carried out the conversion process to eight bits, we still do not have an exact binary equivalent of 0.2. In fact, we can continue this process as long as we want and never get an exact equivalent. The binary number that we come up with will always be slightly less than 0.2.

Many decimal fractions do not have an exact binary equivalent. Decimal integers, however, can always be represented exactly in the binary number system. In the next section we will see how this relates to the internal data representation of integers and reals.

Internal data representation

Computers use the binary number system or some variation of it to represent data in their internal storage. In general, a computer's internal storage is composed of a large number of electronic circuits. The individual circuits are grouped to form *storage locations*. Each storage location is a group of several computer circuits. By setting the circuits in a storage location to a particular pattern of on/off states, a value can be stored. Later the computer can examine the pattern of on/off states to determine what value is stored at the storage location.

As a simple analogy consider a sequence of four light bulbs. In Figure E-1 the light bulbs are shown in the pattern on-off-off-on. Using binary digits this represents 1001 or the decimal number 9. A different pattern of on/off states (i.e., bits) represents different data. Of course computers do not use

Figure E-1. Internal data representation — the light bulb analogy

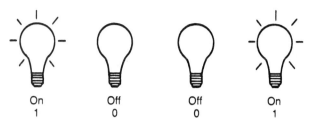

On	Off	Off	On
1	0	0	1

light bulbs for their internal storage, but the idea is the same; a pattern of bits, stored in a series of computer circuits, is used to represent data.

Types of data

Computers can process several types of data, but all data falls into two basic categories — numeric and nonnumeric. *Numeric data* consists of numbers that are manipulated arithmetically. For example, a student's grade point average is numeric data because it results from arithmetic processing and may be used in further calculations. *Nonnumeric data* consists of data that cannot be processed arithmetically. For example, a student's address is nonnumeric. An address usually consists of numbers, letters, and special characters. The numbers in an address are not normally used in arithmetic calculations. Therefore, an address, even though it may contain numbers, is considered nonnumeric data.

In FORTRAN there are two basic types of numeric data — integer and real. *Integer data* is represented in a program without a decimal point. *Real data* has a fractional part and therefore has a decimal point when coded in a program.

Nonnumeric data in FORTRAN includes character data and logical data. *Character data* is represented in a program as a group of characters enclosed in apostrophes. *Logical data* consists of truth values.

Internally, computers represent different types of data in different ways. To process a FORTRAN program, a computer must be able to store numeric and nonnumeric data. This section explains how these types of data are stored in a computer. The system that is used varies with different types of computers. This section only considers the internal data representation used by medium and large-scale IBM and related computers. The basic principles, however, can be extended to almost all computers.

Character data

Character data consists of alphabetic, numeric, and special characters. In an IBM computer a character is stored as a sequence of eight bits. That is, each character is assigned a unique eight-bit code that represents the character.

For example, the letter A is represented by the code 11000001; the letter K is represented by 11010010; the number 5 is 11110101; the decimal point is represented by 01001011. There is a unique eight-bit pattern for each character.

This code is called the Extended Binary Coded Decimal Interchange Code or EBCDIC. There are a total of 256 different configurations of eight bits but not all are used for characters in the EBCDIC code. All of the characters used in FORTRAN, however, have a unique representation in this code.*

Although the EBCDIC code uses binary digits to represent characters, the computer does not confuse a character with a true binary number. For example, if the computer is told that 11000001 represents a character in the EBCDIC code, it interprets it as the letter A. If this pattern of eight bits is interpreted as a true binary number, it is equivalent to the decimal number 193. This is especially important when considering the numeric characters. For example, 5 is represented in the EBCDIC code as 11110101. If this pattern is interpreted as a true binary number, it is equivalent to the decimal number 245. Thus the way in which a series of bits is interpreted depends on whether the bits are supposed to represent character data or numeric data.

In IBM and many other computers, each storage location is composed of eight bits. An eight-bit storage location is called a *byte*. Bytes are the basic building blocks of internal storage and each byte is given a separate *address*. The computer locates data in storage by specifying the address of the byte or bytes where the data is stored. The internal storage capacity of a computer is measured in terms of the number of bytes that it can store.

Integer data

Integer data (also called *fixed-point data*) is the simplest type of numeric data. Internally, integers are represented in the binary number system. Each integer is stored in a fixed number of bits. In an IBM computer each integer is stored in 32 bits. For example, the decimal number 25 is 11001 in binary. As a 32-bit binary number, 25 is represented as follows:

00000000000000000000000000011001

Note that when a binary number does not use all 32 bit positions, leading positions are filled with zeros.

A configuration of a fixed number of bits used to represent a numeric value is called a *word*. In an IBM computer each word is 32 bits. Because internal storage is composed of eight-bit bytes, four consecutive bytes are

---

* Another code that is used on some small IBM computers and on many non-IBM computers is the American Standard Code for Information Interchange or ASCII. In this code each character is represented by seven bits. For example, the letter A is represented by 1000001; the letter K is 1001011; the number 5 is 0110101; the decimal point is 0101110. There are a total of 128 different codes in ASCII.

required to form a word. Thus integer data is stored as a true binary number in a four-byte word.

The difference between numeric and nonnumeric data can be understood more clearly at this point. As a 32-bit binary number, 25 is represented as shown previously. As character data, however, 25 appears as follows:

11110010 11110101

The first byte represents 2; the second byte is 5. In this form, the data cannot be used in arithmetic calculations. It only can be stored in the computer's internal storage and retrieved when needed. As a binary number, however, the data can be used in arithmetic processing.

An integer value can be either positive or negative. As a 32-bit binary number, the sign is represented by the first bit. If the first bit is 0, the number is positive; if the first bit is 1, the sign is negative. In fact, negative numbers are stored in a special manner known as *two's complement form*. To form the two's complement of a binary number, the number is first inverted (that is, all of the 1-bits are changed to 0's and all of the 0-bits are changed to 1's) and then 1 is added. The result is the negative of the original number in two's complement form. For example, -25 is formed as follows:

00000000000000000000000000011001 ($+25$ as a true binary)
11111111111111111111111111100110 (invert the number)
$\underline{ +1 \text{ (add 1)}}$
11111111111111111111111111100111 (-25 in two's
                                      complement)

Note that the first bit (the sign bit) is a 1, indicating a negative number in two's complement form. Internally, all negative integer numbers are represented in two's complement form.

Because the sign bit for a positive number is 0, the maximum integer that can be stored is:

01111111111111111111111111111111

This corresponds to the decimal number $+2,147,483,647$. The minimum negative number in two's complement form is:

10000000000000000000000000000000

This corresponds to the decimal number $-2,147,483,648$.

Real data

Real data (also called *floating-point data*) is represented internally in a different form than integer data. This form, known as *floating-point notation,* involves rewriting the number as a fraction times some power of ten. For example, 27305.85 is written as $.2730585 \times 10^5$. Similarly, .00008356902 is written as $.8356902 \times 10^{-4}$. In writing a number in this way, the decimal point is shifted to the right or left until it is just to the left of the first nonzero digit in the number. Then the exponent for the power of ten is equal to the number of places that the decimal point is shifted. If the decimal point is shifted to the left, the exponent is positive; if it is shifted to the right, the exponent is negative.

In floating-point notation a number is represented by its fraction and exponent. The decimal point, the multiplication symbol, and the number 10 are not necessary because it is assumed that the decimal point is always just to the left of the fraction and that the number is the fraction times ten to the power of the exponent. Thus, in floating-point notation, if the fraction is 2730585 and the exponent is 5, the number is .2730585 $\times$ 10^5 or 27305.85. Similarly, if the fraction is 8356902 and the exponent is -4, the number is .8356902 $\times$ 10^{-4} or .00008356902.

Any real value can be expressed in floating-point notation. It is in this form that real data is stored in the computer's internal storage. The computer converts the number to floating-point notation and stores the fraction and the exponent in the binary mode. In an IBM computer, data is stored in a 32-bit word as shown in Figure E-2. The sign of the number occupies the first bit of the word. The exponent occupies the next seven bits. The last 24 bits of the word are reserved for the fraction. Note that the point to the left of the fraction is called a decimal point only in the decimal number system; in the binary number system it is called a *binary point* and in general it is referred to as the *radix point.*

Because of this representation of real numbers, limitations on the size of numbers are expressed in terms of maxima and minima for the fraction and the exponent. For an IBM computer the maximum exponent is approximately 75 and the minimum is -78. These values express the range of *magnitude* of the number; real numbers must have a magnitude between 10^{-78} and 10^{75}. The fraction is limited to a maximum of approximately seven decimal digits. This gives the maximum *precision* of the number. Thus, there can be a number very large in magnitude (up to 10^{75}) but with only seven digits.

Figure E-2. Internal representation of real data

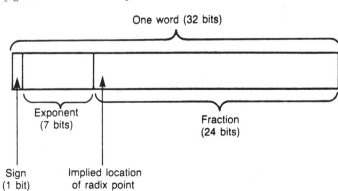

One word (32 bits)

Exponent
(7 bits)

Fraction
(24 bits)

Sign
(1 bit)

Implied location
of radix point

Figure E-3. Internal representation of double-precision data

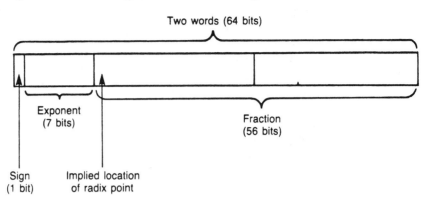

Limitations on the magnitude and precision of a real number as stated here are approximate because they are expressed as decimal numbers. Precise limitations are in terms of binary digits, and their interpretation is beyond the scope of this book; however, the values stated here are sufficiently accurate for programming purposes.

It is possible to extend the precision but not the magnitude of real data. For an IBM computer, two words can be linked together and real data stored in *double precision* form. (See Figure E-3.) The sign of the real number occupies the first bit of the first word. The next seven bits are reserved for the exponent. The fraction occupies the remaining 24 bits of the first word and all 32 bits of the second word. For double precision data the size of the exponent is the same as for the standard real data form. Therefore, the range of magnitude is the same. However, the amount of storage allocated to the fraction increases substantially. In the double precision form the computer can store real numbers up to approximately sixteen decimal digits.

Because real data may contain a fractional part, its representation in floating-point notation may not be exact. In the last section we saw that some decimal fractions do not have an exact equivalent in the binary number system. Hence, in converting a real number to its internal data representation, some accuracy may be lost. Because integers do not have fractional parts, the conversion of an integer to a binary number is always exact.

Logical data

Logical data consists of truth values; that is, *true* and *false*. In an IBM computer, each logical value is stored in a 32-bit word (four bytes). The first byte is used for the truth value and the remaining three bytes are ignored. If the value is *true*, the first byte contains all 1's; if the value is *false*, the first byte is all 0's.

Relationship of internal data representation to FORTRAN

Data processed by a FORTRAN program is stored in the computer's internal storage in one of the forms just discussed. Character, integer, real, double precision, and logical data each has its own internal representation. Within a FORTRAN program we use constants and variable names to identify data. The internal representation of the data is indicated by the type of the constant or variable name.

A numeric constant can be coded in a FORTRAN program with or without a decimal point. When a constant is written without a decimal point it is stored in the computer's internal storage as a true binary number; that is, it is stored as integer data. When a constant is coded with a decimal point, it is converted to floating-point notation and stored as real data. A real constant is stored in the standard real data form (also called *single precision* form). A double precision constant is coded in a program using the exponential form discussed in Appendix F. Such a constant is stored in double precision, floating-point form.

When a variable name is used in a FORTRAN program, a storage location (or perhaps several locations) is reserved for the data to which the name refers. Each time the variable name is used in the program, the computer locates the same storage location. If the variable name is integer (either typed explicitly or implicitly), storage is reserved for integer data. Any time a value is assigned to the variable name by an assignment statement or by an input statement the value is stored in integer form. If an integer variable name is used in an arithmetic expression or an output statement, the value retrieved from storage is integer.

When a variable name is real (either because of explicit or implicit typing), storage is reserved for real data. If a value is assigned to the variable name, the value is stored in single precision, floating-point form. When a real variable name is used in an arithmetic expression or an output statement, the computer retrieves a real value from storage.

A double precision variable name is declared in a DOUBLE PRECISION statement (see Appendix F). When this statement is used it causes extra storage to be reserved for all variable names specified. Any data assigned to a double precision variable name is stored in double precision form.

A character constant is written in a FORTRAN program as a group of characters enclosed in apostrophes. Each character in such a constant is converted to the appropriate code. The entire constant is stored as a sequence of codes in a group of storage locations. A character variable name is declared in a CHARACTER statement. Such a name identifies a group of storage locations each containing a character in the appropriate code. The length is given in the CHARACTER statement. Any use of a character variable name retrieves all of the characters to which the name refers.

A logical constant is coded as .TRUE. or .FALSE. in a FORTRAN program. Such a constant is stored in a storage location in the appropriate logical data form. Any variable name declared in a LOGICAL statement refers to a storage location containing logical data.

In summary, we have seen in this appendix how different types of data are represented in the computer's internal storage. Character, integer, real, double precision, and logical data each have their own internal data representation. The type of data that a constant or variable name refers to in a FORTRAN program is determined by how the constant is coded or the variable name is typed. An understanding of the internal data representation for the computer being used helps the programmer understand and use FORTRAN.

Appendix F

Exponential form and double precision data

In Chapter 2 we discussed real variables and in Chapter 3 we described real constants. We noted that real data is stored in floating-point notation and that there are limits on the exponent and the fraction of the floating-point value. The limits on the exponent express the range of *magnitude* of real data; the limits on the number of digits in the fraction gives the maximum *precision* of the data. (Magnitude and precision of real data are discussed in more detail in Appendix E.) These limitations depend on the computer being used. For example, on one computer the magnitude of a real value may range from 10^{-78} to 10^{75} and the precision is limited to at most seven digits.

So far we have only used real data where the magnitude is not very large or very small. Real data with large or small magnitudes can be used by coding constants in a special form. This form is described in the first section of this appendix. Formatted input and output of very large and small real data is discussed in the second section.

Although the range of the exponent of real data (i.e., the magnitude) usually cannot be extended, the precision can be increased. The third section in this appendix describes how this is done. Formatted input and output of this type of data is discussed in the last section.

Exponential form of real constants

Assume that we need the following real constant in a program:

```
5863000000000000.0
```

Although this is an acceptable way of coding this value, it is cumbersome. Another approach is to write the value as a constant times some power of

10. To indicate the power, we use the letter E followed by the exponent. For example, the previous constant can be coded as:

    5.863E15

This means "5.863 times 10 to the fifteenth power." This is equivalent to the previous value and may be used in a program in exactly the same manner as any other real constant. We call this the exponential form of a real constant.

In general, exponential form requires a basic real constant or an integer constant followed by the letter E and a signed or unsigned integer exponent. For example, the following are valid real constants in this form:

5.8E2	$(5.8 \times 10^2$ or 580.)
.051E-13	$(.051 \times 10^{-13})$
-.39E+7	$(-.39 \times 10^7)$
789.E-25	$(789. \times 10^{-25})$
-6.0E-8	(-6.0×10^{-8})
21.3E+05	(21.3×10^5)
75E+10	$(75. \times 10^{10})$
-138E3	$(-138. \times 10^3)$
6E-35	$(6. \times 10^{-35})$

Notice that an integer constant can be used before the E in the exponential form. The result is still a real constant.

With the exponential form, the exponent must not cause the magnitude of the constant to exceed the maximum real value of the computer being used. For example, the following constant is too large for some computers:

    3.72E85

Real constants in exponential form can be used in any way that a basic real constant can. For example, the following statement shows a valid use of an exponential form real constant:

    A=B+6.25E12

List-directed input data can also be recorded in exponential form. List-directed output data is sometimes printed in an exponential form as discussed in Section 2-3.

E-format code

Formatted input and output of real data of large magnitude can be accomplished with E-format code. The syntax of this code is as follows:

Ew.d

where w is the field width.
d is the number of decimal positions.

For input, this code may be used to describe data in the same format as the F-format code or the input data may be in an exponential form. For example, consider the following statements:

```
   READ (5,10) X,Y
10 FORMAT (E10.2,E12.4)
```

The two input fields described by the E-format codes in the FORMAT statement are 10 and 12 positions in length, respectively. The first field has two positions to the right of the decimal point; the second field has four decimal positions. The input data may be recorded in an exponential form consisting of an integer or real value followed optionally by the letter E and a signed or unsigned integer exponent. For example, assume that the values to be read for the fields are 5.62×10^8 and $-.0321 \times 10^{-25}$. Then the input data may be recorded as follows:

```
123456789..............
     5.62E8  −.0321E−25
```

The letter E may be left out of the field in which case the exponent *must* be preceded by a sign. Thus the following is another way to record the data for the previous example:

```
123456789..............
     5.62+8   −.0321−25
```

It is not valid, however, merely to leave a blank in front of the exponent without a sign or the letter E.

The exponent may be any integer constant within the limits of the computer being used. The exponent should be right-justified because trailing blanks in the field are usually interpreted as zeros.

If the decimal point is left out of the field, the computer uses the number of decimal positions specified in the format code to determine the decimal point's position. The number of decimal positions are counted beginning with the first digit to the left of the exponent. Thus the previous example may be recorded as follows with the same result:

```
123456789...............
|     562+8  |   -0321-25  |
|            |             |
```

When a decimal point is included in the field, its position overrides the position specified in the format code.

For output, the E-format code specifies that the field is to be written in a standardized exponential format. In this format the output data is arranged so that the decimal point appears at the left of the first nonzero digit in the output. Ahead of the decimal point is a zero and, if necessary, a negative sign. The number of digits to the right of the decimal point is the number specified in the format code. The exponent occupies the last four positions of the field. It begins with the letter E followed by a plus sign if the exponent is positive or a minus sign if it is negative. Following this is a two-digit exponent. For example, consider the following statements:

```
    WRITE (6,20) X,Y
 20 FORMAT (1X,E10.2,E12.4)
```

If the values of X and Y are as in the previous example, the printed output is as follows:

```
123456789...............
|  0.56E+09 | -0.3210E-26 |
|           |             |
```

Note in both of the output fields that the exponent has been modified to reflect the shift in the decimal point to the left of the first nonzero digit. Because of this shift and because of the number of decimal positions specified in the format codes, the last digit of the first field is not printed and a zero is added to the second field.

When using E-format code for output, the field must be sufficiently large to accommodate the output data. In general, the field width should be at least seven positions larger than the number of decimal positions. Seven positions are needed for the sign, the lead zero, the decimal point, and the four-position exponent.

Double precision data

Basic real data is sometimes referred to as *single precision* data. Variable names and constants for such data are also called single precision. Real data of greater size is called *double precision* data. The maximum number of digits in the fraction of a double precision value depends on the computer being used. For one computer, the fraction of a double precision value has between eight and sixteen digits. (This range is approximate because the internal representation is in the binary mode. See Appendix E.) For example, the value 28430621.92 is double precision because it contains ten digits in its fraction, whereas the six-digit value 5837.25 is single precision. In this section we discuss double precision variable names and constants.

Double precision variable names

Real variable names, either specified in a REAL statement or typed implicitly, refer to single precision data. To use a variable name to identify double precision data, we must specify the name in a DOUBLE PRECISION statement. The syntax of this statement is as follows:

DOUBLE PRECISION *list*

where *list* is a list of variable names separated by commas.

For example, the following statement identifies the names RATE, X, Y, and NUM as double precision variable names:

DOUBLE PRECISION RATE,X,Y,NUM

As with the REAL and INTEGER statements, the DOUBLE PRECISION statement is a type statement and, as such, must appear at the beginning of the program before the first executable statement.

Double precision constants

To code a double precision constant, we use the exponential form described earlier, but we replace the letter E with the letter D. For example, the following are valid double precision constants:

25.3D7	(25.3×10^7)
1.23456789012D-16	$(1.23456789012 \times 10^{-16})$
-40D+21	$(-40. \times 10^{21})$
.83260547012D27	$(.83260547012 \times 10^{27})$
56204D-08	$(56204. \times 10^{-8})$

Double precision constants can be used in conjunction with double precision variable names to form double precision mode arithmetic expressions. For example, assume that X and Y are double precision variable names. Then the following expression is double precision:

X**2+3.2D5*Y

Mixing single precision and double precision in the same expression is permissible but can yield undesirable results. We can convert from double precision to single precision with the SNGL function, and from single precision to double precision with the DBLE function.

Double precision data for list-directed input can be recorded in the form of a double precision constant. List-directed output of double precision data is printed in the same way real (single precision) data is printed.

Double precision arrays

If an array is to contain double precision data, a DOUBLE PRECISION statement specifies the dimension of the array. For example, the following statement describes a double precision array named W with 50 elements:

```
DOUBLE PRECISION W(50)
```

Double precision functions

A function that returns a double precision value must specify this in its FUNCTION statement. For example, assume that FUND is the name of a double precision function with two arguments. The FUNCTION statement for this function would be

```
DOUBLE PRECISION FUNCTION FUND(A,B)
```

The function name must also be declared in a DOUBLE PRECISION statement in the calling program.

D-format code

Formatted input or output of double precision data is specified by the D-format code. The syntax of this code is as follows:

```
Dw.d

where w is the field width.
      d is the number of decimal positions.
```

For input, the D-format code may describe data in the same format as the F-format code or in exponential form. The exponential form may use the letter E, the letter D, or just a sign to specify the exponent. For example, consider the following sequence of statements:

```
       DOUBLE PRECISION A,B
       READ (5,30) A,B
   30 FORMAT (2D12.4)
```

In this example, two 12-position fields are specified, each with four positions to the right of the decimal point. If the values 53.8721×10^{-8} and 4.3601×10^{25} are to be read and assigned to the variables named A and B, respectively, the input data may be recorded as follows:

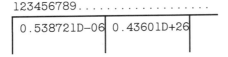

```
   123456789.................
```

| 53.8721D–8 | 4.3601D25 |

When used for output, the D-format code describes a field in the same format as E-format code except that the letter D replaces the letter E. For example, assume that the values of A and B from the previous example are printed with the following statements:

```
       WRITE (6,40) A,B
   40 FORMAT (1X,D13.6,D12.5)
```

Then the output appears as follows:

```
   123456789.................
```

| 0.538721D–06 | 0.43601D+26 |

Appendix G

Answers to selected review questions

Chapter 1

1. input device, output device, internal storage, processor, auxiliary storage
3. input devices: keyboard, card reader; output devices: CRT, printer
5. internal storage, processor
7. magnetic disk, magnetic tape
9. The instructions in the program are stored in internal storage. Each instruction is brought from internal storage to the processor where it is analyzed by the control circuits. The control circuits send signals to the other units based on what the instruction tells the computer to do.
11. A machine language program needs no translation in order to be executed. A high-level language program must first be translated into machine language before it can be executed.
13. Application software consists of programs to solve specific problems (e.g., keep track of sales, determine a rocket velocity). System software consists of general programs that help make the computer easier to use (e.g., a compiler).
15. numeric characters or digits, alphabetic characters or letters, special characters
17. Data is transferred to the CPU from auxiliary storage (input) and from the CPU to auxiliary storage (output).
19. Time-sharing is the means by which a computer interacts with several users at one time by "sharing its time" among those using it.
21. coding
23. Executable statements cause the computer to perform some action; nonexecutable statements describe some characteristic of the program or of the data.
25. blank = + – * / ( ) , . $ ' :
27. A statement longer than one line is continued on a second line and a character other than a blank or a zero is put in column 6 of the continuation line.
29. Comments are placed in a program by putting a C or an asterisk in column 1 of the comment line.
31. System commands or control records tell the operating system what is to be done during the processing of a program. They are not part of the FORTRAN language.
33. Program testing involves the following steps: design the test data; determine the

expected output if the program is run with the test data; run the program with the test data; compare the actual output with the expected output.

35. understand the problem, design the program, code the program, test the program, document the program

Chapter 2

1. In list-directed I/O the format of the input and output data is preset outside of the program. With formatted I/O the format of the data is specified in the program.
3. storage locations; an address
5. a. valid   c. invalid   e. invalid
7. `REAL PRICE,DESC`
   `INTEGER QTY`
8. a. real   c. integer   e. integer
9. Answer depends on computer being used.
11. Values must be separated by a comma or a blank; an integer value must not have a decimal point; a real value must have a decimal point unless there are no digits to the right, in which case the decimal point is optional.
13. `PRINT *,PRICE,DESC,QTY`
15. `PRINT *,I`
    `PRINT *,J`
    `PRINT *,K`
17. `PRINT *,'OUTPUT DATA',A,B`
19. the STOP and END statements
21. `GO TO 100`
23. `READ (*,*,END=999) PRICE,DESC,QTY`
25. It helps make a program more understandable and readable for a human.

Chapter 3

1. a. valid   c. invalid
2. a. real   c. real
3. exponentiation; multiplication and division; addition and subtraction
4. a. $X**2-2.0*X+3.0$ c. $(A-B)/(A+B)$
5. a. 3.0   c. 5.0   e. $-.2$
6. a. real mode   c. mixed mode
7. It causes the value of X to be halved.
9. 27
11. `C=SQRT(A**2+B**2)`
12. a. 5.0   c. 2.0
13. a. 2   c. 4
15. a. -10 c. 1
17. overflow
19. Z = 6, Y = 6, X = unchanged, W = unchanged, V = 5, U = 8, T = 8, S = 8, R = unchanged, Q = unchanged

Chapter 4

1. a. 20.0
2. a. less than or equal to   c. equal to
3. a. false   c. true

5. IF (U.LE.50.0) THEN
       S=0.0
       T=1.0
    ELSE
       S=1.0
       T=0.0
    END IF

7. IF (I.GE.J) THEN
       R=P+Q
    END IF

8. a. A.NE.B   c. P.LE.Q

9. Two-sided approach:

        IF (X.GT.Y) THEN
          Z=X
        ELSE
          Z=Y
        END IF

One-sided approach:

    Z=X
    IF (Y.GT.X) THEN
      Z=Y
    END IF

11. IF (J.EQ.10) THEN
        IF (K.LT.5) THEN
          I=0
        ELSE
          I=1
        END IF
    ELSE
        IF (K.LT.5) THEN
          I=2
        ELSE
          I=3
        END IF
    END IF

13. IF (T.EQ.2.0) THEN
        IF (U.EQ.4.0) THEN
          S=0.0
        END IF
    ELSE
        IF (U.EQ.3.0) THEN
          S=2.0
        END IF
    END IF

15. case selection

17. IF (Y.LE.Z) X=X-2.0

19. IF (X.NE.Y) THEN
        X=X+1
        Z=0
    ELSE
        Z=X+Y
        Y=X
    END IF
    PRINT *,Z

Chapter 5

1. An input loop is controlled by some characteristic of the input data. A processing loop is controlled by some characteristic of the data processed in the loop.

3. A trailer value is an input value that is used to signal the end of the data.

5.
```
      COUNT=0
   10 READ *,I
         COUNT=COUNT+1
      IF (I.NE.100) GO TO 10
      PRINT *,COUNT
```

7. five

9. In a pretest loop, the test to terminate the loop is the first step in the loop. In a posttest loop, the test to repeat the loop is the last step in the loop.

11. a. 6   c. 30   e. 5

13.
```
      DO 100 K=5,15,3
         X=X+K
  100 CONTINUE
```

15.
```
      DO 250 I=21,3,-3
         PRINT *,I
  250 CONTINUE
```

16. a. 10   c. 7

17. a. 15   c. 120

18. a. input loop   c. uncontrolled loop   e. pretest counting loop nested in a DO loop

19. Answer depends on computer being used.

Chapter 6

1. formatted input: READ, FORMAT;   formatted output: WRITE, FORMAT

3. `READ (5,100) PRICE,DESC,QTY`

5. `READ (5,100,END=999) PRICE,DESC,QTY`

7. `WRITE (*,200) PRICE, DESC,QTY`

8. a. I = 9876   c. A = 987654.32, B = 1.12   e. K = 4321, X = .34, Y = 678.9

9.
```
      READ (5,110) ID,STATUS,SALES
  110 FORMAT (I5,7X,I1,20X,F6.2)
```

11.
```
     123456789.............. (print positions)
  a.    765   -321
  c. 123.45 98.7654    -100.
  e. ******
```

13.
```
      WRITE (6,220) A,B
  220 FORMAT (1X,'OUTPUT DATA',2F10.3)
```

15. They cause a blank line to be printed.

16. a.
```
         WRITE (6,240)
     240 FORMAT ('1','FINAL SUMMARY')
```
   c.
```
         WRITE (6,260)
         WRITE (6,260)
         WRITE (6,261)
      260 FORMAT ('0')
      261 FORMAT (' ')
```

17.
```
      READ (5,120) A
      READ (5,120) B
      READ (5,120) C
  120 FORMAT (F6.2)
```

19. Modify the FORMAT statement numbered 200 as follows:
```
      200 FORMAT ('0',I5,5X,F5.1,5X,F5.1)
```

```
21.      READ (5,121) A,B,C
     121 FORMAT (F6.2/F6.2 /F6.2)
         WRITE (6,281) I,J,K
     281 FORMAT (' ',I5/' ',I5/' ',I5)
23.      READ (5,120) A,B,C
     120 FORMAT (F6.2)
         WRITE (6,280) I,J,K
     280 FORMAT (' ',I5)
```

Chapter 7

1. sequence structure, decision structure, loop structure
2. a. decision   c. sequence
3. Because each basic control structure has a single entry point and a single exit point, any structure can be nested in any other structure and the result has a single entry point and a single exit point.
5. static; dynamic
7. Any three of the rules listed at the beginning of Section 7-3 are an adequate answer.
9. stepwise program refinement
11. documenting the program
13. an algorithm
15. false
17. Program testing is the process of determining if there are errors in a program. Debugging is the process of locating and correcting errors once their presence has been determined.
19. Coding involves preparing the instructions for a program in a specific programming language. Programming is the whole set of activities associated with preparing a computer program.

Chapter 8

1. `CHARACTER CNTRY*15,LANG*10`
3. The character data must be enclosed in apostrophes.
5.
```
     READ (5,100) CNTRY,LANG
 100 FORMAT (A15,A10)
     or
 100 FORMAT (2A)
```
7.
```
     WRITE (6,210) CNTRY,LANG
 210 FORMAT (1X,A15,5X,A10)
     or
 210 FORMAT (1X,A,5X,A)
```
9. a. false   c. true   e. false
11.
```
IF (MCODE.EQ.'M') THEN
   NUM=NUM+1
ELSE IF (MCODE.EQ.'D') THEN
   NUM=NUM-1
ELSE IF (MCODE.EQ.'S') THEN
   NUM=0
END IF
```
13. `ID='12345'`
14. a. ABCDE   c. OUTPU
15. `PARAMETER (CNTRY='USA',LANG='ENGLISH')`
16. a. Z123A   c. ABC   e. XYZ1
17. a. 4   c. 8

19. a. ABCXYZ   c. ABCDEF
20. a. true   c. false   e. false   g. true
21. `IF ((I.EQ.5.OR.J.EQ.5).AND.(K.EQ.10)) THEN`
    `    PRINT *,A`
    `END IF`
23. `RESP=.TRUE.`
    `CHCK=A.GT.B`
25. `PARAMETER (CHCK=.FALSE.)`
27. Each logical data value must begin with a T or F optionally preceded by a period. Any characters may follow the T or F.
29.   `READ (5,120) RESP,CHCK`
    `120 FORMAT (L5,L4)`

Chapter 9

1. a. An array is a group of data values identified in a program by a single name.
   c. An array element is a value in an array.
3. `INTEGER S`
   `REAL T`
   `DIMENSION S(50),T(50)`
4. a. 20.5   c. 5.7
5. `REAL U(10:30)`
6. a. invalid   c. valid
7. `U(30)=U(10)*U(11)`
9.   `READ (5,110) S`
   `110 FORMAT (10I5)`
11.   `DO 20 I=1,25`
   `        WRITE (6,210) S(I),S(I+25)`
   `    20 CONTINUE`
   `210 FORMAT (1X,I5,3X,I5)`
13.   `TOTAL=0`
   `    DO 40 I=1,49,2`
   `        TOTAL=TOTAL+S(I)`
   `    40 CONTINUE`
15.   `I=1`
   `    60 IF ((S(I).EQ.R).OR.(I.EQ.50)) GO TO 65`
   `        I=I+1`
   `        GO TO 60`
   `    65 IF (S(I).EQ.R) THEN`
   `            WRITE (6,220) T(I)`
   `        ELSE`
   `            WRITE (6,225)`
   `        END IF`
   `    220 FORMAT (' ',F10.2)`
   `    225 FORMAT (' VALUE NOT FOUND')`
17.

Before			After	
7	7	7	7	7
10	10	6	6	6
6	6	10	4	4
4	4	4	10	10
12	12	12	12	12

     I=1 I=2 I=3 I=4
19. `DATA J,K,L,X,Y/1,2,3,2.5,7.5/`

Chapter 10

1. A one-dimensional array can be thought of as organized in one direction such as a column. One subscript is needed to identify an element. A two-dimensional array can be thought of as organized in two directions such as rows and columns. Two subscripts are required to identify an element.

2. a. 100   c. 96

3. a. REAL A(5,20)

4. a. INTEGER B(0:10,51:75)

5. A(4,20)=A(1,1)+A(3,2)

7.
```
     COUNT=0
     DO 120 J=1,20
        IF (A(1,J).EQ.A(2,J)) THEN
           COUNT=COUNT+1
        END IF
120  CONTINUE
```

9.
```
     DO 160 I=1,5
        J=1
150     IF ((A(I,J).EQ.AVAL).OR.(J.EQ.20)) GO TO 155
        J=J+1
        GO TO 150
155     IF ((A(I,J).EQ.AVAL) THEN
           WRITE (6,800)
        ELSE
           WRITE (6,810)
        END IF
160  CONTINUE
800  FORMAT (' VALUE FOUND')
810  FORMAT (' VALUE NOT FOUND')
```

11.
```
     DO 190 I=1,5
        READ (5,820) (A(I,J),J=1,20)
190  CONTINUE
820  FORMAT (20F4.1)
```

13. The elements must be in order by columns.

15. a. 68   c. 83

16. a. INTEGER C(10,5,6)

17.
```
     DO 230 K=1,6
        DO 220 I=1,10
           DO 210 J=1,5
              C(I,J,K)=K-1
210        CONTINUE
220     CONTINUE
230  CONTINUE
```

19. The elements must be in order by levels, and within each level the elements must be in order by columns.

Chapter 11

1. A main program can be executed by itself. A subprogram can only be executed along with another program.

3. passed; returned

5. A function can only return one value to a calling program; a subroutine can return any number of values to the calling program.

7. the RETURN statement (or the END statement)

9. dummy; actual; number, type, order

11.
```
INTEGER A,B,C,Z
READ *,A,B
C=Z(A,B)
PRINT *,C
STOP
END
```

13.
```
REAL X(25),TOTAL
READ *,X
WRITE *,TOTAL(X)
STOP
END
```

15.
```
SUBROUTINE POWER(X,X2,X3)
REAL X,X2,X3
X2=X**2
X3=X**3
RETURN
END
```

17. The next statement executed is the statement after the CALL statement that called the subroutine.

19.
```
REAL X(25),TOT,AVER
READ *,X
CALL TOTAVE(X,TOT,AVER)
PRINT *,TOT,AVER
STOP
END
```

21. Change the COMMON statement in the subroutine to

```
COMMON /BLK/X,X2,X3
```

Change the COMMON statement in the main program to

```
COMMON /BLK/A,A2,A3
```

23. `AMT=A(1000.00,.1,5)`

25.

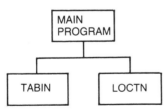

Chapter 12

1. A track is a circle on the surface of a disk along which data is stored. A read/write head is a mechanism in a disk drive (or tape drive) that records data on or retrieves data from a magnetic disk (or magnetic tape).

3. With sequential access, the records in a file are processed in the order in which they are stored in auxiliary storage. With direct access, the records can be processed in any order. Sequential and direct access can be used with magnetic disk. Only sequential access can be used with magnetic tape.

5. output
7. input; output
8. a. OPEN (UNIT=2,FILE='AFILE',ACCESS='SEQUENTIAL',
    1   FORM='FORMATTED',STATUS='NEW')
   c. ENDFILE (UNIT=2)
9. a. OPEN (UNIT=3,FILE='BFILE',ACCESS='SEQUENTIAL',
    1   FORM='FORMATTED',STATUS='OLD')
   c. BACKSPACE (UNIT=3)
11. Data in a master file is the main data used by the organization. Transaction data represents events that have taken place and that need to be reflected in the master file.
13. The records in both the master and transaction files must be in the same order (either increasing or decreasing order) by key field for sequential file updating. The updating algorithm is based on locating matching master and transaction keys. When the keys match, updating takes place.
14. a. 4   c. 6
15. true
16. a. OPEN (UNIT=1,FILE='CFILE',ACCESS='DIRECT',
    1   FORM='FORMATTED',STATUS='NEW',RECL=15)
   c. CLOSE (UNIT=1)
17. a. OPEN (UNIT=4,FILE='DFILE',ACCESS ='DIRECT',
    1   FORM='FORMATTED',STATUS='OLD',RECL=25)
19. In direct file updating, data in a file is changed without creating a new file; with sequential file updating, a new file is created with the updated data. In direct file updating, the master records and transaction data may be in any order; with sequential file updating, the data must be in order by key field.
20. a. 6   c. 3

Index